LEGAL INFORMATION ONLINE ANYTIME

24 hours a day

www.nolo.com

AT THE NOLO.COM SELF-HELP LAW CENTER, YOU'LL FIND

- Nolo's comprehensive Legal Encyclopedia filled with plain-English information on a variety of legal topics
- Nolo's Law Dictionary—legal terms <u>without</u> the legalese
- Auntie Nolo—if you've got questions, Auntie's got answers
- The Law Store—over 250 self-help legal products including Downloadable Software, Books, Form Kits and eGuides
- Legal and product updates
- Frequently Asked Questions
- NoloBriefs, our free monthly email newsletter
- Legal Research Center, for access to state and federal statutes
- Our ever-popular lawyer jokes

Quality LAW BOOKS & SOFTWARE FOR EVERYONE

Nolo's user-friendly products are consistently first-rate. Here's why:

- A dozen in-house legal editors, working with highly skilled authors, ensure that our products are accurate, up-to-date and easy to use
- We continually update every book and software program to keep up with changes in the law
- Our commitment to a more democratic legal system informs all of our work
- We appreciate & listen to your feedback. Please fill out and return the card at the back of this book.

OUR "NO-HASSLE" GUARANTEE

Return anything you buy directly from Nolo for any reason and we'll cheerfully refund your purchase price. No ifs, ands or buts.

An Important Message to Our Readers

5th edition

Tax Savvy for Small Business

Year-Round Tax Strategies to Save You Money

by Attorney Frederick W. Daily

Keeping Up-to-Date

To keep its books up-to-date, Nolo issues new printings and new editions periodically. New printings reflect minor legal changes and technical corrections. New editions contain major legal changes, major text additions or major reorganizations. To find out if a later printing or edition of any Nolo book is available, call Nolo at 510-549-1976 or check our website at http://www.nolo.com.

To stay current, follow the "Update" service at our website at http://www.nolo.com/update. In another effort to help you use Nolo's latest materials, we offer a 35% discount off the purchase of the new edition of your Nolo book when you turn in the cover of an earlier edition. (See the "Special Upgrade Offer" in the back of the book.)

Fifth Edition	AUGUST 2001
Editor	SHANNON MIEHE
Illustrations	MARI STEIN
Cover Design	TONI IHARA
Book Design	TERRI HEARSH
Proofreading	SHERYL ROSE
Index	JULIE SHAWVAN
Printing	CONSOLIDATED PRINTERS, INC.

Daily, Frederick W., 1942-
    Tax savvy for small business : year-round tax strategies to save you money / by Frederick W. Daily.--National 5th ed.
        p.   cm.
    Includes index.
    ISBN 0-87337-718-4
    1. Small business--Taxation--Law and legislation--United States. 2. Tax planning--United States.   I. Title.
KF6491.D35 2001
343.7305'268—dc21   2001030041

For information on bulk purchases or corporate premium sales, please contact the Special Sales Department. For academic sales or textbook adoptions, ask for Academic Sales. Call 800-955-4775 or write to Nolo, 950 Parker Street, Berkeley, CA 94710.

Dedication

To my wife, Brenda, who has brought me everything that is good in life.

Acknowledgments

Trying to translate the tax code into plain English for the small businessperson was a challenge that all but overwhelmed me. Without the help of many others I could not have done it.

Nolo has some of the most caring (and careful) editors on the face of this earth. First and foremost in both categories is Mary Randolph. Other Nolo folks with a hand in the project were Jake Warner, Robin Leonard, Lisa Goldoftas and Steve Fishman. Stephanie Harolde, Ely Newman, Robert Wells and Susan Cornell made valuable contributions in copyediting, proofreading and production. Thank you one and all for putting up with me.

My peers in the tax community contributed immensely and without complaint. The most helpful in making sure the things you need to know were covered: Chris Kollaja, CPA; Dewey Watson, Tax Attorney (all in San Francisco); Lew Hurwitz, EA (Oakland); Steven Mullenniex, EA (Berkeley); Malcolm Roberts, CPA of Roberts Schultz & Co. in Berkeley; and Gino Bianchini, Tax Attorney (Newport Beach). A special thanks to Richard L. Church, CPA (Southwest Harbor, Maine) for his technical expertise.

Table of Contents

Part 2: The Form of Your Business

8 S Corporations

9 Partnerships

10 Limited Liability Companies

11 Personal Service Corporations

Part 3: Thinking Small

12 Family Businesses

13 Microbusinesses and Home-Based Businesses

Part 4: Fringe Benefits

14 Fringe Benefits

15 Retirement Plans

Part 5: Buying or Selling a Business

16 Buying a Business

17 Selling a Sole Proprietorship

Part 6: Dealing with the IRS

18 When You Can't Pay Your Taxes

19 Audits

23 Answers to Frequently Asked Tax Questions

Glossary

Appendix

Index

Introduction to Business Taxes

If mastering the tax code were a prerequisite to starting a business, no one would dare. Luckily, most tax law has little or no application to you, the small businessperson. The basics are right here in this book. And once you grasp the fundamentals, you can pick up the rest as you go along, perhaps with the help of a tax advisor. As the well-worn phrase goes, "It's not brain surgery."

A. Small Business and Self-Employed Taxes

Owning and operating a small business, full- or part-time, has been called the little guy's tax shelter. The self-employed get tax benefits for any number of expenditures not allowed to "wage slaves." In effect, you are sharing expenses (as well as profits) with Uncle Sam.

Small business or independent contractor? One of the most common questions self-employed people (such as independent contractors, freelancers and consultants) ask is whether they are a "business." The answer is, you're both. Whether you run a flower shop or freelance as a graphic artist, you're a small business. When we talk about small businesses in this book, we're talking about all kinds of self-employed people, from independent contractors, consultants and freelancers to the guy who owns the pizza parlor down the street.

Everyone has their own idea on what a "small" business is. The typical U.S. small business grosses less than $1 million and has fewer than ten employees. That's the venture we are mostly talking about in this book, but keep in mind that most of the tax information here applies to any size operation. As you might expect, when the numbers of dollars or employees increase, so do the tax complexities. Still, the book in your hands covers all the tax basics you need to know to get started.

The IRS does not require or issue business licenses. Whether you need any kind of license depends on the state your business is in as well as the local authorities. For more information about business licensing and other small business start-up issues, see *The Small Business Start-Up Kit*, by Peri Pakroo (Nolo).

Tax Advantages for Small-Time Operators

1. Personal expenses can become wholly or partially deductible: your home, car, computer, meals, education and entertainment.
2. Retirement savings plans can shelter part of your venture's income from taxes, accumulate earnings tax-deferred and provide for your retirement at a reduced tax rate.
3. Family members—young and old—can be put on the payroll to shift income to them and reduce a family's overall tax bill.
4. Travel and vacations can qualify in whole or in part as deductible business expenses.

Sound interesting? With all of these possibilities, your business can earn less than if you were working for someone else, and you still can come out ahead. All these and more ways to beat the tax man are covered in this book.

Of course, by going into business you might be trading an eight-hour-a-day job for a 24-hour one. But for many of us, it is worth it. Having your own enterprise might prove disastrous, but it could be especially rewarding if you are doing something that you enjoy.

Our country has 45 million small businesses and self-employed folks that the IRS knows about, and probably many more. Unhappily, U.S. Chamber of Commerce statistics show that a venture has an 85% chance of closing its doors within its first five years. But our entrepreneurial spirit is strong, and many who fail go back and try again.

Four out of five of these brave souls are what the tax code calls sole proprietors—one-person or mom 'n' pop operations. The rest are either partnerships, limited liability companies or corporations. Ten million small businesses provide jobs only for the owners and their families.

Don't Forget About State Taxes

While this book focuses on federal taxes, don't forget your state and local tax laws and agencies. Unfortunately, it can be even more time consuming to comply with state tax laws than with federal tax laws. Especially if your enterprise is a multi-state affair, you might find yourself drowning in paperwork. At the very least, figure state tax compliance into your cost of doing business, including hiring more bookkeeping and accounting help.

State tax enforcement agencies can be even more bureaucratic, tough and downright frustrating to deal with than the IRS. (See *Stand Up to the IRS*, by Frederick W. Daily (Nolo) for advice on dealing with state tax agencies.) Many states have out-of-state enforcement offices, and others use private collection agencies to track you down anywhere in the U.S. So, just because you live in Maryland, don't think the state of California can't get you.

Here are some state tax issues to watch out for if you're a small time operator:

- **Income taxes.** See Chapter 7, Section B2; Chapter 8, Section C (corporate state income tax and franchise tax information); Chapter 10, Section A2 (LLC state income taxes); and Chapter 9, Section B1 (partnership state income tax reporting).
- **Sales taxes.** Just about every state imposes a sales tax on items a business sells. But each state has different rules for collection and exemptions. Usually the seller is responsible for collecting and paying state sales tax, whether it has been collected from the buyer or not.
- **Use taxes.** This is a tax on goods that you purchased out of state that were brought into your state without paying sales tax.
- **Business transfer taxes** (see Chapter 16, Section D). Whenever a business changes hands, your state, county or city may impose a transfer tax on either the buyer, seller or both.
- **Inventory and other property taxes.** Some states and local governments impose an annual tax on the value of the personal (non-real estate) property used in the business. And, most states or localities impose an annual tax on real estate, whether it is used for business or personal purposes.

- **Internet taxes.** There is a federal moratorium on states imposing taxes on Internet transactions. However (as of the date of this writing), the moratorium is due to expire on October 21, 2001. The states are putting a lot of pressure on Congress to allow them to tax transactions over the Internet that are now escaping the state sales tax nets when the goods are shipped out of state. Stay tuned.
- **Payroll taxes.** All states with income taxes have a payroll tax and collection system roughly similar to the federal system.
- **Telecommuter taxes.** New York is one of a growing number of states that tax you when working from home located in another state (for instance, Connecticut), if your main business location is in New York.
- **License fees.** There are myriad state and local licenses that a business must secure to be legal. Whatever they are called, these fees are really just another tax. Check with your local tax agencies, Chamber of Commerce or attorney.
- **Out-of-state taxes.** This is a broad catchall similar to telecommuter taxes, above. For example, as an employer, you can be responsible for withholding state income taxes on your nonresident employees' income in their home states. Recently, a small incorporated consulting business owner came to me with a plan to open satellite offices in two surrounding states. After considering the fact that he would have to learn and deal with three sets of state payroll, corporation and other tax rules, he decided not to expand.
- **Death taxes** (see Chapter 12, Section D). Most states, as well as the federal government, tax the value of all of your assets, including your business, when it becomes part of your estate on your death.

While we can point you in the direction of state tax issues, we don't have room to discuss and explain them all here. To find your state tax and licensing agencies, go to http://www.piperinfo.com/index.cfm for a listing of all the government agencies in your state that are on the Web, or look them up in your local phone book.

No one likes paying taxes or dealing with the IRS, but operating a business without some tax awareness is like skydiving without a parachute—certain to end in calamity. Many failures stem from ignoring the financial and tax side of the operation. Like it or not, the government is always your business partner.

Conversely, tax knowledge has powerful profit potential. It can give you a fatter bottom line than your competitors who don't bother to learn. For instance, there are several ways to write off car expenses. Your choice can mean a few thousand more after-tax dollars in your pocket each year.

What You'll Get From Reading This Book

1. An explanation of the tax benefits of each legal form of business—sole proprietorship, partnership, limited liability company or corporation.
2. Ways to minimize taxes and stay out of IRS trouble.
3. What to do if the IRS ever challenges your business tax reporting or sends you a tax bill you don't agree with.

Four different federal taxes affect small business ventures:

- income taxes (everyone who makes a profit owes these)
- employee taxes (if your business has employees)
- self-employment taxes (Social Security and Medicare taxes), and
- excise taxes (few small businesses are subject to these).

Thousands of federal tax laws, regulations and court decisions deal with these four categories. We will look only at the relatively few rules most likely to affect you, and translate them into plain English.

Do You Need a Tax Professional?

This is not a tax-preparation manual. As much as we'd love to walk you, line by line, through each and every tax form you might have to file, every small business's tax situation is different. Our goal is to explain the IRS rules in plain English so you will have a better understanding of how they apply to your business. As good as we hope this book is, nothing takes the place of a personal tax advisor. Everyone's tax situation is unique, and tax laws change annually. But the more you know, the better you can work with your tax professional (referred to as "tax pro" throughout this book), and the less you will have to pay him or her. (See Chapter 22 for tips on finding and using a tax pro.) Also, take a look at IRS Publication 1 for a summary of your rights as a taxpayer in dealing with the IRS.

B. How Tax Law Is Made and Administered—The Short Course

The following discussion may help put the world of federal taxes into perspective. Think of it as a high school government lesson, only try to stay awake this time—it could be money in your pocket.

The Government. Visualize a three-branched tree. Congress, the legislative branch of the federal government, makes the tax law. The executive branch, which includes the Treasury Department, administers the tax law through the IRS. The judicial branch comprises all the federal courts, which interpret the tax laws and oversees the IRS when it goes beyond the law.

The power to tax incomes was granted by the 16th Amendment to the U.S. Constitution; the first Income Tax Act was passed in 1913. Contrary to what fringe groups and con artists would like you to believe, income tax law and the IRS are legal and are not going to go away.

Tax law begins with the Internal Revenue Code (referred to throughout this book as the IRC). Congress enacts and revises the tax code annually. One major reworking was officially called the Tax Reform Act, but was known to tax pros as the "Accountants' and Tax Attorneys' Relief Act." The funny thing is that it started off as the Tax Simplification Act. Even the merry pranksters in Washington didn't think they could put that one over on us, and changed the title. The tax code is now over 4,500 pages of exceedingly fine print.

The IRS. The Internal Revenue Service (IRS or whatever other name you want to use), a division of the Treasury Department, is headed by the Commissioner of Internal Revenue, a presidential appointee.

IRS tax administration policy is set in Washington, but it is doubtful you will ever deal directly with anyone there. The real work is done at IRS Service Centers and local offices.

The Courts. The United States Tax Court is an arm of the federal court system that decides disputes between the IRS and taxpayers. It is pretty easy to go to Tax Court, even without an attorney. Tax disputes can be also decided in U.S. District Courts and the Federal Court of Claims, but these require payment of the tax first, unlike the Tax Court. All decisions of those courts, for or against you, may be reviewed by higher courts (except "small case" Tax Court decisions; see Chapter 20 for details).

See, that wasn't all that bad, was it? Now, venture forth into the rest of the book and into the entre-preneurial world, and may the small business gods be with you.

⚠ **The tax code changes frequently.** While we have made every effort to keep the material in this book up-to-date as of the time it went to press, Congress is forever tinkering with the tax code. What's more, some changes could be made retroactive to January, others will be effective on the date they are signed into law by the president and still others won't be effective until the new year. Also, federal court decisions, which interpret the tax code, come out regularly and may have an impact on what is written here. Your best strategy is to make sure you have the most current edition of this book and check with your tax advisor to see if anything has changed in your tax world.

C. Sources of Tax Law

How to research tax law questions is covered in Chapter 22, Help Beyond the Book, but here's a brief description of the main sources of federal tax law.

Federal Statutes. Congress enacts tax laws, called codes, which are published as the Internal Revenue Code. Each tax provision (called a "code section") has its own number and title. For example, IRC § 183 refers to tax code section number 183, titled "Activities Not Engaged in for Profit."

Regulations. When Congress makes laws, it paints with a fairly broad brush. It's then up to the Treasury Department (the IRS is a part of it) to fill in the details of how the tax code is to be applied. The details are set forth in Treasury Regulations, called simply "regulations" or "regs." They are numbered to correspond with the IRC sections they explain. Regulations are published in volumes separate from the IRC. Most regs are numbered in the same order as their related tax code sections, but preceded by the numeral "1." For example, the regulation explaining IRC § 183 is designated Reg. 1.183. (Not all IRC sections have corresponding regulations.)

Both the IRC and Treasury Regulations are available at most public libraries, larger bookstores and, of course, IRS offices. You can also find the IRC online at http://www4.law.cornell.edu/uscode/26.

Court Cases. When the IRS and taxpayers go to court, the judges' rulings containing the reasons for their decisions are collected and published in "case reporters," available in law libraries. These written opinions offer guidance on the correct interpretation of the tax code. A federal court may invalidate an IRS regulation or an IRS position taken in court. You can also find a limited number of Tax Court opinions (from January 1, 1999 to the present) on the Tax Court's website at http://www.ustaxcourt. gov/ustcweb.htm.

D. Personal Income Tax Brackets

In our "graduated" tax system, the more money you make, the higher your tax rate. The easiest way to determine the tax effect of additional income or deductible expenses is to find your marginal tax rate—the percentage at which additional income is taxed. For instance, if your marginal tax rate is 31%, 31¢ of every new dollar you earn goes to Uncle Sam. Conversely, you save 31¢ in taxes on every additional dollar qualifying as a deductible expense. If you factor in state and local income taxes and Social Security and Medicare tax, your marginal tax rate on business income may exceed 50%!

The table below illustrates the value of a deduction to an individual. The law works the same for most small business deductions as well.

For higher-income taxpayers, two extra "gotchas" pump your tax rate up another point or two. First, you lose part of your exemptions (a graduated phase-out) if you are married filing jointly and have an adjusted gross income in excess of $199,450—or if you are single and the figure is more than $132,950. And you also lose part of your itemized deductions (mortgage interest, property taxes, medical expenses and other expenses claimed on Schedule A)—if your adjusted gross income is more than $132,950, married or single. Congress giveth

	New Tax Rates	
	2001 Tax Rates	
Bracket	**Married Filing Jointly***	**Single**
15%	up to $45,200	up to $27,050
27.5%	$45,201 to 109,250	$27,051 to 65,550
30.5%	$109,251 to 166,500	$65,551 to 136,750
35.5%	$166,501 to 297,350	$136,751 to 297,350
39.1%	over $297,350	over $297,350

* Tax brackets for heads of households and married people filing separately are somewhat different.

This table does not take into account itemized or standard deductions or personal exemptions that every taxpayer gets.

Note: On June 7, 2001, the Economic Growth and Reconciliation Act of 2001 was enacted. This bill made some sweeping changes to the tax rates which took effect in the middle of the year. So, the rates listed above are a combination of the old rates (which were effective from January 1, 2001 to June 30, 2001) and the new rates (which are effective July 1, 2001 to December 31, 2001). In future years, these tax rates are slated to decrease even more, as follows:

Old Rate	**28%**	**31%**	**36%**	**39.6%**
2001–2003	27%	30%	35%	38.6%
2004–2005	26%	29%	34%	37.6%
2006 and after	25%	28%	33%	35%

Remember, since the lower rates for 2001 only apply for half of the year, the *effective* rate for the year is half a percentage higher than the reduced rate (as we note in the table above). In addition to lowering existing rates, Congress also added a new 10% tax bracket that will apply to the first $6,000 for single people and $12,000 for married couples filing jointly. For more information on how these changes affect you, check with your tax advisor.

and Congress taketh away, but I wish they wouldn't be so sneaky about it.

Note: In 2006, these exemption and itemized deduction phase-outs are slated to decrease and then expire completely in 2010.

E. The Alternative Minimum Tax (AMT)

As if the tax code weren't diabolical enough, there is something called the alternative minimum tax (AMT). The AMT is really a second (alternative) set of tax rates that potentially apply to everyone. The theory of the AMT is that higher-income folks who take "too many" tax code benefits should still have to pay a minimum amount of income taxes. About a quarter of those with incomes between $100,000 and $200,000, and 40% of those earning more than $200,000, are subject to the AMT.

The AMT has been around since 1969, but affected few taxpayers until it was expanded in 1997. Now, everyone must figure their income tax liabilities under both the regular tax rates noted above, and the AMT rates—and pay whichever is the *greater* number. Ouch! The AMT is reported on Form 6251 filed with your individual tax return.

Without getting into details, the AMT works to deny upper-income folks many tax deductions and credits otherwise allowed on their tax returns. The AMT is triggered by such common things as:

- net operating loss in a business
- interest deductions on home equity loans
- large itemized deductions for state and local taxes
- foreign tax credit
- passive income or loss
- certain installment sale income
- unreimbursed employee expenses
- exemptions for dependents
- newly enacted child and education tax credits for Hope scholarships and Lifetime Learning
- interest income on certain tax-exempt bonds, and
- the exercise of incentive stock options.

The AMT is yet another reason for self-employed folks to use a tax pro or a software program like *Turbotax for Business* (Intuit). ■

1

Business Income and Tax-Deductible Expenses

"There is nothing sinister in arranging one's affairs as to keep taxes as low as possible…for nobody owes any public duty to pay more than the law demands."
    —Judge Learned Hand

Every small business owner wants to know how to legally minimize her tax obligations. The key is understanding tax-deductible expenses, which are explained in this chapter. Chapter 2, Writing Off Business Assets, completes the picture; it deals with the rules for deducting assets purchased for your business.

Tax-Deductible Expenses in a Nutshell

1. Just about any expense that helps a business is tax-deductible as long as it is ordinary, necessary and reasonable.
2. Some business outlays can be deducted in the year they are paid. (They are called "current expenses.") Other expenditures must be capitalized—that is, spread out and deducted over several future years.

A. How the Tax Code Focuses on Profit

There are many systems of business taxation in the world. In Europe, the "value added tax," or VAT, is the rule. The VAT taxes the incremental value added to a product at each stage of manufacturing and distribution. Another approach is to tax a business on a percentage of its gross receipts.

The U.S. tax code zeroes in on a business's profits: the more you make, the more you pay. So the American entrepreneur has a strong incentive to keep taxable profits low, while at the same time taking home as much money and benefits as the law allows. Doing this legally means learning your ABCs (and even your DEFs) about how your enter-

prise is taxed. We'll start with some basic tax rules governing how expenses are deducted.

Congress says just about any expense to produce income can be deducted from a business's receipts. But to get the deduction, you must follow the Internal Revenue Code (IRC).

Here's a very simple illustration of how taxable profits are determined.

> **EXAMPLE:** Sam and Jeannie own Smiths' Computer Sales and Service as a sole proprietorship. Because the business is very profitable, Sam and Jeannie are in the highest federal tax bracket (39.1% in 2001). Here is how they determine their taxable profit:

Gross Sales (receipts from sale of computers)	$2,500,000
Less: Cost of Goods Sold (what they paid for the computers)	– 1,900,000
Gross Profit (before operating expenses)	= 600,000
Less: Deductible Business Expenses (rent, wages, supplies, etc.)	300,000
Net Profit (taxable to Sam and Jeannie)	= $300,000

The $300,000 net profit is subject to income tax. How much tax Sam and Jeannie will actually owe on this business income depends on: their other income, losses on any investments, personal deductions such as for home mortgage interest and, as we'll learn, how much they can take out of the business in tax-advantaged fringe benefits.

> **EXAMPLE: Federal Excise Taxes.** Some businesses face federal "excise taxes." For instance, an interstate trucking company may have to pay a federal excise tax on fuels or on each truck. Excise taxes affect few small businesses, so we won't go into detail. Operations most likely to be subject to excise taxes are in transportation

or manufacturing. See IRC §§ 4041 to 5763 to find out whether or not you are affected. Otherwise, you may not discover this special tax until it is too late—when you receive a huge bill for delinquent excise taxes.

B. What Is—And Isn't—Income

What does the tax code means by the term "income"? With a few exclusions discussed below, the tax law doesn't care whether you get it from your business, from wages paid by someone else's business or from an investment: it is taxable to you as an individual.

Actually, the better question is, "What is gross income?" The tax code (IRC § 61) talks in terms of gross income, so we will, too. It reads: "Except as otherwise provided … gross income means *all* income from whatever source derived." You can't get much broader than that, can you?

Goods and services. Income, for tax purposes, doesn't mean just cash; it can take many forms. Goods, property or services received have all been held to be within the definition of income.

If you barter (exchange goods or services for the same), the fair market value of the item or service you received should be included in your tax-reported income. Admittedly, a lot of bartering goes on, and the IRS isn't any the wiser. But getting away with it doesn't make it right.

Anything of value your business (or you individually) receives is income, unless it specifically falls within the exclusions discussed below.

Constructive income. Income also includes anything you have the right to put your hands on but don't for some reason. A legal doctrine called "constructive receipt" says that as soon as money or property is available to you, or is credited to your account, it becomes income—whether you grab it or not. For instance, you can't get a check for your services in November 2001 and hold it for deposit until 2002 without being taxed on it in 2001, the year you received it.

Illegal income. IRC § 61 is morally neutral; it doesn't distinguish between illegal and legal income.

If you earn a living as a hit man for the Mob, you still are earning income as far as the IRS is concerned, and had better declare it on your tax return. Al Capone wasn't sent to prison for murder, bootlegging or racketeering; he was convicted of tax evasion for not reporting the fruits of his labors to the IRS. You don't have to disclose the source of your income in some cases, however.

Worldwide income. Americans are taxed on their worldwide income; no matter where earned it is still taxable in the U.S. One exception: if you earn it and reside outside the United States for most of the year, your foreign income may be excludable. In addition, you may be entitled to a credit towards your U.S. income tax bill if you paid foreign income taxes. These exceptions are beyond the scope of this book. See IRS Publication 54, Tax Guide for U.S. Citizens and Resident Aliens Abroad.

What isn't income: exclusions. Some kinds of income fall into the "except as otherwise provided" exception of IRC § 61. For instance, the tax code specifically excludes gifts and inheritances from taxable income. There is no dollar limitation on how much you can get without tax to you. (Sorry, the $10 million that is being dropped off by the Prize Patrol from Publisher's Clearinghouse is not legally a gift and is taxable.) Thankfully, many so-called fringe benefits provided by businesses to owners and employees are specifically excluded from income. (See Chapter 14, Fringe Benefits.) Specific exclusions from income granted by Congress are found in IRC §§ 101 to 150. See IRS Publication 525, Taxable and Nontaxable Income, for more information.

Return of capital. Of great importance to investors is that the return of a capital investment is not taxable income. For example, to the extent that you sell a business or any asset and get back your investment, you haven't earned any taxable income. Only the profit, if any, is taxed.

EXAMPLE: Toni invests $1,000 in the stock of Ronaldo's Rubber Fashions, a small business corporation, and later sells her stock for $1,500. Only $500 is considered income for tax purposes; the other $1,000 is a return of capital to Toni.

Tax-free withdrawals. If you borrow against an asset, whether it belongs to your business or to you personally, the loan proceeds are not income. This is a valuable tool for taking money tax-free out of an unincorporated business that holds an appreciated asset, such as real estate.

C. What Is Tax-Deductible in Business?

The tax code allows you to deduct costs of doing business from your gross income. What you are left with is your net business profit. This is the amount that gets taxed.

So knowing how to maximize your deductible business expenses lowers your taxable profit. To boot, you may enjoy a personal benefit from a business expenditure—a nice car to drive, a combination business trip/vacation and a retirement savings plan—if you follow myriad tax rules. The balance of this chapter deals with the best ways to get the biggest business expense deduction bang for your buck.

1. Business Operating Expenses

Internal Revenue Code § 162 is the cornerstone for determining the tax-deductibility of every business expenditure. It is fairly lengthy, but the first hundred or so words are the key:

"Internal Revenue Code § 162. 'Trade or business expenses.'

*(a) In general. There shall be allowed as a deduction all the **ordinary and necessary** expenses **paid or incurred during the taxable year** in carrying on any trade or business, including*

(1) a reasonable allowance for salaries or other compensation for personal services actually rendered;

(2) traveling expenses (including amounts expended for meals and lodging other than amounts which are lavish or extravagant under the circumstances) while away from home in the pursuit of a trade or business; and

(3) rentals or other payments required to be made as a condition to the continued use or possession, for

purposes of the trade or business, of property to which the taxpayer has not taken or is not taking title or in which he has no equity."

Section 162 goes on—and on—but the rest of it deals with specific items that can't be deducted. Those with relevance to small businesses are covered later. Other code sections contain specific rules for deducting purchases of assets used in your business —machinery, cars and a thousand other things. We discuss asset write-offs in the next chapter. Right now we are focusing on the day-to-day operating expenses of a business.

In most cases, a legitimate business expense under IRC § 162 is obvious. In some cases, such as outlays for travel, the IRS provides specific instructions for determining whether or not an expense is "ordinary and necessary." This is often done through various IRS publications ("pubs") and "regulations" mentioned above and noted throughout this book.

Like the rest of the tax code, IRC § 162 is far from clear. Starting with trying to figure out what "ordinary and necessary" means, we suspect that things could go wrong for us. The tax code doesn't define either "ordinary" or "necessary." Instead, myriad federal courts have tried to figure out what Congress intended and apply it to a particular set of facts. "Ordinary" has been held by courts to mean "normal, common and accepted under the circumstances by the business community." "Necessary" means "appropriate and helpful." Taken together, the legal consensus is that "ordinary and necessary" refers to the *purpose* for which an expense is made. For instance, renting office space is ordinary and necessary for many business folks, but it is neither unless it is actually used in running an enterprise for profit.

Given these broad legal guidelines, it is not surprising that some folks have tried to push the envelope on "ordinary and necessary" business expenses, and the IRS has pushed back. Sometimes the issue is thrown into a court's lap.

EXAMPLE: Mr. Henry, an accountant, deducted his yacht expenses, contending that because the boat flew a pennant with the numbers "1040," it brought him professional recognition and clients. The matter ended up before the Tax Court. The

court ruled that the yacht wasn't a normal business expense for a tax pro, and so it wasn't "ordinary" or "necessary." In short, the yacht expense was personal and thus nondeductible. (Henry v. CIR, 36 TC 879 (1961).)

Does your deduction pass the laugh test? Tax pros frequently rely on the "laugh test": Can you put down an expense for your business without laughing about putting one over on the IRS? In the example above, the Tax Court laughed the accountant and his yacht out of court.

2. Large Expenses

Because the IRS knows that people don't intentionally overpay for anything, amounts paid aren't usually questioned. However, IRS auditors sometimes object to expenditures deemed unreasonably large under the circumstances.

While the tax code itself contains no "too big" limitation, courts have ruled that it is inherent in IRC § 162. For example, it might be reasonable for a multi-state apparel company to lease a jet for travel between manufacturing plants, but not for a corner deli owner to fly to New York to meet with her pickle supplier.

3. Personal Expenses

The number one concern of the IRS when auditing businesses is whether someone is claiming purely *personal* expenditures as business expenses. For instance, the cost of commuting to work isn't deductible because the tax code says this is a personal, not a business, expense. Ditto with using the business American Express card for a vacation.

Fortunately, as discussed throughout this book, you can often arrange your affairs—legally—in a way that lets you derive considerable personal benefit and enjoyment from business expenditures.

Be careful if you deal with relatives. An IRS auditor will look askance at payments to a family member or to another business in which your relatives have an ownership interest. In tax code parlance, these are termed "related parties." An auditor may suspect that taxable profits are being taken out of your business for direct or indirect personal benefit in the guise of deductible expenses. For example, paying your spouse's father, who is in prison, $5,000 as a consultant's fee for your restaurant business would smell bad to an auditor.

Business Costs That Are Never Deductible

A few expenses are not deductible even if they are business-related, because they violate "public policy." (IRC § 162.) This small category includes:

- any type of government fine, such as a tax penalty paid to the IRS or even a parking ticket
- bribes and kickbacks, foreign or domestic
- any kind of payment made for referring a client, patient or customer, if it is contrary to a state or federal law, and
- expenses for lobbying and social club dues.

D. Current vs. Capitalized Expenses

Tax rules cover not only what expenses you can deduct but also *when*—what year—you can deduct them. Some types of expenditures are deductible in the year they are incurred, but others must be spread out and taken over a number of future years.

The first category is called "current" expenses, and the second "capitalized" expenditures. You need to know the difference between the two, and the tax rules for each type—but there are some gray areas.

"Current expenses" are everyday costs of keeping your business going, such as the rent and electricity bills. Rules for deducting current expenses are straightforward; subtract the amounts spent from your business's gross income in the year the expenses were incurred.

"Capitalized" expenditures are those expected to last and generate revenue in future years—they become assets of the business. As capital assets are used, their cost is "matched" to the business revenue they help earn. Accounting-wise, this allows the business to more clearly account for its profitability from year to year.

It is not always clear what is a current expense and what is a capital one. For instance, normal repair costs, such as fixing a broken copy machine or a door, are obviously currently deductible expenses. On the other hand, the tax code says that the cost of making improvements to a business asset must be capitalized if the enhancement:

- adds to its value
- appreciably lengthens the time you can use it, or
- adapts it to a different use.

"Improvements" usually refers to real estate—for example, putting in new electrical wiring, plumbing and lighting—but the capitalization rule also applies to rebuilding anything, as the following example shows.

EXAMPLE: Gunther uses a die-stamping machine in his metal fabrication shop. After 15 years of constant use, the machine is on its last legs. His average yearly maintenance expenses on the machine have been $10,000, which Gunther has properly deducted as repair expenses. In 2001, Gunther is faced with either thoroughly rehabilitating the machine at a cost of $80,000, or buying a new one for $175,000. He goes for the rebuilding. The $80,000 expense must be capitalized—that is, it can't be taken all in 2001 when the die stamper is rebuilt. The tax code says that metal-fabricating machinery costs must be deducted over five years.

Preview: Chapter 2, Writing Off Business Assets, goes into more detail about tax-deducting capitalized asset purchases. Generally, costs for items with a "useful life" of one year or longer cannot be deducted as current expenses. Rather, asset purchases are treated as investments in your business, and must be deducted over a number of years, specified in the tax code (with one important exception, discussed below). The deduction is usually called "depreciation," but in some cases it is called a "depletion" or "amortization" expense. All of these words describe the process of writing off or depreciating asset costs through a series of annual tax deductions.

There are many rules for how different types of assets must be written off. The tax code dictates both absolute limits on some depreciation deductions, and over how many future years a business must spread its depreciation deductions for all asset purchases. Enterprises, large and small, are governed by these provisions (IRC §§ 167, 168 and 179), which we discuss in detail in Chapter 2.

A super-size tax break creating an exception to the long-term write-off rules is found in IRC § 179. A business can write off in *one* year most types of its capital expenditures, up to a grand total of $24,000 (2001). See Chapter 2, Writing Off Business Assets, for details on how IRC § 179 works.

E. Special Deduction Rules

Certain business expenses have special rules that govern how they must be tax-deducted. Let's start with one of the most common, vehicles.

1. Business-Used Vehicle Expenses

Motor vehicle expenses are one of the greatest small business tax-deductible items. Fine-print tax rules for claiming car and truck expenses for your business are tricky, but well worth mastering; they can provide a jumbo payoff at tax time.

Records. First, make sure you keep the right records to calculate your vehicle expense deduction—and to back you up if you are ever audited. Keep a trip and mileage log (see sample, below).

Business/personal use allocation. Keep in mind that if your automobile is used for both business and pleasure, only the business portion produces a tax deduction. So you must track the use of a dual-purpose vehicle and allocate business/personal use. Do a year-end analysis of your records to come up with the percentage of each use, such as "62% business, 38% personal."

If you own or lease just one car or truck, no IRS auditor will allow you to claim that 100% of its use is business-related. (Some folks get away with as much as 90%, though.) If you have both business and personal vehicles, and one is obviously dedicated to a business use (a minivan with your logo painted on the side), it isn't necessary to do any allocation to claim 100% business use.

Two methods to claim vehicle expense deductions. You have a choice of two ways to calculate and deduct business vehicle expenses: the *standard mileage* and *actual expense* methods. With some qualifications explained below, you may switch between the two methods each year and choose the one that gives you the largest tax benefit. As a rule, if you use a newer car primarily for business, the actual expense method provides a larger deduction. But the mileage method works better for some folks and requires much less recordkeeping.

⚠️ **You can't deduct the cost of commuting to work in your car.** However, trips to a "temporary" job site are deductible as long as you have a permanent regular workplace.

a. Standard Mileage Method for Deducting Vehicle Expenses

The simplest way to write off business vehicle expenses is called the *mileage* or standard mileage rate method. You just total up the number of business miles driven over the year and multiply by 34.5¢ (2001 tax code allowed rate).

Commuting miles (getting to and from your business location) are nondeductible personal miles. However, if your business is home-based, trips from home for a job are considered "business."

You can elect to use the mileage method whether you own or lease your vehicle.

Not everyone can choose the mileage method. If any of the following conditions apply, you must use the "actual expense" method (discussed next):

- You used more than one vehicle simultaneously for business.
- You previously used the actual expense method on this same vehicle and claimed an accelerated depreciation method. (See Chapter 2.)
- You ever claimed IRC § 179 to write off part of the vehicle's purchase price. (See Chapter 2.)

If you choose the mileage method, you cannot also deduct your operating expenses—gas, repairs, license tags and insurance—but you can deduct parking fees, tolls and any state and local property taxes on the car or truck.

> **EXAMPLE:** In 2001, Morris drove 10,000 business miles in his practice of veterinary medicine. He also spent $700 in bridge and highway tolls and for parking garages. Morris's 2001 vehicle expense deduction is $3,450 (34.5¢ x 10,000) + $700 = $4,150. If Morris's practice is incorporated, the business could deduct this sum and reimburse Morris the same amount. However, if the corporation paid Morris a car allowance of $4,800 per year for the use of his personal car for business, the excess over the proper business deduction ($650) would be reportable as income to Morris on his 2001 tax return.

Primary disadvantage of mileage method. If you choose the mileage method to claim auto expenses, you can't take a depreciation deduction on the vehicle—which could be substantial with newer cars. (See Chapter 2, Writing Off Business Assets.) But again, the more miles you drive the more the mileage method may be to your advantage. It pays to figure it both ways, as we shall see.

Recordkeeping for Business-Used Vehicles

No matter which method you use to claim auto expenses, you will need to keep accurate records. The best way to keep auto use records is with a log book, sold at office supply stores. Or just keep a notepad in your glove compartment, or, if you're tech savvy, store the information in a personal digital assistant, such as a Palm Pilot®. However you do it, whenever you drive a personal car for business, record:

- the date of the trip
- your destination
- your mileage (round-trip), and
- who you visited and your business relationship with that person.

Below is a sample page from a logbook, showing vehicle expense entries.

Also, keep vehicle-servicing receipts showing the mileage at the first servicing of the year and at the last servicing. This is one way to prove annual miles driven. If using the actual expense method, you should save all of your other car expense receipts, too.

Vehicle Expense Log

			Odometer Readings			Expenses	
January, 2001							
	Destination	Business			Miles	Type (Gas,	
Date	(City, Town or Area)	Purpose	Start	Stop	this trip	oil, tolls, etc.)	Amount
1/18/01	Local (St. Louis)	Sales calls	8,097	8,188	91	Gas	$18.25
1/19/01	Indianapolis	Sales calls	8,211	8,486	275	Parking	2.00
1/20/01	Louisville	See Bob Smith	8,486	8,599	113	Gas/	16.50
		(Pot. Client)				Repair flat tire	
1/21/01	Return to St. Louis		8,599	8,875	276	Gas	17.25
1/22/01	Local (St. Louis)	Sales calls	8,914	9,005	91		
1/23/01	Local (St. Louis)		9,005	9,005	0	Car Wash	8.50
///	MONTHLY TOTAL	///	8,097	9,005	846	///	$62.50
TOTAL JANUARY, 2001		Business Miles Driven			846	Expenses	$62.50

b. Actual Expense Method for Deducting Vehicle Expenses

The mileage method described above is simplified and works well for some, but doesn't provide the largest deduction available for owning and operating most newer cars. If your auto costs more than $15,800, it is usually better to use the actual expense method, including the depreciation deduction.

Simply total up your car operating expenses—gas, repairs, insurance and so on—and then add the depreciation deduction allowed in the tax code. (See Chapter 2, Writing Off Business Assets.)

> **EXAMPLE:** Sam buys a Plymouth minivan in 2001 for $25,000 and uses it 100% for his business. He drives the van 10,000 miles the first year. The tax code allows $3,060 for depreciation in 2001. Sam's actual operating expenses for gas, maintenance and insurance total $2,600, plus $700 for parking and tolls. Sam can deduct a total of $6,360 for car expenses in 2001, including depreciation. Compare this to the previous example where Morris' using the mileage method was $4,150.

How to Claim Expenses for Autos

A business claiming expenses for car use must file IRS Form 4562, Depreciation and Amortization, with its tax return. This form requires a breakdown listing the business, personal and commuting miles driven during the year. Even if you don't use the mileage method, you still must use this form and report the number of miles driven for business. See Chapter 2, Section C, for a sample filled-out Form 4562.

Do the math before you pick a way to claim auto expenses. Usually, the actual expense method results in higher tax deductions if you own a late-model car, because you can take a depreciation deduction as well as claiming operating expenses. On the other hand, the standard mileage method may be better if you drive a lot of miles in a 50 mpg gas miser or in a faithful old clunker.

Generally, you may switch back and forth between the standard mileage and actual expense methods each year to get the greatest tax deductions. However, if you use the mileage method the first year your auto is placed in service, you are not allowed to take accelerated depreciation deductions in any future years. If you switch, you must take a straight-line depreciation. If you qualify, figure your deduction both ways each year and then choose.

c. Vehicle Deductions for Corporations

Business expenses of vehicles used in businesses that are organized as corporations are claimed in a slightly different fashion. How vehicle expenses are claimed depends on whether the corporation or its employee owns the car.

Company-owned vehicles. Corporations often buy cars and give employees—including shareholder-owners—use of them for both work and play. Records *must* be kept as to how much the car is used for each purpose. With the actual expense deduction method, all car costs are tax-deductible to the corporation, but any personal use of the car must be reported as taxable income to the employee. The amount of income is modest, however, compared to the real cost of owning a newer car. See a tax pro for an accurate determination of your tax consequences here or else wade through IRS Publication 917, Business Use of a Car.

Employee-owned vehicles. To get tax deductions, a corporation doesn't have to own the cars its employees drive. Alternatively, a shareholder/owner or other employee can buy a car and be reimbursed directly by the corporation for all expenses of using the car for business—gas, repairs and so on. Plus, the company can pay the car owner the amount of depreciation allowed in the tax code. (IRC § 168(b)(1).) This expense is deductible to the corporation, and the payment is not income to the employee.

EXAMPLE: Ralph's corporation reimburses him $3,812 for his actual cost of operating his personal car. It also gives him $1,675, the amount of the depreciation deduction allowed under the tax code for the value of Ralph's car. He gets a total of $5,487. (See Chapter 2, Writing Off Business Assets, for how this amount is determined.) Ralph uses his car 90% for business, so he must report 10% of the reimbursements, $548, as extra income from his corporation ($381 + $167 = $548).

The tax result would be the same if all of the car expenses were paid directly by the corporation instead of reimbursed to Ralph. For example, if Ralph used a company check or credit card to pay expenses, he would still be entitled to the corporation reimbursement for depreciation of the $1,675 without paying taxes on it.

d. Miscellaneous Auto and Commuting Expense Rules

You can also deduct a few other vehicle-related expenses.

State vehicle taxes. Any taxpayer—whether in business or not—who itemizes deductions on her income tax return (Schedule A) may deduct any state-imposed personal property taxes on autos. But parking fines and traffic tickets cannot be deducted; to do so would be against "public policy."

Commuting expenses. As noted, commuting expenses—getting to work and back home—are not deductible. Only if you make stops for business en route may you claim a portion of your commuting travel expense as a business expense.

Public transit and other commuter vehicles. Only incorporated businesses may deduct expenses for providing their employees transit passes, cash or vouchers for commuting—up to $65 per month per employee in 2001. This tax-free benefit must be offered to all employees using public transportation or a special "commuter vehicle." (Sorry, your family car probably won't qualify—and even if it does, a shareholder in the company can't be the driver.)

The monthly amount is subject to indexing for inflation. (See IRC § 132 for more details.)

Business-paid employee parking. Parking is tax-deductible for businesses and tax-free for employees, even if given only to some employees and not others. A business can either provide parking or reimburse an employee for parking tax-free, up to $180 per month (2001 figure). Anything more than $180 is taxable income to the employee. The benefit is subject to inflation indexing. If cash is given to those who don't pay to park, it is still deductible to the business, but is taxable to the employee. (IRC § 132.)

Vehicle loan interest. Interest paid on a car loan is deductible in proportion to the business use percentage. Otherwise, car loan interest is a nondeductible personal expense.

⚠ **Special capitalization rules for manufacturers and contractors.** Manufacturers, building contractors and agricultural producers are subject to tax deduction rules known as the "uniform capitalization rules." (IRC § 263A.) Under these provisions, certain costs you might otherwise think are current expenses must be treated as capitalized expenses and added to the tax basis of your product or inventory. In turn, these expenses figure into the "cost of goods sold" formula discussed in Chapter 2. These are complex accounting rules, so if you're in a business that might be subject to these rules, see a tax pro.

2. Costs of Going Into Business

All costs of getting a business started before you actually commence operations are not current expenses but are capital items—including advertising, travel, office supplies, utilities, repairs and employee wages. (IRC § 195.)

This can be a bit of a shock, since these are the costs that can be immediately deducted as expenses once you are open for business. Under the tax code, these start-up expenses must be deducted ratably over the first 60 months you are in business. Technically, the tax code calls these deductions "amortization" of expenses. (For sole proprietors, partners and limited liability company members, these deductions are claimed on IRS Form 4562, Depreciation and Amortization.)

EXAMPLE: Bill and Betty set up Management Consulting Partners (MCP). During the first three months of 2001, they locate and fix up office space (with the help of a handyman) and have brochures printed and mailed to prospective clients. MCP spends a total of $6,000, and on April 1st, it opens for business. Tax result: all of the pre-April costs are capital expenditures and as such are deductible at the rate of $100 per month over the first 60 months MCP is in business. Therefore, in 2001, $900 can be deducted for the nine months the business was open, $1,200 in 2002, and so on until 60 months elapse. Expenses incurred after the business is in operation—April's rent and most other recurring monthly costs—are 100% deductible in 2001.

You can work around this limitation. If it would tax benefit you to deduct start-up costs in the first year rather than pro rata over five years, then consider:

- delay paying pre-opening costs until you start serving customers. (Whether or not your suppliers and workers will allow you this much time to pay is another matter.) The IRS may challenge this tactic if you are audited, however.
- doing a trivial amount of business before you are officially open. That will probably be enough to satisfy an IRS auditor. Make a $75 sale to a friend or give a few people a bargain, just to get some activity on the books.

Before rushing to get take start-up cost deduction all in the first year, make sure it really helps. If, like many businesses, you have low gross receipts or even losses the first few years of operation, you might be better off taking this deduction over 60 months.

Costs of not going into business. What happens if, after incurring start-up expenses, you back out and never go into operation? Your costs may or may not be deductible, depending on the tax rules you fall under. The tax code (IRC § 195) divides expenses of trying, but failing, to establish a business into two categories:

- costs of investigating whether to start a business. Any expenses for a general search or preliminary investigation are *not* deductible.
- costs of attempting to acquire or start a specific business. These are classified as "investment" expenses. All investment expenses are itemized deductions on Schedule A of your individual income tax return. As such, they don't provide as much tax benefit as do "start-up" type expenses. They are not considered start-up expenses because you never went into any business.

3. Education Expenses

Education is a deductible business expense if it is related to your current business, trade or occupation. The tax code (IRC § 162, Reg. 1.162-5) requires that a deductible education expense must be either:

- to maintain or improve skills required in your (present) work, or
- required by your employer or as a legal requirement of your job or profession.

EXAMPLE: The State Contractor's Board requires Jim, a licensed building contractor, to attend 24 hours of continuing education as a condition of renewing his license. In this case, both IRC conditions are met, so the expense is deductible for Jim's business. Any additional educational expenses are also deductible if they qualify under the first rule above.

⚠️ **Education expenses that qualify you for a new job or different business are not deductible under the tax code.** This tax rule has been interpreted rather narrowly by the IRS and courts.

EXAMPLE: Mary, a public school teacher, wants to open up a small private school. Her state requires her to take several college courses before granting her a license. Mary can't deduct the cost of these courses, because they are for a new job or business, even though it's in a related field.

Also see Chapter 14, Section J, for a discussion of education "fringe benefits."

4. Legal and Other Professional Fees

Professional fees for attorneys, tax pros or consultants are deductible if you actually go into business. For instance, fees for forming the business—drawing up a partnership agreement or reviewing license requirements—are immediately deductible.

However, when professional fees clearly relate to future years, they must be deducted over the life of the benefit. Some fees, however, fall into a gray area, and you can choose between deducting them all in the first year or spreading them over future years.

EXAMPLE: Carlos and Teresa's attorney helps them negotiate and prepare a five-year lease for their restaurant. In this case, the lawyer's fees may be deducted either in the current year or in equal amounts over the lease's 60-month period. Carlos and Teresa should figure out which method gives them the best tax benefit. Taking

the expense all in the first year of operation may not be a good idea if they won't have sufficient income to offset it.

Tax assistance and tax return preparation fees are deductible. But again, it can get sticky. Folks usually want tax advice covering both their business and individual taxes, which in most cases are intertwined. You might ask a tax pro how to minimize taxes on income from all sources—your sole proprietorship, stock and real estate investments and your spouse's income. Tax result? The tax pro's fee is deductible in proportion to the business advice given or time spent to prepare the business tax schedule or return. The remaining portion, for tax advice on investments and spouse's income, can be deducted (but not as a business expense—as a personal itemized deduction on Schedule A of your return along with fees for tax preparation).

💡 **Separate bills for business and personal expenses.** When hiring a lawyer or a tax pro, ask that the bill clearly show the extent it relates to your business. The IRS rarely questions the apportionment used, so the advisor can be liberal in putting as much of the expense as possible to the business side.

5. Research and Experimentation Expenditures

Certain enterprises are entitled to a research tax credit equal to 20% of these expenses. A "credit" is more valuable than a deduction, as it comes straight off your tax bill. Very few businesses qualify, however. Check with a tax pro to see whether you can use this credit (chances are you won't qualify), and if it has been extended by Congress to the current year. (Form 6765 and Form 3800 are used to claim this credit.)

6. Business Bad Debts

If you are in business long enough, you will eventually be stiffed by a deadbeat. The resulting bad debt may or may not be a deductible expense. Read on. (IRC § 166, Reg. 1.166.)

⚠️ **If your operation offers services—consulting, medical, legal and so on—you cannot deduct an unpaid bill as a bad debt.** No tax deduction is allowed for *time* you devoted to the client or customer who doesn't pay. The tax code rationale is that if you could deduct the value of unpaid services, it would be too easy to inflate your bills and claim large bad debt deductions—and too hard for the IRS to catch you.

If your business provides goods, however, you can deduct your costs of any goods sold, but never paid for. You cannot deduct any lost profits you would have collected from the sale.

The same rules apply to cash. Say you made a loan to a customer and didn't get paid back. For a bad debt deduction (a) there must have been a business—not personal—reason for the loan, and (b) you must have taken reasonable steps to collect the debt—such as making a written demand for payment, going to court or turning the debt over to a collection agency.

> **EXAMPLE:** In 2000, Ralph and Rhonda's incorporated print shop made a $2,000 loan to Susan, a friend and good customer, to keep her florist business afloat. Despite this help, Susan went into bankruptcy in 2001. Result: As long as Ralph and Rhonda's corporation made the loan to protect their business relationship—and not just to help a friend—the bad debt is deductible for the corporation in 2001.

Nonbusiness bad debts. There are different tax rules for "nonbusiness" bad debts—ones that don't qualify under IRC § 166 discussed above. A bad debt in your personal life can still produce a tax benefit, but under restrictive short-term capital loss rules. Generally, a personal bad debt can be claimed only to offset any capital gains—plus up to another $3,000 in ordinary income. (See Chapter 4, Business Losses and Failures.)

To claim a nonbusiness bad debt deduction, file Schedule D, Capital Gains and Losses, with your tax return. Keep in mind that a loan to Uncle Festus won't fly if it was really a gift to get him into alcohol rehab and you never expected to get the money back. To make it legitimate, get a promissory note from Uncle Festus and make serious efforts to try to collect on it. Note: Auditors are suspicious whenever a child or other relative is the deadbeat you are trying to wangle into a tax deduction.

 A business or nonbusiness bad debt claimed on a tax return may increase your audit chances. Attach a statement to the return referring to the bad debt with the date it became due, the name and address of the debtor and your reason for determining it was worthless—the guy skipped town, died, declared bankruptcy or whatever. Of course, there is no free lunch; if in 2001 you collect the debt previously deducted as worthless, you must then report it as income in 2001.

Note: If your business uses the "accrual" accounting method, you have an alternative way to deduct bad debts. This is too technical to get into here, so see your tax pro or IRS Publication 535, Business Expenses.

7. Promotion and Business Entertaining

Picking up the tab for entertaining present or prospective customers, clients or employees makes the cost partially—but not wholly—deductible.

You may deduct 50% of a business entertainment expense if it satisfies one of two tax code tests. The entertainment must *either* be:

- "directly related" to the operation. Business must actually be discussed during the entertainment. For example, a catered meeting at your office would qualify, or
- "associated with" the business. The entertainment must take place prior to or immediately after a business discussion. No business has to be discussed while having fun. For example, a business meeting is followed by an evening out at a restaurant, play or sporting event.

Transportation to the entertainment event is fully deductible, and is not subject to the 50% limit.

Corporate entertainment expenses. With a C corporation (see Chapter 7), entertaining customers or clients, you can either personally pay the expenses and claim reimbursement, or the corporation can pay these expenses directly. Direct corporate payment is usually better. So use your company credit card and let the corporation pay the bill when it comes due.

If you are not reimbursed by the corporation, claim out of pocket expenses as "unreimbursed employee expenses" on your individual tax return. However, this is not only less advantageous tax-wise, it increases the chances of an audit of your personal return.

Employee parties. Holiday parties and picnics for employees and their families are recognized morale builders. These affairs are not subject to the regular entertainment rule and so are 100% deductible. Don't overdo it, though. Employee parties should be infrequent, and everyone at work must be invited. No business need be discussed to make the event deductible.

Home entertaining. You can get a deduction for home entertaining if you follow the rules. Guests must either be employees or have a business connection—that is, be a present or potential customer or client. If family or social friends are also present, their pro-rata share of party costs is not deductible. You are on the honor system here. If audited, it will help your cause to show you also threw (purely social) parties you did not claim as business expenses.

Business gifts. Gifts to clients and customers are deductible as long as the value does not exceed $25 per person per year. You can also deduct the cost of wrapping, mailing or even engraving the gift, so the real limit is slightly higher than $25. And items costing less than $4 on which your business name is imprinted aren't counted against the $25 limit.

Keep good records of business entertainment. If you have a business party, keep a written guest list, along with your explanation of the business connection or general nature of business discussed. This should satisfy most IRS auditors, unless the amount spent was outrageous. I have never heard of an auditor contacting guests to see whether or not business was really discussed or there was a business tie-in.

When Are Entertainment Expenses Deductible?

General Rule

You can deduct expenses to entertain a client, customer or employee if the expenses meet the "directly related" test or the "associated" test.

Definitions

- Entertainment includes any activity generally considered to provide amusement or recreation, and includes meals provided to a customer or client.
- The type of expense must be common and accepted in your field of business, trade or profession.
- The expense must be helpful and appropriate, although not necessarily indispensable, for your business.

Two tests

"Directly related" test

- Entertainment took place in a clear business setting such as your business premises, or if it didn't, the
- Main purpose of entertainment was the active conduct of business, and
  a. You actually did some business (such as, you talked business during lunch), and
  b. You had more than a general expectation of getting income or some other specific business benefit (such as, it was a long-time customer). However, you don't have to prove that income actually resulted from the entertainment.

"Associated" test

- Entertainment is associated with your trade or business, and
- Entertainment directly precedes or follows a substantial business discussion.

Other rules

- You can deduct expenses only to the extent that they are not lavish or extravagant under the circumstances.
- You generally can deduct only 50% of your business entertainment expenses.
- If your client brings along a spouse, you can bring yours, too, and deduct the cost as an entertainment expense.

8. Business Travel

Pure business travel expenses are tax-deductible if they are "ordinary" and "necessary" for your business. Below is a summary of the rules. Also see Chapter 14, Fringe Benefits, for the rules on combining business and pleasure travel.

Deductible Travel Expenses

Transportation. The cost of travel by airplane, train or bus between your home and your out-of-town business destination (but not commuting to your place of business from home).

Taxi, Commuter Bus and Limousine. Fares for these and other types of transportation between the airport or station and your hotel, or between the hotel and your work location away from home.

Baggage and Shipping. The cost of sending baggage and sample or display material between your regular and temporary work locations.

Car. The costs of operating and maintaining your car when traveling away from home on business. You may deduct actual expenses or the standard mileage rate, including business-related tolls and parking. If you lease a car while away from home on business, you can deduct business-related expenses only.

Lodging. The cost of lodging if your business trip is overnight or long enough to require you to get substantial sleep or rest to properly perform your duties.

Meals. The cost of meals only if your business trip is overnight or long enough to require you to stop to get substantial sleep or rest. Includes amounts spent for food, beverages, taxes and related tips.

Cleaning. Cleaning and laundry expenses while away from home overnight.

Telephone. The cost of business calls while on your business trip, including business communication by fax machine or other communication devices.

Tips. Tips you pay for any expenses listed in this chart.

Other. Other similar ordinary and necessary expenses related to your business travel, such as public stenographer's fees and computer rental fees.

9. Sick Pay

Disability and sick pay to employees (but not to business owners) are deductible business expenses—if they are for health-related work absences under a written "wage continuation plan." The plan doesn't have to be in any particular legal form; any document setting out conditions of sick pay benefits qualifies. Sick or disability pay is fully taxable income to the recipient, just like wages. (IRC § 104, Reg. 1.104-1.)

10. Interest

If, like many folks, you use credit for business purchases, the interest and carrying charges are fully tax-deductible. Ditto if you use the proceeds of a personal loan for your business. In case the IRS comes calling, keep good records showing that the money borrowed went into your enterprise. Otherwise, the interest is a nondeductible personal expense. And if you pay interest for a part-business and part-personal item (such as a car loan for a dual-purpose vehicle), you must pro-rate the interest expense between the two uses.

Mortgage loans. If you own your house and can borrow against it to finance your business, go for it. Mortgage loans always carry lower rates of interest than personal or business loans, longer periods to repay and are usually tax deductible. Check with your tax pro for details.

11. Moving Expenses

You may be able to deduct certain household moving costs that would otherwise be nondeductible personal living expenses. To qualify, you must have moved in connection with your business (or job, if you are an employee of your corporation or someone else's enterprise). The new workplace must be at least 50 miles farther from your old home than your old home was from your old workplace. If you had no former workplace, the new one must be at least 50 miles from your old home.

Technically, moving costs are not business expenses, and so aren't claimed on Schedule C (sole proprietors) or other business entity tax reporting forms. Instead, use Form 3903, Moving Expenses, to claim the deduction, and attach it to your personal 1040 income tax form. The moving expense is taken as a deduction on the first page of Form 1040, line 24. (See IRS Publication 521, Moving Expenses, for details.)

12. Computer Software

As a general rule, software purchased for business must be written off over a 36-month period. But there are three important exceptions:

- When the software is acquired with the computer (and its cost is not separately stated), the software is treated as part of the computer hardware. This means its cost is deducted by taking depreciation over the five-year recovery period for computers and peripherals.
- If you elect it, and all of your equipment purchases are less than $24,000 (2001 figure) for the year, the whole system, including "bundled software," can qualify for a first-year write-off under IRC § 179. (See Chapter 2, Writing Off Business Assets.)
- Software with a useful life of less than one year may be deducted as a business expense in the year purchased. Arguably, with the rapid changes in technology, most software programs are only good for a year or so.

13. Charitable Contributions

A business can't claim a charitable deduction (unless your business is a C corporation). Instead, you must deduct charitable contributions by the business on Schedule A of your personal tax return. Likewise, if you own an S corporation, partnership or LLC, charitable contributions pass through to you to claim on your individual return. (The contribution is shown on the K-1 form that each shareholder or partner receives from the business each year.) Add the business-reported deduction to the rest of your charitable deductions and claim it on Schedule A of Form 1040. (Note: There is an overall charitable deduction limit for individuals of 50% of your adjusted gross income.)

Maximize your charitable deductions by donating business-used items. Giving old computers or office furniture to a school or local nonprofit organization may yield a tax benefit. If, however, you have fully depreciated or used IRC § 179 in the past to write off the item, you can't double-dip—that is, deduct again for something you already wrote off. But if that computer still has some unused depreciation, you may get a deduction for its value, but not greater than its tax basis (the remaining portion of depreciation that hasn't been claimed).

EXAMPLE: Belinda buys a new nailgun for her drywall contracting business and donates her old one to a nonprofit organization. She paid $2,000 for the equipment and has claimed a total of $1,000 in depreciation in the past three years. Unless Belinda is operating as a C corporation, she may claim a $1,000 charitable deduction if the donated equipment is still worth at least $1,000. She cannot claim a deduction of more than $1,000 for it even if that is its fair market value, however, because that exceeds its $1,000 tax basis.

Donating services to charity. You may never deduct the value of your services that you provide free of charge to a charitable organization— whether you're a plumber, doctor or baker. However, you can deduct any out-of-pocket expenses you incur, such as pipe fittings, prescription drugs or flour.

14. Taxes

Various taxes incurred in operating your business are generally deductible. How and when to deduct these taxes in your business depends on the type of tax. Here are a few of the most common.

Sales tax on items purchased for your day-to-day operation is deductible as part of the cost of the items. It is not deducted separately as "taxes." On the other hand, sales tax (or federal luxury tax) on a business asset—such as a truck—must be added to the vehicle's cost basis. This means the sales tax is not all totally deductible in the year the truck was purchased. (See Chapter 2, Writing Off Business Assets.)

Sales taxes that you collect as a merchant and pay over to the state are not deductible (unless you included them in your business's gross receipts).

Excise and fuel taxes paid by qualifying businesses are deductible as separately stated tax expenses.

Employment taxes (FICA) paid by your business on its employees are partially deductible. The employer's one-half share is deductible as a business expense.

Self-employment (SE) **tax** isn't a business-claimed expense. However, the owner can deduct one-half of the SE tax on the front page of her Form 1040 tax return.

Federal income tax paid on your business's income is never deductible.

State income tax can be deducted on your personal federal tax return as an itemized deduction on Schedule A, but is never a business expense.

Real estate tax on business-used property is fully deductible, along with any special local property assessments. However, if the assessment is for improvements (for example, a sewer or sidewalk), it is not immediately deductible; instead, the cost is added to the basis of the property and deducted (amortized) over a period of years. (See Chapter 2.) Real estate tax for nonbusiness property, such as your home, is deductible too but as an itemized deduction on Schedule A of your personal tax return.

Penalties and fines paid to the IRS and any other governmental agencies are never tax-deductible, because this is deemed to be against public policy. Sorry, this includes parking tickets, too.

15. Advertising and Promotion

Advertising your goods or services—business cards, Yellow Page ads and so on—is deductible as a current expense.

Promotional costs that create business goodwill—for example, sponsoring a Peewee football team—are also deductible as long as there is a clear connection between the sponsorship and your business. For example, naming the team the "Southwest Auto Parts Blues" or listing the business name in the program is evidence of the promotion effort. A contest prize given to a customer qualifies as a promotional expense, but not if an employee wins it.

Any cost that is primarily personal is not deductible. For example, you can't deduct the cost of inviting customers or clients to your son's wedding. Also not deductible are costs of lobbying a politico (with a few limited exceptions).

⚠ **The cost of advertising signs, if they have a useful life of over one year, cannot be deducted in one year.** Instead, they must be capitalized, and depreciation deductions taken over seven years.

16. Repairs and Improvements

Upkeep and improvements to your business assets are tax-deductible. However, sometimes an expenditure to keep a business asset maintained can be deducted immediately, and other times it has to be depreciated (taken as a deduction over a period of future years). This is discussed in Chapter 2.

💡 **There are special real estate related deduction breaks for rehabilitating older buildings, improvements for the elderly and disabled and for removing architectural or transportation barriers.** If you can fit into one of these special provisions, you can deduct an improvement sooner than by capitalizing it, or maybe even get a tax credit. However, most small businesses' expenditures don't qualify, so we can't get into details here. Check with a tax pro, or look at the instructions accompanying IRS forms 3800, General

Business Credit; 3468, Investment Tax Credit; and 8826, Disabled Access Credit.

17. Health and Other Fringe Benefits

See Chapter 14, Fringe Benefits, Section H, for the tricky rules of deductibility of health costs for owners and employees of a business.

F. How and Where to Claim Deductions

Although the tax deductibility rules for business expenses are consistent, *how* and *where* you claim the expenses on a tax return often depends on your entity form. The basics are as follows.

Sole proprietors (remember, this includes independent contractors, consultants and freelancers who don't operate through a separate business entity) and *statutory employees* report business expenses on Schedule C of their individual income tax returns (Form 1040). In the eyes of the tax code, a sole proprietor and his business are one and the same. (See Chapter 6.)

S corporations (Form 1120S)**, partnerships and limited liability companies** (Form 1065) file their own returns showing expense deductions. In turn, these entities issue Form K-1s to their owners showing how much profit or loss is reportable by each individual. This amount is reported on Schedule E of their Form 1040s. So, with a few exceptions (called "separately stated" items, discussed in Chapters 8 and 9), an S corporation shareholder, partner or limited liability owner's tax returns won't list any of their business's expenses.

Non-owner employees of businesses who incur out-of-pocket business expenses which are not reimbursed to them can also deduct them, but only under the restrictive "unreimbursed employee expense" rules on Schedule A of their Form 1040s. Tax-wise, a business should always either fully reimburse its employees for their expenses or should pay those expenses directly.

And as mentioned above in Section E, some things, such as business charitable contributions and personal moving expenses for business reasons, are not technically business expenses under the tax code. However, they may be claimed on Schedule A of the business owner's personal tax return, Form 1040.

G. General Business Credit

The general business credit is a dollar-for-dollar credit against income tax, which unfortunately can be taken by a relatively few small business owners. Since so few qualify, we don't go into much detail here, but alert you to the possibilities. If anything below sounds as if it might affect you, check it out on the IRS website, at your local IRS office or with your tax pro.

A taxpayer's general business credit is the sum of the following individual credits:

- investment credit, which is composed of the rehabilitation property, energy and reforestation credits (see Section E16, above and Form 3468)
- welfare-to-work credit for wages paid to long-term family assistance recipients
- low income housing credit (Form 8586)
- alcohol fuels credit
- research (see Section E5 above)
- disabled access
- renewable resources electricity production
- American Indian employment
- contributions to certain community development corporations, and
- work opportunity credit (Form 5884).

There are also a few other really esoteric items, not mentioned above.

To claim any of these credits, file Form 3800, General Business Credit, along with the forms listed above and your annual income tax return. None of these credits are "refundable," meaning that they can't be used to claim a tax refund, only to reduce a tax liability.

Commonly Overlooked Business Expenses

Despite the fact that most people keep a sharp eye out for deductible expenses, it's not uncommon to miss a few. And some folks don't list a deduction because they can't find what category it fits into. Some overlooked routine deductions include:

- advertising giveaways and promotions
- audio- and videotapes related to business skills
- bank service charges
- business association dues
- business gifts
- business-related magazines and books (like the one in your hand)
- casual labor and tips
- casualty and theft losses
- coffee and beverage service
- commissions
- consultant fees
- credit bureau fees
- education to improve business skills
- office supplies
- online computer services related to business
- parking and meters
- petty cash funds
- postage
- promotion and publicity
- seminars and trade shows
- taxi and bus fare, and
- telephone calls away from the business.

 Just because you didn't get a receipt doesn't mean you can't deduct the expense. Keep track of those small items and get big tax savings. Generally, business expenses of less than $75 do not require receipts to be claimed on a tax return.

Resources

- IRS Publication 463, Travel, Entertainment, Gift and Car Expenses. This 50 page booklet is a must-read if you are doing your own tax preparation and need more details than we can provide here.
- IRS Publication 525, Taxable and Nontaxable Income
- IRS Publication 529, Miscellaneous Deductions
- IRS Publication 535, Business Expenses
- *Master Tax Guide* (Commerce Clearing House). A one-volume tax reference book with a lot of tax deduction materials for individuals and small business owners. Many IRS auditors use this book for quick answers to tax questions, too.

- *Small-Time Operator,* by Bernard Kamoroff (Bell Springs). A good small business guidebook, written by a CPA, that has tips on maximizing deductions.
- Small Business Development Centers have small business tax publications and personal counseling available. Contact a federal Small Business Administration office or the nearest large university to find an SBDC near you.
- Ferro, Willett & Thompson offers an inexpensive "non-computer," all paper Small Business Recordkeeping System by mail (406-245-6262).

2

Writing Off Business Assets

"Of all debts, men are least willing to pay the taxes."
—Ralph Waldo Emerson

As a business person, one of the few joys of spending money on a new computer, photocopier or even that great rosewood desk is knowing that the government is paying part of the cost—maybe as much as 50%. Just how much tax benefit you get from acquiring assets depends on your business's earnings and your tax bracket. The more you make, the more your asset purchases are subsidized by Uncle Sam.

Equipment, buildings or other "fixed assets" can't be deducted as ordinary business expenses (see Chapter 1). Instead, you must "capitalize" these asset costs. (IRC § 263.) With one important exception, this means you must spread these expenditures by taking tax deductions (in tax lingo, "depreciate") over a number of years. You recover the costs for these assets as tax benefits as they wear out in future years. (IRC §§ 167 and 168.) Just how many future years depends upon which category of the tax code the particular asset falls into—it may be as few as three or as many as 39 years.

 Important exception to the rule that capital expenditures must be depreciated or recovered over a number of years. Section 179 of the tax code lets you write off or depreciate, immediately, up to $24,000 of most capital expenditures (2001). Read on for more information.

This chapter explains how to best use both IRC § 179 and regular tax code depreciation rules to lower your tax bill. Let's find out how.

Writing Off Business Assets in a Nutshell

1. The tax code divides expenditures for business into "current expenses" and "capital items," and treats each type differently.
2. Capital expenditures for business assets must be deducted over a number of years under regular tax code depreciation rules.
3. A special tax code provision, IRC § 179, allows most business owners to tax-deduct up to $24,000 or more of capital expenditures as if they were current expenses.
4. Typically, assets are tax-deducted using one of two methods, called "accelerated" and "straight-line" depreciation. No matter which method is used, the entire cost of the asset may be written off over a number of years.
5. There are several ways to tax-deduct the business-use portion of an automobile.

A. Some Expenditures Must Be Capitalized

All business expenditures must first be divided up into two categories, called "current expenses" and "capitalized" costs.

Generally, costs of things used up *within a year* are current expenses. These include ordinary operating costs of a business such as rent, equipment repair, telephone and utility bills for the current year. Garden-variety supplies, such as stationery and postage stamps, are also considered expenses even though they may be around from one year to the next. These items can be fully deducted in the tax year they are purchased. (See Chapter 1, Business Income and Tax-Deductible Expenses.)

Capitalized costs, on the other hand, are usually for things the tax code says have a useful life of *more than one year*—equipment, vehicles and buildings are the most common examples. (See Section 3, below, on inventory.) A capital cost may be either to acquire an asset, or to improve one so as to substantially prolong its life or adapt it to a different use. (Chapter 1 explains how to determine whether an expenditure should be categorized as a current expense or capital cost.)

No matter the size and scale of the business, all capital items come under the heading of "business assets." And while almost all provide tax write-offs for a business owner, not all capital expenditures are treated equally by the tax code, as we shall see.

Business Assets That Must Be Capitalized

Buildings
Cellular phones and beepers*
Computer components and software*
Copyrights and patents
Equipment*
Improvements to business property
Inventory
Office furnishings and decorations*
Small tools and equipment*
Vehicles
Window coverings*

(See IRC § 263 and Reg. 1.263 for details about items that must be capitalized.)

[*May be subject to immediate deduction under IRC § 179 at your option. See Section B.]

---

1. Types of Property (Assets)

Almost any kind of property, from a building or a car, can qualify for a tax write-off if it is used in a business.

The tax code categorizes assets as "tangible" or "intangible," and "real" or "personal." These distinctions are important because they dictate how you must calculate and deduct asset costs and how fast you can deduct them from your business income.

Tangible items of property are things that can be touched—for example, warehouses, machines, desks, trucks, vans and tools. The vast majority of property is tangible. *Intangible* property refers to things like trademarks, royalties, franchise rights or business goodwill.

Our legal system divides the world of property into two broad kinds: real and personal property. *Real* property is land and anything permanently attached to it, called "improvements," such as fences, parking lots, buildings and even trees. Everything else in the universe is called *personal* property, such as furniture, equipment, patent rights, cars and paper clips.

These two divisions are recognized in our tax law. The tax code dictates much longer periods to write off real property than personal property. This makes sense. Real property improvements—structures—wear out more slowly than personal property, such as cars and computers. Land itself is considered to never wear out, and so is nondeductible.

2. Tax Basis of Assets

Tax basis, or just plain *basis*, is the amount the tax code says you have invested in an asset—which may be quite a different figure than you think.

Your basis in an asset determines how much you can deduct each year when you write off a business asset. Basis is also used to determine your taxable gain or loss when you sell or dispose of the asset.

IRS Publication 551, Basis of Assets, is a 12-page summary of the law if you want details on basis beyond the summary that follows.

a. Basis of Property Purchase

As a general rule, the beginning tax basis of an item of property is its original cost to you. (IRC § 1012.) So, if Billie Bob pays $3,000 for a dry cleaning machine for his store, Clean World, that's his beginning basis for tax purposes. Related costs, such as $200 for freight to get it to Clean World and $150 for installation by Joe, are added to the beginning basis, making it $3,350.

Basis also includes state and local taxes. Any state or local sales-type taxes paid on assets are deductible along with the item itself. Sales taxes become part of the basis of the asset. A sales tax cannot be completely written off in the year the item was bought (unless it qualifies for IRC § 179 treatment; see Section B, below). For instance, an 8% state sales tax on a truck bought for $10,000 ($800) must be added to its cost ($10,800) and written off over the period the truck is depreciated, usually five years. (See Section C, below.)

b. Basis of Property You Receive As a Gift

If you receive property as a gift, you take the same tax basis as the person who gave it to you had. This is termed a "transferred" basis. (IRC § 1015.)

> **EXAMPLE:** Ralph's father, Josiah, gives him a building worth $60,000. Josiah's tax basis in the property was $15,000; Ralph has a transferred basis the same as his father's—$15,000. So if Ralph immediately sells the building for its fair market value of $60,000, he will owe tax on a $45,000 gain (the sales price, $60,000, less his tax basis, $15,000).

c. Basis of Property You Receive for Services

If you receive property in exchange for your services, your basis in the property is its fair market value. (IRC § 7701.) The value of the property is considered barter income to you and is taxable in the year you receive it. If the property is then used in your business, it may be tax deducted under the depreciation rules for the type of asset it is.

> **EXAMPLE:** In 1998, Woody refinished four antique chests for Zeke; in exchange, he received one of them. Because it could be sold for $250, that was its fair market value, and became Woody's tax basis in the chest. He should have reported $250 as income on his 1998 tax return. When Woody sells the chest for $350 in 2001, he has a further taxable gain of $100 (less any costs of making the sale, such as a newspaper classified ad).

d. Basis of Property You Inherit

If you inherit property and subsequently use it in your business, the tax basis of the property is its fair market value on the date of death of the person who left it to you. (IRC § 1014.)

> **EXAMPLE:** Beth dies and leaves a warehouse to her son, Charles. She bought the property in 1970 for $50,000, and it was worth $200,000 on the real estate market when Beth died. Charles, who has an insurance agency, can't use the warehouse, but needs a small office building for his business. If Charles sells the warehouse for $200,000, he has no taxable gain or loss, because $200,000 was his tax basis. Charles can then buy a new building with the proceeds and begin taking depreciation deductions as soon as he starts using it for his insurance business.

It's not always wise to give away appreciated property during your lifetime. If you leave appreciated property in your estate, instead of giving it away before you die, the tax basis rules can help reduce the recipient's tax bite. For more information on estate planning and making gifts during your lifetime, see *Plan Your Estate*, by Denis Clifford and Cora Jordan (Nolo).

Sales of Business Equipment

There is a special top rate of 20% for long-term capital gains. This means if you own a capital asset for longer than 12 months and sell it at a gain, the gain will not be taxed higher than 20%. If your ordinary income tax rate is lower than 20%, the gain will be taxed at the lower rate. However, gains on most property used in a trade or business are treated differently; they are taxed as ordinary income when sold to the extent that the gain represents recapture of depreciation deductions taken in prior years. Any excess is treated as a capital gain. (IRC § 1231.)

e. Basis of Property You Receive In Exchange for Other Property

If you trade an asset for something else, the new asset's basis is usually the same as the property you traded. This is called "substituted" basis.

EXAMPLE: Janet, a cabinet maker, trades a table saw with a tax basis to her of $250 to Boffo for his industrial shop vac. Her basis in the shop vac is $250.

However, the tax code doesn't allow substituted basis treatment for all types of property exchanges. To be nontaxable, the trade must be for a "like kind" property. For instance, if you give real estate, you must receive real estate. And if you trade tangible property (such as Janet's table saw, above), you can't get intangible property, such as a copyright, in return. The tax code says this is a sale of the table saw (normally resulting in a taxable profit or loss), followed by the purchase of the copyright, and not a tax-free exchange.

f. Basis of Property Exchanged With Money

If you trade property and throw in money to boot, your basis in the property received equals the basis of the asset you exchanged, plus the amount you paid in cash—called, appropriately enough, "boot" in tax lingo.

EXAMPLE: Kevin trades his old Ford pickup (tax basis of $3,000) and $10,000 cash to Truck City for a new Chevy. Kevin's basis in the new truck is $13,000.

Conversely, if you get an asset plus money, your basis in the item is reduced by the cash.

g. Basis of Property You Convert to Business Use

When converting personal, nonbusiness property to business use, you must determine its basis at the time you make the switch. The tax basis of converted property is the lesser of:

- the fair market value of the property on the date it is converted to business use, *or*
- your adjusted basis in that property. (IRC § 167.)

EXAMPLE 1: Jacob bought that $3,500 computer a year ago for fun and games, but now starts using it in his consulting business. The tax basis of the computer is the lesser of Jacob's cost or its current fair market value. Since the computer has undoubtedly lost value, Jacob finds it is now worth $2,000, which becomes its tax basis as a business asset.

EXAMPLE 2: Theresa pays $60,000 to a contractor to have a home built on a lot she bought for $10,000. She lives in the home several years and spends $20,000 for improvements, and one year claims a $2,000 tax deduction for a casualty loss when a runaway car hits her living room. Over time, Theresa's neighborhood becomes a commercial area. The building has a fair market value of $125,000. Theresa moves out and converts the house into a health food store. The tax basis of the building is computed for the business as follows:

	$60,000	cost of building
+	20,000	improvements
-	2,000	deductions taken in prior years
=	$78,000	tax basis

(The $10,000 cost of the land is not part of the basis of the building, and as land it is never depreciable under the tax code.)

Note that Theresa must use the $78,000 tax basis because it is less than the fair market value of $125,000.

EXAMPLE 3: Following along with Theresa, if the building's fair market value had decreased to $50,000 at the time of the conversion, Theresa's basis would have decreased to $50,000 as well. That's because she must use the fair market value as her basis whenever it is lower than her cost. (IRC § 167, Reg. 1.167.)

3. Inventories

Businesses selling goods (rather than services) usually maintain stock, called "inventory." Money spent for goods to sell is not a current business expense. Instead, inventory is considered a business asset and its cost is expensed as it is sold—or discarded.

You must value your "cost of goods sold" using an IRS-approved inventory accounting method. In effect, what you spend for inventory is deducted, as it is sold, from the revenue it generates, to come up with your gross profit. From this figure, your general business expenses are deducted to determine your net profit. It is the net profit that is taxed.

Tax rule. Inventory generally must be listed at the lower of cost or market value.

EXAMPLE: At the end of its first year of operation, Rick's Music Store has an inventory of compact discs that cost him $50,000, and vinyl LP records that cost $30,000. Using the "cost method," Rick has an ending inventory worth $80,000. Here is Rick's cost of goods sold deduction:

	$0	beginning inventory
+	$300,000	purchases
-	$80,000	ending inventory at cost
=	$220,000	cost of goods sold

You may reduce ("write-down") the value of any inventory that has become unsalable. For tax purposes, this needs to be documented. For instance, if you write-down and destroy dead stock, keep evidence of the destruction—photos, videos, receipts or the statement of a reputable third party who can certify the goods were destroyed.

EXAMPLE: At inventory time, Rick knows his inventory of CDs has held its value, but his LP records hardly sell any more. Rick asks a prominent music distributor to appraise the LP inventory and gets a written statement saying the market value is only $8,000. Accordingly, Rick reduces retail prices for the LPs and lowers the inventory on his books by $22,000. Now Rick's cost of goods sold deduction for tax reporting looks like this:

	$0	beginning inventory
+	$300,000	purchases
-	$58,000	ending inventory
=	$242,000	cost of goods sold

The difference between the two examples is the method of valuing the inventory. Using fair market value instead of cost reduces Rick's income for tax purposes by $22,000. It is improper to reduce the book value of the inventory without some evidence of the loss in value and without reducing the retail price of the goods. With the taxes saved from the inventory write-down, Rick can build up his CD inventory or do anything he wants to with the extra money in his pocket.

B. Expensing Business Assets: IRC Section 179

Small business owners don't need to learn the Internal Revenue Code by section number, but know at least one: IRC § 179 allows—but doesn't require—a business owner or C corporation to deduct up to $24,000 (in 2001) of asset purchases each year as current operating expenses. This produces an immediate write-off of capital assets.

Using § 179 is referred to as "expensing an asset," as opposed to capitalizing it under normal tax code rules. Within the $24,000 limit, a business may buy assets and deduct the costs in full—as long as they are "placed in service" in that same year. I once bought, set up and started using a new computer on December 31, for $3,000, and wrote it off completely that year.

EXAMPLE: Hal, a self-employed consultant, buys a computer for $5,000 in early 2001. Hal plans on using IRC § 179 to write off the computer. Hal's business is very profitable and later in the year, while estimating how much he is going to owe in taxes for 2001, Hal finds he will owe $4,000 more than the estimated quarterly tax payments he has made. Hal was planning to buy a $12,000 color printer in 2002. If, instead of waiting, Hal purchases and starts using the printer before December 31, 2001, he qualifies under § 179 to write off a total of $17,000 in 2001 and wipe out most or all of his 2001 tax balance.

It works out like this: Hal is in approximately a 30% combined federal and state income tax bracket and pays self-employment taxes of 15.3%. This means that for Hal's tax bracket every business deduction dollar saves him roughly 45¢ in taxes. So the total tax savings resulting from the $12,000 printer purchase in 2001 wipes out Hal's projected $4,000 tax balance. Of course, Hal had to spend $12,000 to get the tax savings. But Hal would still get the deduction even if he purchased the machine on credit and paid in later years. As long as he needs the printer, this is still the next best thing to a free lunch.

Think twice about taking a § 179 deduction. When would you not want the fast deduction of IRC § 179? Answer: When you don't get much, if any immediate tax benefit from it. For instance, say your business is new and you don't have enough business income to offset the § 179 deduction, but you expect big things in a year or two. In that case, choosing regular depreciation (discussed in Section C, below) and spreading the deduction over future years makes more tax sense.

EXAMPLE: Hal's advertising agency loses money in 2001 when a major account doesn't pay him and then declares bankruptcy after Hal buys a $5,000 computer. The tax code prescribes a five-year depreciation period for computers. Hal doesn't have any outside income, so spreading the deduction over five years makes more sense than writing off the whole cost under IRC § 179 in 2001.

A few other tax code sections let you choose whether to expense all assets similar to IRC § 179 or capitalize certain assets. These special provisions don't affect small businesses except for research (IRC § 174), agriculture (IRC §§ 175, 180 and 193), publishing (IRC § 173) or mining (IRC §§ 615 and 616). (See IRC § 263 and Reg. 1.263 or a tax pro for details.)

Increasing § 179 Deductions

The annual limit on expensing of business assets under IRC § 179 is scheduled to increase as follows:

2001 and 2002:	$24,000
2003 and thereafter:	$25,000

1. When You Can't Use Section 179

For some types of property, and in some circumstances, you can't use IRC § 179's quick write-off. Ineligible property includes:

- real estate
- inventory bought for resale to customers (discussed above)
- property received by gift or inheritance
- property bought from a close relative—grandparent, parent, child, sibling or equivalent in-law—or from another business in which you have an ownership interest, or
- property you already own. It can't be converted from personal to business use under Section 179; instead, it must be depreciated, as explained in Section C, below.

2. Listed Property— Special IRC Section 179 Rules

Using IRC § 179 to write off things designated in the tax code as "listed" property entails special rules. Three typical business assets are termed *listed property*:

- vehicles used wholly or partly for business
- cellular phones, and
- computers and peripherals.

Special rules. Listed property qualifies for IRC § 179 only if it is used 50% or more of the time for business, both in the year acquired and years thereafter.

Typically, listed property items have a potential for personal as well as business usage. And remember, Congress frowns on you deducting personal expenses against your business income. So the IRS enforces strict recordkeeping rules for listed property if also used for personal purposes. (See Chapter 3, Record-keeping and Accounting, Section D, for how to keep such records.)

> **EXAMPLE:** Joan paid $3,000 for a computer in 2001 and uses it 60% of the time for business. She can write off $1,800 as a business expense in 2001 (60% business usage x $3,000 cost) using IRC § 179. But if Joan used it only 45% of the time for business, she could not use IRC § 179. Instead, Joan would have to take depreciation deductions for the business portion ($1,350) over the five-year period the tax code prescribes for computers.

Autos used for business are subject to a different limitation under IRC § 179. The deduction for vehicle depreciation under IRC § 179 is currently limited to $3,060 in the year of purchase—even if the business usage is 100%. For passenger cars costing over $15,300 there is no advantage to choosing IRC § 179 because the $3,060 limit is the same as with regular depreciation rules. (See Section D, below.) There is a clear disadvantage to using § 179 in this instance because it wastes the § 179 deduction that could be used for other business asset purchases.

For heavy vehicles, such as delivery trucks, vans and SUVs, exceeding 6,000 lbs. gross weight, the depreciation limits don't apply; so using § 179 might pay tax dividends.

3. Items Bought on Credit and IRC Section 179

An asset can be bought on credit—that is, not be fully paid for—and still produce a full tax write-off under IRC § 179. This means you can buy on credit and get a tax deduction in that year larger than your cash outlay!

> **EXAMPLE:** With $10,000 down, Jack buys and starts using $34,000 worth of machinery for his tool and die shop. The balance of $20,000 is to be paid over the next five years. Jack is nevertheless allowed to deduct up to $24,000 in the year of purchase (2001), using IRC § 179. Jack can then claim depreciation deductions on the balance of $10,000 in subsequent years. (See Section C, below.) Jack cannot, however, carry over the $10,000 excess and use IRC § 179 to write it off in 2002. (Also, Jack can take a deduction for any interest paid on the unpaid balance of the note each year.)

4. Other Limitations on Using Section 179

Assuming you qualify under all the rules discussed above, there are some tax limitations on using IRC § 179. Does this start to remind you of circumnavigating a maze?

a. Income Limit and Carryforward

Your deduction using IRC § 179 can't exceed your total taxable earnings. However, the earnings don't have to be just from the business for which the asset was purchased. You may also count wages earned as an employee somewhere else. For instance, if

Sonja's part-time parrot training enterprise loses money, she can still use IRC § 179 to offset some of her day job earnings as an undertaker.

If your IRC § 179 expenditures exceed your total earned income from all sources, you can carry the excess over to future years' tax returns. You can then claim the unused portion as long as the total in any one year is $24,000 (2001) or less.

> **EXAMPLE:** Joy is a sole proprietor who establishes an acting school in 2001. After deducting all operating expenses, her earned income is $6,000. Joy buys $15,000 worth of furnishings and stage props in 2001, paying for them from her savings. Result: Joy can deduct at least $6,000 of the costs using IRC § 179. If Joy earned an additional $9,000 in 2001 from managing a health food store, she could deduct the whole $15,000. Otherwise Joy can carry the $9,000 unused excess deduction over to her 2002 tax return and claim it along with any other IRC § 179 expenses—as long as she has enough income in 2002.

b. Limits on Married Couples

Being married works against you when it comes to IRC § 179. A married couple is limited to an annual total write-off of $24,000 (2001). This is true even if both have separate businesses and whether they file tax returns jointly or separately. If they file separately, each is limited to $12,000 in IRC § 179 deductions. This is another example of "marriage penalties" built into the tax code. Congress is presently considering rectifying this inequity.

c. Spending Too Much

IRC § 179 is really just for *small* businesses. You cannot take any IRC § 179 write-off if your business spends $219,000 (2001) or more per year. You can still take normal long-term depreciation deductions. (See Section C, below.)

d. More Than One Owner

Partners, limited liability company members or shareholders in an S corporation can use IRC § 179 in proportion to their ownership share. The $24,000 limit applies to the business as a whole. So if a four person operation buys $30,000 of qualified IRC § 179 equipment, each owner can claim only one-fourth ($6000) of the $24,000 (2001) deduction on his or her individual tax return.

There are other limitations for multiple owners:
- owners who are married to each other, as discussed above, and
- with C corporations, only the corporation (and not the shareholders) can take the IRC § 179 deduction.

e. Not for Passive Investors

Owners may use IRC § 179 if they are *active* in the business. They can't use it if they are passive investors, unless they are employed or active in some other business.

> **EXAMPLE 1:** W & W Partnership buys a $16,000 injection molding machine for manufacturing plastic toys. The partnership allocates $8,000 of the IRC § 179 deduction to each of the two partners, Wanda and Willie. Since they are both active in the business and earn at least $8,000, each can write off $8,000 against earned income.

> **EXAMPLE 2:** Willie becomes disabled. He is still a partner in W & W, but gets no income from the partnership. Instead, he lives on his Social Security and monthly payments from the state lottery. He can't take an IRC § 179 deduction of any amount.

> **EXAMPLE 3:** Willie takes an outside job as a part-time toy designer for ToyCo and earns $12,000. He can take his share of the § 179 deduction of $8,000 from the W & W Partnership.

f. Minimum Period of Business Use

You must use equipment written off under IRC § 179 in your business for *at least* the period over which it should have been depreciated. Also, remember, the asset must be used for business purposes at least 50% of all of that time.

If you don't meet these two rules, you face "recapture"—meaning you must report as income an IRC § 179 deduction taken in a prior year. You don't report the entire deduction, just the portion that would remain if you had depreciated the equipment instead of using § 179. Perhaps an example is in order.

> **EXAMPLE:** In 2001, Hal used IRC § 179 to write off a $4,000 computer for his business. On January 1, 2002, he got a new computer and took the year-old computer home for video games. Hal must report recapture income of $3,600 in 2001. The amount of depreciation deduction Hal would have gotten had he not used IRC § 179 in 2001 is $400. So he must "give back" $3,600 of the deduction on his 2001 tax return.

IRS auditors usually look at your purchase contracts and proofs of payment, but they rarely check whether or not equipment is currently being used for business. Let your conscience be your guide.

g. Trade-In Limitation

The Section 179 deduction is reduced by any trade-in allowance toward the new asset purchase.

> **EXAMPLE:** Sacajawea buys new showcases for her Indian crafts store in 2001. The total cost is $24,800. She is allowed a trade-in credit of $9,750 on her old cases. She may claim an IRC § 179 deduction of $14,250 (2001 IRC § 179 limit of $24,000 minus $9,750 trade-in). The balance of her cost can be taken as depreciation deductions over a period of seven years. (See Section C below.)

5. Combining IRC Section 179 and Depreciation Deductions

After using IRC § 179 to immediately write off the first $24,000 (2001) of assets purchased, you can claim regular depreciation deductions for the balance.

> **EXAMPLE:** In 2001, Miranda bought and started using a $34,000 instant printing press for her graphics business. She elected IRC § 179 and took the maximum deduction of $24,000 in the first year. She can claim the remaining $10,000 as depreciation expenses in the following years. (See Section C, below.)

Section 179 deductions are reported on IRS Form 4562, Depreciation and Amortization. See Section C, below.

C. Depreciating Business Assets

Typically, small business owners look first to IRC § 179 to write off asset purchases. But you must go with depreciation deductions instead of IRC § 179 if:

- you don't have other business or nonbusiness earned income to offset the IRC § 179 deduction
- the asset doesn't meet IRC § 179 qualifications (see Section B, above), or
- you've already used up your IRC § 179 dollar limit that year.

1. What Is Depreciation?

Almost everything wears out over time. So assets used in a trade or business or held for the production of income are entitled to an annual tax deduction called "depreciation." This is commonly called a "write-off" or "cost recovery." For a few special assets, this deduction is called "amortization" or "depletion."

A tax deduction for depreciation works like this. Derek buys and uses a copy machine in his business.

Under the tax code a copy machine is assigned a (rather arbitrary) five-year life expectancy. (IRC § 168, Reg. 1.168.) This means Derek can write off *part* of the cost of the copier in the year he bought it and the balance in each of the following five years, by taking annual deductions. (Yes, I know this is a total of six years, not five, as the tax code seems to indicate.) Eventually, the whole cost of the copier has been deducted from his business income if he sticks around that long. Just how much Derek can take each year, and how to claim the deduction, are explained next.

⚠ **An important exception to the normal depreciation rule:** Land costs can *never* be deducted. Special rules also apply to deducting business inventories and natural resources. (See Chapter 1.)

Keeping Up With Changing Depreciation Rules

Congress changes the depreciation rules frequently —five times in the last two decades. The good news is that if the rules change after you acquire something, the old rules still apply. The bad news is that you will have to use the new rules for any new assets. So, you may end up tracking depreciation of different business assets—computers, buildings or whatever—under several sets of rules. A tax pro can keep the process straight and even compare different depreciation methods available to see which one produces the best results for you. Software (such as Turbotax for Business (Intuit)) also can compare and track depreciation under multiple schedules.

---

2. Depreciation Categories

The tax code establishes depreciation categories for all business assets. Each category is assigned an arbitrary "useful life," meaning the time period over which the cost of an asset can be deducted—for example, five years for a computer.

In tax lingo, this is called the "recovery period." IRS Publication 534 lists the categories and the depreciation periods for different assets.

Most assets fit into one of four "classes." Here is a summary of classes:

- **3-Year Property:** Manufacturing equipment (plastics, metal fabrication, glass).
- **5-Year Property:** Cars, trucks, small airplanes, trailers, computers and peripherals, copiers, typewriters, calculators, manufacturing equipment (apparel), assets used in construction activity and equipment used in research and experimentation.
- **7-Year Property:** Office furniture, manufacturing equipment (except types included in 3- and 5-year categories above), fixtures, oil, gas and mining assets, agricultural structures and personal property that doesn't fit into any other specific category.
- **Real Estate (varying periods):** Business-use real estate is depreciated over 39 years using the straight-line method only (discussed below) if placed in service after May 31, 1993. Residential rental real estate is allowed a 27.5-year recovery period. Some types of land improvement costs (sidewalks, roads, drainage facilities, fences and landscaping) are depreciable over 20 years.

There are also classes of 10, 15 and 20 years, if your business is agricultural or unusual, like breeding horses or operating tugboats. See IRC § 168 and IRS Publication 534 for more information on all asset classes or check with your tax advisor.

3. Methods of Depreciation

Once you find the correct tax category for an asset, you must determine the most advantageous depreciation method to use. You may or may not have a choice, depending on the type of asset.

Depreciation methods fall into two general types:
- **straight-line depreciation,** and
- **accelerated depreciation.**

The tax code makes it a little more complicated by offering four principal methods of depreciating most business assets—one straight-line and three accelerated—all of which result in the same total amount of deductions in the end. An additional method, for farm equipment only, isn't covered here. (See IRS Publication 946.)

a. Straight-Line: The Slowest and Simplest Tax Depreciation Method

The straight-line method allows the cost of an asset to be deducted as a depreciation expense in equal amounts every year, *except* for the first and last years. In those two bookend years, you get only half of a year's tax deduction.

For instance, with a $10,000 business machine, straight-line tax code depreciation allows these deductions:

Year 1	$1,000 (one half year)
Years 2, 3, 4 & 5	$2,000 each year
Year 6	$1,000 (one half year)
Total deductions	$10,000

Assuming you own and use the machine for six years, you can deduct 100% of its cost.

Note Section 4b, below, for special first-year depreciation rules, which may limit the amount of your tax deduction in the first year depending on the month of the year you acquire an asset.

b. MACRS: The Fastest Accelerated Tax Depreciation Method

The present tax code accelerated depreciation system is known by the acronym MACRS (pronounced "makers" by tax folks). This stands for "modified accelerated cost recovery system."

Technically, MACRS covers all of the accelerated depreciation methods. Typically it is a shorthand reference to the most widely chosen method: MACRS 200% Declining Balance. This is the very fastest—most "accelerated"—way to write off assets (but don't overlook using IRC § 179, described above).

MACRS allows greater deductions in early years of ownership of an asset than in later ones. For instance, using this accelerated method to depreciate a $10,000 business machine produces $7,120 in depreciation deductions in the first three years, versus $5,000 with the straight-line method.

To find the exact yearly deduction amounts, refer to the IRS tables that show the deduction as a percentage of the cost for each year of ownership. MACRS tables are found in your annual Form 1040 instruction booklet, IRS Publication 946, the IRS website (http://www.irs.gov) and annual tax preparation guides. Tax software such as *Turbotax for Business* (Intuit) will automatically compute these amounts, too, or leave it to your tax pro.

c. Special Depreciation Rules for Motor Vehicles

Special tax code depreciation rules and limits apply to motor vehicles used in business. The technical name for these rules is "alternative ACRS depreciation."

These rules favor trucks (including some SUVs) over passenger cars. Adjustments must be made if the vehicle is partly used for pleasure and partly for business, which is often the case with small-time operators.

However, there are caps (annual dollar limits) on motor vehicle depreciation deductions, as shown in the table below. The total depreciation for the first three years is $11,110 if the car is 100% used for business. Note that the annual depreciation deduction after the third year of ownership drops to only $1,775 per year. The net effect is to extend the period for deducting the cost of most newly purchased vehicles to five years or more.

As long as you use the vehicle for business more than 50% of the time, then you can take accelerated depreciation deductions. If you use it for business less than 50% of the time, slower straight line depreciation rules apply. But the annual cap is the same, regardless of whether you use the accelerated or straight-line depreciation method. Don't forget that the percentage of personal use reduces the amount of depreciation deduction each year.

Figuring depreciation can get a little tricky. IRS tables guide you, but tax software like *Turbotax for Business* (Intuit) is better. (See Chapter 1, Business Income and Tax-Deductible Expenses, Section E1, as well as Section D1, below for details on depreciating business vehicles.)

⚠️ **The fastest depreciation method may not be the best.** Don't automatically conclude that the quicker you can take a deduction, the better. If your business is quite profitable, you are probably right. But most start-up businesses are not immediate money-makers, so they don't benefit by using accelerated depreciation. For them, the straight-line method, with smaller deductions in their formative years, gives the best long-term tax benefit.

Depreciation Limits for Vehicles

The tax code imposes absolute dollar maximums on depreciation deductions for each year that you own a passenger car used for business—no matter how much it costs; but see the exception for heavy vehicles in Section B2 above. For 2001, you are limited to depreciation deductions of:

1st year	$3,060
2nd year	$5,000
3rd year	$2,950
4th and subsequent years	$1,775

These amounts are adjusted annually for cost of living changes. (IRC § 280F.) New electrically powered vehicles enjoy significantly higher limits, though.

💡 **Should you lease?** Because of these limits, it may take longer than your life expectancy to fully write off a Mercedes-Benz or other valuable business asset. Section E, below, describes leasing versus buying business assets. Leasing often provides the biggest tax deduction.

4. Mechanics of Depreciation

Whether you use a straight-line or accelerated depreciation method, here's what you must have to claim depreciation deductions:

a. Basis for Depreciation

The asset's *tax basis* must be established before you can claim a deduction for depreciation on it. Section A, above, tells you how to figure out your tax basis in a business asset. Basis is typically the same as your cost, but not always.

b. First-Year Depreciation Rules

1. Placed in Service

Asset depreciation starts when it is "placed in service." This means that you must start using it before you may claim a depreciation deduction. This rule may require you to keep track of the date of first use. In other words, if you acquire an asset in 2001 but don't take it out of the box until 2002, you may not take a deduction for it in 2001.

2. The Half-Year Convention

When during the year does the depreciation period begin? Generally, assets are treated in the tax code as if you bought them in the middle of the year—July 1—for depreciation purposes. This rule is called the "half-year convention." Bottom line: You get only one-half year's depreciation deduction in the first year. Your final tax deduction comes in the year following the last year of the asset's useful life. So the final year of deductions for five-year property, such as a computer, is really the sixth year. In case I've lost you, the example should help.

EXAMPLE: In April 2001, Julie buys a color copier to use at her boutique for $2,000. If Julie depreciates it over five years on a straight-line basis, her deduction for 2001 is $200. ($1/2$ year x $2,000 x $1/5$.) In each of the next four years she takes a $400 deduction, and takes the remaining $200 in the year 2006, the sixth year. (200 + 400 + 400 + 400 + 400 + 200 = $2,000.)

3.   The Last Quarter Limitation

Another tax quirk can further reduce your first-year depreciation deduction. If you make more than 40% of all your asset purchases in the last three months of a year, you get only 1.5 months of depreciation on the last-acquired portion. So unless you are using IRC § 179 (see Section B, above), don't buy equipment near the end of the year.

> **EXAMPLE:** Julie, in the example above, also purchases $25,000 of new display cases—classified as "five-year" property—in May 2001. If she uses the straight-line method of depreciation, the tax write-off for 2001 is $200 for the copier and $2,500 for the cases. In November, Julie buys $20,000 of racks and shelving (also five-year property). Since Julie's November purchase is more than 40% of the total assets bought during the year, she can write off only $500 of it the first year (1.5 months of 60 months of depreciation of the racks and shelving). But Julie can still write off $2,700 for the copier and display cases purchased in 2001.

c.   How to Report Depreciation and IRC Section 179 Deductions

Whether you choose depreciation methods, IRC § 179 or combine the two, you list the deduction on IRS Form 4562, Depreciation and Amortization. Sole proprietors, partners, LLC members and S corporation shareholders file Form 4562 with their individual returns, and C corporations with their income tax returns.

Form 4562 must be used if you are either:
- depreciating any assets acquired that year
- depreciating certain types of assets (such as vehicles, computers, cellular phones and a few others named in the tax code) acquired in a previous year, or

- operating as a C corporation and are depreciating any assets.

A sample Form 4562 is shown below. For original forms, see the IRS's website at http://www.irs.gov or call the IRS and request forms by mail.

Show the IRS how you figure depreciation. Attach a separate "depreciation schedule" or worksheet to your tax return whenever claiming depreciation or IRC § 179 deductions. This shows the IRS how the deduction was calculated. If the schedule looks okay, it may ward off a further IRS inquiry or audit. It indicates that you are careful and aware of the tax rules on depreciation. If you are doing taxes yourself, tax preparation software like TurboTax for Business makes depreciation schedules and the required tax forms and worksheets.

The sample forms are for illustrative purposes only. Throughout this book we provide sample, filled-out IRS forms so you can see what they might look like for a typical small business. However, keep in mind that these forms are just that: examples. Your completed, filled-out tax form will probably look a lot different. If you're unsure of how to complete any of the tax forms we discuss in this book, see a tax pro.

Form **4562**

Department of the Treasury
Internal Revenue Service   (99)

Depreciation and Amortization
(Including Information on Listed Property)
▶ See separate instructions.   ▶ Attach this form to your return.

OMB No. 1545-0172

2000

Attachment
Sequence No. **67**

Name(s) shown on return	Business or activity to which this form relates	Identifying number
Fields of Flowers	Retail Florist	10-1787889

Part I **Election To Expense Certain Tangible Property (Section 179)**
Note: *If you have any "listed property," complete Part V before you complete Part I.*

1	Maximum dollar limitation. If an enterprise zone business, see page 2 of the instructions . .	**1**	$20,000
2	Total cost of section 179 property placed in service. See page 2 of the instructions	**2**	30,145
3	Threshold cost of section 179 property before reduction in limitation	**3**	$200,000
4	Reduction in limitation. Subtract line 3 from line 2. If zero or less, enter -0-	**4**	-0-
5	Dollar limitation for tax year. Subtract line 4 from line 1. If zero or less, enter -0-. If married filing separately, see page 2 of the instructions	**5**	20,000

(a) Description of property	(b) Cost (business use only)	(c) Elected cost	
6			

7	Listed property. Enter amount from line 27	**7**	20,000	
8	Total elected cost of section 179 property. Add amounts in column (c), lines 6 and 7 . . .	**8**	20,000
9	Tentative deduction. Enter the smaller of line 5 or line 8	**9**	20,000
10	Carryover of disallowed deduction from 1999. See page 3 of the instructions	**10**	-0-
11	Business income limitation. Enter the smaller of business income (not less than zero) or line 5 (see instructions)	**11**	20,000
12	Section 179 expense deduction. Add lines 9 and 10, but do not enter more than line 11 . .	**12**	20,000
13	Carryover of disallowed deduction to 2001. Add lines 9 and 10, less line 12 ▶	**13**	-0-	

Note: *Do not use Part II or Part III below for listed property (automobiles, certain other vehicles, cellular telephones, certain computers, or property used for entertainment, recreation, or amusement). Instead, use Part V for listed property.*

Part II **MACRS Depreciation for Assets Placed in Service Only During Your 2000 Tax Year (Do not** include listed property.)

Section A—General Asset Account Election

14	If you are making the election under section 168(i)(4) to group any assets placed in service during the tax year into one or more general asset accounts, check this box. See page 3 of the instructions . . . . ▶ ☐

Section B—General Depreciation System (GDS) (See page 3 of the instructions.)

(a) Classification of property	(b) Month and year placed in service	(c) Basis for depreciation (business/investment use only—see instructions)	(d) Recovery period	(e) Convention	(f) Method	(g) Depreciation deduction
15a 3-year property		3,000	5 years	MQ	200DB	750.00
b 5-year property						
c 7-year property						
d 10-year property						
e 15-year property						
f 20-year property						
g 25-year property			25 yrs.		S/L	
h Residential rental property			27.5 yrs.	MM	S/L	
			27.5 yrs.	MM	S/L	
i Nonresidential real property			39 yrs.	MM	S/L	
				MM	S/L	

Section C—Alternative Depreciation System (ADS) (See page 5 of the instructions.)

16a Class life		2345	•	•	S/L	43.80
b 12-year			12 yrs.		S/L	
c 40-year			40 yrs.	MM	S/L	

Part III **Other Depreciation (Do not** include listed property.) (See page 5 of the instructions.)

17	GDS and ADS deductions for assets placed in service in tax years beginning before 2000 .	**17**	4,813.32
18	Property subject to section 168(f)(1) election	**18**	
19	ACRS and other depreciation	**19**	

Part IV **Summary** (See page 6 of the instructions.)

20	Listed property. Enter amount from line 26	**20**	340.00
21	**Total.** Add deductions from line 12, lines 15 and 16 in column (g), and lines 17 through 20. Enter here and on the appropriate lines of your return. Partnerships and S corporations—see instructions	**21**	25,947.12
22	For assets shown above and placed in service during the current year, enter the portion of the basis attributable to section 263A costs . .	**22**	-0-	

For Paperwork Reduction Act Notice, see page 9 of the instructions.   Cat. No. 12906N   Form **4562** (2000)

Form 4562 (2000)   Page **2**

Part V   **Listed Property** (Include automobiles, certain other vehicles, cellular telephones, certain computers, and property used for entertainment, recreation, or amusement.)

Note: *For any vehicle for which you are using the standard mileage rate or deducting lease expense, complete **only** 23a, 23b, columns (a) through (c) of Section A, all of Section B, and Section C if applicable.*

Section A—Depreciation and Other Information (Caution: *See page 7 of the instructions for limits for passenger automobiles.*)

23a Do you have evidence to support the business/investment use claimed? ☐ **Yes** ☐ **No**   **23b** If "Yes," is the evidence written? ☐ **Yes** ☐ **No**

(a) Type of property (list vehicles first)	(b) Date placed in service	(c) Business/ investment use percentage	(d) Cost or other basis	(e) Basis for depreciation (business/investment use only)	(f) Recovery period	(g) Method/ Convention	(h) Depreciation deduction	(i) Elected section 179 cost
24 Property used more than 50% in a qualified business use (See page 6 of the instructions.):								
USA 280F Van	11-16-00	100 %	24,800	6,800	5	200DB/MQ	340.00	20,000
		%						
		%						
25 Property used 50% or less in a qualified business use (See page 6 of the instructions.):								
		%				S/L –		
		%				S/L –		
		%				S/L –		

26 Add amounts in column (h). Enter the total here and on line 20, page 1 . . . . . . | **26** | 340.00

27 Add amounts in column (i). Enter the total here and on line 7, page 1 . . . . | **27** | 20,000

Section B—Information on Use of Vehicles

Complete this section for vehicles used by a sole proprietor, partner, or other "more than 5% owner," or related person.
If you provided vehicles to your employees, first answer the questions in Section C to see if you meet an exception to completing this section for those vehicles.

	(a) Vehicle 1		(b) Vehicle 2		(c) Vehicle 3		(d) Vehicle 4		(e) Vehicle 5		(f) Vehicle 6	
28 Total business/investment miles driven during the year (**do not** include commuting miles—see page 1 of the instructions)												
29 Total commuting miles driven during the year												
30 Total other personal (noncommuting) miles driven												
31 Total miles driven during the year. Add lines 28 through 30.												
	Yes	No	Yes	No	Yes	No	Yes	No	Yes	No	Yes	No
32 Was the vehicle available for personal use during off-duty hours?												
33 Was the vehicle used primarily by a more than 5% owner or related person?												
34 Is another vehicle available for personal use?												

Section C—Questions for Employers Who Provide Vehicles for Use by Their Employees

Answer these questions to determine if you meet an exception to completing Section B for vehicles used by employees who **are not** more than 5% owners or related persons. See page 8 of the instructions.

		Yes	No
35	Do you maintain a written policy statement that prohibits all personal use of vehicles, including commuting, by your employees?	✓	
36	Do you maintain a written policy statement that prohibits personal use of vehicles, except commuting, by your employees? See page 8 of the instructions for vehicles used by corporate officers, directors, or 1% or more owners	NA	
37	Do you treat all use of vehicles by employees as personal use?	NA	
38	Do you provide more than five vehicles to your employees, obtain information from your employees about the use of the vehicles, and retain the information received?	NA	
39	Do you meet the requirements concerning qualified automobile demonstration use? See page 8 of the instructions . .	NA	

Note: *If your answer to 35, 36, 37, 38, or 39 is "Yes," do not complete Section B for the covered vehicles.*

Part VI   **Amortization**

(a) Description of costs	(b) Date amortization begins	(c) Amortizable amount	(d) Code section	(e) Amortization period or percentage	(f) Amortization for this year
40 Amortization of costs that begins during your 2000 tax year (See page 8 of the instructions.):					

41 Amortization of costs that began before 2000 . . . . | **41** |

42 **Total.** Add amounts in column (f). See page 9 of the instructions for where to report . . . | **42** |

Form **4562** (2000)

Depreciation Worksheet

Description of Property	Date Placed in Service	Cost or Other Basis	Business/ Investment Use %	Section 179 Deduction	Depreciation Prior Years	Basis for Depreciation	Method/ Convention	Recovery Period	Rate or Table %	Depreciation Deduction
Computer	3/31/01	3,200	100%	3,200	0	0	200DB/MY	5	20%	0
Cellular Phone	6/26/01	300	40%	0	0	120	SL/MY	5	10%	12
Chevy Pick-Up	11/1/99	10,500	20%	0	525	2,100	SL/MQ	5	20%	420
Total				3,200						432

Watch Out for Depreciation Recapture!

Depreciation deductions may come back to bite you if you quit using business property that has given you past tax benefits. In certain circumstances you must report as ordinary income some of your past tax deductions for depreciation (called "recapture") when an asset is no longer used for business. (IRC §§ 1245, 1250.) Maybe you just stop using the property in your business or dispose of it.

EXAMPLE: Rusty, a self-employed flooring contractor, closes his shop in 2001 and sells his 100% business-used Dodge pickup for $7,500. The truck cost $11,000, and Rusty took $4,200 of depreciation deductions in past years. He must report $700 as recapture income (the difference between his tax basis of $6,800 and the sale price of $7,500) on his 2001 tax return. Rusty should use IRS Form 4797, Sales of Business Property, to report the sale and the recapture income.

However, there are several ways to avoid the tax recapture. For instance, if you trade a business asset for another of like kind, no recapture results.

EXAMPLE: Rusty's business is going great. So instead of selling his truck, he trades up to a $20,000 truck and is allowed a $10,000 trade-in for his old pickup. There is no recapture income to worry about because this was a like-kind exchange.

Another exception to recapture is if the asset had been damaged, stolen or destroyed, and the loss was covered by insurance. In this case (called "in-voluntary conversion"), there is no recapture as long as all of the insurance proceeds are used to replace the asset.

EXAMPLE: Rusty wrecks the old pickup, and it is declared a total loss. Allsnake Insurance pays him $9,000 ($2,200 more than his tax basis in the truck). As long as he buys a replacement truck for at least $9,000, there is no recapture. But if Rusty buys a used truck for $5,000, he must report $2,200 as recapture income.

D. Depreciating Some Typical Business Assets

These days, hardly any small business is without a computer, and most also need vehicles. Here are some special rules for tax depreciating these items and a few other common business assets.

1. Business Vehicles

The cost of operating and owning a car or truck you use in business is deductible. (See Chapter 1, Business Income and Tax-Deductible Expenses, for details on how to claim operating expense deductions on vehicles used for business.) The following summarizes Chapter 1 in most respects.

- If your car is used exclusively for business, the entire costs of the vehicle are deductible, including depreciation. The tax code imposes a dollar ceiling on the amount of annual depreciation you may claim for business use of a car. For cars placed in service in 2001, the limits are $3,060 for the first year, $5,000 for the second year, $2,950 for the third year and $1,775 for every year thereafter.

- If you use the vehicle for business less than 100% of the time, the maximum depreciation limits must be reduced to reflect the business-use percentage. (But, as shown in Chapter 1, you may not be able to claim auto depreciation deductions in all cases.)

- What happens when you no longer want your business vehicle? If you sell it, the difference between its tax basis and the sale price produces either a (taxable) gain or a loss. (But if the car was used for both business and pleasure, you report only the allocable business portion as a gain or loss. See Chapter 4 for information on taking losses for tax purposes.) As a practical matter, because of the stingy tax code limits on depreciation deductions, it is more often than not a loss instead of a gain. However, the tax rule is different if you trade in your car for another business-used one. In this case, your tax basis in the new car is increased by the remaining basis of the old one. So there isn't any gain or loss to report with a trade-in. (See Chapter 1 for details and examples.)

Major League Loophole for Big Sport Utility Vehicles (SUVs) & Trucks

Buying a truck or heavy sport utility vehicle (gross vehicle weight when loaded of over 6,000 pounds) gets around the tax deduction limitations discussed above. Road yachts such as Toyota Land Cruiser or a Mercedes-Benz MLS, among others, qualify. Lighter SUVs, such as Ford Explorers and Lexus RX300s do not qualify—check the manufacturer's specifications. If your business vehicle falls into this category, you may fully write it off in six years. For example, if you start using the SUV in the first nine months of the year, you may take 20% of the cost as depreciation (assuming business use is 100%) that year. Then, claim 32% in year two, 19.2% in year three, 11.52% in years four and five, and 5.76% in year six. If you don't buy an SUV until the last three months of the year, however, you only get a 5% deduction that first year.

Three more tax benefits:

1. SUVs are exempt from the federal "luxury" tax on new vehicles over $36,000
2. IRC § 179 allows a hefty $24,000 first year (2001) write-off if you elect it; and
3. SUVs are exempt from the IRS lease table income "add-backs." (See Section E, below.)

EXAMPLE: Benecia buys a heavy $44,000 SUV and uses it 60% of the time for her property management company. She also uses the vehicle for weekend family camping trips to off-road destinations. Benecia has the option of deducting $24,000 (2001) under IRC § 179, and then writing off the balance of $2,400 over six years ($44,000 x 60% business use = $26,400 - $24,000 = $2,400). Otherwise, using regular depreciation rules it would take Benecia about 14 years to fully write off the same vehicle.

2. Writing Off Business and Home Computers

Most entrepreneurs use computers at home. The tax code allows you to deduct the costs of business-used computers no matter where they are kept.

Section B, above, discusses how to get a fast write-off using IRC § 179. If you decide instead to go for a long-term write-off of a computer used in your office or at home, here's the deal. The tax code says computers have a five-year depreciable life, and you can use the MACRS 200% Declining Balance method to write it off (explained above in Section C3).

 If you use your computer for personal as well as business purposes, keep a diary or log. Record the dates, times and reason the computer was used, to distinguish the two uses in case an IRS auditor comes calling. Keep a simple paper log next to your computer or use you daytimer to keep track of your computer use.

3. Other Items—Stereo, Camcorders, Etc.

Things not ordinarily tax-deductible can be, under the right circumstances. I have a great stereo system in my home office, and if the volume is cranked up enough, it sounds throughout the rest of the house, too. My clients and I enjoy the background music while we ponder their tax problems. It sounds even sweeter knowing that I tax-deducted the entire cost. My home office also contains two aquariums, oriental rugs and pricey furniture. All these are 100% tax-deductible if used in your business.

> **EXAMPLE:** Herb owns and operates "Olde Tyme Quilts" to sell quilts that he makes and takes on consignment from other quiltmakers. To improve his skills, he buys and uses a VCR to watch tapes on quilt-making. Later Herb buys a camcorder to make tapes of quilt designs at craft shows, a video catalog of his stock and him doing a quilt-making demonstration. These items are all depreciable or deductible under IRC § 179. But if he also uses the VCR and camcorder for vacations to Hawaii, he must apportion between business and personal use.

⚠ **You might have to defend asset purchases at an audit.** You are on the honor system when it comes to claiming suspicious business asset purchases— no one from the IRS is watching to see how you really use your camcorder. But if some expenditures are questionable, be ready to prove how the items were used for business. Otherwise, an auditor can reclassify them as (nondeductible) personal expenses.

E. Leasing Instead of Buying Assets

To conserve cash, consider leasing equipment or autos instead of buying them. There may be a tax advantage to leasing as well. Lease payments are deductible as current business expenses, like electricity or office supplies. (See Chapter 1, Business Income and Tax-Deductible Expenses.)

There are some special tax code rules for leasing.

1. Vehicles Used for Business

Both tax and non-tax considerations determine whether it's best to buy or lease a business vehicle.

Here are some tax angles that apply to any form of enterprise, from sole proprietor to C corporation.

a. Keeping Track of Personal Use

If you, like most small business people, use your car both for business and personal transport, the tax code requires records tracking each use. This is true whether you lease or buy. (See Section D, above.) A simple log for keeping track of this data can be obtained from office supply stores or tax pros.

b. Tax Rules Favor Leasing

Because of the tax code rules, the tax advantage of leasing starts when your business usage is 50% or more and the vehicle cost exceeds $15,300. Part of the reason is that if you buy instead of lease, your tax write-off period for depreciation extends beyond five years for most vehicles under the law. For instance, it might take 20 years to fully write off a $60,000 Lexus if you buy it. People rarely keep cars that long. In effect, leasing gets around the stingy depreciation deduction limits for most newer vehicles.

Auto lease payments are deductible business expenses without the tax limitations placed on purchased vehicles. (See Section D1, above.) In addition, the tax code, in its oblique fashion, favors leasing over buying more expensive passenger cars, through its leasing "inclusion" tables. It works like this: You are required to include extra income, as stated on the table, on your tax return if you lease a business-used car costing more than $15,300. This is true even when the car is used 100% for business with no personal driving at all. This may sound unfair, but the extra imputed income is relatively insignificant, as shown in the example below.

> **EXAMPLE:** Phil, an independent sales representative for a furniture manufacturer, leases a $40,000 BMW in 2001. Assuming 100% business use, the IRS lease table directs Phil to report only $175 of extra income for 2001 and $384 for 2002.

Phil can deduct his lease payments in full as a business expense as long as the car is 100% used for business. If Phil uses the car 20% of the time for business calls, he would discount the lease "inclusion amount" by 20%, meaning he would report only $307 (80% x $384) as additional income in 2002. Even if he were in the highest tax bracket, Phil's additional income tax would be less than $130 in 2002.

The IRS tables are adjusted annually for cost of living changes. Many computer tax programs can make the lease inclusion calculations for you.

To further complicate the matter, in weighing a lease versus a purchase, you must also consider the tax benefits from deducting the interest on a business-used car loan. For instance, if you buy a car and pay $2,000 in interest over a year and drive 80% for business, $1,600 is deductible. The other $400 is nondeductible personal interest.

c. The Mileage Method

Alternatively, you may elect the "mileage method" (see Chapter 1, Section E1a) for leased vehicles. The rate (2001) is 34.5¢ per mile. However, once you start using the mileage method, you must continue using it for the remaining term of the lease. If your business miles exceed 20,000 per year you should compare the tax deduction allowed under the mileage method with the regular lease deduction rules (see Subsection b, above).

d. End of the Lease

Leasing also avoids some tax issues from disposing of an owned car or truck. That's because turning in a leased car is a non-taxable event. By comparison, trading in an owned car will likely increase your basis in the new car, meaning an even longer period for claiming depreciation deductions. Additionally, selling the owned car means a tax loss or gain depending on the sale price and the car's tax basis at the time.

💡 **Leasing should not be just a tax decision.** First, do a purely economic analysis of the lease. Start with the stated "gross capitalized cost" (value or purchase price of the vehicle). Then find the stated "residual value" (what the car will be worth) at the end of the lease. Next, see a tax pro, or try a "buy vs. lease" computer software program (check the Internet—many car sites have these kinds of programs). Analyzing leases is a little simpler now than in previous years, due to a recent federal law mandating clarity in lease disclosures. While leasing costs are still far more complex than purchasing, they can produce big tax savings so it is often worth the effort to investigate it.

While there is no standard car lease, all limit the total miles you can drive and all punish you for terminating the lease early. Manufacturers frequently have the best lease deals, so start there. Never rely on a car salesperson for advice on "lease or own." Additionally, salespeople push leases because they receive higher commissions, and dealers like leases because they can disguise the true sales price in the lease agreement mumbo-jumbo.

2. Leasing Assets to Your C Corporation

A business doesn't have to own all of its operating assets. Leasing your personally owned property—your building, vehicle or equipment—to your C corporation business may provide a tax savings. Generally, this strategy will not work unless your enterprise is a regular or "C" corporation.

Alternatively, an asset leased to your C corporation may be owned by another corporation, a partnership or a family business in which you have an ownership interest. (As discussed in Chapter 12, Family Businesses, such arrangements can result in "income shifting"—transferring income to people in lower tax brackets to reduce overall taxes for the family unit.)

💡 **Leasing assets can protect your business.** Apart from taxes, business people—especially in endeavors where lawsuits are a hazard—don't want their corporation to hold assets. Leasing insulates assets from potential creditors of the corporation's business.

To be legal, lease terms between an individual and his corporation must be "arm's length" deals, not merely tax-motivated schemes. Lease payments are deductible expenses to the corporation. Lease income is taxable to the asset's owner, who in turn deducts costs of ownership—mortgage interest, property taxes, maintenance, repairs and depreciation. The overall result may a "wash"—no money savings, but in some cases, it might work, as the following example shows.

> **EXAMPLE:** Sam bought a store building in June 2000 for $100,000. The land has a fair market value of $20,000, and the structure $80,000. Sam does some minor repairs and leases it to Sam Smith, Inc., a C corporation, in 2001 for $16,000 per year. Sam's out-of-pocket expenses of ownership are $15,000, and he is entitled to a $2,052 depreciation deduction in 2001 (the second year's write-off of the building allowed in the tax code). Tax result: Sam is ahead $1,000 in cash after expenses on his investment ($16,000 - $15,000), which is canceled out by his $2,052 depreciation deduction. Sam has a "tax loss" of $1,052. This paper loss "shelters" Sam's other earned income in 2001, such as his salary from Sam Smith, Inc. Before structuring his affairs in this manner, Sam sat down with his tax advisor—and so should you.

F. Tax Errors in Depreciation

Because tax rules are so complex, it isn't uncommon to misfigure your depreciation deductions. The good news is that if you catch a mistake after you have filed a tax return, it can be corrected. This could result in a tax refund, or tax bill—depending on which direction the error was made. Make the correction by filing Form 3115, or an amended tax return. It is best to have a tax pro do this for you.

Resources

- IRS Publication 946, How to Depreciate Property
- IRS Publication 463, Travel, Entertainment, Gift and Car Expenses
- IRS Publication 551, Basis of Assets
- IRS website, http://www.irs.gov. Here you can download the latest tax forms and publications in Adobe Acrobat® format.
- *Master Tax Guide* (Commerce Clearing House). This manual contains a good explanation of the depreciation process, covered in more detail than in this chapter. Although it's intended for tax professionals, it's more readable than the IRS materials.
- *Small-Time Operator*, by Bernard Kamoroff (Bell Springs). This CPA-written self-help book covers the fundamentals of depreciating business assets and keeping depreciation records.

Bookkeeping and Accounting

"The income tax has made more liars out of the American people than golf has."

—Will Rogers

Most ventures are started by enthusiastic people with ambition. Whether they are hoping to build the next Fortune 500 company or simply supplement their day job, it's what the business will buy, sell, make or fix that drives them. They aren't intrigued by the paperwork, but the law mandates some basic recordkeeping know-how.

The good news is that the IRS does not require business records to be kept in one uniform fashion. Any format is okay, as long as it paints a true picture of income and expenses. Since no two enterprises are alike, no two recordkeeping systems are exactly alike. Never forget that the IRS (and state tax agencies too) has the right to audit you and inspect your records.

This chapter outlines the minimum recordkeeping required, how to set up and maintain a good system and alerts you to basic accounting principles.

Recordkeeping in a Nutshell

1. The IRS doesn't prescribe any particular format for keeping your business's records, as long as they clearly reflect your income and expenses.
2. You can choose a manual or computerized recordkeeping system, but a computer saves time and is more accurate.
3. Small businesses are usually required to keep records and tax report on a calendar-year basis.

A. Why You Need a Bookkeeping System

Some fledging entrepreneurs think that if there is money in their business checking account at the end of the month, they must be making a profit. But only if you keep accurate records will you really know if your business is making or losing money. A recordkeeping system is also crucial for preparing your annual federal and state income tax returns.

The first commandment of the tax code is thou shalt keep "records appropriate to your trade or business." (IRC § 6001.) Most records don't have to be kept in any particular form, but they must be accurate. (Reg. 31.6001-1(a).)

Good records can also serve as an early warning system to let you know whether changes need to be made in your enterprise. Indeed, operating without good business records is like flying in dense fog with no instruments. You may be thinking, "I think I'll skip this chapter; I hate bookkeeping. After all, if my business takes in enough money, all these paperwork matters will resolve themselves. If they don't, I'll hire someone to clean them up." Think twice, please.

⚠ Take recordkeeping seriously. If you only get one thing out of this book, go away knowing that ignoring recordkeeping is inviting disaster. If the IRS ever audits you or your business and finds insufficient records or significant mistakes, it can disallow significant deductions and impose hefty fines and penalties, possibly forcing you out of business and wiping out your life savings as well.

Recordkeeping must become part of your everyday business routine, just like opening your doors each morning. Believe me, I am not an accountant and I hate paperwork as much as any of you. I also hate shaving every morning, keeping fat out of my diet and carrying out the garbage in the rain, but these tasks never seem to go away. But as we shall see, recordkeeping doesn't need to be drudgery, and you don't need to keep track of every last penny.

Random Business Record Inspections

You may be audited after written notice, but there are no "IRS inspectors" roaming around spot-checking to see that records are being kept. In many states, however, employment or sales tax auditors do show up unannounced and demand to see records. So, just like the Boy Scouts, "be prepared."

B. Should You Hire a Bookkeeper?

When it comes to keeping small business records, you can either do it yourself, or hire someone. But don't make the mistake of doing this job badly or hiring the wrong person to do it.

Maybe you can't afford to pay someone when starting out, but once you are on more solid financial footing, consider bookkeeping help. Some folks actually like doing other people's paperwork, leaving you with more time to focus your talents on your business.

Typically, bookkeepers charge $15 to $50 per hour and can take care of a business for as little as $50 to $100 a month. Because this is a tax-deductible expense, keep in mind that Uncle Sam is paying part of the bookkeeper's salary.

Don't just hire the first person who comes along claiming to be a bookkeeper. Check references and learn enough about your records so that you can periodically review them to see that things are done right. Accountants can usually recommend a book-keeper to you, or they may have folks on staff to do the job for your business. Whomever you choose, keep in mind that the IRS holds *you* responsible for any bookkeeper screw-ups—so choose wisely. If you don't believe us, following is a sad but true story of an entrepreneur who didn't pay attention to what his bookkeeper was up to, and paid the price.

EXAMPLE: Barney owned an auto body shop. He had no patience for bookkeeping, so he hired Lorraine, a prim and proper type, to do it for him. She came in once a week to do his books, pay the bills and file various tax reports. Lorraine was a faithful worker, and so Barney was upset when she suddenly quit after two years and moved to parts unknown. Shortly thereafter, an IRS collector came calling about unfiled and unpaid payroll taxes. Barney discovered that sweet Lorraine had embezzled $38,000, including unpaid federal taxes. Barney had to go into his savings for the unpaid taxes—plus hefty penalties—or face padlocking of his body shop by the IRS. Note: It may be possible to insure your business from a bookkeeper's dishonesty. Check with your insurance agent.

Run it by a tax pro. Have a tax pro review your system early on to make sure it is registering all necessary data. This can avoid headaches when it comes time for filing tax returns. And the tax pro's fees are tax-deductible business expenses.

C. Manual or Computer System?

There are two ways to keep business records: manually—the pencil and paper way; and with a computer—the indisputably better way. The IRS has no preference for either system, as long as your system accurately reflects your business's transactions. If you don't have any system, or just throw papers in a shoebox and forget them, consider yourself an audit waiting to happen.

Whether you use a computer or pencil, the basics of bookkeeping are the same. You must keep accounts showing your enterprise's financial activities. "Accounts" refer to the places where the transactions are noted in your records; they are simply categories —such as "advertising," "rent" and "utilities"—in which the day-to-day income and expenses are written or entered into a computer.

A microbusiness, such as a home-based consultant, independent contractor or freelancer, might get by with a check register, adding machine tapes and an accordion file for paid bills.

Organize your receipts by category. Contrary to how a lot of folks do it, paid business receipts should be organized by category—rent, entertainment, travel, equipment and so on—and not by week or month. This way you can go directly to totaling up the different types of expenses at the end of the year for tax preparation.

Every time you spend money in the business (or once a week or month), note in your records the following:

- the amount
- the date
- a brief description of the business purpose of the transaction (office rent, new stapler, gas, etc.), and
- whom you paid (Chevron, Kinko's).

Details on how to keep a good manual or computer system follow below.

1. Manual Bookkeeping System

If you have enough gumption to go into business, you should be able to pick up enough about recordkeeping to start off on the right foot. The manual system works fine for very small enterprises and costs only $5 to $20 for ledger paper or a simple business record booklet at an office supply store.

Keep income and expense records using ledger sheets listing income and expense items. This columnar paper (usually light green like those eyeshades the money counters wear) is found in office supply stores. A sample ledger sheet is shown below.

At the top of the columns, list categories of expenses or income. The chart below is called an "expense journal." Gross receipts are recorded on an "income journal," which is very similar.

As the "Jumbalaya Enterprises" example below illustrates, an expense journal first lists your business's different types of expenditures—such as cash, credit card and check payments.

Next is the date when an expense was paid or incurred. Going across the top of the paper are headings for listing the category of each type of expenditure, such as "rent," "supplies" or "utilities." (Ideally, every item of expense listed should be taken from an invoice, receipt, cash voucher, check register or other document showing it was incurred by the business.)

Jumbalaya Enterprises—Expense Journal—April 20XX

Ck	Cash	Cred	Date	Transaction	Advert	Util	Supplies	Rent
		VISA	4/1	Daily News	48.00			
122			4/15	Prop. Mgmt. Serv.				782.75
	$		4/21	Office World			62.44	
123			4/30	City Electric		91.50		
124			4/30	KFOO Radio	95.00			
April 20XX				TOTALS	143.00	91.50	62.44	782.75

After each item of current expense or income is entered under its proper heading, all of the columns are periodically totaled. Typically, totals are run weekly or monthly. Finally, the 12 months are added up at the end of the year for tax reporting.

Make up your ledger sheets at least once a month. It's better to do it more often—daily or weekly, when everything is fresh in your mind and before data is misplaced.

Keep old records. Ledger sheets (and your receipts for expenses and canceled checks) should be kept at least three years after you file your tax return. This is the period in which the IRS or state tax agency is most likely to audit your business. Keep them six years if space permits. And if you ever sell your business, a buyer may want to see old records to verify its financial history.

2. Computerized Bookkeeping System

Recordkeeping on a computer works on the same principles as the manual system, but the computer automates the process. A simple software program like Quicken (Intuit) or MS Money (Microsoft) eliminates the need for a handwritten set of books. With Quicken or MS Money, you can print out records, like a profit and loss statement, in a flash. Quicken or MS Money ($50 or less) are fine for most small service businesses. I use Quicken in my law practice. For businesses with inventories, a more sophisticated software program like QuickBooks or Peachtree Accounting, is necessary.

It works like a checkbook register, as shown below. Each transaction, usually a business expense or an item of income, is typed in as either a check out of, or deposit into, your bank account. (You can also record "cash" and "credit card" expenses in Quicken or MS Money using separate accounts as shown in the illustration below.)

Sample Quicken Check Register (Along With Credit Card and Petty Cash Registers

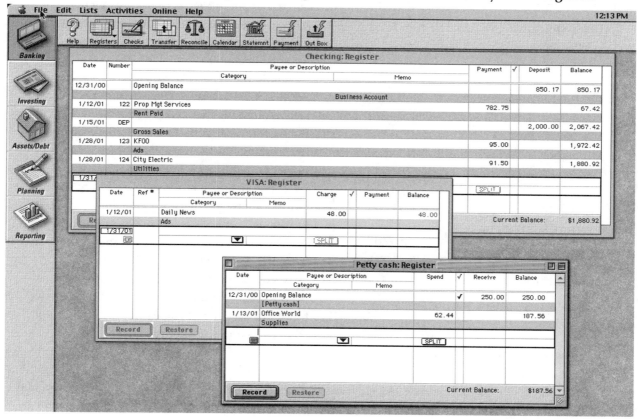

Assign a number or category name to each transaction and type it in. For instance, call "201" office rent, or type "rent," which tells the computer to group together all rent payments. Category 202 could be "supplies," and so on. Track "advertising" as category 301, or break it into subcategories such as 302 for "ads—Yellow Pages," 303 for "ads—newspaper." Quicken groups the entries like a manual system ledger sheet system and does the math. You are now only a keystroke away from up-to-date expense journals, which are the heart of your bookkeeping system.

Sample Quicken Income Statement

Jumbalaya Enterprises
Income Statement

1/1/01 Through 1/31/01

Category	1/1/01- 1/31/01
Inc/Exp	
Income	
Gross Sales	2,000.00
Total Income	2,000.00
Expenses	
Ads	143.00
Rent Paid	782.75
Supplies	62.44
Utilities	91.50
Total Expenses	1,079.69
Total Inc/Exp	920.31

Take it from someone who did not grow up in the computer age—Quicken and MS Money are easy to use, even if you type like a snail. An hour should get you up and running, no kidding. No more math errors that always plagued me when I kept books by hand.

Avoiding computation mistakes isn't the best reason to use Quicken or MS Money—the categorization feature is my favorite. It eliminates the chore of going through (or paying someone to organize) a jumble of paper. A computerized system allows you to see your income and expenses—by category—instantly. Your "profit & loss" statement is only a keystroke or two away, so you can whip out a financial statement for a bank or creditor at any time. (See Sample Quicken Income Statement above.)

With the push of a button, you'll also have at least 90% of the data needed to prepare your business's annual tax schedule or return. If you do your own tax preparing, this feature is a godsend. Quicken and MS Money are compatible with tax preparation programs like TurboTax for Business (Windows and Macintosh). These excellent computer programs published by Intuit will prepare any type of business tax return: sole proprietor, C or S corporations, partnerships or limited liability company. You can move your financial data from Quicken or MS Money into those tax return programs, without having to reenter the same figures. These programs can also track your personal finances, too, by using separate accounts.

Simple programs like Quicken or MS Money are not adequate for some small businesses, namely sellers of goods that maintain an inventory. Quick-Books (Intuit) handles more complex small business bookkeeping tasks and sells in the $100 to $200 range, depending on the features needed.

A tiny sideline business may not justify a computer, but if you are serious, then you should come into the 2000s. Not only is a computer a nearly foolproof bookkeeping tool, it can also churn out professional-looking letters, bills and invoices. At the end of the year, computers take minutes instead of hours to produce data for a tax return. Don't take my word for it; talk to fellow businesspeople about their computers and software programs.

EXAMPLE: Jack Johnson is a medical technology consultant with only one client who pays him monthly. So keeping track of gross receipts is no problem. Expenses are more troublesome. Jack maintains an office, and occasionally hires support staff. He travels in the U.S. and abroad, drives his car for business, pays insurance and so on. Over the course of a year, Jack incurs hundreds of different expenses, so he needs an expense recordkeeping system. Jack keeps a business checking account in addition to his personal account. He writes business checks or uses his business-only credit card. Jack is an ideal candidate for Quicken, MS Money or another computerized system.

D. What Kinds of Records to Keep

Business records can be divided into three categories: *income*, *expenses* and *capital expenditures*. Income and expenses are pretty much self-explanatory, but "capital expenditures" (Chapter 2) may be new to you. We'll go over each in order.

1. Income Records

Your operation may take in money from one or many sources, depending on your line of work. Most inflows are termed "gross" receipts—for goods or services sold. Business records should distinguish all types of payments received and the source of each item—for instance, "retail sales" and "cash." Identifying payments received is necessary because money you put into your business's bank account may not always be taxable income—for example, a loan to the business from a relative or a tax refund check.

There are numerous ways to track gross receipts. Retail stores typically use cash registers with tapes or printouts of sales. Service businesses use bank deposit records, keeping copies of deposit slips identifying the monies put into a business bank account, as well as the monthly bank statements. Deposit slip copies indicate the form and source of items deposited—cash, checks, credit card payments —which are not detailed on the bank statements.

Part

1

The Basics

Commonsense Tips on Keeping Business Records

File paid bills, canceled checks and other business documents in an orderly fashion and keep them in a safe place. Some people use manila folders or an accordion file divided into "car," "utilities," "entertainment" and so on. At a minimum, stuff receipts in the proper folders throughout the year and total them up at tax time. Staple the adding machine tape to each folder or stack of receipts. If this works, good for you. You aren't required to keep records in a formal "set of books."

A perfectly adequate recordkeeping system for a small business might include some or all of the following:

- Check register—preferably from a separate bank account for your business
- Summary of receipts of gross income— totaled daily, weekly or monthly
- Monthly summary listing of expenses
- Disbursements record (check register or expense journal) showing payments of bills
- Asset purchase listing (equipment, vehicles, real estate used in business)
- Employee compensation record (if you have workers).

Keep track of where your money comes from. Make notes explaining the origin of *all* money put into both your business and personal bank accounts. Write down the source of the deposit on the slip or in your checkbook while it is fresh in your mind.

When the IRS audits, they want to see bank statements, deposit slips and canceled checks. If you don't furnish bank records voluntarily, they can get them from your bank—and you can't stop it. If bank deposits are greater than your reported income, you must show why, otherwise the auditor will assume the difference was unreported income —and assess tax, interest and penalties.

There may be a valid explanation of why a deposit is not taxable income. For instance, say you transferred $10,000 from your personal bank account into your business bank account to buy inventory. Or maybe you sold a personal item or put inherited money in your business. So keep notes to explain bank deposits.

Income from services reported on 1099 forms. If you had income from selling your services to another business, you should receive Form 1099s from the payors showing how much you were paid in a year. Include this 1099 income on your tax return—the IRS computer routinely matches Form 1099 and W-2 reported payments to tax returns. If the 1099 is wrong, make sure you get the issuer to send a corrected form to you and the IRS.

> **EXAMPLE:** Dr. No was snagged by the IRS on a computer check of 1099-form payments. He had claimed less gross income than Medicare alone reported to the IRS they paid him—not even taking into account his other patients! (How Dr. No thought he could get away with this is beyond me.) He was audited and heavy penalties and interest were added to his audit bill. Dr. No could have also been (but lucky for him, wasn't) charged criminally with tax evasion.

2. Expense Records

As the old saying goes, to make money in your venture you have to spend money. The good news is that "ordinary and necessary" business expenditures are deductible against your gross receipts. (This is discussed in detail in Chapter 1.) And business asset purchases are deductible, but under different rules. (See Chapter 2, Writing Off Business Assets.)

Recording expenses is only part of the job. You also need proof the business-related expenditures were made—such as receipts, invoices, credit card charge slips, canceled checks or lease agreements. Microbusinesses can get by with saving paid bills and invoices in accordion folders or envelopes by expense category ("supplies," "travel" and so on).

Get organized. Everyone selling services should keep a daily organizer to serve as a business diary and calendar. Something like a Franklin Day Planner or Palm Pilot® not only keeps your schedule straight, it also serves as a permanent tax record of expense items. An organizer lists appointments, helps you note tax-related things like travel, names of business contacts entertained, out-of-pocket cash expenses for bridge tolls and parking.

Canceled checks and paid receipts. These are the standard documents that back up your business expenses. The IRS now accepts statements from financial institutions showing check clearing or electronic funds transfers, without the actual canceled checks or charge slips in most cases. This rule covers credit card statements and banks that do not return canceled checks. To satisfy an IRS auditor, the financial institution's statement must show the date, name of the payee and amount of expense. However, you may have to produce copies of the charge slips or canceled checks if the auditor is not satisfied with the statement. (My advice is to keep your original credit card slips, especially for travel and entertainment expenses. See "Business Entertainment, Meals and Travel Records," below.)

Proof of payment by itself does not establish a business expense deduction. If audited, you also need to show *how* the expense was related to the business. Many items (rent, advertising) are pretty much self-explanatory. For others, not obviously business-related (travel, entertainment), you should make notes when incurred—in your business records or diary, or on the receipt—to explain the business purpose. (See "Business Entertainment, Meals and Travel Records," below.)

Business Entertainment, Meals and Travel Records

With certain expenses, the tax code requires more stringent recordkeeping. Primarily, these are business expenses for travel, meals and entertainment. (IRC § 274.) In tax lingo, these are "T&E" items.

For each T&E expense you must document five elements:

1. Date
2. Amount
3. Place
4. Business purpose, and
5. Business relationship.

Get in the habit of making notes of these five items on the back of receipts and in your business diary or calendar. For example, write on your calendar or appointment book, "Lunch with Bill Jones, client, to discuss new advertising campaign. Ritz Restaurant, $60 with tip." If you used your American Express card, write "Bill Jones" and the topic discussed ("television advertising on Channel 5") on the back of the charge slip.

No receipts are necessary for expense items less than $75. The IRS no longer requires at audit any paid receipts, canceled checks, bills or other proof of single-expense items of less than $75 each. However, the cost itself must appear reasonable, ordinary and necessary for your business to the auditor. There is one exception: For lodging expenses, you must have a receipt regardless of the amount.

3. Asset Records

Whenever a business acquisition provides a benefit beyond the year incurred—a fax machine, building, car or office furniture, and so forth—the IRS classifies it as a business "asset" or "capital" item which must be tracked separately from current business expense records. Accountants call purchased assets records the "fixed asset schedule" or "asset log." You don't have to know the terminology—just keep a separate file for each item or category of business assets. Show the date of purchase and the type of asset—computer, truck, machinery and so on. And unless

Sample Travel and Entertainment Diary Form

Date	Type of Expense	Place	Business Purpose	Amount				
				Travel	M & E	Other	Mileage	Reimbursed
			Totals 1/2001					

it is obvious, write a short explanation of how the asset is used in the business.

Long-term assets must be tax-deducted differently from everyday operating expenses like rent or telephone bills. Generally, you can't deduct the whole cost in the year of purchase; instead, you must take "depreciation" or "amortization" deductions over several years. There is one important exception to this rule: Up to $24,000 (2001) worth of assets may be written off in the year of purchase under a special tax code provision, IRC § 179. (See Chapter 2, Writing Off Business Assets, for details.)

Life is much simpler for leased assets. With the limited exception of leased vehicles, you simply deduct lease payments instead of maintaining an asset log for them.

a. How to Keep Asset Records

For business assets, keep records showing:

1. A *description* of each item, the date acquired and how you acquired it, usually by purchasing it. Typically, all this information is shown on an invoice or receipt from the seller. A description is important because the tax code has different rules for different assets. For instance, office furniture is deductible over seven years, but computers over five. (These categories are discussed in Chapter 2, Writing Off Business Assets.)

2. *When* you started using the asset—the month and year it was "placed in service." Ordinarily you start using something as soon as you acquire it, but not always, so note it.

3. Your tax *basis* in the asset. Usually, this is how much you paid for it, including sales tax, installation and delivery. But the basis could be greater if you later spent money on improvements or modifications—such as a larger hard drive added to a computer. (See Chapter 2 for a discussion of determining the basis of assets.) Conversely, there may have been reductions in the basis over the life of the asset. For instance, depreciation deductions

taken on your past years' tax returns, if you used the equipment in a prior venture.

4. The sales price of the asset when you *dispose* of it or, if it becomes worthless or obsolete, the date you discarded it.

5. Any *costs of selling* the asset—for instance, a newspaper ad for your old computer.

Keep track of assets and their tax bases either manually, using ledger sheets or asset log books, or with a computer program such as QuickBooks, discussed above.

b. Special Records for Listed or Mixed-Use Property

"Listed" or "mixed-use" property are tax terms for certain assets, such as cell phones and laptop computers. This category was concocted by Congress for items with a high potential for personal as well as business use. If you use listed property strictly for business and keep it on the premises, then this special recordkeeping rule does not apply to you. But if there is any personal benefit, or if you keep the property at your home, you must record all personal use. As you might expect, you can't claim any tax benefit for the personal use portion.

Listed property includes:

1. Autos, airplanes and other forms of transportation.

2. Entertainment-type property such as VCRs, cameras and camcorders.

3. Cellular telephones and similar communications equipment.

4. Computers and related peripheral equipment (if not used exclusively at a regular business location).

Satisfy this rule by keeping a log book showing dates, times and business purpose. Or write notes in a calendar or business diary. (For more information on listed property see IRS Publication 946, How to Depreciate Property.)

EXAMPLE: Joan bought a laptop computer. She uses it 60% of the time for her direct marketing business. Her son, Jason, uses it the rest of the time for school projects and games. Joan should keep a log by the computer, showing the times it was used for her business and for personal purposes, in case the IRS comes calling.

IRC § 179 Rule. If you want to immediately deduct the cost of listed property under IRC § 179, you can if records show that it is used more than 50% for business. (See Chapter 2 for a full explanation of IRC § 179.)

> **EXAMPLE:** Joan paid $3,000 for her computer. Because she uses it 60% for business, she can write off $1,800 as an IRC § 179 expense. But if Joan only used it 45% of the time for business, she could not claim it as an IRC § 179 write-off. (She would have to take depreciation deductions instead over five years.)

Recordkeeping If You Have Several Small Businesses

If you report income from more than one business on a tax return—say, you are a part-time coin dealer and own a bicycle shop, and your spouse has a sideline home decorating business—keep three sets of records, because each venture requires separate tax reporting. Three businesses operated as sole proprietorships require three IRS Schedule C forms with your tax return each year. (See Chapter 6, Sole Proprietorships.)

E. How Long Records Should Be Kept

The IRS normally has three years to audit you and your business, starting from the date you file a tax return. (Note that if you never file a return for a given tax year, all bets are off—you can be audited forever.) So, three years is the absolute minimum period for record retention. However, for serious

tax reporting misstatements, the IRS can go back six years—and for outright fraud, it can go back an unlimited period of time.

Your state tax agencies can inspect your records, too. Some state agencies have statutes of limitations for auditing that are longer than the IRS's. Considering all the laws here, the best thing to do is keep your regular tax-related documents—receipts, invoices, bank statements—for six years.

Asset records are an exception, meaning equipment, vehicles and sometimes real estate. For assets like these, acquisition records should be kept for six years after the asset has been disposed of. If a tax agency audits your business, the issue of annual depreciation deductions of a long-term asset may be questioned. Only by having the original acquisition documents can the starting tax basis be proven.

> **EXAMPLE:** In 1986, Calista bought a building for her insurance agency operation. She tax deducted all expenses of maintaining the building and took depreciation deductions. Calista sold her agency, including the real estate, in 1998. She filed her tax return reporting the sale of the business on 4/15/99. Calista should keep her 1986 documents on the purchase of the building until at least April 15, 2002 (three years from the date of the tax return), or better, for six years, to April 15, 2005.

F. Bookkeeping Methods of Tracking Income and Expenses

There are two manual methods for keeping your books, called "single-entry" and "double-entry" bookkeeping.

If you are doing books by hand and don't have a lot of transactions, the single-entry method is okay. A better way is the double-entry method because it is inherently more accurate. Let's briefly look at each manual method, and then move quickly into the advantages of using a computer instead of a manual system.

1. Single-Entry System

Single-entry bookkeeping is the easiest way to go and is perfectly acceptable to the IRS. Single-entry, like it sounds, means you write down each transaction once indicating the type of expense or income. Use ledger paper or just a lined notebook.

Single-entry bookkeeping records the flow of income and expenses by keeping a running total of money taken in (gross receipts) and money paid out (disbursements.)

Gross receipts figures are typically summarized daily and weekly, and along with summaries of expenses, totalled monthly. At the end of the year the 12 monthly summaries of income and expenses are totalled up. You are ready for tax time. Easy, huh?

A single-entry system, however, does not work for tracking inventory, loans, assets and liabilities. For this, you need a double-entry system, discussed below.

2. Double-Entry System

Many small businesses start out with a single-entry method, but later convert to *double-entry*. Like it sounds, this bookkeeping system requires two entries for each transaction. A double-entry system has checks and balances to assure accuracy. Each transaction requires an entry once as a "debit" and the second time as an equal "credit." For instance, you buy a Palm Pilot for $500. It will be recorded as a "debit" on one side of your records because you spent money, and a "credit" on the other side since you've acquired an asset.

A double-entry system is time-consuming if done by hand, because everything is recorded twice. And, if done manually, this method requires a formal set of books—"journals" and "ledgers." As illustrated below, all transactions are first entered into a journal, then are totaled and posted (written) on a ledger sheet—the same amount is written on a line in the journal and then again in the ledger by category.

Typical ledger account categories are *income*, *expenses*, *assets* and *liabilities* (debts). There also may be an account called "net worth," which shows the amount by which total assets exceed total liabilities, or vice versa if you are in the hole. The "net worth" account is not required for IRS purposes, but it is a good measure of your success, nonetheless.

Income and expense accounts are totaled up in the ledger and this data is used for tax preparation. Your books are "closed" at the end of each tax year, new books are begun for the new business year. Asset, liability and net worth accounts, however, are "open" as long as you are in operation and carry over from year to year.

Computers make it easy. If you are using a computer program, the double-entry is done automatically for you. You only enter the new data once, and the computer makes the second entry. Programs such as Quicken (Intuit) and MS Money (Microsoft) work this way.

If you want to try it manually after all, here is a sample of a double-entry system, showing a payment of rent by Sam's Computer Shop.

General Journal of Sam's Computer Sales & Service

Date	Description of Entry	Debit	Credit
10/5/01	Rent Expense	$1000	
	Cash		$1000

As you can see, payment of rent resulted in two separate journal entries—a debit to rent expense of $1,000, and an equal credit to cash of $1,000. The debits in a double-entry method (here, $1,000) must always equal the credits ($1,000). If they don't, you know there is an error somewhere. So, double-entry allows you to "balance your books," which you can't do with the single-entry method.

With a computer, the $1,000 rent expenditure is input as an expense (a debit), then automatically posted to the "rent" account as a credit. The computer eliminates the extra step or the need to comprehend debits and credits—and it doesn't make math errors.

G. Timing Methods of Accounting: Cash and Accrual

Besides recordkeeping systems, there are also two *accounting methods* for recording the income and expenses called the "cash" and "accrual" methods. These are two sets of tax accounting rules for the timing of income and expenses.

The general proposition is that a venture's income and expenses must ordinarily be tax-reported in the year in which they occur. Normally the period is a calendar year, but for a few businesses it may be a non-calendar fiscal year.

> **EXAMPLE:** Monique buys $7,000 in supplies for her hairdressing salon in January 2002. But Monique hasn't filed her 2001 income taxes yet —can she deduct the $7,000 expense on her 2001 tax return? No, because the expense was incurred in 2002. Monique cannot shift it to another year. This is true no matter which accounting method is applied.

Less clear-cut is the question: What if Monique had bought the supplies in 2001, but didn't pay for them until 2002? In which year does Monique take the deduction? To answer, you need to know the difference between cash and accrual methods of accounting and which one Monique's business is using.

1. Cash Method Accounting

The term "cash method" refers to recording an expense when it is paid or income when it is received—not how it is paid. So, don't take the word "cash" here literally; it covers any kind of payment— checks, barter, credit cards, etc.—as well as the green stuff.

Most businesses selling *services* use the cash method of accounting for income and expenses. The cash method makes sense even to us non-accountants. You simply report income in the year you receive it and an expense in the year you pay it.

⚠ **The cash method seems simple, but there are a few special tax rules to watch out for.** One is the legal doctrine of "constructive receipt," which requires counting some items as income before you actually receive them. This means you have income, for tax purposes, as soon as it is available or credited to your account—even if you don't take it.

> **EXAMPLE:** Ray gets a $3,000 check for consulting in early December 2001, but doesn't deposit it until January 2002. Because Ray could have cashed it in 2001—the banks were open and the check was good—2001 is the tax year in which Ray "constructively received" the $3,000.

The corollary of the constructive receipt rule is that you are not allowed a deduction in the current year for items paid for but not yet received.

> **EXAMPLE:** Ray got a special deal on *Consulting Times*, a monthly business publication. He paid $360 for a three-year subscription in July of 2001. He can tax-deduct only $60 in 2001 ($1/6$ of the total); the balance must be prorated over the term of the subscription and deducted $120 ($1/3$) in 2002, $120 ($1/3$) in 2003 and $60 ($1/6$ in 2004.

Watch the calendar. There is some flexibility allowed by the IRS for prepaying some expenses at the end of the year. The last week of every December, I review the income and expense figures of my law practice to see if I can shave some money off my tax bill. For instance, if I pay January's office rent on December 27, I'll get the deduction a year earlier. As long as I don't prepay an expense more than 30 days in advance, I'm okay. Or, if I had an especially good year (meaning a big tax bill), I can stock up on office supplies or buy new equipment to write off under IRC § 179. And in some years the converse is true—my late December accounting shows a disappointing year. Then I put off new purchases or paying creditors until January.

2. Accrual Method Accounting

Many C corporations, manufacturers and businesses with inventories of goods *must* use the *accrual method* of accounting. The accrual method requires some getting used to.

With accrual accounting, income is treated as received when it is earned—regardless of when it is actually received. On the other side, an expense is recorded at the time the obligation arose—which is not necessarily when it is paid.

In accountant's lingo, business expenses and income accrue the moment they become "fixed." Don't fret; though it sounds complicated, the example below shows that this is not rocket science.

Accrued income and expenses must meet what the tax code calls the "all events" test to become fixed. This means that everything required—all events —to secure a right to receive the income, or to cause a liability for the expense, must have happened. At that point in time it becomes fixed, whether or not any cash has changed hands.

> **EXAMPLE:** George's Foundry, which uses the accrual method, receives a $4,500 deposit in 2001 for custom ironwork to be manufactured in 2002. George won't report $4,500 as income in 2001 because it hasn't been earned yet. On the expense side, if the foundry incurs a $250

charge in 2001 for lawyer's fees relating to the contract, it is accrued and tax deducted in 2001—even if not paid for until 2002.

Get help setting up accrual accounting. If your operation keeps inventories, manufactures goods or is a C corporation, consult a tax pro before setting up your accounting system. Find a tax pro familiar with your industry, whether it is a gas station, a loan company or a medical practice. In addition, most software programs accommodate accrual accounting.

3. Hybrid and Special Accounting Methods

Some businesses may choose a combination of the cash and accrual methods of accounting. For instance, Waldo's electronics store may sell items and repair them, too. Waldo may use the *cash* method for repairs, but Waldo's inventory, under tax code rules, must be accounted for on an *accrual* basis. So both methods may be used, creating a hybrid accounting system.

Other special accounting methods, beyond the scope of this book, apply to farmers and certain businesses working on long-term contracts, manufacturers and building contractors.

You usually need to get permission from the IRS before adopting a hybrid or special method of tax accounting. (See a tax pro or IRS Publication 538, Accounting Periods and Methods.)

4. Changing Accounting Methods

A business must choose an accounting method and notify the IRS which one it is using on its tax return (a box on the form must be checked). Once chosen, that method must be used in all subsequent tax returns unless the IRS grants you permission to switch to another method.

The IRS is concerned that whenever an accounting method is changed the business could obtain an unfair tax advantage—or some expenses or income could get "lost" in the transition. So, if you want to change your venture's accounting method, ordinarily you need permission from the IRS. However, if there is a fundamental change in the operation of your business—say, from selling goods to only offering services—then IRS permission is not required.

> EXAMPLE: Kate's Lamp Repair Service, which has been using the cash method, starts stocking and selling lamps. She now has an inventory, so she must use an accrual accounting method for the retail portion of the business. Permission from the IRS is not required because there was a fundamental change in operation. However, if Kate's remains just a repair shop but wants to change accounting methods, she must get written permission from the IRS.

To get IRS permission for changing methods, file Form 3115, "Application for Change in Accounting Method." File it within 180 days before the end of the year for which you want to make the change. There is a $500 application fee, but the IRS may waive the fee in some circumstances. (See Rev. Proc. 97-27 or a tax pro for further details.)

H. Accounting Periods: Calendar Year or Fiscal Year

All enterprises must keep their books based on accounting periods, called "tax years." For John and Jane Taxpayer, individuals, the tax year is the same as the good old calendar year—starting on January 1 and ending on December 31. Most small businesses are required to use the calendar year, too.

Some enterprises may choose an alternative tax-reporting period called a "fiscal year." This is defined as any one-year period that does not end on December 31.

A business notifies the IRS of its accounting period by checking the designated box on its annual tax return form. Once chosen, the accounting period usually cannot be changed without written approval from the IRS.

Regardless of which accounting tax year is used, a business's payroll taxes must be reported on a calendar year basis. Individual taxpayers are *never* allowed to report on a fiscal year basis.

1. Calendar Year

Sole proprietors, partnerships, limited liability companies, S corporations and personal service corporations must report as calendar-year entities, *unless* they can convince the IRS they qualify for an exception. (See Section 2, below.)

2. Fiscal Year

A minority of small enterprises may legally use a "fiscal year" instead of a calendar tax year. A fiscal year is a one-year period ending on the last day of any month *except* December. The fiscal year is not favored by the tax code for small businesses, and when allowed it is usually for C corporations. Other entities can use a fiscal year only by showing a business reason for it, such as a cyclical or seasonal business—for instance, farming. For IRS permission, file Form 8716, Election to Have a Tax Year Other Than a Required Tax Year. Consult a tax pro first to see if this really makes sense.

3. Short Tax Years

A "short tax year" occurs whenever a business starts up during a calendar year on any day but January 1. For instance, if Sandra's Sunshades opens on July 15 and uses a calendar tax year reporting period, her first tax year is only five and a half months and ends on December 31. Likewise, a short year occurs if Sandra closes her doors at any time other than the year end. This may require Sandra to prorate certain tax deductions, such as depreciation of assets, to match the short period in that first year of operation.

Resources

- IRS Publication 552, Recordkeeping for Individuals. Helpful especially if you are new in business or are keeping your own books, as it contains examples.
- IRS Publication 583, Starting a Business and Keeping Records, Publication 551, Basis of Assets; Publication 946, How to Depreciate Property; Publication 538, Accounting Periods and Methods; and Publication 535, Business Expenses. These booklets can get fairly technical, but if you are hungry for tax knowledge or are bent on tackling tax return preparation, this is stuff you must know.
- *Keeping the Books*, by Linda Pinson and Jerry Jinnett (Upstart Publishing). A primer for those of you keeping your books without a computer.
- *Small-Time Operator*, by Bernard Kamoroff (Bell Springs Publishing). A wealth of practical recordkeeping and accounting tips from a long-time CPA.
- *Business Owner's Guide to Accounting & Book-keeping*, by Jose Placencia, Bruce Welge & Don Oliver (Oasis Press). A more detailed and complex small business accounting book for those who are really serious about the subject.
- *Accounting and Recordkeeping Made Easy for the Self-Employed*, by Jack Fox (John Wiley & Sons). This book offers case studies, worksheets and sample forms to help you work through basic accounting in a small business.
- Basic accounting system information is available free through the Small Business Administration (SBA). Send for the Resource Directory for Small Business Management: SBA, Mail Code 7111, 409 Third St., SW, Washington, DC 20416 or go to the SBA's website at http://www.sba.gov.

Business Losses and Failures

"There is no such thing as justice—in or out of court."
—Clarence Darrow

The term "risky business" comes to mind whenever I see another brave soul take the plunge into a new venture. Most operations lose money during their start-up phase. Some folks hang in there until the business turns the corner, while most others throw in the towel after a year or two. A significant number will go under because they lose money—and a few of these will have done so badly that they will be forced to file for bankruptcy.

Fortunately, the tax code softens the blow for people who lose money in business. Congress has long believed that one way to encourage new enterprises is to give a tax break to those who try. After all, when the business flourishes, the government shares in profits, so why shouldn't it absorb part of the losses as well? The help that you will get from Uncle Sam, however, depends on whether or not your business is incorporated, and whether you are active in the business operation or just an investor. The basics on taking tax benefits from business losses are the subject of this chapter. By "losses," we are not talking about bad debts that you incur in your business operation. For the tax treatment of bad debts, see Chapter 1.

Business Losses in a Nutshell

1. The law allows, but limits, tax losses that can be claimed by owners and investors in a business.
2. Your ability to claim a tax benefit for a business loss may depend on whether or not your business is incorporated.
3. Because a C corporation is a separate tax entity, its operating losses belong to the corporation, not the shareholders.
4. C corporation shareholders get a tax break for their business's losses, but only in the year that the corporation fails, or when they sell their stock at a loss.

A. Unincorporated Businesses

Congress extends a helping hand by allowing struggling sole proprietors, partners, limited liability company members and shareholders of S corporations to reap a tax benefit from business operation losses. Complex rules dictate how much and when you can claim business operating losses for a tax break.

1. Owners' Business Operating Losses

Owners of an unincorporated business—a sole proprietorship, partnership or limited liability company—can claim business operating losses on their individual tax returns. This loss is called a "net operating loss" or NOL. It can be used to offset other income to lower the total amount subject to income tax. However, NOL can't reduce a taxpayer's income to below zero for tax purposes. So the law allows unused losses to be taken in other tax years, as we explain below.

EXAMPLE: John Jones Hardware, a sole proprietorship, shuts its doors in 2001. The business had profits in its first two years, 1999 and 2000, but lost $100,000 in its third and final year of operation. In 2001, John's wife, Jean, worked at the phone company to keep the family afloat and earned $25,000. The Joneses also sold mutual funds they had owned for several years at a $10,000 gain, so their total family taxable income was $35,000. The Joneses can claim $35,000 of the hardware store net operating loss on their tax return in 2001. The balance of $65,000 must be used to offset income in other tax years.

The following is a summary of the NOL rules:
- An NOL is first taken to offset your other income in the year it occurred.
- If your business operating loss (NOL) exceeds your other total income for the year, you can amend as many as two past tax returns and perhaps qualify for a tax refund. An unused

loss must first be carried back two years and the tax return amended to show the loss. From there, any unused business loss is carried forward to each of the preceding two years. (The example below should help make this clear.)

- If there's still more loss, you can carry it forward to 20 years, but any unused NOL expires after 20 years. The overall effect is to spread out the tax benefit of business losses over as many as 23 years.

EXAMPLE: Harry started Nebula Graphic Designs in 2001 and lost $40,000 that year. Harry also worked as a printer's representative, netting $12,000 in commissions. Harry claims $12,000 of the loss to wipe out his commission income in 2001. Then Harry must carry the balance of the net operating loss of $28,000 back two years to 1999 to offset income and hopefully entitle him to a refund of taxes paid that year. If he still has any unused loss, Harry will amend his 2000 return. He can keep claiming the loss against income until it is fully used up or the 20-year period expires.

⚠ Be sure to claim your business operating losses. You must notify the IRS on your tax return that you intend to carry over your outfit's net operating loss. Either attach a written statement to the loss year's tax return, or attach IRS Form 3621, Net Operating Loss Carry-Over. Use this form to determine how much loss is left over after the first tax year. See a tax pro if you're not sure what to do.

2. Investors—Different Rules

If you are an investor in someone else's unincorporated enterprise (sole proprietorship, partnership or limited liability company), the tax result is different than if you operated the business yourself. An investor is *not* entitled to any tax benefit from operating losses of an ongoing business. Sorry—it's the law.

However, if the venture goes bust, you can deduct some of these losses. Here are the rules:

- You can claim a loss on the investment to offset other your income for that year.
- You can carry any excess loss forward to future years.
- You *cannot* carry the investment loss to past years. Your loss is termed "capital loss" and is treated under different rules than operating losses (NOLs) for business owners discussed in Section A1, above. (IRC § 1212.)

More rules for capital losses. Capital losses are first deducted dollar-for-dollar from your other capital gains, if any. A *capital gain* results from an investment held for more than one year—for example, a $10,000 capital gain from selling Microsoft stock. Any excess capital loss (after offsetting your capital gain) can then be deducted against ordinary income (compensation earned from your labor), but only up to $3,000 in any year. Any capital loss left over can be carried forward until your death. If we've lost you, let's go to another example.

EXAMPLE 1: Jake and Mona Willow invest $45,000 in Jake, Jr.'s, digital imaging business. The business fails in 2001, and the Willows lose their entire investment—a $45,000 capital loss. If they have other income but no capital gains to offset this loss, it will take them 15 years (at $3,000 per year) to tax-deduct the whole amount.

EXAMPLE 2: The Willows sold stock in Microsoft in 2002, realizing an $8,000 capital gain. They can claim $11,000 of the investment loss from Jake Jr.'s digital imaging business (the $8,000 capital gain plus $3,000 of ordinary income). After taking $3,000 as a tax loss in 2001 and $11,000 in 2002, the Willows have $31,000 in capital losses remaining to be taken in future years. They will only be able to deduct $3,000 per year against ordinary income unless they have some more capital gains.

Three Tax Rules That Might Limit Your Loss Deductions

In addition to the normal tax rules for deducting operating business losses, there are three more hurdles to clear before you are home free with a tax break. However, with the possible exception of the "hobby loss rules," none of these three sets of laws affect the average working small-time operator, so we won't go into much detail about them. The rules apply to sole proprietors, partners, limited liability company members and to S corporation (but not C corporation) shareholders.

- **Hobby Loss Rules.** You cannot deduct a loss from a venture unless it was operated with a "profit motive." (See Chapter 13, Microbusinesses and Home-Based Businesses, for a full explanation of how this rule works.) This tax law is primarily aimed at wealthier folks who race cars or yachts, breed show horses and claim tax loss benefits—but it has been applied to us common folk as well.

- **At-Risk Rules.** You may deduct no more than your economic investment in the venture. This law targets the tax games played with so-called "tax shelter" investments. For instance, Manny puts $5,000 cash into ABC Partners along with a $10,000 nonrecourse promissory note—a promise to put more money into the partnership in the future. Manny is given a one-third partnership interest for his contributions. By signing a "nonrecourse" note, Manny doesn't have personal liability to the ABC partnership. The note was to be paid out of Manny's share of the profits of ABC. He may never make good on the note, and in fact, Manny doesn't ever pony up because there aren't any profits. The business goes belly up and Manny's tax loss is limited to $5,000. The at-risk rules are also tied into the passive activity loss rules discussed next.

- **Passive Activity Loss Rules.** If you have ownership in, but do not "materially participate" in the conduct of a business venture, you may be subject to the very complicated "passive activity loss" rules. In essence, nonworking investors subject to these rules may not tax deduct an operating loss from the investment in excess of the income produced by the business. For example, ABC partnership takes in $30,000, but spends $40,000. Manny, a nonworking one-third partner, doesn't get the benefit of a loss of $3,333 on his tax return that year. Manny can, however, carry over that loss and take it in a future year in which he does participate. (Note: There is a separate set of passive activity loss rules for closely held C corporations, and exceptions to this rule for rental real estate investments. Both of these topics are beyond the scope of this book.)

⚠️ **Foreclosure of business property by a lender can result in "cancellation of indebtedness" taxable income.** See a tax pro if you have any questions.

📖 **There is a way to get beyond these limitations** —if the business is incorporated. See Section B, below.

B. Corporations

Whether tax benefits from a corporation's losses can be taken by the shareholders individually, or only by the corporation, depends on several factors, discussed below.

1. Shareholder Losses When a Business Fails

One tax code provision you should know by number if you incorporate is IRC § 1244. This provision allows stockholders in small business corporations— whether they are active in the business or not—to deduct their investment loss in the year the business fails, or when they sell their stock. This option is available if, when the corporation was formed, the total money or property it received in return for stock was less than $1 million.

This means that most individual shareholders may take losses *beyond* the $3,000 annual limit that applies to individual investors in unincorporated businesses. (See Section A, above.) Section 1244 allows a tax loss up to $100,000 (for a married couple filing jointly or a single taxpayer), or $50,000 for a married person filing separately. The loss may be claimed against the shareholder's ordinary income in the year of the loss, reducing or eliminating their tax bill.

And, any excess loss (over $100,000) can be carried forward and claimed in future years. However, in future years, the $3,000 per year limit applies; over that amount, the loss can be used only to off- set any other capital gains from investments, not ordinary income from earnings.

EXAMPLE: Gordon and Joella Hall buy $150,000 in stock in LowTech, a § 1244 corporation. LowTech does poorly (customers apparently wanted high-tech), and in 2001, the Halls sell their stock for $20,000, losing $130,000 of their investment. If they have income of at least $100,000 in 2001, the Halls can offset $100,000 of their investment as a tax loss in 2001.

The remaining $30,000 of the Halls' loss is classed as a "capital loss carry forward." It must be claimed on the Halls' future tax returns. However, if the Halls don't have any capital gains in future years to absorb the loss carryforward, they are limited to an annual loss deduction of $3,000 per year. In this case, it takes the Halls ten years to use up the excess capital loss of $30,000.

💡 **Make sure your corporation qualifies for § 1244 treatment.** The details on forming a § 1244 corporation are in Chapter 7, C Corporations.

If you take a loss under IRC § 1244, you must file a statement with your individual tax return telling the IRS this is what you are doing. If the IRS audits and finds that IRC § 1244 wasn't applicable, your loss is treated instead under "capital loss" rules, discussed in Section A, above. This means you can't take your loss against ordinary income beyond the $3,000 capital loss annual limit, and you will face an audit bill for the disallowed loss claim.

IRC § 1244 stock sales between related parties are suspect. If you claim a tax loss from a transaction with someone related to you, an IRS auditor can disallow it. "Related parties" means parents, children and in-laws, as well as other businesses controlled by family members. To be safe, deal with a non-relative, if possible. For instance, if the corporation stock you own is worthless, sell it to a friend for a dollar. Your buddy has nothing to lose by helping you out—except the dollar.

2. C Corporation Operating Losses

C corporation operating losses are *not* passed through annually to the individual shareholders, as with an S corporation. The losses are "locked" in the C corporation, a separate tax entity from its shareholders.

As with most S corporations, very few small business C corporations pay corporate income taxes; instead, their shareholders typically take out all corporate profits as salaries, bonuses and fringe benefits. (See Chapter 7, C Corporations.) The ideal tax result is to break even. And if corporate income taxes must be paid in one year, it may be possible to get them refunded in a future year that the corporation loses money. This is called a corporate net operating loss (NOL). (Net operating loss is discussed in Section A, above.)

Alternatively, a corporate NOL can be carried back to get refunds of corporate income taxes paid in the past. Keep in mind that any tax refunds go to the corporation, not to its shareholders.

 The fastest way to get a C corporate tax refund is to file IRS Form 1139, Corporation Application for Tentative Refund. The IRS is required to process this form within 90 days, and issue a refund. If your corporation hasn't yet filed its prior year's tax return, use Form 1138, Extension of Time for Payment of Taxes by a Corporation Expecting a Net Operating Loss Carryback instead.

Resources

All of the following IRS publications shed light on the topic of reaping tax benefits from business losses.

- IRS Publication 550, Investment Income and Expenses
- IRS Publication 925, Passive Activity and At-Risk Rules
- IRS Publication 536, Net Operating Losses
- IRS Publication 541, Partnerships
- IRS Publication 908, Bankruptcy Tax Guide

■

5

Tax Concerns of Employers

"If there isn't a law, there will be."

—Harold Farber

Chances are if your venture is successful, you won't be able to do all the work yourself. If you can do it all on your lonesome, skip this chapter.

Being an employer carries a whole new set of tax responsibilities. With employees, the IRS (and the state agency that monitors employees) will be looking over your shoulder to see if you are timely filing payroll tax returns and making required tax deposits.

Using independent contractors (ICs) instead of employees avoids payroll taxes and hassles of paperwork. The IC is responsible for making quarterly estimated tax payments to the IRS and is subject to the self-employment tax (See Chapter 6.) However, the IRS or your state may audit you to see if anyone you call an "independent contractor" rather than an "employee" is classified correctly. If you lose, the consequences can be very expensive, as we shall see.

Every employer must:

- withhold payroll taxes from employees' wages
- remit withheld taxes, together with the business share of employment taxes, to the IRS and your state, and
- make periodic employment tax reports to the IRS (IRC § 3509) and your state.

According to the IRS, the majority of small businesses fall behind in filing reports or making federal tax deposits at one time or another. While many of these employer delinquencies are oversights—like missing a deadline—others reflect poor office management or misunderstanding of complicated employer tax obligations.

It is tempting, in a "cash crunch," to pay rent, utilities and key suppliers instead of making a payroll tax deposit. Folks rationalize that since it takes the IRS months (if not years) to find out, employment taxes can wait. Too often, however, the venture keeps struggling or goes under altogether, but the tax obligation survives.

⚠️ **Under all circumstances, pay your payroll taxes, in full and on time.** If you don't, the IRS will knock at the door, and it won't be a tap. The IRS tacks on interest and large penalties to delinquent payroll taxes. The bill can skyrocket so fast that often, businesses fail as a result. And unlike ordinary debts, payroll taxes survive the death of the business or bankruptcy of the enterprise. Payroll taxes, by law, are personal liabilities of business owner(s) or their heirs. (IRC § 6502.) (See Chapter 18, When You Can't Pay Your Taxes, for strategies to deal with a tax debt.)

Employer Tax Concerns in a Nutshell

1. If your business has employees, you must withhold taxes and file payroll tax reports.
2. IRS auditors are on the alert for businesses that misclassify employees as independent contractors, and they can levy heavy penalties on violators.

A. Payroll Taxes

The term "payroll taxes" covers three different types of taxes that every employer is responsible for:

- **Income tax withheld** from each employee's paycheck throughout the year. You must send an IRS W-2 form to each employee showing all payments and all withholdings from their wages. W-2 forms must be furnished by January 31 of each following year. By February 28, employers must also file IRS Form W-3 (summary and transmittal form) and copies of all the W-2s to the Social Security Administration, which transmits the data to the IRS.

- **Social Security and Medicare tax (FICA).** The employee's share is withheld from each paycheck; the employer must match this amount. The total FICA tax rate is 15.3% of wages paid up to $80,400 (2001). All income over this amount is taxed at 2.9% for Medicare.

- **Federal Unemployment Tax (FUTA).** This tax goes to the unemployment insurance system and is paid by the employer. The employee pays no part of FUTA.

IRS Publications 15 and 15-A, Circular E, Employers' Tax Guide show you how to figure tax withholding for employees. Form W-4 (Employee's Withholding Allowance Certificate) helps an employer determine how much to withhold from employees' paychecks for federal income tax purposes. But one look at Circular E (64 pages of fine print) might convince you to hire a payroll tax service or get your accountant to do the calculations—at least the first time around.

Verify Social Security numbers. Employees do not always give their correct Social Security numbers (SSN) when filling out a Form W-4. It is a good idea to call the Social Security Administration (SSA) to verify they are using a correct number. You can contact the SSA at 800-772-1213.

Generally, each employee's withheld income and FICA taxes are paid to the IRS monthly, by making federal tax deposits at specified banks. (If the total owed is $2,500 or less, the deposits are due quarterly.) An IRS Federal Tax Deposit coupon (Form 8109-B) must be submitted with each payroll tax payment.

If your total annual payroll tax obligation exceeds $200,000, you must make electronic deposits. Call the IRS at 800-555-4477 or 800-945-8400 for details, and see IRS Publication 966.

Employment tax deposits are reported to the IRS on Form 941, Employer's Quarterly Federal Tax Return. This form is due one month after the end of each calendar quarter that you have employees. Form 941 shows how many employees you had, how much you paid them and the amount of Social Security, Medicare and federal income tax withheld during the three-month period. (A sample Form 941 follows.) Alternatively, you can file Form 941 Telefile by using a touch-tone telephone. Call the IRS at 800-829-1040 or visit the IRS's website at http://www.irs.gov for more information.

There is also an annual unemployment tax report detailing FUTA taxes due (Forms 940 or 940EZ). This form shows how much federal unemployment

tax is owed. A credit is allowed for any state unemployment taxes paid. (You don't get any credit unless you paid the state unemployment tax on time.) FUTA is 100% paid by the employer, with no contribution or deduction from an employee's wages.

Payroll tax obligations are based on a "trust fund" theory. The employer initially acts as a tax collector by holding employees' taxes in trust until paid to the IRS. Violation of this trust can bring on both civil and criminal punishments to the employer. Although the IRS seldom throws anyone in jail, it can—and often does—seize a business's assets and force it to close down if it owes back payroll taxes.

States Have Payroll Taxes, Too

Most states that tax income also require employers to withhold employees' taxes similar to the federal law. Some cities, such as New York City, have payroll taxes, too.

1. Personal Responsibility for Payroll Taxes

The IRS and most states can hold people associated with a small business *personally responsible* for payment if the operation fails to meet its payroll tax obligations. This draconian power is authorized by the Trust Fund Recovery Penalty. (IRC § 6672.)

To enforce this law, a Revenue Officer—an experienced IRS collector—investigates people associated with an active business (or, more likely, a defunct one). Anyone found responsible has the "trust fund" portion of unpaid payroll taxes treated as a personal debt.

The "trust fund" portion is the income tax that should have been withheld from an employee's wages, *plus* one-half of the FICA tax (7.65% of the first $80,400 (2001) of wages paid). The other half of the FICA tax (7.65%) and the employer's federal unemployment tax (FUTA) are not trust fund taxes, and so are not personal debts.

Form **941**		**Employer's Quarterly Federal Tax Return**			OMB No. 1545-0029

Form **941**
(Rev. January 2001)
Department of the Treasury
Internal Revenue Service

Employer's Quarterly Federal Tax Return
► See separate instructions for information on completing this return.
Please type or print.

Enter state code for state in which deposits were made **only** if different from state in address to the right ► [:   ] (see page 2 of instructions).

Name (as distinguished from trade name)
Peter Cone
Trade name, if any

Address (number and street)
362 Main Street

Date quarter ended
December 31, 2001
Employer identification number
10-1234567
City, state, and ZIP code
Pinetown, VA 23000

OMB No. 1545-0029

T	
FF	
FD	
FP	
I	
T	

If address is different from prior return, check here ►

IRS Use

1 1 1 1 1 1 1 1 1 1   2   3 3 3 3 3 3 3   4 4 4   5 5 5
6   7   8 8 8 8 8 8 8   9 9 9 9 9   10 10 10 10 10 10 10 10 10 10

If you do not have to file returns in the future, check here ► [ ]   and enter date final wages paid ►
If you are a seasonal employer, see **Seasonal employers** on page 1 of the instructions and check here ► [ ]

1	Number of employees in the pay period that includes March 12th . ►	**1**			
2	Total wages and tips, plus other compensation			**2**	19500	00
3	Total income tax withheld from wages, tips, and sick pay			**3**	1820	00
4	Adjustment of withheld income tax for preceding quarters of calendar year			**4**		
5	Adjusted total of income tax withheld (line 3 as adjusted by line 4—see instructions) . . .			**5**	1820	00

6	Taxable social security wages	**6a**	19500	00	× 12.4% (.124) =	**6b**	2418	00
	Taxable social security tips	**6c**			× 12.4% (.124) =	**6d**		
7	Taxable Medicare wages and tips . . .	**7a**	19500	00	× 2.9% (.029) =	**7b**	565	50

8	Total social security and Medicare taxes (add lines 6b, 6d, and 7b). Check here if wages are not subject to social security and/or Medicare tax . . . . ► [ ]	**8**	2983	50
9	Adjustment of social security and Medicare taxes (see instructions for required explanation) Sick Pay $ _____ ± Fractions of Cents $ _____ ± Other $ _____ =	**9**		
10	Adjusted total of social security and Medicare taxes (line 8 as adjusted by line 9—see instructions)	**10**	2983	50
11	**Total taxes** (add lines 5 and 10)	**11**	4803	50
12	Advance earned income credit (EIC) payments made to employees	**12**		
13	Net taxes (subtract line 12 from line 11). **If $2,500 or more, this must equal line 17, column (d) below (or line D of Schedule B (Form 941))**	**13**	4803	50
14	Total deposits for quarter, including overpayment applied from a prior quarter	**14**	4803	50
15	**Balance due** (subtract line 14 from line 13). See instructions	**15**		
16	**Overpayment.** If line 14 is more than line 13, enter excess here ► $ _____ and check if to be: [ ] Applied to next return **or** [ ] Refunded.			

- **All filers:** If line 13 is less than $2,500, you need not complete line 17 or Schedule B (Form 941).
- **Semiweekly schedule depositors:** Complete Schedule B (Form 941) and check here . . . . ► [ ]
- **Monthly schedule depositors:** Complete line 17, columns (a) through (d), and check here . . . . ► [X]

17	Monthly Summary of Federal Tax Liability. Do not complete if you were a semiweekly schedule depositor.			
	(a) First month liability	**(b)** Second month liability	**(c)** Third month liability	**(d)** Total liability for quarter
	1847.50	1478.00	1478.00	4803.50

Sign Here

Under penalties of perjury, I declare that I have examined this return, including accompanying schedules and statements, and to the best of my knowledge and belief, it is true, correct, and complete.

Signature ► Peter Cone
Print Your Name and Title ► Peter Cone, owner   Date ► 2/5/02

For Privacy Act and Paperwork Reduction Act Notice, see back of Payment Voucher.   Cat. No. 17001Z   Form **941** (Rev. 1-2001)

Form **940-EZ**

Department of the Treasury
Internal Revenue Service   (99)

**Employer's Annual Federal
Unemployment (FUTA) Tax Return**

► **See separate Instructions for Form 940-EZ for information on completing this form.**

OMB No. 1545-1110

20**00**

T		
FF		
FD		
FP		
I		
T		

Name (as distinguished from trade name)

Peter Cone
Trade name, if any

Calendar year

2000

Address and ZIP code   *362 Main Street
Pinetown, VA 23000*

Employer identification number

10 : 1234567

Answer the questions under **Who May Use Form 940-EZ** on page 2. If you cannot use Form 940-EZ, you must use Form 940.

A   Enter the amount of contributions paid to your state unemployment fund. (See separate instructions.) . . . ► $ *630.00*

B   (1) Enter the name of the state where you have to pay contributions . . . . ► ....*Virginia*...........

(2) Enter your state reporting number as shown on your state unemployment tax return ► *0-0000000-0*

If you will not have to file returns in the future, check here (see **Who Must File** in separate instructions), **and complete and sign the return.** ► ☐

If this is an Amended Return, check here . . . . ► ☐

Part I   **Taxable Wages and FUTA Tax**

1	Total payments (including payments shown on lines 2 and 3) during the calendar year for services of employees	**1**	*78000*	*00*
2	Exempt payments. (Explain all exempt payments, attaching additional sheets if necessary.) ► ----------------------------------- ---	**2**		
3	Payments of more than $7,000 for services. Enter only amounts over the first $7,000 paid to each employee. Do not include any exempt payments from line 2. (See separate instructions.) The $7,000 amount is the Federal wage base. Your state wage base may be different. **Do not use your state wage limitation**	**3** *57000* *00*		
4	Total exempt payments (add lines 2 and 3)	**4**	*57000*	*00*
5	**Total taxable wages** (subtract line 4 from line 1) . . . . ►	**5**	*21000*	*00*
6	**FUTA tax.** Multiply the wages on line 5 by .008 and enter here. **(If the result is over $100, also complete Part II.)**	**6**	*168*	*00*
7	Total FUTA tax deposited for the year, including any overpayment applied from a prior year	**7**	*149*	*60*
8	**Balance due** (subtract line 7 from line 6). Pay to the **"United States Treasury"** . . . . ►	**8**	*18*	*40*
	If you owe more than $100, see **Depositing FUTA tax** in separate instructions.			
9	**Overpayment** (subtract line 6 from line 7). Check if it is to be: ☐ **Applied to next return or** ☐ **Refunded** ►	**9**		

Part II   **Record of Quarterly Federal Unemployment Tax Liability** (Do not include state liability.) **Complete only if line 6 is over $100.**

Quarter	First (Jan. 1 – Mar. 31)	Second (Apr. 1 – June 30)	Third (July 1 – Sept. 30)	Fourth (Oct. 1 – Dec. 31)	Total for year
Liability for quarter	*149.60*	*18.40*	*–0–*	*–0–*	*168.00*

Under penalties of perjury, I declare that I have examined this return, including accompanying schedules and statements, and, to the best of my knowledge and belief, it is true, correct, and complete, and that no part of any payment made to a state unemployment fund claimed as a credit was, or is to be, deducted from the payments to employees.

Signature ►   *Peter Cone*   Title (Owner, etc.) ►   *Owner*   Date ►   *1/25/01*

For Privacy Act and Paperwork Reduction Act Notice, see separate instructions.   Cat. No. 10983G   Form **940-EZ** (2000)

DETACH HERE

Form **940-EZ(V)**

Department of the Treasury
Internal Revenue Service

Form 940-EZ Payment Voucher

Use this voucher only when making a payment with your return.

OMB No. 1545-1110

20**00**

Complete boxes 1, 2, 3, and 4. Do not send cash, and do not staple your payment to this voucher. Make your check or money order payable to the **"United States Treasury"**. Be sure to enter your employer identification number, "Form 940-EZ", and "2000" on your payment.

1 Enter the first four letters of your last name (business name if partnership or corporation).	**2** Enter your employer identification number.	**3** Enter the amount of your payment.
		$

Instructions for Box 1

—Individuals (sole proprietors, trusts, and estates)—
Enter the first four letters of your last name.

—Corporations and partnerships—Enter the first four characters of your business name (omit "The" if followed by more than one word).

4 Enter your business name (individual name for sole proprietors)

Enter your address

Enter your city, state, and ZIP code

How to Get a Tax ID Number

If your sole proprietorship has employees or if your business is a partnership, limited liability company or corporation, you must get a federal "employer identification number" (EIN). If you are a sole proprietorship without employees, your tax ID number can be either your Social Security number or an EIN. You will use this number on all business-related forms you send to the IRS.

To get an EIN, send IRS Form SS-4, Application for Employer Identification Number, to the IRS address in the instructions to the form. This form is available in Adobe Acrobat" format on the IRS's website at http://www.irs.gov or at all IRS and Social Security offices.

If you apply for your EIN by mail, it usually take several weeks to process your application. If you need the number more quickly, you may call the Tele-TIN number listed for your area and request an EIN over the phone (make sure you fill out the form first; you'll have to read the answers to the representative over the phone). You will then send the filled-out SS-4 form to the IRS.

There is no charge to get an EIN. If any tax filings are due before you get your number back, write "applied for" on the filing in the space for the EIN.

If you have more than one business, you need a different EIN for each. If you change the form of your entity, such as from a sole proprietorship to a corporation, or from a partnership to a limited liability company, you must get a new EIN. AN EIN is always a nine-digit number in the following format: "12-3456789."

The IRS legally has ten years to collect payroll (or any other federal) taxes after they become due. This is true whether the debtor is a business or individual. (IRC § 6502.) The IRS can seize almost anything you own—bank accounts, wages, cars and even your home. You can't wipe out a payroll tax debt even with bankruptcy.

To hold you *personally* liable for the Trust Fund Recovery Penalty (TFRP), the IRS must find that: (1) you were responsible for making the missed payments, and (2) you acted willfully in not seeing that payroll tax obligations were paid.

⚠ Business owners are almost always held personally responsible for unpaid payroll taxes. They can seldom avoid the TFRP if the taxes aren't paid. The TFRP is primarily applicable to incorporated businesses. Sole proprietors, LLC members and partners have direct liability for payroll tax obligations, so the IRS does not have to invoke the TFRP to find them liable.

If a staff member or outside accountant screws up—or worse, steals the money that should have gone to the government—the owner(s) is still on the hook. The IRS reckons that whoever chose the person responsible for tax reporting and paying has the duty of supervising them. (On rare occasions, however, an owner of a business may escape liability for payroll taxes if the IRS finds that someone else acted without the owner's knowledge and beyond their control.)

When it comes to pinning on the personal responsibility tag, the IRS does not always stop with the head people. Non-owner employees, such as a bookkeeper or office manager, can also be held responsible. Even outside accountants and attorneys for the business may be found responsible.

Because the IRS is eager to find as many people responsible as possible, its officers are given wide latitude in assigning personal responsibility for payroll taxes. The IRS may question anyone it remotely suspects may be responsible. In determining who is to blame for the missed payments and filings, the IRS looks at a number of factors, primarily:

- Who made the business's financial decisions?
- Who signed, or had authority to sign, checks? (This is the factor the IRS seems most impressed with.)
- Who had power to direct payment (or non-payment) of bills?
- Who had the duty of tax reporting?
- Was the non-payment willful?

Form SS-4

(Rev. April 2000)

Department of the Treasury
Internal Revenue Service

Application for Employer Identification Number

(For use by employers, corporations, partnerships, trusts, estates, churches, government agencies, certain individuals, and others. See instructions.)

▶ Keep a copy for your records.

EIN

OMB No. 1545-0003

Part 1

The Basics

Please type or print clearly.

1 Name of applicant (legal name) (see instructions)

Alpha Bean Cromwell

2 Trade name of business (if different from name on line 1)

ABCD Plumbing

3 Executor, trustee, "care of" name

4a Mailing address (street address) (room, apt., or suite no.)

1234 Rooter Place

4b City, state, and ZIP code

Nowheresville, CA 95555

5a Business address (if different from address on lines 4a and 4b)

1234 Rooter Place

5b City, state, and ZIP code

Nowheresville, CA 95555

6 County and state where principal business is located

Somewherestown, California

7 Name of principal officer, general partner, grantor, owner, or trustor—SSN or ITIN may be required (see instructions) ▶

Alpha Bean Cromwell

8a Type of entity (Check only one box.) (see instructions)

Caution: *If applicant is a limited liability company, see the instructions for line 8a.*

- [X] Sole proprietor (SSN) 555 55 5555
- [ ] Partnership
- [ ] REMIC
- [ ] State/local government
- [ ] Church or church-controlled organization
- [ ] Other nonprofit organization (specify) ▶
- [ ] Other (specify) ▶

- [ ] Personal service corp.
- [ ] National Guard
- [ ] Farmers' cooperative

- [ ] Estate (SSN of decedent)
- [ ] Plan administrator (SSN)
- [ ] Other corporation (specify) ▶
- [ ] Trust
- [ ] Federal government/military (enter GEN if applicable)

8b If a corporation, name the state or foreign country (if applicable) where incorporated

State

Foreign country

9 Reason for applying (Check only one box.) (see instructions)
- [X] Started new business (specify type) ▶
- [ ] Hired employees (Check the box and see line 12.)
- [ ] Created a pension plan (specify type) ▶
- [ ] Banking purpose (specify purpose) ▶
- [ ] Changed type of organization (specify new type) ▶
- [ ] Purchased going business
- [ ] Created a trust (specify type) ▶
- [ ] Other (specify) ▶

10 Date business started or acquired (month, day, year) (see instructions)

1/01/01

11 Closing month of accounting year (see instructions)

December

12 First date wages or annuities were paid or will be paid (month, day, year). **Note:** *If applicant is a withholding agent, enter date income will first be paid to nonresident alien.* (month, day, year) . . . . ▶ N/A

13 Highest number of employees expected in the next 12 months. **Note:** *If the applicant does not expect to have any employees during the period, enter -0-. (see instructions)* . . . . ▶

Nonagricultural	Agricultural	Household
1	0	0

14 Principal activity (see instructions) ▶ Plumbing

15 Is the principal business activity manufacturing? . . . . [ ] Yes [X] No
If "Yes," principal product and raw material used ▶

16 To whom are most of the products or services sold? Please check one box.
- [X] Public (retail)
- [ ] Other (specify) ▶
- [ ] Business (wholesale)
- [ ] N/A

17a Has the applicant ever applied for an employer identification number for this or any other business? . . . . [ ] Yes [X] No
Note: *If "Yes," please complete lines 17b and 17c.*

17b If you checked "Yes" on line 17a, give applicant's legal name and trade name shown on prior application, if different from line 1 or 2 above.
Legal name ▶   Trade name ▶

17c Approximate date when and city and state where the application was filed. Enter previous employer identification number if known.

Approximate date when filed (mo., day, year)	City and state where filed	Previous EIN

Under penalties of perjury, I declare that I have examined this application, and to the best of my knowledge and belief, it is true, correct, and complete.

Business telephone number (include area code)
(415) 555-5555

Fax telephone number (include area code)
(415) 666-6666

Name and title (Please type or print clearly.) ▶ Alpha Bean Cromwell

Signature ▶ Alpha Bean Cromwell

Date ▶ 1/1/01

Note: *Do not write below this line. For official use only.*

Please leave blank ▶	Geo.	Ind.	Class	Size	Reason for applying

For Privacy Act and Paperwork Reduction Act Notice, see page 4.

Cat. No. 16055N

Form **SS-4** (Rev. 4-2000)

Willfulness—one of those legal terms that keep lawyers and judges fully employed—is what the IRS is searching for. You were willful if you knew payroll taxes were owed and didn't do anything about it—even if you never intended to cheat the IRS. In short if you're responsible for making payments, the IRS regards your failure to do so as a willful act.

💡 **Protect yourself from co-owners' carelessness or misdeeds.** If you share financial responsibilities with others—that is, you're a partner, limited liability company member or corporation shareholder—get a written agreement with the other owners that contains a payroll tax "indemnification clause." This obligates your co-owners to reimburse any payroll tax penalty assessed against you personally, plus any costs of fighting the IRS.

A suitable clause looks like this:

"All co-owners (or shareholders) agree to indemnify any of the others that may be held liable for any unpaid payroll tax liabilities of the business that are proposed or assessed against them personally, together with legal costs in contesting the taxes, except amounts in proportion to their ownership (shares) in the business."

Even with this indemnification clause, you are still liable to the IRS for the whole thing if the others don't pay. This clause simply obliges them to pay you back some of what the IRS takes out of your hide. It helps as long as the other owners are still solvent (or become so).

2. If You Get Behind on Payroll Tax Payments

If your enterprise gets behind in payroll taxes, the obvious advice is to catch up as fast as possible. If you can't do it all at once, first bring payments up to date for the *current* tax quarter—if you still have employees. Then start paying the older quarters' payroll taxes. Paying current quarterly taxes on time stops interest and heavy penalties from accumulating. More importantly, the IRS is much more likely to work with you for past quarters of delinquencies if you've made your current quarter's payroll tax deposits.

Whenever paying *past due* employment taxes, tell the IRS specifically how you want back payments credited—the type of tax and tax periods. This is called "designating" the application of your payments. Designating ensures payments don't get misapplied to a different tax account, such as your personal income taxes. Also, if the payments don't cover the whole past due payroll tax bill—which is frequently the case—state that you want the "trust fund portion" of payroll taxes credited first. Here's how to designate your payments:

Step 1. Write a letter, like the one below, to the IRS office where you file your employment tax returns. If you're in doubt as to where to send it, call the IRS at 800-829-1040 to speak to a taxpayer service representative.

Sample Letter to the IRS

XYZ CORPORATION

September 15, 2001

Dear IRS:

Please apply the enclosed payment of $1,529 to the account of XYZ Corporation, EIN 94-5555555, for payroll tax Form 941 liability, 3rd Quarter of 2000. Apply to Trust Fund portion only.

Yours truly,

Sandra Shoestein

Sandra Shoestein, President

Encl. Check

Step 2. Enclose your check. Write in the lower left hand corner: "Apply to Trust Fund portion only." Under this, write your employer identification number, the tax type and period the payment is for, such as: "EIN 94-5555555, for payroll tax Form 941 liability, 3rd quarter, 2001."

Step 3. Send the letter and check to the IRS by certified mail.

 Get your IRS payroll tax records. If you're in doubt as to whether the IRS has given you proper credit for all your payroll tax payments, order a printout of your account. Call the IRS at 800-829-1040 and ask for your "BMF," or Business Master File. Tell them the specific tax periods you want, such as "3rd and 4th quarters of 2001." You should receive this information by mail within a week or two. Compare the IRS records with yours. If the printout is too full of strange codes, call the IRS to ask for an explanation, or show it to a tax pro.

3. If You Are Found Personally Liable for Payroll Taxes

If you are found personally liable for payroll taxes, you may appeal. Maybe you don't believe you are liable, or you just want to delay the collection process. IRS Appeals Officers can reverse a TFRP finding. And if you lose the IRS appeal, you may take the IRS to court, but this will be very costly. (See Chapter 20, Appealing IRS Audits.)

Payroll taxes cannot be legally discharged in bankruptcy. You will either have to pay, or live with a payroll tax debt hanging over your head for ten years.

 One way to reduce a payroll tax debt is through a negotiation process called an Offer in Compromise. The IRS will sometimes accept an Offer if it is convinced that you don't have the assets or adequate income to pay in full. (See Chapter 18, When You Can't Pay Your Taxes.)

B. Employee or Independent Contractor?

Individuals who perform services for your business are usually classified as either *regular employees* (in legalese, "common law employees") or *independent*

contractors (usually meaning they are "self-employed" for tax purposes).

A small percentage of people are in two other categories: "statutory employees" and "statutory non-employees." We talk about all of these classifications below.

It may not make much difference to a business owner how someone is classified, as long as the work gets done. The distinctions, however, are very important to the IRS, and can be very costly if you don't pay attention to them. Let me warn you: the law is muddled here, and legal experts regularly disagree as to whether someone is an employee or an independent contractor.

Congressional Dithering

In recent sessions, Congress has repeatedly failed to pass bills which would have greatly simplified the question of just who is an employee and who isn't. Sooner or later, Congress will again try for clarification—we hope.

So far we've learned that business owners have payroll tax withholding and reporting obligations for all of their employees. Report your employees' earnings to the IRS on quarterly 941 forms and again on W-2 forms issued annually to each employee.

On the other hand, with a true independent contractor, business owners don't have any withholding or contributions for payroll taxes. Your only reporting duty to the IRS is to issue a 1099 form once a year to each worker. (There are 11 versions of the 1099 form; the "1099-Misc." is the one issued to an independent contractor.)

You don't have to report to the IRS if (1) you pay the independent contractor less than $600 a year, (2) the services were performed for you personally and not for your business or (3) if the service provider was incorporated. (See Section D, below, for the filing deadlines and details on reporting workers to the IRS.)

⚠ **The employee/independent contractor determination is crucial.** The most important advice in this book might turn out to be this: Always make a determination (hopefully, a correct one) of whether or not the person you hire is an employee or independent contractor before the work begins.

Calling someone an independent contractor is very advantageous to a business—it saves a lot of time complying with IRS reporting requirements. Even better, you won't have to make the employer's share of the FICA contributions of 7.65% (2001) for each worker. You won't have to pay unemployment compensation tax (FUTA), either. But the IRS is *very aware* of the benefits of misclassifying an employee as an independent contractor, and has wide powers to make life miserable for all those it catches doing it. (See Section C, below.)

Business Owners. Sole proprietors, limited liability company members and partners are neither employees nor independent contractors of the business. These owners don't have to fool with payroll tax withholding and paying. Instead, the owners must pay their own quarterly estimated taxes. The same amount of tax is being withheld, but with a lot less IRS paperwork required. (See Chapter 6, Section E.) However, working shareholders/owners of corporations—C or S type—are employees and subject to payroll tax rules.

⚠ **No other classifications of workers are recognized by the IRS.** Many employers mistakenly believe that a short-term worker is not an employee. Sorry, whether part-time or temporary, called a consultant or subcontractor, a worker must fit into one of the four categories discussed below for tax reporting purposes.

1. Common Law Employees

Anyone who performs services that can be controlled by an employer (what work will be done and how it will be done) is termed a "common law employee" or just plain "employee." Even if an employer doesn't actually exercise control, but gives the worker freedom of action, she is the employee. As long as an employer has the legal *right* to control the method and result of the work done, there's an employer-employee relationship. Under this definition, most working people who do not own their businesses are common law employees.

Here are more factors the IRS says that show a worker is a common law employee:

1. The worker can be required to comply with instructions about when, where and how to work.
2. The worker is trained by the employer to perform services in a particular manner.
3. The worker's services are integrated into the business operation, or a continuing relationship exists.
4. The worker is required to render services personally.
5. Assistants to the worker are hired by the business, not the worker.
6. The worker has set hours of work.
7. The worker is required to devote substantially full time to the employer.
8. Work is done on business premises.
9. The worker is required to submit reports regularly.
10. The worker is paid by the hour, the week or month, unless these are installments of a lump sum amount agreed for the job.
11. The business pays the worker's business or travel expenses.
12. The business furnishes tools, equipment and materials.
13. The business has the right to fire, and the worker has the right to quit at will.

2. Independent Contractors

The IRS says that people in business for themselves —not subject to control by those who pay them— are *independent contractors*, not employees. When you hire an independent contractor to accomplish a task for your business, you don't have an employer-employee relationship and don't, therefore, have to pay employment taxes. Independent contractors

(ICs) are responsible for their own tax reporting and are treated as business owners themselves.

The IRS says these factors tend to show a person is an IC:

1. The worker hires, supervises and pays her assistants.
2. The worker is free to work when and for whom she wants.
3. The work is done on the worker's premises.
4. The worker is paid by the job or on straight commission.
5. The worker has the risk of profit or loss.
6. The worker does work for several businesses at one time.
7. The worker's services are available to the general public.
8. The worker can't be fired except for breach of contract.

 Protect yourself from potential IRS claims that you misclassified workers. All independent contractors you hire should be:

- paid by the job, not by the hour
- working off your premises
- holding business licenses and workers' compensation insurance coverage (if applicable) and showing it to you acknowledging they are independent contractors, and
- signing a contract spelling out the terms of the relationship. (See "Contracts With Independent Contractors," below.)

Contracts With Independent Contractors

If an IRS auditor attempts to reclassify a worker from independent contractor (IC) to employee, a written contract with the IC may sway the auditor. A signed contract won't help if the worker in question is obviously an employee, but it can be persuasive in borderline situations. A written agreement with an independent contractor should acknowledge that he or she is an IC and spell out his or her responsibilities. (Pay attention to the IRS list of factors.) Include a clause stating that all payments to the IC will be reported to the IRS on Form 1099. If you will be using any independent contractors, develop blank contract forms and have each IC sign one before they start performing any services. (See "Resources" at the end of this chapter for sources of IC contracts.)

3. Statutory Employees

In addition to common law employees and independent contractors, federal law automatically classifies some people as "statutory employees." (IRC § 3121(d)(3).)

Statutory employees are subject to tax withholding by businesses that pay them, in *all* cases; they can never be treated as independent contractors.

Employers must issue W-2 forms to statutory employees; however, these people are allowed to tax-deduct all business expenses from their statutory employee income. This is a tax break not granted to common law employees, who receive W-2 forms. Workers who fall in this odd category include:

- corporate officers who provide services to the corporation
- delivery drivers of food, laundry and similar products, even if they are paid strictly on a commission basis
- full-time, business-to-business salespeople, who may be paid on commission—such as manufacturer's representatives and other traveling salespeople, who do not sell directly to the public
- full-time life insurance agents working primarily for just one company, and
- home workers who do piecework according to a business's specifications and are provided the materials.

> **EXAMPLE:** Mary is an on-the-road salesperson for RoofCo, a roofing materials manufacturer selling to building contractors. She works out of her car and an office at home, visiting the RoofCo headquarters only twice a month, to pick up samples and commission checks. RoofCo has little control over how and where Mary does her work. Although her work meets some requirements of an independent contractor, Mary is classified as a statutory employee.

A statutory employee reports wages and expenses on Schedule C, the same form used by sole proprietors. (See Chapter 6.)

4. Statutory Non-Employees

The fourth tax code category for working people is the "statutory non-employee," sometimes called an "exempt employee." (IRC § 3508.) Primarily, this classification covers two types of salespeople:

- licensed real estate agents working on commission only, or

- direct (to the customer) sellers of consumer products—if the sales took place somewhere other than a retail store or showroom.

These individuals are tax-treated as self-employed independent contractors, and are not subject to tax withholding of FICA taxes. A true statutory non-employee's income must be directly related to sales—not to hours worked.

> **EXAMPLE:** Lorenzo runs a wholesale cosmetics business and tax-reports that his salespeople are statutory non-employees. This will stand up to an IRS audit as long as all sales were made off the premises, to consumers of the cosmetics, and the salespeople were paid strictly on commission.

Statutory non-employees report tax on Schedule C, the same as sole proprietors. (See Chapter 6.)

C. Misclassifying Employees as Independent Contractors

Small businesses often run up against IRS auditors when they classify workers as independent contractors instead of employees. The interests of the business person and the IRS are diametrically opposed: the IRS wants to collect employment taxes for as many workers as possible, and the business person wants to keep employment taxes at a minimum.

A small business can save a bundle by not having employees. According to the U.S. Chamber of Commerce, it costs a business 20% to 40% more per worker to treat them as employees. Because most business people can't operate without help, some try to be creative in their hiring practices, which can be disastrous.

1. Penalties for Misclassification

If your business is audited for any reason, the IRS typically asks about payments to independent contractors. Also, special IRS teams search for misclassified workers under the ETE (employment tax examina-

Employee or Independent Contractor?

The following is a summary of the IRS rules on this question.

An employer must generally withhold income taxes, withhold and pay Social Security and Medicare taxes and pay unemployment taxes on wages paid to an employee. An employer does not generally have to withhold or pay any taxes on payments to independent contractors.

Common law rules. To determine whether an individual is an employee or an independent contractor under the common law, the relationship of the worker and the business must be examined. All evidence of control and independence must be considered.

Facts that provide evidence of the degree of control and independence fall into three categories: behavioral control, financial control and the type of relationship of the parties as shown below.

Behavioral control. Facts that show whether the business has a right to direct and control how the worker does the task for which the worker is hired include the type and degree of:

- **Instructions the business gives the worker.** An employee is generally subject to the business's instructions about when, where and how to work. Even if no instructions are given, sufficient behavioral control may exist if the employer has the right to control how the work results are achieved.

- **Training the business gives the worker.** An employee may be trained to perform services in a particular manner. Independent contractors ordinarily use their own methods.

Financial control. Facts that show whether the business has a right to control the business aspects of the worker's job include:

- **The extent to which the worker has unreimbursed business expenses.** Independent contractors are more likely to have unreimbursed expenses than employees. Fixed ongoing costs that are incurred regardless of whether work is currently being performed are especially important. However, employees may also incur unreimbursed expenses in connection with the services they perform for their business.

- **The extent of the worker's investment.** An independent contractor often has a significant investment in the facilities he or she uses in performing services for someone else. However, a significant investment is not required.

- **The extent to which the worker makes services available to the relevant market.**

- **How the business pays the worker.** An employee is generally paid by the hour, week or month. An independent contractor is usually paid by the job. However, it is common in some professions, such as law, to pay independent contractors hourly.

- **The extent to which the worker can realize a profit or incur a loss.** An independent contractor can make a profit or loss.

Type of relationship. Facts that show the parties' type of relationship include:

- **Written contracts describing the relationship the parties intended to create.**

- **Whether the business provides the worker with employee-type benefits, such as insurance, a pension plan, vacation pay or sick pay.**

- **The permanency of the relationship.** If you engage a worker expecting the relationship to continue indefinitely, rather than for a specific project or period, this is indicative that your intent was to create an employer-employee relationship.

- **The extent to which services performed by the worker are a key aspect of the regular business of the company.** If a worker provides services that are a key aspect of your regular business activity, it is more likely that you will have the right to direct and control his or her activities. For example, if a law firm hires an attorney, it is likely that it will present the attorney's work as its own and would have the right to control or direct that work. This would indicate an employer-employee relationship.

IRS help. If you want the IRS to determine whether a worker is an employee, file Form SS-8, Determination of Employee Work Status for Purposes of Federal Employment Taxes and Income Tax Withholding, with the IRS.

Excerpt from IRS Publication 15-A, Employer's Supplemental Tax Guide.

tion) program. Typically, these ETE audits focus on industries where abuses are suspected. Recent targets include temporary employment agencies, nursing registries and building contractors. Enterprises can be selected for filing many 1099 forms for independent contractors.

The IRS can order offenders to pay all employment taxes that should have been paid, plus a special penalty that ranges from 12% to 35% of the tax bill. The *Wall Street Journal* reported that in one six-year period, the IRS performed more than 11,000 audits of companies using independent contractors. The results: 483,000 reclassifications (independent contractor to employee status) and $751 million in back taxes and penalties. Ouch!

The IRS is very selective in its enforcement of work classification rules. It picks on small businesses while major corporations often flout the worker classification rules. Two of the largest local employers in the San Francisco Bay Area frequently hire independent contractors. These corporate giants furnish offices, require regular work hours and treat these so-called independent contractors like their regular employees—except they do not pay employment taxes or give the workers any benefits. I have reported these companies to the IRS, but nothing ever comes of it; politics, I guess.

Here's how easily a small business person can get in trouble.

YOU OWE DOUGH!

EXAMPLE: Ray, who wholesales American-made bathing suits, faces stiff competition from cheap imports. To survive, he must keep prices low by cutting overhead to the bone. Ray decides to classify his secretary, warehouse person, delivery person and two inside salespersons as independent contractors, to save some money:

- administrative work—filing quarterly tax-reporting forms, withholding employees' pay and making federal tax deposits
- Social Security and Medicare tax matching. Unlike employees, with independent contractors there is no obligation to pay 7.65% of their wages for the employer's share of Social Security and Medicare taxes.
- federal and state unemployment tax costs, and
- non-tax expenses like workers' compensation insurance and employee benefits such as sick leave and vacation pay.

Ray is saving a hefty sum by calling these individuals independent contractors. The problem is that Ray's workers are legally employees, not ICs.

Let's say the IRS audits Ray and reclassifies his secretary, Faye, as an employee. Faye was paid $20,000 per year for the past three years. Ray's audit bill, with interest and penalties, could be as much as $30,000 if the auditor decides that Ray intentionally disregarded the law. If, however, the IRS auditor concludes Ray made an "innocent" mistake, the tax bill could be half that amount. It's a judgment call, but either way it is still a lot of money.

State employment tax agencies also get into the employee classification act. Suppose a worker who was misclassified as an independent contractor is laid off and makes a claim for unemployment benefits. This triggers a state agency inquiry, and the state may turn the employer in to the IRS. Of course, if the state reclassifies an IC as an employee, the business owner will owe state payroll taxes plus penalties, in addition to any federal payroll taxes and penalties.

IRS Classification Settlement Program

The IRS offers an olive branch to small business owners found misclassifying employees. It's called the Classification Settlement Program (CSP). This is a relatively inexpensive way to settle with the IRS over past misclassification of workers. To qualify for CSP, a business owner must:

1. have an open case with the IRS at the time, either in an audit or in appeals. (In other words, don't volunteer for the program; you must have first been selected for audit.)

2. specifically request a CSP deal.

3. be in compliance with § 530 of the 1978 Revenue Act (known as the Safe Harbor Rule). That means an employer must have:

   • filed all tax returns, including 1099 forms showing independent contractor payments

   • treated all similarly situated workers as independent contractors

   • had a reasonable basis for misclassification, such as: reliance on court decisions, IRS ruling or written IRS advice; a past audit that resulted in no employment tax liability for workers in positions substantially similar

to the workers in question; or a long-standing practice of a significant segment of your industry.

Qualifying employers will be offered one of three settlement deals:

1. no tax assessment for past misclassifications

2. pay the most recent year of taxes for worker classification deficiencies and the IRS will drop demands for assessments for prior years, or

3. pay 25% of the latest audit year deficiency.

And in all three cases, you must agree to classify the workers as employees in the future. The IRS says it will monitor your business for five years to make sure you don't fall back into your old ways.

Which one of the three deals you get depends on the judgment of the auditor or appeals officer—and your ability to convince them you acted "reasonably" but incorrectly in misclassifying workers. Excuses that may work: your reliance on the advice on an attorney or tax pro; industry practice, even if not widespread; or your misinterpretation of the 20 IRS factors.

Always issue a 1099 to each independent contractor. Some sly types will tell you it isn't necessary to give them a 1099. Undoubtedly these folks aren't playing it straight with Uncle Sam. The IRS can penalize you $50 for each 1099 not issued when you make payment of more than $600 in the year to an individual. Of much more importance, you can be assessed all of the income taxes not paid on the earnings from you for each individual not given a 1099—if they are later classified as employees instead of ICs. This could be thousands of dollars if you had a lot of workers over a three-year period. There is no penalty for filing a 1099 if it was not required, so if in doubt, file one for each IC. If you have questions on issuing Form 1099 (or a W-2 Form) call a special IRS number: 304-263-8700.

Leasing Employees

Larger businesses may sidestep employee classification challenges—and save on employee fringe benefits—by leasing workers. The lease company, not you, withholds and does payroll tax reporting. It is all legal as long as you deal with a bona fide employee leasing company.

Weigh whether the cost markup of leasing is worth any fringe benefit or administrative savings for your business. Generally, this idea makes sense only for certain types of successful businesses with fluctuating needs for workers.

2. Should You Ask the IRS to Classify Your Workers?

If you are in doubt as to how to classify a particular worker, you can ask the IRS to determine the worker's status. Fill out and send to the IRS Form SS-8, Determination of Employee Work Status for Purposes of Federal Employment Taxes and Income Tax Withholding. The IRS will respond within several months, which may be impractical for most small-time operators.

Think twice before you ask the IRS to classify workers. The IRS is very likely to rule them employees no matter what the circumstances are. And by using Form SS-8, you have put yourself on record. This can work against you if you decide not to follow the IRS's determination and are audited.

3. Appealing a Ruling That You Misclassified Workers

Since the IRS starts off biased towards classifying workers as employees, it shouldn't be a surprise that business owners usually lose on this issue at audits. Fortunately, just as with any audit issue, you may appeal a misclassification finding. (See Chapter 20 on how to appeal an IRS ruling.) What's more, the IRS now allows you to appeal a worker classification issue even before the rest of the audit of your business is complete. (Rev. Proc. 96-9). You may also take an IRS reclassification of your workers to the U.S. Tax Court for review (IRC 7436).

There are four possible grounds for winning your appeal:

1. The IRS didn't properly consider all the factors.
2. The "safe harbor" rule may apply. Even if the IRS properly classified a worker as an employee, you can claim "industry standard" relief in your independent contractor treatment—if you did what at least 25% of the other businesses in your industry are doing (§ 530 of the Revenue Act of 1978).
3. You can raise the "previous audit" defense if you were audited at any time in the past and no IRS challenge was made to how you classified your workers—assuming you are still in the same line of business with similar workers.
4. If you still can't convince an Appeals Officer you are right on the first three, offer to change your business's classification of disputed workers to employees in all future years, if the IRS will forget the past years. This "future compliance" offer might be accepted if your workers are in a gray area and the Appeals Officer is concerned that you might win in court. (For more on negotiating strategy, see Part 6, Dealing with the IRS.)

It might be worthwhile to consult a tax pro before you start your appeal. At tax pro can help you analyze your position.

D. IRS Filing and Payment Requirements for Employers

As should be clear by now, the IRS imposes a lot of form filing duties on employers. If you fail to file a required form—or file it late—at the very least you'll get annoying inquiries from the IRS, and at worst expensive penalties. If you miss a due date it will almost certainly cost you extra. Following is a list of tax dates to mark on your calendar. Make sure that either you or your staff, accountant or payroll service meets these deadlines.

Note: For any due date, the "file" or "furnish" requirement is met if the form is properly addressed, mailed first class and postmarked on or before the due date. If any deadline falls on a weekend or legal holiday, use the next business day.

If you don't use a tax pro, get IRS Publication 15 and tax forms from your local IRS office or call 800-829-FORM (3676) to order by mail. You can also get forms online at the IRS's website, http://www.irs.gov; see Chapter 22, Help Beyond the Book for more information.

- **Each Payday: Withhold Income Taxes and Employees' Share of Social Security and Medicare.** See Section A, "Payroll Taxes," above. No separate report needs to be made to the IRS at the time of the withholding. (Make federal tax deposits either quarterly, monthly or more often, depending on the size of your payroll.)
- **Annually on January 31: Reporting of W-2 and 1099 Payments to Workers, FUTA.** January 31 is a key date for businesses with employees or independent contractors. That is the deadline for mailing workers either a Form W-2 to report wages (any amount) paid for the prior year or Form 1099-Misc. to report independent contractor payments to individuals ($600 or more only).

  Copies of the 1099s and W-2s you issue must be sent to the IRS, along with Form W-3, by the last day of February (see below). Follow the instructions in IRS Publication 15, Circular E, Employer's Tax Guide, if you are not using a tax pro or payroll tax service.

  Also, Form 940 (or 940EZ), Employer's Annual Federal Unemployment Tax Return, is due on January 31, along with payment of any balance due.

- **Annually on February 28: Forms 1099 (and 8027) to IRS.** Mail copy "A" of all any Form 1099 you issued to workers on January 31, along with Form 1096, Annual Summary and Transmittal of U.S. Information Returns, to your IRS Service Center. If applicable, also file Form 8027, Employer's Annual Information Return of Tip Income.
- **Annually on February 28: Forms W-2 to Social Security Administration.** Mail copy "A" of all the Forms W-2 you issued, along with Form W-3, Transmittal of Wage and Tax Statements, with the Social Security Administration (address on the forms). Alternatively, you may file electronically. Go to the Social Security Administration website at http://www.ssa.gov/employers for more information.

Deposit penalties are severe. The IRS charges a penalty of 2% for late tax deposits that are one to five days late and up to 15% for payments not received within ten days of an IRS notice and demand.

E. Recordkeeping Requirements on Service Providers

You must keep records on workers—whether employees or independent contractors—who provided services to your business. The IRS and state tax agencies can demand to see these records as part of a regular audit or a special employment tax audit. Keep these records at least three years, but six years is advisable. Basic employer records should show:

- your Employer Identification Number (EIN) document issued by IRS
- amounts and dates of wage and pension payments to workers
- names, addresses, Social Security numbers, occupations, dates of employment for everyone paid for their services
- fringe benefits and goods or services provided in addition to cash to workers
- employee tips reported (if applicable)
- Forms W-2 and 1099 showing payments to workers, including any that were returned by the post office as undeliverable
- income tax withholding certificates completed by each worker (Forms W-4)
- federal and state payroll tax deposit forms with dates and proof of payment (deposit slip, canceled check or financial institution receipt)
- federal Forms 940 (annual) and 941 (quarterly) and corresponding state payroll tax forms
- income tax returns of yours or the business entity on which payments to workers were claimed, and
- FICA (Social Security & Medicare) and FUTA (unemployment) taxes paid for each worker.

Resources

- IRS Publication 505, Tax Withholding and Estimated Tax. A 48 page booklet which greatly expands on the information in this chapter.
- IRS Publication 509, Tax Calendar for 2001
- Notice 931, Deposit Requirements for Employment Taxes
- IRS Publication 15-A, Employer's Supplemental Tax Guide. Every employer should be familiar with this publication; it shows how to fill out employment tax forms.
- IRS Publication 15, Circular E, Employer's Tax Guide. This is a useful booklet with forms and charts for determining how much to withhold from employees' paychecks if you do not use an accountant or payroll service.
- *Hiring Independent Contractors: The Employer's Legal Guide*, by Stephen Fishman (Nolo). Every-thing you need to know about federal and state laws for working with independent contractors.
- *Stand Up to the IRS*, by Frederick W. Daily (Nolo). This book should be helpful in contesting adverse IRS decisions.
- *The Employer's Legal Handbook*, by Fred Steingold (Nolo). This book details all the legal issues involved with being an employer.
- IRS Forms and Publications. Call 800-920-3676 to order current and prior year tax forms, instructions and publications. You should receive your order in about ten days. Alternatively, download the latest forms from the IRS's website at http://www.irs.gov.
- SSA Wage Reporting Specialist. If you have a wage reporting problem, call 800-772-1213 for help.
- SSS website. For SSA-related information go to http://www.ssa.gov/employers.

Sole Proprietorships

"The most enlightened judicial policy is to let people manage their own business in their own way."
**—Oliver Wendell Holmes, Jr.,
U.S. Supreme Court Justice**

A "sole proprietor" is an individual (or husband and wife) who owns and operates a business. A "business" is any enterprise operated with a profit motive. The term "sole proprietor" also covers self-employed freelancers, independent contractors and consultants who provide services to other businesses who don't run their operation through a separate legal entity. (See Chapter 5.)

Independent contractors, freelancers and consultants can run their business through a separate entity. There's no rule that an IC must run her business as a sole proprietor. Many ICs decide to incorporate or operate their business through a limited liability company. In fact, many businesses to whom you provide services may *want* you to incorporate your business to reduce the risk of the IRS reclassifying you as an employee. If you are an IC and operate your business through a separate legal entity, see Chapter 7 (C corporations), Chapter 8 (S corporations), Chapter 9 (partnerships), Chapter 10 (limited liability companies) and Chapter 11 (personal service corporations) for more information on your business taxes.

The IRS estimates that there are 15 to 20 million sole proprietorships in the U.S., comprising over 80% of *all* businesses. No wonder—it is the easiest, fastest and cheapest way to go into business.

For tax and most legal purposes, a sole proprietor and her business are indistinguishable. Business profits (or losses) are reported on the owner's Form 1040 tax return every year. The sole proprietor is personally responsible for business debts, including all taxes. And when the owner dies, a sole proprietorship terminates by law—unlike a corporation or limited liability company. Unpaid tax liabilities also attach to any assets the deceased sole proprietor leaves behind.

Sole proprietorships may offer any type of goods or services, have multiple employees (or no employees) and lose or make millions. You can start a sole proprietorship by simply putting up a sign offering your goods or services. Get a local business license and possibly a sales tax permit as well, but that's about it—you are a sole proprietorship, or a "solo" as we call you.

Taxes and Sole Proprietorships in a Nutshell

1. A sole proprietorship is not a separate entity from its owner, so the business does not file its own tax return. Its income or loss is reported on Schedule C, which is filed with the owner's tax return.
2. Sole proprietors, as self-employed individuals, must pay quarterly estimated income taxes, as well as self-employment tax for Social Security and Medicare contributions.
3. Most small businesses begin as sole proprietorships, but many eventually convert to a partnership, limited liability company or corporation.

A. Business Expenses

You can tax-deduct business expenses under the same rules whether you operate a sole proprietorship or a major corporation. The types of expenses and rules for deducting them are covered in Chapters 1 and 2. For home-based business, also see Chapter 13, Microbusinesses and Home-Based Businesses, for special rules.

B. Profits Left in the Business

The following comes as a shock to most sole proprietors: You are taxed on all profits in the year they are earned—whether you take the money out of the business or not. Any profits remaining in a business at the end of the year are taxed as if you had put them in your pocket. Remember, under the tax code a sole proprietor and her business are one.

For retailers and small manufacturers, this rule means if you put profits into building your inventory —which is often the case—you first will be taxed on them. In other words, you must use "after-tax" dollars to expand your sole proprietorship business.

> **EXAMPLE:** Jose made a net profit of $85,000 in his magic and novelty shop last year. He took $50,000 out of the business bank account for living expenses and spent the remaining $35,000 on inventory. Jose pays income and self-employment tax on the full $85,000.

💡 **By incorporating, you may save tax on profits put into inventory.** This is because owners of C corporations do not report profits left in the business on their personal tax returns, even if they are the only shareholder. Although profits left in a corporation are taxable to the corporation, initial rates of taxation are lower than for most individuals, producing a tax saving for most small businesses. (Before trying this, however, see Chapter 7, C Corporations, for the tax advantages and disadvantages of incorporation.) Note that this doesn't apply to S corporations (see Chapter 8).

Start-Up Permits

Although it is easy to start a sole proprietorship, certain businesses and professions (restaurants and attorneys, for example) need state or local licenses before beginning operation. For more information, see *The Small Business Start-Up Kit*, by Peri Pakroo (Nolo) and *Small-Time Operator*, by Bernard Kamoroff (Bell Springs).

C. How Sole Proprietors Tax-Report

For tax purposes, a sole proprietorship starts the day an individual begins receiving income for goods or services. No IRS licensing or even form-filing is required to start off. A sole proprietorship and its owner (or married couple filing a joint tax return) are one and the same for tax purposes. The following also applies to independent contractors, statutory employees and statutory non-employees who don't provide services through a separate legal entity.

1. Schedule C (or Schedule F, for Farming)

Business income and expenses are reported on a separate "schedule" (form) attached to the sole proprietor's annual Form 1040 individual tax return. Either Schedule C or C-EZ, Profit or Loss From Business (Sole Proprietorship), or Schedule F if your business is farming. You must enter your principal business code number (see instructions for Schedule C) to report to the IRS the type of business you own or run.

File Schedule C if your *net* income (after deducting expenses) from all sole proprietorship ventures exceeds $400. But you should file one even if you make less than $400 or even lose money. One reason for filing is that if you have a loss, it may produce a tax benefit. Also, filing starts the statute of limitations (the period during which the IRS legally can audit you) running.

> **EXAMPLE:** In December 2001, Sam and Jeannie Smith open Smith's Computer Sales and Service as a sole proprietorship. The Smiths just about break even that year. Even though they didn't make or lose money, prudence dictates that by April 15, 2002, they should file their 2001 individual income tax return, including a Schedule C or Schedule C-EZ for the business.

A sample Schedule C is shown below. Pay particular attention to lines eight through 27 for categories of deductible expenses common to most businesses. Refer back to Chapters 1 and 2 for rules on these items. Items that don't seem to fit into a category name can be put on line 48 as "other expenses."

The Form of Your Business

SCHEDULE C (Form 1040) Department of the Treasury Internal Revenue Service (99)	**Profit or Loss From Business** (Sole Proprietorship) ▶ **Partnerships, joint ventures, etc., must file Form 1065 or Form 1065-B.** ▶ **Attach to Form 1040 or Form 1041.** ▶ **See Instructions for Schedule C (Form 1040).**	OMB No. 1545-0074 20**00** Attachment Sequence No. **09**

Name of proprietor *John Stephens*	Social security number (SSN) 465 : 00 : 0001

A	Principal business or profession, including product or service (see page C-1 of the instructions) *Tax Preparation*	**B** Enter code from pages C-7 & 8 ▶ 7 6 3 3

C	Business name. If no separate business name, leave blank. *Stephens Tax Service*	**D** Employer ID number (EIN), if any

E   Business address (including suite or room no.) ▶   *821 Union Street*
      City, town or post office, state, and ZIP code   *Hometown, IA 52761*

F   Accounting method: **(1)** ☒ Cash   **(2)** ☐ Accrual   **(3)** ☐ Other (specify) ▶ ....

G   Did you "materially participate" in the operation of this business during 2000? If "No," see page C-2 for limit on losses   . ☒ **Yes**   ☐ **No**

H   If you started or acquired this business during 2000, check here . . . . ▶ ☐

Part I   Income

1	Gross receipts or sales. **Caution.** If this income was reported to you on Form W-2 and the "Statutory employee" box on that form was checked, see page C-2 and check here . . . . . . ▶ ☐	**1**	34,280
2	Returns and allowances	**2**	0
3	Subtract line 2 from line 1	**3**	34,280
4	Cost of goods sold (from line 42 on page 2)	**4**	0
5	**Gross profit.** Subtract line 4 from line 3	**5**	34,280
6	Other income, including Federal and state gasoline or fuel tax credit or refund (see page C-2) . . .	**6**	0
7	**Gross income.** Add lines 5 and 6 . . . . ▶	**7**	34,280

Part II   Expenses. Enter expenses for business use of your home **only** on line 30.

8	Advertising	**8**	250		19	Pension and profit-sharing plans	**19**	
9	Bad debts from sales or services (see page C-3) . .	**9**	1,266		20	Rent or lease (see page C-4):		
					a	Vehicles, machinery, and equipment .	**20a**	
10	Car and truck expenses (see page C-3)	**10**			**b**	Other business property . .	**20b**	
11	Commissions and fees . .	**11**			21	Repairs and maintenance . .	**21**	
12	Depletion	**12**			22	Supplies (not included in Part III) .	**22**	253
13	Depreciation and section 179 expense deduction (not included in Part III) (see page C-3) . .	**13**	3,100		23	Taxes and licenses	**23**	
					24	Travel, meals, and entertainment:		
					a	Travel	**24a**	310
14	Employee benefit programs (other than on line 19) . . .	**14**			**b**	Meals and entertainment 512		
15	Insurance (other than health) .	**15**	750		**c**	Enter nondeductible amount included on line 24b (see page C-5) . 256		
16	Interest:							
a	Mortgage (paid to banks, etc.) .	**16a**			**d**	Subtract line 24c from line 24b .	**24d**	256
b	Other	**16b**	200		25	Utilities	**25**	347
17	Legal and professional services	**17**	350		26	Wages (less employment credits) .	**26**	
18	Office expense	**18**	600		27	Other expenses (from line 48 on page 2)	**27**	267

28	**Total expenses** before expenses for business use of home. Add lines 8 through 27 in columns . ▶	**28**	7,949
29	Tentative profit (loss). Subtract line 28 from line 7	**29**	26,331
30	Expenses for business use of your home. Attach **Form 8829**	**30**	1,462
31	**Net profit or (loss).** Subtract line 30 from line 29. ● If a profit, enter on **Form 1040, line 12,** and **also on Schedule SE, line 2** (statutory employees, see page C-5). Estates and trusts, enter on Form 1041, line 3. ● If a loss, you **must** go to line 32.	**31**	24,869
32	If you have a loss, check the box that describes your investment in this activity (see page C-5). ● If you checked 32a, enter the loss on **Form 1040, line 12,** and **also on Schedule SE, line 2** (statutory employees, see page C-5). Estates and trusts, enter on Form 1041, line 3. ● If you checked 32b, you **must** attach **Form 6198.**	**32a** ☐ All investment is at risk. **32b** ☐ Some investment is not at risk.	

For Paperwork Reduction Act Notice, see Form 1040 instructions.   Cat. No. 11334P   **Schedule C (Form 1040) 2000**

Schedule C (Form 1040) 2000   Page **2**

Part III **Cost of Goods Sold** (see page C-6)

33 Method(s) used to value closing inventory: **a** ☐ Cost   **b** ☐ Lower of cost or market   **c** ☐ Other (attach explanation)

34 Was there any change in determining quantities, costs, or valuations between opening and closing inventory? If "Yes," attach explanation . . . . ☐ Yes   ☐ No

35 Inventory at beginning of year. If different from last year's closing inventory, attach explanation	35	
36 Purchases less cost of items withdrawn for personal use	36	
37 Cost of labor. Do not include any amounts paid to yourself	37	
38 Materials and supplies	38	
39 Other costs	39	
40 Add lines 35 through 39	40	
41 Inventory at end of year	41	
42 **Cost of goods sold.** Subtract line 41 from line 40. Enter the result here and on page 1, line 4	42	

Part IV **Information on Your Vehicle.** Complete this part **only** if you are claiming car or truck expenses on line 10 and are not required to file Form 4562 for this business. See the instructions for line 13 on page C-3 to find out if you must file.

43 When did you place your vehicle in service for business purposes? (month, day, year) ► ____ / ____ / ____ .

44 Of the total number of miles you drove your vehicle during 2000, enter the number of miles you used your vehicle for:

a Business _____ **b** Commuting _____ **c** Other _____

45 Do you (or your spouse) have another vehicle available for personal use? . . . . ☐ Yes   ☐ No

46 Was your vehicle available for use during off-duty hours? . . . . ☐ Yes   ☐ No

47a Do you have evidence to support your deduction? . . . . ☐ Yes   ☐ No

b If "Yes," is the evidence written? . . . . ☐ Yes   ☐ No

Part V **Other Expenses.** List below business expenses not included on lines 8–26 or line 30.

48 Total other expenses. Enter here and on page 1, line 27 . . . . | 48 | |

Schedule C (Form 1040) 2000

The Form of Your Business

2. Schedule C-EZ

A tiny side business may use a simplified form, Schedule C-EZ. You are eligible if you:

- have gross receipts under $25,000
- claim less than $2,500 in business expenses
- have no inventory
- have no employees
- use the cash method of accounting
- don't claim IRC §179 or depreciation expenses to write off any assets, and
- don't have an overall loss in operation.

Businesses worthy of the name can usually claim much more than $2,500 in business expenses. Since it is only a little more effort to fill out a regular Schedule C form, I recommend it in most cases.

More Than One Sole Proprietorship

If you and your spouse operate more than one sole proprietorship, you must file a different Schedule C, or C-EZ, for each business. You might have multiple Schedule Cs filed with one tax return if you or your spouse have your fingers in many pies.

EXAMPLE: Jeannie and Sam Smith own Smith's Computer Sales and Service. Besides helping run their business, Jeannie has an Amway distributorship, and Sam buys and sells sports trading cards. The Smiths file one 1040 form, with three Schedule Cs. Since the sports card venture incurs more than $2,500 in expenses, they must use a regular C form, even though the other, smaller ventures might qualify for the EZ form.

3. How Sole Proprietor Income Is Taxed

Schedule C, line 31, shows the bottom line—profit or loss—from your sole proprietorship. This figure is entered on the front page of your Form 1040 tax return. It is added to your income (or losses) from all sources—regular jobs, dividends, capital gains and so on to reach the figure at the bottom of the page called you "adjusted gross income."

After deducting your personal exemptions and itemized or standard personal deductions on Form 1040, the result is taxed at your tax bracket ranging from 10% to 39.1% (2001).

Sole proprietors are also pay self-employment taxes (discussed in Chapter 13) of 15.3% of the first $80,400 of your net self-employment income and 2.9% of everything over $80,400 (2001 rate).

If your sole proprietorship loses money, you can use that loss to offset your other earnings in that year—even earnings from a regular job.

If you don't have enough other earnings, you may carry the so-called net operating loss over to the following year's tax return. If the venture makes

a profit in a future year, you can use the previous year's losses to offset it and reduce your taxes. (See Chapter 4, Business Losses and Failures, for details.)

All of a sole proprietor's net profits are subject to "self-employment" tax (Social Security and Medicare). This is equivalent to the payroll tax for employees.

The SE portion of the Social Security tax stops when your total earned income (from all sources) reaches $80,400 (2001). (IRC § 1401.) This amount is subject to annual cost of living adjustment. You are subject to tax only on the Medicare portion of the SE tax (2.9%) on all further earned income.

> **EXAMPLE:** Wing, who is self-employed, earns $97,700 total this year. The first $80,400 is taxed at the rate of 15.3% ($12,301) and the next $17,300 at 2.9% ($502), for a total SE tax of $12,803.

Spouse's Self-Employment Taxes

Spouses who co-own a sole proprietorship are taxed as one on income of the business. However, they are treated as two individuals for purposes of self-employment tax (SE). (IRC § 1402 (a)(5)(A), Reg. 1.1402(a)(8).) So a separate SE tax form must be filed—and taxes paid—based on an allocation of each spouse's share of the net income. The allocation should be based on how much each spouse contributed to the operation. Beware: This rule has more significance than just filing another form. Listing your spouse as a co-worker in a sole proprietorship can cost you extra taxes if the business profit exceeds $80,400 (2001). (See Chapter 12, Section C, for an explanation of how this tax provision works against you.) To save this expense, you might list only one spouse as an owner. The other spouse can be treated as an unpaid "volunteer."

You are still liable for the SE tax on business income even if you are currently drawing Social Security or Medicare benefits.

 Paying self-employment taxes produces a tax break on your individual tax return. One-half of these self-employment taxes is deductible. (IRC § 164.) This deduction is not claimed on the business schedule of your tax return. Instead, it is deducted on the first page of your Form 1040 tax return from your total "adjusted gross income."

> **EXAMPLE:** Carol quits her job and operates Carol's Catering as a full-time business. During her first year she makes a profit and pays self-employment taxes of $1,102. She is in the 28% bracket. Carol can deduct one-half of her SE taxes, $551. This shaves $154 (28% x $1,102 x 50%) off her income tax bill.

However, a one-time job may not be subject to self-employment tax. For example, John, a retired mechanic, took a short-term job—less than a month—installing windows in an office building. The Tax Court held that this did not establish John in a "trade or business," so he wasn't liable for the self-employment tax. Of course, the income was subject to income tax, though. (*John A. Batok*, TC Memo 1992-727.)

D. Estimated Tax Payments = Pay As You Go

In addition to paying self-employment taxes, sole proprietors are required to make income tax payments, called "estimated taxes," four times a year.

If you wait until April 15 to pay all at once, expect an IRS penalty for failing to make timely estimated tax payments. The penalty is a percentage of the tax due and is typically equal to 8% annually, close to the interest rate on a bank loan. The rate is subject to change quarterly, by law. You must make estimated tax payments if you expect to owe at least $1,000, and any tax withheld will be less than:

- 90% of the tax you'll owe, or
- 100% of last year's tax bill.

To make the quarterly estimated tax payments, use IRS Form 1040-ES. The four equal payments are

The Form of Your Business

due on April 15, June 15, September 15 and January 15 (of the following year).

Estimated tax payments cover self-employment taxes (better known as SE or Social Security and Medicare taxes) as well as plain old income taxes.

In effect, you must predict how much you will earn for the whole year ahead of time or risk a penalty. To avoid the estimated tax penalty, you should make payments equal to your tax liability for the previous year. For example, if you paid $5,000 in income taxes in 2000, you should make four estimated tax payments of $1,250 each during 2001. Tax-preparation programs print out the forms with how much you should pay each quarter to avoid the penalty.

⚠️ **Estimated tax payments are higher if you have a higher income.** If your income exceeds $150,000, you must make estimated payments in 2001 of at least 90% of your tax bill or 110% of your 2000 tax, whichever is smaller.

If estimated tax payments are too small or aren't made on time, the IRS will assess an underpayment of estimated taxes penalty. Skipping quarterly ES payments, waiting to pay in one lump sum with your annual Form 1040 income tax return, may find you short of funds at tax time. And if you don't catch up by paying all the estimated taxes by April 15, the IRS will tack on another heavier tax penalty and interest for paying late.

Most states also require quarterly estimated income tax payments from self-employed folks. Get forms and information from your state's tax agency.

E. Employee Taxes

Sole proprietorships are not necessarily one-person or mom-and-pop affairs. Hiring employees means paying federal employment taxes and withholding employees' income taxes.

Employment taxes cover Social Security and Medicare for the employees as well as federal unemployment compensation insurance (FUTA). (IRC §§ 101, 3111.)

Any business, including a sole proprietor, with employees must follow these employment tax rules:

- report federal payroll tax information quarterly (Form 941)
- make federal payroll tax deposits regularly, usually once a month
- report and pay federal unemployment tax (FUTA) annually (Form 941)
- report wages for employees annually (Form W-2s), and
- report payments to independent contractors annually (Form 1099-Misc.).

All these rules are explained in Chapter 5, Tax Concerns of Employers.

Sole proprietors (including a husband and wife team) are technically not employees of their business, so no payroll taxes are due on their income. Instead, as discussed in Section E, above, sole proprietors pay quarterly estimated taxes, which include self-employment taxes for Social Security and Medicare.

F. Recordkeeping

Poor recordkeeping—such as scribbling cash expenses on scraps of paper, trusting your memory, or mixing up personal and business records—is the chief tax bugaboo of the self-employed. Without accurate records, however, you will never really know, let alone properly tax-report, your income and expenses.

Basic recordkeeping is the same for all businesses, including sole proprietorships. Of course, bookkeeping becomes more complex (and time-consuming) as your business grows.

To summarize Chapter 3, a business must keep track of its income and expenses, using a system to accurately record its transactions. The IRS doesn't dictate any particular way to do it—just that records be kept and available for an audit.

Note: If your business sells goods and you maintain stock on hand, you must keep inventory records—meaning you count up the goods on hand at least once every year on the last day of the tax year.

Beware of mixing business and pleasure. Segregate business records from your personal ones. Sole proprietors tend to run the loosest ships, keeping everything in the same pot. If you mix things up, you will have a mess at tax preparation time, not to mention at an audit. If you haven't set up a real recordkeeping system, at least maintain a separate checking account and credit card just for business. If you take money from the business for personal use, write a check from your business to your personal account. Alternatively, use a computer program such as Quicken (Intuit) or MS Money (Microsoft), to distinguish business from personal items in one or more checking accounts. Quicken or MS Money also track credit card and even cash expenditures.

For more on keeping business records for tax purposes and computer recordkeeping programs, see Chapter 3, Recordkeeping and Accounting.

G. Outgrowing a Sole Proprietorship

While most businesspeople start and finish their business lives as sole proprietors, others take on partners, incorporate or form a limited liability company later on down the road. For example, if your business wants the maximum fringe benefit packages, it may make tax sense to incorporate. But incorporating can pose tax problems, too. For instance, if you shut the business down, you must formally liquidate a corporation, which might bring extra tax costs that a sole proprietor wouldn't face. (See Chapter 7, C Corporations.) The point is that there are no simple solutions in the world of taxes—no one "right" form of business entity.

Tax reasons alone will rarely justify changing the legal structure of your business. More often, entrepreneurs growing out of sole proprietorship are influenced by non-tax issues, such as the shield from personal liability for business debts that corporations and limited liability companies offer. Also, partnerships, corporations and limited liability companies allow bringing co-owners into the business. And some proprietors believe the letters "Inc." in a business name may impress customers, investors and lenders, and so they incorporate without even bringing in any co-owners.

Don't forget about new expenses. Don't change the form of your sole proprietorship business without factoring in the added costs of accounting and legal services that will probably be needed. On the other hand, the processing fees will be 100% deductible.

H. Ending the Business

Just as the sole proprietorship is the easiest business to start, it is also the easiest to end. For tax purposes, simply stop doing business. File a Schedule C for the final year of operation with the words "Final Return" across the top, along with your 1040 return.

However, things aren't so simple when it comes to disposing of your enterprise's assets. You may need to report a gain (or loss) on your tax return. (See Chapter 17, Selling a Sole Proprietorship, for the tax consequences of selling a business or its assets.)

I. Death and Taxes

If you die owning a sole proprietorship, the business dies with you in the eyes of the tax law (except when a husband and wife are co-proprietors). Your business is an asset of your estate. There may be estate tax and probate consequences depending on how large your estate is. (See Chapter 12, Family Businesses, for a brief discussion of estate planning for a small business.)

If your heirs (or your spouse) carry on the proprietorship after your death, they will report its income and expenses on Schedule C of their own tax returns. They will need a new Employer Identification Number from the IRS, unless your spouse is the only owner.

For more information about estate planning for sole proprietors, including avoiding probate, see *Plan Your Estate*, by Denis Clifford (Nolo).

The Form of Your Business

Resources

- Publication 334, Tax Guide for Small Business (For Individuals Who Use Schedule C or C-EZ). This is a must-read for those of you doing your own tax return preparation.
- If you are a farmer, see Publication 225, Farmer's Tax Guide; if you are a commercial fisherman, see Publication 595.
- IRS Publication 505, Tax Withholding and Estimated Tax
- IRS Publication 533, Self-Employment Tax

- IRS Circular E, Employer's Tax Guide. This booklet gives a detailed explanation of the payroll tax process and the forms used.
- IRS Form 1040, Schedule "C" and Schedule "SE"

Several good books thoroughly discuss factors to consider when choosing the legal form for your business. Two of the best are:

- *Legal Guide for Starting & Running a Small Business*, by Fred Steingold (Nolo).
- *Small-Time Operator*, by Bernard Kamoroff (Bell Springs).

■

C Corporations

"You can have a lord, you can have a king, but the man to fear is the tax collector."

—Sumerian Proverb

The word "corporation" brings to mind IBM, GM or AT&T—businesses so big and familiar we know them by their initials. But corporations don't have to be huge; anyone can form one. Incorporating is more popular than ever in the U.S.; in 1997, 798,917 new businesses incorporated, which was an all-time high.

Big business obviously has a great deal of say in Congress. So, our tax code favors corporate America. Fortunately, small incorporated businesses qualify for many corporate tax breaks unavailable to partnerships, LLCs and sole proprietorships. Incorporating offers potential tax savings, but any tax advantages must be balanced against other factors, including the more complex tax rules corporations must follow.

A corporation is the most costly way of doing business. You must pony up an initial incorporation charge, as well as annual fees to the state, to maintain a corporation—whether or not it is active or makes a profit. Additional accounting costs and fees can put a significant dent in a new business's cash flow. Professional help will be needed to deal with federal and state corporation tax reporting forms in future years.

Most corporate tax breaks involve fringe benefits. This means that only solidly profitable businesses stand to gain a tax advantage by incorporating. Typically, small enterprises don't reap tax advantages from incorporating and the simplicity of a sole proprietorship, limited liability company or partnership is preferable. Later, if the business grows as you hope it will, you can always incorporate.

C Corporations in a Nutshell

1. A C corporation is a completely separate tax entity from its owners who work in the business; they are treated as employees of the corporation for tax purposes.
2. C corporations are subject to corporate income taxes, but most small business C corporations can legally avoid paying corporation income taxes.
3. C corporations are the most formal business entity to set up, and they have greater tax reporting responsibilities than other entities.
4. C corporations allow profits to be kept in the business for expansion or inventory buildup. Retained profits are taxed, but at lower rates than for businesses that are not incorporated.

⚠ **Tax considerations are only one factor in deciding whether to incorporate.** For most businesses, other reasons—primarily the personal liability shield a corporation provides—are more important. For instance, if your building demolition business carries high risks that can't be adequately covered by insurance, a corporation protects your personal assets from business creditors or a judgment. Don't get so carried away with the tax aspects of the different forms of business that you overlook these other issues.

A. Types of Taxable Corporations

For federal tax purposes, most business corporations are classified as either "C" or "S" types. These two letters refer to subchapters of the tax code in case you were wondering. This chapter discusses tax treatment of "C" corporations; "S" corporations are covered in Chapter 8. The "professional corporation" is covered in Chapter 11, Personal Service Corporations. Nonprofit corporations are beyond the scope of this book.

Most business corporations begin life as C corporations. After incorporating, the shareholders may

How to Set Up a Corporation

Small business corporations are chartered by the 50 states, not the federal government. While there are differences in the details, state incorporation procedures are remarkably similar. However, foreign and tax-exempt corporations are beyond—way beyond—this book.

Some states, such as Delaware and Nevada, have very low incorporation fees, seemingly making them more attractive than your home state. These two states do not tax corporations unless they are doing business in that state.

Be warned: Though another state's incorporation rules may seem attractive, there is a very big catch. For starters, your home state probably requires out-of-state corporations to register and pay a fee before doing business in the state. For instance, California charges the same fee for an out-of-state corporation as it does to a native California corporation. So a California resident forming a Nevada corporation must pay two annual corporation fees, if the company does any business in California. What's more, any income from the Nevada corporation paid to the California stockholder is subject to California's state income tax. In this case, there is a tax cost, not a savings, for incorporating out of state. However, there may be other non-tax advantages (such as the right not to disclose the names of corporate shareholders) by incorporating in other states. Check with a knowledgeable business attorney if you're interested in doing this.

If you are tempted to form a corporation in a state such as Nevada or Delaware and then do business in your home state without registering, you should know this is a poor idea. The back taxes, fees and penalties your home state might assess against you if you get caught are not worth it. Further, many states do not permit unregistered "foreign" (out-of-state) corporations to sue in their state courts until the foreign corporation registers and pays the required fees. That means if you have a grievance with someone and need to sue, you'll probably have to pay these fees anyway.

Incorporating is not difficult. You can do it yourself using a self-help book containing forms and instructions. A private incorporation service (check your Yellow Pages) or software can prepare the forms for you. Or you can hire a local business lawyer, the best—but most expensive—way to go.

First, choose your corporate name (after making sure it is available by checking with your state's corporate filing office). Next, prepare a document called the "Articles of Incorporation," usually available as a fill-in-the-blanks form. In the articles, state the name of your corporation, its address, its general purpose and the name of the person to be served with legal papers in case of a lawsuit. (Many of these forms are available directly from your state's Secretary of State or Corporations Department websites. Visit http://www.piperinfo.com/index.htm for links to these agencies in your state.)

Send this paperwork to your state's corporate filing office, along with the filing fee—usually $50 to $1,000. You will get back your corporate charter and, congratulations, you are officially incorporated.

After getting your state charter, you must hold a meeting of stockholders and adopt "bylaws"—rules that govern the corporation's operation. Again, you can use fill-in-the-blanks preprinted bylaws forms. Nolo sells corporate form books for California, New York and Texas. (See "Resources" at the end of the chapter.) "Corporate kits" with blank stock certificates and form minutes of corporate meetings are available in office supply and stationery stores. After the initial meeting, you must hold annual corporation meetings to maintain your legal status as a corporation.

⚠ Keep a corporate records book to prove to the world (including an IRS auditor) that you really are a corporation, or you may lose any benefits of corporate status.

The Form of Your Business

choose S corporation status if they want the business to be taxed more like a partnership than like a standard C corporation. (Read Chapter 8 as well as this chapter to fully understand your options.)

B. How C Corporations Are Taxed

A corporation is legally termed an "artificial person." Legally, and for tax purposes, it is an entity distinct from its owners, who are called "stockholders" or "shareholders." As a separate entity, a corporation may own property, enter into contracts, borrow money and sue and be sued, just like an individual. In most states, corporations are allowed to exist with just one stockholder, who can also serve as the manager of the corporation's business. This person is called a "director," and he will likely name himself as the "president" as well as take on other corporate titles.

Closely Held Corporations

The corporations discussed in this chapter are referred to in the tax code as "closely held" corporations. Most small business corporations fall into this category. A closely held corporation is defined as one that:

- sells stock privately and has 75 or fewer shareholders, and
- has shareholders who all work in the business, or are closely related to people who do, or are experienced investors.

If a corporation offers shares to the public or has more than 75 investors, it is not closely held—and more complicated state and federal tax and securities laws come into play.

If your business operates as a corporation, you will be its employee. A shareholder of a corporation who is active in the business is not self-employed in the eyes of the tax law. Consequently, throughout this chapter, the term "employee" usually includes owners (the stockholders).

EXAMPLE: Sam Smith and his wife Jeannie incorporate Smith's Computer Sales & Service. All stock is owned by Sam, Jeannie and two key employees, all of whom are actively involved in the operation.

For most legal purposes, including paying taxes, the Smiths and their business are now separate entities. Both the Smiths and their corporation must file separate annual income tax returns. This is a huge change from when Sam and Jeannie were sole proprietors; then the Smiths and their business were legally one.

1. Avoiding Double Taxation

A "C" corporation is subject to federal and state corporation income tax laws. These rules are totally different from those for sole proprietorships, limited liability companies or partnerships.

Theoretically, before any profits are paid to shareholders, a C corporation must pay income tax at the corporate rate. (See Section 3, below.) Any profits that are distributed to shareholders via dividends are then subject to individual income tax. This amounts to *double taxation*, with business profits taxed at both the corporate and personal levels—not a good thing.

In the real world, small C corporations can easily avoid income taxes. All or almost all of a small C corporation's earnings typically are paid out to its employees as wages and fringe benefits. After everyone is paid for their labor, there is usually no income for the small business corporation to owe tax upon—unless the shareholders want there to be taxable profit (see Section 3, below, for more information).

EXAMPLE: Ned's corporation, Men's Den, Inc., earns $70,000 one year. But after the corporation pays Ned $50,000 as a salary, provides him with $10,000 in tax-free fringe benefits, including retirement plan contributions and gives him a year-end bonus of $10,000, the corporation has no taxable net profit; so it owes no federal corporate income tax. Ned, however, pays personal income taxes on $60,000 of earned income. Ned's fringe benefits of $10,000 aren't subject to tax. Note that the corporation may still be subject to state income taxes depending on that state's tax code.

If any corporate income is left in the business, it is usually tied up in inventory or retained to fund future growth. It is taxed, but at corporate tax rates that are, in most cases, lower than personal income tax rates.

EXAMPLE: Instead of giving Ned a year-end bonus of $10,000, Men's Den, Inc., retains it all for expansion in the next year. This amount is subject to federal corporate income tax at 15%, resulting in a $1,500 tax bill to the corporation. Ned pays taxes on $50,000 of earned income at his individual income tax rate.

Although double taxation of C corporations is usually avoidable, it can occur. For instance, if some shareholders are just investors and don't work for the business, they can't take salaries and fringe benefits. The only way to get profits from the corporation and to these investors/shareholders is by paying dividends. However, dividends are not deductible corporate expenses like wages. Dividends come out only after corporate income taxes are calculated. Dividends are therefore taxed (again) to the recipients on their individual tax returns. (See Section F, below, for a discussion of dividends.)

EXAMPLE: Ned's sisters, Shirley and Sally, each invest $100,000 in Men's Den, Inc., in return for 100 shares of stock each. Sally is a salesperson for the business and receives a yearly salary of $50,000; Shirley is retired and plays a lot of golf. After paying all wages and all other business expenses, Men's Den, Inc. has $30,000 in profits. Its directors decide to pay out $30,000 as dividends to shareholders. First, the corporation

must pay income tax of $4,500 (15% corporation tax rate x $30,000), leaving $25,500 for the dividends. The dividend each of them receives is subject to income tax on their individual tax returns.

💡 **Dividend double taxation is no problem.** For example, call corporate payments to a non-active shareholder who is a "consultant" compensation, not dividends (but make sure she actually does some consulting, otherwise the IRS could recharacterize the payments as dividends and the corporation would lose its deduction). However, there is a trade-off: the consultant and the corporation both must pay FICA (Social Security and Medicare) taxes on compensation paid to that shareholder. Alternatively, the consultant may be treated as an independent contractor, and in that case she would be liable for the self-employment tax on this income from the corporation. The point is to weigh the tax consequences to both shareholders and the corporation to determine whether to pay salaries or dividends. If you are in this situation, have a tax pro run the figures.

No Shareholder Benefit for C Corporation Losses

Just as C corporation profits belong to the business and don't flow through directly to shareholders, neither do losses. Instead, losses of a C corporation in one year can be offset against future or past years' profits. So, individual shareholders can't claim operating losses of a C corporation business. Recall that the corporation is a separate tax entity from its shareholders.

EXAMPLE: Men's Den, Inc., loses $20,000. Ned received no compensation for his year's work, but Ned had a second job. The corporation's loss provides no tax benefit to Ned when he files his individual tax return. The business operating loss can be used to offset any corporate profits in future years, however.

The Form of Your Business

2. Tax Reporting for C Corporations

C corporations file annual tax returns, either IRS Form 1120, U.S. Corporation Income Tax Return, or IRS Form 1120A (the short form). The due date is the 15th day of the third month after the close of their tax year. So if the corporation uses a calendar year, its tax return is due every March 15.

A corporation gets an automatic six-month extension to file its tax return (using IRS Form 7004). The return will be due September 15 assuming a calendar year reporting schedule. (See Chapter 3, Section H.) If any corporate tax is owed, it must be paid along with the extension filing to avoid penalty and interest charges.

Corporations must make quarterly estimated tax payments similar to self-employed individuals, only if the corporation will owe taxes. (But, as discussed in Section B1, small business corporations usually do not owe income taxes.)

States require annual corporate tax filings as well, on separate state corporate return forms. Unlike the IRS, most states require a minimum amount of corporate tax be paid each year to maintain the corporate charter.

 A corporation must file an income tax return every year whether or not it has any income.

3. C Corporation Income Tax Rates and Retained Earnings

As discussed, most small corporations aren't concerned with corporate tax rates because all profits are paid out as tax-deductible salaries and fringe benefits. But sometimes draining the business of cash isn't desirable. An enterprise may need money to expand or build up an inventory.

Fortunately, C corporation profits kept in the business are taxed, but at an initial tax rate of 15%—usually lower than the individual tax rates of its owners/shareholders. (IRC § 11.) This ability to "retain earnings" at a lower tax cost is an advantage that growing small C corporations have over their unincorporated counterparts. (But see Section G2 below for the limitation on the amount of earnings that a corporation can retain.)

Federal Corporate Tax Rates	
Net Income	**Tax Rate**
First $50,000	15%
Next $25,000	25%
Next $25,000	34%
Next $235,000	39%
Everything else	34%-38%

Note: Many states also impose corporate income taxes.

EXAMPLE 1: Henry's engine-rebuilding corporation, Top Value Motors, Inc., plans to expand. To do so, it retains $100,000 of net profit in the business bank account. Top Value owes corporate income taxes on the profit as follows:

$50,000 x 15%	=	$ 7,500
$25,000 x 25%	=	$ 6,250
$25,000 x 35%	=	$ 8,500
Total tax		$22,250

This is a blended tax rate of 22¼%. By contrast, if Top Value paid Henry this $100,000, depending on his tax bracket, as much as $39,600 could be added to his personal tax bill.

Form **1120-A**	**U.S. Corporation Short-Form Income Tax Return**	OMB No. 1545-0890
Department of the Treasury Internal Revenue Service	For calendar year 2000 or tax year beginning................, 2000, ending ...., 20...... See separate instructions to make sure the corporation qualifies to file Form 1120-A.	**2000**

A Check this box if the corp. is a personal service corp. (as defined in Temporary Regs. section 1.441-4T—see instructions) ☐

Use IRS label. Otherwise, print or type.

10-2134567 DEC00 5995
Rose Flower Shop, Inc.
38 Superior Lane
Fair City, MD 20715

Employer identification number

Date incorporated 7-1-82

Total assets (see page 8 of instructions)
$ 65,987

E Check applicable boxes: **(1)** ☐ Initial return **(2)** ☐ Change of address

F Check method of accounting: **(1)** ☐ Cash **(2)** ☒ Accrual **(3)** ☐ Other (specify) ▶

Income

1a	Gross receipts or sales 248,000 **b** Less returns and allowances 7,500 **c** Balance ▶	1c	240,500
2	Cost of goods sold (see page 14 of instructions).	2	144,000
3	Gross profit. Subtract line 2 from line 1c	3	96,500
4	Domestic corporation dividends subject to the 70% deduction	4	
5	Interest	5	942
6	Gross rents	6	
7	Gross royalties	7	
8	Capital gain net income (attach Schedule D (Form 1120))	8	
9	Net gain or (loss) from Form 4797, Part II, line 18 (attach Form 4797)	9	
10	Other income (see page 8 of instructions)	10	
11	**Total income.** Add lines 3 through 10 ▶	11	97,442

Deductions (See instructions for limitations on deductions.)

12	Compensation of officers (see page 10 of instructions)	12	23,000
13	Salaries and wages (less employment credits)	13	24,320
14	Repairs and maintenance	14	
15	Bad debts	15	
16	Rents	16	6,000
17	Taxes and licenses	17	3,320
18	Interest	18	1,340
19	Charitable contributions (see page 11 of instructions for 10% limitation)	19	1,820
20	Depreciation (attach Form 4562) 20		
21	Less depreciation claimed elsewhere on return 21a	21b	
22	Other deductions (attach schedule)	22	3,000
23	**Total deductions.** Add lines 12 through 22 ▶	23	62,800
24	Taxable income before net operating loss deduction and special deductions. Subtract line 23 from line 11	24	34,642
25	**Less: a** Net operating loss deduction (see page 13 of instructions) . 25a		
	b Special deductions (see page 13 of instructions) 25b	25c	

Tax and Payments

26	**Taxable income.** Subtract line 25c from line 24	26	34,462
27	**Total tax** (from page 2, Part I, line 8)	27	5,196
28	**Payments:**		
a	1999 overpayment credited to 2000 28a		
b	2000 estimated tax payments . 28b 6,000		
c	Less 2000 refund applied for on Form 4466 28c ( ) Bal ▶ 28d 6,000		
e	Tax deposited with Form 7004 28e		
f	Credit for tax paid on undistributed capital gains (attach Form 2439). 28f		
g	Credit for Federal tax on fuels (attach Form 4136). See instructions . 28g		
h	**Total payments.** Add lines 28d through 28g	28h	6,000
29	Estimated tax penalty (see page 14 of instructions). Check if Form 2220 is attached . . ▶ ☐	29	
30	**Tax due.** If line 28h is smaller than the total of lines 27 and 29, enter amount owed . .	30	
31	**Overpayment.** If line 28h is larger than the total of lines 27 and 29, enter amount overpaid . . .	31	804
32	Enter amount of line 31 you want: **Credited to 2001 estimated tax** ▶ 804 | **Refunded** ▶	32	

Sign Here

Under penalties of perjury, I declare that I have examined this return, including accompanying schedules and statements, and to the best of my knowledge and belief, it is true, correct, and complete. Declaration of preparer (other than taxpayer) is based on all information of which preparer has any knowledge.

▶ George Rose
Signature of officer

2-15-01
Date

▶ President
Title

Paid Preparer's Use Only

Preparer's signature ▶		Date	Check if self-employed ☐	Preparer's SSN or PTIN
Firm's name (or yours if self-employed), address, and ZIP code	▶		EIN	
			Phone no. ( )	

For Paperwork Reduction Act Notice, see page 1 of the instructions.

Cat. No. 11456E

Form **1120-A** (2000)

The Form of Your Business

Form 1120-A (2000)   Page **2**

Part I — Tax Computation (See page 17 of instructions.)

1	Income tax. If the corporation is a qualified personal service corporation (see page 17), check here ▶ ☐	**1** 5,196
2	Alternative minimum tax (attach Form 4626)	**2**
3	Add lines 1 and 2	**3** 5,196
4a	General business credit. Check if from Form(s): ☐ 3800 ☐ 3468 ☐ 5884 ☐ 6478 ☐ 6765 ☐ 8586 ☐ 8830 ☐ 8826 ☐ 8835 ☐ 8844 ☐ 8845 ☐ 8846 ☐ 8820 ☐ 8847 ☐ 8861	**4a**
b	Credit for prior year minimum tax (attach Form 8827)	**4b**
5	**Total credits.** Add lines 4a and 4b	**5**
6	Subtract line 5 from line 3	**6** 5,196
7	Recapture taxes. Check if from: ☐ Form 4255 ☐ Form 8611	**7**
8	**Total tax.** Add lines 6 and 7. Enter here and on line 27, page 1	**8** 5,196

Part II — Other Information (See page 19 of instructions.)

1 See page 21 and enter the: **a** Business activity code no. ▶ 5995
    b Business activity ▶ Flower Shop
    c Product or service ▶ Flowers

2 At the end of the tax year, did any individual, partnership, estate, or trust own, directly or indirectly, 50% or more of the corporation's voting stock? (For rules of attribution, see section 267(c).) ☒ Yes ☐ No
If "Yes," attach a schedule showing name and identifying number.

3 Enter the amount of tax-exempt interest received or accrued during the tax year . . . . . ▶ |$ -0- |

4 Enter total amount of cash distributions and the book value of property (other than cash) distributions made in this tax year . . . . ▶ |$ -0- |

5a If an amount is entered on line 2, page 1, enter from worksheet on page 14 instr.:

(1) Purchases . . . . . ▶	134,014
(2) Additional 263A costs (attach schedule)	
(3) Other costs (attach schedule) .	9,466

b If property is produced or acquired for resale, do the rules of section 263A apply to the corporation? . . . . . ☐ Yes ☒ No

6 At any time during the 2000 calendar year, did the corporation have an interest in or a signature or other authority over a financial account (such as a bank account, securities account, or other financial account) in a foreign country? . . . . . ☐ Yes ☒ No
If "Yes," the corporation may have to file Form TD F 90-22.1.
If "Yes," enter the name of the foreign country ▶ _____

Part III — Balance Sheets per Books

		(a) Beginning of tax year	(b) End of tax year
Assets	1 Cash	20-540	18,498
	2a Trade notes and accounts receivable		
	b Less allowance for bad debts	( )	( )
	3 Inventories	2,010	2,530
	4 U.S. government obligations	13,807	45,479
	5 Tax-exempt securities (see instructions)		
	6 Other current assets (attach schedule)		
	7 Loans to shareholders		
	8 Mortgage and real estate loans		
	9a Depreciable, depletable, and intangible assets . . .		
	b Less accumulated depreciation, depletion, and amortization	( )	( )
	10 Land (net of any amortization)		
	11 Other assets (attach schedule)		
	12 Total assets	36,877	65,987
Liabilities and Shareholders' Equity	13 Accounts payable	6,415	6,079
	14 Other current liabilities (attach schedule)		
	15 Loans from shareholders		
	16 Mortgages, notes, bonds payable		
	17 Other liabilities (attach schedule)		
	18 Capital stock (preferred and common stock) . . .	20,000	20,000
	19 Additional paid-in capital		
	20 Retained earnings	10,462	39,908
	21 Adjustments to shareholders' equity (attach schedule) .		
	22 Less cost of treasury stock	( )	( )
	23 Total liabilities and shareholders' equity	36,877	65,987

Part IV — Reconciliation of Income (Loss) per Books With Income per Return (Note: The corporation is not required to complete Part IV if the total assets on line 12, column (b), Part III are less than $25,000.)

1	Net income (loss) per books	29,446	6 Income recorded on books this year not included on this return (itemize) _____	
2	Federal income tax	5,196		
3	Excess of capital losses over capital gains . .		7 Deductions on this return not charged against book income this year (itemize) _____	
4	Income subject to tax not recorded on books this year (itemize) _____			
5	Expenses recorded on books this year not deducted on this return (itemize)		8 Income (line 24, page 1). Enter the sum of lines 1 through 5 less the sum of lines 6 and 7	34,642

Form **1120-A** (2000)

Disbursing some corporate profits to shareholders and keeping the rest in the business amounts to "income splitting." (See Section C1, below.) But once a corporation reaches the $100,000 profit level (after paying salaries and benefits), retaining earnings produces smaller, if any, tax savings. This is because corporate profits between $100,001 and $335,000 are hit with a 5% tax surcharge, effectively eliminating the benefits of the initial lower tax rates.

> **EXAMPLE 2:** Top Value Motors, Inc. retains a $200,000 net profit after paying salaries and fringe benefits. The corporation owes $61,250 tax to the IRS ($22,250 on the first $100,000 and $39,000 on the second $100,000). This is an average tax rate of about 31%.
>
> By contrast, if all the money had been paid to the only shareholder, Henry, as salary, he most likely would have been in the top individual tax bracket (39.6%). If Henry's income had exceeded $300,000 before this addition, he would have had to pay an extra $79,950 in income taxes. The tax savings thus were $17,950 ($79,200 – $61,250).

For more in-depth information about income splitting, see *Save Taxes With Corporate Income Splitting*, by Anthony Mancuso (Nolo), a downloadable eGuide available at http://www.nolo.com.

A C corporation faces three other potential federal taxes that other business entities don't have to worry about:

- the accumulated earnings tax
- personal holding company tax, and
- the corporate alternative minimum tax.

All of these are discussed in Section G, below.

Get help with corporate tax matters. This chapter covers only the basics—not the details—of corporate tax rules. Because the learning curve to master corporate tax intricacies is steep, always involve a tax pro in corporate tax matters.

Another Incorporation Advantage: Fewer Audits

One of the best unofficial tax reasons for incorporating a small business is that it lowers your audit odds. Corporations reporting under $100,000 of gross receipts per year are audited at one-third the rate of unincorporated businesses with the same income. Only when a business brings in over $1 million per year do the audit odds turn against corporations. The IRS keeps threatening to step up small corporation audits, but never quite gets around to it.

C. Tax Benefits of C Corporations

C corporations offer several tax planning benefits, but not until the venture is very profitable. Let's look at a few tax opportunities.

1. Income Splitting

A C corporation may engage in "income splitting"— that is, dividing income between the corporation and the shareholders in a way that lowers overall taxes. This benefits shareholders in the higher tax brackets. (See Section B3, above.)

2. Fringe Benefits

Maybe the best tax reason for a C corporation is to get the greatest tax-favored fringe benefits of all business entities. New ventures typically can't afford fringes, so this is not an advantage for start-ups. But once your business is thriving, seriously consider a C corporation.

A fringe benefit is any tax-advantaged benefit allowed a business owner or employee. A fringe benefit is either partially or totally tax-free to the recipient and tax-deductible to the business.

The Form of Your Business

Two C corporation fringe benefits worth considering are retirement and medical plans. While any business owner can establish a tax-advantaged retirement plan, C corporations offer greater contribution limits and flexibility.

For instance, sole proprietors, partners and limited liability company members can deduct only 60% (2001) of their medical insurance premiums. A C corporation with a medical plan can deduct 100% of insurance premiums. On top of that, a C corporation can adopt a medical reimbursement plan. With a medical reimbursement plan, the C corporation reimburses the employee for any medical expenses not covered by insurance and then deducts these amounts as expenses. This is usually far more tax advantageous than taking the same medical expense deductions on the shareholders'/employees' individual income tax returns.

The principal drawback of corporate fringe benefits is that ordinarily they must be given to most, if not all, employees of the corporation—not just the owners of the business. (See Chapter 14, Fringe Benefits, and Chapter 15, Retirement Plans, for details.)

3. Business Operating Losses of C Corporations

While no one enjoys losing money in a venture, it happens. When it does, it is only natural to look for a tax break to cushion the blow. There are essentially no tax restrictions on the capital or operating losses of a C corporation that may be carried over to other corporate tax years.

By contrast, sole proprietors, partners and limited liability company owners are subject to restrictive rules for claiming tax benefits from losses. For instance, in most circumstances, an individual cannot claim an annual capital loss greater than $3,000 unless he has offsetting capital gains. (See Chapter 4, Business Losses and Failures, for details.)

4. Dividends Received From Other Corporations

Another tax break reserved for C corporations is the "dividends received" exclusion. This rule won't affect many of you, but it should be kept in mind if your corporation is cash-heavy and you don't want to take out profits right away. This rather strange rule says that a C corporation may receive dividends from stock it owns in another unrelated corporation 70% tax-free. In other words, while you as an individual would have to pay taxes on 100% of a $1,000 corporate stock dividend, a C corporation is taxed on only $300. This could produce a savings if your corporation is investing in other corporations' stock. But don't try this without seeing your tax pro first; there are some highly technical rules at play.

Limited Liability: A Non-Tax Reason to Incorporate

Most small business owners who incorporate do so to limit their personal liability for debts of their business—not for tax purposes. The U.S. is the most "sue-happy" place in the world. If you are in business long enough you will be sued, and if you lose, life as you know it could be over.

Incorporating provides a "corporate shield" that separates your business assets and liabilities from your personal finances. For instance, if a customer is injured on your premises, she can sue only your corporation—not you personally. If she wins, she can collect only from corporate assets—not your house or personal bank account. Ditto if your business fails and can't pay its creditors. Of course, you lose this protection if you personally guarantee corporate obligations to suppliers.

So deciding to incorporate (and whether to be a C or S corporation) involves weighing pros and cons. The *Legal Guide for Starting & Running a Small Business*, by Fred Steingold (Nolo), discusses the non-tax issues involved in choosing a business entity. Then sit down with a tax pro to confirm whether your choice makes good tax sense.

D. Incorporating Your Business

While you may jump right into operation as a C corporation, most folks wisely wait to see if the venture will succeed. Incorporating can complicate things. Remember, a corporation is a separate tax entity from its owners, and normally when two taxpayers transfer assets between themselves there are potential tax issues. The tax code, however, allows a going business to incorporate without tax consequences if certain rules are followed. (IRC § 351.) Just know what you are getting into before incorporating. We discuss some of these start-up issues below.

1. Putting Cash Into a New Corporation

Typically, incorporators (who become shareholders) put money into a corporate bank account in return for shares of stock. While there is no minimum investment required for federal tax purposes, there might be under your state's law. Most states require corporations to have sufficient cash or other assets to show that they are not empty "shells." In legalese, this is called "adequate capitalization."

⚠ Always adequately capitalize your corporation. To protect your limited liability, you need to make sure there is a reasonable amount of money in the corporation to meet its expenses and pay its debts as they come due. Otherwise, the IRS or a creditor might successfully argue that the corporation is a sham and hold you personally liable for corporate debts.

Whether you are buying shares of Microsoft or starting your own Minisoft corporation, there are no immediate tax consequences of acquiring stock. You are making an "equity" investment. The taxes come later, if and when you sell or otherwise dispose of your stock at a profit.

EXAMPLE: Marty incorporates her newsletter business and puts $10,000 into its bank account. In return, Marty, Inc., issues Marty 1,000 shares of stock. This is an equity investment with no tax consequences. Later, when Marty sells her shares or dissolves Marty, Inc. and distributes its assets to herself, she will be taxed only if she has a gain—that is, she receives more than her $10,000 tax basis in the stock.

2. Lending Money to Your New Corporation

You may want to put money into a new corporation as a loan, not as a purchase of stock. For tax purposes, this would mean the first money that shareholders (investors) take out of the business is a repayment of their loan. In effect, they would receive a tax-free return of their investment. Sorry—this technique no longer works.

The tax code frowns on shareholder loans to fund a corporate start-up. There must be a cash or property investment for stock, and a shareholder cannot take back any corporate debt (promissory notes) for his contributions. (IRC § 351.)

However, once the corporation is established and profitable, a shareholder can legally make loans to fund a corporation's operation or expansion. (See Section F, below.) Later, the corporation can pay back the loan to the shareholder without any tax consequences.

3. Putting Assets Into a New Corporation

You may transfer property other than cash—such as a building, vehicle or patent you own—to a corporation in exchange for its stock. There may be a tax trap, however. Let's look at how to avoid these tax pitfalls.

The Form of Your Business

a.   When IRC § 351 Can Help

Transferring an asset with a fair market value greater than your tax basis in it to a corporation in exchange for stock is *potentially* taxable. Thankfully, a special elective tax code provision, IRC § 351, lets you defer or postpone any taxes that otherwise would be due.

With IRC § 351, no taxes are imposed unless you sell the stock received in exchange for the property at a profit. Alternatively, you may be taxed if the corporation is dissolved and you receive assets worth more than your investment.

> **EXAMPLE:** Mario transfers his warehouse (which he has owned for ten years and which has a tax basis of $50,000), to Mario Brothers, Inc., in exchange for stock. (See Chapter 2 for an explanation of how the tax basis of property is determined.) At the time of the transfer, the warehouse has a fair market value of $100,000.
>
> Without IRC § 351, the tax code treats this transfer as Mario selling his warehouse to his corporation. This produces a taxable gain to Mario of $50,000—the difference between his $50,000 basis and the $100,000 market value. Fortunately, Mario can elect *nontaxable* treatment of the transfer by invoking IRC § 351.

b.   When Not to Use IRC § 351

Section 351 is not mandatory; it is elective. If property transferred to a corporation has gone down in value, IRC § 351 may not be the way to go, because electing IRC § 351 treatment takes away the tax benefit of a loss. A shareholder may not claim a taxable loss when transferring property to his own corporation. IRC § 351, in effect, makes all transfers "tax-neutral."

> **EXAMPLE:** In the previous example, suppose Mario bought his warehouse for $50,000, its value has dropped to $30,000 when he decides to incorporate. In effect, Mario has lost $20,000

on paper. IRC § 351 does not allow a tax loss on a transfer of a shareholder's property to his corporation. So if Mario elected § 351, he would not get a tax benefit of the $20,000 loss in value if he transfers the warehouse to Mario Brothers, Inc.

c.   Selling Property to Your Corporation

Selling an asset to your corporation and claiming a loss on the sale on your individual tax return is generally a no-no. The "related party" rules (IRC § 267) prohibit claiming tax losses on transactions between shareholders and their corporation if they own 50% or more of its stock. According to the IRS, you and your corporation are related parties.

> **EXAMPLE:** Mario, in the previous example, can claim a $20,000 tax loss resulting from the warehouse's decline in value only by selling the warehouse to an unrelated party—not to his corporation. If Mario Brothers Inc. needs the warehouse, Mario could lease it back from the new owner after the sale.

d.   How to Meet the Conditions of IRC § 351

Generally, if you are transferring property that has appreciated since you acquired it, elect IRC § 351. To do so, four conditions must all be met:

1. **The corporation must receive property in exchange for stock.** Real estate and equipment are the most common types of property transferred, but it could also be just about anything of value.
2. **Shareholders must receive only stock in exchange for the property.** Transferors can't take back cash, bonds, corporate promissory notes or more complicated instruments like stock warrants or stock options. And each shareholder must receive stock in direct proportion to the fair market value of the property he or she transfers.

EXAMPLE: Joe transfers $20,000 fair market value of equipment and Jill transfers $20,000 worth of real estate to Joe & Jill, Inc. Each must get an equal number of shares of stock in return.

If any transferors get anything else but stock, the value of these items is taxable income to that shareholder. For instance, if in addition to stock, Joe receives a $10,000 promissory note from Joe & Jill, Inc., $10,000 of income is taxable to him.

3. The shareholders who transfer property must be in control. Taken as a group, shareholders who transfer property for stock must own at least 80% of the new corporation's shares after the transfer. Since the stock of most small business corporations is held by only a handful of investors, ordinarily this restriction is not a problem.

EXAMPLE: Paul, Ringo and John want to incorporate using IRC § 351. Paul and Ringo transfer $170,000 in biotech research equipment, previously used by the P & R partnership, in return for 75% of the shares of Bio Research, Inc. John, who is retired and does not intend to work in the business, is internationally known in this field; the corporation gives him 25% of the shares outright on condition that it can advertise his name as a shareholder. This transaction fails IRC § 351 rules because after the transfer, Paul and Ringo own less than 80% of the stock.

4. No stock may be given in exchange for future services. This condition of IRC § 351 causes the most problems. The "no work for stock" rule precludes folks short on cash from start-up ownership. Any shareholders who got stock for their promise of service owe income tax on the value of the stock received.

EXAMPLE: Wanda and Perry form Galaxy Inc. to help businesses advertise on the Internet. Perry contributes $100,000. Wanda, who is broke, promises to apply her skill with online networks. They each receive 250 shares of Galaxy Inc. Wanda's stock doesn't qualify under IRC § 351, so she is taxed on $50,000, the value of her half of the corporation's stock. Perry is not taxed, because he is qualified under IRC § 351. Given this result, Wanda may not want to become a stockholder of Galaxy, Inc.

e. Value of Stock in an IRC § 351 Transfer

The shares of stock received for property transferred have the same tax basis the property had. In tax lingo, this is "substituted basis." It follows that the value of your stock equals the value of the property exchanged for it. For tax purposes, you have the same amount invested in the stock as you did in the asset transferred for it.

EXAMPLE: When he forms Jones, Inc., Jason transfers a building he owns for stock. Jason's tax basis in the building, valued at $110,000, was $75,000, so his basis in his Jones, Inc. stock is $75,000. Jason substituted the building for the corporate stock. The actual fair market value of the building is irrelevant to Jason's basis in his stock.

f. IRS § 351 Filing by Corporations and Shareholders

A corporation *and* each shareholder must tax report all IRC § 351 transfers. A "351 statement" listing all property transferred must be attached to the tax returns of the individual shareholders, and of the corporation its first year of operation. There is no IRS preprinted form for this, so get help from a tax pro here. (Reg. 1.351-3.)

Record IRC § 351 transfers from shareholders in the corporate minutes book. Each individual shareholder should also keep records of assets transferred —for as long as they own their shares, and for at least three years after they dispose of them (just in case the IRS comes calling).

The Form of Your Business

Transfers to a corporation may be taxed under state and local laws. IRC § 351 is a federal tax rule. State and local laws may treat transfers of shareholder assets as taxable sales to the corporation. For example, a retail clothier who transfers clothing racks and his inventory of men's suits to his new corporation may be subject to his state's 5% sales tax. Check this out with a local tax pro before attempting an IRC § 351 transfer.

There may be other unexpected state tax issues from an IRC § 351 transfer. For instance, real estate transferred may trigger a property tax reassessment. For instance, in California, transferring appreciated real estate to a corporation usually means a property tax hike. So see a tax pro or contact state and local tax agencies before transferring property to a corporation. You might be better off leasing your real estate to your corporation. (See Section F4, below.)

E. Issuing IRC § 1244 Stock to Benefit Shareholders If the Business Fails

A small business C corporation should always issue so-called "Section 1244 stock." (S corporations don't qualify for IRC § 1244—see Chapter 8.) This enables shareholders to get better tax treatment if they lose money on their investment in C corporation stock. (See Chapter 4 for an explanation of business losses.) There is no downside and it is easy to qualify stock in a corporation for IRC § 1244 treatment if you follow the rules—none of which should be a problem for most folks:

1. IRC § 1244 corporate shares may be issued only in return for money or property. Meaning that you can't exchange stocks or bonds from another corporation, or contribute services in return for IRC § 1244 stock. And 1244 stock can't be issued in return for canceling a prior debt to the shareholder.

2. Investors must be individuals—not other business entities, such as partnerships or other corporations.

3. No more than 50% of the corporation's gross receipts during the preceding five years (or the life of the corporation, if less than five years) was "passive" income. Passive income includes royalties, dividends, interest, rents, annuities or gains from securities or stock. So IRC § 1244 corporation losses must be from active business operations, not investments.

4. The total money or property received by the corporation for IRC § 1244 stock cannot exceed $1 million.

5. The corporation must be a domestic (U.S.) company.

6. The shareholder must be the original purchaser of the stock.

 Subsequent investments in the corporation by an IRC § 1244 shareholder. Folks seldom risk putting big bucks into a start-up venture. But an investor can't claim IRC § 1244 treatment for any contributions made *after* the initial shares were issued. You can solve this dilemma by treating any money later contributed as payment for IRC § 1244 stock that was "authorized but not issued." The example below shows how to do this.

> **EXAMPLE:** HairCo, a new corporation, authorized 1,000 shares of IRC § 1244 stock be issued to Morey who agreed to buy them at $100 per share. At the time HairCo was formed, Morey paid $40,000 for 400 shares. The next year Morey paid $60,000 for 600 authorized shares, a total of $100,000. All of Morey's stock is IRC § 1244 stock.

Always adopt a written corporate resolution at the time the corporation first issues stock, stating that it is IRC § 1244 stock. You might get by without a written resolution if you meet the other conditions, but why take the risk? Even a postdated resolution (made after the stock was issued) will work.

Neither the corporation nor shareholders have to file the resolution with the IRS. Just keep it in your corporate records book in case the IRS decides to question the investment loss during an audit. A sample IRC § 1244 resolution is shown below.

Sample IRC § 1244 Resolution

The Board next considered the advisability of qualifying the stock of this corporation as IRC § 1244 stock as defined in the Internal Revenue Code, and of organizing and managing the corporation so that it is a Small Business Corporation as defined in that section. Upon motion duly made and seconded, it was unanimously

RESOLVED, that the proper officers of the corporation are, subject to the requirements of federal law and the law of this state, authorized to sell and issue shares of stock in return for the receipt of the aggregate amount of money and other property, as a contribution to capital and paid in surplus, which does not exceed $1,000,000.

RESOLVED FURTHER, the sale and issuance of shares of stock shall be conducted in compliance with IRC § 1244 so that the corporation and its shareholders may obtain the benefits of that section.

RESOLVED FURTHER, that the proper officers of the corporation are directed to maintain such records as are necessary pursuant to IRC § 1244 so that any shareholder who experiences a loss on the transfer of shares of stock of the corporation may determine whether he or she qualifies for ordinary loss deduction treatment on his or her individual income tax return.

Since there was no further business to come before the meeting, on motion duly made and seconded, the meeting was adjourned.

_____   _____
Date   Secretary

An IRC § 1244 stock investment loss is claimed on IRS Form 4797, which is filed with your individual income tax return after the year of the loss.

F. Taking Money Out of a C Corporation

A C corporation offers great flexibility for a shareholder/owner in taking money out of a business. Never forget that a corporation is a separate legal and tax entity from its owners—unlike a sole proprietorship, limited liability company or partnership. This is valuable because you and your corporation may engage in beneficial financial dealings—such as loans—between each other.

 Pay attention to corporate formalities; the IRS does. Always prepare corporate minutes (records) of any significant corporate financial transactions—loans, compensation of officers and so forth. IRS auditors often inspect corporate minutes. If you haven't kept up your corporate paperwork, an auditor may not recognize your business's corporate status. Tax benefits can be disallowed because corporate minute books were not up-to-date, or some state filings for the corporation were not made.

1. Compensation for Services

If you work in your incorporated business, you are *not* self-employed in the eyes of the IRS. You are an employee of your corporation earning wages, just like any other individual working for the business.

 Small corporations may benefit from putting the owner/shareholder's spouse and kids on the payroll too. Spreading family business income over lower tax brackets is legal as long as everyone does real work and isn't overpaid. (See Chapter 12, Family Businesses.)

In theory, the tax law limits the wages you can receive from your C corporation. (IRC §§ 162, 274.) Corporations paying "unreasonable compensation for personal services" can have this (otherwise deductible) wage expense disallowed on an IRS audit. In reality, this rarely ever happens.

An IRS auditor can also assess a 25% penalty on certain excessive salaries. This penalty applies to officers, directors and family members of closely held corporations. (Again, this is not really a concern for small business corporations.) Publicly traded corporate officers are not subject to this penalty, which doesn't seem quite fair. What's more, an additional 200% penalty is added if the excessive part isn't promptly repaid to the corporation. Also, the same penalties can be applied if corporate assets are transferred at large discounts instead of cash. If you're worried ask your tax pro when it comes time to determine compensation for officers, directors and corporate employees.

One case that allowed a million-dollar annual salary should give all high flyers solace. Here the principal stockholder was the CEO, who designed products sold by the company. The Tax Court found that the products he designed were responsible for increased sales, so he in effect performed more than one job. The $1 million corporate compensation was not unreasonable under these circumstances. (*PMT Inc. v. CIR*, TC Memo 1996-303.)

Be ready for an IRS audit challenge for "unreasonable compensation." Assuming you do significant work for your corporation, draw up an employment contract stating your salary and duties. This shows that your pay was a well-thought-out business decision.

Keep your stated salary fairly consistent from year to year—even if the corporation does not always have enough funds to pay it. Otherwise, if your salary is tied to profits, it looks more like a corporate dividend on your investment, and not wages. If the corporation has a down year and can't pay your scheduled salary, get a promissory note from the corporation. Then take funds when they're available in future years as payment on the note. Document compensation decisions in the minutes of the corporation and by corporate resolutions.

2. Dividends Double Taxation

A C corporation may pay dividends to shareholders if it has enough current and retained earnings to also pay its debts and remain solvent. Paying dividends brings up the bugaboo of double taxation —the corporation is taxed on its profits before the dividend is paid, and the recipient shareholder is taxed again on the same income. While it seldom makes sense for a small corporation to pay dividends, it may be done to compensate shareholders who don't work in the business.

Consider putting inactive shareholders on the payroll. You may be able to use them as consultants or elect them as corporate directors and pay for their services. This technique avoids double taxation.

3. Loans to Shareholders

A *profitable* C corporation may lend money to its shareholders. A loan from your C corporation isn't taxable income to you, and doesn't have tax consequences to the corporation. Interest received on the loan is income to the corporation, of course.

Shareholder loans must be "bona fide." The borrowers must obligate themselves in writing to repay the loan at a specific date, and the loan should be secured by pledging property, which will be turned over to the corporation if the loan is not repaid.

Loans to shareholders of less than $10,000 can be interest-free. Larger loans must carry a commercially reasonable rate of interest—at least the minimum legal interest rate. (See "How to Make Sure a Loan From a Corporation Is Treated as Legitimate by the IRS," below.)

The IRS knows shareholders are tempted to label all withdrawals from their corporation as "loans," because loans are not taxable income to the shareholders. Even worse, if payments are called dividends, taxes result to both the corporation and shareholders. So, if a loan doesn't look legitimate an IRS auditor can rename it and tax it as compensation or a dividend payment to the shareholder.

Checklist: How to Make Sure a Loan From a Corporation Is Treated As Legitimate by the IRS

The more a loan to a shareholder meets the criteria of a bank loan, the less likely an IRS auditor will challenge it. And not only must the loan look legitimate, the parties must abide by its terms. The corporation shouldn't give the shareholder any breaks—such as forgiving interest on the loan—that a bank wouldn't give. Specifically, loans between corporations and shareholders should meet these requirements:

- The corporate minutes should reflect all loans.
- The shareholder should sign a promissory note for a specific amount.
    - The note should obligate the shareholder to repay the loan unconditionally on a specific date or in regular installments.
    - The corporation should charge at least the minimum legal interest rate. The Treasury Department sets this rate once a month; call the nearest Federal Reserve Bank office to get the current rate. If a corporation doesn't charge at least this rate, an IRS auditor can attack it as a "below market" loan (IRC § 7872) and the borrower will be taxed as receiving the value of the undercharged interest.
- The note should be legally transferable by the corporation to a third party.
- The loan should be secured by collateral such as a bank account, real estate or other shareholder property.
- The note should stand on equal footing with debts of others to the corporation.
- The note should give the corporation the right to sue and take the collateral if the shareholder does not repay the loan on time.
    - The shareholder should make all interest and principal payments when due.

4. Leasing Property to Your Corporation

Leasing your individually owned assets to your corporation is another way to extract profits—without paying dividends or worrying about the "unreasonable compensation" issues discussed earlier.

Real estate is the most common kind of property leased to a corporation by shareholders. However, leasing can work tax-wise for things like equipment or machinery.

Renting real estate to your corporation may produce a tax loss for you, the shareholder. Typically, this results from your taking a depreciation deduction on the property. Or leasing may produce an out-of-pocket loss if cash expenses exceed cash income. Either type of loss offsets or "shelters" other income on your individual tax return.

> **EXAMPLE:** On January 1, 2001, Bart buys a building and land for $100,000. He immediately leases it to his C corporation, Homer, Inc., at the market rate of $12,000 per year. The building is worth $80,000 (the lot is worth $20,000). Bart is allowed to take tax code depreciation deductions of $2,051 per year. (See Chapter 2, Writing Off Business Assets.) Bart incurs annual expenses for real estate taxes, maintenance and mortgage interest on the building totaling $11,400. After applying the rent payments from Homer, Inc., Bart has an overall loss of $1,451, which he claims on his individual 2001 tax return. ($12,000 income - $11,400 expenses - $2,051 depreciation = $1,451 tax loss.) In reality, Bart ends up with $600 in his pocket, because most of his "tax loss" was from the depreciation deduction.

 To pass IRS audit muster, a lease between a shareholder and the corporation must be a realistic deal. The lease payment must be close to fair market value. Since rents for similar properties can vary considerably, you can charge your corporation a bit more (or less) than you might get from others. How much depends on several factors. A 25% discrepancy is usually defensible—especially if you can back it up with a written opinion from a real estate professional that the rent your corporation pays is within the market range.

EXAMPLE: Brenda owns a storefront building and rents it to her incorporated bakery business. The building might rent for $500 a month on the open market, but its size, amenities and location are unique, making precise valuation difficult. Brenda is probably safe renting it to her corporation for $625 a month, but $2,000 is not likely to fly at an IRS audit. Brenda would jack up the rent only if she wanted to take more money out of the corporation without having it taxed as compensation to her. It would be rental income to her, though. The tax savings would result from a reduction in the payroll tax for Brenda.

Leasing property limits your liability. A good non-tax reason for leasing your property to your corporation (rather than having the business own it) is to protect your personal assets from corporate liabilities. For instance, suppose your corporation is successfully sued for sexual harassment. The judgment can be collected against the corporation's property, but your assets are safe. Even if the corporation declares bankruptcy, the leased property is not a corporate asset; it still belongs to you.

5. Selling Your Corporate Stock

A share of corporate stock—a fractional ownership interest in a business—is an asset. As with any asset, its sale is a taxable event, usually producing a gain or loss to the seller.

a. Capital Gains

A gain on stock owned in a C corporation business held longer than one year is taxed at special tax code capital gains rates when sold. (See Chapter 2, Writing Off Business Assets, for an explanation of capital gains rates.)

EXAMPLE: Robin forms RRR, Inc., and transfers his warehouse to the corporation in exchange for stock. Robin elects IRC § 351 treatment, so the transfer is not a taxable event. (See Section D3, above.) His basis in the warehouse—$75,000—becomes his basis in his stock.

Two years later, when the fair market value of the warehouse is $125,000, Robin sells his stock to Wanda for $175,000. Robin has a taxable gain of $100,000 ($175,000 minus his basis in his stock of $75,000). The capital gains tax on Robin's profit is a maximum of 20% (IRC § 1(h)), making his tax liability $20,000. (Robin's state tax agency will probably want a cut of the action, too.) Without the capital gains tax rate, Robin's tax could have been as high as $39,600.

b. Capital Losses

Losses on the sale of stock are treated under more restrictive tax rules than are gains. Unless the corporate stock is qualified under IRC § 1244 (discussed in Section E, above), a shareholder's capital losses can only partly offset his ordinary income in any one year. His capital losses may, however, fully offset any of the shareholder's capital gains. (See Chapter 4, Business Losses and Failures, for a detailed explanation.)

Tax Breaks for Qualified Small Business Corporation Investors

Investors in C corporations formed after August 10, 1993, may be eligible for a special tax break if they sell their stock at a gain. Fifty percent of any gain on the sale of stock in these "qualified" corporations is not taxed if held for more than five years.

What corporations qualify? The rules are complex, but one is that at least 80% of the corporation's assets must be used in the active conduct of the business. This eliminates corporations with significant income from investments. Corporations that sell services, or a mix of goods and services—for example, hotels or restaurants—are excluded. See IRC § 1202 for details.

G. Tax Pitfalls of C Corporations

When you operate as a C corporation, you are treated like the big boys. Mind-boggling corporate tax complexities occasionally trap small business people. One worry—double taxation—has been discussed; here are three others.

1. Personal Holding Company Tax

There is a special penalty tax on C corporations the IRS deems "incorporated pocketbooks." This provision targets corporations that derive 60% or more of their income from investments, such as dividends and royalties.

This "personal holding company" tax doesn't affect typical small businesses, which aren't just passive investment entities. For more information, see IRC § 541 and following sections.

2. Accumulated Earnings Tax

An advantage of a C corporation over other business entity forms is its ability to accumulate earnings (roughly meaning "profits") to fund future growth. These earnings are taxed to the corporation—but at lower rates than if they had been distributed to the shareholders.

If, however, a C corporation keeps too much profit in its coffers, it incurs an "accumulated earnings" tax of 39.6%. Smaller C corporations can breathe easy—this tax does not kick in until accumulated earnings exceed $250,000. (IRC § 531.)

3. Corporate Alternative Minimum Tax

A corporation that takes advantage of certain tax code provisions to lower its income taxes can't avoid income taxes altogether. C corporations are subject to the "corporate alternative minimum tax." (IRC § 55-58, Reg. 1.56-.58.) However, few small business corporations ever have to worry about this tax, so we won't bore you with too many details.

The tax breaks that cause the corporate alternative minimum tax to come into play are called "tax preference" items. They include out-of-the-ordinary things like income from life insurance or from a corporation spreading its tax liabilities into the future by using the installment method of tax reporting.

H. Dissolving a C Corporation

How your corporation legally goes out of business depends on your state's law—just as its formation did. Generally, a corporation can close down voluntarily by agreement of its shareholders if more than 50% of the shareholders vote to quit.

A corporation can also cease to exist involuntarily "by operation of law"—such as from a deadlock of shareholders or nonpayment of annual corporation fees. Neglecting to keep up with state filings and fees is the most common way small corporations die.

The Form of Your Business

While it is relatively easy to dissolve a corporation, if you suddenly stop filing corporate income tax returns, expect the IRS or your state taxing agency to notice—and investigate. Special tax code provisions deal with corporate liquidations or dissolutions. The specter of "double taxation" arises if a C corporation has assets that are distributed to the shareholders. Or, a sale of the business's assets and a distribution of the proceeds to the shareholders may mean the corporation owes tax on any gain on the sale. Moreover, shareholders may owe tax again on the money received.

Keep in mind that if the corporation has ever claimed any tax benefits (such as depreciation) on its assets, the corporation's basis in these assets may be very low or even zero. Technically, corporate tax depreciation deductions previously taken may be "recaptured" on dissolution and are now taxable. The result may be unexpected taxable gain even when the corporation disposes of assets for minimal amounts. If the business failed miserably and the shareholders all took a bath, it may be that no one has a taxable gain. Dissolving a corporation is probably one time you'll want to bring in a tax pro for you and the corporation.

Consider switching to S corporation status on your way out. One way around any double taxation problems may be for a dissolving C corporation to elect S corporation status before it liquidates—but don't try this without first consulting a good tax pro.

IRS Form 966, Corporate Dissolution or Liquidation, must be filed with the IRS whenever a corporation is terminated. (For more information, see IRC § 331 and following sections (recipients), 336 and following sections (corporations), Reg. 1.331, 336.)

Resources

- IRS Publication 334, Tax Guide for Small Business. This is an indispensable book for any small business, including C corporations.
- IRS Publication 542, Tax Information for Corporations. This booklet is especially useful if you are preparing and filing corporate tax forms without professional assistance.
- IRS Form 1120, U.S. Corporation Income Tax Return and Instructions
- How to Form Your Own Corporation (California, Texas and New York editions), by Anthony Mancuso (Nolo). This book takes you through the incorporation process step by step. The forms are also available on disk.
- The Corporate Minutes Book, by Anthony Mancuso (Nolo). These books show you how to write up minutes of corporate meetings and document corporate decisions and transactions, which are often important to withstand IRS scrutiny.
- Legal Guide for Starting and Running a Small Business, by Fred Steingold (Nolo). This excellent book deals with all of the ramifications of operating as a C corporation.

S Corporations

*"Corporations cannot commit treason, nor be out-
lawed, nor excommunicated, for they have no souls."*
                                    —Sir Edward Coke

Before tackling this chapter, take a look at the
previous one (Chapter 7) on C Corporations.
That's because all corporations are born as C
corporations under the tax code. Becoming an S
corporation requires an extra step—called an
"election"—with vital tax implications. This chapter
explains the tax treatment of S corporations and
how to become one.

S Corporations in a Nutshell

1. All corporations begin as C corporations, but
   may elect S status with the IRS.
2. S corporations are treated much like partnerships, for tax purposes. S corporations don't
   pay taxes; instead, shareholders pay taxes on
   business income, at their individual tax rates.
3. Electing S corporation status means forgoing
   some of the tax benefits available to a C corporation.
4. Because business start-ups typically lose money
   in their early years, electing S corporation status
   is advantageous. S corporation shareholders
   can claim business losses directly on their
   personal tax returns.

A. An Overview of S Corporations

The tax code recognizes numerous types of corporations, including nonprofits, financial institutions
and personal service corporations. But for most
businesses the choice is a so-called "C" or "S"
corporation.

C and S corporations (the letters refer to subchapters of the Internal Revenue Code) are distinguished by *how* their income is reported.

In broad outline, S corporations "pass" income
through to their shareholders, who then pay tax on
it according to their individual income tax rates. C
corporations, as explained in Chapter 7, are separate
tax entities that may be liable for corporate income
tax on profits. (Taxation of professional corporations
for certain, mostly service professions—such as
doctors and lawyers—is explained in Chapter 11,
Personal Service Corporations.)

Electing S corporation status eliminates the possibility of double taxation on business profits. (C
corporations may pay income tax at the corporate
level, and then the shareholders may be taxed again
when that income is put into their hands.) Because
S corporations are tax-termed "pass-through" entities,
their profits are taxed directly to the shareholders,
the business's owners. S corporations pay no separate corporate income tax, but must file annual tax
returns.

Similarly, S corporation shareholders take most
business operating losses on their individual returns
since losses "pass through" as well. (There are some
restrictions on loss-taking by shareholders who aren't
active in the business; see Section D, below.) By
contrast, C corporation losses remain in the corporation, so their shareholders cannot claim them on
their individual tax returns.

Business income and losses passing through to S
corporation shareholder/owners retain their tax
"characteristics." For instance, S corporation profits
are *ordinary income* to shareholders, and S corporation capital gains are *capital gains* to the shareholders. This is beneficial because capital gains are
generally taxed at a lower rate than is ordinary
income.

Although an S corporation business is not a tax-
paying entity, it is most definitely a tax-reporting
entity. An annual corporation tax return, Form
1120-S, showing income and expenses and the
resulting profits or losses, must be filed. Individual
S corporation shareholders then report the
business's income (or loss) on their individual tax
returns.

An S corporation must file and pay employment
taxes on its employees just like a C corporation. (See
Chapter 5 for an explanation of employment taxes.)

S corporations generally must file state tax returns, too.

B. Should You Choose S Corporation Status?

Most people incorporate for *non*-tax reasons—usually to shield their personal assets from business obligations. Corporate shareholders, unlike partners and sole proprietors, aren't personally liable for business debts. The S corporation combines this limited liability with pass-through tax treatment—allowing business income and loss benefits to flow directly to shareholders. This is the same tax result as with a sole proprietorship, partnership or limited liability company.

S corporation status offers shareholders tax benefits from business losses, common in a business's start-up phase. S corporations (unlike C corporations) allow shareholders active in the business to take annual operating losses against their other income.

New enterprises often elect S corporation status for the early years and when profitable, convert to a C corporation. If the business becomes profitable, they can get C corporation fringe benefit tax-savings. (See Chapter 14, Fringe Benefits.)

EXAMPLE: Jeannie Smith works as a loan officer for First Bank, earning $25,000 in 2001. She and her husband, Sam, also run a small S corporation business selling computers. The Smiths file tax returns jointly. The computer business loses $15,000 in 2001. By offsetting this $15,000 operating loss against Jeannie's $25,000 salary, the Smiths' total taxable income is reduced to $10,000. After taking into account their exemptions and personal deductions, the Smiths probably won't owe any income taxes. If this had been a regular C corporation, the business loss of $15,000 wouldn't have had any effect on the Smiths' personal tax return.

Consider an alternative to S corporations, the limited liability company. If an S corporation sounds good, consider a limited liability company (LLC), too. This relatively new form of business entity, like an S corporation, provides a "pass through" of business income and losses to individual owners. LLCs also offer the personal liability shield of corporations, but are simpler to form and operate than S corporations. (See Chapter 10, Limited Liability Companies.)

1. Small Business Eligibility for S Corporation Status

If an S corporation is for you, you must first form a corporation by filing Articles of Incorporation with your Secretary of State or Department of Corporations. The corporation will probably—but doesn't necessarily have to—be formed in the state you are living and operating in. In all likelihood, you will qualify for S status with the IRS, but before you form your corporation, check these technical rules to make sure your corporation is eligible:

- It is a U.S. corporation with no more than 75 shareholders. This eliminates public corporations. (A husband and wife are considered one shareholder if they own their stock jointly.)
- All shareholders are individual U.S. citizens or resident aliens. In 1997, other S corporations, and a new kind of tax code-recognized entity called an "electing small business trust," also became eligible to own S corporation shares.
- The corporation has only one "class" of stock. There can't be any "preferred" or other types of shares that give special privilege to some shareholders—for example, one class of stock with voting rights and another without.
- The corporation doesn't own 80% or more of the shares of stock in another corporation.
- All shareholders consent in writing to S corporation status by signing a form filed with the IRS. (See Sample Form 2553, below.)

The Form of Your Business

Form 2553
(Rev. January 2001)
Department of the Treasury
Internal Revenue Service

Election by a Small Business Corporation
(Under section 1362 of the Internal Revenue Code)
▶ See Parts II and III on back and the separate instructions.
▶ The corporation may either send or fax this form to the IRS. See page 1 of the instructions.

OMB No. 1545-0146

Notes:
1. This election to be an S corporation can be accepted only if all the tests are met under **Who May Elect** on page 1 of the instructions; all signatures in Parts I and III are originals (no photocopies); and the exact name and address of the corporation and other required form information are provided.
2. Do not file **Form 1120S**, U.S. Income Tax Return for an S Corporation, for any tax year before the year the election takes effect.
3. If the corporation was in existence before the effective date of this election, see **Taxes an S Corporation May Owe** on page 1 of the instructions.

Part I — Election Information

Please Type or Print	Name of corporation (see instructions) XTC Incorporation	**A** Employer identification number 94 : 000 0000
	Number, street, and room or suite no. (If a P.O. box, see instructions.) 123 Main St.	**B** Date incorporated 1/1/01
	City or town, state, and ZIP code Anytown, CA 90210	**C** State of incorporation CA

D Election is to be effective for tax year beginning (month, day, year) . . . . ▶ / /

E Name and title of officer or legal representative who the IRS may call for more information

   Jose Smegola, President

F Telephone number of officer or legal representative
   (555) 555-5555

G If the corporation changed its name or address after applying for the EIN shown in **A** above, check this box . . . . ▶ ☐

H If this election takes effect for the first tax year the corporation exists, enter month, day, and year of the **earliest** of the following: (1) date the corporation first had shareholders, (2) date the corporation first had assets, or (3) date the corporation began doing business . . . . ▶ 1 / 1 / 01

I Selected tax year: Annual return will be filed for tax year ending (month and day) ▶ 12/31

If the tax year ends on any date other than December 31, except for an automatic 52-53-week tax year ending with reference to the month of December, you **must** complete Part II on the back. If the date you enter is the ending date of an automatic 52-53-week tax year, write "52-53-week year" to the right of the date. See Temporary Regulations section 1.441-2T(e)(3).

J Name and address of each shareholder; shareholder's spouse having a community property interest in the corporation's stock; and each tenant in common, joint tenant, and tenant by the entirety. (A husband and wife (and their estates) are counted as one shareholder in determining the number of shareholders without regard to the manner in which the stock is owned.)	**K** Shareholders' Consent Statement. Under penalties of perjury, we declare that we consent to the election of the above-named corporation to be an S corporation under section 1362(a) and that we have examined this consent statement, including accompanying schedules and statements, and to the best of our knowledge and belief, it is true, correct, and complete. We understand our consent is binding and may not be withdrawn after the corporation has made a valid election. (Shareholders sign and date below.)		**L** Stock owned		**M** Social security number or employer identification number (see instructions)	**N** Shareholder's tax year ends (month and day)
	Signature	Date	Number of shares	Dates acquired		
Jose Smegola 123 Main St. Anytown, CA 90210	Joe Smegola	2/10/01	100	1/1/01	123-45-6789	12/31
Francine Schwatzkopf 666 B. St. Anytown, CA 90000	Francine Schwatzkopf	2/15/01	100	1/1/01	987-65-4321	12/31

Under penalties of perjury, I declare that I have examined this election, including accompanying schedules and statements, and to the best of my knowledge and belief, it is true, correct, and complete.

Signature of officer ▶ Francine Schwatzkopf   Title ▶ Secretary   Date ▶ 2/28/01

For Paperwork Reduction Act Notice, see page 4 of the instructions.   Cat. No. 18629R   Form **2553** (Rev. 1-2001)

2. S Corporation Disadvantages

S corporations offer advantages to many small business owners, but not for everybody. Here are some potential tax disadvantages to consider.

a. No Retained Earnings

A successful corporation may want to squirrel away some profits for future growth. Profits remaining in corporations are called "retained earnings." An S corporation, however, cannot retain earnings. Remember, S corporation profits pass through to the shareholders even if not taken out of the business. A C corporation, on the other hand, can keep its profits in the business in return for paying a relatively small amount of tax. (See Chapter 7, C Corporations, for details.)

> **EXAMPLE:** Sam and Jeannie Smith's incorporated computer retail store earns a $50,000 profit after paying the Smiths $200,000 in salary. They keep $50,000 in the business bank account at the end of the tax year. If the business were a C corporation, it would pay income tax of $7,500 ($50,000 at a rate of 15%). By contrast, as an S corporation, the $50,000 is taxed at the Smiths' personal income tax rate. The Smiths' rate might be 39.6%, meaning an additional tax bill of $19,800.

b. Limited Employee Fringe Benefits

S corporations can't provide the full range of fringe benefits that C corporations can. Rarely can new businesses afford fringes anyway, so this is a big deal only for more mature corporations. Nevertheless, once a business has substantial earnings, a C corporation offers tax-savings opportunities over an S corporation. (Chapter 14, Fringe Benefits, and Chapter 15, Retirement Plans, discuss tax-advantaged fringe benefits.)

c. Converting From a C Corporation

It is possible to change a C corporation to an S corporation; however, tax bugaboos pop up. This is more than a little complex, but a converted S corporation will have a tax bill under any of the following three circumstances if:

- the C corporation has passive income
- it used the last-in-first-out (LIFO) method to report inventory, or
- it had gains related to depreciated assets of the C corporation.

Before converting your C to an S corporation, *always* see a savvy tax pro. My advice here is not optional.

C. Tax Reporting for S Corporations

An S corporation must file U.S. Corporation Income Tax Form 1120-S for every year of its operation— whether or not it has any income. Typically, the tax year is the calendar year, so the return is due on March 15. If a company uses a different tax (fiscal) year, the return is due on the 15th day of the third month following the close of its tax year.

To get a six-month extension to file, submit IRS Form 7004, Application for Automatic Extension of Time to File Corporation Income Tax Return, before the return's original due date.

A filled-in 1120-S form is shown below to give you an idea of the kinds of things that must be reported to the IRS. This is *not* to suggest that you prepare your corporation tax return yourself. To the contrary, corporate returns are the stuff that tax pros were made for. If you insist on doing it yourself, however, at least do it with tax software such as Turbotax for Business (Intuit).

Form **1120S**	**U.S. Income Tax Return for an S Corporation**	OMB No. 1545-0130
Department of the Treasury Internal Revenue Service	► Do not file this form unless the corporation has timely filed Form 2553 to elect to be an S corporation. ► See separate instructions.	**2000**

For calendar year 2000, or tax year beginning _____ , 2000, and ending _____ , 20 ___

A Effective date of election as an S corporation	Use IRS label. Other- wise, print or type.	Name	C Employer identification number
12-01-99		StratoTech, Inc.	10 : 4487965
B Business code no. (see pages 29–31)		Number, street, and room or suite no. (If a P.O. box, see page 11 of the instructions.)	D Date incorporated
5008		482 Winston Street	3/1/75
		City or town, state, and ZIP code	E Total assets (see page 11)
		Metro City, OH 43705	$ 771,334

F Check applicable boxes: (1) ☒ Initial return   (2) ☐ Final return   (3) ☐ Change in address   (4) ☐ Amended return
G Enter number of shareholders in the corporation at end of the tax year . . . . ► 6

Caution: *Include **only** trade or business income and expenses on lines 1a through 21. See page 11 of the instructions for more information.*

Income	1a	Gross receipts or sales	1,545,700	**b** Less returns and allowances	21,000	**c** Bal ►	**1c**	1,524,700
	2	Cost of goods sold (Schedule A, line 8)	**2**	954,700
	3	Gross profit. Subtract line 2 from line 1c	**3**	570,000
	4	Net gain (loss) from Form 4797, Part II, line 18 *(attach Form 4797)*	**4**	
	5	Other income (loss) *(attach schedule)*	**5**	
	6	**Total income (loss).** Combine lines 3 through 5 . . . . ►	**6**	570,000

Deductions (see page 12 of the instructions for limitations)	7	Compensation of officers	**7**	170,000
	8	Salaries and wages (less employment credits)	**8**	138,000
	9	Repairs and maintenance	**9**	800
	10	Bad debts	**10**	1,600
	11	Rents	**11**	9,200
	12	Taxes and licenses	**12**	15,000
	13	Interest	**13**	14,200
	14a	Depreciation *(if required, attach Form 4562)*	**14a**	15,200
	b	Depreciation claimed on Schedule A and elsewhere on return .	**14b**	
	c	Subtract line 14b from line 14a	**14c**	15,200
	15	Depletion **(Do not deduct oil and gas depletion.)**	**15**	
	16	Advertising	**16**	8,700
	17	Pension, profit-sharing, etc., plans	**17**	
	18	Employee benefit programs	**18**	
	19	Other deductions *(attach schedule)*	**19**	78,300
	20	**Total deductions.** Add the amounts shown in the far right column for lines 7 through 19 . ►	**20**	451,000
	21	Ordinary income (loss) from trade or business activities. Subtract line 20 from line 6	**21**	119,000

Tax and Payments	22	**Tax: a** Excess net passive income tax *(attach schedule)* . . .	**22a**	
	b	Tax from Schedule D (Form 1120S)	**22b**	
	c	Add lines 22a and 22b (see page 15 of the instructions for additional taxes)	**22c**	
	23	**Payments: a** 2000 estimated tax payments and amount applied from 1999 return	**23a**	
	b	Tax deposited with Form 7004	**23b**	
	c	Credit for Federal tax paid on fuels *(attach Form 4136)* . . .	**23c**	
	d	Add lines 23a through 23c	**23d**	
	24	Estimated tax penalty. Check if Form 2220 is attached . . . . ► ☐	**24**	
	25	**Tax due.** If the total of lines 22c and 24 is larger than line 23d, enter amount owed. See page 4 of the instructions for depository method of payment . . . . ►	**25**	
	26	**Overpayment.** If line 23d is larger than the total of lines 22c and 24, enter amount overpaid ►	**26**	
	27	Enter amount of line 26 you want: **Credited to 2001 estimated tax ►** _____	**Refunded ►**	**27**	

Sign Here

Under penalties of perjury, I declare that I have examined this return, including accompanying schedules and statements, and to the best of my knowledge and belief, it is true, correct, and complete. Declaration of preparer (other than taxpayer) is based on all information of which preparer has any knowledge.

► *John H. Green* | 3-10-01 | ► President
Signature of officer | Date | Title

Paid Preparer's Use Only	Preparer's signature ►		Date	Check if self-employed ☐	Preparer's SSN or PTIN
	Firm's name (or yours if self-employed), address, and ZIP code	►		EIN	
				Phone no. ( )	

For Paperwork Reduction Act Notice, see the separate instructions.   Cat. No. 11510H   Form **1120S** (2000)

Form 1120S (2000) Page **2**

Schedule A Cost of Goods Sold (see page 16 of the instructions)

1	Inventory at beginning of year	1	126,100
2	Purchases	2	1,127,000
3	Cost of labor	3	
4	Additional section 263A costs (attach schedule)	4	
5	Other costs (attach schedule)	5	
6	**Total.** Add lines 1 through 5	6	1,253,100
7	Inventory at end of year	7	298,400
8	**Cost of goods sold.** Subtract line 7 from line 6. Enter here and on page 1, line 2	8	954,700

9a Check all methods used for valuing closing inventory:

(i) ☒ Cost as described in Regulations section 1.471-3

(ii) ☐ Lower of cost or market as described in Regulations section 1.471-4

(iii) ☐ Other (specify method used and attach explanation) ▶ --------------

b Check if there was a writedown of "subnormal" goods as described in Regulations section 1.471-2(c) . . . . ▶ ☒

c Check if the LIFO inventory method was adopted this tax year for any goods (if checked, attach Form 970) . . . . . ▶ ☒

d If the LIFO inventory method was used for this tax year, enter percentage (or amounts) of closing inventory computed under LIFO . . . . **9d** | |

e Do the rules of section 263A (for property produced or acquired for resale) apply to the corporation? . . . . ☐ Yes ☐ No

f Was there any change in determining quantities, cost, or valuations between opening and closing inventory? . . ☐ Yes ☐ No
If "Yes," attach explanation.

Schedule B Other Information

		Yes	No
1	Check method of accounting: **(a)** ☐ Cash **(b)** ☒ Accrual **(c)** ☐ Other (specify) ▶--------		
2	Refer to the list on pages 29 through 31 of the instructions and state the corporation's principal: **(a)** Business activity ▶ _5008 Distributor_ **(b)** Product or service ▶ _heavy equipment_		
3	Did the corporation at the end of the tax year own, directly or indirectly, 50% or more of the voting stock of a domestic corporation? (For rules of attribution, see section 267(c).) If "Yes," attach a schedule showing: **(a)** name, address, and employer identification number and **(b)** percentage owned.		X
4	Was the corporation a member of a controlled group subject to the provisions of section 1561?		X
5	Check this box if the corporation has filed or is required to file **Form 8264,** Application for Registration of a Tax Shelter . . . ▶ ☐		
6	Check this box if the corporation issued publicly offered debt instruments with original issue discount . . ▶ ☐ If so, the corporation may have to file **Form 8281,** Information Return for Publicly Offered Original Issue Discount Instruments.		
7	If the corporation: **(a)** filed its election to be an S corporation after 1986, **(b)** was a C corporation before it elected to be an S corporation **or** the corporation acquired an asset with a basis determined by reference to its basis (or the basis of any other property) in the hands of a C corporation, and **(c)** has net unrealized built-in gain (defined in section 1374(d)(1)) in excess of the net recognized built-in gain from prior years, enter the net unrealized built-in gain reduced by net recognized built-in gain from prior years (see page 17 of the instructions) . . . . ▶ $ _37,200_		
8	Check this box if the corporation had accumulated earnings and profits at the close of the tax year (see page 18 of the instructions) . . . . ▶ ☐		

Note: If the corporation had assets or operated a business in a foreign country or U.S. possession, it may be required to attach **Schedule N (Form 1120),** Foreign Operations of U.S. Corporations, to this return. See Schedule N for details.

Schedule K Shareholders' Shares of Income, Credits, Deductions, etc.

	(a) Pro rata share items		(b) Total amount
1	Ordinary income (loss) from trade or business activities (page 1, line 21)	1	119,000
2	Net income (loss) from rental real estate activities (attach Form 8825)	2	
3a	Gross income from other rental activities	3a	
b	Expenses from other rental activities (attach schedule)	3b	
c	Net income (loss) from other rental activities. Subtract line 3b from line 3a	3c	
4	Portfolio income (loss):		
a	Interest income	4a	4,000
b	Ordinary dividends	4b	16,000
c	Royalty income	4c	
d	Net short-term capital gain (loss) (attach Schedule D (Form 1120S))	4d	
e	Net long-term capital gain (loss) (attach Schedule D (Form 1120S)):		
	(1) 28% rate gain (loss) ▶ ---------------- (2) Total for year ▶	4e(2)	
f	Other portfolio income (loss) (attach schedule)	4f	
5	Net section 1231 gain (loss) (other than due to casualty or theft) (attach Form 4797)	5	
6	Other income (loss) (attach schedule)	6	

(left margin: Income (Loss))

(right margin: The Form of Your Business)

Form **1120S** (2000)

State S Corporation Tax Rules

Most states recognize S corporation status, but state corporation tax rules may differ from the federal tax law. Check with a local tax pro or your state's corporation office to find out how an S corporation files state returns. Typically, states impose a minimum annual corporate tax or franchise fee that applies whether your corporation's business is active or inactive. You may also face a state corporation tax on S corporation income. California, a particularly tax-hungry state, imposes a 2.5% tax on S corporation profits—in addition to a minimum annual franchise tax of $800 after the corporation's first year (no tax is due the first year). The bright side (if you can call it that) is that you can deduct any state and local taxes as business expenses on your federal corporate tax return.

D. How S Corporation Shareholders Are Taxed

S corporation profits and losses do not always flow though to shareholders. The tax code adds a twist, but one that is generally beneficial to shareholders of S corporations: Some items of S corporation income, loss or deductions are "separately stated" on the shareholder's tax return.

For instance, if an S corporation sells an asset at a gain, and the item qualifies for capital gain treatment, this is a separately stated item so the shareholder gets the more beneficial capital gain tax treatment of individuals. Another example is when the corporation is entitled to use the accelerated write-off of assets under IRC § 179 (see Chapter 2, Writing Off Business Assets); the Section 179 deduction flows through to each shareholder as a separately stated item. (IRC § 1366.)

An S corporation reports each stockholder's proportionate share of its profit (or loss) on annual IRS "K-1" forms. K-1s are filed with the IRS by the corporation, and copies are given to each shareholder. In turn, each shareholder reports the K-1 income and separately stated item information on her annual individual Form 1040 tax return. As we all know, April 15 is the date for filing your individual income tax return, which includes this K-1 data.

The law provides a four-month extension to August 15 and a further two-month discretionary extension until October 15 to file.

In addition, S corporations must pay employment (SE) taxes on all employee wages (but not dividends), whereas sole proprietors, LLC members and partners pay self-employment taxes individually on their 1040 returns on all income. (See Section E, below, for more information.)

1. Profits

Typically, S corporation shareholders take profits out of their business either as compensation for services or, less often, as dividends on their investment in the corporation. Either way—or even if all profits are retained by the S corporation instead of being paid out—the earnings are taxed directly to the shareholders as ordinary income. In this regard, an S corporation business owner is like a sole proprietor, partner or limited liability company member.

> **EXAMPLE:** Rusty's S corporation, Rustco, makes a profit of $17,000 in 2001. It issues a Form K-1 to Rusty, who owns 100% of its stock, reporting $17,000 of income. Rustco owes no income tax. Instead, Rusty enters the $17,000 on the first page of his 2001 Form 1040 income tax return, and pays income taxes according to his overall income tax bracket.

2. Losses

S corporation operating losses are similarly passed through to shareholders, and can offset their other taxable income.

The business's operating loss is claimed on the front page of the S shareholder's individual tax return, just like a profit.

There is one limitation, however. A shareholder may not tax-deduct as a loss more than the amount of her tax "basis" in their stock. Generally, a shareholder's tax basis is the total of money and property she put into the corporation for shares of stock. Also, added to the basis are any direct loans to the corporation from the shareholder. An example is in order.

EXAMPLE: Jerrie paid $5,000 for 100% of the stock in her S corporation, JerriCo. In its first year of operation, the business lost $7,000, which was reported on the corporate income tax form and on Jerrie's Form K-1. Jerrie can claim only $5,000 as a loss, because this is the amount of her basis (investment) in her S corporation stock.

Material Participation

For an S corporation shareholder to deduct losses against other income, she must "materially participate" in the business. Being an investor in an S corporation doesn't cut it; you must also be active in the operation. If challenged by the IRS at an audit to show material participation, you'll be okay if:

- you put in at least 500 hours per year working in the business
- you worked at least 100 hours, if no other shareholder puts in more time, or
- the "facts and circumstances" show that you worked on a regular, continuous and substantial basis. (IRC § 469 and Reg. 1.469.)

E. Social Security and Unemployment Taxes

The tax code intends that *all* small business owners —no matter what the form of their business—pay the same amount of Social Security and Medicare,

generally called self-employment or FICA taxes. (See Chapter 6, Sole Proprietors, on how SE taxes are computed and paid.)

Nevertheless, there is a potential tax loophole here for S corporation shareholders. While salaries and bonuses paid by an S corporation to employees are subject to employment taxes, corporate dividends are "investment" income and are not subject to employment tax.

Here's the tax planning opportunity: If you work in your S corporation, you must take a salary if the business is profitable. However, taking a combination of salary and dividends typically reduces an owner's self-employment (SE) taxes, as the example below illustrates.

EXAMPLE: Gordon manages his S corporation, Wham Bam Inc. and pays himself an annual salary of $40,000. He pays self-employment taxes of 15.3% on this compensation ($6,120). Gordon also takes $14,000 from Wham Bam as a dividend on his stock in the corporation. If the $14,000 were instead labeled as salary or a bonus, Gordon would have had to pay an additional $2,142 in employment taxes (15.3% of $14,000).

⚠ **IRS auditors may question low S corporation owner salaries.** It hasn't escaped the notice of the IRS that S corporation owners minimize their SE taxes by taking "dividends." If you are audited, and the IRS claims your dividends were really wages, you'll have to show your salary was reasonable. One way to show this is to compare compensation paid to managers of similar businesses.

F. Electing S Corporation Status

If you decide to choose S corporation status after you have incorporated, run it by a tax pro first. But generally speaking, the process includes the following steps:

The Form of Your Business

SCHEDULE K-1 (Form 1120S)	**Shareholder's Share of Income, Credits, Deductions, etc.**	OMB No. 1545-0130
Department of the Treasury Internal Revenue Service	► **See separate instructions.** For calendar year 2000 or tax year **beginning** _____ **, 2000, and ending** _____ **, 20** ___	**2000**

Shareholder's identifying number ►	Corporation's identifying number ► 10 : 448 7975
Shareholder's name, address, and ZIP code John H. Green 4340 Holmes Parkway Metro City, OH 43704	Corporation's name, address, and ZIP code Strato Tech, Inc. 482 Winston Street Metro City, OH 43705

A Shareholder's percentage of stock ownership for tax year (see instructions for Schedule K-1) . . . . ► ....45.... %

B Internal Revenue Service Center where corporation filed its return ► ...Cincinnati, OH...............................

C Tax shelter registration number (see instructions for Schedule K-1) . . . . ► ....

D Check applicable boxes: **(1)** ☐ Final K-1   **(2)** ☐ Amended K-1

	(a) Pro rata share items		**(b)** Amount	**(c)** Form 1040 filers enter the amount in column (b) on:
Income (Loss)	**1** Ordinary income (loss) from trade or business activities . . .	**1**	53,550	See pages 4 and 5 of the Shareholder's Instructions for Schedule K-1 (Form 1120S).
	2 Net income (loss) from rental real estate activities	**2**		
	3 Net income (loss) from other rental activities	**3**		
	4 Portfolio income (loss):			
	a Interest	**4a**	1,800	Sch. B, Part I, line 1
	b Ordinary dividends	**4b**	7,200	Sch. B, Part II, line 5
	c Royalties	**4c**		Sch. E, Part I, line 4
	d Net short-term capital gain (loss)	**4d**		Sch. D, line 5, col. (f)
	e Net long-term capital gain (loss):			
	(1) 28% rate gain (loss)	**4e(1)**		Sch. D, line 12, col. (g)
	(2) Total for year	**4e(2)**		Sch. D, line 12, col. (f)
	f Other portfolio income (loss) (attach schedule)	**4f**		(Enter on applicable line of your return.)
	5 Net section 1231 gain (loss) (other than due to casualty or theft)	**5**		See Shareholder's Instructions for Schedule K-1 (Form 1120S).
	6 Other income (loss) (attach schedule)	**6**		(Enter on applicable line of your return.)
Deductions	**7** Charitable contributions (attach schedule)	**7**		Sch. A, line 15 or 16
	8 Section 179 expense deduction	**8**	10,800	See page 6 of the Shareholder's Instructions for Schedule K-1 (Form 1120S).
	9 Deductions related to portfolio income (loss) (attach schedule) .	**9**		
	10 Other deductions (attach schedule)	**10**		
Investment Interest	**11a** Interest expense on investment debts	**11a**		Form 4952, line 1
	b (1) Investment income included on lines 4a, 4b, 4c, and 4f above	**11b(1)**	1,350	See Shareholder's Instructions for Schedule K-1 (Form 1120S).
	(2) Investment expenses included on line 9 above	**11b(2)**	9,000	
Credits	**12a** Credit for alcohol used as fuel	**12a**		Form 6478, line 10
	b Low-income housing credit:			
	(1) From section 42(j)(5) partnerships for property placed in service before 1990	**12b(1)**		
	(2) Other than on line 12b(1) for property placed in service before 1990	**12b(2)**		Form 8586, line 5
	(3) From section 42(j)(5) partnerships for property placed in service after 1989	**12b(3)**		
	(4) Other than on line 12b(3) for property placed in service after 1989	**12b(4)**		
	c Qualified rehabilitation expenditures related to rental real estate activities	**12c**		
	d Credits (other than credits shown on lines 12b and 12c) related to rental real estate activities	**12d**		See page 7 of the Shareholder's Instructions for Schedule K-1 (Form 1120S).
	e Credits related to other rental activities	**12e**		
	13 Other credits	**13**	2,700	

For Paperwork Reduction Act Notice, see the Instructions for Form 1120S.   Cat. No. 11520D   **Schedule K-1 (Form 1120S) 2000**

	(a) Pro rata share items		(b) Amount	(c) Form 1040 filers enter the amount in column (b) on:
Adjustments and Tax Preference Items	**14a** Depreciation adjustment on property placed in service after 1986	**14a**		See page 7 of the Shareholder's Instructions for Schedule K-1 (Form 1120S) and Instructions for Form 6251
	b Adjusted gain or loss	**14b**		
	c Depletion (other than oil and gas)	**14c**		
	d **(1)** Gross income from oil, gas, or geothermal properties	**14d(1)**		
	(2) Deductions allocable to oil, gas, or geothermal properties	**14d(2)**		
	e Other adjustments and tax preference items *(attach schedule)*	**14e**		
Foreign Taxes	**15a** Name of foreign country or U.S. possession ▶			
	b Gross income sourced at shareholder level	**15b**		
	c Foreign gross income sourced at corporate level:			
	(1) Passive	**15c(1)**		
	(2) Listed categories *(attach schedule)*	**15c(2)**		
	(3) General limitation	**15c(3)**		
	d Deductions allocated and apportioned at shareholder level:			Form 1116, Part I
	(1) Interest expense	**15d(1)**		
	(2) Other	**15d(2)**		
	e Deductions allocated and apportioned at corporate level to foreign source income:			
	(1) Passive	**15e(1)**		
	(2) Listed categories *(attach schedule)*	**15e(2)**		
	(3) General limitation	**15e(3)**		
	f Total foreign taxes (check one): ▶ ☐ Paid ☐ Accrued	**15f**		Form 1116, Part II
	g Reduction in taxes available for credit and gross income from all sources *(attach schedule)*	**15g**		See Instructions for Form 1116
Other	**16** Section 59(e)(2) expenditures: **a** Type ▶			See Shareholder's Instructions for Schedule K-1 (Form 1120S).
	b Amount	**16b**		
	17 Tax-exempt interest income	**17**	2,250	Form 1040, line 8b
	18 Other tax-exempt income	**18**		
	19 Nondeductible expenses	**19**	7,358	See pages 7 and 8 of the Shareholder's Instructions for Schedule K-1 (Form 1120S).
	20 Property distributions (including cash) other than dividend distributions reported to you on Form 1099-DIV	**20**	29,250	
	21 Amount of loan repayments for "Loans From Shareholders"	**21**		
	22 Recapture of low-income housing credit:			
	a From section 42(j)(5) partnerships	**22a**		Form 8611, line 8
	b Other than on line 22a	**22b**		
Supplemental Information	**23** Supplemental information required to be reported separately to each shareholder *(attach additional schedules if more space is needed)*:			

- File IRS Form 2553, Election by Small Business Corporation. You'll find a filled-in sample in Section B. Get the current form by calling 800-829-FORM (1040), by downloading it from the IRS's website at http://www.irs.gov or by going to an IRS office, your tax pro or a corporation self-help book.

- Meet the filing deadlines. File Form 2553 with the IRS no later than the 15th day of the third month after your corporation's taxable year begins—whether your corporation is brand new or is a longtime C corporation. In 1997, the IRS adopted a procedure allowing an additional six months to elect, if you can show "good cause" for missing the deadline. If you miss the deadline in one year, you can elect S status in the next year. Don't file Form 2553 until your corporation charter has been granted by the state of incorporation.

- Have Form 2553 signed by whoever is authorized to sign the corporation's tax returns—usually the president or other corporate officer.

- Get written consents from all shareholders (or known prospective shareholders) by having each sign Form 2553 at the appropriate place. Unless every shareholder signs, your S election is invalid. In a newly forming corporation, have every possible shareholder sign. There is no penalty if someone who signs doesn't ever become a shareholder.

- Mail your completed Form 2553 to the IRS Service Center where you file your individual tax returns. The IRS should send you a written acknowledgment that you are an S corporation within 30 days.

G. Revoking S Corporation Status

Once elected, S corporation status continues until revoked by shareholders (holding more than 50% of its shares). In addition, the IRS can unilaterally revoke your S corporation status for various corporate misdeeds, such as failing to file tax returns or keep corporate records. If a corporation loses S status—voluntarily or involuntarily—it cannot be reinstated for five years. Once S corporation status is revoked, the corporation is taxed as a C corporation. (See Chapter 7, C Corporations.)

There is no IRS form to revoke S status. Instead, send a "Revocation of S Status" letter to the IRS Service Center where you filed your S election form. State the name of the corporation, the tax identification number and the number of shares outstanding. Have the letter signed by all of the shareholders. A sample letter is shown below.

Letter Revoking S Corporation Status

To: Your IRS Service Center

Dated: 12/20/01

Re: Revocation of S Corporation Status of Bone Corporation
Federal Identification Number #94–0000000

1. Bone Corporation hereby voluntarily revokes its prior election to be treated as an S corporation under IRC § 1362 (a).

2. The revocation is to be effective January 1, 2002.

3. At the time of revocation there are 1,000 shares outstanding in the corporation.

Statement of Consent

The following shareholders, who own all of the shares of the corporation, under penalty of perjury, consent to the revocation of the election of S corporation status:

Hamilton Bone
111 Main St., Juneau, AK
SSN 555-55-5555
1,000 shares acquired 1/1/87

Hamilton Bone
Hamilton Bone
Shareholder

H. Dissolving an S Corporation

When your S corporation calls it quits, the tax code says it is "liquidated." Shareholders receive whatever money or property the corporation owns.

Gains and losses on any assets in the corporation are passed through to shareholders—just as profits and losses from the operating business were. Each shareholder is then taxed on the difference between the fair market value of each asset and the basis of his or her stock. The shares of stock are returned to the corporation and canceled.

> **EXAMPLE:** Ted, the only shareholder of TYVM, Inc., an S corporation, decides to close up shop in 2001 and move to Costa Rica. After selling its inventory and paying its bills, TYVM's remaining asset is a patent on an injection molding tool. The patent rights, with a tax basis of $1 million, are sold for $2 million. The $1 million gain is "passed through" to Ted and is taxed at a 20% capital gains rate, resulting in $200,000 income tax. Ted may owe state income taxes as well.
>
> The tax consequences of the liquidation don't stop with the tax on the patent sale. The pass-through to Ted of the $1 million gain causes an increase in Ted's tax basis in his corporation stock. Let's say Ted's tax basis in his corporation stock is $500,000 before the property sale, so Ted's basis becomes $1,500,000 after. (Be careful not to confuse TYVM's tax basis in the building with Ted's tax basis in his TYVM stock. Remember, the tax code considers the corporation a separate entity from Ted—even though tax benefits and burdens pass through in an S corporation to Ted.)
>
> If Ted received only the $1 million from the liquidation of TYVM, then the $200,000 tax is all he pays.
>
> It would be worse for Ted if TYVM had been a C corporation. Then, there would have been "double taxation" on the liquidation. First, the gain on the sale of the patent rights would be taxed to TYVM at the corporate rate of 34%, and then again to Ted at his capital gains rate of 20%.

Ending a corporation business often has hidden tax consequences. A tax return marked "final" also increases your audit odds. See a tax pro whenever dissolving your S corporation, and take special care to file an accurate return.

The Form 1120S tax return filed for the final year of operation should state "Final Return" across the top of the first page. Also, check the box on the first page noting this is the final return. Otherwise, the IRS may keep the corporation in the tax reporting system for future years.

Resources

- IRS "S" Corporation Income Tax Package (annually updated). Includes most of the current year's tax forms and instructions. This form is available at IRS offices, from the IRS website (http://www.irs.gov) or by telephone at 800-829-1040.
- IRS Publication 542, Corporations
- Instructions for Form 1120S, U.S. Corporation Income Tax Return
- IRS Form 2553, Election by a Small Business Corporation and Instructions
- *Taking Money Out of Your Corporation*, by John Storey (John Wiley & Sons). This book, written by a savvy business owner, discusses a number of tax-wise techniques for taking money out of both S and C corporations.

The Form of Your Business

Partnerships

"We must not read either law or history backwards."
—Helen M. Cam

Partnerships in a Nutshell

1. Partnerships do not pay taxes; they pass profit and loss through to individual partners. Partnerships must file annual tax returns.

2. Profits and losses in a partnership may be allocated unequally among partners, so as to distribute tax benefits favorably.

3. Partnership accounting and tax law is very complex, and seeing a tax pro early on may prevent headaches later.

4. Contributing services in return for a partnership interest creates a tax problem, but there may be a way to get around it.

5. Terminating a partnership may result in tax liability for the partners.

We are all familiar with the general partnership—two or more people (or legal entities) running a business and splitting the profits or losses. Typically, partners begin by contributing money or property and their efforts to form a partnership. Legally a partnership agreement doesn't have to be in writing, but of course, it is always a good idea.

Each partner is *personally* responsible for *all* of the debts and liabilities of the business, not just their proportionate share. An exception to the rule of personal liability is the limited partnership—however, most active small businesses are necessarily "general," not "limited," partnerships. (See "General and Limited Partnerships," below.)

From a tax standpoint, partners are much like sole proprietors; both report their share of the business's profits or losses on their personal tax returns and partners pay self-employment tax (Social Security and Medicare) on their share of the partnership's income. Partnerships also bear a tax resemblance to S corporations and limited liability companies. All three are "pass-through" entities, which means that the business owners—not the entity—pay taxes on business income. Nevertheless, all three entities must file their own annual tax returns.

There is no federal partnership law; each state's law governs partnership formation and operation. However, all states have adopted the Uniform Partnership Act and Uniform Limited Partnership Act, so partnership laws are very similar in each state.

General and Limited Partnerships

Partnerships come in two varieties: general and limited. The vast majority of small business partnerships are general, where each partner has a voice in the management of the business. Each partner can obligate the partnership to any contract, debt or other transaction within the scope of the partnership business. Each general partner is responsible for all of the debts of the partnership—liability is not limited just to the partner's proportionate interest in the partnership.

The law is different for limited partnerships (LPs), which are primarily used to raise money from "passive" investors (the limited partners) who will not be active in the business. LPs must have two categories of partners: one (or more) general partners, who are personally liable for all partnership obligations, and one (or more) limited partners, who have no liability for partnership debts.

LPs may have to register with the state agency that regulates securities (in most states, the Secretary of State or Department of Corporations), and in some cases with the federal Securities and Exchange Commission as well. LPs are most often found in the small business world as family limited partnerships. (See Chapter 12, Family Businesses.)

The following examples illustrate the primary difference between the two flavors of partnership.

EXAMPLE 1: Serendipity Partners, a limited partnership (LP) formed to design and market 1970s sportswear, incurs debts of $17,000 to various creditors. Raul, the general partner of the LP, is personally liable for the whole $17,000 if Serendipity goes under. Chessie, a limited partner who invested $6,200 into the partnership is not liable for any of the debt. Her liability is limited to the $6,200 she invested.

EXAMPLE 2: If Serendipity was a general partnership, both Raul and Chessie would be each liable for the whole $17,000. Creditors could go after each partner's personal assets to collect the entire debt, not just $8,500 each. Of course, the creditors would not be entitled to collect more than a total of $17,000.

A. Partnership Tax Status

Partnership provisions of the tax code apply even when two people go into business on a handshake and never sign a formal partnership agreement. As long as costs and profits of a venture are split, a partnership exists as far as the IRS (and your state's partnership law) is concerned.

There is an exception for spouses who operate an unincorporated business together. The spouses may report either as partners or as co-sole proprietors. If they choose partners they must file a partnership tax return. As long as they file a joint individual tax return, their tax income liability is the same either way. A partnership provides no tax benefits to a married couple.

Since a partnership requires extra paperwork and tax filings, most spouse-partners report as co-sole proprietors on Schedule C of their tax return. If spouses file tax returns separately, though, usually to keep their tax liabilities separate, they might want to tax-report as a partnership. Filing separately seldom results in a lower overall income tax liability. However, check it out with a tax pro who knows your complete family tax picture and can run the numbers both ways.

Get help with partnership tax decisions. When forming a partnership, you face tax-related decisions including choosing a method of accounting, the tax year and the depreciation method to adopt. Depending on your needs and the tax code, some tax decisions may be changed as your partnership goes along. Other decisions cannot be, so take care. See a tax pro. (See Chapter 3, Recordkeeping and Accounting.)

Put your agreement in writing. Set down the basics: the ownership interest of each partner (for instance, 1/3 or 22%), and the investment each partner has in the business. Lawyers typically charge about $500 to $2,500 to form a partnership and draw up a partnership agreement. Alternatively, you can try it yourself using a guide book or software. (See the "Resources" list at the end of the chapter.) An economical approach is to use a self-help resource to draft an agreement, and then have it polished by an experienced small business lawyer and reviewed by a tax pro.

B. Tax Reporting by Partnerships

A partnership is a tax-reporting entity separate from its owners, but it is not a federal *tax-paying* entity. (IRC §§ 701, 761.) Instead, a partnership's profit or loss passes through to the individual partners. Each partner must report his or her share on an individual Form 1040 tax return (or joint return, if filing with a spouse).

A partnership must record its income and expenses, just like any business. A partnership must obtain its own tax ID number and file its tax returns annually, for as long as it is in operation. States may require separate tax reporting and ID numbers, in addition to federal ones. (See "State Partnership Taxes," below.)

Part 2 — The Form of Your Business

1. Annual Partnership Tax Return

Even though it pays no federal income tax, a partnership must file its annual partnership tax return, showing the venture's income and expenses. The report is made on IRS Form 1065, U.S. Partnership Return of Income.

The annual due date is the 15th day of the fourth month after the end of the partnership tax year—April 15 for most partnerships, the same date individual income returns are due.

Form 1065 is an "information" return. Nevertheless, the IRS can penalize you for not filing it on time. The late filing penalty is $50 per month for each partner, to a maximum of $250, and applies to each year the partnership is delinquent. An extension to file is available if you can't file by the deadline.

State Partnership Taxes

Most states treat partnerships like the federal government does—that is, they tax individual partners, not partnerships. A state partnership tax return, similar to Form 1065, must be filed annually. Partnerships may have to pay an annual tax or fee for the privilege of operating in the state. Check with your state tax department or ask a tax pro what forms and fees are required.

---

2. Partner's Profit or Loss Statements

Active business partnerships must issue an IRS Form K-1 to each partner annually (with a copy to the IRS). As discussed in Section C, below, the K-1 shows each partner's share of income or loss, deductions and credits. The K-1 report is entered into IRS computers to keep track of the income of individual partners and to make sure it gets reported on the partners' personal tax returns.

3. Partnership Federal Identification Number

A partnership gets a tax ID number, called the federal Employer Identification Number (EIN), from the IRS. The terminology might lead you to believe that you need an EIN only if you have employees, but this is not the case. This ID number is required for *all* partnerships and is used on annual partnership tax returns and K-1 forms. (Instructions on how to get a tax ID number are in Chapter 5.)

EXAMPLE: Brenda and Betty apply to the IRS for a tax ID number. They are assigned 94-1234567 as the Employer Identification Number of the B & B partnership. They must use the number on all tax returns and K-1 form filings. They will most likely be required to use this same EIN for state tax filings, although their state may use its own ID number.

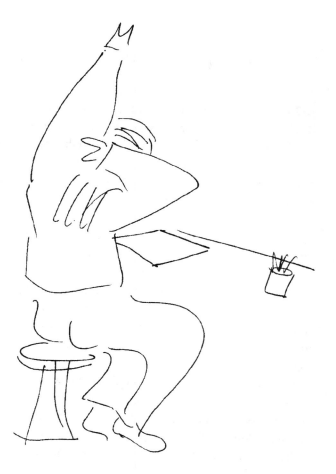

Form 1065
Department of the Treasury
Internal Revenue Service

U.S. Return of Partnership Income

For calendar year 2000, or tax year beginning .... , 2000, and ending .... , 20.....
► See separate instructions.

OMB No. 1545-0099

2000

A Principal business activity Retail	**Use the IRS label. Otherwise, print or type.**	Name of partnership AbleBaker Book Store	**D** Employer identification number 10 9876543
B Principal product or service Books		Number, street, and room or suite no. If a P.O. box, see page 13 of the instructions. 334 West Main Street	**E** Date business started 10-1-79
C Business code number 594		City or town, state, and ZIP code Orange, MD 20904	**F** Total assets (see page 13 of the instructions) $ 45,391

G Check applicable boxes: **(1)** ☐ Initial return **(2)** ☐ Final return **(3)** ☐ Change in address **(4)** ☐ Amended return
H Check accounting method: **(1)** ☐ Cash **(2)** ☒ Accrual **(3)** ☐ Other (specify) ► ....
I Number of Schedules K-1. Attach one for each person who was a partner at any time during the tax year ► ....2........

Caution: *Include **only** trade or business income and expenses on lines 1a through 22 below. See the instructions for more information.*

Income

1a Gross receipts or sales	**1a**	409,465	
b Less returns and allowances	**1b**	3,365	**1c** 406,100
2 Cost of goods sold (Schedule A, line 8)			**2** 267,641
3 Gross profit. Subtract line 2 from line 1c			**3** 138,459
4 Ordinary income (loss) from other partnerships, estates, and trusts (attach schedule)			**4**
5 Net farm profit (loss) (attach Schedule F (Form 1040))			**5**
6 Net gain (loss) from Form 4797, Part II, line 18			**6**
7 Other income (loss) (attach schedule)			**7** 559
8 **Total income (loss).** Combine lines 3 through 7			**8** 139,018

Deductions (see page 14 of the instructions for limitations)

9 Salaries and wages (other than to partners) (less employment credits)			**9** 29,350
10 Guaranteed payments to partners			**10** 25,000
11 Repairs and maintenance			**11** 1,125
12 Bad debts			**12** 250
13 Rent			**13** 20,000
14 Taxes and licenses			**14** 3,295
15 Interest			**15** 1,451
16a Depreciation (if required, attach Form 4562)	**16a**	1,174	
b Less depreciation reported on Schedule A and elsewhere on return	**16b**		**16c** 1,174
17 Depletion **(Do not deduct oil and gas depletion.)**			**17**
18 Retirement plans, etc.			**18**
19 Employee benefit programs			**19**
20 Other deductions (attach schedule)			**20** 8,003
21 **Total deductions.** Add the amounts shown in the far right column for lines 9 through 20			**21** 89,648
22 **Ordinary income (loss)** from trade or business activities. Subtract line 21 from line 8			**22** 49,370

Sign Here

Under penalties of perjury, I declare that I have examined this return, including accompanying schedules and statements, and to the best of my knowledge and belief, it is true, correct, and complete. Declaration of preparer (other than general partner or limited liability company member) is based on all information of which preparer has any knowledge.

► *Frank W. Able* ► 3/12/01
Signature of general partner or limited liability company member Date

Paid Preparer's Use Only

Preparer's signature ►	Date	Check if self-employed ► ☐	Preparer's SSN or PTIN
Firm's name (or yours if self-employed), address, and ZIP code ►		EIN ►	
		Phone no. ( )	

For Paperwork Reduction Act Notice, see separate instructions. Cat. No. 11390Z Form **1065** (2000)

Form 1065 (2000)
Page **2**

Schedule A — Cost of Goods Sold (see page 17 of the instructions)

1 Inventory at beginning of year	1	18,125
2 Purchases less cost of items withdrawn for personal use	2	268,741
3 Cost of labor	3	-0-
4 Additional section 263A costs (attach schedule)	4	-0-
5 Other costs (attach schedule)	5	-0-
6 **Total.** Add lines 1 through 5	6	286,866
7 Inventory at end of year	7	19,225
8 **Cost of goods sold.** Subtract line 7 from line 6. Enter here and on page 1, line 2	8	267,64

9a Check all methods used for valuing closing inventory:

    (i) ☐ Cost as described in Regulations section 1.471-3

    (ii) ☒ Lower of cost or market as described in Regulations section 1.471-4

    (iii) ☐ Other (specify method used and attach explanation) ▶ ---

  b Check this box if there was a writedown of "subnormal" goods as described in Regulations section 1.471-2(c) . . . . ▶ ☐

  c Check this box if the LIFO inventory method was adopted this tax year for any goods (if checked, attach Form 970) . . ▶ ☐

  d Do the rules of section 263A (for property produced or acquired for resale) apply to the partnership? . . ☐ **Yes** ☒ **No**

  e Was there any change in determining quantities, cost, or valuations between opening and closing inventory? ☐ **Yes** ☒ **No**
    If "Yes," attach explanation.

Schedule B — Other Information

	Yes	No
1 What type of entity is filing this return? Check the applicable box:		
a ☒ Domestic general partnership **b** ☐ Domestic limited partnership		
c ☐ Domestic limited liability company **d** ☐ Domestic limited liability partnership		
e ☐ Foreign partnership **f** ☐ Other ▶ ---		
2 Are any partners in this partnership also partnerships?		X
3 During the partnership's tax year, did the partnership own any interest in another partnership or in any foreign entity that was disregarded as an entity separate from its owner under Regulations sections 301.7701-2 and 301.7701-3? If yes, see instructions for required attachment		X
4 Is this partnership subject to the consolidated audit procedures of sections 6221 through 6233? If "Yes," see **Designation of Tax Matters Partner** below		X
5 Does this partnership meet **all three** of the following requirements?		
a The partnership's total receipts for the tax year were less than $250,000;		
b The partnership's total assets at the end of the tax year were less than $600,000; **and**		
c Schedules K-1 are filed with the return and furnished to the partners on or before the due date (including extensions) for the partnership return.		
If "Yes," the partnership is not required to complete Schedules L, M-1, and M-2; Item F on page 1 of Form 1065; or Item J on Schedule K-1		X
6 Does this partnership have any foreign partners?		X
7 Is this partnership a publicly traded partnership as defined in section 469(k)(2)?		X
8 Has this partnership filed, or is it required to file, **Form 8264**, Application for Registration of a Tax Shelter? . .		X
9 At any time during calendar year 2000, did the partnership have an interest in or a signature or other authority over a financial account in a foreign country (such as a bank account, securities account, or other financial account)? See page 19 of the instructions for exceptions and filing requirements for Form TD F 90-22.1. If "Yes," enter the name of the foreign country. ▶ ---		X
10 During the tax year, did the partnership receive a distribution from, or was it the grantor of, or transferor to, a foreign trust? If "Yes," the partnership may have to file Form 3520. See page 19 of the instructions		X
11 Was there a distribution of property or a transfer (e.g., by sale or death) of a partnership interest during the tax year? If "Yes," you may elect to adjust the basis of the partnership's assets under section 754 by attaching the statement described under **Elections Made By the Partnership** on page 7 of the instructions		X
12 Enter the number of Forms 8865 attached to this return . . . . ▶ -------------		

Designation of Tax Matters Partner (see page 19 of the instructions)

Enter below the general partner designated as the tax matters partner (TMP) for the tax year of this return:

Name of designated TMP ▶	Identifying number of TMP ▶
Address of designated TMP ▶	

Form **1065** (2000)

C. Tax Obligations of Partners

Partners are technically *not* employees of their business. They don't get wages, and the business does not pay payroll taxes on partners' income. Typically, partners take out business profit through periodic "draws" or "distributions."

At the end of each tax year, each partner's share of business profits (or losses) is computed and reported on IRS Form K-1. This form shows each partner's "distributive share" of income or loss, credits, deductions and various other tax items. In turn, partners enter the K-1 information on the front page and other pages of their individual Form 1040 income tax returns. A sample K-1 form is shown below.

1. Estimated and Self-Employment Taxes

Partners must make quarterly estimated income tax payments on their share of the partnership income, just like sole proprietors. These four "estimated tax payments" are due on April 15, June 15, September 15 and January 15.

If the partnership loses money and makes no distributions, no estimated taxes are due. (And, as explained below in Section 2, withdrawing money from a partnership is not always equivalent to taking taxable income.) Partners use Form 1040-ES to report and pay these estimated taxes. (See Chapter 6, Sole Proprietorships, for information on this form.)

Estimated tax payments must also cover each partner's self-employment taxes (Social Security and Medicare). All general partners are subject to self-employment tax on their share of the partnership profits, which is reported on Form SE filed annually with their 1040 tax return. Limited partners (investors) are not subject to the self-employment tax, so aren't required to file this form.

2. Reporting a Partner's Income

The tax code makes calculating a partner's taxable income or loss a challenge. For instance, the cash a partner takes out isn't necessarily the same as that partner's taxable income from the business. We explain this in more depth in the remainder of this section. (After reading this section, you may decide that a partnership is not for you, and we wouldn't blame you one bit.)

a. The Distributive Share

The law taxes a partner on the amount she is *deemed* to have gotten from the partnership under complex tax accounting rules. (IRC § 704.) This is called a partner's "distributive share." (IRC § 703.)

A distributive share is normally calculated based on the percentage of the partnership each partner owns—from 1% to 99%. Unless a partnership agreement says otherwise, the tax code presumes all partners have an equal interest in the business. So, if two people are in business together without any written agreement, it's considered a 50-50 partnership.

> **EXAMPLE:** Brenda and Betty's partnership agreement calls for each to get 50% of the profits (or losses) of the B & B partnership. If B & B makes a profit of $70,000 in 2001, each partner has a distributive share of $35,000 to report on her individual 1040 tax return. In reality, Brenda may have taken $40,000 and Betty may have taken $30,000 out of the partnership. This is between them: they still must tax-report 50-50. The next section on Special Allocations explains how this could be handled to reflect the reality of the distributions taken.

b. Special Allocations

If a written partnership agreement authorizes it, unequal distributive shares, called "special allocations," may be made. A special allocation is a tax code term for any distribution of profits or losses that is *not* proportionate to a partner's ownership.

For instance, giving 65% of profits to one 50-50 partner and 35% to the other is a special allocation.

SCHEDULE K-1 (Form 1065) Department of the Treasury Internal Revenue Service	**Partner's Share of Income, Credits, Deductions, etc.** ▶ See separate instructions. For calendar year 2000 or tax year beginning , 2000, and ending , 20	OMB No. 1545-0099 **2000**

Partner's identifying number ▶ 123-00-6789   **Partnership's identifying number** ▶ 10:9876543

Partner's name, address, and ZIP code	Partnership's name, address, and ZIP code
Frank Able 10 Green Street Orange, MD 20904	Able Baker Book Store 334 West Main Street Orange, MD 20904

A This partner is a ☒ general partner ☐ limited partner
☐ limited liability company member

B What type of entity is this partner? ▶ Individual

C Is this partner a ☒ domestic or a ☐ foreign partner?

D Enter partner's percentage of:
    (i) Before change or termination   **(ii)** End of year

Profit sharing . . . . % ..50.. %
Loss sharing . . . . % ..50.. %
Ownership of capital . . . . % ..50.. %

E IRS Center where partnership filed return: Philadelphia

F Partner's share of liabilities (see instructions):
Nonrecourse . . . . $ ------------------
Qualified nonrecourse financing . $ ------------------
Other . . . . $ .10,900.........

G Tax shelter registration number . ▶ ....N/A............

H Check here if this partnership is a publicly traded partnership as defined in section 469(k)(2) . . . . . ☐

I Check applicable boxes: **(1)** ☐ Final K-1 **(2)** ☐ Amended K-1

J Analysis of partner's capital account:

(a) Capital account at beginning of year	**(b)** Capital contributed during year	**(c)** Partner's share of lines 3, 4, and 7, Form 1065, Schedule M-2	**(d)** Withdrawals and distributions	**(e)** Capital account at end of year (combine columns (a) through (d))
14,050		24,460	(26,440)	12,070

	(a) Distributive share item		**(b)** Amount	**(c)** 1040 filers enter the amount in column (b) on:
Income (Loss)	**1** Ordinary income (loss) from trade or business activities . . .	**1**	24,685	See page 6 of Partner's Instructions for Schedule K-1 (Form 1065).
	2 Net income (loss) from rental real estate activities	**2**		
	3 Net income (loss) from other rental activities	**3**		
	4 Portfolio income (loss):			
	a Interest	**4a**		Sch. B, Part I, line 1
	b Ordinary dividends	**4b**	75	Sch. B, Part II, line 5
	c Royalties	**4c**		Sch. E, Part I, line 4
	d Net short-term capital gain (loss)	**4d**		Sch. D, line 5, col. (f)
	e Net long-term capital gain (loss):			
	(1) 28% rate gain (loss)	**4e(1)**		Sch. D, line 12, col. (g)
	(2) Total for year.	**4e(2)**		Sch. D, line 12, col. (f)
	f Other portfolio income (loss) *(attach schedule)*	**4f**		Enter on applicable line of your return.
	5 Guaranteed payments to partner	**5**	20,000	See page 6 of Partner's Instructions for Schedule K-1 (Form 1065).
	6 Net section 1231 gain (loss) (other than due to casualty or theft) .	**6**		
	7 Other income (loss) *(attach schedule)*	**7**		Enter on applicable line of your return.
Deductions	**8** Charitable contributions (see instructions) *(attach schedule)* . .	**8**	325	Sch. A, line 15 or 16
	9 Section 179 expense deduction	**9**		See pages 7 and 8 of Partner's Instructions for Schedule K-1 (Form 1065).
	10 Deductions related to portfolio income *(attach schedule)* . . .	**10**		
	11 Other deductions *(attach schedule)*.	**11**		
Credits	**12a** Low-income housing credit:			
	(1) From section 42(j)(5) partnerships for property placed in service before 1990	**12a(1)**		
	(2) Other than on line 12a(1) for property placed in service before 1990	**12a(2)**	75	Form 8586, line 5
	(3) From section 42(j)(5) partnerships for property placed in service after 1989	**12a(3)**		
	(4) Other than on line 12a(3) for property placed in service after 1989	**12a(4)**		
	b Qualified rehabilitation expenditures related to rental real estate activities	**12b**		
	c Credits (other than credits shown on lines 12a and 12b) related to rental real estate activities.	**12c**		See page 8 of Partner's Instructions for Schedule K-1 (Form 1065).
	d Credits related to other rental activities	**12d**		
	13 Other credits	**13**		

For Paperwork Reduction Act Notice, see Instructions for Form 1065.   Cat. No. 11394R   **Schedule K-1 (Form 1065) 2000**

Schedule K-1 (Form 1065) 2000 — Page **2**

(a) Distributive share item		(b) Amount	(c) 1040 filers enter the amount in column (b) on:
Investment Interest			
14a Interest expense on investment debts	**14a**	44,685	Form 4952, line 1
b (1) Investment income included on lines 4a, 4b, 4c, and 4f . .	**14b(1)**		See page 9 of Partner's Instructions for Schedule K-1 (Form 1065).
(2) Investment expenses included on line 10	**14b(2)**		
Self-employment			
15a Net earnings (loss) from self-employment	**15a**		Sch. SE, Section A or B
b Gross farming or fishing income	**15b**		See page 9 of Partner's Instructions for Schedule K-1 (Form 1065).
c Gross nonfarm income	**15c**		
Adjustments and Tax Preference Items			
16a Depreciation adjustment on property placed in service after 1986	**16a**		
b Adjusted gain or loss	**16b**		
c Depletion (other than oil and gas)	**16c**		See page 9 of Partner's Instructions for Schedule K-1 (Form 1065) and Instructions for Form 6251.
d (1) Gross income from oil, gas, and geothermal properties . .	**16d(1)**		
(2) Deductions allocable to oil, gas, and geothermal properties	**16d(2)**		
e Other adjustments and tax preference items (*attach schedule*)	**16e**		
Foreign Taxes			
17a Name of foreign country or U.S. possession ▶ -----------------			
b Gross income sourced at partner level	**17b**		
c Foreign gross income sourced at partnership level:			
(1) Passive	**17c(1)**		
(2) Listed categories (*attach schedule*)	**17c(2)**		
(3) General limitation	**17c(3)**		
d Deductions allocated and apportioned at partner level:			
(1) Interest expense	**17d(1)**		Form 1116, Part I
(2) Other	**17d(2)**		
e Deductions allocated and apportioned at partnership level to foreign source income:			
(1) Passive	**17e(1)**		
(2) Listed categories (*attach schedule*)	**17e(2)**		
(3) General limitation	**17e(3)**		
f Total foreign taxes (check one): ▶ ☐ Paid ☐ Accrued . . .	**17f**		Form 1116, Part II
g Reduction in taxes available for credit and gross income from all sources (*attach schedule*)	**17g**		See Instructions for Form 1116.
Other			
18 Section 59(e)(2) expenditures: **a** Type ▶ -----------------------			See page 9 of Partner's Instructions for Schedule K-1 (Form 1065).
b Amount	**18b**	25	
19 Tax-exempt interest income	**19**		Form 1040, line 8b
20 Other tax-exempt income	**20**		
21 Nondeductible expenses	**21**		See pages 9 and 10 of Partner's Instructions for Schedule K-1 (Form 1065).
22 Distributions of money (cash and marketable securities) . . .	**22**		
23 Distributions of property other than money	**23**		
24 Recapture of low-income housing credit:			
a From section 42(j)(5) partnerships	**24a**		Form 8611, line 8
b Other than on line 24a	**24b**		

Supplemental Information

25 Supplemental information required to be reported separately to each partner (*attach additional schedules if more space is needed*):

Schedule K-1 (Form 1065) 2000

A partnership agreement could also provide different ratios for splitting losses and profits, such as an 80-20 split for losses and 65-35 split for profits.

Partnership agreements may allow special allocations for any number of reasons. For instance, one partner may work full-time and others only part-time, or one partner may have special skills or generate more income.

> **EXAMPLE:** Betty plans to work more hours for B & B partnership than Brenda, who intends to spend part of her time authoring a travel book. The two agree in writing that Betty will receive 70% of the partnership's profits. Now Betty's distributive share of the $70,000 profit is $49,000, and Brenda's is $21,000. These are the amounts shown on their respective K-1 forms and reported on each of their individual tax returns.

A partner's personal income taxes depend on her overall tax situation—not just on what she gets from the partnership. It's unlikely that two partners will pay the same amount of taxes. Special allocations may be used to sprinkle different tax benefits to different partners.

> **EXAMPLE:** In its second year, Brenda and Betty's partnership makes a profit of $70,000. By the terms of their partnership agreement, Brenda is entitled to a special allocation of a 60% distributive share of the profits, or $42,000. Taking into account her other income, exemptions and deductions, Brenda falls into the 28% tax bracket. Her federal income tax on the B & B income is $11,760.
>
> Betty, on the other hand, has investment income besides her partnership income. Her share of the partnership profits puts her into the 39.1% tax bracket, so the tax due on Betty's 40% distributive share ($11,088) is almost as much as Brenda's tax on her 60% share. Without a special allocation there would have been a 50-50 division of partnership profits. Brenda would have paid $9,800 and Betty $13,860 in taxes—$23,660, a total of $812 more in taxes paid to the IRS.

Special allocations rules are tricky. This discussion and example don't take into account other highly technical tax code rules. Make sure you are on firm ground before making special allocations. Check out the law with a tax pro. (IRC §§ 703, 704 and Regs. 1.703, 1.704.)

c. Money Left in the Partnership

If a partnership keeps profits in the business at the end of the tax year for any reason, the partners are still taxed on that money. It doesn't matter that they never, as individuals, got their hands on the funds.

If your business needs to retain profits, consider incorporating. Forming a C corporation may be the best way to keep profits in your business for future expansion or to expand your inventory. Remember that partnerships (as well as S corporations and limited liability companies) are tax pass-through entities. This means that any profits left in the partnership bank account—or as inventory—are taxed at each business partners' tax individual tax rate. C corporations offer some relief from this tax bite. (See Chapter 7, C Corporations, to see how this works.)

D. Partnership Losses

For tax purposes, partnership *losses* are similar to profits—they pass through to each partner in proportion to her ownership share. This is true unless a different scheme is written into the partnership agreement. Tax-reporting partnership losses is, however, more complicated than reporting profits. Generally, a partner can deduct her share of a partnership loss on a current—or future—year's tax return. This can lower her tax bill by offsetting her other income, and may even produce a tax refund. (See Chapter 4, Business Losses and Failures, for an explanation of the rules of loss carryovers.)

> **EXAMPLE:** Betty and Brenda formed the B & B Partnership in 2001. The operation lost $40,000 that year, largely because their bed and break-

fast inn was not yet listed in travel guides. Brenda gets a distributive share of 60% of the loss ($24,000) under their partnership agreement. In the year before, 2000, she earned $70,000 working for HotelCo, and paid taxes in the 28% tax bracket. By amending her 2000 individual tax return to claim the 2001 partnership loss, Brenda can get a tax refund. It should be about $6,700 (28% x $24,000), plus interest. Brenda uses IRS Form 1040X. If everything is in order, she'll get a refund in two to three months.

Passive Partners

If you are only a "money" partner—that is, you invested in a general partnership business but are not involved in its day-to-day operations—you are termed a "passive" investor. Tax rules limit your claiming partnership losses of more than $25,000 per year on your individual tax return for passive investment losses. (IRC § 469, Reg. 1.469.) If your partnership investment losses are greater, the balance can be carried forward to claim on future years' tax returns. The $25,000 limit applies each year.

Typically, you might be affected by the passive loss rules if you invest in—but are not otherwise involved in—a real estate partnership or a business run by one of your children.

E. Partnership Contributions

When folks form a partnership, they typically throw a combination of money, property and services into the pot. These contributions may have unexpected tax consequences, however, to the individual partners.

Tax and accounting rules for partnerships are especially baffling to those of us who are not accountants. We are nearing deep waters, but will stop before we are over our heads. If your situation strays beyond the ones covered here, head for the resources listed at the end of this chapter or see a tax pro.

1. Keeping Track of Partners' Contributions

Each partner's money and property contribution to the partnership is recorded in that partner's "capital account." This is a listing of contributions and withdrawals of each partner, including her annual distributive share of income or losses from the partnership. Think of each partner's capital account as their financial history, starting at the beginning and continuing through the life of the partnership.

A partnership interest is an asset—an investment in the business. For tax purposes, you need to establish and track the investment you have in your partnership interest for as long as the partnership is in operation or holds any assets.

You must keep track of your partnership contributions to figure out the tax consequences of taking money or property out of the partnership. No income tax is due from you on money or property taken out of the partnership until your capital account is reduced to zero. You are just recouping your investment. Another way of stating this principle is that your capital account balance is equal to your tax basis in your partnership interest. Your tax basis in your partnership interest is reduced by your distributive share. And until you recover your tax basis by taking distributions from the partnership, you don't have any tax liability.

The following example illustrates this point and one made earlier (in Section C): that cash you take out of a partnership is not necessarily the same as your taxable income from the business.

EXAMPLE: Moe contributes $14,000 and six seltzer bottles worth $200 to the Stooges Partnership in 2000. That means $14,200 is the amount of Moe's capital account balance and his tax basis in his partnership interest.

In 2001, Moe takes $12,000 as his distributive share from the partnership. He has no tax liability because he has not recovered all of his investment in the partnership.

a. Cash Contributions

When everyone contributes just cash for their partnership interests, then things are simple, tax-wise. Each partner's capital account equals the cash contributed.

EXAMPLE: Moe puts $14,000 cash (nothing else) into the Stooges partnership. His capital account balance is $14,000.

b. Asset Contributions

If you transfer anything other than money—such as real estate, vehicles or copyrights—to the partnership, more complicated tax rules come into play. Your existing tax basis in the property transferred to the partnership becomes your tax basis in the partnership interest. As long as property has the same value from the time you acquired it to the date you contribute it to the partnership, your tax basis is clear-cut.

EXAMPLE: Ken transfers an office condominium he owns to VideoPro, a partnership that he and Barbara are setting up to sell video conferencing equipment. Barbara contributes $50,000 cash. In exchange for the office condo, Ken receives a 50% share of VideoPro partnership. At the time of its transfer, Ken had owned the condo for just a few months, and his tax basis in it (what

he paid, minus depreciation, plus the value of his improvements) was $50,000. This was also its fair market value, so Ken's tax basis in his partnership share is $50,000. Barbara's basis is the same as her interest.

Real life is often more complex than this example. For instance, if real estate owned and contributed by a partner has changed in value between the date acquired and date contributed (very likely), the tax result changes as well. Your basis in your partnership interest remains the same. But now, you face "built-in gain" taxes on any increase in value of the asset prior to the date of contribution. The good news is that there isn't any immediate tax bite. Instead, taxes to you are delayed until the property is disposed of by the partnership or when the partnership is dissolved.

EXAMPLE: Instead of $50,000 (Ken's basis), suppose Ken's office condo is worth $100,000 when contributed to VideoPro partnership. Barbara, Ken's partner, puts $100,000 cash into VideoPro's bank account for her one-half share. Two years later, VideoPro has outgrown the office and sells it for $140,000. There are two tax results. First, Ken is taxed on $50,000 of the profit (difference between his basis and value at time of contribution). Second, Ken is taxed on $20,000 of the $40,000 increase in value after the contribution and Barbara is taxed on the remaining $20,000 gain.

c. Contributions of Services to the Partnership

Often one partner has cash, while another has the expertise to make the business go. This may create a tax problem because "services" are not considered "property" when contributed to a partnership. The tax code imposes a tax cost if you take ownership in a partnership in return for a promise to work in the business. If you get a partnership share without putting in property, you are liable for income tax in that year on the value of your ownership interest.

Becoming a profits partner can get around this problem. A "profits partner" clause can be inserted into your partnership agreement to reward someone who wants to work but can't make a financial contribution. This clause states that the individual contributing services has no ownership, but gets a share of partnership profits—if any—in exchange for his work. (This doesn't prevent that partner from buying into the partnership later and becoming a full partner.)

EXAMPLE 1: Brenda and Betty form the B & B partnership to operate a bed & breakfast inn. Betty has $100,000 in cash but no business experience. Brenda has 20 years in the hospitality field but no money. If they are both 50% partners, Brenda is taxed the fair market value of her share in the partnership. Since Betty contributed $100,000, and Brenda (who the IRS views as contributing nothing) got a 50% interest, Brenda owes tax on $50,000 income.

EXAMPLE 2: Brenda and Betty draw up their partnership agreement stating Brenda is entitled to 50% of the profits. Brenda is now only a "profits partner," and there is no tax to pay.

Two additional tax code rules restrict the rights of profits partners:

- A profits partner can't sell her profits interest in the partnership within two years of receiving it.
- A profits partner can't be promised any fixed amount of money; she must bear a genuine risk of getting nothing if the partnership doesn't make a profit. (IRS Rev. Proc. 93-27.)

The legal status of profits partners for non-tax purposes is unsettled. Whether or not a profits partner has legal liability for partnership debts depends on the law of your state.

A tax disadvantage to being a profits partner is that if the partnership suffers a loss, a profits partner—who may have put blood, sweat and tears into the business—can't deduct any of the loss on her tax return. Partnership tax losses can pass through only to the "real" partners, not "profits" partners.

Partnership tax accounting rules are very complex. This discussion and examples are necessarily oversimplifications of the process. When in doubt, consult a tax pro.

2. Adjustments to Partners' Capital Accounts

Once a partnership venture is up and running, continual accounting adjustments must be made for each partner's capital account. These adjustments are necessary for accurate tax reporting and for making any financial statements of the partners and partnership. Numerous circumstances require adjustments to each partner's capital account. Here are a few of the common ones:

- A partner contributes cash or property to the partnership. If you have been with me so far, you know that contributions increase a partner's basis in his capital account.

EXAMPLE: Midway in the first year of business, the Sylvester & Son partnership needs operating capital. Sylvester puts in another $10,000 (beyond his $50,000 initial investment). Starting in year two, Sylvester's tax basis in his capital account is $60,000.

- A partner is allocated his annual "distributive share" of partnership profit or loss. These amounts are passed through to the individual partners and then reported on their personal tax returns. A profit increases a partner's tax basis; a loss decreases their basis.

EXAMPLE: Assume the Sylvester & Son partnership earns a small profit of $2,000 in its first year. Sylvester is a 50% partner. Thus, his $50,000 capital account is increased by $1,000 to $51,000, by including 50% of the partnership's profit.

Not all financial transactions of the partnership change a partner's basis. For instance, the tax basis of a partner's capital account is not usually affected by his share of partnership liabilities. Let's say the partnership borrows $10,000 from a bank and so incurs a liability to repay the loan. It follows that each partner bears a share of $10,000 debt in proportion to their percentage ownership of the partnership. However, the cash (or asset acquired with the loan) now is in the business, so each partner's share of assets will increase proportionately by the same amount. The net result is zero change.

> **EXAMPLE:** Sylvester & Sons partnership borrows $15,000 from Bus Bank to buy factory equipment. In the partnership books an asset of $15,000 is added, but it is offset by a $15,000 liability. Because of this "wash," Sylvester's capital account is unaffected.

F. Money Withdrawn From a Partnership

Since you went into business to put cash in your pocket, let's look at the tax effect of taking money or property from your partnership. Again, the tax bogeyman makes this more complicated than you would suspect.

1. Taxation of Withdrawals

The tax effects of withdrawals by partners has been mentioned above. Let's recap. Each partner has a unique tax basis capital account—maybe it's $100 or $10 million. This figure represents the value of her investment in the partnership business for federal tax purposes.

The tax basis in the capital account for each partner is continually adjusted through the life of the partnership, as a result of different financial transactions. Withdrawals by the partner decrease her tax basis; contributions by the partner increase it.

Withdrawals from a partnership are first treated as a non-taxable return of your investment. Only after you have recovered your entire investment (meaning that your basis in your partnership interest has been reduced to zero), are withdrawals taxable to you.

> **EXAMPLE:** Sylvester puts $50,000 into Sylvester & Sons partnership. The operation is profitable and Sylvester is entitled to a distributive share of $10,000 at the end of the year. If Sylvester withdraws—say $60,000—he will owe income tax on $10,000, the amount he received in excess of his basis ($50,000). In effect, Sylvester got back all of his contributions to Sylvester & Sons, plus his share of the firm's income. So, his basis in his partnership interest (capital account) is reduced to zero.

2. Loans to Partners

Partnerships are separate entities and can lend money to their partners. This presents an opportunity to get money out of your partnership—at least for the short term—without it being taxed. Loans aren't income if there is a legal obligation to repay them. Moreover, borrowing from your partnership doesn't affect your tax basis in your partnership interest.

A true loan must meet tax code requirements. You must sign a written, legally enforceable obligation to repay the partnership at a determinable date and at a reasonable rate of interest. (See Chapter 7, C Corporations, for all of the legal requisites of a corporate loan, which apply to partnerships, too.)

G. Partnership Expenses

Tax rules for deducting expenses of a partnership are the same as for other businesses: an expenditure related to the trade or business can be deducted if it's ordinary and necessary. (See IRC § 162 and Chapter 1, Business Income and Tax-Deductible Expenses.) Expense deductions are taken each year on the partnership's tax returns (Form 1065), not on the individual partners' returns.

Partnership start-up expenses—money spent before a business begins operating—are *not* deductible in the year incurred. Instead, these costs must be capitalized and deducted equally over the first five years of operation. If the partnership dissolves before five years is up, any balance not yet deducted can be taken all in the final year. (IRC § 709.)

Delay some expenses until your doors are open. As soon as your partnership begins taking in money, you are officially in business. This means you can begin deducting expenses that might otherwise be considered of the start-up variety. So, engineer a way to open up—take in a little money—as soon as possible. Delay incurring and paying expenses until you open, if possible. Otherwise you'll have to wait out the next 60 months to fully deduct all of your start-up costs.

H. Selling or Transferring a Partnership Interest

Only diamonds are forever, so eventually you will either die or dispose of your partnership interest. Naturally, there are tax ramifications.

1. Selling Your Interest in a Partnership

If you sell your partnership interest to another partner—or to anyone else—there is no tax impact on the partnership. It's like a shareholder selling stock in a corporation—it doesn't affect the corporation one way or the other.

On the other hand, for the selling partner there is likely a taxable gain or loss. Your basis in your partnership interest determines the amount of your taxable gain or loss. Again, this is similar to selling a share of stock.

Your gain is computed by subtracting your tax basis in your interest from money and/or property you receive in exchange for your partnership interest. If you have owned your interest for over a year, your gain qualifies for "capital gains" tax rates—a top tax rate of 20% on your profit. (See "Favorable Capital Gains Tax Rate," below, and IRC §§ 704, 706, 732.)

EXAMPLE: Ken sells his VideoPro partnership interest to Jackie for $75,000. Ken initially put $40,000 into VideoPro, and contributed another $15,000 when the business needed cash for expansion. Ken also took out $50,000 over several years, which represented his distributive share of earnings. All told, Ken's basis in his partnership interest was $5,000 when he sold to Jackie.

> $40,000 original basis
> + $15,000 additional investment
> - $50,000 withdrawals
> = $ 5,000 adjusted basis

So Ken has a taxable gain of $70,000 when he sells to Jackie ($75,000 received, less this $5,000 basis).

When a partnership interest is sold or exchanged, the partnership reports the sale or exchange to the IRS on Form 8308, Report of a Sale or Exchange of Certain Partnership Interests. This form is filed with the annual partnership tax reporting on IRS Form 1065.

2. When the Partnership Buys Out a Partner

If the partnership itself buys out your interest, your tax result is usually the same as selling to anyone else. The tax code calls this a "retirement."

Payments you receive for the retirement are treated first as a distribution of your partnership capital account. In other words, you first get back your investment—with no tax consequences. Anything more is a taxable gain to you, and anything less than your investment is a taxable loss. A retirement has no effect on the basis of the remaining partners in the partnership.

EXAMPLE: Starsky retires from the Starsky & Hutch partnership in return for $60,000. Starsky's tax basis in his partnership interest is $80,000. So, the first $60,000 Starsky gets is just a return on his investment. The balance, $20,000, is treated as a loss on his investment in the partnership. (See Chapter 4, Business Losses and Failures.)

Part 2

The Form of Your Business

Death of a partner is discussed in Section I, below.

Favorable Capital Gains Tax Rate

Profits on investments are currently taxed at a maximum capital gains rate of 20% (in the year 2001), as long as they have been held for more than 12 months. Most other income, including gains on investments held less than one year, is termed "ordinary income" and is taxed at an individual's tax bracket rate, which ranges from 10% to 39.1%. If an individual's ordinary income tax rate is lower than 20%, then the lower rate will apply. For those in the 15% tax bracket, the capital gains rate is now 10%. Some state income tax laws follow the federal law on taxing capital gains at a reduced rate, but some do not.

3. Special Rules to Watch Out For

Two more tricky tax rules come into play when you transfer a partnership interest. One deals with "relief of debt" for the transferring partner, and the other applies to partnership income to the partner for the year of sale.

a. Relief of Debt—Phantom Income

For tax purposes, the amount of income you realize when you sell your partnership interest includes—in addition to cash and any property you receive—your share of any partnership liability you are leaving behind.

For instance, if a three-person equal partnership owes $150,000 to its creditors when you withdraw, you are treated as receiving $50,000 because you no longer owe that portion of partnership debt. This "relief of debt" income is not obvious to most of us. But it can produce an unexpected tax bill, even exceeding the amount you get from selling your interest.

EXAMPLE: Brenda, a 50% partner in the B & B partnership, retires. Brenda takes partnership assets—a car worth $10,000 and $25,000 cash—in return for her share. Brenda is also relieved of half of the $40,000 owed by B & B to its creditors. The tax code says Brenda got a total of $55,000 for her partnership interest. How much, if any, is taxable gain for her is determined by Brenda's basis in the partnership.

b. Date-of-Sale Adjustment

When you sell a partnership interest, your basis in your interest is subject to a final adjustment for any partnership gains or losses for the year to date. Of course, if you sell at the last day of the partnership's tax year, this is not an issue. Any operating partnership profit must be reported on your individual tax return as ordinary income—not capital gain on the sale. On the other hand, if the year-to-date figure is a loss, it is deducted from your basis.

EXAMPLE: On July 1, Betty sells her 50% partnership interest for $100,000. Her basis is $50,000 and she had been in the partnership for ten years. The B & B partnership has a profit of $40,000 so far during the year. Betty must report $20,000, half of the profit, as her distributive share for that year—plus any gain or loss on the sale of her partnership interest. She owes regular income tax on the partnership profits ($20,000) at a rate as high as 39.1%. Betty's gain on her partnership share, however, is taxed at the capital gains tax rate of 20%.

I. Ending a Partnership

Unless a written agreement provides otherwise, a partnership terminates on the death or withdrawal of a partner. All partnership assets—equipment, inventory and any other property—are considered distributed to the individual partners. (IRC § 708(b).) The value of the property is tax-reported by each recipient in the year distributed. Tax is due on the difference between the partner's tax basis and the property's fair market value (the gain), whether the partner sells or retains the property. If there is a loss instead of a gain, the loss may be claimed on the partner's individual tax return.

A deceased partner's share goes into her estate, where it may be subject to tax depending on the size of the estate.

If property is sold before ending the partnership, the proceeds are divvied up among the partners and taxed to them individually if there was a gain.

> **EXAMPLE:** Ken dies, and his VideoPro partnership with Barbara terminates. Barbara takes the business equipment (a value of $120,000) to use in a new business. Ken's estate takes the partnership bank account of $120,000. At the date the partnership ends, Barbara's basis in her partnership interest is $50,000. So Barbara has a taxable gain of $70,000 ($120,000 value of equipment less her basis of $50,000). Whether or not Ken's heirs will have to pay estate taxes on this distribution will depend on Ken's basis in the VideoPro partnership and the overall size of his estate. (See Chapter 12, Family Businesses, for an explanation of estate tax.)

 You may need cash to pay your tax liability if you receive property when a partnership ends. Implicit in the above example is the danger of a tax liability for Barbara without receiving the cash to pay it. If you take non-cash assets—like real estate, that is hard to liquidate, or that you want to keep—make sure you have enough to pay the tax man.

Partnerships and IRS Audits

Small general partnerships are audited only about one-third as often as sole proprietorships with the same income. The IRS apparently reasons that since partnerships don't pay taxes (partners do, remember), auditing them won't directly result in more revenue. Of course, if a business partner's tax return is audited, chances are the IRS will look at the partnership's tax return, too. And if problems are found—such as an improper tax deduction taken on the partnership tax return—it can lead to the audit of all of the other partners' income tax returns as well.

Resources

- IRS Publication 541, Partnerships
- IRS Form 1065, U.S. Partnership Return of Income, and instructions
- *The Partnership Book,* by Denis Clifford and Ralph Warner (Nolo). Contains a wealth of details about setting up and running a partnership business.
- IRS Publication 505, Tax Withholding and Estimated Tax
- IRS Publication 533, Self-Employment Tax

■

Limited Liability Companies

"I stay within the law only because the law is maneuverable, it can be manipulated."
— **William M. Kunstler**

An increasingly popular way to organize a small business is the "limited liability company" (LLC for short).

An LLC offers potential non-tax advantages over a partnership or a corporation. Unlike general partnerships, LLCs give owners (called "members") personal protection from business creditors. Individual LLC members' liability for business debts is limited to their ownership interest in the business—hence the name "limited liability." And all LLC members can take an active role in the operation of the business without exposing themselves to personal liability—unlike limited partners.

Limited Liability Companies in a Nutshell

1. The limited liability company offers a personal liability shield to its owners, much like a corporation does.
2. State law regulates the formation and operation of LLCs.
3. LLCs are taxed by the IRS like general partnerships; the LLC does not pay taxes, but instead passes its profits and losses through to its individual owners. However, an LLC may choose to be taxed like a corporation.
4. The LLC is a relatively new form of business entity, and some tax and legal issues are not yet resolved.

A. Limited Liability Company Income

The LLC, like a partnership or S corporation, is normally a pass-through tax entity. Owners ("members") report and pay taxes on LLC income on their individual tax returns and are responsible for filing estimated taxes like sole proprietors and partners. (See Chapter 9, Section C1.)

1. Federal Tax Reporting

Because LLCs—like partnerships and S corporations—do not pay federal income taxes, LLC income is taxed at a single level—to the members. LLC members report their portion of the LLC's business income or loss on Schedule C of their individual income tax returns.

The LLC must file Form 1065, U.S. Partnership Return of Income, unless the LLC elects to be taxed as a corporation. The LLC must also annually issue each member IRS Form K-1, showing her share of the business's profit or loss. The LLC must file all K-1 forms with its tax return every year. The same K-1 forms are used by partnerships and S corporations. Members also pay self-employment tax on earnings (Social Security and Medicare) if they are working in the LLC, but not if they are just passive investors.

Single-member LLCs are treated like sole proprietorships and must report income on Schedule C (see Chapter 6) unless the LLC elects to be taxed as a corporation.

Not all states permit single-member LLCs. As of this writing, Massachusetts and the District of Columbia do not allow single-member LLCs. This may change, however—check with an attorney if you want to form a single-member LLC in either of these places.

Unless they elect to be taxed as a corporation, an LLC and its owners don't face the prospect of double taxation that C corporations do. But there's a downside. A C corporation can keep some of its earnings in inventory or in cash for future growth. These retained earnings are taxed, but at corporate tax rates that are 15% for the first $50,000, which is lower than shareholders' tax rates. LLC members, on the other hand, can't leave profits in the business without first paying taxes on these profits at their individual tax rates, which might be as high as 39.1%. (See Chapter 7, C Corporations.)

2. State Taxes on LLCs

Your state may impose income taxes on LLCs even though the IRS doesn't. For example, in California, LLCs are subject to annual fees and taxes that range from $800 and $4,500. In addition, most states require annual tax reporting on their own forms for LLCs (as well as corporations and partnerships).

B. Comparing LLCs With Other Entities

Most folks are attracted to LLCs because it combines the pass-through taxation of a partnership with the limited liability of a corporation. That means if the business is sued or incurs obligations it can't meet, a creditor can only go after the assets of the business —not property belonging to the members. One exception: the IRS (and probably your state tax authority, too) can collect delinquent LLC payroll taxes directly from members. (See Chapter 5, Tax Concerns of Employers.)

> **EXAMPLE:** Alex and Cathy form Fishworld, LLC, to wholesale tropical fish. Two years later, their main customer declares bankruptcy, owing Fishworld $70,000. At about the same time, most of their fish stock die from an outbreak of para-sites. The LLC owes $43,000 in general debts and $8,000 in payroll taxes. It has no cash but owns $10,000 of equipment. Fishworld's creditors can sue and get the equipment to satisfy their claims, but that's it. Alex and Cathy, however, will be personally, jointly liable to the IRS for the $8,000 in employees' payroll taxes.

This limited liability feature, *not* taxes, is the reason most folks choose an LLC. Here's a summary of how LLCs stack up against other entities:

- **Sole proprietorship.** The IRS has ruled that an LLC can be a one-man band, but as noted, Massachusetts and the District of Columbia still require at least two members to form an LLC. A spouse could be the other owner. However, Massachusetts and the District of Columbia will probably drop this rule on for-mation of one-person LLCs in the near future.
- **General partnership.** For tax purposes, an LLC usually elects to be treated like a partnership. But LLC owners aren't personally liable for non-tax business debts as are general partners. In the Fishworld, LLC example, above, if Alex and Cathy had been general partners, they would be responsible for the $43,000 in business debts out of their personal assets— bank accounts, autos or just about anything they owned.
- **Limited partnership.** There is no tax benefit of limited partnerships over LLCs. While limited partners are shielded from personal liability for business debts, they can lose this protection if they participate in the management of the business; limited liability company members have no restrictions on participation. And each limited partnership must by law have at least one general partner with full liability for busi-ness debts.
- **S corporation.** LLCs and S corporations are both tax "pass-through" entities, so profits and losses flow through the business to its owners. LLCs, however, enjoy fewer state organization restrictions, fewer formalities and are generally cheaper to operate than S or C corporations. LLCs can allocate income and expenses to their members disproportionately, but S corporations must allocate according to share ownership. (See Section C5, below.)
- **C corporation.** As with S corporations, because they are separate entities from their owners, C corporations offer shareholders protection from creditors. However, C corporations—unlike all of the other entities—are taxpaying entities. So there could be a double taxation of profits. Liquidation of C corporations may trigger a corporate and shareholder tax, but LLC liqui-dations will usually only have tax consequences to the members.

 Since LLCs are relatively new, a lot of legal and tax issues are not yet settled. Here are some murky areas:

Part 2

The Form of Your Business

- Converting a corporation to an LLC may have unwanted tax consequences. (See Section C2, below.)

- Legal uncertainties. Just as a new model of car might have some problems, LLCs might be more likely to have legal difficulties, at least until the law is settled. This is a risk, albeit a small one.

Professional Limited Liability Partnerships and LLCs

Some states now allow certain professionals to form LLCs, while a few states (such as California) allow professionals to form something similar to an LLC, called a Limited Liability Partnership (LLP). In states that don't allow professional LLCs or LLPs, the alternative is the personal service or professional corporation. (See Chapter 11.) Only certain state-licensed occupations—such as doctors, lawyers and accountants—may form these LLCs or LLPs. (For example, in California only accountants, lawyers or architects may form LLPs. A California LLP is a special kind of partnership that is registered with the state, on a provided form, with the payment of a $70 fee.)

The designations "LLP" or "RLLP" ("Registered Limited Liability Partnership") become part of the firm name and must be used in all legal transactions and advertising to the public. Once registered, the partners of the LLP do not have liability for the malpractice of the other partners, but remain liable for their own acts. This limited liability feature—not taxes—is the primary reason why professionals form LLPs.

If you provide professional services, check with your state or attorney for LLC and LLP restrictions and requirements.

C. Forming and Operating a Limited Liability Company

As with most business entities, limited liability companies are creatures of individual state laws.

While these laws tend to be similar, there is not yet a "Uniform Limited Liability Company Act," so LLC laws, procedures, paperwork and expenses vary from state to state.

1. Formalities

If you don't hire an attorney to form an LLC, you'll need to prepare written "Articles of Organization" (some states call this a "Certificate of Formation") and send them to your state's filing office, often called the Secretary of State. The articles may be just a simple one-page form, similar to Articles of Incorporation. The filing fee depends on your state and ranges from $50 on up. (Tax-hungry California charges $800. New York's fee is $200.) Most states provide a blank articles form on their Secretary of State or Department of Corporations website.

A written agreement (called an "operating agreement") may also be required by your state. These are similar to partnership agreements or bylaws that govern a corporation.

The operating agreement sets out the internal rules for governing the LLC: voting rights, check-signing authority and other vital matters. Even if a written LLC operating agreement is not required by your state, it is certainly a good idea. It should help avoid or settle disputes about the management of the LLC business later down the road. See *Form Your Own LLC,* by Anthony Mancuso (Nolo), for some examples of operating agreements.

Most states' LLC statutes don't require corporate formalities such as keeping minutes, passing resolutions and holding annual meetings. However, you may want to formally document some of the LLC's actions, just so you have a written record of important decisions, such as electing to be taxed as a corporation or entering into an executive employment agreement.

Some states require a few extra steps before your LLC can start business. In New York, for instance, you must publish notice of your LLC formation in a newspaper.

To qualify for pass-through taxation, LLCs used to have to jump through a number of hoops set up by the IRS. The goal was to distinguish LLCs from corporations. The IRS dumped these requirements when it adopted its 1997 rules that allowed LLCs to choose either pass-through taxation or to be taxed like a corporation. (It's fairly unusual for an LLC to elect to be taxed like a corporation, however.) If you're interested, see IRS Form 8832, Entity Classification Election.

For federal tax purposes, the only step after forming the LLC is to get a new federal identification number (EIN) for the LLC from the IRS. (See Chapter 9, Partnerships, for details on how to get an EIN.)

Where to Get Help

Check with your Secretary of State's office for LLC fee and filing rules. Some states may provide sample LLC articles or fill-in forms. See the "Resources" box at the end of this chapter for recommendations on legal self-help references. Business lawyers can help you form an LLC, and tax pros can do the IRS and state tax reporting. Attorneys' fees should be about the same as for forming a partnership or corporation—ranging from $500 to $2,500.

If you are forming a one-person LLC, you should be able to do it without a lawyer, but get help if others will be involved.

2. Converting a Corporation to a Limited Liability Company

Before converting an existing corporation to an LLC, consider the tax consequences.

⚠ **Changing an existing S or C corporation business to an LLC may carry too heavy a tax price.** A corporation must be formally "liquidated" under tax code rules before its assets may be put into an LLC. Corporate liquidations of successful, active companies are complex. For instance, converting a C corporation with significant assets might mean taxes for the corporation, because this is treated as a sale of the corporation's assets. Then the funds from the sale of assets are deemed to have been distributed to the shareholders, who are taxed again. (See Chapter 7, C Corporations.) Whatever is left after taxes goes into the LLC.

If you convert an S corporation to an LLC, you'll fare slightly better, because any taxes on liquidation are placed only on the shareholders. There is no double taxation, as with C corporations.

A relatively new corporation, or one that has not been successful or that has minimal assets may be able to convert to an LLC without a tax cost. Bottom line: If you are tempted to convert to an LLC, see a tax pro first.

Part 2

The Form of Your Business

3. Restrictions on Limited Liability Company Membership and Rights

The tax code does not restrict the number or types of owners (members) an LLC can have. By contrast, an S corporation may have no more than 75 shareholders, including individuals and estates. And S corporation shareholders can't be nonresident aliens —which rules out any foreign shareholders. Because LLCs aren't under the ownership restrictions of S corporations, it may be easier for them to bring in more owners to raise capital.

Unlike general partners or S corporation owners, LLC members may be legally excluded from managing the business, as long as the LLC operating agreement states this and the powerless member agrees. In this respect, an LLC member is like a limited partner or the holder of nonvoting corporate stock. This kind of member is likely just an investor in the LLC. However, there are some rights an LLC member *cannot* waive (such as the right to vote to dissolve the LLC). Check your state's LLC statute or with your legal advisor for these non-waivable rights.

4. Transferring Ownership by Sale or Death

Membership interests are called "shares" of the LLC, similar to a partnership interest or shares of corporate stock. In the absence of prohibitions or restrictions in the operating agreement, transferring an LLC ownership interest is relatively easy—the current owner simply assigns his membership interest in the LLC to the buyer or transferee and the buyer or transferee gets all the rights (and obligations) of the departing member.

The tax consequences to the selling or transferring member are the same as with a partnership—the gain or loss is determined by the member's tax basis in his share. (See Chapter 9, Partnerships.)

However, most small business owners don't want a co-owner forced on them without their approval. So, your LLC operating agreement should contain restrictions on transfers of LLC shares. Typically, the members will agree that a retiring or departing member of an LLC must first offer his share to the remaining members before selling to anyone else. Usually, a predetermined price for a share or a formula for valuing it is set out in the operating agreement. These buy-sell provisions should bind all members and should be part of the LLC formation process.

Apart from non-tax reasons (to avoid disputes between members as to the value of a share if one member wants to sell out), the IRS will stick its ugly nose into the picture when a member dies. That's because an LLC membership interest will be an asset in the estate of the dearly departed member, so there may be an estate tax for heirs to worry about. Valuation of business interests is a Number One concern to an IRS estate tax auditor. Many executors end up in IRS battles over just what a small business interest is worth. (See *Stand Up to the IRS,* by Frederick W. Daily (Nolo), for more information about estate tax audits and business valuations.)

The good news is that the IRS usually respects the terms of a well-drafted buy-sell agreement for fixing a fair price of a member's share. If the LLC members don't provide for some valuation formula, the estate might hire an (expensive) appraiser. If the IRS audits, it may not accept the professional appraiser's opinion. On the other hand, if there was a valuation formula (or maybe even a fixed price) for a member's LLC share, the IRS may just go along with it. However, this price or valuation method may be questioned by an IRS auditor if it is deemed to be unreasonably low. See *How to Create a Buy-Sell Agreement and Control the Destiny of Your Small Business,* by Anthony Mancuso and Bethany Laurence (Nolo), for more information on setting a fair price for LLC membership interests.

5. Passing Profit and Loss Through to Members

LLC profits and losses "pass through" the LLC and are allocated and taxed to the LLC owner or owners at the end of each LLC tax year. Or put another way, the LLC owners, not the LLC itself, are responsible for paying income taxes on business profits on their individual returns. In a co-owned LLC, the percentage of income or loss allocated to each LLC member at the end of the year is as specified in the LLC's operating agreement. In a one-member LLC, of course, all income will pass through to the sole owner.

Unlike an S corporation, an LLC may make distributions of profits (or losses) disproportionately to the owners' shares in the business—if authorized in the LLC agreement in a way that the IRS approves.

Like a partnership, however, an LLC can distribute profits unequally only if it meets some technical tax code rules. Usually, this entails including some "magic language" in your LLC operating agreement that will satisfy the IRS rules. See a partnership tax attorney if you are interested in making special allocations of profits or losses in your operating agreement.

D. Terminating a Limited Liability Company

Generally, the procedure for terminating or dissolving an LLC is similar to closing up a partnership. It is governed by the state law and is typically provided for in the LLC operating agreement.

For tax purposes, tax treatment of the members is the same as if they were general partners. (See Chapter 9, Partnerships.)

Resources

- *A Guide to Limited Liability Companies* (Commerce Clearing House) and *The Limited Liability Company*, by James Bagley (James Publishing). These are technical books written for CPAs and attorneys.
- *Limited Liability Companies*, by Robert W. Wood (John Wiley & Sons). This book discusses in depth the implications and mechanics of converting existing small businesses to LLCs.
- *Form Your Own Limited Liability Company*, by Anthony Mancuso (Nolo). This book provides step-by-step forms and instructions for setting up an LLC without costly legal fees.
- *Your Limited Liability Company: An Operating Manual*, by Anthony Mancuso (Nolo). This book provides ongoing help on running your LLC, as well as numerous minutes and resolution forms.
- *LLCMaker* software, by Anthony Mancuso (Nolo). This interactive computer program takes you, step by step, through the LLC formation process and helps you create articles of organization that meet the requirements for your state, as well as a comprehensive operating agreement.
- IRS Form 8832, Entity Classification Election and Instructions

Part

2

The Form of Your Business

11

Personal Service Corporations

"There is no magic in parchment or in wax."
—**William Henry Ashhurst**

Professionals—physicians, lawyers, accountants and others—are treated as small businesses under the tax code. Most are sole proprietorships or partnerships, and go by the same tax rules as these entities. However, certain professionals who offer services may form and operate a special entity, called a "professional corporation." Moreover, state laws require specified categories of professionals, if they want to incorporate, to do so as a professional corporation. A professional corporation has shareholders, who perform services for the corporation as employees.

Most professional corporations are classified by the federal tax code as "personal service corporations" (PSCs) and taxed similarly to C corporations, with a few twists.

Limited Liability Partnerships are now allowed in many states. (See Chapter 10.) This new form of business provides an alternative to the PSC in states that allow LLPs.

Personal Service Corporations in a Nutshell

1. In most states, certain specified professionals who want to incorporate must form "professional corporations."
2. The IRS recognizes specified professional corporations as separate tax entities called personal service corporations (PSCs).
3. For a successful professional, incorporating offers a few tax advantages, including a greater range of fringe benefits.

A. Professional Corporations That Qualify as Personal Service Corporations

Each state licenses and regulates various professions, and determines who may—or may not—form a professional corporation. For example, a group of attorneys and paralegals may not form a single professional corporation if under their state's law a non-lawyer can't hold stock in a professional legal services corporation.

A professional must be incorporated under a state's law to be treated as a personal service corporation under the federal tax code. But as you shall see, a professional corporation isn't always treated as a PSC. (IRC § 448.) If it doesn't, it is treated under the tax code as a general partnership. (See Chapter 9, Partnerships.)

A PSC is defined as a state-formed corporation in which substantially all of the activities involve services in the fields of "health, law, engineering, accounting, architecture, veterinarians, actuarial science, performing arts or consulting."

IRS regulations elaborate on the occupations. For example, "health care" professionals include physicians, nurses, dentists and others, but not folks who operate health or exercise clubs. "Consulting" covers someone who gives advice, but not a salesperson or any kind of broker. "Performing arts" covers actors, entertainers and musicians but not their promoters or managers. Interestingly enough, professional athletes are not allowed to form PSCs. (Reg. 1.448-1T(e)(4).)

The IRS imposes two tests a corporation must meet to qualify as a personal service corporation. These tests focus on what the corporation does (the "function test") and how it's owned (the "ownership test").

1. Function Test

Substantially all of the activities of the PSC must involve rendering personal services. IRS regulations say that "substantially all" means 95% or more of work time expended by employees. (Reg. 1.448-IT(e).)

> **EXAMPLE:** Jack and Jill are fresh out of law school, but they cannot find full-time work as attorneys. To keep bread on the table, they form an S corporation, Sweetstuff, Inc., to operate a yogurt store. In addition, they find part-time employment, about ten hours a week, with a law firm. Can they convert their S corporation into a PSC? No, because Sweetstuff, Inc., employees don't devote 95% of their time to providing legal services.

2. Ownership Test

Substantially all stock in a PSC must be held directly or indirectly (through one or more partnerships, S corporations or other qualified PSCs) by either:

- employees performing professional services for the corporation
- retired employees who performed services in the past
- the estates of such individuals, or
- any person who acquired stock by reason of the death of any such persons.

As with the function test, "substantially all" ownership means 95% of the value of all outstanding stock.

> **EXAMPLE:** Ralph and Connie are physical therapists who are approached by Gino, the owner of Costa La Health Spa, to offer services at the spa. If Ralph and Connie will incorporate as a professional corporation with him, Gino will invest $20,000 in return for some stock. They incorporate, with Ralph and Connie owning 75% of the stock and Gino 25%. This may qualify as a professional corporation, but it fails the PSC 95% ownership rule, because Gino, who is not a health professional, owns more than 5% of the stock.

B. Taxation of Personal Service Corporations and Shareholders

In theory, a PSC is federally taxed at a flat rate of 35% of its net income. In practice, as with most small corporations, the shareholders take out all profits as tax-deductible (to the corporation) salaries, bonuses and fringe benefits. So, typically the shareholders pay income taxes on their individual tax returns and the PSC, with no net income, pays nothing.

Non-Tax Benefits of Professional Corporations

Professionals find that incorporating is beneficial for a variety of non-tax-related reasons. For instance, like any corporation, a PSC has perpetual existence. So if one shareholder dies or withdraws, a PSC business can carry on with minimal legal disruption.

Professional corporations also offer shareholders limited personal liability. (The extent of this protection depends on state law.) However, an incorporated professional can't legally escape personal liability for her own negligent acts—for this you need professional liability insurance. But a PSC shareholder practicing with other professionals can usually avoid personal liability for *other* shareholders' misdeeds.

> **EXAMPLE:** Allison and Bill, both psychiatrists, form a professional corporation, sharing a receptionist and other common expenses. If Dr. Bill loses a malpractice lawsuit, both the corporation's assets and Dr. Bill's, personally, can be in jeopardy. However, Dr. Allison will not be personally liable—meaning her house and savings cannot be grabbed to pay the judgment. If, on the other hand, their business were a general partnership, Dr. Allison would be personally liable for Dr. Bill's acts in their practice of medicine.

C. Special Tax Rules for Personal Service Corporations

For tax purposes, a PSC is a separate entity from its owners, similar to a C corporation. So, it must file its own corporate tax return every year. A PSC may also offer many of the fringe benefits available to a C corporation. (See Chapter 14, Fringe Benefits, and Chapter 15, Retirement Plans, for a discussion of corporate fringe benefits.)

Technically, a PSC may elect to be an S corporation, but if it does, it won't qualify for corporate fringe benefits discussed below. (See Chapter 8, S Corporations.) Moreover, the tax code does not provide the same flow-through tax treatment to PSC shareholders as S corporation shareholders get, so PSCs seldom elect S status.

A PSC may adopt IRC § 1244 status when it is formed (if it has not elected to be an S corporation). This allows advantageous tax treatment to shareholders if they ever sell their stock in the PSC for a loss. (See Chapter 4, Business Losses and Failures.)

A PSC can give its professional shareholders/employees some corporate fringe tax benefits not available to unincorporated professionals. This advantage is discussed next.

1. Greater Contributions to Retirement Plans

A PSC may establish corporate retirement plans and a 401(k) plan, allowing greater contributions than plans available to unincorporated professionals. (See Chapter 15, Retirement Plans.)

2. Health and Life Insurance Benefits

A PSC with three or more shareholders may establish a "Voluntary Employees' Beneficiary Association" (VEBA). This allows the PSC to tax-deduct and provide health and life insurance coverage to all PSC employees and shareholders as a tax-free benefit. VEBAs are usually administered by banks or insurance companies. (See IRC § 501(c)(9) for details, or consult a tax or pension professional.)

3. Other Fringe Benefits

Generally, PSCs can offer tax-advantaged life and disability insurance, death benefits, dependent care and other fringes, without establishing a VEBA. (See Chapter 14, Fringe Benefits.)

4. Tax Year Election

A PSC must keep its records on an annual basis, either a calendar year or fiscal year. (See Chapter 3, Recordkeeping and Accounting.) While a PSC can tax-report on a non-calendar fiscal year basis, it may be more trouble than it is worth. A PSC must get IRS permission to use a fiscal year by showing a "business purpose" for it. (Rev. Procs. 87-32 and 87-57 have details and examples.) To apply for permission from the IRS to use a fiscal year, file IRS Form 1128. However, it's better to have a tax pro do this for you.

5. Accounting Method Elections

A PSC may choose either the "cash" or "accrual" method. (See Chapter 3.)

Alternatives to the Professional Corporation

Some states recognize professional limited liability companies (LLCs) as an alternative to the professional corporation. At this time, these states are Arizona, Kansas, Louisiana, Minnesota, Oklahoma, Texas, Utah and Virginia. Other states (California, Delaware, Louisiana and Texas) allow professionals to form a similar business entity called a limited liability partnership (LLP). See Chapter 10, Limited Liability Companies, for more information about the pros and cons of forming an LLC or LLP.

D. Potential Tax Problems With Personal Service Corporations

A few tax villains may creep up on an unsuspecting PSC shareholder. They are rarely encountered, but I'll mention them briefly.

1. Passive Loss Limitations for Non-Active Shareholders

Tax code "passive loss limitations" may restrict some PSC shareholders from taking tax deductions for corporation losses. This is not a problem unless the PSC loses money in its operation and wants to pass the loss along to non-active shareholders. In reality, most PSCs are composed of active owners and few lose money. This rule means the majority of PSC shareholders must actively perform services for the corporation—they can't be part-timers or shareholders who have retired. (IRC § 469.)

2. No Income Splitting and Retained Earnings

A C corporation is a separate tax entity that may divide its income between the corporation and its shareholder to take advantage of their different tax rates. (See Chapter 7, C Corporations.) However, income splitting between PSCs and their shareholders is not allowed.

A flat 35% PSC tax applies to any profits left in the corporation at the end of the year. A tax savvy PSC doesn't have any net earnings at year end, however. That's because retaining earnings in a PSC rarely makes tax sense. (See Section B, above.)

E. Transferring Shares or Dissolving a Personal Service Corporation

State laws typically prohibit transferring PSC stock to a non-professional. So PSC shares usually can't be left to a spouse or other family member when you die; this also violates the PSC requirement that "substantially all" stock be held by those who are performing services.

PSCs typically have written agreements, binding on both the shareholders and their estates, requiring purchase of deceased shareholders' stock by the PSC. Often, this "cross purchase" agreement is funded by a life insurance policy. The PSC takes out life insurance policies on its members and uses the death benefit to purchase the deceased owner's share from his or her estate.

A PSC may be ended voluntarily, by a majority vote of the shareholders, or dissolved involuntarily by the state or as a result of legal action against it. The tax results from dissolving a PSC are roughly the same as for a C corporation. (See Chapter 7, C Corporations.) The important thing to know is that a taxable gain (or loss) for each shareholder results when a corporation folds. Again, see a tax pro for guidance through this process.

Resources

- IRS Publication 542, Corporations
- *How to Form a California Professional Corporation*, by Anthony Mancuso (Nolo). While this book is geared for California, much of it applies to other states, too, and it contains many valuable professional corporation forms.

12

Family Businesses

"Don't tax you, don't tax me; tax the fellow behind the tree."

—Senator Russell B. Long

Many small businesses get the whole family involved. Parents bring children into a business for help and to teach the kids money-making skills. When the children grow up, they may take over the family business and maybe even pass it on to their offspring.

Most tax provisions apply whether the family is involved or not. However, some restrictions and tax-saving opportunities are inherent in family businesses. When it comes to passing ownership on to the next generation, the law contains both tax traps and opportunities.

Family Businesses in a Nutshell

1. Family businesses allow "income splitting" to reduce the family's overall tax bill.
2. It is okay to hire your spouse and kids and take tax deductions for their paychecks, as long as they do real work and their pay is reasonable.
3. A corporation or a family limited partnership allows a transfer of valuable family business to a younger generation over time, while reducing or eliminating estate tax.

A. The Legal Structure of a Family Business

A husband and wife can own a business together and still be a sole proprietorship for tax purposes. But if other family members share ownership, too, the operation must be organized as a partnership, limited liability company or corporation.

Happily, these more complex forms of doing business offer families both tax and non-tax advantages. Partnerships, limited liability companies and corporations allow more tax and estate planning flexibility than do sole proprietorships. For instance, incorporating allows family members to receive ownership benefits (such as stock dividends) even if they don't work for the enterprise. (See Section B, below.) Forming a family limited partnership makes it easier to transfer business ownership to family members gradually over time and save both income and estate taxes.

Another, more exotic, alternative is to combine several different organizational forms to best distribute tax benefits. For instance, a partnership consisting of several children can own and rent a building to a corporation owned by their parents. Whether or not multiple entities make sense depends on the tax situations of all the family members. If this sounds intriguing, check it out with a top tax pro, preferably a CPA or tax attorney. Generally, whether the complications of forming several entities results in significant tax savings hinges on the "income splitting" ideas discussed below—shifting income from family members in the highest tax brackets to those in the lowest.

B. Income Splitting to Lower Taxes

Family members often pool their efforts and resources to run small businesses. For many, this provides not only a good living, but also a sense of security and closeness. As a bonus, family ventures can also bring tax savings for the family unit.

A tax planning technique known as "income splitting" shifts income from higher bracket taxpayers —usually parents—to lower ones—usually children or retired grandparents. Obviously, these strategies depend on cooperation and trust between family members. If done carefully and legally, real tax savings can result.

It's perfectly legal to hire the family. Court decisions have supported operators who hire even minor children as long as they give them real work to do. By and large, employing relatives is not a problem at IRS audits—as long as some work was done and pay wasn't outrageous. Following are the basic tax code rules on hiring your children or parents.

1. Tax Benefits of Hiring Your Kids

Putting your children to work in your business can reduce your income taxes. Paying your kids reduces the amount of business profits subject to taxation at your tax rate, which will always be higher than your kids' rate.

The tax code says that no FICA (Social Security and Medicare) taxes are due for services performed by a child under 18 in the employ of her or his parent. Further, there is an exclusion from FUTA (federal and state unemployment tax) for a business paying the owner's child who is under 21. This means no payroll taxes are incurred for putting junior on the payroll. (IRC § 3121(b)(3)(A), IRC § 3306(c)(5).) Assuming that the child saves up or uses the money for things the parents would be buying anyway, this is money in the family piggy bank.

> **EXAMPLE:** Laura, a single mother and the sole proprietor of PhotoLand, a wholesale film processing company, earns $300,000 per year, putting her in the top tax bracket (39.1%) (2001). Her 17-year-old daughter, Louisa, helps out after school, on weekends and all summer. Louisa is paid $20,000 over the year, which puts her in the 15% tax bracket (2001). The overall tax on the family unit is reduced about $7,000. This is because of the difference in the mother's and daughter's tax rates. It works out like this:
>
> Louisa files a tax return, taking her personal exemption and claiming the standard deduction. She owes $1,582.50 (10% on her first $6,000 of taxable income and 15% on the remainder) in income taxes and no FICA tax. If Laura doesn't hire Louisa, and instead took the $20,000 in income herself, she'd pay extra taxes of $8,400 ($7,820 income taxes based on her tax bracket of 39.1% plus an additional $580 in self-employment taxes of 2.9% for Medicare).
>
> Total family tax savings: almost $7,000 (this would be even more if they lived a state that imposed an income tax). The tax deal can be even better if Louisa opens an IRA. (See below.)

⚠️ **These tax exclusion provisions apply only to unincorporated businesses.** Consult your tax pro for more information.

💡 **Save even more with an IRA for your child.** An Individual Retirement Account can be established for any working child who earns wages. Up to $2,000 of earnings can be put aside each year tax-deferred—meaning that Junior may earn $6,300 ($4,300 plus $2,000) before incurring any income tax liability. Income earned by the child over that is taxed starting at the lowest income tax rate, 10% (2001).

Putting money into an IRA can make tax sense even if the child takes it out long before retirement, say for college. (See Chapter 15, Retirement Plans, for details on new IRA contribution limit rules.)

Part

3

Thinking Small

Tax Rules When Your Children Work for You

- **Child labor laws.** I've never heard of any agency applying child labor laws against parents putting their own minor kids to work. Of course, if you hire underage kids other than your own, you are breaking the law.

- **Taxation.** A minor child can earn up to $4,300 without any income tax liability. After that, the tax rate starts at 10% (2001). As long as the income is earned by the child performing services for the family business, the "kiddie tax" (tax on a child's investment income, discussed in Section 2, below) doesn't apply.

- **Real work.** Courts have okayed kids as young as seven getting paid for simple chores like taking phone messages or cleaning the office windows. (I don't know about your kids, but I shudder at the thought of a seven-year-old answering my business phone.) Children can be paid a reasonable sum for their work, depending on the facts and circumstances of each case. I'd say don't try to pay and deduct more than $3,000 per year to any of your children under age 12.

    EXAMPLE: Dr. Moriarty (his real name—not Sherlock Holmes's nemesis), hired his four teenagers to do clerical work for his medical practice. An IRS auditor said this was a mere subterfuge to deduct the kids' allowances as a business expense. The U.S. Tax Court overruled the IRS, saying it was all legal as long as the kids did real work and were paid reasonable wages. (*James Moriarty*, TC Memo 1984-249.)

Type of work. The kind of work done by the child—such as washing the company car, filing or going to the mailbox—doesn't matter, as long as it's a task a business customarily would pay someone else to do. Duties should reflect the age and training of the children. While it is fine to pay a 16-year-old to do computer inputting, it wouldn't wash for an eight-year-old. But it's okay to hire your precocious 13-year-old to do filing even if you might not hire someone else's 13-year-old for the job.

Rate of pay. Generally, don't pay your child more than you would a stranger, but there is some wiggle room. If you pay little Susie $7 per hour, and you could realistically find someone else to do it for $5.50, an auditor will likely let it pass. But you are pushing the envelope if you pay Susie $20 per hour.

When paid. The payments to your kids should match up to a work schedule. This can be tied to school vacations, after-school time or holidays. If you make only one or two lump sum payments in a year, an auditor might think that you are trying to fudge on your taxes instead of legitimately employing Junior.

2. Making Your Kids Co-Owners

Another strategy to shift business income from higher-bracket family members to lower ones is by giving them stock in your incorporated business or through a family limited partnership; see Section D, below. Children are not required to work in the family business with this income-splitting technique.

For tax purposes, stock ownership is treated as an investment in the business by the family member, even if they didn't pay for it. The primary drawback is that you must irrevocably transfer the stock to the family members. You have no legal right to take it back later. If you are the cautious type, transfer only shares of non-voting stock. Otherwise, older children holding stock will have a vote in the management of the business—including whether they will get any dividends each year.

> **EXAMPLE:** Wally and Wanda incorporate their business, House of Shoes, and give their three children each $20,000 worth of stock every year ($10,000 from each parent). The gift is not subject to federal gift tax. (See the discussion in Section D about estate and gift tax basics.) The children's stock is non-voting, so Wally and Wanda maintain control of the management of the House of Shoes.

Children who own stock can receive dividends on their ownership interests in the business. Dividends are taxed according to how old the kids are. This is classed as "investment income" under the tax code. Here are the rules:

- **Under 14 Rule.** An under-14-year-old child's "net unearned income"—such as stock dividends from a family-owned corporation—is taxed at the parent's tax rate. This is the so-called "kiddie tax," which forecloses income splitting when kids are very young and don't work in the business. However, the first $1,500 of the child's income is exempt from the kiddie tax in 2001.
- **Over 14 Rule.** If your child is 14 or over and gets dividends from the family corporation,

the child is taxed on all income at her tax bracket rate. (Don't ask me why 14 is the magic age.) The family unit may get an advantage because the child is in a lower tax bracket than the parents, thereby lowering the family tax bill.

 A corporation can pay your kid for services and also pay them dividends on stock ownership. As long as a child's tax bracket remains lower than his parents', an overall income tax saving results. However, watch out for double taxation. A family C corporation paying dividends may have already incurred corporate income tax on this money, so overall tax savings may vanish in the process. Have a tax pro run the numbers to see whether it makes sense for your family. (See Chapter 7, C Corporations, for a discussion of the taxation of corporations.)

3. Putting Older Parents on the Payroll

An income-splitting strategy can also work with retired parents and their grown children in business. For example, a builder who might otherwise help his retired father financially could hire his dad part-time. Not only does the business benefit from the expense deduction, but the father's pay is likely to be taxed in a lower bracket.

Shifting income to parents makes sense only if they are in a lower tax bracket and need the income. In addition, before hiring mom, see what effect earnings will have on her Social Security benefits. If a retiree is under age 65, her Social Security benefits are reduced in the following year if earned income is over $10,800. Social Security benefits are reduced only as a result of so-called earned income from working. Other income—investments, annuities, private pensions, unemployment, gifts and rents—don't count toward the $10,800; see "How Working Reduces Social Security Benefits," below.

Note: Compensation received by a person on Social Security is still subject to FICA (Social Security and Medicare) in addition to normal income taxes.

How Working Reduces Social Security Benefits		
Age	Annual Earnings Limit	Reduction in Benefits
62 through 64	$10,800	$1 for every $2 earned

(These amounts are for 2001, and are subject to an annual adjustment in subsequent years.)

> **EXAMPLE:** Marina started drawing Social Security benefits at age 62. She went to work for her son, Manny, at his Motel Five as a part-time desk clerk. In 2000, Marina earned $13,200. In 2001, she will lose $1,200 in Social Security benefits under the tax code rules ($13,200 – $10,800, divided by 2 = $1,200).
>
> Also, Marina's $1,200 in wages are subject to Social Security and Medicare taxes. If Marina continues to work after age 64, she won't lose any Social Security benefits, no matter how much she makes.

Don't enlarge a parent's large estate. Think twice before paying your parent if she has an estate that is large enough to be subject to federal estate tax at her death. The federal estate tax threshold is $675,000 in 2001; it will increase to $3.5 million by 2009 and be phased out completely by 2010. Federal estate tax starts at 37% and goes up to 55% (although this top rate is scheduled to decrease to 45% in the coming years, until the tax is repealed in 2010). (IRC § 2001.) It might be better for an older parent to work for a low wage or else as a volunteer. That way, the business gets the value of the senior's labor, but his or her estate doesn't grow too big.

C. A Spouse in the Business

When spouses work together, the tax implications are quite different than for their children. Instead of putting spouses on the payroll, taxes are saved by keeping them off—even though they do work. The reason is that *all* employees—except owners' children under 18—are subject to payroll taxes.

In 2001 Social Security and Medicare taxes add 15.3% to the cost of wages, up to $80,400, and 2.9% over that. Spouses employed by spouses aren't subject to federal unemployment taxes, however. Plus, when a spouse is on the payroll, other expenses are incurred, such as state unemployment and disability taxes, and workers' compensation insurance.

 There are two ways to get around the added expenses of a spouse on the payroll:
- let your spouse volunteer, or
- share ownership.

Let's take a closer look at both options.

1. Let Your Spouse Volunteer

You won't have extra payroll tax and employee expenses if your spouse doesn't get a paycheck. I have never seen any government agency, including the IRS, try to force a working—but unpaid—spouse onto the payroll. However, "volunteers" can't get employee benefits—except when benefit plans cover their owner-spouses.

> **EXAMPLE:** Susie Sanders earns $100,000 from her SS Personnel Services business. Susie hires Jocko, her hubby, as a consultant and pays him $20,000 a year. Putting Jocko on the payroll increases the Sanders' joint tax bill by $3,060 (Social Security and Medicare tax of 15.3% x $20,000). By contrast, if Jocko had done the work and not been paid (thereby increasing Susie's income by $20,000), the family would have come out ahead about $2,500 ($3,060 minus $580, the amount of Medicare tax that Susie would have had to pay on the extra $20,000 income.) Note: This example assumes Susie and Jocko file a joint tax return.

⚠️ **Watch out for Social Security issues.** An unpaid spouse won't get Social Security account credit. This is not a problem if the spouse has already qualified for coverage from a former job. Also, he or she may be eligible for Social Security survivor benefits if the other spouse dies first and the marriage lasted ten years or more. However, survivor benefits are smaller than those paid on primary Social Security accounts.

2. Share Ownership

A husband and wife in a family business can legally be co-owners. Most spouses tax-report as co-sole proprietors (by listing both names on Schedule C of their joint tax return), and the IRS considers them both owners, not employees. The husband and wife team commonly puts the business income into the family pot.

Because neither co-owning spouse is legally an employee, there aren't any employment taxes. (See Chapter 5, Tax Concerns of Employers.) However, co-owners are subject to and must pay their own self-employment taxes (Social Security and Medicare).

Alternatively, the two spouses could form a partnership. This doesn't normally change the overall income tax consequences for either partner, but in a few instances, it may allow income splitting and estate tax savings. (See Section D, below, and Chapter 9, Partnerships.) Couples in a partnership must file annual partnership tax returns in addition to their own joint or separate tax returns. When considering a formal partnership with a spouse, see a tax pro first to determine if the extra expenses and effort are worth it.

💡 **Co-owning spouses can write off business travel.** Spouses co-owning an enterprise may get a tax break for out-of-town travel. If both travel together—to conventions or on other business—the expenses of both are tax-deductible. By contrast, if one is not an owner, but an off-the-books volunteer, her or his travel costs aren't deductible. (See Chapter 14, Fringe Benefits.) Paying the spouse a small salary might be worth the tax trade-off if you do a lot of business travel with social overtones.

D. Preserving a Family Business

This book deals with the day-to-day tax issues of a small business. We can only touch on some of the larger issues in the vital tax topic called "estate planning"—how to pass on a business, at death, to minimize or avoid probate fees and taxes. Everyone with a business should be concerned about:

- keeping the operation going after the owner dies, and
- preventing estate taxes from taking a huge chunk of money from surviving family members or forcing the liquidation of the business.

Choosing an Estate Tax Strategy

Lawyers and financial planners can often find loopholes in the tax code to avoid or greatly reduce estate taxes. This may be accomplished through sophisticated trusts, such as marital by-pass trusts, charitable trusts and other types of trusts called by acronyms such as GRITS, GRATS and QTIPS. This area is fraught with tax peril; the best strategy for you will depend on the details of your personal and financial situation. Don't make a move without having a tax pro or lawyer guiding you.

1. Death and Taxes

A successful small family enterprise often becomes very valuable over time. The flip side is that significant federal estate taxes may be due after the death of the owners if the business is included in their estates. The federal estate tax begins on all estates with a value in excess of $675,000 (2001). Roughly speaking, your taxable estate is everything you own at your death. The estate tax exemption will increase to $3.5 million by 2009 until it is phased out completely in 2010. However, unless Congress reauthorizes these changes, the estate tax will automatically reappear in 2011, consult your estate planner for details of these changes.

> **EXAMPLE:** Stella, a single woman, dies in 2001. Her estate has a net value, after debts, of $900,000. In 2001, $675,000 can be passed tax-free, so Stella's estate is taxed on the balance ($225,000). Her estate will owe a federal tax bill of almost $90,000, and may also owe estate taxes to her state.

Estate taxes can be murderously high. To pay them, family members may even be forced to sell the business or its assets. To prevent this outcome, Congress has granted qualifying family-owned businesses and farms an additional estate tax exemption.

Qualified Family Owned Business Deduction

Your estate may be eligible for a $1.3 million exemption from federal estate tax. This is called QFOBI (Qualified Family Owned Business Interest). To get this break, you and your family members must meet stringent requirements. For example, the business can be left only to certain family members or long-term employees—and if they sell the business within ten years, part or all of the estate tax savings must be repaid to the IRS. If you want to take advantage of this new estate tax exemption, check with a tax pro. Also note that this exemption will become obsolete once the estate exemption reaches $1.5 million in 2004.

The tax code provides one other break that lets families avoid business liquidations on the owner's death: a long-term estate tax payment plan at a 2% interest rate on tax for the first $1 million taxable due and 4% on any balance. An estate with a small business worth at least 35% of the estate's total value qualifies to pay estate taxes over 14 years. And for the first five years, the estate is allowed to pay interest only. (IRC § 6166.)

> **EXAMPLE:** Jorge suddenly dies with a will but no other estate planning. Jorge's Plumbing Supplies, his sole proprietorship, is worth several million dollars. Jorge's will leaves the business to his two sons, but there isn't enough money for the estate taxes. Choosing the installment payment option, Jorge's sons can keep the business. They can pay the estate tax out of future profits over 14 years at a favorable interest rate of 4%.

Although the installment plan helps business owners' families, a better way may be through estate planning. Jorge might have been able to eliminate estate taxes altogether.

Don't overlook state death taxes. Most states also impose death taxes by either an estate or inheritance tax. Partial tax relief is provided by a federal estate tax credit for any state death taxes paid. (IRC § 2011.) Under this provision, combined federal and state death taxes usually don't exceed the federal tax alone. A few states impose estate taxes higher than the federal credit—but the extra state tax is insignificant in all but multi-million-dollar estates. If this worries you, check with an estate planning professional. You may want to change your state of residence if your state's death taxes are particularly onerous.

2. Keeping the Business Going With Minimal or No Estate Taxes

Now that you see the estate tax trap, let's look for ways to step around it. Strategies for keeping a family business include involve forming a corporation or family limited partnership. Each requires pre-planning; "deathbed" transfers won't pass IRS muster.

a. A Family Business Corporation

Incorporating a business makes it easier to pass it on and continue operation after the owner's death. And incorporating also provides a way to beat—or

Estate and Gift Tax Basics

Estates

Federal estate taxes are due if you leave an estate valued at over $675,000 in 2001. In future years, these amounts will increase. Here are the numbers:

Year	Personal Estate Tax Exemption
2002-2003	$1 million
2004-2005	$1.5 million
2006-2008	$2 million
2009	$3.5 million
2010	estate tax repealed
2011	$1 million unless Congress extends repeal

One break for married couples is that when the first dies, all property left to the survivor (if a U.S. citizen) is tax-free. This is called the unlimited marital deduction. Of course, when the surviving spouse dies, the estate is fully taxed if it's over the threshold amount. Estate taxes, like income taxes, are graduated —the bigger the estate, the higher the tax rate. The bite begins at 37% and quickly ascends to 55% (although this top rate is also scheduled to decrease gradually to 45%, until the estate tax is repealed in 2010).

There is no federal inheritance tax; beneficiaries of an estate do not owe tax on anything they inherit. Instead, the estate is liable for any federal estate tax. The tax is supposed to be paid before the property is distributed to the people who inherit it. If it isn't, the IRS can come after the beneficiaries.

Gifts

Gifts made during someone's lifetime are considered, for estate tax purposes, the same as property in her estate at the time of her death, with one major exception. Under the "annual exclusion" rule, you may give $10,000 (in property or cash) to as many folks as you like, each year, without it being taxed to your estate. Recipients of inheritances and gifts are not taxed on your largess, either. The $10,000 annual exclusion was made subject to annual cost of living adjustments after January 1, 1998 in $1,000 increments.

A few other kinds of gifts are tax-free as well, regardless of amount:

- gifts to your spouse (limited to $100,000 if the recipient is not a U.S. citizen)
- gifts to tax-exempt charities, and
- gifts for tuition or medical expenses.

If you give more than $10,000 in cash or property away to someone, the excess is subtracted from your lifetime estate tax exclusion. You must file a gift tax return for that year, but no tax is due—until you have given away more than the exempt amount, not counting the nontaxable gifts.

EXAMPLE: John & Julie Johansen have an estate of $2 million. They want to transfer it to their heirs tax-free. They decide to reduce their estate by gifting money annually to their two kids, two nephews, one grandchild and one old friend. The Johansens can give away $120,000 each year to these folks (6 x $10,000 for John and 6 x $10,000 for Julie) under the "annual exclusion" rule. These annual gifts don't count against each spouse's estate tax exemption. Over a number of years the Johansens, or the survivor of the two, should be able to reduce their estate to below the estate tax threshold.

The above example is an oversimplification and is not necessarily the recommended approach for everyone. Read on for some other ideas.

at least minimize—estate and death taxes that is not available to partners or sole proprietors, if it is planned correctly.

With a corporation, an owner can give his kids part ownership of the business over time by transferring stock in a series of annual gifts. (See Section B, above.) (IRC § 2503.) As long as the value of the stock given to each recipient each year is no more than $10,000, the gift is not taxable to either the giver or the recipient. This is true whether the business is an S or C corporation. For a very valuable business, this is obviously a long-term planning device, due to the annual $10,000 limitation. Married co-owners can combine their $10,000 annual gift limits for a total of $20,000 per recipient, which helps a little.

Giving corporate stock is more complicated than giving cash. Each time a business owner makes a gift of corporate stock, she must determine its fair market value. Valuing a private company's stock requires the help of a CPA or other business appraisal specialist. If the IRS ever audits, it is doubtful it will just take your word for the value—the auditor will want to see the backup.

⚠ Joint tenancy ownership doesn't avoid estate taxes. There is a widespread misconception that joint ownership of property avoids estate and gift taxes. Sorry, it doesn't. Adding a child's name to a deed or stock certificate as a "joint tenant" may avoid state probate expenses, legal fees and delay, but doesn't remove an asset from the reach of the federal estate tax.

 Giving away small business corporation stock doesn't mean relinquishing control of the business. An owner may transfer stock but keep the voting rights of the shares. A parent-owner could put children's stock in a trust and reserve the right to vote the shares. Again, call in a good business attorney to help you.

This advice bears repeating: Whenever transferring a business to family members, get an accountant or business appraisal expert to make a written valuation. Keep these appraisals handy in case you are ever audited by the IRS.

b. Family Limited Partnerships (FLPs)

Instead of incorporating your family business, you may form a family limited partnership (FLP). An FLP operates under the tax rules for a limited partnership. Typically, parents form an FLP and transfer their assets, such as an existing business, to this entity. A venture can, however, be formed as an FLP right from the start. (See Chapter 9, Partnerships, for a discussion of limited partnerships.)

FLPs can minimize or avoid estate taxes, but FLPs can also help business owners shift current business income to (lower bracket) family members. (Section B, above, discusses splitting income to lower taxes for the family group.)

In a family limited partnership, the parents are usually the "general" partners. Children are "limited" partners, with an ownership interest in—but no right to manage—the operation.

As with corporation stock, each child can receive a limited partnership interest worth $20,000 per year (from a set of two parents) as a gift, without tax consequences to anyone. (See "Estate and Gift Tax Basics," above, about the "annual exclusion" rule for gift taxes.) Limited partners may also work in the business and earn wages, but they don't have to.

With a FLP (as with a corporation), business owners can pass ownership of a business to others (usually children) over a period of years to lower the estate tax bite. This can be a tax boon if the business is appreciating in value. Given enough time, as much as 99% of the parents' FLP ownership can be transferred to the children tax-free, leaving little or nothing subject to estate tax. As general partners, Mom and Pop are in full control, deciding how annual profits are to be split among their limited partner kids. An FLP can be a win-win tax deal for the family business.

EXAMPLE: Wally and his wife Wanda, who are in the highest income tax bracket (39.6% in 2001), form an FLP to own and operate North Oxon Pottery. They give each of their three children—who are all in the lowest income tax bracket—limited partnership interests in the business annually over a number of years. (If

Tax-Discounting the Value of a Family Business

The tax law—as interpreted by various federal courts—allows "discounts" of the value of small business interests when transferred by gift or on death. Reduced valuations produce tremendous gift and estate tax savings, or eliminate these taxes altogether. This is particularly true when ownership is passed from one generation to the other. The reduction is called a "marketability" or "minority" discount. It applies to family corporation stock, family limited partnership or limited liability company shares.

Small enterprises are inherently difficult to value. If the business is incorporated, chances are its stock is not sold on any public exchange and seldom changes hands at all. As a practical matter, outsiders are not eager to get part ownership of any small business; they want control. But since anything will sell if the price is right, a 20% to 40% discount might entice someone to settle for a piece of the action. Large discounts (as high as 50%) have been upheld where the interest is minority, corporate stock without voting rights or a limited partnership interest.

The size of discount a transferor of a business interest can claim is determined by as many as ten factors; one or more might apply to your situation. A 1995 Tax Court case (*Bernard Mendelbaum v. Commissioner*, TC Memo 1995-255), involving a family-owned S corporation, discussed the factors. My comments (in parentheses) follow each point as to its importance in justifying a large discount:

1. Whether or not the stock has been traded publicly (insignificant; hardly ever the case in a small business).

2. Financial statement analysis (fairly important; best done by an experienced tax pro, mainly to see how profitable the business is; if only average or marginal, a larger discount can be taken).

3. Dividend policy of the business (usually insignificant; most small corporations don't pay dividends).

4. Nature, history and industry position of the business (not too significant; how the business is positioned for competition and like factors).

5. Strength of company management (important; successful businesses depend heavily on personalities).

6. Degree of control in the transferred shares (very important; if the transferor maintains control after the transfer—typical with small businesses—large discounts can be justified).

7. Stock transfer restrictions (very important; for example, "first refusal" clauses, which require offering shares to family member on favorable terms, make it very difficult to sell partial ownership).

8. Required holding period of stock (important; a stock transfer restriction; see comments on #7 above).

9. Stock redemption policy of the company (important; if the business has not historically redeemed stock of shareholders, this factor allows larger minority discounts).

10. Public offering costs (insignificant; few businesses worth less than $10 million ever consider a public offering).

EXAMPLE: Juan, a widower, owns 70% of the stock of Star-Tar, Inc., which manufactures Spanish guitars. Juan's five children, all active in the business, own the other 30%. A business valuation expert values Juan's corporation at $2.3 million. If Juan starts on an estate plan to give each of the children $10,000 worth of stock every year, after 12 years he will have probably given away a majority interest in the corporation. Because of the discount allowance for family corporate stock, the value of Juan's new minority stock interest could be discounted. Depending on the value of his other assets, Juan's estate may not owe any estate taxes. (The same analysis holds true if Juan forms a family limited partnership instead of a corporation.)

Part

3

Thinking Small

the interest given by the parents to each child is worth under $20,000 each year, there is no gift tax liability.) The children, as limited partners, have no say in the day-to-day affairs of the business. Over 25 years, Wally and Wanda give most of North Oxon Pottery FLP ownership to their kids, while controlling the business until they are ready to step down. If planned right, when Wally and Wanda have both died, their remaining partnership interest is minimal, and their estates won't owe estate tax on the entire value of the business.

You can't use a family limited partnership solely as a device to beat estate tax. An FLP must have a "business purpose" when used for estate planning. It must carry on an active for-profit venture, as opposed to holding a family investment. For example, an FLP formed to own a family-used vacation home doesn't meet this business purpose test. Likewise, an FLP that holds an investment portfolio of marketable securities, with the expectation of gain, is not considered active business.

FLPs also have the non-tax feature of protecting the personal assets of the limited partners from any business creditors. Limited partners can lose only the value of their partnership interest to creditors— not their homes or bank accounts. Every limited partnership, by law, must have at least one general partner, however, who is fully liable to creditors.

See a tax pro. If you are considering forming an FLP for tax advantages, by all means see an estate planning attorney. Unless your business is worth at least $1 million, an FLP may not justify the legal and accounting fees and state-imposed costs. Additionally, the valuation issues can get tricky, and you will probably need some help.

c. Employee Stock Ownership Plans (ESOPs)

Another tax-wise option for passing a small business to the next generation is the Employee Stock Ownership Plan, ESOP for short. The ESOP is often offered as an employee benefit by big corporations, but it also can work for a small corporation.

The main drawback of an ESOP for small businesses is that it cannot discriminate against (keep out) long-term employees who aren't family members. Tax code ESOP rules under IRC § 404 are very complex; we can only skim the surface here.

Small business ESOPs typically work like this: The corporation makes annual contributions of its stock (or cash) to an ESOP trust. The trust is set up under tax code rules for profit-sharing plans, similar to corporate retirement plans discussed in Chapter 15. Over an extended period, ownership passes to the beneficiaries of the trust, the company employees, through the ESOP. Employees have account balances in the ESOP in proportion to their salaries.

> **EXAMPLE:** Blowhard Corporation stock has a value of $1 million. It pays out $500,000 in salaries to employees in 2001. The company establishes an ESOP in 2001. The tax code allows Blowhard to make an annual contribution up to 25% of salaries to the ESOP, a total of $125,000 to purchase corporate stock. This represents 12.5% of the stock of the company that the ESOP trust now owns. Joe Blowhard, Jr., got a $120,000 salary in 2001, so he has 3% of Blowhard stock allocated to his ESOP account at the end of the year (120/500 x 12.5%).
>
> Blowhard, Inc. gets a tax deduction for the value of the stock contributed, and it is not income to the beneficiaries of the ESOP. If the company had simply given the stock to the employees, without using an ESOP, the stock would have been taxable income to the recipients.

ESOPs are not do-it-yourself items. First, only a C corporation, the most complex way to do business, can set up an ESOP. You'll need a sharp CPA and probably a tax attorney (but their fees will be deductible to the company). Figure in the costs of annual appraisals of the value of the company while an ESOP is in place. Generally, owners should be approaching retirement, say in five to ten years, for an ESOP to make the most sense, with a business worth $1 million or more.

Resources

- IRS Publication 554, Older Americans Tax Guide
- IRS Publication 950, Introduction to Estate and Gift Taxes
- IRS Publication 929, Tax Relief for Children and Dependents
- *Plan Your Estate*, by Denis Clifford and Cora Jordan (Nolo). This is a thorough overview of estate planning options and strategies, including federal and state estate taxes.
- *Make Your Own Living Trust*, by Denis Clifford (Nolo). This book contains forms and instructions for creating two kinds of trusts: simple living trusts that avoid probate and a more complicated "AB" trust to reduce estate taxes.
- *Living Trust Maker* software (Nolo). This program lets you make a simple probate-avoidance living trust.
- *Social Security, Medicare and Pensions*, by Joseph L. Matthews with Dorothy Matthews Berman (Nolo). This book explains, among other things, the rules that govern taxation of Social Security benefits.

Part

3

Thinking Small

13

Microbusinesses and Home-Based Businesses

"Of course there's a different law for the rich and the poor; otherwise who would go into business?"

—E. Ralph Stewart

According to *Time* magazine, big business of the future will consist of a relatively small core of central employees and a mass of smaller firms working for it under contract.

Millions of Americans already operate very small businesses, many of them home-based. Quite a few of these ventures supplement a regular job or another business. Most tax rules are the same whether your business has 500 employees and is based in its own building or it's just you, working alone from home. Nevertheless, a few tax code restrictions are aimed at home-based and other small enterprises that look more like hobbies than businesses to the IRS.

This chapter focuses on sole proprietorships, but most of these principles apply to any type of unincorporated business. If your business is incorporated, see Chapter 7, C Corporations, and Chapter 8, S Corporations.

Microbusinesses and Home-Based Businesses In a Nutshell

1. Business expenses are deductible no matter where they are incurred. But to deduct part of your home rent or depreciation for a home office, you must meet strict tax law requirements.

2. Losses from home-based and sideline businesses can be claimed against your other income to reduce your overall individual tax bill.

3. If you claim losses from your small business, an IRS auditor may challenge you, saying your business was really a hobby. Defend your business loss by showing a "profit motive."

4. Unless you run the very smallest of businesses, you are responsible for making estimated tax payments and paying self-employment taxes.

A. Business Expenses Incurred at Home

Most expenses related to your business are tax-deductible, no matter where they are incurred—at home, on the road or in a traditional office or shop.

Tax-deductible home office expenses include: office supplies, materials, professional and trade memberships and dues, travel, business use of your auto, meal and entertainment expenses, insurance premiums for business assets, local and long-distance telephone calls on the home phone (but not the cost of the basic monthly service), maintenance and repair of office computers and other equipment, depreciation (or IRC § 179 write-off) of furniture and other business assets, interest on business debts, employee wages and benefits, publications and software, advertising. (See IRC § 162, Reg. 1.162 and Chapter 1, Business Income and Tax-Deductible Expenses, for details and examples of other expenses.)

You can claim home-based business expenses without a home-based office. You may deduct all of the above kinds of home-based business expenses whether or not you qualify for the "home office" deduction discussed below.

B. Deducting Part of the Cost of Your Home

If you operate out of your home, you may (or may not) qualify to tax-deduct part of your rent or take a depreciation deduction. This tax break is commonly called the "home office" deduction. Regardless of what you might have heard, the home office deduction is alive and well. About 1.6 million folks claim a home office deduction each year, according to the IRS. Undoubtedly, more people could legally claim the deduction, but don't know how or are scared they will be audited if they do.

A house, apartment, condominium, mobile home, motor home, boat or just about anywhere else with *sleeping and cooking* facilities can qualify for the home office deduction.

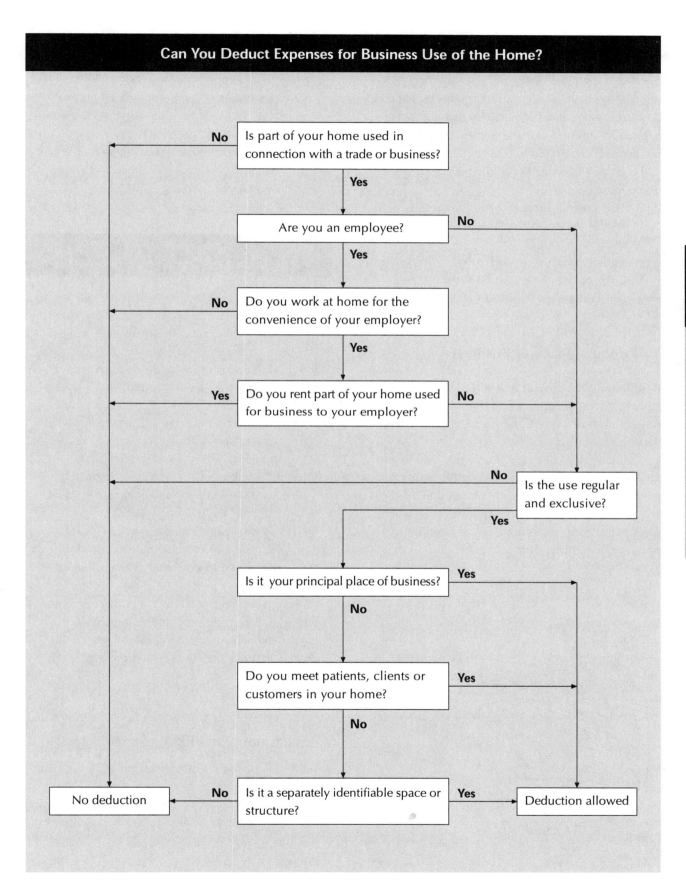

Can You Deduct Expenses for Business Use of the Home?

Is part of your home used in connection with a trade or business? — No →

Yes ↓

Are you an employee? — No →

Yes ↓

Do you work at home for the convenience of your employer? — No →

Yes ↓

Do you rent part of your home used for business to your employer? Yes ← / No →

Is the use regular and exclusive? — No →

Yes ↓

Is it your principal place of business? — Yes →

No ↓

Do you meet patients, clients or customers in your home? — Yes →

No ↓

Is it a separately identifiable space or structure? — No → **No deduction** / Yes → **Deduction allowed**

Part 3

Thinking Small

Calculating the amount of rent or depreciation to deduct is discussed in Section C below. First, you need to know whether or not you qualify to take the deduction at all. If you don't, your housing costs are nondeductible personal living expenses (except for home mortgage interest and real estate tax deductions available to every home owner).

To claim a home office deduction, your home office must be:

- the principal place of your business
- a separately identifiable space in your home, and
- regularly and exclusively used for business.

All three of the rules must be satisfied, and are discussed in detail next. (IRC § 280A.)

1. Principal Place of Business

Determining whether or not your home is the "principal place" of your business is not as simple as it sounds. And if it is not, there's no tax deduction for depreciation or rent.

If your only jobsite is at home, and you spend most of your working hours there, it is your principal place of business. But if you conduct the business at a site outside your home and just bring home work sometimes, the home may or may not qualify as the principal place of business.

EXAMPLE: Jake, a plumber, works out of his home office. He keeps a full-time employee there to answer phones and do bookkeeping. Jake is working at his home office ten hours a week and in the field 40 hours a week. As of January 1, 1999 he is entitled to a deduction for rent or depreciation, and can deduct all other ordinary business expenses, such as the salary of his employee working at his house.

Taxpayers Win:
Soliman Overturned by Congress!

Beginning Jan. 1, 1999, Congress expanded the meaning of *principal place of business*. Congress undoubtedly recognized the advances in technology favoring the home office and current business trends of downsizing and outsourcing. Now a home office deduction is available if:

1. You use the home office to conduct "administrative or management activities" of a trade or business.
2. There is no other "fixed location of the trade or business" where you conduct "substantial administrative or management activities" of the trade or business.
3. You meet the rest of the home office rules discussed below requiring a separately identifiable space and regular and exclusive use.

So now service providers and professionals, as well as outside sales persons and tradespersons who spend most of their time at job sites, are entitled to the home office deduction.

---

2. Separately Identifiable Space

Assuming your home is the principal place of your business, let's move on to the second rule. The space in which you work must be separate from the rest of your home to qualify for the home office deduction.

A completely separate structure works best as proof of a legitimate home office to the IRS—for example, a detached garage converted to an office. But most self-employed people just convert a spare bedroom to a legitimate home office by removing the bed and personal items. To pass IRS muster, if your home office is not physically divided by walls, some kind of demarcation should be evident between the business and personal space.

3. Regular and Exclusive Use

If you passed tests one and two, then let's go to the last hurdle. The tax code requires "regular" business use, which is, admittedly, vague. If you meet business customers or do paperwork at your home office, it should satisfy the regular use test. Keeping a record of use or appointments, in case you're ever questioned by an IRS auditor, is wise.

"Exclusive use" is more straightforward. It means you can't use the space for any other reason than business. This eliminates the kitchen table, or the room in which you watch TV with the kids, as your home office. This rule is akin to the "separately identifiable space" rule above. An office should look like a pure work space if the IRS ever comes calling.

Don't be afraid of a legitimate home office deduction. Claiming a home office depreciation or rent expense on your tax return usually increases your audit risk. A home office deduction is reported separately on IRS Form 8829, attached to your tax return, so it is easy to spot.

However, even if taking the deduction doubled your chances of audit, statistically, there's less than a one in 40 chance of an IRS confrontation. You would lose only if you failed to meet the home office qualifications discussed above. If audited, you will have plenty of time to make sure your home office appears "office-like." Take some photographs of the home office to show the auditor. Rarely will the auditor make a personal visit.

C. Calculating Your Home Office Deduction

If your home office qualifies, calculate your deduction on IRS Form 8829, Expenses for Business Use of Your Home. This form is filed with your individual income tax return. (See sample below.)

This form can be intimidating, and can take considerable time and patience to complete. But if you don't use Form 8829, and claim the home office deduction anyway, you risk an IRS inquiry.

The overall home office deduction is limited. The deduction cannot be greater than the profit generated by your home-based business. For instance, if your business made a profit of $2,700 before taking into account a home office deduction, the deduction can't be larger than $2,700.

When calculating your home office deduction, first divide the number of square feet used for your home business by your home's total square footage. The resulting percentage of business use (for instance, 27%) determines how much of your rent or depreciation is deductible each year. Other home related expenses are deductible too, as discussed in 3 below.

Note: If the business use of the home is for less than 12 months, you must prorate to the nearest month. For instance, three months business use means $3/12$ of the home office is deductible.

1. Renters

If you rent, figuring up your home office deduction is simple. Take the percentage of the total space occupied for business and multiply it by your rent payments for the period you are in operation.

> **EXAMPLE:** Lois, who makes and sells ceramic frogs at home, rents a 900-square-foot apartment. The room that contains a kiln and working tables is 200 square feet. She pays $8,000 rent per year. Lois is entitled to deduct 22% (200/900)

Part 3

Thinking Small

of her yearly rent—$1,778—as a home office expense, assuming 12 months of business use. In addition, 22% of her utility and renter's insurance expenses are also deductible business expenses. Lois must file Form 8829 showing this allocation of expenses to her home business.

2. Owners

Just like renters, homeowners must figure the percentage of their home's square footage used for business. But then an extra step is necessary: you need to separate the value of the building from the value of the land it rests upon. Use either your local property tax assessor's breakdown, or, if it produces a higher deduction, you are probably safe allocating 80% of your property's value to structure and 20% to land. In most parts of the country, this is roughly the case. Allocation is mandatory, because you cannot tax-deduct the cost of the land. Land never depreciates in the eyes of the tax code.

Find the tax code depreciation rules in effect in the year you bought your home or call your tax pro. For instance, after 1987, you must use straight-line depreciation instead of accelerated methods. And from 1987 to 1994, the period for taking the depreciation deduction was 31.5 years. Since 1995 it is 39 years, meaning you get 1/39 of the value of the home every year multiplied by the business use portion. (See Chapter 2, Writing Off Business Assets, for an explanation of depreciation rules and methods.)

EXAMPLE 1: Katie uses 22% (400 feet) of her home's 1,800 square feet for Katie's Krafts. Katie bought her home for $100,000 in 1987 and started her business in 1992. The local property tax assessor says the lot her home is on is worth $20,000 and the structure $80,000. The $20,000 land portion can't be as a depreciation deduction.

Katie calculates her depreciation deduction by first dividing 31.5 years into $80,000 = $2,540 per year. This sum ($2,540) is then multiplied by the business usage fraction, 22%, which

gives the figure of $559. That's Katie's home office deduction each year she is in business. If Katie started business in 1998, she would use 39 years instead of 31.5.

EXAMPLE 2: Since she bought her home, Katie has made improvements costing $10,000, so her basis for depreciation is increased from $80,000 to $90,000. (How to figure the basis of business property is discussed in Chapter 2, Writing Off Business Assets.) This increases her home office depreciation deduction to $629 per year.

3. Other Home-Related Deductible Expenses

Form 8829 requires separating all of your home-related business expenses into two categories: "direct" and "indirect." The part of your home that is used exclusively for an office is a *direct* expense area. All other costs, such as your home's light bill, are *indirect* home office expenses.

Direct Expenses. Take a full tax deduction for anything spent directly for the home office. Examples: insurance on equipment or for decorating, modifying, furnishing or hiring maid service for your office portion.

Indirect Expenses. Tax deduct a pro rata share of the utilities, repairs, taxes and insurance expenses for all of your home as indirect home office expenses. Single-line telephone service to your home is not deductible, but any business long-distance charges or a second phone line for business qualifies. (IRC § 262(b).)

These indirect expense deductions are based on the same percentage of your home occupied by the business that you calculated earlier.

EXAMPLE: Katie, from the previous example, spent a total of $2,110 for gas, electricity and homeowner's insurance in 2001. She also doled out $820 to modify and repaint the office space. Tax result: Katie can write off 22% of the $2,110 ($464) for the indirect overall home expenses and all of the $820 in direct home office

Form **8829**	**Expenses for Business Use of Your Home**	OMB No. 1545-1266
Department of the Treasury Internal Revenue Service (99)	▶ File only with Schedule C (Form 1040). Use a separate Form 8829 for each home you used for business during the year. ▶ See separate instructions.	**2000** Attachment Sequence No. **66**

Name(s) of proprietor(s)	Your social security number
John Stephens	465 00 0001

Part I   Part of Your Home Used for Business

1	Area used regularly and exclusively for business, regularly for day care, or for storage of inventory or product samples. See instructions	1	200
2	Total area of home	2	2,000
3	Divide line 1 by line 2. Enter the result as a percentage	3	10 %

• For day-care facilities not used exclusively for business, also complete lines 4–6.

• All others, skip lines 4–6 and enter the amount from line 3 on line 7.

4	Multiply days used for day care during year by hours used per day	4	hr.
5	Total hours available for use during the year (366 days × 24 hours). See instructions	5	8,784 hr.
6	Divide line 4 by line 5. Enter the result as a decimal amount	6	.
7	Business percentage. For day-care facilities not used exclusively for business, multiply line 6 by line 3 (enter the result as a percentage). All others, enter the amount from line 3 ▶	7	10 %

Part II   Figure Your Allowable Deduction

8	Enter the amount from Schedule C, line 29, **plus** any net gain or (loss) derived from the business use of your home and shown on Schedule D or Form 4797. If more than one place of business, see instructions		8	26,331

	See instructions for columns (a) and (b) before completing lines 9–20.	(a) Direct expenses	(b) Indirect expenses		
9	Casualty losses. See instructions	9			
10	Deductible mortgage interest. See instructions	10		4,500	
11	Real estate taxes. See instructions	11		1,000	
12	Add lines 9, 10, and 11	12		5,500	
13	Multiply line 12, column (b) by line 7	13		550	
14	Add line 12, column (a) and line 13				14	550
15	Subtract line 14 from line 8. If zero or less, enter -0-				15	25,781
16	Excess mortgage interest. See instructions	16			
17	Insurance	17		400	
18	Repairs and maintenance	18	300	1,400	
19	Utilities	19		1,800	
20	Other expenses. See instructions	20			
21	Add lines 16 through 20	21	300	3,600	
22	Multiply line 21, column (b) by line 7			22	360
23	Carryover of operating expenses from 1999 Form 8829, line 41			23	-0-
24	Add line 21 in column (a), line 22, and line 23				24	660
25	Allowable operating expenses. Enter the **smaller** of line 15 or line 24				25	660
26	Limit on excess casualty losses and depreciation. Subtract line 25 from line 15				26	25,121
27	Excess casualty losses. See instructions			27	
28	Depreciation of your home from Part III below			28	252
29	Carryover of excess casualty losses and depreciation from 1999 Form 8829, line 42			29	
30	Add lines 27 through 29				30	252
31	Allowable excess casualty losses and depreciation. Enter the **smaller** of line 26 or line 30				31	252
32	Add lines 14, 25, and 31				32	1,462
33	Casualty loss portion, if any, from lines 14 and 31. Carry amount to **Form 4684**, Section B				33	
34	Allowable expenses for business use of your home. Subtract line 33 from line 32. Enter here and on Schedule C, line 30. If your home was used for more than one business, see instructions ▶				34	1,462

Part III   Depreciation of Your Home

35	Enter the **smaller** of your home's adjusted basis or its fair market value. See instructions	35	75,000
36	Value of land included on line 35	36	15,000
37	Basis of building. Subtract line 36 from line 35	37	60,000
38	Business basis of building. Multiply line 37 by line 7	38	6,000
39	Depreciation percentage. See instructions	39	4.2 %
40	Depreciation allowable. Multiply line 38 by line 39. Enter here and on line 28 above. See instructions	40	252

Part IV   Carryover of Unallowed Expenses to 2001

41	Operating expenses. Subtract line 25 from line 24. If less than zero, enter -0-	41	
42	Excess casualty losses and depreciation. Subtract line 31 from line 30. If less than zero, enter -0-	42	

For Paperwork Reduction Act Notice, see page 4 of separate instructions.   Cat. No. 13232M   Form **8829** (2000)

Part **3**

Thinking Small

expenses. With Katie's depreciation deduction of $559 (Section 2, above), her total home office deduction is $464 + $820 + $559 = $1,843. The only limitation on this deduction is that Katie's home-based business must have made a profit of at least $1,843 to claim it in full.

D. Home Office Tax Recapture When Selling Your Home

The other shoe drops when selling a home on which you have claimed home office depreciation deductions. After May 6, 1997, you owe taxes for "recapture" of depreciation deductions previously taken on the home portion claimed for business.

Sorry, you can't use the $250,000 per person "exclusion of profits" on the sale of a home to offset the recapture gain. If you took a total of $20,000 in home office depreciation deductions over the past ten years, you will be taxed on $20,000 in the year of the home sale. The top tax rate on this $20,000 recapture is limited to 25% or $5,000.

For renters, there is no tax recapture for previous home office deductions. Because of recapture, home owners may want to think twice about taking a home office deduction. However, it is still beneficial to get a tax break today that you don't have to repay until perhaps far into the future. Who knows —the tax law may have changed in your favor by the time that day of reckoning comes.

E. A Microbusiness as a Tax Shelter

The vast majority of home-based businesses are sole proprietorships; if you are organized in another form, then also check out the specific chapter dealing with that entity.

Hopefully, your home business will be a money maker. But even if it doesn't pan out, it may provide a "tax shelter." This tantalizing term doesn't refer just to gold mining schemes, ostrich farms or oil wells. A venture becomes a tax shelter simply by applying its cash and paper losses to offset your

taxable income from other sources, such as a regular job. There is no minimum amount of time or money you must invest in the business to qualify for this tax benefit, as long as you had a profit motive at the outset.

Never go into a sideline business with the intention of just creating a tax shelter. Ignore the con artists peddling schemes for slashing your tax bill with a sideline business.

IRS Audits of Microbusinesses

Rumors to the contrary, home-based businesses are not guaranteed IRS audit-bait. Historically, the odds against a small business being audited are about 30-to-one in any year. However, tax returns with business losses—home-based or not—are audited more often. The more years of losses, the more likely you'll be audited. The size of the loss is probably the biggest factor; a $50,000 loss is more likely to blip on IRS radar than a $5,000 one. (See Chapter 19, Audits.)

1. How Business Losses Can Cut Income Taxes

A tax loss is not necessarily a cash loss. For instance, depreciation deductions for equipment and real estate are not out-of-pocket expenses, but are often referred to as "paper losses."

A "loss" in tax code terms may feel like a gain to you personally. This is the best of both worlds: more cash to spend and a lower tax bill. Here are some examples:

- Assets purchased wholly on credit (no cash out of pocket) can still be written off at tax time as long as they are used for business. Home computers, furniture, VCRs, camcorders, TVs and stereos all can qualify. (See Chapter 2, Writing Off Business Assets.)
- If you meet the qualifications for a home office deduction, you can deduct some of your rent

or depreciation, utilities and home upkeep expenses. These are expenses you would have paid anyway, but would not have been able to tax-deduct.

EXAMPLE: Carol, a clothing store manager who enjoys cooking, forms Carol's Catering as a sideline. Carol's big catering client declares bankruptcy and she ends the year with a loss. Carol throws in the towel, having spent $18,500 for food, supplies and equipment against revenues of $16,000.

On her tax return, Carol claims a cash operating loss of $2,500 plus $2,200 for depreciation and automobile expenses. Carol's total business loss of $4,700 offsets wages from her regular job, trimming about $1,500 off her income taxes. Carol's $2,500 out of pocket operating paper loss becomes a $1,000 after-tax out-of-pocket loss.

2. The Profit Motive Requirement

To use your business as a tax shelter, it must look legitimate to the IRS. The tax law roughly defines a business as "any activity engaged in to make a profit. You don't actually have to make a profit to be considered a business—you must just make an honest effort to do so. This "loophole" invites imaginative people to claim tax losses for hobbies and other pleasurable money-losing activities. As you may expect, the tax man is lying in wait.

To discourage folks from claiming business losses from fun things like speedboat racing or stamp collecting, the tax code prohibits claiming losses for "activities not engaged in for profit." (IRC § 183.) Expenses of enterprises without a realistic profit motive can be deducted only up to the amount of income produced from these activities. In other words, losses from a non-business can't be claimed against your income from a real job. (This is called the "hobby loss" provision, but a truer description would be the "no hobby loss" rule.)

EXAMPLE: Carol, of Carol's Catering, is audited. The IRS auditor claims she was only indulging her cooking hobby, not running a business with a profit motive. Her $4,700 cash and paper losses are disallowed—it can't offset Carol's income from her regular job. (Carol can appeal this decision; see Chapter 20.)

Whether Carol ultimately wins or loses depends on whether or not she can show her business motive. How can Carol demonstrate that she engaged in business with the clear purpose of making a profit?

a. The "3 of 5" Test

One way to determine whether a particular enterprise has a profit motive is by applying a mechanical tax code test. If a venture makes money in three out of five consecutive years, it is legally presumed to possess a profit motive. (IRC § 183(d).) The IRS relies heavily on this test when auditing small businesses that lose money.

The "3 of 5" test is not the final word, even for perpetual money-losers. For one thing, the tax code doesn't say how much profit must be made. A struggling business might pass the test by forgoing deductions and reporting a profit in any given year. For example, a business that loses $10,000 in years one and five and reports a profit of $5 in years two, three and four technically satisfies this test.

Of more importance is that even if you flunk the 3 of 5 test, you can still claim business losses. It may just be a little harder to justify them if you are audited. Courts have held that even an activity that never makes a profit is still a business. The Tax Court upheld one long-suffering taxpayer who claimed small business losses for 12 straight years! (*Lawrence Appley*, TC Memo 1979-433.) So don't give up taking losses on your tax return just because your business doesn't pass the 3 of 5 test. As you'll see in subsection b, below, it is only one factor and not the last word on profit motive—no matter what an IRS auditor may tell you.

Part

3

Thinking Small

EXAMPLE: Let's return to Carol and her struggling catering operation. This time, assume she keeps her business going, but at the end of her second year, she is still losing. Carol has several tax options:

1. She can throw in the towel, close her business, take tax losses in both years and hope she isn't audited.

2. She can continue to run her business and take any future losses on her return. If Carol does this, her likelihood of an audit goes up with every year that she reports a loss—but she may never face an audit.

3. She can close her catering business and go into a new sideline venture, which starts the 3 of 5 rule period over again.

4. If the prospect of an audit keeps her awake at night, Carol can continue her catering business but stop claiming losses on future tax returns.

The IRS provides Form 5213, Election to Postpone Determination That Activity Is For Profit, which gives you an extra year to show a profit under the 3 of 5 test. For instance, say you lost money in the first three years of operation, but believe you'll turn the corner soon. Filing this form gives you a sixth year to overcome the presumption that your business is a hobby. Few people ever do this, and for good reason. It draws the IRS's attention and may invite an audit.

Appeals of unfavorable audit findings on a profit motive issue are frequently successful. If you really tried to make a profit—but can't convince an auditor—you can usually appeal or go to Tax Court. There is a good chance you'll get at least part of your claimed loss deduction restored. Courts have allowed gentlemen farmers, stamp collectors, garage-based inventors and many other unsuccessful venturers to claim business loss deductions over IRS objections. (See Chapter 20, Appealing IRS Audits.)

EXAMPLE: Gloria, an amateur artist, painted at home in her spare time and tried, mostly in vain, to sell her paintings. She lost money every year for many years, and was audited. Her painting business losses were disallowed by the IRS for lack of a profit motive. The Tax Court heard Gloria's story and, finding that she had made a serious effort to sell her art, overruled the IRS. (*Gloria Churchman*, 68 TC 696.)

b. Other Ways to Show Profit Motive

Another way to show a profit motive—and withstand an audit challenging a business operating loss—is by demonstrating that you ran your venture in a businesslike manner. So be prepared to show an auditor:

- **Business records.** Bank statements, canceled checks and receipts that back up your expenses.
- **Advertising.** Flyers, business cards, stationery, ads and listings on the Internet to promote your business.
- **Your business diary or calendar.** Show the names of people contacted for business and any business use of your car or home. An entry might look like this:
  "3/1/01 12:30 p.m. Met Don Skinner, buyer for Bargain Basements, at Fabio's Restaurant, Kalamazoo. Discussed sale of 10,000 Tonya Harding T-shirts. Lunch: $27.42 with tip. Cab fare: $12 round trip." (See Chapter 3, Recordkeeping and Accounting.)
- **Licenses and permits.** Show that you followed your state and local licensing laws by obtaining a fictitious business name registration, an occupational license and a sales tax permit if required.

EXAMPLE: Carol had flyers advertising her catering service printed and mailed to 2,000 local businesses. She passed out business cards at social events. Carol kept track of her marketing efforts and business expenses rather informally in a spiral notebook. She kept most receipts for expenses, but never got around to getting a business license. Even though Carol did not do everything perfectly, these items should go a long way in establishing a profit motive to an auditor.

Try to look like a business. Just fooling around at something—woodworking, bird breeding or sewing—may reap a tax benefit by being "business-like." Inexpensive indicia of profit efforts, such as business cards, stationery and classified ads in local "shoppers" frequently sway auditors that you're not just indulging in a hobby. As they say, "Walk the walk and talk the talk."

F. Estimated Tax Rules

If your operation is profitable you must make quarterly estimated (ES) tax payments. (See Chapter 6, Section E.) The IRS form submitted with each payment is 1040-ES. (See IRS Publication 505, Withholding and Estimated Taxes.) If you don't make estimated tax payments four times a year, the IRS will hit you with an "underpayment of estimated taxes" penalty—currently a 9% annual charge.

It's difficult to figure estimated tax payments precisely because you won't know your profit (or loss) until the year is over. Generally, as long as at least 90% of your tax liability is paid in four equal installments during the year, you won't incur this penalty. However, if your adjusted gross income exceeds $150,000, to avoid the penalty you must pay at least 105% of last year's tax.

There is no penalty if the total tax liability for the year, reduced by any withheld tax and estimated tax payments, is less than $2,500 (2001 limit).

Resources

- IRS Publication 505, Withholding and Estimated Taxes
- IRS Publication 587, Business Use of Your Home
- IRS Publication 946, How to Depreciate Property
- *Being Self-Employed*, by Holmes Crouch (Allyear Tax Guides). This little book contains some practical tips from a self-educated small businessman.
- *Small-Time Operator*, by Bernard Kamoroff (Bell Springs). This CPA-authored book contains a wealth of information for very small businesses.
- *The Home Business Bible*, by David R. Eyler (John Wiley & Sons). This book has answers to common tax—and non-tax—questions, and also comes with a disk with small business accounting software.

■

Part

3

Thinking Small

Fringe Benefits

"When I hear artists and authors making fun of businessmen I think of a regiment in which the band makes fun of the cooks."

—H. L. Mencken

Everyone has heard of "fringe benefits," "fringes" or "perks," but exactly what are they? The term fringe benefit is mentioned—but not actually defined—in the tax code. Generally, fringes are things of value a business provides owners and employees over and above their wages and bonuses.

A fringe either isn't taxable to the recipient, or is tax-deferred, or is partially taxable or is taxable but at an advantageous rate. From the business owner's point of view, fringe benefit expenses are usually tax-deductible expenses. (See Chapter 1, Business Income and Tax-Deductible Expenses.) Congress is a spoilsport—it doesn't let businesses run amok with fringes.

Fringe Benefits in a Nutshell

1. A business can offer its owners and workers a variety of fringe benefits, which may be wholly or partially tax-free or tax-deferred.
2. The widest selection of fringe benefits can be offered by a regular C corporation business, but fringes alone are seldom a reason to incorporate.
3. Retirement plan benefits offer the greatest short- and long-term potential tax savings of any fringe benefit.

A. How Fringe Benefits Save Taxes

The tax code starts by making all fringe benefits taxable. A fringe benefit is tax-free or tax-advantaged only if Congress grants a specific exemption somewhere in the IRC. This chapter discusses the most popular fringe benefits favored by small businesses. Most of the specific "exclusions from income" covering fringes are found in IRC §§ 101 to 137, and are noted below. (See IRS Publication 15-B.)

The reason fringe benefits are popular is simple. When you take cash profits out of your business, you receive taxable income. If your business provides a fringe benefit such as professional education courses, you and your employees get something of value without paying any tax on it.

A fringe benefit may be:

- **Totally tax-free to the recipient.** For example, if an employer provides medical insurance, employees pay no tax on the value of the coverage.
- **Partly tax-free to the recipient.** For example, if an employee uses a company-provided car partially for personal purposes, some of the value of the car may be includable in the employee's income.
- **Tax-deferred—that is, not taxed until a later date.** For example, if an employee receives an option to buy company stock at a below-market price, no tax is due until the stock or option is sold.
- **Fully taxable to the recipient in the year provided.** Such benefits may nevertheless be desirable if an owner or employee can get something cheaper than if they had to buy it on their own—for example, a group disability insurance policy.

Tax breaks for some fringes are available only to C corporations. Sole proprietors, limited liability company members, S corporation stockholders and partners are out of luck. When folks first hear that corporations enjoy advantageous tax treatment, they naturally think about incorporating. However, the decision to incorporate should rarely be made based on the availability of fringe benefits alone. In reality, very few businesses are profitable enough to afford the full range of corporate-type fringe benefits.

⚠ Follow the rules on benefit plans or risk the consequences. The IRS can audit benefit plans separately or as part of a regular examination. If plans are not in compliance with all aspects of the tax law, then previous tax deductions or contributions to the plan can be disallowed. The business loses the deductions, and the benefit recipients will have to pay taxes on the benefits—an all-around disaster.

A business may offer employees an option of taking cash instead of fringe benefits through a "cafeteria" or flexible benefit plan. However, the employees should know that cash is taxable income in that year. Qualifying benefits under a cafeteria plan include group term life insurance, health, accident and disability insurance, dependent care assistance and certain 401(k) plans. See a benefits plan specialist for help in setting up a cafeteria plan.

Tax-Free Benefit Requirements

For a fringe benefit to be totally tax-free, all of the following requirements must be met:

- **The tax code must specifically allow it.** Unless a fringe benefit is excluded from income by a special provision of the tax code, its value is taxable income to the recipient.
- **It may have to be in writing.** Certain types of fringes—such as 401(k) plans—must be set out in a document that conforms with tax law rules, usually called an employee benefit plan. An unwritten policy probably won't satisfy the tax law.
- **It must have an indefinite life.** The benefit plan can't expire next year, or when an employee reaches a certain age or for most any other reason.

---

retirement funds to accumulate tax-free until it is withdrawn in later years. In the meantime, the fund is invested, and any income it produces is also not taxed. Retirement plans are available to corporations, partners, limited liability company members and sole proprietors under a variety of names. Chapter 15 is devoted entirely to the fringe benefit of retirement plans.

C. Motor Vehicles

Car ownership is the average American's third largest expenditure, after housing and food. Happily, the tax code helps share the cost of car expenses for business owners and employees. Autos can be a fringe benefit if, like most small business owners, you use the same vehicle for both business and personal transportation.

B. Retirement Benefits

Dollarwise, the most valuable tax-deductible fringe benefit is—by far—a retirement plan. Business owners and employees can deduct and put away money in

There are several tax-approved methods of providing autos as fringe benefits; some choices depend on whether or not the business is incorporated. Rules for deducting auto expenses on cars used for business are in Chapter 1, Business Income and Tax-Deductible Expenses, and Chapter 2, Writing Off Business Assets.

D. Meals

If a business pays for meals of owners and employees, the cost may be at least partly tax-deductible. Meals are also tax-free to the recipient if they serve a "business purpose" and are provided in the "course of employment." (IRC § 119.) Rules vary, depending on where and when the meal takes place. Here are the basics:

- Free meals are 100% deductible to the business and tax-free to the employee if given "for the convenience of the employer." This rule covers people working late or attending company meetings through the meal hour. In 1998 a condition was added to the law to require that no more than one-half of the business's employees be provided free meals in order to qualify for this benefit.

    EXAMPLE: Reggie, the owner of a small incorporated wholesale drapery business, orders food from local restaurants for employees working late. This expense is "for the convenience of the employer," and is deductible and tax-free to the employees, including Reggie.

- Inexpensive meals—but not free food—can be provided to employees on a regular basis from a company facility. Prices employees pay must cover at least the company's direct costs. Such subsidized meals are tax-free to the employees, and the cost is tax-deductible to the business.

- Off-the-premises meals and drinks for employees are deductible to the business and nontaxable to the employee, but *only* if business is discussed and such events are occasional

rather than every day. (See Chapter 1, Business Income and Tax-Deductible Expenses.)

EXAMPLE: Reggie takes her sales manager and a top salesperson out to dinner once a month. They discuss plans for future promotions. Reggie usually spends about $100 for drinks, meals and tips. There should be no problem for Reggie claiming this as a business expense.

E. Travel, Conventions and Lodging

Most of us like to go out of town occasionally, even if it's for work. If the business pays and we can sightsee or visit friends along the way, all the better.

When you travel on business, the enterprise can deduct all of your lodging costs, but only if you go far enough from home to "require rest." Fifty percent of your travel meal costs are deductible. It's not 100% because you would have presumably eaten if you had stayed home (and home-cooked dinners aren't deductible). (IRC § 132.)

1. Mixing Business and Pleasure Travel

If your business pays for a vacation—not a business trip—it must add the cost to your income reported to the IRS. The company then deducts the cost as additional compensation for your services. That said, let's see how a business can pay—and tax-deduct—at least some of your vacation expenses *without* it being taxed to you.

Have you noticed that more trade shows are held in resorts and destinations like San Francisco than in cities like Des Moines? Convention planners, aware of this fringe benefit opportunity, know they can build attendance with meetings in fun places.

To be tax-deductible—and not count as income—the trip's *primary* purpose must be business. Travel for political, investment or social conventions cannot be tax-deducted as a business expense. Commerce doesn't have to be the *sole* purpose—if you have some fun on the side, it's okay with those junketeers in Congress who write the tax laws.

How do you prove your trip had a clear business purpose? Obvious cases—say you are a car dealer and go to Detroit to meet with factory representatives, or you own a bookstore and travel to a booksellers' trade show—shouldn't be questioned by an IRS auditor. On the other hand, if you're a plumber and go to Hawaii to see how they insulate pipes, or own a water-ski shop in Florida and travel to Aspen to check out whether snow skis might be adaptable to your business, expect to be quizzed if you are audited. There are few hard-and-fast rules: If you use your common sense and don't push too far, your mixed-purpose travel will pass tax muster.

Here are some special tax code rules for business meetings, trade shows and conventions:

- **In the United States.** If you travel to a trade show within the U.S., your expenses are deductible to the business. There's no problem as long as you go straight there and come back as soon as the show is over.

- **In the rest of North America.** If you go to a trade show in Canada, Mexico, Puerto Rico or most of the Caribbean Islands, travel is tax-free; expenses may be business deductions only if you stay away no longer than a week and spend at least 75% of your time on business. If not, you must allocate the expenses between business and pleasure. Keep a log of how your time is spent in case an auditor comes calling.

- **Outside North America.** Travel outside North America is deductible only if you can show a valid business reason for the trip—something you could not accomplish in the U.S. Researching tropical fruit processing in Paraguay for your frozen food operation sounds okay, but studying high technology there doesn't.

- **Cruise ships.** Once I attended a tax seminar on a Hawaiian cruise ship and got a nice business deduction. The whole cruise is tax-free and deductible in full as long as:
    a. there is a bona fide program related to your business
    b. the majority of the days are spent in attendance
    c. the ship is registered in the U.S.

d. it stops only at U.S. ports (or U.S. possessions), and

e. the trip costs less than $2,000.

However, because of federal laws and union rules, few cruise ships are of U.S. registry. Generally, only companies operating in Hawaii and on the Mississippi River qualify.

Weekend stayovers after business are deductible if you fly. Most airlines require a Saturday night stayover for the lowest fare. So, if the total costs of air, weekend hotel and meals on a business trip are less than the cost of air without a Saturday night, the whole shebang is deductible. This means coming back home on Sunday or Monday for the next flight out. Note for your records both the excursion and regular airfares in case you're audited.

Temporary Assignment Travel

Business may take you away from home for up to one year, with company-paid (or reimbursed) travel and living expenses. While there is no limit on how much your business can pay and deduct, it must be "reasonable under the circumstances." A multi-million-dollar business can put you up at the Ritz-Carlton for six months, but if you are a struggling consultant, the Motel 6 would be easier to pass by an IRS auditor. After the first year, living expenses paid by your company are income to you—but are still tax-deductible, as compensation, by the business. (IRC § 162, Rev. Rule. 93-86.)

2. Family Travel for Business

Family travel brings more tax rules into play. If you take the spouse and kids, you can't deduct greater business expenses than if you were traveling alone. Happily, your entire car expense for a business trip can be deducted if relations ride along (even though the additional weight probably cuts your gas mileage). The same with hotels; if your family stays in one standard room, the entire cost is tax-deductible. Look out for two-for-one or "bring along the family" hotel and airline fare discounts without passing the cost break along to the IRS.

EXAMPLE 1: Sam, a computer retailer, his wife Jeannie, Sam Jr. and daughter Sandra fly to Anaheim, California, so Sam can attend the Worldwide Computer Show. He finds out about the latest technology while Jeannie and the kids go to Disneyland. Expenses for Sam (only) are fully deductible.

EXAMPLE 2: Sam and his family drive to Anaheim instead of fly. The entire car expense is deductible, even if the back seat is wall-to-wall kids. Once in California, Sam squeezes everyone into a regular room at the Holiday Inn, so the hotel cost is also deductible. The business can't, however, deduct the expense of family meals or tickets for Disneyland. And if everyone lingers for more sightseeing, none of the after-convention expenses are deductible, even for Sam.

The law formerly allowed a spouse's travel expenses to be deducted if his or her presence served a business purpose. Now, only a spouse who is a bona fide employee of the business can have his or her expenses paid and deducted.

Make a paper trail, too. Keep a copy of pro grams and workbooks from trade shows along with all receipts for your expenses in case the IRS ever audits. (See Chapter 3, Recordkeeping and Accounting, for the kinds of records to keep.)

3. Lodging at Your Workplace

Owners and employees of relatively few types of businesses (such as motels and funeral homes), where someone should be present 24 hours a day, can live there tax-free. The business can also deduct costs of the owners' or employees' meals if eaten on the premises. To qualify, three conditions must be met:

1. Living on the premises must be an express condition of employment.
2. It must be primarily "for the convenience of the employer."
3. There must be a legitimate need for someone to be at the business around the clock. (IRC § 119.)

What About Frequent Flyer Miles?

If you are like me, you love free trips from airline and credit card frequent flyer miles. The IRS has threatened to tax the receipt of these freebies if the awards resulted from deductible business travel and credit card charges. The IRS reasons that this is like a rebate that either should be taxed or should lower the amount of the original business deduction. Luckily for us, the IRS hasn't yet figured out how to tax this (unofficial) fringe benefit, and Congress hasn't pressed the issue.

F. Clubs and Athletic Facilities

Entertaining at private clubs or athletic facilities can qualify for tax deductions, as long as it serves a business purpose. However, membership fees for these facilities may not be deductible. The tax code has become more restrictive in recent years, so be aware of some special rules. (IRC §§ 132, 274, Reg. 1.132, 1.274.)

- **Clubs and Associations:** Dues for some private clubs are not deductible or tax-free benefits— even if the membership is used primarily for business. (Reg. 1.274-2.) Associations where a business purpose is obvious—chamber of commerce, real estate board, business leagues and public service clubs like Rotary and Lions— are deductible. Purely social organizations— country clubs, athletic clubs and the like—are

Part 4

Fringe Benefits

not deductible, but 50% of business entertainment expenses that take place there —such as greens fees and 19th hole libations —are deductible.

- **On-Premises Athletic Facilities:** A business can provide athletic facilities on the business's premises, but only if they are open to all employees. This might be a NordicTrack in an unused storeroom, or a full company gym and swimming pool. Outside athletic clubs don't qualify as tax-free fringe benefits.

G. Association Dues and Subscriptions

Business owners and employees can get tax-free trade association memberships and subscriptions to business publications. These are business-deductible expenses if the organizations is not primarily social in nature. (IRC § 162, Reg. 1.162-6, 1.162-15.)

> **EXAMPLE:** Jessica, owner of a motorcycle parts business, pays $200 per year for membership for her and her employee, Joy, in the Motorcycle Parts Retailers Association. They go to its annual convention. This is a deductible business expense and is a tax-free benefit, no matter how much champagne they drink at the affair.

H. Health Benefits

Providing group hospitalization and medical insurance are a hot fringe benefit. Tax rules for health benefits vary, depending upon whether or not your business is incorporated. C corporations get a better shake.

1. Unincorporated Businesses

Tax rules for business-paid health benefits are different for owners than for their employees— unless the operation is incorporated.

a. Owners

Sole proprietors, partners, limited liability company members and S corporation shareholders active in a business can deduct 60% (2001) of the health insurance premiums paid by them—not the business— for themselves and their families. (IRC § 162(*l*).)

The deduction is claimed on a special line for "medical insurance premiums" on the front page of your individual tax return.

⚠ **Owner's health insurance is not a business expense.** It can't be claimed on the business tax return or schedule unless the business is a C corporation.

EXAMPLE: Jack, a sole proprietor, pays $3,200 for an annual health insurance policy for himself and his family. Jack can deduct 60% of the premium ($1,920) on his individual tax return. Depending on Jack's tax bracket, his tax savings will range from $300 to about $420.

The annual limit on deducting health insurance premiums for self-employed individuals is being increased annually in stages: 60% in 2001 and goes to 70% in 2005 and 80% in 2006 and later years.

Medical Savings Accounts

Business owners and their employees may qualify for a Medical Savings Account (MSA). To qualify for an MSA, you or your business (up to 50 employees) must adopt and purchase a medical insurance plan. The insurance must have an annual deductible of at least $1,500 (for an individual) or $3,000 (for a family). Then you can make tax-deductible contributions to the MSA, similar to an IRA retirement plan. Money put into an MSA by a business or employee builds up tax-free in the plan. MSA investments must be managed by an insurance company or financial institution, similar to an IRA. MSA contributions produce an immediate tax deduction—up to 65% of the insurance plan's deductible portion for individuals or 75% for families. The MSA deduction is taken on the first page of your tax return, close to where IRA contributions are claimed.

Alternatively, employers can put money into their employees' MSAs, and the contributions are not included in the income of the employees. Once the funds are in the MSA, they can be distributed only for medical expenses that were not covered by insurance. Similar to the health insurance premium deduction for self-employed folks discussed above, the deduction is claimed by the individual business owner as a personal—not business—deduction.

b. Non-Owner Employee Health Benefits

In a sole proprietorship, limited liability company, partnership or S corporation, health benefits for *non-owner employees* are tax-free to them and deductible to the business. As discussed above, owners can presently deduct only 60% of their health insurance premiums.

EXAMPLE: Rosemary, a sole proprietor, purchases a group health plan for herself and her two employees. The $4,998 annual insurance premiums are deductible to the business in full. The portion attributable to Rosemary, however, $1,666, is taxable income to her—but she can deduct 60% ($999) on her individual income tax return. (See example 1a above.)

Hire your spouse and get fully deductible health benefits for yourself. A tax loophole allows any small business to *fully* tax-deduct health insurance and doctor's bills if a spouse is working and on the payroll. (IRC § 105.) The other spouse (owner of the business) can get medical benefits not as an owner, but as a spouse of an employee. The business deduction is 100%—not the 60% for self-employed folks.

However: (1) any other employees of the business have to be given the same health benefits, (2) there are offsetting tax costs (Social Security, Medicare and unemployment taxes) of putting a spouse on the payroll and (3) he or she can't be a co-owner and must do real work for the enterprise, part- or full-time. This loophole requires a written "medical reimbursement plan" that complies with IRC § 105. Before trying it, see a tax pro.

2. C Corporations

For C corporation businesses, a health plan has even greater tax advantages. Medical insurance premiums paid for owners and employees are entirely tax-deductible to the corporation and tax-free to the recipients. This beats the stingy 60% insurance premium deductibility limit for owners of unincorporated businesses. It is also better taxwise than claiming deductions for medical expenses other than insurance premiums on an individual tax return. (You can deduct medical expenses only to the extent that they exceed 7.5% of your adjusted gross income. This rule effectively eliminates medical deductions for higher-income individuals.)

> **EXAMPLE:** If Lois's Pets 'R Us, Inc., is a C corporation, the whole amount for her health insurance ($3,000) is tax-deductible to the business and tax-free to Lois—even if she is the only person eligible for the plan. Depending on Lois's tax bracket, this could produce a federal tax saving of as much as $1,200. Whether or not this will offset the added expense of being incorporated is another question.

Health benefits don't have to be from a group plan. Instead, an owner/employee of a C corporation can pick a health policy and be reimbursed by the business, without it counting as extra income.

Also, C corporations can establish a "medical reimbursement plan" which pays for—and deducts —medical costs not covered by insurance for employees, their spouses and dependents. A reimbursement plan must cover 70% or more of the employees, and everyone must benefit equally— except employees under age 25, part-time or seasonal or on the job for less than three years can be excluded. (IRC § 105(h).)

> **EXAMPLE:** Fred and Ethel's incorporated business, Sitcom Writers, Inc., adopts a medical reimbursement plan. Ethel has a frontal lobotomy that costs $25,000; their individual medical insurance policy covers $20,000. If the corporation pays the additional $5,000, it can deduct it—whether paid directly to the medical provider or to Ethel. The payment is tax-free to Ethel either way.

Even if your corporation doesn't have a health plan, the cost of physical checkups by an employee's doctor can be paid and be deductible by the business. To qualify, there should be a written employment contract between the corporation and employee stating that annual checkups are a condition of employment. (IRC § 162.)

I. Day-Care Benefit

Any business can establish and deduct the cost of a dependent or day-care assistance plan for its employees' children under age 13.

Payments up to $5,000 per worker annually are tax-free to the parent. (If the employee is married but files taxes separately, the maximum is $2,500.) However, the business can deduct all payments, even if over $5,000. (IRC § 129.) The excess is taxable income to the employee.

An incorporated business can add up to $5,000 to an employee/parent's salary for dependent care tax-free. This benefit must be given to every parent on the payroll, except that the corporation may exclude the following four types of workers:

- employees under age 21
- those with less than one year of service
- leased employees, or
- employees covered by a collective bargaining agreement. (IRC § 129.)

Some businesses without a dependent care plan (perhaps because it would be too expensive to cover all employees) may still qualify for the "dependent care income tax credit." This tax break for working parents is rather complex. (For details, see IRC § 21.)

J. Education Benefits

Businesses can get a tax break for helping employees, or owners, with educational expenses if they follow strict tax code rules.

1. Directly Related Education

Any business can pay—and deduct—an owner's or employee's education expenses if directly related to her job. Deductible costs include tuition, fees, books, course supplies, lodging and similar education expenses. There is no upper limit to the education benefit, but the expenses must be reasonable, taking into account the financial circumstances of the business. For instance, sending the cook for your café to a local cooking course is okay, but not if she goes to Paris for two years to attend a culinary academy.

2. Traditional Education

A business can also pay and tax deduct up to $5,250 per year for each employee's education expenses even if not directly related to the job. However, this must be traditional education—hobby-type courses don't qualify. In other words, English literature, yes; astrology, no. (See IRC § 127, Reg. 1.127, for details.) The business must adopt a written Educational Assistance Plan (EAP). Payments or reimbursements are tax-free to the employee. An EAP can cover tuition, books and supplies.

Expenses paid for graduate-level courses are ineligible for this exclusion. If the business pays for graduate education, the amounts paid are income to the worker, but are still deductible expenses to the business.

K. Gifts, Rewards, Discounts and Free Services

Relatively small tax-free benefits can be deducted and given to employees tax free if they fit into one of six categories.

1. Small Gifts

Gifts to employees—totaling under $25 per year per recipient—are nontaxable. Trinkets are considered a "de minimus fringe" and fly below the IRS radar. (IRC § 132, Reg. 1.132.) The proverbial Thanksgiving turkey for employees is probably tax-free to your employees and deductible to the business. This $25 limit applies to all business entities, and it isn't subject to an annual inflation adjustment. Employers often can be more generous with qualified award plans (discussed below).

2. Achievement Awards

With a "qualified award plan," a business can give and deduct gifts valued up to $1,600 each year—gift certificates, watches, TVs and the like—tax-free to employees. Such awards must be for special achievement, length of service or safety efforts. Sorry, awards can't be in cash, given to more than 10% of all employees or favor highly compensated employees. (See IRC §§ 74 and 274 for more details.)

If your business doesn't have a qualified award plan, you still may give special employees "good habit" rewards, up to a value of $400 per employee per year. Again, no cash payments qualify; cash is taxable income to the employee.

3. Free Services

Certain businesses—such as hotels, airlines and cruise lines—can provide their services or facilities tax-free to employees and their families. This must be an "excess capacity" service—something that would remain unused if not given to the employee. It's easy to see how this fringe applies to empty airplane seats and hotel rooms, but not many other things qualify. (IRC § 132, Reg. 1.132.)

4. Employee Discounts

Discounts on goods or services may be given by a business to employees and families tax-free. You can provide anything your business makes or sells at a reduced price, but never below cost. Discounts must be given across the board to employees and families (or even retired employees), not just to higher-paid people.

Part

4

Fringe Benefits

There are a few items specifically prohibited from being discounted without being taxed to employees—primarily, real estate and investment property. (IRC § 132, Reg. 1.132.)

5. Employee Parking or Cash

A business can either provide free parking for employees or reimburse parking expenses, or it can give cash without strings up to $180 per month (2001). The monthly stipend is indexed for inflation annually. However, if cash is chosen, it is taxable to the employee, but deductible to the business. (IRC § 132.)

6. Miscellaneous Minor Benefits

Some fringe benefits are so small that even the IRS doesn't require a business to keep track of them separately. Things that fly below IRS radar include use of the company copy machine, having a personal letter typed by a secretary, coffee and donuts, local telephone calls or an occasional theater or sporting event ticket. However, petty cash can't be given tax-free, unless it's used for occasional meals for employees working late or given for local transportation expenses (under $1.50).

Look out for taxable fringes. More valuable perks—season tickets to sporting events, the use of an employer-owned or leased vacation facility or a company car used for commuting—are taxable income to the recipient. The fair market value of these benefits must be shown on an employee's W-2 form along with wages. While these items may never be caught by an IRS auditor, you should be aware of the letter of the law here. (IRC § 132(d), Reg. 1.132.) The expense of these items given to employees is still deductible to the business, however.

L. Special Benefits for C Corporation Employees

The tax rules for fringe benefits discussed so far generally apply to all business entities. But C corporations also qualify for special tax breaks for certain fringe benefits. As you read this, keep in mind that owners of C corporations who work in the business can get these perks too.

1. Financial and Tax Planning

A C corporation (only) can provide tax-free financial planning and income tax preparation help to employees. To be tax-free, such benefits must be part of a written employee benefit plan and available to all employees, not just the owners. (See IRC § 127, Reg. 1.127-2, for details on qualifying.)

If your corporation doesn't adopt a plan, there's a less advantageous way to provide this tax benefit: The corporation may add the cost of financial or tax counseling (say $500) to an employee's taxable pay. Then the employee claims $500 on his or her individual tax return on Schedule A as a "miscellaneous" deduction. (Rev. Rul. 73-13.) The downside is that the employee cannot get a full tax break, but instead a deduction under the more limited itemized deduction rules.

2. Disability Benefits

C corporations can deduct insurance premiums paid for disability (wage continuation, sickness and accident policies) for employees, including owners. However, payments are reportable as income to employees. Payouts for disability claims are also taxable income to the recipients, except in the case of permanent or total disability. (IRC § 104, Reg. 1.104, and IRC § 105, Reg. 1.105.)

3. Group Life Insurance

C corporations can provide employees with group life insurance coverage and deduct the premium costs. (IRC § 79.) Sorry, sole proprietors, partners, limited liability companies and S corporations can't qualify for this fringe.

Only group term life insurance qualifies as a tax-free benefit. Individual policies, or those that accumulate cash reserves—called whole life or universal life—are not eligible.

Death proceeds for group life beneficiaries are limited to $50,000. If greater coverage is provided, the cost is still deductible to the business, but the excess coverage cost is taxable to the employee. IRS tables show the taxable portion of the premium for excess coverage, depending on the recipient's age and amount of insurance. The IRS income table "inclusions" are below the actual costs, so even if some of the premium is taxable, there is a savings benefit.

To qualify for this fringe, C corporations must cover all full-time workers, and can't require physical exams. The business doesn't, however, have to give the same coverage to everyone. The death payoff can be greater for owners, subject to the $50,000 limit per person.

4. Loans to Shareholders

A shareholder can borrow up to $10,000 from his or her C corporation, interest-free. A shareholder borrowing over $10,000 must either pay interest to the corporation or pay tax on the minimum amount of interest he should have paid. The minimum interest rate is determined by IRS tables. (IRC § 7872.)

This tax-free loan benefit is *not* available to sole proprietors, partners, limited liability company members or S corporation shareholders.

⚠ Observe loan formalities. Chapter 7, C Corporations, covers loan rules. For example, your corporate records must show the loan was authorized, and there must be a written promissory note to the corporation. Otherwise, an IRS auditor may rule that the shareholder loan is really a disguised dividend, making it taxable income to the borrower.

5. Entertainment Facilities

Businesses can't deduct the cost of acquiring and maintaining facilities used purely for the entertainment of owners and employees—ski cabins, yachts, hunting lodges and so forth. (IRC § 274(a).) These facilities costs can be claimed as business expenses for the periods solely used for business, however.

The value of vacation (no business) stays in business-owned properties is taxable income to the employees unless the business is reimbursed for the lodging. A business can provide very favorable rental rates to owners and employees, though.

A ski lodge used primarily for business meetings and incidentally for pleasure is not a prohibited entertainment facility. But before you designate that cabin a corporate sub-office, keep in mind that someday you might have to prove business usage to an IRS auditor.

 A shareholder who owns a facility may rent it to his corporation to wine and dine customers or for company meetings. This is tax-okay as long as rent is reasonable and the facility is available for rental for others besides your company. The corporation may even lend the shareholder funds to acquire the facility. The shareholder is entitled to tax write-offs for interest, depreciation and other expenses of ownership of the facility. If you are intrigued by the possibilities, have a tax pro run the numbers for you. There may be no tax savings if all you are doing is taking money from one pocket and putting it in the other.

6. Corporation Job Placement Assistance

Helping former employees find new jobs is a tax-free benefit and deductible for C corporations. Assistance must be provided to everyone, and the former employees can't be offered the choice of job placement services or cash. (IRC § 132(d), Rev. Rul. 92-69.)

Resources

- *The McGraw-Hill Small Business Tax Advisor*, by Cliff Roberson (McGraw-Hill). This book explains most of the fringe benefits described in this chapter, in greater detail.
- IRS Publication 560, Retirement Plans for the Self-Employed
- IRS Publication 502, Medical and Dental Expenses
- IRS Publication 503, Child and Dependent Care Credit
- IRS Publication 15B, Employer's Tax Guide to Fringe Benefits
- *Business Entity Analysis* (Troutdale, Oregon). This software compares the tax benefits of fringe benefits—including retirement plans—for the different business entities chosen, and is primarily intended for accountants.

Final thought:

"Money is a sixth sense, without which it is impossible to enjoy the other five."

—W. Somerset Maugham

■

Retirement Plans

"No man who knows what the law is today can guess what it will be tomorrow."

—Alexander Hamilton

Only the most wide-eyed optimist believes that Social Security will provide enough money for our "golden years." Indeed, as the ratio of workers to retirees shrinks, the trend is to effectively reduce benefits by taxing recipients with outside income. Create your own retirement plan to close the gap.

Fortunately, Congress helps business owners and their employees save for a secure retirement. Any kind of business—corporation, partnership, sole proprietorship or limited liability company—can set up one or more tax advantaged retirement plans. If you don't have a retirement plan, you are missing one of the greatest tax benefits of being in business!

Tax rules on retirement plans are very complicated. This explains why only a third of small businesses have retirement plans, compared to five-sixths of major companies.

This chapter presents a broad outline of retirement plan options available to businesses. After reading this, you'll probably want an expert in helping you cope with retirement planning. Stock brokerages, banks and insurance companies offer retirement plan advice, mostly to sell their investment products. Also, independent pension consultants, CPAs and tax attorneys and planners will help, for a fee. First, understand the retirement plan basics, and then go to these resources to establish a good plan.

⚠ Expect continuing changes in the law when it comes to retirement plans. Rarely does a session of Congress go by without significant changes being made. If the book in your hand is more than a year old, beware! Also, please note that while we've included information about some of the major changes Congress made to many of the retirement plan rules in 2001 (especially contribution limits) you should consult your tax advisor for specific details).

Retirement Plans in a Nutshell

1. One of the best tax reasons for being in business is to have a retirement plan.
2. Plans allow businesses to tax-deduct contributions to accounts that accumulate tax-deferred until they are finally distributed.
3. Businesses with full-time employees usually must include all employees in their retirement plans, which can be expensive.
4. All small businesses can take advantage of retirement plans, but some options are available only to incorporated businesses.
5. Federal law heavily regulates retirement plans, and professional guidance for setting up and maintaining plans is advisable.

A. Tax-Advantaged Retirement Plans

Retirement plans qualified under the Internal Revenue Code have these tax attributes:

1. Your contributions as an owner or employee are tax-deductible from current income, thus reducing your present income taxes.

   A contribution to a tax-advantaged retirement plan must be based on earned income, meaning compensation for work. An investor in a business who isn't active in it can't deduct contributions to its retirement plan. Neither can a landlord contribute to a plan based on his rental income.

2. Income generated by investments in your retirement plan accumulates tax-free until it is withdrawn, usually at a specified age.

3. The tax code imposes penalties for taking money out of a plan before retirement, but some early withdrawals are allowed.

4. When you retire, withdrawals from your plan are usually taxed at a lower rate than when you were working, as your overall income will probably be diminished.

Clearly, retirement plans are a deal that is hard to refuse. Not only can you put aside money before it's taxed, but as long as you keep your hands off it, it will compound tax-free from corporate dividends and appreciation.

Plan participants contributing $5,000 to $8,000 a year can build up $150,000 to $400,000 over a ten- to 20-year period, depending on how plan investments perform. If you contribute for 20 to 40 years, or own a very successful business and make maximum contributions, you might be able to accumulate several million dollars.

The keys to retirement plan success are to start early, make the largest contributions you can and take full advantage of all that the law allows.

What if you don't have the funds to make a contribution? A retirement plan contribution is the only way I know to do any "tax reduction planning" after the year has passed. But many folks find themselves unable to come up with the bucks to put into a plan, and lose the opportunity. If it comes time to make your annual contribution to a retirement plan, and you come up short, get creative. Borrow money from wherever you can—even a credit card advance—because chances are the long-term tax savings will out-weigh short-term borrowing costs. Or liquidate any non-retirement investments and use the funds for the plan contribution. Again, even if there is tax to pay from selling an investment, the retirement plan benefits will likely outweigh it.

B. Types of Retirement Plans

There are numerous rules for who can get into which kinds of plans and how much money can be put into them.

This can get confusing fast. If you want more information, see IRS Publication 560, Retirement Plans for the Self-Employed; it is one of the better-written IRS publications, and it's free.

The table below shows the most common retirement plans for businesses. You may have several plans running at the same time. And there is no limit to how many plans you can accumulate over your working life. For instance, someone who has held several corporate jobs and who also has been self-employed over her lifetime may have Individual Retirement Accounts, a Keogh plan, Simplified Employee Pensions, 401(k) plans and a corporate pension and profit-sharing plan.

Part 4

Fringe Benefits

Retirement Plans for Small Business Owners

	IRA	SIMPLE IRA	SEP	KEOGH	401(K)
Sole Proprietorship	Y	Y	Y	Y	N
(with employees other than owner)	Y	Y	Y	Y	Y
Partnership	Y	Y	Y	Y	N
(with employees other than owners)	Y	Y	Y	Y	Y
Limited Liability Company	Y	Y	Y	Y	N
(with employees other than owners)	Y	Y	Y	Y	Y
S corporation	Y	Y	Y	N	N
(with employees other than owners)	Y	Y	Y	Y	Y
C corporation	N	Y	Y	N	Y

Where to Go for a Pension Plan

Picking the right retirement plan is one of the most important financial decisions you will make. Find a reputable financial services institution or a pension consultant. Ask your banker, accountant or attorney for their recommendations. Perhaps a friend or business associate has worked with a retirement planner. Speak to several outfits and compare what they have to offer.

For most folks, a "ready-made" prototype plan offered by a mutual fund company, bank or brokerage is fine. Standard plans are cheap to set up and maintain. Fidelity Investments and Charles Schwab are two low-cost financial families that offer retirement plans.

A pension consultant costs more, but you get more personalized attention. This might make sense if your business is very prosperous. Expect to pay $100 or more per hour for a professional's assistance in customizing a pension plan, or several plans. Or the pro may quote a flat fee. In most cases, the fee should not run more than $1,500 and is tax-deductible. One caution: Many pension pros push plan investments that carry hefty sales commissions. Some people decide to put investment decisions into the hands of a money manager. The fee is usually around 1% per quarter based on the value of your retirement accounts.

Once you set up the plan or plans, you must decide who will take care of the annual paperwork and investments. With off-the-rack plans, it will be Fidelity, Schwab or a similar institution. For custom plans, it could be your pension pro, a professional plan administrator or a money manager. Ask to see how their plan investments have performed, and their references. Check if their clients are pleased with their services, meeting deadlines and answering questions.

Keep an eye on your retirement plan's performance. Most plans issue monthly or quarterly reports. Monitor how well the investments in the plan are performing. Change the investments or move to a new administrator if you aren't happy.

Contribute to retirement plans as early in the year as you can. Typically, folks contribute to their retirement plans at the last minute, just before they file their tax returns. This may be more than a year after you were legally allowed to contribute—that is, on January 1. You not only miss a full year of tax-free compounding, but also incur taxes on earned interest or dividends on that same money in your non-retirement accounts.

C. Retirement Plans for Sole Proprietors, Partners, S Corporation Shareholders and Limited Liability Company Members

Over 95% of small business owners are sole proprietors, partners, S corporation shareholders or limited liability company (LLC) members. While the one remaining form of doing business, the C corporation, offers a greater range of retirement plan options, it does so at a cost. For most folks, the added expense and complexity of operating as a C corporation don't justify this choice.

Small business owners who don't choose the C corporation can select one, or maybe more, of three varieties of tax-advantaged retirement plans: Individual Retirement Accounts (including new variations such as the SIMPLE IRA, Roth IRA and Education IRA), Simplified Employee Pension plans (SEPs) and several different types of Keogh plans. All plans offer the same benefits to participants, putting away part of your earnings before it is taxed in an investment account, where it accumulates tax-free until withdrawn.

A sole proprietorship, partnership, S corporation or LLC with employees can add the increasingly popular 401(k) plan, which allows participant borrowing in addition to other retirement plan features.

1. Keogh Plans

The Keogh plan, named after the New York Congressman who proposed it, is the oldest retirement savings plan for the self-employed. A Keogh can be set up by a sole proprietor, partner or limited liability company member.

A corporation shareholder who works in the business can't establish a Keogh. Likewise, neither may an employee of a business have her own separate Keogh plan; she must work for a business with a Keogh and participate in it.

Keogh contributions are typically made by an owner for herself and the business's participating employees. Because some types of Keoghs allow larger annual contributions (up to $140,000 in 2001) than other retirement plans, they are popular with high-earning business owners.

Keoghs can be set up by folks with either profitable full-time or sideline businesses. As long as you have self-employment income, you can have a Keogh even if you are covered by a retirement plan from a present or past job. And you can close other plans and roll them into a Keogh if you leave a job (voluntarily or involuntarily) and go into business for yourself.

There are two varieties of Keoghs:

- *defined-contribution* plans, and
- *defined-benefit* plans.

An individual may have one or both of them.

a. Defined-Contribution Keogh Plans

The defined-contribution plan (DCP) is the most common Keogh plan. How much you get back from a defined-contribution plan in benefits depends on the total amount put into the plan as well as the earnings on the investments. That means that if retirement is quite a few years away, with a DCP you can make only a rough estimate of how much will be in your pot on retirement. Retirement planning software, such as Quicken's Financial Planner (Intuit), will help you with this projection.

Keogh DCPs can further be subdivided into two types: profit-sharing plans (PSPs) and money purchase plans (MPPs).

Profit-Sharing Defined-Contribution Plans (PSPs). For a business owner, PSP contributions are, as the name implies, normally made from the business's profits. A PSP (unlike an MPP) doesn't require any annual contribution; it is entirely voluntary. The owner of the business decides each year whether or not to make a contribution both for herself and for her employees.

EXAMPLE: Bartoleme's Bakery, a sole proprietorship, has a Keogh PSP. Ludwig is the owner. Lisa, his only employee, is paid $25,000 per year. In 2001, the business has a net profit of $150,000. Ludwig chooses to contribute to the plan for himself and Lisa. In 2002, the business loses $20,000, so no contribution is made to the PSP. Technically, a contribution still could be made for Lisa if Ludwig can come up with the money, but as a practical matter that is doubtful.

Money Purchase Plans (MPPs). MPPs differ from PSPs in that annual contributions are mandatory—whether the business makes a profit or not. Once you set up an MPP, a fixed percentage of everyone's pay (no more than 20% for an owner or 25% for an employee) must be put into the retirement plan

Part

4

Fringe Benefits

every year. For this reason, MPPs are usually found in older businesses with reliable cash flow. The reason why someone would choose an MPP—requiring annual contributions come hell or high water—is that MPPs allow larger tax-deductible contributions than do PSPs. (The limits and rules are provided in Section d, below.)

If you are a business owner in an MPP and don't have the funds to contribute one year, you must ask the IRS for permission to postpone it and catch up in a later year.

> **EXAMPLE:** Drake's Poultry, a sole proprietorship, adopts a maximum contribution Keogh MPP. Drake, the owner, and Lark, an employee, are the only workers. Lark earns $28,000 per year. In 2001, the business has a net profit of $100,000, so $7,000 (an amount equal to 25% of Lark's pay) must be contributed for her. Drake must contribute $20,000 (20% of his earnings) for himself.
>
> In 2002, the business loses $50,000, but Drake still must contribute $7,000 for Lark to the MPP. If he gets IRS permission, Drake will not be forced to make a contribution for himself, since the business lost money.

b. Keogh Defined-Benefit Plans (DBPs)

With a Keogh Defined-Benefit Plan (DBP), you can set a target for receiving a specific monthly amount, or a lump sum, on retirement. The amount of the payment is usually tied to a preestablished formula, such as 40% of your average compensation, based on the highest three years of salary. The goal of a DBP is to have enough funds in the plan at retirement to provide a fixed sum, such as $1,500 per month, for life.

Setting up a DBP requires finding a pension consultant and a specialized financial analyst called an "actuary." The actuary is necessary to satisfy IRS requirements for calculating life expectancy of participants and forecasting DBP performance expect to pay $2,000 or more for these professionals' services in the first year, and a slightly lesser amount each year the DBP is in place.

The amount the business contributes each year on behalf of each employee depends on the individual employee's age, length of employment and amount of annual compensation from the business. Age is the most critical of these factors. Generally, DBPs work out best for those over age 50. Annual tax-deductible contributions of $80,000 or more to DBPs are not unusual. This is a far greater contribution than is allowed by non-DBP Keoghs or SEP-IRAs and 401(k) plans.

As with other Keogh plans, employer contributions for younger employees must be made. However, if there are wide age discrepancies between owners and employees, the employer's cost is typically much less than required for Keogh defined-contribution plans.

> **EXAMPLE:** Julia, Atmose Company's owner, is 55 and Bert, Atmose's office manager, is 25 when the company adopts a DBP Keogh. The business makes contributions sufficient to provide a 10%-of-average-pay monthly retirement check beginning at age 65. A pension plan professional determines that this will require an annual contribution of $9,800 for Julia, but only $2,900 for the younger Bert. (These figures are hypothetical, are used for illustration only and are subject to change annually.)

The Keogh DBP allows business owners who start late on retirement planning to catch up by making large annual contributions. A DBP offers the highest tax-deductible contributions of all pension plans, translating into fantastic tax breaks for self-employeds who earn enough to make maximum contributions. I have a DBP, but they are not common, primarily because DBPs are the most complex (and costly) of all retirement plans to establish and administer.

c. Keogh Participation Rules

Generally, all of a business's employees must be included in its Keogh plan—but some may be excluded if they don't qualify. Here are the basic rules:

- Full-time employees age 21 or older with the business for one year must be covered.
- Part-timers may be excluded if they don't work at least 1,000 hours during the year (about 20 hours a week). (By contrast, SIMPLEs and SEPs which are discussed in Sections 3 and 4, below, require many part-time employees to be covered.)
- A Keogh participant departing from the business may leave his Keogh account balance in the plan (and wait for retirement to take whatever benefit he is entitled to), or immediately withdraw the funds. If he takes the money before retirement age, he may be subject to early withdrawal penalties and income taxes. (Section G, below, discusses retirement plan withdrawal rules and rolling over funds to other plans.)

d. Keogh Contribution Rules

There is both a *dollar* limit and a *percentage of income* limit on how much you can put into a Keogh plan every year. This is not as straightforward a calculation as it might seem, so pay close attention to the specifics here. And the limits apply differently to employees than to owners. To get the maximum allowable Keogh contribution, most folks establish both a Keogh money purchase plan and a profit-sharing plan, called a "paired plan" (both discussed above).

- **Keogh profit-sharing plan (PSP).** If you are a business owner, you may contribute to a PSP and deduct up to 13.04% of your gross earned income, or $25,500, whichever is less. (The same limits apply with a SEP.) This means your business must earn $192,168 to get the full deduction.

  The maximum contribution rate for an *employee* to a PSP is 15%, up to $30,000 per year.

- **Keogh money purchase plan (MPP).** The tax code seems to say that a business owner can contribute 20% of a business's profits, up to $30,000. However, an owner's net earnings

from self-employment must first be reduced by one-half of the self-employment tax you paid, so the real limit is closer to 18%. *Employees*, on the other hand, may contribute up to 25% of their compensation, with a maximum of $30,000 per year.

Paired Plans. When you establish both types of Keogh defined-contribution plans—as many people do—the overall limits are the same as with just the MPP. In effect, by having both plans (or just the MPP), you can contribute up to $4,500 more per year to a retirement plan than with a SEP.

There is, however, a hidden price to pay for being able to contribute more to a Keogh than to a SEP. Once you establish an MPP, annual contributions are mandatory as long as there is gross earned income from your business. With a PSP, on the other hand, it is always discretionary whether or not to make an annual contribution.

If you have paired plans, you must fund the MPP every year. Most folks make the mandatory contribution amount the smaller of the two Keogh accounts by designating fixed percentages when paired plans are established. For example, a "paired plan" may provide for a 5% MPP and a 15% PSP contribution, a total of 20% maximum allowed for an owner.

Make use of your computer. Good tax preparation software, such as Turbotax for Business (Intuit), computes retirement plan contribution limits, so you don't have to work out these complex calculations.

e. Setting Up and Administering a Keogh Plan

Establishing a Keogh involves adopting either a "custodial" ("account type") or a "self-trusteed" (individually designed or prototype) Keogh plan.

Account type plans are fine for average small business owners. They are offered by banks, brokerages, mutual fund and insurance companies and are the most economical choice. Custodial plans conform to IRS requirements, and are typically in one- or two-page documents prepared by the investment company. Sometimes called "prototype" plans, they conform with the law by using broadly applicable language.

Account plan annual fees for administrators typically range from zero to about $100 per year per participant. Many institutions build their fees into the investments they sell you for your account.

Self-trusteed are individually designed plans which may offer more to businesses with highly compensated owners and multiple employees. As with a tailor-made garment, this is a more expensive way to go than buying off-the-rack. Call a pension consultant for details on setting up a self-trusteed plan to see if it might be for you.

Formalities and Rule Changes

A qualified Keogh plan requires either an IRS Letter of Determination or Letter of Notification under IRC § 401, or both. A pension professional or financial institution usually gets this for you. Also, these folks make sure your Keogh plan is amended as the law changes. You must have an Employer Identification Number to tax-report your Keogh plan contributions; you can't use your Social Security number.

f. Taking Money Out of a Keogh

Tax rules for Keogh distributions are in Section G, below. Caution: You may never borrow from your Keogh plan—unlike 401(k) and corporate pension plans. Don't ask why—it's the law.

2. Individual Retirement Accounts (IRAs)

Anyone in business can open an Individual Retirement Account, commonly called an IRA. (IRC § 408.) Yes, an IRA is okay, even if you have other tax code retirement plans, as long as you are working and earning. And unlike other retirement savings plans, a business owner can establish an IRA regardless of what her employees do about their retirement plans.

IRAs were highly touted when they started in the early 1970s. Since then, the low contribution limits ($2,000 per year) coupled with restrictions on deductions for higher earning folks have caused the IRA to lose its luster. But given that many self-employed people have no retirement plan at all, the IRA fills a gap—it's much better than nothing. In fact, thanks to tax-deferred compounding, a couple with two IRAs and 30 years of $2000 contributions could amass more than a million bucks with moderately successful investments.

Since 1997, IRAs can also be used to help meet shorter-term savings goals: your children's education and first-time home ownership.

a. New IRA Eligibility and Contribution Rules

The 1997 Tax Act created new IRA options, called the "Roth IRA" and the "Education IRA." First, let's go over the new eligibility and contribution rules for what we'll call the "Traditional IRA."

Spousal IRA Rules. IRA contributions for non-working spouses is now a maximum of $4,000 per year. To get the maximum IRA deduction per married couple, the working spouse must earn at least $4,000.

Increased IRA Eligibility and Phase-Out Limitations. If you are not covered by another tax-advantaged retirement plan, you can deduct up to $2,000 each year (2001). But if you are participating in another qualified retirement plan, the tax deduction for IRA contributions begins to disappear ("phase out," in tax lingo) at the $33,000 income level for singles and $53,000 for married couples (2002 figures). The deduction was completely eliminated for those making over $43,000 (single) and $63,000 (married couple). The phase-out limits increase each year so that by 2005 they don't start until $50,000 for singles, and two years later (2007), they start at $80,000 for married couples. (This presumes that

Congress doesn't strike again in the interim, of course.)

Other Rules for Traditional IRAs. You may make an IRA contribution based only on earnings from your labor. It cannot be based on "unearned" income such as clipping coupons or collecting rents.

Withdrawals are taxed in the year made, much like any retirement plan withdrawal. (See Section G, below.) Until that time, your IRA earnings on investments are tax-deferred. However, some "qualified special purpose" withdrawals from IRAs can be made without penalty. They are discussed below in Section 2e.

IRA contribution limits will increase. Congress has finally increased the amount you can contribute to your IRA. These amounts are slated to increase over the next few years as follows:

2002-2003	$3,000
2005-2007	$4,000
2008 and thereafter	$5,000

If you're over 50, you get to contribute more—$500 more from 2002 to 2005, and $1,000 more from 2006 and afterward.

b. The Roth IRA (IRA Plus)

You may contribute to a new *non-deductible* IRA Plus, more commonly called a Roth IRA after Senator Roth, its sponsor. (IRC § 408(a).) Why would you ever want to make a non-deductible contribution to a retirement plan? The answer lies in a feature unique to the Roth IRA: the funds are not taxed on withdrawal. So any earnings made on your IRA investments are withdrawn tax-free.

The tax dilemma inherent here is whether to take the tax break now (from the deduction provided by a traditional IRA), or later with a tax-free withdrawal from a Roth IRA. It is not an easy call, and one that you may want to discuss with a tax pro before making the choice. Annual contributions to a Roth IRA are subject to adjusted gross income limits of $110,000 for single workers and $160,000 for married couples.

EXAMPLE: Marston sets up and contributes $2,000 to a Roth IRA for five years. He is in a combined federal and state tax bracket of 45%. Upon retirement at 59½, Marston begins withdrawals from the IRA when his bracket has dropped to 20%. In this case, Marston would probably have been better taking the $900 per year tax savings ($2,000 x 45%) with a traditional IRA. If, however, in the less likely event that Marston's tax bracket remained about the same on retirement, the tax-free buildup of earnings in a Roth IRA may make more sense.

The longer the time before retirement—generally ten years or more—the greater the potential advantage of the Roth IRA over the traditional IRA. This is especially the case if the IRA investments perform at a 12% or better clip during this period.

Unlike traditional IRAs, a Roth IRA can be set up after you turn 70½.

c. The Education IRA

The Education IRA (IRC § 530), like the Roth IRA, is a non-tax-deductible plan. It allows you to make a maximum annual contribution of $500 for educational expenses of "designated family beneficiaries" in 2001.

Generally, in 2001, you can withdraw contributions and earnings tax-free if family beneficiaries use them to pay for expenses of higher education (or, beginning in 2002, elementary or secondary school expenses). You can set up an Education IRA in addition to a traditional (deductible) IRA or Roth IRA. Education IRA investments can be in any of the ones allowed by law for any IRA fund (see below).

Education IRA contributions are allowed only for a beneficiary under age 18. Contributions may not be made by married taxpayers whose adjusted gross income exceeds $150,000 (or $95,000 for singles). If the funds are not used before the beneficiary's 30th birthday, the IRA becomes taxable unless rolled over to another beneficiary in the same family.

Part

4

Fringe Benefits

EXAMPLE: Dr. Estarch and her husband have annual adjusted earnings of $240,000. Her office manager, Leslie, makes $35,000. Dr. Estarch can't set up an Education IRA for her kids, but Leslie, who also has two tots, can have two plans, and contribute a total of $1,000 to them each year. When Leslie withdraws funds for the kids' education, it will all be tax-free, including any earnings in account investments.

Congress recently made some significant changes to the Education IRA rules, however. Beginning in 2002, the maximum contribution amount is $2,000, a boon to parents trying to save for expensive education costs. In addition, elementary and secondary school expenses now qualify as expenses that can be paid tax free from the Education IRA, including tuition, fees, books, supplies and even a computer and Internet access. The income phase-out range has been increased from $190,000 to $220,000 for married filers. Consult your tax advisor for more information.

d. Opening an IRA

All IRAs must be established at a financial institution. You can't just call any old investment-type account your IRA. Most banks, mutual fund companies and stockbrokers can set up any kind of IRA. They charge small fees, $25 or so, to set up an IRA, and then similar annual maintenance fees.

IRA investments are usually self-directed—you make investments among things such as stocks, CDs, mutual funds or bullion. The investments may be changed at your discretion, but some restrictions and penalties may be imposed by the financial institution.

e. IRA Withdrawal Rules

The rules for withdrawing money from all types of retirement plans, including IRAs, are set out in Section G, below. Generally, IRA withdrawals may

not be made without penalty before you turn age 59½. However, special rules may allow you to take money earlier, in addition to the new "qualified special purpose" rules below.

Qualified special purposes. Withdrawals from any type of IRA may be made for certain "qualified special purposes," meaning two circumstances:

- **First-Time Home Buyers.** First-time home buyers, or their close family members, may withdraw up to $10,000 for acquisition costs within four months of the purchase.
- **Higher Education.** Withdrawals may be made for higher education expenses for a taxpayer or his immediate family. Not to be confused with the Education IRA, this is only for college-level expenses.

⚠ **Regular IRA withdrawals are still taxable in the year taken.** These two exceptions only eliminate the early withdrawal penalty of 10%.

3. Savings Incentive Match for Employees (SIMPLE) IRAs

The SIMPLE plan, as you will see, it is not exactly true to its acronym. SIMPLEs come in two distinct varieties: SIMPLE IRAs and SIMPLE 401(k)s. (SIMPLE 401(k)s are discussed in Section D, below.) Unlike the traditional IRA, SIMPLE IRAs require a contribution by the employer as well as the employee.

a. Contributions

Basically, business owners and workers may direct that up to $6,500 (2001) of their compensation be put into a SIMPLE IRA. The business owner must then either match the employee's contribution (up to 3% of the employee's wages) or make a flat contribution equal to 2% of her pay. The boss can even match his own contribution. Once money is in the plan, it is like a traditional IRA account, subject to the same rules for withdrawals. (See 2b above.)

SIMPLE IRA contribution limits will increase over the next few years as follows:

2002	$7,000
2003	$8,000
2004	$9,000
2005	$10,000

In addition, anyone over 50 can make additional "catch-up" contributions each year as follows:

2002	$500
2003	$1,000
2004	$1,500
2005	2,000
2006 and beyond	$2,500

b. Tax Deductions

Money put into a SIMPLE IRA is fully deductible to the employer as compensation, and earnings in the account are tax-deferred until withdrawn. Although the employee doesn't take a deduction, it works out the same—money put into the SIMPLE plan by the employer is not taxed as income to the employee.

> **EXAMPLE:** Scone, the owner of Dundee Company, an S corporation, earns $40,000. Leotis, his employee, earns $25,000. With a SIMPLE IRA, Scone can contribute up to $7,200 to his plan ($6,000 plus 3% of $40,000); Leotis decides to contribute $500, 2% of her wages. Scone must match 100% of Leotis's contribution because it is less than 3% of her wages, so the total put into Leotis' SIMPLE IRA is $1,000. All contributions to both SIMPLE IRAs are tax-deductible to Dundee Company.

c. Eligibility and Participation

Employers can impose some age and service restrictions on employee participants in SIMPLE IRA plans. For instance, any employee who doesn't earn at least $5,000 per calendar year can be excluded from a SIMPLE IRA. Employees can be required to earn $5,000 or more in any two prior years as well.

A SIMPLE IRA may cover as many as 100 of a business's eligible employees, but there is no minimum percentage of employees who need to contribute.

 SIMPLE IRAs offer a more flexible, less costly alternative to SEPs. SEPs force businesses to cover more employees and to contribute greater amounts than with SIMPLE IRAs. When contributions must be made by owners for employees, they can be unequal amounts. This is because employer contributions are strictly based on whatever the employee contributes; if the employee contributes zero, the business owner has nothing to match, and so is off the hook. SEPs are discussed next.

d. Setting Up a SIMPLE IRA

If you want to create a SIMPLE IRA, talk to a financial institution—a bank or brokerage house. Some offer both traditional and SIMPLE IRAs.

4. Simplified Employee Pensions (SEPs)

The Simplified Employee Pension or SEP is also called a SEP-IRA because it is governed by similar rules, but with higher contribution limits. SEPs are still good choices because of their higher contribution limits.

The SEP is Congress's response to complaints that Keoghs and corporate-type retirement plans were too rule-heavy and that IRAs did not allow large enough contributions.

A SEP can be either a primary or a supplemental retirement account. It can cover both self-employed people and their employees who work full- or part-time. A SEP is the first plan I established for my law practice. The fact that my wife, Brenda, works for a mega-corporation and is in its pension, profit-sharing and 401(k) plans doesn't affect my SEP (or my Keogh and DBP) plans at all. And if Brenda had time for a sideline business, she could set up her own SEP and keep her company plans, too.

How good a tax deal are SEPs? If you socked away $5,000 each year in a SEP earning 8%, your nest egg would reach $247,115 in 20 years. That is about $150,000 more than going with $2,000 IRA contributions. Over a longer period, and if your investments perform better, your SEP could top $1 million.

A separate SEP account is opened for each business owner or employee—unlike a Keogh, where everyone is in one account. In a SEP, the owner contributes for herself and her employees, so a SEP is a "non-contributory" plan for employees.

a. SEP Contribution Limits and Deductibility Rules

How much can be put into a SEP and tax-deducted each year? The answer depends on whether you are an owner or employee of a business. Contribution limit rules are tricky, so pay close attention. It will be worth the effort when tax bill time comes each year, and again when retirement finally rolls around.

Business Owners. For 2001, business owners can contribute a maximum of $25,500, or 13.04% of the business's earned income. SEP contributions for a business owner can be made annually by any *profitable* business—sole proprietorship, partnership or limited liability company.

> **EXAMPLE:** Manfred, owner of Pillpushers Pharmacy, puts $5,216 into his SEP in 2001. This is 13.04% of his business's net income of $40,000. It is tax-deductible to Manfred, saving him $1,000 or more in taxes, depending on his marital status, other income and overall tax bracket.

Employees (Non-Owners). After 1996, employers who continue to contribute to a SEP account for themselves must make contributions for their employees. Employees may continue to make contributions only to a pre-1997 SAR-SEP. Many business owners with both a SEP and employees have converted to the less costly SIMPLE IRA. As noted, a SIMPLE IRA is an employee "contributory" plan. (See Section 3, above.)

If there are employee participants in the SEP, the owner must contribute the same percentage of pay for his employees as for himself. The top contribution that can be made for an employee is 15% of compensation, up to $25,500 per year. Contributions may be made for employees but not for owners, in the discretion of the owner, even if the business doesn't turn a profit. In real life, I can't see this happening, but it is allowed.

⚠ **Congress has made some changes to these contribution limits** for 2001 and beyond. Check with your tax advisor for more information.

b. Participation Requirements

Everyone working in the business who is over 20 years old, has been with the company three of the last five years and makes $500 or more per year must be included in the SEP plan. If these folks' SEPs aren't funded by the business owner, he can't contribute to his own SEP account.

> **EXAMPLE:** Melissa, owner of Superfast Delivery Service, has three long-time regular employees. She contributes 5% of Superfast's business profit, $2,500, to her SEP. She must also contribute 5% of wages to each eligible employee's SEP. This could be expensive, and so Melissa may want to consider a SIMPLE IRA instead of a SEP.

c. Other SEP Rules

Only business earned income qualifies for SEP contributions. Capital gains, interest, dividends and other sources are not "earned income," and so you can't base a SEP contribution on these items.

> **EXAMPLE:** Manfred, in the example above, made a profit of $32,000 from the sale of property and inherited $3,400 in 2001. Neither amount was earned, so they don't affect his maximum SEP contribution. It is still $5,216.

⚠ **Be careful not to overcontribute to a SEP.** There is a 10% tax on any excess unless you withdraw the funds right away. This can easily happen if you make your SEP contribution before finalizing your tax return.

d. SEP Tax Reporting

You have up to the date of filing your tax return to contribute to a SEP. Normally this means by April 15, or if you get an extension to file, the last date of the extension to make a SEP contribution—either August 15 or October 15.

You decide every year whether or not to put anything into a SEP if your operation is profitable, up to the maximum allowed—but you can't play catch-up for any past years in which you didn't contribute.

Even though your SEP contributions are not taxed as income until withdrawal, they are still treated as income for payroll or self-employment tax purposes each year. This means that Social Security and Medicare taxes (ranging from 2.9% to 15.3%, as discussed in Chapter 5, Employer Tax Concerns) must be paid on earnings each year on contributions to a SEP. In contrast, annual contributions to corporate plans, discussed in Section E below, are not subject to Social Security and Medicare taxes. Not fair, but it's the law nonetheless.

e. How to Establish a Simplified Employee Pension Plan

Set up a SEP through a bank, insurance company, brokerage house or mutual fund company. They handle the paperwork for a small fee, or for free if you make your investments through them. Fidelity Investments and Charles Schwab are two discount brokerage firms that offer stock and mutual funds for SEPs.

You may freely change investments within the SEP. Transaction fees are often waived if you keep your retirement plans with these institutions, although some charge annual SEP account maintenance fees of $10 to $100 per year.

You may have an unlimited number of SEP accounts, as long as your total contributions don't exceed the annual limits. I accumulated six different SEP accounts over the years, all with different mutual fund families. I have since consolidated these SEPs, since it was too much trouble to keep track of all of them.

f. SEP Withdrawal Rules

See Section G1, below.

SEP-IRA, Keogh or SIMPLE IRA?

By now, you are probably thoroughly confused. Which is the best plan for your small business? Well, I can try to cut through the thicket and make some comparisons to try to help with the decision.

IRAs and SEPs are a little simpler to set up and maintain than Keoghs. But Keoghs allow the largest tax-deductible contributions and are worth it if you are able to take advantage. Keoghs and SEPs are attractive for businesses with few or no workers other than the owners. Otherwise, the expenses of covering employees may offset the overall tax advantages. New SIMPLE IRAs overcome this cost factor by requiring low (or no) contributions by the business owner for employees. And the traditional IRA dictates no employer contributions for employees, but the owner and spouse can put in a maximum of $4,000 for themselves.

> **EXAMPLE:** Merillee earns $200,000 as a self-employed executive recruiter. With a traditional IRA, she could contribute $2,000 to a retirement plan. With a SIMPLE IRA she could contribute $12,000. With a Keogh Profit-Sharing Plan, Merillee could contribute $25,500, and if she adds a Keogh Money Purchase Plan, she could contribute $30,000.

Part 4

Fringe Benefits

Key Self-Employment Retirement Plan Rules (Non-Corporate)

Type of Plan	Last Date for Contribution	Maximum Contribution	Time Limit to Begin Distributions
IRA	Due date of income tax return (NOT including extensions)	Smaller of $2,000 or taxable compensation	April 1 of year after year you reach age 70$\frac{1}{2}$

COMMENT: Good for sideline businesses and those with limited funds available for contributions. *Note:* Keep an eye on contribution limit increases.

SEP-IRA	Due date of employer's return (plus extensions)	**Employer** Smaller of $25,500 or 15% of participant's taxable compensation	April 1 of year after year you reach age 70$\frac{1}{2}$
		Self-Employed Individual Smaller of $25,500 or 13.0435% of taxable compensation	April 1 of year after year you reach age 70$\frac{1}{2}$

COMMENT: Better choice than IRAs for business owners with moderate income, because they allow larger contributions than IRA.

Keogh	Due date of employer's return plus extensions) (To make contributions to a new plan in a given year, the plan must be set up by the last day of the employer's tax year.)	**Defined-Contribution Plans**	
		Employer *Money Purchase.* Smaller of $35,000 or 25% of taxable compensation	April 1 of year after year you reach age 70$\frac{1}{2}$
		Profit-Sharing. Smaller of $25,500 or 15% of employee's taxable compensation	April 1 of year after year you reach age 70$\frac{1}{2}$
		Self-Employed Individual *Money Purchase.* Smaller of $35,000 or 20% of taxable compensation	April 1 of year after year you reach age 70$\frac{1}{2}$
		Profit-Sharing. Smaller of $25,500 or 13.0435% of self-employed participant's taxable compensation	April 1 of year after year you reach age 70$\frac{1}{2}$
		Defined-Benefit Plans	
		Amount needed to provide an annual retirement benefit no larger than the smaller of $140,000 or 100% of the participant's average taxable compensation for his or her highest three consecutive years	April 1 of year after year you reach age 70$\frac{1}{2}$

COMMENT: Best choice for mature businesses with enough cash flow to make larger contributions than allowed with SEP-IRAs.

D. 401(k) Deferred-Compensation Plans for Businesses With Employees

IRC § 401(k) provides that any enterprise *with employees* can have a deferred-compensation plan. This is commonly called a "401(k) plan," or a "salary reduction plan."

A partnership or limited liability company with or without employees can also establish a 401(k), along with a corporation in which only the owner is an employee. Any business except a one-person sole proprietorship (or husband and wife team) can establish a 401(k) plan. I know, it's not fair, but it's the law.

"Deferred compensation" means not taking income earned this year until some future year. Why would you want to do that? Because, if you take income now, it is fully taxed. If instead, you put part of your earnings into a tax-advantaged retirement plan, it not only reduces your tax bite this year, it will accumulate earnings tax-free over future years.

A typical deferred-compensation 401(k) plan provides that an employee makes an annual contribution. The employer may fully or partially match the 401(k) contribution. Or less often, the employer may make all of the 401(k) contribution. It is up to the employer, since the law doesn't require the owner to contribute for employees.

> **EXAMPLE:** Dennis, owner of a management consulting firm, DenCo, is in the 36% tax bracket. His corporation puts $9,000 into his 401(k) plan in early 2001. The $9,000 is immediately tax-deductible to DenCo as an expense, but is not income to Dennis in 2001. If the $9,000 earns $1,000 during 2001, Dennis's total income tax savings are $3,600 (36% tax savings on the $9,000 contribution, and 36% of the $1,000 the investment earned).

A great feature of 401(k) plans is that participants can decide each year whether—and how much—they want to contribute (within tax code limits).

Another incentive for making 401(k) contributions is that many companies partially match the contributions made by the employees.

1. 401(k) Contribution Limits and Drawbacks

The tax code never allows too much of a good thing. There are both dollar and percentage-of-income limits on how much can be annually contributed to retirement plans—including 401(k) plans. For 2001, the maximum contribution to a 401(k) is the lesser of 25% of earnings or $10,500. (IRC § 402(g).)

You don't have to contribute every year to a 401(k) or your can put in less than the maximum. Typically, 401(k) participants contribute 2% to 10% of earnings. A married working couple can contribute a total of $21,000 to separate 401(k) plans, or to the same plan if they are both employed by the same company.

One tax drawback is that Social Security and Medicare taxes are still imposed on the 401(k) contributions in the year made. So you pay anywhere from 2.9% to 15.3% of taxes on income put into a 401(k) that you don't get until some years later (same rule with SEPs). For some folks, this extra reduction in take-home pay is a reason not to contribute to a deferred-compensation plan. This can cause many people to miss a tax-saving opportunity.

401(k) contribution limits are increasing. As with IRA contributions, Congress has decided that we can put more money in our 401(k)s in the coming years. Contribution limits are slated to increase as follows:

2002	$11,000
2003	$12,000
2004	$13,000
2005	$14,000
2006 and thereafter	$15,000

If you're over 50, you can put more in with "catch-up" contributions (on top of the standard contribution amounts. These are as follows:

2002	$1,000
2003	$2,000
2004	$3,000
2005	$4,000
2006 and thereafter	$5,000

2. 401(k) Participation Rules

A 401(k) plan can't be just for the business owners alone. It must be open to any full-time employee who is 21 or older and has worked at least one year in the business.

The ratio of participation of "highly compensated" employees must be close to that of lower-rung workers (though it may be slightly higher). For instance, for a business owner to contribute 6% of his salary, his employees must kick in at least 4% of their wages to the 401(k) plan.

If the top brass put in too much relative to the rank and file, the excess must be returned to them (and taxed). Because owners can't force their employees (who tend to be younger and less concerned with retirement) to contribute to a 401(k) plan, this can pose a problem. As an incentive for the little guys to join its plan, some businesses match 401(k) contributions of all participants in the plan—although matching is not required by the tax code. Typically, businesses make a partial match, such as 3% if an employee contributes 6%. It is a tax deductible business expense, as long as the annual maximum is not exceeded.

3. Getting Into a 401(k) Plan and Investment Limitations

A 401(k) should be set up by a pension pro or a financial institution. There is more paperwork than with most other retirement plans. A 401(k) plan may be too expensive to administer for small businesses with just an owner and a few employees. Before choosing a 401(k) for your business, check on the cost of establishing it and the annual charges thereafter.

Another drawback of 401(k) plans is that they usually limit your investment choices. Your control over 401(k) plan investments is restricted by Department of Labor regulations that don't apply to Keoghs, SEPs or IRAs. For instance, you may only invest in certain bonds, stocks, mutual funds or money market funds. You are allowed to mix investment choices, but you may only be able to switch your plan money around a few times a year.

A few 401(k) plans now permit participants to freely play the stock market. Whether or not this is wise in a retirement savings plan is another question. Mutual funds are the usual choice for 401(k) plans.

The SIMPLE 401(k) Plan

Congress recently brought forth yet another retirement plan option, called the Savings Incentive Match for Employees 401(k) or SIMPLE 401(k), for short. This is a slimmed-down 401(k) but still is subject to most of the heavy 401(k) tax code rules described above. At first glance, there may not seem to be much of a difference between a SIMPLE 401(k) and a SIMPLE IRA. Both have the same contribution limit of $6,000, the 2% non-elective contribution and the 3% matching option for employers. But there are very significant differences in the two SIMPLE plans. Unlike the SIMPLE IRA, the SIMPLE 401(k) requires a pooled trust to be formally administered, annual Form 5500 reporting to the IRS, issuing of participant statements of accounts and more—everything that a small business person fears most.

The SIMPLE 401(k) tax rules here are horrendously complicated. I suspect very few of these plans are being adopted. I can't say whether this new plan fills a need that can't be met with other tax code retirement plans. If you are interested in finding out more, SIMPLE 401(k) prepackaged plans are offered by stock brokerage firms, banks and insurance companies. Also, private pension consultants can advise you whether a SIMPLE 401(k) is worth the effort.

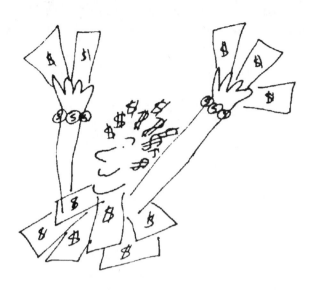

At one time, "corporate retirement plans" offered significant advantages over other business entities. Although the gap has narrowed today, a wider range of options and larger contribution limits make corporate plans attractive for cash-rich enterprises. One tax savings with corporate plans is that annual contributions aren't subject to Social Security and Medicare taxes—unlike with unincorporated entities.

Another potential advantage is that you can borrow from a corporate savings plan, unlike most other plans. If you have medical bills or need a down payment for a home, for example—it is comforting to know the plan money is there for you.

Keep in mind that if your business is incorporated, then you are an employee—perhaps the only one. So whenever you see the word "employee" here, it means working shareholders as well as anyone else on the payroll.

4. Taking Money Out of a 401(k)

An advantage of 401(k) plans over SEPs, Keoghs and IRAs is that you can borrow from your 401(k), but can't from the other non-corporate plans. Section G below explains the rules for loans and for withdrawals from all types of retirement savings plans, including 401(k)s.

5. Annual Tax Reporting

Businesses with 401(k) plans must file IRS Form 5500 each year. Most plan administrators, such as financial service firms, assist in the preparation of Form 5500. The fees are tax-deductible.

E. C Corporation Retirement Plans

If you're a sole proprietorship, partnership, limited liability company or S corporation, this material will be of interest only if you are considering becoming a C corporation.

1. Federal Law: ERISA

The Employee's Retirement Security Act (ERISA) is a complex set of federal laws governing benefit and retirement plans for certain employees of mostly mega-type businesses. ERISA has been revised by Congress more times than I can count. ERISA provisions are enforced by both the Department of Labor and the IRS.

Whenever you see the term "qualified plan," it means that it is an employee benefit plan governed by ERISA. ERISA retirement plans provide tax advantages similar to the Keogh, IRA and other smaller business retirement plans discussed in this chapter.

The Pension Benefit Guarantee Corporation, a federal agency, also gets into the regulatory act for corporate *defined-benefit plans only*. This agency protects plan participants from fraud or theft of plan assets. However, most smaller businesses aren't covered because few have defined-benefit plans. (See Section C1, above, for an explanation of defined-benefit plans.)

ERISA rules generally prohibit discriminating among corporate employees. For instance, plan benefits can't favor business owners and officers of

Part

4

Fringe Benefits

a corporation over other employees. Having to include the rank and file makes ERISA plans too expensive for all but a few small businesses. A common dilemma is presented when a business can't afford to cover all employees, but wants benefits for the owners. The law grants some leeway—for instance, employees can be excluded from corporate ERISA retirement plans until after they have stuck around long enough to be valuable. (See Section 2, below.)

The IRS can audit retirement plans to see if they are complying with ERISA rules. If a violation is found that can't be easily fixed, the plan can be terminated and/or heavy penalties assessed. Penalties could wipe out the plan—a financial disaster. If you suspect your ERISA plan is not in compliance with the law, and don't want to risk the IRS finding out in an audit, you should come clean. You can report and correct defects in a pension plan and pay only relatively small IRS compliance fees. (Rev. Proc. 98-22.)

Taking Cash Instead of a Retirement Plan

An ERISA "cafeteria" or "flexible benefit" plan gives employees a choice between taking cash or selecting among fringe benefits. This choice may include retirement plans that are contributed to by the business. If the employee takes cash, it is *fully taxed*. Whatever the employee chooses, it is a deductible expense for the business. Like most ERISA plans, a flexible benefit plan must be in writing and can't discriminate in favor of highly paid employees.

---

2. Types of Corporate Retirement Plans

ERISA covers several types of retirement savings plans. The most useful of these for smaller corporations are discussed below. Depending on the type of plan, contributions can be made by the business, the employee or both.

Tax Advantages of an ERISA Retirement Plan

- Contributions to an employee's retirement plan are tax-deductible expenses to the corporation, thus reducing its taxable income.
- Contributions to a retirement plan are made with "pre-tax dollars." This reduces a participant's annual taxable income while increasing the amount he or she can save in a plan.
- Retirement plan investments earn income without being taxed as long as they remain in the plan.
- Withdrawals from a corporate plan can begin as early as age 55, but can be delayed until age $70\frac{1}{2}$. Withdrawals are taxed at the retired participant's then-current tax bracket, which is likely lower than when she was working.

Participants in corporate retirement plans don't have to stay with the same company until retirement age to get their benefits. Whether they leave voluntarily or not, they have a "vested" right to whatever they contributed to the plan as of the date they leave. However, participants might not be entitled to contributions by their employer, unless they have worked a minimum period, typically two to six years. And the plan can require participants to reach retirement age before the right to collect the benefits kicks in. (Section G, below, discusses taking money out of retirement plans.)

Corporate retirement plans are of two types, called *defined-contribution* and *defined-benefit* plans. (IRC §§ 414, 415.) Let's look at each one in more detail.

a. Corporate Defined Contribution (DC) Plan

The Defined Contribution (DC) plan is the most popular type of corporate plan because it allows definitely determinable annual contributions to be made by the business. Here, a percentage of each participating employee's pay is contributed and put into an investment account by the business.

Employees can either participate in pooled accounts, in which the plan trustees (generally the employer) choose the investments, or, with certain formal notice requirements, contribute to segregated accounts, in which the employee selects the investment and assumes the risk. Segregated accounts give the participant a voice in his investments (IRC § 404(C).)

Defined Contribution plans can be either profit-sharing plans (PS), or money-purchase (MP) plans. The concept and difference between the two was discussed above under Section C1a, so we won't repeat it here. The basic difference is that a profit-sharing plan doesn't mandate annual contributions and has a contribution limit of 15%.

Cash-rich, mature small business corporations should combine both PS and MP plans to get the maximum tax bang for the buck. As noted, unlike a profit-sharing plan, a money-purchase plan creates a hard and fast long-term obligation on the corporation for annual funding. Don't adopt a MP plan without knowing what you are getting into. See a tax or pension pro first.

The DC plan contribution is always made by the business, not the employees, with the exception of a 401(k) plan. The corporation decides on the contribution each year as a percentage of total payroll and contributes that amount before filing its tax return. Typically, the contribution allocated to each eligible employee's account in proportion to his or her compensation. With a profit-sharing plan, the maximum is 15%. If there is a money-purchase plan, either by itself or in combination with a profit-sharing plan, the maximum can be stretched to 25%, with a maximum of $30,000. Five percent to 8% of wages is a typical contribution.

> **EXAMPLE:** Sierra Corporation contributes $15,000 to its DC plan—a profit-sharing plan. Margaret, the owner (sole shareholder and a corporate employee), has an annual salary of $50,000. Her two eligible employees, Jason and Pam, are paid $25,000 each. The contribution is thus allocated $7,500 to Margaret and $3,750 each to Jason and Pam. Had Sierra Corporation also adopted a money-purchase plan, it could have contributed an additional $10,000.

It is also possible to allocate DC plan contributions to favor owners slightly over employees. This involves complicated "permitted disparity" rules which are best left to a tax or pension pro. (IRC 401(l).)

The payouts in a DC plan, as with most retirement plans, depend on how much has been contributed and how well plan investments have performed. Nothing is guaranteed to a DC participant, unlike a Defined Benefit (DB) plan discussed below (Section b).

> **EXAMPLE:** Jobe contributes an average of $3,000 per year to Jobe, Inc.'s, Defined Contribution plan for 30 years. Jobe's investments perform well, and build up to $450,000. Josephine puts the same amount into Josephine Inc.'s DC plan, but there were too many losers in the plan portfolio, and she ended up with only $125,000 on retirement.

b. Corporate Defined Benefit (DB) Plan

The traditional corporate retirement plan is called a Defined Benefit (DB) Plan. A DB plan promises a specific monthly benefit for life on retirement. Alternatively, a lump sum may be taken, with some restrictions. (Similar Keogh Defined Benefit Plans are also available to other entity business owners; see Section C1b above.)

DB plans are more expensive to set up and maintain because they require the expertise of a pension pro and an actuary on an ongoing annual basis.

Each DB plan participant has the comfort of knowing how much they will get every month with a DB plan. In general, the longer an employee is with the company, the larger the monthly benefit on retirement. The maximum annual limit on retirement payouts is $125,000. The following example illus-

Part

4

Fringe Benefits

trates some of the numbers that work in a typical DB plan that conforms with tax code rules.

> **EXAMPLE:** Ramona, age 56, goes to a pension consultant and adopts a Defined Benefit plan for her C corporation. The plan provides a benefit of 45% of her three highest years of compensation. There is also a pro-rata reduction if she retires with less than 30 years of employment under the plan. Ramona is allowed to apply her previous time spent as a sole proprietor to satisfy the 30-year rule. Based on Ramona's life expectancy and the projected balance in the plan on her retirement, the plan's actuary calculates her benefit as follows:

Benefit Percentage: 45 % (benefit percentage chosen in the plan)

x $100,000 (highest average 3 years of pay)

Benefit: $45,000 per year ($3,750 per month) on retirement

In practice, the benefit percentage formula is more complex than in Ramona's example. Until Ramona's retirement, projected at age 62, the actuary must annually recalculate the amount needed to fund the $3,750 per month benefit. If we assume that Ramona is just starting her plan at age 56, and has not had other plans in the past, her first year retirement contribution (and legally allowed tax deduction) would be about $85,000! If it turns out that her plan investments perform well, or she decides on a later retirement age, the future required contributions under the plan will be less.

 As shown in Ramona's case above, the DB plan works well with highly compensated professionals. This is especially true for those who start late in the retirement plan game—because of its generous contribution limits. As mentioned, I have a DB plan and am overjoyed at the large tax deduction I get every year for my contribution.

3. Corporate Plan Distributions

For a discussion of corporate plan distributions— that is, taking money out of retirement plans— please see Section G3, below.

4. Setting Up and Administering Corporate Retirement Plans

A huge industry has emerged to help businesses set up, find and service benefit plans. If you are with me so far, you may have some inkling of just how complicated all of the rules are. Pension consultants, life insurance companies, banks and mutual funds all are in the retirement plan business. They do the paperwork and make annual tax reports, so you don't have to know much. Some institutions work with independent pension consultants, but most "bundle" these services. Unfortunately, this may leave you to your own devices and an 800 number. Institutions are better at explaining their investment products than fitting a corporate retirement plan to your needs.

F. IRS Problems With Retirement Plans

Most retirement plans are overseen by financial institutions or professional administrators so there are rarely any IRS difficulties. When problems do arise, they usually are uncovered in IRS audits of the business or its owners. Here are some things to watch out for.

1. Technical Violations

Since the IRS knows just how complex the retirement plan law is, audits are conducted by specially trained agents. Targets are selected from an IRS review of Forms 5500, which benefit plans must file annually.

A violation occurs when, for example, an eligible employee was not included in the retirement plan, or an investment was made in a prohibited asset, like a sugar futures contract.

Under the IRS's Voluntary Compliance program, a business can report violations before the IRS initiates contact and hence avoid penalties. The IRS responds with a "compliance statement" showing how to fix things, such as giving the forgotten employee benefits or selling the improper investment.

2. Over-funded Defined-Benefit Plans

Corporate plan investment accounts (defined-benefit plans only) can become "too fat" under ERISA rules. The account balances have become too high relative to projected pay-outs. For instance, say the plan investments grow at 12%, where the projections only called for 9%. In this case, the company can't make any further contributions to the plan until things balance out. Complex IRS formulas determine when a plan is overfunded.

Since most of you won't have a defined-benefit plan, I'll skip the details. If your company does have a DBP, you should be working with a pension professional to see that overfunding doesn't occur.

3. Excess Contributions

The most common tax problems arise when excess contributions are inadvertently made. As discussed, there are strict percentage-of-compensation and absolute dollar limits on contributions for each year.

For instance, if contributions are made throughout the year, they may not match up with the business's profits, which aren't known until the year ends. If there is a contribution shortage, there is no tax problem (unless it is a defined-benefit plan). However, if there is an overage, it must be given to the plan participants and the returned funds become taxable income to each participant. If excess contributions aren't removed and the IRS discovers it, stiff tax penalties are assessed against the retirement plan account.

G. Taking Money Out of Retirement Plans

This is the part we all wait for, the retirement plan payoff. Here is how it plays out, tax-wise.

Withdrawals mean income tax is finally due on the earnings that accumulated over the years (except for Roth IRAs; see Section C2b). Money taken out of any retirement plan becomes taxable income (except in the case of loans from certain types of plans, as discussed later in this section).

Withdrawals are taxed at your income tax bracket in the year taken. Typically, your income tax bracket will be lower in retirement than when you were working. This could mean a drop from as high as 39.6% (2001) to as low as 15% (2001) (plus your state tax bite). It depends on your total income at that time and further tax law tinkering by Congress.

 See the introduction, Section D, for the new income brackets for 2002 and beyond.

Follow retirement plan withdrawal rules carefully. If you don't follow the rules when pulling money out of your retirement account, you'll incur not only income tax on the withdrawals but a special 10% penalty tax as well.

There is a 20% IRS withholding of tax on retirement plan withdrawals. If you do owe taxes, it doesn't necessarily follow that you owe 20% in taxes on the distribution. Depending on your other income, exemptions and deductions you may owe nothing, or you may owe more than 20%. The withholding tax requirement is an incentive for you to keep filing tax returns after retiring (sorry)—especially if you are due a tax refund.

Pension accounts may consist of both taxable and nontaxable contributions. This would be true if you had a nondeductible IRA or made both deductible and nondeductible contributions to the same plan. (See Section C2, above.)

Be careful to identify distributions from mixed contribution plans so that you don't pay tax on the same income twice. Unfortunately, this process isn't as easy as it might appear if, as most folks do, you take plan distributions over a number of years. You should prorate each distribution payment between taxable and nontaxable each year, and additional account earnings must be prorated as well. IRS Publication 575, Pension and Annuity Income, has a formula for doing this. Another alternative is to ask the IRS to do the calculation for you. There is a $50 fee for this service; IRS Publication 939, Pension General Rule, explains how to apply for it.

> **EXAMPLE:** Sherman made deductible IRA contributions of $40,000 and nondeductible contributions of $15,000. His IRA is worth $90,000 at retirement. Only $75,000 would be taxable to Sherman, beginning when he started taking distributions. Sherman would find it easier if he established separate IRA accounts in the first place but he didn't.

Withdrawal rules are different for just about every type of plan. For instance, some plans allow you to take a lump sum distribution on retirement and defer taxes on it over the succeeding five or ten years, depending on the year you were born. If in doubt, check with a tax or pension pro before taking any money out of a retirement plan.

Move to a low/no-tax state on retirement. States can no longer tax pensions of former residents who have retired elsewhere. So, moving from tax-hungry states like New York or California to sunny Florida or Nevada could save you up to 12% on your retirement plan state payout taxes. You still owe the IRS, of course.

1. IRA, SEP and Keogh Plan Withdrawals

There are five basic rules for taking money out of your IRA, SEP or Keogh retirement plan:

1. Generally, a distribution before age 59½ triggers a 10% premature withdrawal penalty tax, unless:

- You become permanently disabled at any age. In this case, there is no withdrawal penalty.
- Withdrawals are part of a series of withdrawals over at least five years, or until age 59½, whichever is longer.

2. A withdrawal is reported on your next filed tax return, and is subject to income tax at your tax bracket rate. The balance in your plan continues to accumulate tax-deferred income.

3. You must start withdrawing money by age 70½ or face 50% penalty tax! The IRS publishes tables showing the minimum annual withdrawals required, based on your life expectancy.

4. You can spread the tax liability out over a period of five or ten years with a *lump sum* withdrawal from a corporate plan, 401(k) or Keogh—but not with a SEP or IRA.

5. On your death, any funds still in your SEP, Keogh or IRA pass to your named beneficiary or estate. The plan automatically terminates unless your spouse is the beneficiary. A surviving spouse may continue the plan and accumulate earnings tax-deferred. Alternatively, the widow or widower can transfer the account into a new SEP or IRA and name younger family members as beneficiaries—stretching the tax deferral benefits even further. Check with a tax pro on this.

Loans may be taken from 401(k) and corporate plans (if the plans allow it) subject to tax code rules, but never from SEP, IRA or Keogh plans.

2. 401(k) Plan Withdrawals

To get money out of a 401(k) plan without being penalized, you must:

- be retired and at least 59½ years old
- have left the business and be at least 55 years old

- have died (meaning your heirs or named beneficiaries take it)
- be disabled, or
- take a loan from the plan, if specifically allowed under the plan documents. You must provide collateral (which can be done by pledging the balance of your 401(k) account). You can't borrow more than 50% of your plan balance, or $50,000, whichever is less. Generally, you must repay the loan, with interest, at commercial loan rates, within five years. But for home purchases, you may extend the repayment schedule to 30 years.

Premature Withdrawals. It's okay to take distribution for a qualifying "hardship," but you will be charged a premature withdrawal penalty. So, if the plan allows it, take a loan instead. Hardships include medical expenses, school tuition for a family member or buying a home. See Reg. 1.401(k)-1(d)(2) or check with a tax or pension pro before going the hardship route.

If your withdrawal doesn't meet these rules, you will be assessed a penalty tax of 10% plus income tax at your tax bracket rate. The withdrawal is reportable and the tax is due on your next filed tax return.

> **EXAMPLE:** Jocko takes a $10,000 withdrawal from his 401(k) to buy a car. This reason doesn't meet tax code rules. This will cost Jocko $1,000 as a penalty tax, plus income tax at his tax bracket (which will range from 15% to 39.6%), meaning a total tax cost of $2,500 to $4,960. Jocko should have taken a loan if the plan allowed it. There is no tax cost to Jocko with a loan unless he doesn't repay it.

3. Corporate Plan Withdrawals at 55

Corporate plan distribution rules are more liberal than non-corporate plans. First, you can start taking out money without penalty as early as age 55. Before 55, the 10% premature penalty tax kicks in.

With most other plans, 59½ is the earliest you can take money out.

Like all other retirement savings plans, you must start withdrawing funds by age 70½—except for those who continue to work past age 70½. These hearty folks can put off withdrawals, as long as they don't own more than 5% of the stock of the corporation.

Minimum withdrawals each year after attaining age 70½ are based on IRS life expectancy tables. The intent of the law is that your retirement account is zeroed out on the day you die—even though this is hardly likely for anyone except Dr. Kevorkian's patients.

4. Rolling Over Retirement Plan Funds

You may keep your retirement funds in a corporate account when quit, if the corporate plan allows it. (Alternatively, you can switch your account balance to a new employer's plan if you keep on working.)

However, there is a third choice. Many folks roll over (transfer) their retirement funds into an IRA when leaving their employer. This allows you to keep accumulating earnings tax-deferred and to self-manage your investments, unlike with a corporate plan.

⚠ **Be careful rolling a corporate plan into an IRA if some of your plan funds were from nondeductible contributions.** For instance, if your pension account has $120,000 in it, with $18,000 from your after-tax contributions, you can roll over only $102,000. If you transfer the whole amount, you will not only incur a penalty tax, but you will end up paying tax twice on the $18,000 you contributed.

Final thought:

"The trouble with retirement is that you never get a day off."

—Jack Patterson

Part

4

Fringe Benefits

Resources

- IRS Publication 590, Individual Retirement Arrangements (SEPs & IRAs)
- IRS Publication 560, Retirement Plans for the Self-Employed
- *IRAs, 401(k)s & Other Retirement Plans: Taking Your Money Out*, by Twila Slesnick and John C. Suttle (Nolo). A comprehensive guide to various retirement plans that helps you make sense of the rules governing distributions and contains detailed information on avoiding or minimizing the taxes and penalties that can crop up when you start taking distributions.
- *Create Your Own Retirement Plan*, by Twila Slesnick and John C. Suttle (Nolo). A self-employed person's resource for setting up a retirement plan. Contains a thorough discussion of the various options and helps you weigh the pros, cons and costs of each.

- *Social Security, Medicare and Pensions*, by Joseph L. Matthews with Dorothy Matthews Berman (Nolo). As the title indicates, this book covers the whole realm of retirement income, not just retirement plans, from a recipient's point of view.
- *Everyone's Money Book*, by Jordan E. Goodman and Sonny Bloch (Dearborn Financial Publishing). This encyclopedic book includes a worthwhile discussion of tax-wise options in taking money from different kinds of retirement plans.
- *How to Pay Zero Taxes*, by Jeff Schnepper (Addison-Wesley). Although the title over-promises, the book includes some innovative tax twists on using retirement plans.
- *Retirement Savings Plans*, by David A. Littell (John Wiley & Sons). This is a fairly technical book written for tax professionals. It contains a number of forms, examples and sample plans.

■

16

Buying a Business

"The rule of my life is to make business a pleasure, and pleasure my business."

— Aaron Burr

Instead of starting from scratch, you can usually find someone with a business who wants to sell. Buying an established enterprise may be more costly—but less risky—than starting a new one. There's a lot to be said for taking over a proven business with a customer base and established location.

Buyers do have tax worries not faced by those who start from the ground up, such as:

- outstanding tax liabilities that come with the business, and
- potential tax audits of the business for prior years.

This chapter covers the tax concerns of buying a business. The flip side, selling a business, is covered in Chapter 17. Take a look at both chapters, no matter which side of the fence you are on, to get a well-rounded tax picture.

Whether you want to acquire a service, retail, wholesale or manufacturing business, the tax issues are remarkably similar. Once you are aware of them, you must ferret out any tax land mines.

Buyers need professional advice. When buying an existing business, look out for undisclosed tax and other debts, overstated earnings, employee problems, overvalued inventory and pending or potential lawsuits, to name a few. Hidden liabilities can lurk in all areas—from land contaminated with toxic chemicals to accounts receivable that prove to be uncollectible or inventory that's defective or dated.

A business-savvy attorney should be on your team for all but the smallest business acquisitions. A lawyer can represent you or just answer questions. She can act as an escrow agent or recommend a company to handle the exchange of money. Many attorneys are not familiar with the tax aspects of business transfers, so run the deal by a tax pro, too. (See Chapter 22, Help Beyond the Book.) All professional fees here are tax-deductible and if a professional advisor screws up, he may be liable for any losses you suffer as a result of the bad advice.

If you are buying more than just a small business's "hard" assets (such as the business's name, or a trademark), consult a business appraiser, too. Find someone with expertise in valuing businesses in the same industry. This can help not only in coming up with a fair purchase price but in establishing an equitable tax basis for the business assets.

Buying a Business in a Nutshell

1. A buyer and seller must assign a value to all business assets (including any covenant not to compete) transferred and report it to the IRS on their respective tax returns.
2. A buyer can write off goodwill and other intangible business assets purchased over 15 years.
3. Buyers should be wary of outstanding tax liabilities. Always check for tax liens, and require the seller to agree to indemnify you for any tax debts that may attach to assets transferred.
4. There is no federal tax on the purchase of a business, but states and localities may impose transfer taxes.

A. Buying the Assets of a Business

A business is simply a collection of assets, in the eyes of the tax code. Someone offering a business for sale is trying to sell all these assets together. A buyer may not want all of them, however. For instance, Dayna wants to buy Sal's Pizza Parlor for its prime real estate, but she doesn't want Sal's business name or the old pizza ovens and furniture. If Dayna makes Sal a good enough offer, he may sell just the building to her and sell the rest of the items to other folks.

How the business is legally structured—sole proprietorship, partnership, limited liability company or corporation—also has important tax consequences to both the buyer and seller, as we'll see.

1. Unincorporated Businesses

If you buy a partnership, limited liability company or sole proprietorship, you are purchasing its *assets*—a store lease, inventory, customer list and so on. Normally, you don't agree to take over business-related *liabilities*, including tax debts. Contracts of sale typically require the seller to pay all debts before closing, or out of escrow. If not paid, then the business's debts may remain the seller's personal responsibility after the transfer. However, debts that attach to specific assets—such as equipment—are the responsibility of the new owner.

Tax debts. The IRS never releases the seller from unpaid business-related taxes when the business is transferred. Buyers normally don't have to worry about the seller's tax debts, however, unless the IRS or state taxing agency has filed a tax lien against the seller's assets. Such liens are not secret and normally appear on the public record in the name of the business or the owner. See Section B1, below, for how to find out whether tax liens have been filed.

> **EXAMPLE:** Angelo, a sole proprietor, sells his profitable business, Korner Mart, to Luigi. Angelo has not filed or paid income taxes for the past three years. The IRS hasn't caught on to Angelo—yet. Luigi takes the business assets free of any tax liability. Angelo, of course, remains personally liable for taxes he should have paid on the business income before he sold the business.

You are not required to notify the IRS *before* purchasing or selling a business. However, state and local agencies may have to be notified and a notice to creditors published under your state's Bulk Sales Act.

2. Corporations

The tax situation is more complex when buying someone's incorporated business. Whether you buy corporate shares or the corporation's assets is a crucial choice, because:

- If you buy only a corporation's *assets*, you ordinarily don't assume its liabilities, including taxes.
- If you buy a corporation's shares of *stock*, however, you end up with both its assets and liabilities—including known and unknown taxes. An example of an unknown tax debt would be one from an IRS audit that has not yet begun. Legally, a seller of corporate shares is released from all corporate debts unless he personally guarantees them or agrees in writing to be liable for them after the transfer.

Why, then, would you ever consider buying a corporation's stock, given the potential for legal trouble? Because some owners will sell only if a buyer takes the stock. There are several valid reasons why a seller may insist. One, as mentioned, is to rid himself of any potential tax liabilities, since the buyer assumes these along with the stock. More likely is that the seller had a tax savings motive for selling corporate stock instead of its assets. (See Chapter 17, Selling a Sole Proprietorship.)

B. Buying Shares of Stock

Buyers of the stock of a corporation take over any tax debts of the business—disclosed or not—along with its assets. For instance, a potentially devastating tax bill can be inherited from a corporation that misclassified its employees as independent contractors and so did not file payroll tax returns or make payments to the IRS.

> **EXAMPLE:** Renate buys all of the stock of XTC corporation from Kendra. Unbeknownst to Renate, XTC's employment tax returns were not filed or taxes paid two years ago. When Renate bought the stock, no tax liens had been filed. When the IRS catches on, the corporation will be held liable for the old payroll taxes—whether Renate knew about them or not. She may have a claim against Kendra for not disclosing the tax delinquency, but this is no concern of the IRS. Kendra will also be held liable to the IRS for the payroll taxes.

Part

5

Buying or Selling a Business

Well-drafted business sale contracts include a guarantee from the sellers that the corporation doesn't owe taxes and that the sellers are liable to the buyer (in legal lingo, the sellers agree to "indemnify" the buyer) if this turns out not to be true. (And if past employment taxes aren't paid, the IRS can go after the former owners, too. See Chapter 5, Tax Concerns of Employers.)

If you must buy corporate shares in a small business, see a tax pro and ask about the potential for undisclosed tax liabilities. Do some investigating (discussed just below). But know that even with the best investigation of a corporation and its owners, it's impossible to predict some future tax problems. No one knows whether the IRS (or any state taxing agency) will audit tax returns the corporation filed before you bought its shares.

1. Investigation

Hire a business attorney or tax pro to help check out a seller. Get copies of all business income tax returns and employment tax returns of the business for the last three years. Demand proof from the seller that taxes have been paid. Copies of filed tax forms, along with canceled checks, should be forthcoming. Contact the seller's accountant and tax preparer.

Your expert should look for unreported income, unfiled tax returns and unpaid taxes. Is there anything that doesn't jibe with what corporation records should show? If a red (or at least a pink) flag is raised, probe further. Exactly what to look for depends on the type of business you are buying. For instance, if independent contractors are used in the business, check whether Form 1099s were filed and other IRS reporting rules were met. (See Chapter 5, Tax Concerns of Employers.) If a corporation's tax returns look strange to your tax pro, ask why. If items catch his attention, they might interest an IRS auditor as well.

A well-drafted stock purchase agreement should provide for an inspection of the business books, and the right to back out if irregularities are found. Require selling shareholder(s) to furnish a personal credit report; be suspicious if they won't. Tax liens against the shareholders may show up on their personal credit reports; tax liens against their corporation, however, will not.

 Put a disclosure requirements clause in the purchase contract. It's too late after the agreement is signed. Use a clause something like this one: "Seller agrees to furnish copies of all business income and employment tax returns for the past three years within ten days of acceptance of this offer. Seller will give full access to all business records to buyer or his representative, for the purposes of verifying that there are no present or potential tax liabilities. Seller will provide a copy of a current credit report on all of the majority shareholders of the corporation."

IRS Information. Sellers are not always honest about business income and expenses; they may even show you dummied-up tax returns. Without confirmation from the IRS, you won't know whether or not the returns are the real thing. So, require in your purchase agreement that the seller give you a signed IRS Disclosure (Form 2848D) for the individual shareholders as well as the business. This allows you, or your attorney or tax pro, access to their IRS tax records. Allow at least several weeks for the IRS to send computer printouts showing a business owner's (or corporation's) tax filing and payment history, and if any taxes are owing. Pay particular attention to whether employment tax returns were filed. Compare the tax disclosures the seller provided against the IRS records.

IRS printouts are free, but may be in IRS code and difficult to decipher. Ask a tax pro to read them, or call the IRS and ask for an explanation.

Public Records. Your county records office has books or computer files showing recorded federal and state tax liens against a business or its owners. If taxes are owed, the IRS may have recorded a "Notice of Federal Tax Lien" under the tax ID number (either the Social Security or Employer Identification Number) of the business or its owners. This is not foolproof—the IRS doesn't always file lien notices on tax debtors.

Look up the names of the owners and the business's name in your County Recorder's Office or Land Registry Office. Search records by computer, microfiche readers or handwritten record books. Ask a clerk for help, or hire a credit bureau, title company or attorney to search the records for you.

> **EXAMPLE:** Harold wants to know if Alco Motors, Inc., or Al Coors, its principal shareholder, has any past tax liabilities. He goes to the county records office and searches the name index for "Alco Motors, Inc." and for "Al Coors." Harold looks back ten years, because this is how long a tax lien is normally valid. No liens appear. This is a positive sign, but not a guarantee that Alco Motors or Al Coors doesn't owe taxes—it just means that no liens appear on the records.

State Records. Check for liens with your state's Secretary of State or Department of Corporations (official titles vary from state to state). As with searching local records, you can do it yourself or hire an expert.

One good way to get state info is to send Form UCC-3 to your Secretary of State's office with a small fee. ("UCC" means Uniform Commercial Code, a set of laws that has been adopted in most states.) Forms are usually available from your Secretary of State's office (many of these agencies have their own websites from which you can download forms) or from stationery stores, reference libraries, business attorneys or accountants.

You should get back a UCC filing report showing state tax liens (although these don't always show up), judgment liens and financing liens on business equipment.

2. Indemnification

In an ideal purchase agreement, the seller of stock should promise to pay any taxes and other corporation liabilities discovered after the closing. While this "indemnification clause" obligates the seller to pay any hidden tax liabilities, if he disappears or can't pay, the pledge will be worthless. Your corporation will be stuck with any tax liabilities.

3. Holdbacks and Offsets

Your best protection from unknown tax liabilities when buying stock is to require the seller to keep part of the purchase price (perhaps 5% to 30%) in an account with an escrow company, attorney or bank after closing.

"Holdback" money is earmarked to pay any corporate liabilities, including taxes discovered after the sale. The longer money is held back for contingencies, the better. Understandably, many sellers won't agree to holdbacks for longer than a few months. However, sellers may agree to a longer period if the holdback account pays interest to them.

Alternatively, if you aren't paying for the stock in full (some cash paid up front with an installment promissory note for the balance), you should include an "offset" clause in your agreement. This will let you reduce promissory note payments by the amount of any undisclosed taxes or debts discovered after closing.

C. Assigning a Price to Business Assets

As you negotiate the purchase of a business, you should be evaluating each of its major assets. The tax code requires buyers and sellers to jointly agree on allocations of the purchase price to each business asset or group of assets. Amounts allocated must be at the "fair market value" and be reported to the IRS by each side on identical tax forms.

You will also use these same values to calculate your tax depreciation deduction for each asset, and to figure the taxable gain or loss when you later sell or dispose of the asset or the whole business.

Do not take lightly this valuation of business assets. Consult a tax pro and bring in a professional appraiser for real estate or other valuable assets. Important tax implications are often overlooked in valuing assets. The overall price paid for a business or its assets usually reflects how eager the parties are to make a deal, not how much each item is really worth. Asset value allocations have tax significance to both parties—but especially to a buyer.

Back up major asset valuations with appraisals. Professional appraisals, though not strictly required by the IRS, are recommended, especially for businesses sold for over $100,000. If either side is ever audited, the IRS may question the asset valuations and allocations. If the numbers are not in line with fair market values, the IRS can refigure them. This may result in longer depreciation periods for the assets, which decreases a buyer's annual tax write-offs—and produces an audit bill for the IRS's efforts.

> **EXAMPLE:** Tony buys Ace Tool & Die from Jim for $95,000. After hiring an appraiser to determine the fair market value of each asset, Jim and Tony agree to allocate the purchase price as follows: $65,000 for machinery, $10,000 for goodwill and $20,000 for a patent right. This allocation is reported to the IRS by both sides when they file their tax returns. If either Tony or Jim is audited, they can produce a report from the appraiser backing up their allocations.

1. Classifying Assets for the IRS

The allocation of the business purchase price is reported on Form 8594, Asset Acquisition Statement.

Both buyer and seller file this form along with their individual income tax returns in the year after the transaction.

The IRS allocation reporting process has two steps. First, you must classify the assets into three categories, discussed below. Second, you must assign dollar values to each category according to tax code rules.

Tax code allocation rules create three distinct categories of business assets. (IRC § 1060(a).) The buyer and seller must jointly determine that each asset transferred belongs in one of three tax categories:

- cash and cash-like assets
- tangible property, or
- intangible property.

Let's go through each in some detail.

a. Cash and Cash-Like Assets

Cash and cash-like assets include:

- money, such as petty cash on hand (if any)
- bank and money market accounts (usually the seller cleans these accounts out)
- notes and accounts receivable (money owed to the business when it's sold, if taken over by the new owner). These receivables may be subject to a discounted value if their collectibility is in doubt. Often, buyers do not purchase a business's accounts receivable, so this may not be an issue.
- marketable securities (stocks in other corporations that are readily salable), rarely ever the case in small business transfers.

Cash-like assets is the easiest category, as valuations are usually obvious, with the possible exception of notes and accounts receivable.

b. Tangible Property

Loosely defined, "tangible" means anything you can touch. As applied to business assets, this tax code category includes:

- **Merchandise inventories.** You'll need to determine whether or not all the goods are salable. If some are out-of-date, the value reported may be lowered (discounted) or even listed at no value.
- **Land, leases and buildings.** Get a written opinion of a real estate agent or appraiser for the value of land, leases and buildings. The greater the value of these items, the more expertise is required—you may need to hire a more expensive certified appraiser.
- **Machinery.** For valuable equipment, get a written appraisal or estimate by a dealer who handles this type of machinery.
- **Office furniture and fixtures.** This includes computers and other electronic gear. Unless the items have trivial value, get written estimates from used computer or furniture dealers, if not professional appraisers.

c. Intangible Property

In general, an "intangible" thing can't be touched or physically possessed. Instead, it usually is a legal *right*, which is recognized in a document. Examples are patents, copyrights, trademarks, client or customer lists, trade secrets and covenants not to compete (promises from the seller that he won't go into a similar business for some time in the future). The most common intangible asset of a going concern is "goodwill," which is defined and explained below.

Intangible assets are extremely difficult to value. Significant intangibles should be evaluated by accountants or other experts. But even among experts, opinions of value may vary widely.

The tax code allows a buyer to tax deduct the cost of intangibles over a period of 15 years. So the allocated value for goodwill, customer lists and covenants not to compete is written off (amortized) at the rate of $^1/_{15}$ per year. (IRC § 197.) Accelerated depreciation methods are not allowed for intangible property, meaning it will take a buyer a long time to get the tax benefit for items of intangible property purchased.

What Is Goodwill?

"Goodwill" comprises the reputation and customer relationships of an existing business. If the price paid for a going concern exceeds the fair market value of all the rest of the assets, the IRS considers the excess was paid for goodwill.

EXAMPLE: Sam pays $100,000 for Honest John's Network Communications Emporium. The cash and tangible assets of the business add up to $69,000: $1,000 in the cash drawer, $15,000 in inventory on hand, $3,000 worth of machinery and a building worth $50,000. Why is Sam willing to pay $31,000 above the value of all of its identifiable assets? Because Honest John's has a good location and has made a decent profit for several years. Sam thinks that a lot of John's customers will stick with the business, so he pays this premium for the business's goodwill.

---

2. Assigning Dollar Values to Categories

After buyer and seller have divided assets into the three categories discussed above, each must jointly assign dollar values to each group. These valuations will be used to figure the buyer's tax basis for depreciation—how much tax write-off he gets—and to determine his gain or loss when he later disposes of these assets. (See Chapter 2, Writing Off Business Assets, for details.) Again, this is a good time to bring in a tax pro.

The buyer and the seller must go through a four-step allocation process to complete IRS Form 8594, Asset Acquisition Statement:

1. Subtract the total value of *cash and cash-like* items received (category one, above) from the purchase price.
2. Subtract the fair market values of the *tangible* assets.
3. Allocate any amount of the purchase price remaining to *specifically identifiable intangibles* such as patents, franchises, agreements

not to compete and trademarks, at their fair market values.

4. If there's any amount still not allocated, label it *goodwill*, the last kind of intangible asset.

EXAMPLE: Gunter, a sole proprietor, owns a geothermal energy consulting firm. Kinte agrees to buy his business for $100,000. They make the following asset allocations:

- $1,000 in the business's bank account at the time of the transfer is allocated to "cash."
- $14,500, the fair market value of office equipment included in the deal, goes in the second category, "tangible assets."
- $42,000 is assigned to Gunter's patent on a small geothermal measurement instrument (professionally appraised) and ascribed to the third category, specifically identifiable "intangible assets."
- $42,500, the remaining sum, is attributed to the only category left, "goodwill."

Get the most from asset allocations. A buyer and seller should agree on the allocation of purchase price of assets as part of negotiating the agreement to purchase the business. Because there is almost always flexibility in valuing assets, the buyer should propose the allocation of purchase price in a way that provides the most tax benefit. A tax pro can help you make the analysis.

Typically, you'll want to allocate as much of the purchase price of an established business as possible to assets with the fastest tax write-offs—that is, those with the shortest depreciation periods. If realistic, attribute the lion's share to business equipment. Typically, equipment and fixtures can be tax code depreciated over three, five, seven or ten years.

Conversely, smaller values should be assigned to intangible assets, because they have 15-year tax write-off periods. Commercial real estate, with a depreciation period of 39 years, also means a long time to write off your costs.

If the business has been a loser, you are likely buying its tangible assets only; there won't be any good-

will or an intangible asset allocation to worry about. (See Chapter 2, Writing Off Business Assets.)

D. State and Local Laws

The state, county or city where the business or its assets are located may impose a transfer tax on either the buyer or the seller. This is common whenever real estate changes owners. If the tax is on the seller, then your agreement should provide that it be paid out of escrow at closing. Be aware that if the seller doesn't pay a transfer tax, the taxing agency can usually come after you or the business assets.

Also, some states or localities impose taxes, such as annual personal property taxes, on business fixtures and equipment or on inventory. Make sure that these types of taxes are not delinquent, or are paid at the time of closing—or else you may inherit them.

Finally, check your state's Bulk Sales Law for requirements on notifying creditors of business asset sales (see Chapter 17 for details).

Resources

- IRS Form 8594, Asset Acquisition Statement and Instructions. The instructions provide more details on allocating business assets. A copy of the form is in the Appendix.
- *Legal Guide for Starting & Running a Small Business*, by Fred Steingold (Nolo). This self-help book has a lot of non-tax pointers on buying a business.
- *Tax Guide for Buying and Selling a Business*, by Stanley Hagendorf and Wayne A. Hagendorf (Knowles Publishing, 800-299-0202). This is a fairly sophisticated manual intended for tax professionals.

Selling a Sole Proprietorship

"The business of America is business."

— Calvin Coolidge

This chapter focuses on the consequences of selling a sole proprietorship. The flip side, buying a business, is covered in Chapter 16. To get a well-rounded tax picture, take a look at that chapter, too.

While 85% of all businesses are sole proprietorships, if you are not, go to these other chapters:

- The tax aspects of transferring a partnership (or limited liability company interest) are covered in Chapter 9, Partnerships.
- Selling a corporation's shares is covered in Chapter 8, S Corporations, and Chapter 7, C Corporations.

Congress, realizing that there are opportunities for people to play tax games on business transfers, has enacted laws to ensure that Uncle Sam gets his cut. To pass IRS muster, the sale of a business must be bona fide—that is, the price and terms must be realistic in the business world. If you sell to a stranger, chances are the deal is fair, and the IRS won't bother you as long as you report it and pay any taxes due. But if you deal with a relative or close friend, an IRS auditor may find that the sale terms weren't realistic and hit you with a tax bill.

Selling a Business in a Nutshell

1. Selling a business or its assets is a taxable event, meaning that it usually produces a gain or loss to the seller.
2. Tax rules for sales of a business interest may depend on whether the business is a sole proprietorship, partnership, limited liability company or S or C corporation.
3. A business is a collection of assets. The IRS requires the buyer and seller to allocate the purchase price to specific groups of assets.
4. Transfers of businesses between related parties look suspicious to IRS auditors.

A. Selling Assets of a Sole Proprietorship

A business is just a collection of assets—typically, things like equipment, inventory and goodwill. The tax code requires that sellers and buyers assign a specific value to each asset or groups of similar assets. (The process and rules for allocating the purchase price of a business to specific assets are covered in Chapter 16, Buying a Business.)

Whenever you sell a business asset, you might have a taxable gain, and Uncle Sam wants his share of it. On the other hand, if you have a loss from the sale, there may be a tax savings for you.

> **EXAMPLE:** Harry sells his business, Bagel World, to Sally for $45,000. They agree that the kitchen equipment and ovens are worth $30,000, the furniture $2,000, computers and cash registers $3,000, the store lease $9,000 and the goodwill of the business $1,000. Harry's taxable gain or loss must be figured on each of these items, as discussed below.

You must report the sale of your business to the IRS by attaching Form 8594, Asset Acquisition Statement, to that year's income tax return. Also, you will report any gain or loss on your sale of business assets on Form 4797, Sales of Business Property on that same tax return.

1. Figuring Gain or Loss

Whenever a sole proprietorship business is sold, each asset or group of assets transferred must be analyzed separately for tax consequences.

> **EXAMPLE 1:** Don, who owns Don's Trucking, sells a diesel engine rebuilding machine to Bruce for $15,000. Don paid $30,000 for it and had taken depreciation deductions totaling $20,000 in past years. These deductions reduced Don's tax basis in the machinery to $10,000. (See Chapter 2, Writing Off Business Assets, for an explanation of how basis is determined.) Since

Don sells the machine for $5,000 more than his tax basis, he has a taxable gain of $5,000—even though he sold it for less than he originally paid for it. In a sense, Don is repaying the government for a prior tax deduction taken.

EXAMPLE 2: Now assume Don's machinery is in bad shape and he gets only $8,000 from Bruce—$2,000 less than his tax basis. Don has a loss of $2,000 for tax purposes. His loss produces an additional tax deduction for him.

EXAMPLE 3: Don's machinery became worthless due to technological advances and the unavailability of parts. Don's tax basis is $10,000 when he sells the machinery to Giuseppe, a scrap metal dealer, for $1. Don has a tax loss of $9,999. Don could junk the equipment himself and take a $10,000 tax write-off. However, a documented sale to a third party looks better in case the IRS ever audits.

2. How Gain or Loss Is Taxed

When a sole proprietor sells business assets, the resulting gain or loss is treated like any other business profit or loss. *The tax code's special capital gain and loss rules don't apply when the operating assets of a sole proprietorship are sold.* Any gain is taxed at a sole proprietor's personal tax rate. Likewise, any loss reduces his or her total taxable income.

Save taxes by using an installment sale.
Sellers facing a large taxable gain on the sale of their business might consider selling on the installment plan.

For example, a sale with 20% down and the balance paid over five years (with interest, of course), will spread the tax on the gain over five years. This is a way to, in effect, "income average." Sellers will likely be in a lower tax bracket for each year by structuring the deal as an installment sale. Of course, there is always the risk that the buyer may default. See IRC § 453 for other rules on installment sales, or ask a tax pro whether or not there

would be a tax reason for making an installment sale.

B. The Importance of an Arms-Length Deal

If a business or its assets change hands for an artificially low price, the IRS usually loses out. But sometimes the true sales price is not clear because business transfers may involve exchanges, promissory notes or unusual terms dreamt up by attorneys and accountants.

Even when the sale price looks fair, the terms may not be "commercially reasonable" in the IRS's eyes. For instance, a business sold for no money down and paid off over 50 years at an interest rate of 3%, is not a deal any seller would make without an ulterior motive—most likely, tax avoidance. Such deals often mean a son, daughter or other relative is the buyer. "Sweetheart" deals look more like gifts than business transactions.

The IRS is legally empowered to look past the stated terms of the deal and rewrite it to reflect its true "economic substance."

However, if you make an "arms-length" deal with an unrelated party, the IRS normally doesn't question it. After all, why would you help a stranger? On the other hand, if you sell your business to a family member—directly or indirectly—you could face an IRS audit adjustment. While the IRS doesn't routinely monitor sales of businesses, if an auditor raises the issue, it's your burden to prove this was a bona fide business transaction. The IRS can disregard your figures and terms if the auditor is not convinced, and if doing so would result in an increased tax bill.

EXAMPLE: Bill, a sole proprietor nearing 70 and in poor health, sells his coffee shop chain, Moonbucks, to his son Junior for $100,000. This price equals Bill's tax basis in the business assets of Moonbucks. It doesn't include any value for the tremendous amount of goodwill the business has built up. Any other buyer would be glad to pay $1 million for Moonbucks. So by selling to

Junior at the bargain price, Bill is avoiding income taxes, and estates as well (see below). If Bill were audited, the IRS would hit him with taxes on an additional $900,000 of income, because this was not an arms-length deal.

The Estate Tax Angle

Income taxes aren't the IRS's only concern when family members are involved. The IRS is also looking ahead to collecting federal estate taxes someday. As discussed in Chapter 12, Family Businesses, everyone may leave $675,000 (2001) free of estate tax. Over the next few years the estate tax exemption will gradually increase to $3.5 million by 2009, and the estate tax will be repealed entirely in 2010. However, this repeal "sunsets" or expires in 2010 unless Congress renews it, so stay in touch with your tax advisor for the latest changes. Until repeal of the estate tax, anything over the exempt amount may be taxed starting at 37% and going as high as 55% (although this top rate will gradually decrease to 45%, until the estate tax is repealed in 2010). To avoid estate tax, older business owners have a strong incentive to sell to relatives for bargain prices, or on special terms.

EXAMPLE: After he sells Moonbucks (worth $1 million) to his son for $100,000, Bill's total estate is valued at $500,000—well below the amount that can be passed at his death tax-free. However, if Bill owned Moonbucks at his death, his estate would be $1,400,000, producing a hefty federal estate tax. So, besides beating the income tax law by selling Moonbucks to Junior for $100,000, his estate escapes estate tax as well. (See Chapter 12, Family Businesses, for some tax advantageous but legal ways to minimize estate taxes when transferring businesses to family members.)

C. How to Protect Yourself From IRS Challenges

There is no way to "IRS-proof" yourself when selling your business, but you can do several things to reduce the odds of an IRS attack.

1. Set a Reasonable Price and Terms

Except in very small deals, have your business assets evaluated by an expert in the field. Valuation specialists include accountants and business brokers. A seller of new or used equipment or a dealer in the same type of merchandise can evaluate your assets or make offers. Keep the written opinion or offer of these experts in case the IRS auditor comes calling.

 If you are making a special deal to family or friends, there are some legitimate steps to save taxes. For instance, transferring your business over several years instead of all at once may be a tax planning opportunity (or loophole, if you like). The tax law recognizes a "minority interest" discount. It works likes this: Whenever you sell less than all of your business—for instance, a one-third interest to your brother-in-law—you are allowed to discount the value of this sale of a minority interest for tax reporting. The larger the discount, the less taxable gain to you from the sale. Reductions of 40% off the value of a minority interest in a business have been upheld in the courts against IRS attacks. (See Chapter 12, Family Businesses, and run this by a tax pro before claiming a minority interest discount.)

2. Observe the Formalities

Selling an enterprise doesn't require any special formalities. The deal can be written on the back of a napkin, for all the IRS cares. The IRS's only interest is whether it is losing any taxes that should have been paid on the transaction, so you will have to report the sale.

Just the same, the more "legal" a deal appears to be, the less likely the IRS is to challenge its tax implications at an audit. That doesn't mean you can make anything fly with a lot of legal boilerplate and neat typing, but you are ahead of the game if you can show you followed normal business formalities.

IRS auditors are fairly unsophisticated about business practices, but some develop a keen sense of smell when something isn't quite right. Using an attorney and producing a raft of supporting documents lends an air of legitimacy to the deal. For all but the smallest deals, have a business attorney by your side. A tax pro should be consulted as well if the size of the deal justifies the expense. Keep in mind the professional fees are tax deductible—which makes them easier to swallow.

3. Allocate Asset Values Fairly

When a business—or substantially all of its assets—is sold, both the buyer and seller must assign values in writing to assets being transferred. Usually the IRS accepts the valuations, but an auditor may question whether the overall price is fair and if the parties are related (as discussed above.)

The seller and buyer must attach an identical Form 8594, Asset Acquisition Statement, to their tax returns. If the forms aren't identical, an IRS computer cross-check might discover the discrepancy and audit the buyer or the seller or both. (See Chapter 16, Section C, for details on this form and for tips on allocating values to business assets.)

⚠ Bulk Sales Notice. All states require that sellers of a business or a major portion of its assets notify all creditors of the business before the sale. This notification is a formal process called a "Bulk

Sale" in most states, which may require publication in a local newspaper. Check with your legal advisor to make sure you are in compliance.

4. Keep Your Records After the Sale

Business good records will help you market your enterprise, but don't turn original records over to the buyer. The reason is that you remain responsible for an IRS audit bill for the period up until the business was sold. Normally, you have three tax years after the year the business is sold to worry about an audit; to be on the safe side, keep records six years. (See Chapter 19, Audits.)

Resources

- IRS Publication 537, Installment Sales.
- IRS Publication 544, Sales & Other Dispositions of Assets
- IRS Form 4797, Sales of Business Property
- IRS Form 8594, Asset Acquisition Statement and Instructions. The instructions provide more details than are given here. (A copy of the form is in the Appendix.)
- *Legal Guide for Starting & Running a Small Business*, by Fred Steingold (Nolo). This self-help book has a lot of non-tax pointers for sellers of a business.
- *Tax Guide for Buying and Selling a Business*, by Stanley Hagendorf and Wayne A. Hagendorf (Knowles Publishing, 800-299-0202). This is a fairly sophisticated manual intended for tax professionals.

Part

5

Buying or Selling a Business

When You Can't Pay Your Taxes

"Creditors have better memories than debtors."
— Benjamin Franklin

The IRS has enormous legal powers to collect past due taxes—it is tougher than any other bill collector you're ever likely to face, with the possible exception of the Mafia. The IRS can seize just about anything that you own, including your bank account, home and wages. The IRS doesn't need a court order or judgment before closing your business and grabbing your property. In most cases, the IRS only has to send you a "demand letter" before it acts—and in some circumstances, it isn't compelled to give you any warning at all. The IRS can even close your business down by seizing your assets or padlocking your doors.

The awesome IRS collection machine won't crush you if you know how it works and you know your legal options. For instance, you can bargain for more time to pay or maybe for a reduction of the amount owed. If your financial situation is truly dire, you can request to be put "on hold" while the IRS bothers other poor souls.

One crucial thing to remember, if you're behind on taxes and want to stay in business, is to keep in touch with the IRS. A business is a sitting target; it can't run. The worst thing you can do when you get behind in your taxes is to bury your head in the sand. The IRS might leave you alone for a while, but usually not for long.

Father Time is especially cruel to tax debts—they grow larger every day with mounting interest and penalties. Unless you are out of business, flat broke, unemployed and likely to remain that way, IRS tax collectors will be hovering.

On the plus side, the IRS collection machine is slow to start and react, which gives you time to plan your next move. You'll get a raft of computerized tax bills and maybe IRS telephone calls, too. It might be months or even several years before you have to confront the IRS face-to-face. With limited personnel, the IRS tries everything before assigning a real person to your case. Don't get too comfortable, though, just because no one knocks on your door. Every year the computerized IRS collection system gets bigger, faster and meaner. Computer-generated tax liens and levies can make your life every bit as miserable as human collectors can.

IRS Collections in a Nutshell

1. The IRS has legal powers that no other debt collector has; it can seize bank accounts and just about anything else that you own—sometimes without warning.
2. You don't have to disclose financial information to an IRS collector unless you are formally served with a summons.
3. The IRS can, but rarely does, shut businesses down—usually for unpaid payroll taxes.
4. Tax debtors may pay off old tax bills in monthly installments, but interest—and maybe penalties, too—is always running.
5. Some folks can make a deal with the IRS to settle a tax bill for pennies on the dollar through the Offer in Compromise process.
6. If you file for bankruptcy, you may be able to hold off the IRS and wipe out some tax debts—but you can never wipe out payroll tax debts.

The strategies discussed in this chapter are covered at length in *Stand Up to the IRS*, by Frederick W. Daily (Nolo).

A. If You Owe Less Than $25,000

If you owe less than $25,000, chances are your account is a fairly low IRS priority. It may be a lot of money to you, but it's small potatoes to the IRS. Often, the IRS won't assign a case to a collector if the balance due is less than $25,000—but will hound you by mail and telephone.

⚠ If you owe business payroll taxes, there is no minimum threshold for vigorous collection efforts. Chapter 5, Tax Concerns of Employers, explains how the IRS pursues business owners who fall behind on payroll taxes.

B. Getting More Time to Pay

Generally, if you can't pay a tax bill you have received, the first thing to do is call or write to the IRS at the number or address on the bill and request more time. A request for a 30- to 60-day delay is usually honored if you haven't called more than once or twice before. If asked, explain why you need the extra time—for example, because you are applying for a loan or waiting for a customer to pay up.

💡 Request more time to pay even if you won't be able to meet the new deadline. It is easier to get several short extensions—a month or two— than one long one. This is the way the IRS operates, presumably to keep the pressure on you.

If you are granted a reprieve by phone, you may not get anything in writing from the IRS to confirm your deal. A new due date will be entered into the computer, but don't expect a reminder from the IRS when the time is up. Note the new deadline on your calendar; then contact the IRS before it is up if you still need more time. You may have to make a partial payment to get more time.

C. Paying in Installments

If you need more than a few months, ask the IRS for an installment payment agreement. If it's granted, you pay the IRS monthly, like a credit card balance. And, as with your Visa or MasterCard, an interest charge is added. The IRS also imposes a $43 "user fee" for setting up an installment plan. A monthly payment plan relieves you of the worry that the IRS will seize your wages or assets—as long as you make payments.

You have no legal right to pay overdue taxes in installments, but the IRS usually agrees to monthly payments. The hitch is that you must show you can't pay your bill in full from your present resources. Indeed, the Taxpayer Bill of Rights (IRS Publication 1) says that you have the right to propose an installment agreement, and that the IRS must fairly consider it.

To request to pay in installments, call or write to the IRS. If writing, send a copy of the tax bill or, even better, file IRS Form 9465, Request for Installment Payments. If you have already been in contact with a name at the IRS, direct your request directly to her. If the IRS agrees, you'll get written confirmation and monthly payment vouchers. For more information, see *Stand Up to the IRS*, by Frederick W. Daily (Nolo).

As mentioned above, the IRS is tough on payroll tax delinquencies, and may not allow you a long-term payment plan for this type of tax debt.

Time Limit on IRS to Collect Tax Debts

There is some justice, even in the tax world. The law limits the IRS to ten years from the date a tax is assessed to collect it. (IRC § 6402(a).) After that, you are home free! However, taking certain actions—filing for bankruptcy, making an Offer in Compromise or signing an IRS extension form— can lengthen the time limit beyond ten years. Nevertheless, since a business failure or other catastrophe can put you into a very deep tax hole, it is comforting to know that there is some light at the end of the tunnel.

Part
6

Dealing With the IRS

1. Interest and Penalties

There is no free lunch with the IRS. A major downside to paying the IRS on the installment plan is that interest and late-payment penalties keep adding up. Recently, interest and penalties run at a combined rate of 12–14% per year. If your installment payments are low and the unpaid balance sufficiently large, you may find the balance owing the IRS is increasing every month.

> EXAMPLE: Brenda is audited and is found to owe the IRS $40,000 for back payroll taxes from her failed graphic design studio. The IRS determines Brenda can pay a maximum of $400 per month. She is also charged 14% interest and penalties, adding $5,600 per year to her bill. One year later, after paying $400 per month, Brenda owes $40,800, which is $800 more than her original bill! (Brenda has some other alternatives in dealing with the IRS, discussed below.)

2. Under $25,000 Payment Plans

If you owe less than $25,000, chances are that you can get an installment payment plan. Generally, your proposed payments must be sufficient to pay the bill in full within 36 months. Monthly payments must be equal. Interest, around 8%–9% annually, and late payment penalties of ¼% per month, will be running. You can always make larger payments than called for in the plan, but if you send less, the plan can be canceled. If you can't make a full payment, call the IRS to ask for permission.

The IRS is tougher on payroll taxes. If you owe back payroll taxes—in any amount—the IRS may not allow you to use the IRS Form 9465 procedure for requesting an installment plan. It may require detailed financial information and faster payoffs.

3. Over $25,000 Payment Plans

If you owe over $25,000, your monthly payment amount is whatever the IRS perceives as your "maximum ability" to pay. This is determined by the IRS's evaluation of the financial information it has gotten from you and recorded on its "collection information statements." (These forms are discussed in Section D, below.)

The IRS rarely accepts less than $50 per month; payment plans can be as high as $5,000 per month—it all depends on your financial circumstances. The IRS welcomes any payments over the agreed-upon amount. Prepaying cuts down the interest and penalty charges that always continue to run during the installment plan.

If the IRS asks for more in monthly payments than you can afford—as is frequently the case—you can attempt to negotiate. How successful you are may depend on your powers of persuasion.

 Make sure your requests get to the right IRS department. When writing about a bill, always send the IRS a copy of the notice, using the bar-coded IRS return envelope that came with it. This ensures that your request for more time or an installment agreement gets to the right department in time to keep things from getting out of hand.

4. If You Fall Behind on Your Payments

If you get into an installment plan, make the payments faithfully each month. If you don't, the IRS can void the agreement and start seizing your bank accounts and other property without further notice.

If you just can't make a payment, call and write to the IRS and explain your circumstances. Ask that the agreement not be defaulted. If it is reinstated, you may be charged an additional fee of $24 for this privilege. Promise to catch up in the next month or request that the monthly amount be lowered because of an unexpected reversal of fortune. The IRS may be sympathetic and go along if you stay in touch.

D. What to Expect When the IRS Gets Serious

If you get behind on taxes, a raft of threatening past due notices and many months may pass before the IRS gets serious. If you owe more than $10,000 in income taxes, or payroll taxes in any amount, you may be called or visited by an IRS Revenue Officer—the elite collectors of the IRS. These folks are to be both feared and respected for their powers.

1. The Sneak Attack

Revenue Officers usually show up at your business or home unannounced, often before 9 or after 5. The collector will start grilling you right then and there.

Keep calm and resist the urge to curse your luck or the IRS. Instead of talking to the IRS Officer on the spot, say that you need time to get financial information together. Emphasize that you want to deal with your tax problems and will meet her at the IRS office within a week or two. Most Revenue Officers will go along if you seem sincere. Avoid making any financial commitments to pay at this time unless you are absolutely certain you can follow through.

2. Meeting With the Collector

At the interview, the IRS Officer will ask for information about your business and personal finances. This data is usually recorded on two IRS Collection Information Statement forms: Form 433-A is used for your personal finances, and Form 433-B for your business's assets, liabilities, income and expenses. After these forms are completed, you will be asked to read, verify and sign them.

It is a good idea to know what information the IRS wants before the meeting with the Revenue Officer. Obtain copies of Forms 433-A and 433-B from IRS offices, at http://www.irs.gov, or by calling 800-829-1040. They are also reprinted in *Stand Up to the IRS*, by Frederick W. Daily (Nolo).

Don't be rushed into signing a 433 form. Data on these forms is the key to further IRS collection efforts, so their importance can't be overemphasized. A misstatement on these forms—intentional or not—is not easy to correct, and you'll lose vital credibility with the tax collector. She has a great deal of discretion whether to hammer you or cut you some slack.

Resist pressure from a Revenue Officer to complete and sign the financial forms at the first interview. Ask to take them home and return them later. Expect her to resist, but hold your ground! Explain that you want to be sure everything is correct and your memory is not good enough to do it right then and there; you need to check your records first.

Beware of the "necessary living expenses" trap. When filling out IRS Form 433-A, pay strict attention to the "necessary living expenses" questions. This is the crucial area in the IRS determination of how big your payments must be (or what kind of Offer in Compromise it will accept, as discussed in Section E, below). The IRS expects you to sacrifice by keeping a minimal lifestyle until the tax debt is paid off. Showing expenses for private schools, trips to Hawaii or Champagne-and-caviar grocery bills won't be tolerated.

Don't underestimate your family's living expenses—list where every penny goes every month. Write in the "comments" section on the 433-A form if your expenses will increase in the near future (a baby is on the way, your car needs a new transmission and so on). If your income is likely to decrease, your spouse is about to be laid off or one of your major customers has declared bankruptcy, mention that as well. Paint it black.

Part

6

Dealing With the IRS

Are Your Personal Assets at Risk?

Whether or not the IRS can come after your personal assets for business-related taxes—or for your business assets when you owe personal taxes—depends on the form of your business entity and the type of taxes owed.

If you operate as a *sole proprietorship*, there is no legal distinction between your business and you. Accordingly, the IRS can grab just about anything you own for any kind of tax debt.

If you are in a *partnership* or *limited liability company*, the IRS can go after your share in property owned by the company. The IRS can also tag the personal assets of any general partner for 100% of a tax debt of the partnership.

If your business is *incorporated*, your personal assets may or may not be shielded. Conversely, because a corporation is a separate tax entity from its owners, the IRS can't seize corporation assets for bills owed by its shareholders. However, if shareholders are using the corporation just to keep assets away from the IRS, the IRS may be able to reach them. (That's why it's critical to observe corporate formalities.) If, however, a corporation owes payroll taxes, the IRS can go directly after personal assets of all responsible shareholders (as discussed in Chapter 5, Tax Concerns of Employers).

On the other side of the coin, while the IRS can't take corporate assets to satisfy your personal tax debts, it can seize your shares of stock in a corporation. But since stock of a small business corporation is difficult to sell, the IRS rarely bothers to take it.

3. Actions the Tax Collector Can Take

Entrepreneurs are natural-born optimists. Typically, when small business people get behind on their bills—including taxes—they believe that things will "turn around" any day and they'll pay back everyone.

IRS collectors, however, are born pessimists. They want their money now, not pie in the sky. If you don't pay, the IRS will ask for a list of everyone who owes you money (your business's accounts receivable), and the name of your bank. This gives the IRS a road map for places to go to seize assets—which can force you out of business real fast.

After analyzing your finances, a Revenue Officer can proceed in one or more of the following ways:

- Demand immediate payment of the full amount if she believes you can pay without much difficulty.
- Ask you to apply for a loan from at least two financial institutions.
- Tell you to sell any assets not currently used in your business, or personal items she considers extravagant—for example, a second home or a pleasure boat.
- Propose an IRS installment agreement allowing monthly payments. (See Section C, above.)
- Suggest you submit an Offer in Compromise (see Section E, below) to settle the tax bill for less than the balance due.
- Begin "enforced collection" against your business—and maybe personal—assets. This means seizing bank accounts, accounts receivable, equipment and other things you own. (See Section F, below.)
- Report your file as "currently uncollectible," if she can't locate enough assets or income for even a nominal payment. Even the IRS has heard about getting blood from turnips. In IRS lingo, this is called "53-ing" a case. If you are in desperate straits, a collector can submit IRS Form 53 to her superiors. If approved, IRS collection efforts are suspended, but interest and penalties continue to mount.

Suspension doesn't last forever—every six to 18 months, the IRS computer will bring up your account. You may be contacted and asked to update your financial situation. If you rejoin the ranks of the employed while on 53 status, the IRS expects you to notify them—but they won't find out automatically.

Regardless of which course the IRS collector pursues, she will demand that—if your business is still operating—you are current on all required tax filings. These include personal income tax returns and business payroll tax returns (if you have employees). If you are taking income from your sole proprietorship, limited liability company or partnership, you will be required to make quarterly estimated tax payments as well. She will want to see evidence that these filings are current or else she won't cut you any slack.

⚠️ **If you don't pay payroll taxes, your business is in jeopardy.** The IRS will aggressively move to shut down a business with employees if it is operating without making current payroll tax deposits. You may be allowed to keep your doors open if you owe payroll taxes for past periods, but only if you keep current on new taxes. You can then agree to a payment plan for old ones. Otherwise the IRS will shut you down to stop the tax losses to the government from growing.

Will the IRS Close Down Your Business?

Revenue Officers will do whatever it takes to scare you into coming up with money to pay your back taxes. But their bark is often worse than their bite. In fact, at the IRS, padlocking the doors of a delinquent taxpayer's business is considered an admission of failure, not a badge of honor. It doesn't usually result in revenue for the government, because auction sales of business equipment typically don't bring much in—often not enough to cover the costs of seizing, storing, advertising and selling the items. Realistically, a shutdown is unlikely because it is simply too much trouble and paperwork. The effort required keeps the collectors from working on more potentially productive cases.

4. Cooperating With the Collector

As mentioned, IRS collectors typically ask where you bank and for a list of the business's accounts receivable. Obviously, the IRS can use this information to start grabbing. While lying to any IRS employee is a crime, not answering questions is legal. If you don't provide financial data, the IRS won't beat you with rubber hoses or throw you in jail. The worst that can happen is that an IRS collector may issue a summons—a legally enforceable order requiring you to appear and provide information under oath. If a collector issues a summons, it usually means she suspects you of hiding assets. However, the IRS doesn't issue summonses very often.

If you do receive an IRS summons, don't ignore it. This could get you hauled in front of a federal judge and jailed. If you have few assets, or the IRS already knows about them, you probably have little to lose by cooperating. If you are still in business and have substantial assets, talk to a tax attorney before answering a summons.

E. Dealing With a Monster Tax Bill

Sad to say, lots of people have huge tax bills and little hope of ever being able to pay.

> **EXAMPLE:** The Smiths' computer store was faced with a new deep-discounting competitor across the street. Trying to keep their business afloat, the Smiths ran up $800,000 in debts— including $300,000 to the IRS for payroll taxes— before calling it quits. Sam Smith went to work as a salesperson, earning $25,000 per year, and Jeannie Smith now earns $15,000 a year as a part-time bank teller. The Smiths' combined earnings are less than the annual IRS interest and penalties on their $300,000 tax bill. Even if they cut expenses to the bone, they will probably never be able to pay off their tax bill. What should the Smiths do? Hint: The answer is not "move to Brazil."

Part

6

Dealing With the IRS

Take heart—there are ways to reduce or even eliminate gargantuan tax bills. One way is the Offer in Compromise. For some folks, another solution is bankruptcy. Let's look at both possibilities.

1. The Offer in Compromise

Under its Offer in Compromise program, the IRS sometimes accepts a few cents on the dollar and calls things square. (IRC §§ 57(10)1, 7122.) For example, in 1994, after hounding country singer Willie Nelson since 1980, the IRS accepted a final compromise settlement of $9 million on a $32 million tax bill. The IRS claims to now accept over half of the Offers in Compromise that are properly submitted and not ridiculous.

Don't think that the IRS takes the forgiving of any tax debt lightly. It will accept less only if it is doubtful more will be collected later. To get the IRS to accept an Offer in Compromise, you must demonstrate to the IRS that it's in its—not your—best interests.

An Offer in Compromise *must* be made on IRS Form 656. It must be accompanied by a completed IRS Form 433-A (individual) and, if you are still in business, Form 433-B (business) financial statements. (These are the forms used in all IRS collection situations, discussed in Section D, above.)

If your offer is deemed processable, you'll be asked to provide verification—such as bank statements for the past three to 12 months, expense receipts, vehicle titles, mortgage notes, rental and lease agreements and a list of outstanding debts. A collector may even want to see your home or business, so she can observe your assets and lifestyle firsthand.

EXAMPLE: The Smiths, whose failed computer business left them with $300,000 in tax debts, make an Offer in Compromise. They give a Form 433-A and documentation to verify their poor financial state. Form 433-B is not necessary, because the Smiths are no longer in business. After losing most of their assets to creditors, the Smiths' financial form is relatively simple. They offer the IRS $25,000, to be provided by Jeannie's mother. Will the IRS accept this? I think the Smiths have a good shot.

For details on how to present an Offer to the IRS, see Chapter 6 of *Stand Up to the IRS*, by Frederick W. Daily (Nolo).

2. Bankruptcy

Bankruptcy laws may be changing. As of this writing, Congress has overhauled the bankruptcy code. This bill is currently in committee where the House and Senate versions are being reconciled. When it emerges, it will probably be signed by the president. If these laws go into effect, they will make bankruptcy much less attractive—and more onerous—for bankruptcy filers. Go to Nolo's Debt & Bankruptcy Law Center at http://www.nolo.com for the latest information.

Bankruptcy offers another way out to some small business owners who have impossibly large bills. Despite IRS misinformation to the contrary, it is possible to wipe out certain business and personal federal tax debts—but not all kinds of taxes—through the federal bankruptcy courts. Although the details of bankruptcy are beyond the scope of this book, let's briefly review the tax effects of a filing a petition under the U.S. Bankruptcy Code.

The Automatic Stay

One of the most alluring features of filing for bankruptcy is the "automatic stay." It works like this: The moment you file a bankruptcy petition, all creditors—including the IRS—are stopped cold. No further seizures, or even threats, can be made by the IRS for as long as your case is pending. Some folks file bankruptcy just to buy time, without ever intending to follow through—simply to stop the IRS from seizing property or otherwise putting them out of business.

A variety of bankruptcy code options are available to small business people. These are usually referred to by the number given to their location in the federal bankruptcy code: Chapter 7, Chapter 11, Chapter 12 and Chapter 13. As you will see, each chapter allows you to get a different kind of "relief" from your tax problems.

a. Chapter 7

Straight liquidation bankruptcy, called Chapter 7, allows anyone to wipe out unsecured debts—including older income taxes. However, payroll taxes or Trust Fund Recovery Penalty taxes can never be wiped out in bankruptcy.

The rules get complicated fast, but bankruptcy may be the answer to your prayers if you qualify.

Income taxes due more than *three* years ago can be wiped out in a Chapter 7 bankruptcy, if:

- tax returns for these debts were filed at least two years ago, and
- the tax bill has been on the IRS's books (assessed) for at least 240 days.

EXAMPLE: As a result of the failure of their business in 1998, Tom and Barbara Keene owe $500,000 to general creditors and $300,000 in payroll taxes to the IRS. They owe another $20,000 for their jointly filed individual income taxes for 1998, which they weren't able to pay when the return was filed on April 15, 1999. This is added to the $70,000 they owe the IRS from an audit of the 1993 tax return, completed January 15, 2002.

The Keenes file a Chapter 7 bankruptcy in May 2002. The general creditor bills of $500,000 can be wiped out. The $300,000 in payroll taxes are not dischargeable. The $20,000 of 1998 individual taxes are dischargeable after April 15, 2001 (three years after they were due). The added $70,000 audit debt does not qualify for discharge because the bankruptcy wasn't filed more than 240 days after January 15, 2001.

Obviously, bankruptcy is not for everyone. See *Bankruptcy: Is It the Right Solution to Your Debt Problems?*, by Robin Leonard (Nolo) for more information.

b. Chapter 13

Bankruptcy repayment plans for wage earners and self-employed folks are known as Chapter 13 plans. This provision permits any debtor (except a corporation) to repay debts monthly, including any kind of taxes. There are some restrictions on who can use Chapter 13. (Chapter 12 gives farmers a repayment option similar to Chapter 13.)

When filing for Chapter 13, you propose a plan based on the amount of income you have to pay creditors on a monthly basis. Repayment plans usually last three years, but the bankruptcy judge may allow up to five years. A plan must provide for full payment of some types of debts, but other debts can be reduced or even wiped out in the discretion of the court. Tax bills arising within three years must be paid in full through the plan—but interest and penalties stop accruing once the petition is filed. If the income tax bill is over three years old, it may be reduced or even eliminated by the judge in a Chapter 13 plan.

A Chapter 13 bankruptcy can cover up to $250,000 of unsecured debts (this includes tax debts) and $750,000 of secured debts (such as a mortgage).

> **EXAMPLE:** Jim and Jackie Jones owe creditors a total of $90,000, including $40,000 in income taxes which are more than three years old. The Joneses file for Chapter 13 bankruptcy and propose a debt repayment plan of $500 per month to the court. If the bankruptcy judge approves the plan, they will be ordered to make monthly payments to a bankruptcy trustee for a period of 36 to 60 months.
>
> After that time, the balance of the debts, including those owed to the IRS, can be discharged by the court. The reason the IRS does not have to be paid in full is because the taxes were for periods of more than three years before the Chapter 13 was filed.

c. Chapter 11

Chapter 11, called a bankruptcy "reorganization," is similar to Chapter 13 in that it requires at least partial repayment of debts. Chapter 11 works for those with debts in excess of Chapter 13 limits. Chapter 11, while open to individuals or any type of business, is too complicated and expensive for most small businesses. A "fast-track" Chapter 11 procedure, for small businesses with debts up to $2 million, simplifies the procedures somewhat, but you still will need a good bankruptcy attorney by your side.

F. When the IRS Can Take Your Assets

If you and the IRS don't agree on payment of back taxes, or you don't file for bankruptcy, you face what the IRS calls "enforced collection." This usually means a tax *lien* and *levy.*

1. Federal Tax Liens

If you owe a tax bill, the IRS may record a "notice of federal tax lien" in the public records in your county. (IRC § 6323(f).) A recorded lien shows the world, or at least anyone who bothers to look, that you have a federal tax debt and the original amount you owe. Lien notices are often picked up and reported in local newspapers and business publications. Credit bureaus collect and report tax lien information and sell it to interested parties.

A tax lien becomes a legal charge against your property, much like a mortgage or deed of trust on real estate. A tax lien is usually the kiss of death to a credit rating. Congress grants the IRS the right to take just about any property that you own to satisfy a tax lien. Lenders will shun you, and others may fear that the IRS might grab their money or goods in your possession.

Ordinarily, the IRS records a tax lien if you owe more than $10,000 and you don't agree to pay it off within a year. The IRS doesn't always file a tax lien notice; it is hit or miss. Whenever you are dealing with a collector, request the IRS not to file a lien. Once on your records, it is very difficult to get a tax lien removed without making full payment to the IRS.

2. Federal Tax Levies: Seizing Property

A tax lien notice doesn't take any of your property —a tax levy does. A levy occurs when the IRS physically seizes your property to satisfy a tax debt. The IRS may grab something directly from you (such as your office equipment), or it may make a written demand to someone holding your property (your bank, for example). A levy may follow closely behind a tax lien notice, or happen without a tax lien being filed, or it may never happen at all.

Property seizures are most likely when you refuse to deal with the tax problem or can't be located by the IRS. When you hear about the IRS padlocking a business or taking someone's home, you can bet it didn't come out of the blue. The IRS first warns the individual or business owner of its intent.

Once the IRS has your property, it is not easy to get it back. You'll need to show it's in the IRS's best interest to release it. For instance, you might get back an essential business asset if losing it means you will have to close your doors, and thus be deprived of any means to pay your tax debt.

> **EXAMPLE:** Harry, owner of Pavco, a road contracting business, owes $75,000 in back payroll taxes. The IRS seizes his paving trucks, effectively putting Harry out of business. He might offer to pay $10,000 per month for the next five months if the IRS will release the trucks. With his trucks back, Harry can stay in business. Otherwise, the IRS will auction off Harry's trucks and use the proceeds toward his tax debts.

a. What the IRS Can Take

The IRS usually seizes bank accounts first, because it just takes the push of a button. A computer-generated levy form is sent to any financial institution that the IRS even suspects holds money for you. The next most popular IRS target is your wages—even if due from your own corporation. And if you are self-employed and have received payments in past years that show up on their computer (usually on Form 1099), the IRS can send levy notices to the payors.

The IRS can also intercept any money owed you for goods or services. Tax refunds from the IRS or states are taken automatically. If he can find it, an officer can grab money or property held for you by relatives or friends.

Most anything you own is subject to IRS levy, including your residence—no matter what your

state homestead laws provide—as well as your pension plans. Thankfully, the IRS does not aggressively go after homes and retirement plans because of the political heat and bad publicity generated. The IRS wants to be perceived as tough, but not heartless. The IRS won't usually levy until it has tried, and failed, to get your cooperation by a payment plan, selling assets or taking other positive steps to deal with your tax debt.

 It can make sense to stonewall an IRS request for information, at least in the short term. Never lie to an IRS collector about anything. Instead, say something like, "I intend to pay the money I owe as soon as possible. I take my debt seriously and am sincerely trying to make the necessary money. I'm sorry, but for my own peace of mind, I can't divulge private information about my bank accounts or other assets." The collector won't be overjoyed, but she won't throw you in chains, either. Use the time to plan on how to deal with your tax problem. The IRS isn't going to go away.

b. What the IRS Cannot Take

Some of your assets are exempt from IRS seizure by law. The IRS won't take the shirt off of your back or the clothes in your closet. Unfortunately, the assets that are exempt from IRS levy have fairly low dollar values.

The IRS can't touch your family's wardrobe, personal effects (under $2,500 in value), tools of your trade (up to $1,250 in value) or a portion of your wages as determined by IRS tables. (IRC § 6334(a).)

> **EXAMPLE:** Brian and Wynona, a married couple with two small children, had a retail seafood business that failed. They are now working for Wal-Mart. If they don't negotiate a deal—such as a payment plan—and the IRS levies their wages, they'll be allowed to keep only about $250 per week, total. The balance goes to the IRS. Unless the couple owns valuable assets (a

race car, vacation home, boats and so forth), the IRS is highly unlikely to seize any of their personal property.

Before seizing assets from your business premises, the IRS will ask for your permission. If you refuse, the IRS can legally remove things from the public areas of the business, such as the cash drawer, furniture and equipment. However, the IRS must get a court order to seize anything in non-public areas.

The IRS cannot come into your home to seize assets, unless you agree or the officer has a court order. As a practical matter, the IRS rarely seeks court orders.

EXAMPLE: The IRS levies on Yick Wo's Chinese restaurant's assets. It can empty out the cash register, but can't remove the woks from the kitchen—unless Yick Wo agrees or the IRS has a court order.

3. Getting Liens and Levies Released

To remove a tax lien from your property, the IRS usually wants at least partial payment. A typical scenario for small business folks is when they find a buyer for their business assets, but the IRS has recorded a tax lien. Typically the IRS won't approve the transfer free of the tax lien unless it receives virtually all of the proceeds of the sale. The collector must also be convinced that the assets are being sold for their market value.

EXAMPLE: Valjean, who owns a motorcycle repair shop he operates as a sole proprietorship, owes a $40,000 tax audit bill. The IRS collector threatens to shut the operation down and sell off the contents of the shop. Booger, Valjean's mechanic, offers to buy the shop's tools and equipment for $20,000. To get the IRS to go along with the sale and grant a partial release of the tax lien, Valjean must convince the IRS that $20,000 is as much as they could get at an auction. Valjean won't get any money from the sale, but will get a $20,000 reduction of his tax bill.

Resources

- IRS Publication 594, *Understanding the Collection Process*. This is a short, relatively clearly written pamphlet.
- *Stand Up to the IRS*, by Frederick W. Daily (Nolo). This book discusses solving IRS collection problems in greater detail than is given in this chapter. It also contains many useful forms for dealing with the IRS.
- *Bankruptcy: Is It the Right Solution to Your Debt Problems?*, by Robin Leonard (Nolo). This book explains bankruptcy alternatives and how to handle your own Chapter 7 bankruptcy case.
- *Chapter 13 Bankruptcy: Repay Your Debts*, by Robin Leonard (Nolo). This book explains how to use Chapter 13 of the bankruptcy code to pay off your tax debts.

Audits

"It is not the thief who is hanged, but one who was caught stealing."

— **H. L. Mencken**

An audit is an IRS examination of you as well as of your tax return. The IRS's goal is to verify that your tax return accurately reflects your income and tax-deductible expenses. Besides looking at your records, auditors make subjective decisions about your honesty.

As a small business owner, you are four times more likely to be audited than other folks. Although odds are low in any one year, if you stay in business very long, chances are you'll be audited at least once. And if irregularities are found, audit lightning is likely to strike again. Indeed, a few business owners with a record of being fast and loose are audited every year or two.

How to prepare for, avoid and defend yourself in an audit is covered in detail in *Stand Up to the IRS* by Frederick W. Daily (Nolo). The fraud and criminal chapters there may be of interest as well. If you're facing an audit, this book is an invaluable resource.

Audits in a Nutshell

1. In a small business audit, you must convince the IRS that your business reported all of its income and was entitled to any deductions the IRS questions.
2. Delaying an audit usually works to your advantage; the IRS is under pressure to finish its cases.
3. You may keep the IRS from holding an audit at your place of business.
4. You may hire a tax pro to handle an audit and not have to meet the IRS auditor face to face.
5. Don't expect to come out of an audit without owing something—the odds are against you.
6. Talk to the auditor's manager if you are being treated unfairly.
7. If you lost receipts or records, try to reconstruct them by other means.
8. If you are worried about tax fraud, bring in a tax pro to handle the audit.

A. Who Gets Audited?

Audit victims are no longer selected randomly. Small businesses and their owners are pulled from the IRS audit hopper in several very deliberate ways, discussed next.

1. Computer Picks

Computer scoring is the most likely way a small business becomes an audit candidate. At least 80% of small businesses are sole proprietorships. Their owners report their business income on "Schedule C" of their Form 1040 individual tax returns. An IRS computer program, known as the DIF scoring process, scans every Form 1040 and assigns it a numerical grade. The highest scores, roughly 10% of all individual tax returns, are human-reviewed for "audit potential."

Business partnerships, limited liability companies and small corporations all file returns, too. However, the audit rate of these three entities is about half that of sole proprietorships.

How the DIF program works is a highly guarded IRS secret, but here is what former IRS employees have told me. The most important scoring factor is the *ratios* of a business's income to various types of its expenses. For instance, if the IRS computer data shows restaurants in your area report food costs as 32% of gross sales on average, and yours claims 55%, you will get a higher DIF score. However, it may take more than just one item, such as one ratio variance, to get you audited.

2. Special Projects and Market Segment Specialization Programs

Every year the IRS targets certain businesses, professions and industries for audit. These campaigns are called "industry specialization" or "market segment specialization programs." Recent victims range from funeral home operators, car dealers, attorneys and airline pilots to plastic surgeons.

The IRS zeroes in on certain businesses because experience has shown a high degree of noncompliance with the tax laws. For instance, in 1993 the IRS completed a study of attorneys. It found that criminal and immigration lawyers were less likely to report all of their income than other kinds of attorneys. Another study found that airline pilots, as a group, were prone to investing in questionable "tax shelters." And undoubtedly, the IRS reasons that lawyers, pilots and other high earners are the ones most likely to be able to pay audit bills.

3. Informants' Tips

Tips to the IRS—from disgruntled former business associates, employees or ex-spouses—can trigger an audit. But don't be overly concerned about someone on your enemies' list. The IRS knows that many tips result from spite or jealousy, so only 2% of all audits come from tip-offs. Anonymous tips are usually ignored altogether.

However, if other people know things—you're keeping two sets of books or paying your house painter with a business check, or you skim cash from the till—be at least a little worried. Cheating on your taxes is not a good idea, but if you try it, at least be discreet. Today's bookkeeper can become tomorrow's tax squeal and cause you trouble, particularly if he can document your tax cheating to the IRS.

4. Follow-Up Audits

Audits of other individuals or businesses can lead to your being targeted. For instance, if one of your business partners gets audited, you may be next. If you have your finger in many pies, you may be hit with a "package audit" of all your enterprises—corporations, investment groups and trusts. The IRS looks askance at folks who operate in myriad business forms, suspecting income may be shifted or hidden among the entities.

5. Prior Audits

If you were audited once and flunked, your odds of a return visit go up greatly. Folks who were once overly aggressive—claiming phony tax deductions or not reporting income—are likely to try it again, the IRS reasons.

On the other hand, some business people lose audits badly, yet never hear from the IRS again. The IRS audit machine operates in hit-or-miss fashion, so don't assume the worst.

6. Governmental Investigations

Law enforcement and IRS criminal investigations can lead to an audit. For instance, when a police agency makes an arrest and finds a lot of cash in someone's possession, it may contact the IRS. Similarly, if you are charged with embezzlement or drug dealing, it may be brought to the IRS's attention. However, the information flow between law enforcement agencies and the IRS is very spotty.

7. Amended Returns and Refund Claims

You may file amended tax returns—for example, if you later discover an overlooked deduction. Generally, you have 36 months after the original due date of the return to amend it to lower your tax liability. (Form 1040X is used for this purpose.) While the IRS has discretion to reject any amended tax return, it usually will accept it.

Most people file amended returns to get a refund. And, as you most surely know, the IRS is not in business to give money back. So, not surprisingly, the audit likelihood for amended returns is rather high—about one in three. If an amended return is audited, the original tax return—not just the items amended—is opened up for inspection.

Computer-Generated IRS Bills and Notices

The IRS often sends computerized notices about some suspected problem with your individual or business tax filings. The notice may look like a bill at first glance. For instance, the IRS claims you forgot to report $400 in interest from your savings account. The notice says that you did not report it on your tax return, and may state how much additional tax you owe—on the assumption that they are right.

This notice is not an audit; it is an IRS "automated adjustment," usually designated as a CP-2000 letter. If the IRS is right—you did forget the $400 interest—then consider it a bill.

But what if the IRS computer is wrong—you really did report the $400 on your return, but listed it under "dividends" instead of interest? In this case, call or mail a letter and documentation to the IRS. Make sure to send a copy of the notice to the IRS office address on the notice. Don't go to your local IRS office; they didn't send the notice and won't help you.

B. How Long Do You Have to Worry About an Audit?

Generally, a tax return can't legally be audited after 36 months from the date it was filed. Note that the time limit (called a "statute of limitations") starts to run *only* if and when you actually file a tax return. Years in which you never file a tax return are open to IRS scrutiny forever.

Audit notices are usually sent out between 12 and 18 months after you file your tax return. Typically, if you haven't heard from the IRS within 18 months, you won't be audited.

However, some circumstances give the IRS more time to audit:

- If you understate your income by at least 25% on a tax return, the audit deadline is extended to six years.
- If you file a fraudulent tax return, there is no time limit. Tax fraud, as explained below, is more than just a little fudging. Luckily, the IRS rarely tries to audit anyone after six years, even if fraud is suspected.

Once an audit is started, the Internal Revenue Manual directs it to be wrapped up within 28 months—beginning on the date you filed your tax return. Legally, as mentioned, the IRS has 36 months. The 28-month cutoff is an internal rule to give the IRS time for potential appeals processing after an audit. (See Chapter 20, Appealing IRS Audits.)

Bottom line. These statutory and internal IRS time limits mean the auditor is under pressure to close out your audit file. So, the older an audit case gets, the more anxious the IRS is to bring it to a conclusion. The auditor can close a case more easily if you agree and sign the audit report; her job performance is partially judged on getting your agreement. This opens up the possibility of negotiating, as explained in Section K, below.

Part

6

Dealing With the IRS

Auditors look for personal expenses disguised as business deductions. With small businesses, the IRS auditor is ever on the lookout for people who bury personal expenses in their business. Cars, travel and entertainment are often targets. In these areas, particularly, it pays to keep good records.

C. How the IRS Audits Small Businesses

The IRS audits small businesses and their owners by "office audits" and "field audits." The difference is not only where the audit is held, but the intensity of the process.

1. Office Audits

If your operation is audited and is a sole proprietorship grossing less than $100,000 per year, the IRS is likely to request you "come on in." Usually, only one year's tax return is selected for an office audit. Just as it sounds, you go to the IRS offices with your box of records (see below for what you must bring). A business office audit with a tax examiner runs two to four hours.

A typical business taxpayer emerges owing additional taxes of about $4,000, but there's always the possibility of a larger bill from an office audit.

2. Field Audits

With a partnership, corporation or a sole proprietorship with gross annual receipts over $100,000, the audit is usually held outside the IRS office. Called a "field audit," this process is much more intensive than an office audit. Field auditors are called Revenue Agents, and are much better trained in accounting than are IRS office tax auditors.

The average field audit "adjustments"—meaning additional tax, penalty and interest assessed—total over $17,000. The IRS may devote as much as 40 hours (including time to write a report) to a field audit of a small business.

 Conduct your audit away from your premises. You have the right to keep an IRS field auditor away from your business premises—even if the IRS requests to do the audit there. You can legally keep the auditor away if her presence would interfere with your operation. Demand that the audit be held elsewhere—at the IRS office, or if you have a tax pro represent you, at her office.

Most audits should be held elsewhere, even if it is not an inconvenience to your operation. It might be easier to have the IRS is up to. But first, consider what the IRS is up to. The auditor can observe your operation and form an opinion as to whether it is more successful than your tax return indicates. And while there, the auditor might question your employees and get the wrong ideas about any number of things.

> **EXAMPLE:** An IRS auditor sees a picture of a vacation house on the desk of Benny, owner of Benny's Burgers. Since he reported only $15,000 to $20,000 in income for the past six years, the auditor asks how he can afford this luxury item. If Benny can't come up with a satisfactory answer, the auditor will look hard for evidence of unreported income. Things could get much worse for Benny.

Another reason to have the audit off your premises is to better control records that are made available. The auditor may ask for additional records, but they are back at the business. Since this would delay the audit, and the auditor is often in a hurry, she may drop the request. And even if she insists on seeing the documents later, you'll have a chance to review them first and perhaps edit out material she is not entitled to see.

D. The Auditor's Powers

Forget about being innocent until proven guilty in America. The tax law specifically places the burden of proof on you to back up what is in your tax return. Proving the correctness to an auditor is not all that easy. The IRS wins over 80% of all audits, often because people can't verify data on their returns. Recordkeeping—not outright cheating—is the downfall of most audit victims.

Congress gives the IRS broad, but not unlimited, powers in auditing. The IRS, in the course of an audit, may:

- inspect your business premises
- view your home office
- scrutinize your records, and
- summon records held by others.

Let's look more closely at each of these.

1. Inspecting Business Premises

Even though you can have an audit conducted outside your business (see above), an auditor neverthe-

less may enter your premises if they're open to the public. This is common practice with a field—not an office—audit.

The auditor cannot go into your business's private area such as a storeroom or your private office, unless invited. Just because you can keep the IRS out of these areas doesn't necessarily mean that you should. If you have nothing to hide, then don't just be obstinate—it may arouse their imaginations. It's better to give agents a guided tour rather than let them wander around on their own.

2. Viewing Home Offices

Legally, you don't have to let an auditor into your home unless she has a court order. If you claimed a home office deduction on your tax return, photographs and diagrams of the business space will probably be enough to satisfy an auditor.

Occasionally, though, auditors request to see home offices. If you don't show her, she will probably disallow your home office depreciation or rental expense because you haven't sufficiently proven there is a home office. Remember, in an audit, the burden of proving deductions taken on a tax return is always on you.

3. Scrutinizing Your Records

Whether the audit is at the IRS office, your business or your tax pro's, the auditor will expect to see records. If they are on a computer, she will ask for a printout. She will want to see check registers, bank statements, canceled checks, receipts and invoices. If you keep a formal set of books, you must show those as well. If you don't produce something, the auditor may give you a written "document request" with a date to comply. If she still isn't satisfied, the auditor can issue a summons to you (just like the "third-party summons" discussed below).

In the end, if you never come up with acceptable records, the auditor is legally authorized to create her own figures—meaning that deductions will be disallowed and unreported income may be added.

Part

6

Dealing With the IRS

⚠️ **Do your records contain a smoking gun?** If there is evidence of something incriminating in your records, you may withhold them by claiming your Constitutional right against "self-incrimination." This is a judgment call that should be discussed with an attorney, and not with your accountant.

4. Summoning Records Held by Others

To get your financial information, an auditor can require records from your tax preparer, banks, suppliers, customers and others. Demands are made by an IRS order called a "third-party" summons. Usually an auditor won't issue a summons without first attempting to get this information directly from you. For example, she'll first ask you for bank statements and canceled checks or invoices. Usually, you should be cooperative, as these are things an auditor can get with a third-party summons anyway.

E. Should You Get Audit Help?

If you fear that some serious irregularity may come to light, at least consult a tax pro before meeting the auditor. For the typical office audit, hiring a tax pro may not be cost-effective. It is okay to go it alone if yours is an office audit and you have nothing to hide. But when it comes to the field audit, think hard about bringing in a tax pro from the get-go, for several reasons:

- Field audits produce much larger tax bills (on average four times greater) than do office audits. So it's a lot easier to justify the expense of a tax pro. Her fees are a tax-deductible business expense to boot.
- The IRS uses its most experienced personnel for field audits. So it's more likely that you will be outmatched if questions come up about documents or tax law.
- If you hire a representative, the field audit can be conducted at her office—not yours.

If you are worried about a serious problem or criminal charges, always bring in a professional, preferably a tax attorney. (See Chapter 22, Help

Beyond the Book.) An authorized representative must be an attorney, Certified Public Accountant, Enrolled Agent or the preparer of the tax return in question and must have your written Power of Attorney (IRS Form 2848).

Tax attorneys are the most expensive (expect to pay $125 to $400 per hour for their time); CPAs may charge slightly less. Enrolled Agents charge about $50 to $150 per hour. Professional time for a small business field audit ranges from ten to 50 hours. You do the math.

By law, you may take anyone with you to an audit that you like. Your tax preparer or bookkeeper can explain the business receipts and records. Of course, you can take along a tax pro, such as a CPA or tax attorney. Or you can bring along a friend to lend moral support.

You do not have to personally attend an audit, in most cases. Bookkeepers, managers or any other employee with knowledge of the business's tax affairs can go to the audit instead of the owner. But if you don't want to show your face, it's best to have a tax pro show up for you.

There is no legal requirement that you ever have to meet the auditor—*unless* they issue a summons to you. Keeping out of the picture means that there is no possibility of you giving damaging answers to the auditor's questions. A tax pro speaks the same language as the auditor and may have dealt with her before, and have an idea of what makes her tick. If tough questions are raised, a tax pro can say, "I don't know, let me check with my client." This may cause the auditor to adjourn the audit so you and the pro can talk things over.

Perhaps most important of all, a tax pro can spot an auditor going into problem areas—for example, expenses on which you didn't keep good records, or ones that look more like personal, than business, deductions.

Never forget that it's your job to prove to the IRS auditor the accuracy of your tax return, what lawyers call the "burden of proof." It is not up to the IRS to disprove anything. Typically, you'll have to verify an expense deduction claimed on your tax return. For instance, can you produce an invoice showing that you incurred the expense? Can you prove that you paid it with a cash receipt, check or credit card statement? Can you show it was business-related?

> **EXAMPLE:** An auditor challenges a deduction that Ethan, owner of Ethan's Travel Service, took as a business entertainment expense of $300. Ethan's first job is to prove he incurred the expense—he didn't just make it up. So Ethan comes up with a Visa receipt, his monthly Visa statement and his canceled check. Next, Ethan shows notations written on the charge slip and in his business diary that the expense was for taking Harry, a longtime customer, and his fiancee out to dinner at the Ritz-Carlton. They discussed a worldwide cruise for their honeymoon. This should satisfy the auditor that Ethan was entitled to claim this expense as a business deduction whether Harry and his fiancee take that cruise or not.

Tax Fraud and How to Avoid It

Careless mistakes, or even overstating a deduction on a tax return, is not tax fraud. Fraud is roughly defined as a deliberate attempt to evade taxes. To put your mind at rest, tax fraud is charged in less than 5% of all audits. Nevertheless, a fraud penalty of 75% can be tacked on to any tax found owing. And in very serious cases, where the fraud covers three or more years (found in less than 1% of all audits), the IRS may call in its Criminal Investigation Division.

If you have major skeletons in your tax closet —income you didn't report or phony business deductions—see a tax pro before the audit starts. Talk to the pro before the fraud has been discovered. It is dangerous to try to explain your way out of it once it has been uncovered. Instead, find a good tax pro, preferably an attorney.

F. Preparing for Your Audit

If you go it alone, before meeting the auditor, thoroughly review the tax returns being audited. Be ready to explain how you—or a tax return preparer —came up with the figures. If you can't, then head for the preparer or another tax pro. Pinpoint problems backing up income sources or expense deductions. Research tax law, if necessary. You'll need to legally show your right to take tax deductions or other tax benefits claimed on your return.

Find all records that substantiate your tax return. As discussed, the IRS has a right to look at any records used to prepare your tax return. Organize your records for the auditor in a logical fashion.

Neatness counts. Forget about dumping a pile of receipts before an auditor and telling her to go at it. Messy records mean more digging, and the more gold the IRS expects to mine. Conversely, auditors frequently reward good record-keepers by giving these folks the benefit of the doubt if any problems arise. Neatness builds your credibility with the auditor even if you are not really all that honest. (Order probably appeals to an accountant's mentality.) Also, pre-audit organization of receipts, checks and other items refreshes your recollection for the audit meeting.

G. What to Bring to an Audit of Your Small Business

Be prepared to show that your tax return is based on good business records. Audit success means documenting your expenses. Proof should be in writing, though auditors can accept oral explanations. A list of items the auditor wants to see usually accompanies your audit notice.

At a minimum, the IRS will expect you to produce the following documents:

- **Bank Statements, Canceled Checks and Receipts.** The auditor will want to see bank records—both personal and business— from *all* your accounts. As a rule, don't discard any business-related canceled checks or invoices or sales slips. If you paid some expenses with cash, keep the paperwork (handwritten notes, receipts or petty cash vouchers) showing the payments.

- **Electronic Records.** Most banks don't return canceled checks anymore, and many business expenses are charged on credit or debit cards. Bank and charge card (Visa, MasterCard, American Express) statements are now accepted by the IRS as proof of payment. They must show the name, date, amount and address of the payee.

  Since charges and statements don't show the business nature of the expense, you can't rely on them as your only records.

- **Books and Records.** The auditor will ask to see your "books." As explained in Chapter 3, Recordkeeping and Accounting, the tax code doesn't require small businesses to keep a formal set of books; don't let an auditor tell you otherwise. If you keep records with only a check book and cash register tapes, so be it. If you maintain more formal records—such as ledgers and journals—the auditor is entitled to see them. If your data is on computer, the auditor will want to see a printout.

  ⚠️ **Don't make the IRS guess.** If you don't produce adequate records, the auditor is legally permitted to estimate your income and/or expenses—plus impose a separate penalty for your failure to keep records.

- **Appointment Books, Logs and Diaries.** Businesses that offer services typically track activities and expenses using calendars, business diaries, appointment books and logs. An entry in a business diary helps justify an expense to an auditor—as long as it appears to be reasonable.

  Additionally, you must keep special records for certain equipment, called "listed property," if used for both business and personal purposes. (IRC § 280F.) (See Chapter 3, Recordkeeping and Accounting.) Computers kept at home but used for business, cellular phones, and vehicles used for both business and pleasure are designated as listed property. Purely business equipment is not in this category—for example, mechanic's tools, a lathe or a carpet loom—and no records of usage are required. But when assets are put to both business and personal use, the auditor can demand records of usage. For example, if you use a computer for business email and to play solitaire, keep track of the business portion. One way is with a note pad next to the computer.

  If you haven't kept usage records of listed property, reconstruct them by memory or reference to projects that you worked on during the year.

- **Auto Records.** As mentioned, a vehicle can be "listed property" if it's used for personal purposes as well as business. So business use of your personal auto requires detailed records showing the work portion. A log is the best way to keep track, but is not strictly required by the tax code. Alternatively, keep all gas and repair receipts in an orderly fashion with notations of trips showing how the car was used for business. A less accurate way to keep records is to add up the gas bills and divide by the number of miles per gallon that your car averages. Show the auditor your auto trip receipts and explain how they link up to sales trips by your business diary or calendar notations.

- **Travel and Entertainment Records.** By law, out-of-town business travel and entertainment expenses (T & E, in auditor lingo), require greater recordkeeping than most other expenses.

  You *must* have a written record of the specific business purpose of the travel or entertainment expense, as well as a receipt for it. (IRC § 267.)

  A good way to document T & E expenses is with an appointment book or log, noting each time you incur a business expense, and the reason. Most folks aren't disciplined enough to write down every expense as it is incurred. It is okay to put together a log or diary after you have received an audit notice. But be up-front about it—don't insult the auditor's intelligence by trying to pass off wet-inked paper as an old record. Remember, it's key to develop and maintain credibility with the auditor.

BOARDING GATE 221
DEPARTURES ⇨

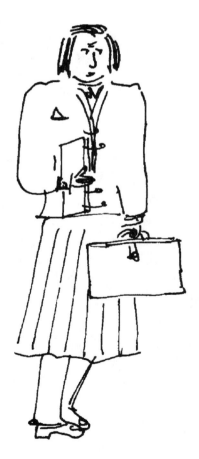

EXAMPLE 1: Bianca, a self-employed designer, reconstructs a calendar book with a notation for June 18, 2001, as follows, "Round-trip cab fare to office of John Johnson, prospective client. $14 (no receipt). Lunch at Circle Restaurant. Discuss proposal to decorate new offices at 333 Pine St. $32 (Visa charge) plus cash tip of $6 (no receipt)." Bianca can also give the auditor details, if asked. The auditor will probably be satisfied if it appears reasonable.

EXAMPLE 2: Sam (the owner of the computer store, remember) went to an out-of-town computer retailers' convention. He spent $1,800 and claimed it as business travel expenses on his tax return. On audit, Sam produces charge card statements to prove the $1,800 was spent for hotels, meals and convention registration. The auditor wants more and asks Sam to justify the business purpose of this trip. Sam produces an ad for the convention, an agenda of events and notes he took at programs. If it looks legitimate, and Sam's explanation of why it was important for him to be there is convincing, the auditor should allow the deduction in full.

- **Expenses for Renting or Buying Property.** To prove business rental expenses, bring in a copy of your lease, or if you own the property or equipment, bring in the purchase contract. This establishes grounds for claiming these expenses as well as a beginning tax basis of the property, if you claim depreciation expenses.

Part

6

Dealing With the IRS

What You Need to Prove Certain Business Expenses

| | Expense | | | |
	Travel	Entertainment	Gift	Transportation (Car)
Amount	Amount of each separate expense for travel, lodging and meals. Incidental expenses may be totaled in reasonable categories, such as taxis, daily meals for traveler, etc.	Amount of each separate expense. Incidental expenses such as taxis, telephones, etc., may be totaled on a daily basis.	Cost of gift.	Amount of each separate expense, including: (1) Cost of the car (2) Mileage for each business use of the car, and (3) Total miles for the tax year.
Time	Date you left and returned for each trip, and number of days for business.	Date of entertainment. For meals or entertainment directly before or after a business discussion, the date and duration of the business discussion.	Date of gift.	Date of the expense or use.
Place	Name of city or other destination.	Name and address or location of place of entertainment. Type of entertainment if not otherwise apparent. Place where business discussion was held if entertainment is directly before or after a business discussion.	N/A	Name of city or other designation if applicable.
Description	N/A	N/A	Description of gift.	N/A
Business Purpose	Business reason for travel or the business benefit gained or expected to be gained.	Business reason or the business benefit gained or expected to be gained. Nature of business discussion or activity.	Business reason for giving the gift or the business benefit gained or expected to be gained.	Business reason for the expense or use of the car.
Business Relationship	N/A	Occupations or other information—such as names or other designations—about persons entertained that shows their business relationship to you. If all people entertained did not take part in business discussion, identify those who did. You must also prove that you or your employee was present if entertainment was a business meal.	Occupation or other information—such as name or other designation—about recipient that shows his or her business relationship to you.	N/A

What to Do About Missing Documents

Myth: Every deduction must be proven, or it won't be allowed.

Fact: Courts say that taxpayers can't be expected to keep perfect records. If your tax documentation is incomplete (which is often the case with small business people), don't despair. You are required to demonstrate to the IRS only that you are in "substantial compliance" with the tax laws. The substantial compliance rule has been interpreted to mean you may do any of the following when you don't have original documentation for an audit:

- offer oral explanations to auditors in place of missing records
- reconstruct records, or
- approximate expenses.

EXAMPLE: Elijah produced a small music festival and rented tents from a traveling carnival company, which insisted on payment in cash. Elijah lost the receipt for the payment of $800, and the carnies moved on to parts unknown. Elijah can reconstruct this receipt with his oral explanation, a picture of the tents from the local paper and a letter from a ticket taker who saw him make the $800 cash payment. The auditor also asked to see Elijah's office utility bills for the year under audit. He could come up with only nine months of bills, and the utility company could not provide duplicates because its computer broke down. Elijah can approximate the missing expense data by averaging out the other nine months of bills.

Even if you can't figure out a way to document an expense, make your own paperwork and tell the auditor this is what you have done. For instance, write a repair receipt with the name and address of the person who did the work, the date and amount paid.

For missing items, you may be able to invoke the Cohan rule for expenses—other than travel and entertainment. A court case (*Cohan v. Commissioner of the Internal Revenue*, 39 F.2d 540, 2nd Cir. 1930) allowed George M. ("Give my regards to Broadway") Cohan to "approximate" his business expenses in an IRS audit. The case stands for the proposition that estimations of business expenses are acceptable—as long as it is reasonable to believe that some amount was spent, and there is a good reason why records are not available. Typical excuses are that records were lost or destroyed, or the transactions were not the type that receipts are normally given for, such as cab fares or tips.

If less than $75 each, business-related travel and entertainment expenses don't require substantiation, as long as they are believable to the auditor and not excessive under the circumstances. (Regulation 1.274-5T.)

H. Don't Rush a Field Audit

Most people want to get an audit over as quickly as possible. I don't blame them. With an office audit this may not be a bad idea, but with a *field* audit, faster isn't always better.

Slowing down an audit often works to your advantage. Extra time to get records together or delaying for any other plausible reason is both permissible and wise.

The older an audit file gets, the more anxious the IRS is to close it out, for several reasons. Auditors are most concerned about the statute of limitations, discussed above, which normally gives the IRS only three years to audit you. Also, the IRS has internal rules requiring its auditors to complete their work within 26 to 28 months after a return is filed. After an auditor is finished, her report must still be processed, reviewed and formally approved, all of which eats up time. So, an auditor is under pressure to close your case.

Making the auditor watch the calendar isn't the only reason to delay. Since you never can be too well prepared for an audit, it often makes sense to ask for extensions of time as a matter of course. Most folks need time to dig out papers from the recesses of their garage or storeroom and put them into some semblance of order. Contact your bank to get missing copies of checks or other items. After getting it all together, you may run it by a tax pro. Assuming you work for a living, this project takes a lot of your spare time to do right.

Your annual family reunion may be set at the time the audit is scheduled, or you become ill, are too busy or have some other excuse for a delay. If you need a postponement, call the IRS and tell them. In most cases, your wish will be granted and the appointment reset for a month or two.

Cash Transactions Catch the IRS's Attention

The IRS is suspicious of all businesses that are inherently "cash intensive." Bars, game arcades, restaurants, mini-marts, pawnshops and laundromats are frequent audit targets. So are waiters, car dealers, cab drivers, gambling industry workers, bellhops and immigration lawyers. The IRS knows the nature of your operation because it's on your tax return. Occupations must be stated both in plain English and by listing a four-digit code on 1040 forms. It is a crime to misstate the nature of your business on a tax return—a prostitute was once convicted of tax fraud for telling the IRS she was in "public relations."

If yours is a predominantly cash operation, an IRS auditor will be particularly interested in your lifestyle. Sports cars, rental property, vacation homes, boats and low reported income could mean an intense audit or, worse, an IRS criminal investigation.

All businesses—including financial institutions—must report transactions of cash over $10,000. Not just greenbacks, but also "cash equivalents"—traveler's checks, money orders and bank drafts—must be reported to the IRS on Form 8300. Personal checks of any amount are not within the cash reporting requirement. While aimed at money launderers and drug dealers, this law applies to legitimate business persons, too.

Structuring a transaction to avoid this law—say, making three cash deposits of $4,000 on three different days—is also required to be reported on Form 8300. Penalties for not following cash reporting rules range from fines to audits and even jail. (See IRS Publication 1544, Reporting Cash Payments of Over $10,000, for details and a copy of Form 8300.)

This law doesn't apply to non-business cash transactions. So, for instance, a parent giving a child more than $10,000 in cash doesn't have to file Form 8300. (But there is a federal gift tax filing requirement.)

I. What Auditors Look for When Examining a Business

First and foremost, the IRS training manual tells its auditors that they are examining *you*, not just your tax return.

The auditor wants to see how you match up with the income reported on your return—"economic reality" in IRS-speak. If your business is audited, the IRS will likely investigate these issues:

- **Did you report all of your business sales or receipts?** If you "forgot" to report significant business income—$10,000 or more—strongly consider hiring a tax pro to handle the audit. Remove yourself from the process altogether. If the auditor finds evidence of large amounts of unreported income, and it looks intentional, he may call in the IRS criminal investigation team. However, if there is any kind of half-way plausible explanation ("someone must have forgotten to record September's sales"), then don't worry about jail. The auditor will probably just assess the additional tax you should have paid in the first place, plus interest and a 20% penalty.

- **Did you write off personal living costs as business expenses?** Let's face it, every small-time operator has claimed a personal expense as a business one. For little things—a few personal long-distance calls on the business telephone line—the IRS won't get too excited. But if you deducted $2,000 in repairs on your motor home during a trip to Yellowstone, an auditor may figure this out by looking at your receipts—and disallow it, with penalty added.

- **Does your lifestyle square with your reported income?** An auditor sizes you up for dress style, jewelry, car and furnishings in your home or office if given a chance to make these observations. Someone who looks like a Vegas high roller, with a tax return of a missionary, will cause any auditor to dig deeper.

- **Did you take cash—or otherwise divert income into your own pocket—without declaring it?** Expect the auditor to suspect skimming if your business handles a lot of cash. (See "Cash Transactions Catch the IRS's Attention," above.)

- **Did you write off personal auto expenses as business?** Personal use of your business-deducted set of wheels is so common that auditors expect to find it. That doesn't mean they will accept it, however. Auditors don't believe you use your one-and-only auto 100% for business and never to run to the grocery store or the dentist. If you operate your car for both business and pleasure and claim a high percentage of business usage, keep good records—preferably a mileage log.

- **Did you claim personal entertainment, meals or vacation costs as business expenses?** Travel and entertainment business expenses are another area where the IRS knows it can strike gold. Document all travel and entertainment deductions. Taking buddies to the ball game and calling it business won't fly if you can't explain the business relationship in a credible fashion.

- **If you have employees, are you filing payroll tax returns and making tax deposits?** Employment taxes are a routine part of every audit of a small enterprise. See "Employment Classification: A Hot Issue," below, and Chapter 5, Tax Concerns of Employers.

- **And last but not least, if you hire people you call "independent contractors," are they really employees?** (Again, see "Employment Classification: A Hot Issue," below, and Chapter 5.)

This list is by no means complete—these are just the most likely things an IRS auditor looks for.

Part

6

Dealing With the IRS

Employment Classification: A Hot Issue

Auditors are on the lookout for employees misclassified as independent contractors. Once the IRS raises this issue, it's up to you to prove that the workers were truly independent contractors. The IRS auditor may talk to the people in question and take other steps to find out if workers have been properly classified. You can't legally stop her. It is okay to give workers the afternoon off when the IRS comes calling.

So far, you know that unreported income, poor business recordkeeping and mixing business and personal use of property are obvious IRS audit concerns. You'll next want to focus on areas in which your tax returns are most vulnerable. Here are some things to watch for.

1. The Income Probe

The number-one issue auditors are trained to sniff out in business audits is unreported income—especially if your operation is cash-intensive (see "Cash Transactions Catch the IRS's Attention," above). Expect an auditor to start with the "income probe." Anticipate questions like, "Did you report all of your income?" Another favorite is, "Do you keep a lot of cash around?" Don't conclude that big brother IRS has secret knowledge here. Auditors ask everyone these questions. This puts you on the defensive early in the game.

Next comes the "bank deposit analysis." Office auditors seldom do this, but field auditors routinely add up all your bank deposits to see if the total is more than your reported income. Auditors also ask to see *all* of your personal bank account records to check that the deposits are consistent with your business receipts. If you don't produce bank records voluntarily, the auditor will likely get them from your bank. If you cover up bank accounts, or otherwise lie to the auditor, you risk being investigated for tax evasion.

Audit your bank accounts in advance. Do your own bank deposit analysis before meeting with a field auditor. If deposits exceed the income reported, you need to come up with explanations. Don't invent sources; many deposits aren't taxable income. Loans, sales of assets (only the gain, if any, is taxed), transfers from other accounts, inheritances and money held for relatives are but a few legitimate explanations.

2. Is It a Legitimate Business Expense?

Next, the auditors move on to verifying business expenses. Remember, the tax code makes you prove that deductions were for profit-making purposes; it's not up to the IRS to disprove them. Any expense may be questioned, but certain ones are zeroed in on. The auditor is searching for deductions which were nondeductible personal expenses in whole or part:

- travel and entertainment (see chapter 1 and discussion above)
- home office (see chapter 13)
- asset purchases (see chapter 2) and
- auto expenses (see Chapter 1).

Review these chapters for the rules on deductibility to see if you are on firm ground before the audit begins.

J. How to Behave at an Audit

Auditors know very little about you before the meeting. Your auditor won't have other years' tax returns, but may have some computer data for two other years. She will have the tax return under audit and a printout of all W-2s and 1099s from outfits that are required to report wages and certain financial transactions. A field auditor may also have a listing of real estate and vehicles registered in your name.

The Internal Revenue Manual says the first taxpayer interview is the most important phase of an audit. Let me repeat, whether you handle this interview or have a tax pro go for you, remember that both you and your business are under the microscope. Take a tip from Shakespeare and be true to thine own self. If you lay bricks for a living, don't try to act or look like a lawyer, and vice versa. Here are some other words to live by.

1. Keep Chit-Chat to a Minimum

Talking with the auditor about the weather or football is okay, but mum is the word about your business and personal affairs. Because audits are so stressful, many of us cover our nervousness by talking. IRS auditors rely on this natural tendency and listen for clues or admissions. For instance, if you fill in a silence by remarking how jet-lagged you are from a trip to Bora Bora, the auditor may wonder how you can afford it. After all, she may earn about what you say you do, but can't swing the bus fare to Omaha. Don't be surprised if she asks point-blank how you did it. Expect idle talk about your kids' private school or an expensive hobby to raise suspicions, if you own a one-chair fingernail salon. If you feel like talking, ask the auditor about herself—to take the focus off you.

2. Answer Questions Concisely

When the auditor asks a direct question, the preferred comeback is "yes" or "no." Resist the temptation to overexplain, ramble on or answer questions that weren't asked. If you are in doubt, say, "I don't know," or "I'll get back to you on that," or "I'll have to check my records," or "I'll ask my accountant." The auditor may let it go. If she doesn't, at least you slowed the process down, usually to your advantage.

> EXAMPLE: The auditor asks Sue what percentage of sales in her Clothes Horse boutique were for cash. Sue doesn't keep separate figures for cash sales apart from credit card and check sales. Sue might make a fairly accurate guess, or she could go into a long explanation of how

most customers pay for clothes with credit cards or checks. But, why should Sue risk giving an answer that may be misinterpreted by an auditor who knows little about small business practices? Sue should simply say, "I have no idea because I don't keep those kinds of records." Or, if the auditor pushes it, "If you give me time, I can review my records, come up with an accurate answer and get back to you."

It's Okay to Ask for Time Out

You have the right to stop or recess an audit for just about any good reason—a bathroom or lunch break, or to call it a day if you feel ill or need to confer with a tax pro. IRS Publication 1, Your Rights as a Taxpayer, states your right to get tax advice or bring in a representative at any time during the audit. If you are in over your head, confused or can't answer a question, firmly tell the auditor that you need a recess. Auditors are tightly scheduled and may not have time to meet again soon. Use the delay to regroup and consider your next step rather than do something you might regret.

3. Don't Be Hostile or Phony

What about trying to charm the auditor with your wonderful personality or good looks? Up to a point, this is fine. All rumors to the contrary notwithstanding, auditors are human. The IRS also gives its auditors wide latitude; a lot of judgment calls are made. If you are pleasant and run an honest-looking business, you may get the benefit of the doubt if the auditor uncovers problems. Conversely, if you come in radiating hostility, you are daring the auditor to reciprocate. Nevertheless, don't try too hard to ingratiate yourself. Auditors abhor folks who think sucking-up is a way to get ahead.

Part 6

4. Complain If the Auditor Is Abusive

Most auditors are straightforward and professional, but a few delight in giving taxpayers a hard time. You may run into an auditor who is impolite, hostile or downright nasty. Perhaps you upset her or she is just having a bad day.

The Taxpayer Bill of Rights entitles you to courtesy from the IRS. If necessary, remind her of this and ask her politely to lighten up. If she persists, tell her you are too upset and want to call off the audit for the day. Or say that you want to consult a tax pro before going further, another privilege in the Taxpayer Bill of Rights. Threatening this can reform an auditor's attitude, because she is under time pressure. Or demand to speak with her manager about the unfair treatment. If all else fails, simply walk out. Send a tax pro to the next appointment in your place, or appeal the audit result. (See Chapter 20, Appealing IRS Audits.)

> ⚠️ **Never offer favors to an auditor.** If an audit takes place at your office—or your tax pro's—it's fine to give an agent a cup of coffee. Don't go beyond that, whether it is lunch or a small discount at your store. IRS agents have an excellent record for honesty. Bribery attempts (or threats, for that matter) are reported and can result in an especially thorough audit, if not a criminal investigation.

K. How to Negotiate With an Auditor

Despite IRS claims that auditors can't negotiate, give-and-take is part of the audit process. An auditor's job performance is judged largely based on how many cases she closes marked "agreed." She wants you to consent to her findings and not appeal or go to Tax Court. So the auditor is told to get your consent. This gives you negotiating power.

It doesn't mean an auditor wants your signature so badly she will allow bogus business expenses or overlook unreported income. But it does give the auditor incentive to negotiate. Here are some negotiating strategies.

1. Don't Just Sit There

Keep asking the auditor about disallowances she is considering as the audit progresses. If you don't ask, she won't tell you what's on her mind, so you will be in the dark until you get her Examination Report. Don't let an auditor take the easy way out—make her face you and justify her decisions. In turn, you can argue your position right then and there. Or if she is making an adjustment because you didn't produce records, you can ask for time to find or reconstruct the documents.

> **EXAMPLE 1:** The auditor tells Sue, owner of the Clothes Horse boutique, that she is disallowing a $400 expense paid to Helena, a fashion consultant. Sue showed a canceled check but hasn't produced anything else showing the nature of Helena's services. Sue could ask for time to get a statement from Helena describing the work, and bring or mail it to the auditor.

> **EXAMPLE 2:** The auditor isn't convinced that it was necessary for Paul to buy a $40,000 airplane for his plumbing subcontracting business. Paul could then get a letter from Morgan, the general contractor who hired him, saying that he hired Paul to work a project in a remote area inaccessible by car.

> **EXAMPLE 3:** The auditor tells Barbara, a direct mail consultant, that she is disallowing her deduction for the theft of a computer. Her reason is that there is no documentation of the loss. Barbara could get a copy of the police report of the theft and send it to the auditor.

2. Talk Percentages, Not Dollars

Auditors don't talk about the dollars you will owe from an audit, but will discuss "adjustments." For instance, your auditor wants to disallow a $500 deduction. Don't reply, "Would you take $300?" Instead, talk in terms of percentages, based on whether the adjustment should be made in the first place. Although this amounts to the same thing, percentages, not dollars, is the language of IRS auditors.

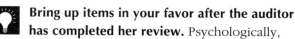 **Keep in mind the difference between arguing and negotiating.** When you argue, you are usually disputing an auditor's conclusion ("It was really a business trip"). By contrast, negotiating is the art of meeting in the middle. ("Perhaps the trip can be viewed as both for business and pleasure, so how about agreeing that 70% of expenses were deductible for business and 30% nondeductible for non-business?")

Or let's say you lost all paperwork for an $820 office supply deduction. The auditor proposes to disallow 100% of the deduction. You could counter by suggesting 50% along these lines: "Since I made a decent profit and obviously worked hard to earn it, I must have bought some office supplies. I lost the receipts, but my reconstruction of expenses is reasonable. I should be allowed at least half."

EXAMPLE: Bertha is a part-time wedding consultant with a small downtown office. At an audit, Bertha was asked to produce paperwork showing she paid $932 in cash for parking at a nearby garage. Bertha didn't bother to keep parking receipts. The auditor says, "No deduction." Bertha could counter by saying, "You know that I live 12 miles away and there is no public transportation to my office, so I must have driven and there is no street parking. However, I will agree to your disallowing 25% of parking expenses just to get it over with."

3. Arguing Issues

Most audit issues fall into two broad categories: *verification* and *justification*. So far we have focused on verification problems, such as lost paperwork. In the previous example, the auditor didn't question Bertha's legal right to claim a parking expense, but whether it was verifiable.

A justification issue, on the other hand, arises if the auditor questions whether Bertha's wedding consulting really was a profit-seeking, legitimate business—or if it was a social pastime. If primarily for pleasure, Bertha wasn't entitled to claim *any* parking expense. (See Chapter 13 for a discussion of why a hobby is not a business for tax purposes.) Unlike verification issues, justification or legal issues (such as whether or not your corporation is valid) may require a tax pro. If a legal issue comes up, ask for a recess to do some research or confer with a tax pro.

4. Adjustments in Your Favor— Taking the Offensive

An audit is not a one-way street. The Internal Revenue Manual says auditors *must* make adjustments in your favor whenever found. Even the most hard-nosed auditor knows that folks occasionally make mistakes in the IRS's favor or overlook claiming tax benefits on their returns. This is another good reason to go over your return and records with a fine-toothed comb before the audit. If you find any missed deductions or if you were too conservative—for instance, you didn't take a deduction for entertainment because you were afraid of raising an audit flag—then bring it up now. You no longer have anything to lose.

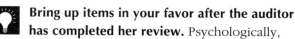 **Bring up items in your favor after the auditor has completed her review.** Psychologically, it's better not to raise anything in your favor until after the auditor has decided on all adjustments

Part

6

Dealing With the IRS

against you. If you bring them up earlier, the auditor may look harder for offsetting items. But if you wait until after she is locked in, she has no choice but to consider your positive change items.

5. Don't Try to Negotiate Based on Inability to Pay

The worst way to negotiate is by telling an auditor you can't afford the extra taxes. Once you concede an adjustment, attempts to throw yourself on the auditor's mercy effectively end the audit. *Whether you ever pay the tax bill from the audit is not the auditor's concern. His job is to audit you.* After the audit is finished, your case goes to the IRS Collection Division, a completely separate department.

Take heart—there are ways to reduce audit bills. It may be possible to negotiate an audit bill down by using the IRS Offer in Compromise procedure. Alternatively, your debt may qualify under one of the provisions in the bankruptcy law. Or, if all else fails you can usually get an installment payment plan. (See Chapter 18, When You Can't Pay Your Taxes, for details.)

L. Your Options After Getting an Audit Report

After the auditor is finished, you will be handed or mailed an IRS Examination Report. The IRS considers the audit completed, but the report may still be modified if you act quickly enough. You have three choices after getting the report.

1. Agree

You may throw in the towel by signing the report. It's all over, and generally speaking you can't change your mind. If tax is due, you will get a bill with interest and penalty (if any) included. The audit report is not officially a tax bill. The final bill is issued by the IRS Service Center a month or two after the IRS audit file is closed.

Check your bill. Sometimes, statements from the IRS Service Centers differ from those given by auditors. Don't ask me why, it just happens. If the bill is for more than the auditor's report, complain to the Service Center. If less, then you may have lucked out.

Getting an Audit Payment Plan

The audit is over and you (reluctantly) agree with the IRS that you owe some money. Naturally, your thoughts turn to how you are going to pay. The auditor may ask if you can pay on the spot. If you can't, she may offer to help you set up a payment plan. Alternatively, you may raise the subject. You don't have to discuss payment at all with an auditor; it's optional. You can wait until you are contacted by the IRS collection division, with no harm done except that the IRS interest meter is running. If you want to pay the IRS in installments, it usually will be granted, if:

- the total owed is under $10,000
- all of your tax returns due have been filed, and
- all current year's tax payments are made (such as quarterly estimated taxes for self-employed people).

If you owe more than $10,000, the auditor may process the forms to request an installment agreement, but it is up to the collection division to grant or deny the request.

It's okay not to commit to pay at the end of an audit. You may need time to think it over, or ask a relative for a loan, or whatever. Your case will simply be shipped off to your IRS Service Center for billing.

2. Argue

Examination Reports aren't chiseled in stone. If you don't think an audit report is fair, call the auditor and tell her why. If she can't be persuaded and you feel your argument is a good one, ask to speak to her manager. *Don't be shy—you have rights as a taxpayer. Take the problem over the auditor's head.* The manager does not have to meet with you, but she should give you a chance to make your key points on the phone. Tell her just where you think the auditor missed the boat. Politely let her know you will continue to fight (see next chapter on how to do this) if she won't intercede. This call may be for naught, but you don't have anything to lose by trying.

> **EXAMPLE:** Phil, a full-time college professor and part-time jazz musician at small clubs on weekends, was audited. The IRS disallowed expenses in Phil's music business for piano lessons of $675 and opera singing lessons of $290. The auditor didn't agree that these lessons were business-related, since Phil was a drum player. Phil called her manager and explained that both types of lessons enhanced his musical abilities. He offered to accept disallowance of the opera lessons ($290) if the IRS allowed the piano lesson ($675) deduction. The manager agreed.

3. Do Nothing

Eventually, IRS audit reports become final—with or without your signature. However, the IRS may sit on your case for weeks or months after sending you the report before closing the case. If you really have no points to negotiate or money to pay, choose the "do nothing" option. It will greatly delay your final audit bill, but interest is mounting.

M. When Your Audit Is Final

Whether you continue to argue with or simply don't respond to the IRS, you will eventually be notified that the audit report is final. If you sit tight, the IRS will send a document informing you that you can either:

- appeal within 30 days (see the next chapter on how to appeal an audit), or
- contest the audit in the U.S. Tax Court. You must act within 90 days of the date of the letter to stop the audit from being finalized. (See the next chapter, Appealing IRS Audits.)

Resources

- *Stand Up to the IRS*, by Frederick W. Daily (Nolo). This self-help book discusses IRS audit, appeal and Tax Court strategies in more detail than covered here.
- *Representing the Audited Taxpayer Before the IRS*, by Robert McKenzie (Clark Boardman Callaghan). As the title suggests, this book is written for tax professionals, but much of it is understandable to laypeople as well.
- IRS Publication 1, Your Rights as a Taxpayer. This pamphlet is clearly written and is a must-read for all taxpayers.
- *Surviving an IRS Tax Audit*, by Frederick W. Daily (Nolo).

Part

6

Dealing With the IRS

Appealing IRS Audits

"Nor shall any person ... be deprived of life, liberty, or property, without due process of law."

— Fifth Amendment, Constitution of the United States

You don't have to accept an IRS audit report. In most instances, you can appeal it within the IRS. If you are not given a chance to appeal, you can always go to federal Tax Court. (IRC §§ 9011, 9041.) An audit appeal is simple to initiate, and for small Tax Court cases—under $50,000—you can do it yourself.

IRS statistics reveal that 85% of taxpayers who appeal are able to reduce their audit bill. The average appeals settlement produces a 40% reduction of the tax bill from the auditor's Examination Report. Many folks do even better. And even if you don't win your appeal, you will have delayed the final tax bill for many months.

Appealing IRS Audits in a Nutshell

1. If you can't live with an audit result, you can usually appeal within the IRS—and you always have the right to go to court.
2. The majority of audit appeals are successful in reducing tax bills.
3. Collection of your audit bill is greatly delayed if you appeal, but interest and penalties still keep accumulating.
4. Prepare for an appeal hearing by carefully organizing your records, researching basic tax law and, perhaps, getting advice from a tax pro.
5. Filing in Tax Court is simple; most folks do it without a lawyer when contesting $50,000 or less in taxes and penalties for any one tax year.

Appealing an audit is discussed in much greater detail in *Stand Up to the IRS*, by Frederick W. Daily (Nolo).

A. IRS Appeals

If you don't sign off on an auditor's Examination Report, in most cases the IRS mails you a "30-Day Letter." This is your invitation to go to the IRS Appeals Office, which is completely separate from the audit division. Until and unless this letter is received, you cannot appeal.

The IRS is not required by law to let you internally appeal an audit, and sometimes it doesn't. But don't worry—the IRS always must notify you in writing of your right to contest the audit in the U.S. Tax Court. (See Section B, below.)

1. Writing an Appeal Letter

An appeal is begun by writing a "protest" letter to the IRS. (If you owe less than $2,500 for the audit, you can simply tell the auditor that you want to appeal; but play it safe and put it in writing.) A sample protest letter is shown below. It should include:

- Your name (or name of your business, depending on which one the audit report specifies) and your taxpayer identification number (either your Social Security number, if you are a sole proprietor without employees, or federal Employer Identification Number for other entities).
- A statement that you are appealing an Examination Report.
- The specific findings in the report that you dispute—something like this: "I disagree with the auditor's disallowance of business expense for travel in the amount of $797," or "I disagree with the finding by the auditor that my dog obedience business was not carried on for profit."
- A brief explanation of why the report is wrong. For example, "The trip in question was necessary to see a potential customer who lived in South Dakota," or, "I operated in a businesslike manner and trained many dogs to be responsible members of the community."

- Your signature, date and these magic words: "Under penalty of perjury, I declare that the facts presented in this protest and in any accompanying documents are, to the best of my knowledge and belief, true, correct and complete."

Attach a copy of the Examination Report and the 30-Day Letter from the IRS. Send the letter to the IRS office that audited you, addressed to the "District Director." Your letter will be processed and forwarded to the IRS Appeals Office.

Sample Protest Letter

October 1, 20xx

District Director
Internal Revenue Service
Your town, Your state 99999

Protest of Sam Smith
SSN 666-66-6666

Dear Sir/Madam:

I wish to appeal from the Examination Report of 9/5/xx, a copy of which is attached. I request a hearing. The tax year protested is 20xx.

I disagree with the disallowance of business expense deductions shown on Schedule C of $13,937 and penalties and interest in the amount of $2,817.

The adjustments were incorrect because the deductions were for legitimate expenses of advertising, promotion, travel and entertainment and were reasonable and necessary for my business.

Under penalty of perjury, I declare that the facts presented in this protest and in any accompanying documents are, to the best of my knowledge and belief, true, correct and complete.

Sincerely,

Sam Smith

Sam Smith

cc: IRS auditor
Enclosed: Copy of IRS 30-Day Letter
           Examination Report

2. Settling Without a Hearing

Within a few months after requesting an appeal, you'll get a call or letter from the IRS Appeals Office asking you to come for a meeting. Or an Appeals Officer may offer to handle the case just by phone or correspondence. This is worth a try. Send in explanations, copies of documents, citations to legal authority, affidavits of witnesses or whatever else you believe supports your position. A tax pro can help put things together if you are unsure.

If the Appeals Officer calls out of the blue and wants to discuss your case by phone and you are ready, go ahead. A better idea is to request a later time to talk when you can be fully prepared. (See Section 3, below, on how to present a case to an Appeals Officer.) If you feel that you could do a better job in person, then insist on a meeting. Most things go better when done face-to-face, but maybe you are more comfortable at a distance.

It's time to consult a tax pro. Even if you handle your IRS appeal yourself, consider seeing a tax pro for some advice. A good one can offer insights on what went wrong at the audit and how to approach the appeal in a professional manner. Appeals Officers appreciate a well-prepared presentation and are more likely to settle when they see their opponent is not just shooting from the hip.

3. The Appeals Hearing

If you don't get anywhere with an Appeals Officer by phone or mail, ask for a face-to-face meeting. Some IRS offices don't have Appeals Officers, so you may have to travel to another city.

Your hearing will probably be one-on-one with the Appeals Officer in a small meeting room. Auditors or other IRS personnel seldom attend. No formal or electronic recordings of Appeals Hearings are made, so take notes.

Most folks find Appeals Officers much easier to deal with than auditors. Even though Appeals Officers work for the IRS, they are not there to just rubber-stamp auditors' decisions. Their aim is to mediate a settlement to keep your case from ending up in court. Use this second chance to sell your position that your tax return was correct—or closer to it than the auditor's report says.

Expect an appeal hearing to last an hour or two. Start with a brief explanation of why you think the Examination Report is wrong. Show any documents supporting your position. Emphasize any material you didn't have at the audit, such as new documents

or a reconstruction of lost items. If you can't produce any missing documents, explain why.

You are trying to convince the Appeals Officer that you have some chance—no matter how small—of winning if you were to go to court. An Appeals Officer can't make a purely "nuisance" settlement—that is, give in just so you will go away. Some evidence—even if only substitute records to replace missing ones—can provide the Appeals Officer with a hook on which to hang a compromise settlement. (Chapter 19, Audits, explains how reconstructed records can be used.)

Almost any kind of auditor's adjustment—other than a dumb mistake like a math error—is subject to appeals negotiation. Common small business appeal issues include entitlements to a home office deduction, travel and entertainment expenses and advertising and business car write-offs.

Making a deal on appeal is often done by "trading" issues. Get the Appeals Officer to see that you have an arguable point on at least one issue and you are on your way to a compromise.

Don't expect total victory in an appeal, although it is certainly possible. It's better to stay flexible; give-and-take is the proper attitude.

> **EXAMPLE:** Rusty is an independent building materials sales rep. He regularly calls on customers in his car, and wines and dines his larger accounts. But an IRS auditor disallowed Rusty's auto expenses of $1,740 as well as his business entertainment expenses of $820, due to spotty recordkeeping and missing receipts.
>
> Rusty can argue to the Appeals Officer that he needs his car to make calls and that it is customary for salespersons in his business to buy customers lunch or take them to baseball games. Rusty lost his receipts but can back up his claims with signed statements from customers acknowledging that he has bought them a meal or entertained them while on business. To settle, Rusty might offer to trade issues by accepting the disallowance of the entertainment expenses if the Appeals Officer allows his automobile expense deduction, or offer to accept a 50% disallowance of each.

Mention your Tax Court option. If the Appeals Officer is not amenable to any kind of settlement, tell him politely you will have to go on to Tax Court. If he thinks you are serious, he may make a last-ditch effort to work things out.

4. Payment After an Appeals Settlement

If and when you reach a settlement, Appeals Officers will request—but cannot insist on—immediate payment of any tax due. They can also process a monthly payment plan request. The amount you owe will be treated as a separate issue from how you are going to pay. An Appeals Officer is not supposed to make any settlement conditioned on your immediate payment or acceptance of a payment plan.

B. Contesting an Audit in Court

You aren't required to go through the IRS appeals process before contesting an audit in court. If you don't appeal—or do but aren't happy with the way it comes out—you can go to one of three courts: United States Tax Court, United States District Court or the Court of Federal Claims.

Almost everyone chooses Tax Court, for two good reasons: First, the District and Claims courts require you to first pay the tax and then sue for a refund. Second, few people succeed in these two courts without lawyers.

Tax Court, on the other hand, allows you to contest an audit for a filing fee of $60, and offers a reasonable chance of success without a lawyer.

1. About Tax Court

The U.S. Tax Court is an independent federal court, not part of the IRS. (IRC §§ 7441-46.) Contesting an audit in Tax Court requires filing a "petition," which is simple if yours qualifies as a small case. (See Section 2, below.)

The chances of at least partial victory are good: over half of those filing in Tax Court either settle

with the IRS lawyers before trial or get some reduction in court. For instance, the judge may uphold the IRS on a tax adjustment, but drop a penalty of hundreds or even thousands of dollars.

In cases under $10,000, 47% of taxpayers win at least partial victories over the IRS auditor. In larger cases, 60% of all petitioners come out ahead! However, less than 10% win a total victory in Tax Court.

2. Can You Do It Yourself in Tax Court?

Whether or not you want to go it alone in Tax Court should depend on how much money is at stake. Most Tax Court disputes involve factual issues—not complex tax law points. Many individuals without law degrees come out just fine representing themselves in Tax Court.

To go to Tax Court, you must have first received an IRS "Statutory Notice of Deficiency," also called a "90-Day Letter." Expect this letter within one to six months after your audit, assuming you did not sign off the Examination Report. The notice is sent by certified or registered mail. If you move during this time, make sure the auditor has your new address.

a. Under $50,000: Informal "S" Cases

The Tax Court allows cases disputing less than $50,000 (per tax year audited) to be treated under rules much like a Small Claims Court. These "S," or small case, procedures are informal. You simply present your case to one judge in your own words, without using legal jargon.

b. Over $50,000: Regular Cases

If yours is a regular case (more than $50,000 per year is in dispute), you may need a lawyer. (A small number of CPAs and Enrolled Agents are also approved to practice in Tax Court.) If you go in without a lawyer, the judge will expect you to know tax law and court procedures. A compromise solution may be to use a tax lawyer as a legal coach, but who doesn't appear in court. Some Tax Court judges are tolerant of "pro se" petitioners (people without lawyers), but others may throw you out of court for not knowing court procedures and law.

Filing a petition is a wise move. Often, just filing a Tax Court case produces a settlement. If not, you can always chicken out before going into court, and all you will be out is the $60 filing fee. Alternatively, you can file and try to settle it yourself, and then bring in a lawyer if you fail. At the very least your petition delays the final tax bill for many months (although the interest continues to run).

3. Filing Your Petition in Tax Court

It is easy to get a small (under $50,000 per year) case before the Tax Court. First, call or write to:

Clerk of the U.S. Tax Court
400 Second Street, NW
Washington, DC 20217
202-606-8754

or go to the Tax Court's website at http://www.ustaxcourt.gov/ustcweb.htm.

Request or download a petition form and pamphlet explaining the court's small case rules. If you request the information by mail, the staff of the Tax Court is very efficient and will get these items to you within a few days. Don't expect any advice on winning your case from the clerk, however.

Carefully follow the instructions for filling in the forms. Mail the petition (via U.S. Postal Service, certified mail, Return Receipt Requested). Enclose your check or money order for the filing fee. You'll get an acknowledgment letter and case number from the clerk in about a week. The clerk sends the IRS attorneys a copy of your petition. You are on your way!

4. Tax Court Pre-Trial Procedure

Within a few months after filing, you'll hear from someone at the IRS, either an Appeals Officer or lawyer. This is an important contact, since most tax court cases are settled by these folks without going to court. You might even settle your case by phone or through the mail without ever meeting these people. (See the discussion in Section A, above, on how to negotiate an appeal.)

If you reach a settlement, a Stipulated Tax Court "Decision" is prepared for your signature. It is sent to the IRS and then to a judge for approval. It takes a few months to complete the paperwork, so don't be concerned if you don't get anything back right away. (The only thing to worry about now is paying the bill.)

If no compromise is reached, you'll get a notice of a trial date, which will be in six to 12 months after you file. Trials are held in about 100 of the largest cities. You may have to travel several hundred miles to court—another reason to settle before trial.

5. Settling Before Trial

IRS lawyers frequently agree to a last-minute deal—even in the hallway outside the courtroom—minutes before your trial is to begin. If they don't bring it up, you should. Try something new—such as agreeing to some adjustment that you previously did not accept. Fewer than 10% of all folks get a total victory in a Tax Court trial, so be realistic.

> **EXAMPLE:** Karen's auto parts business was audited, and additional taxes of $5,100 were found, including $1,300 for disallowed business expenses. Karen could offer to accept $1,300 in taxes if the IRS will concede the balance of $3,800. This might tip the scales with the IRS attorney, or might bring a counteroffer. It doesn't cost Karen anything to try.

6. Your Tax Court Trial

How your trial will be conducted may depend on whether you qualify for the simplified Tax Court procedures for small cases (less than $50,000 contested per tax year).

a. All Cases

On the date you are scheduled for trial, show up on time. Typically, many other IRS victims will be there, and the clerk will start by calling roll. Chances are your case won't be heard on that day; more likely you'll be assigned a time and date later in that week (or the next one) for trial.

The judge sits on a wooden throne (like on TV), or at the end of a conference table if there is no formal courtroom available. Once your case is called, come forward and sit at a table facing the judge. The IRS attorney will be at another table.

Bring all papers you want the judge to see. If you have witnesses, have them sitting nearby. Address the judge as "your honor."

The judge will not be very familiar with the facts of your case. He has only the Tax Court file, consisting of your petition, the IRS's response (called an "answer") and a copy of the audit report. The judge does *not* have the IRS's file or any of the documents that you submitted to the auditor or Appeals Officer. You are starting with a clean slate.

You and your witnesses will be sworn to tell the truth. You may sit or stand, according to the instruction of the judge, as you present your case. A table will be provided for you to lay out your documents and sit at when the IRS attorney is presenting his case.

Start by asking the judge if you can give a brief explanation of why you disagree with the IRS, but don't go into the details just yet. Next, either ask permission to start calling your witnesses, or begin by presenting your documents (whatever you want the judge to consider). Bring an extra copy of everything you give the judge for the IRS's attorney —and don't forget to keep originals.

Briefly explain the significance of each document. For instance, "Your honor, this is a bill from Jake, the plumber who fixed the pipes, which the IRS auditor would not allow as a business expense deduction." Expect the judge and the IRS attorney to ask you questions. Questioning is relatively informal, especially if yours is an "S" case. Speak and show documents as if you were trying to convince a friend about your case.

EXAMPLE: Thom's Hardware store was damaged by a flood. Thom quickly hired Jim, an out-of-town handyman, to make emergency repairs. Jim insisted on payment of $3,800 in cash, and Thom agreed. Thom got a receipt from Jim for payment but lost it in the confusion. Jim is now in parts unknown after his parole officer came looking for him. An IRS auditor disallowed the $3,800 deduction—not because this type of expense was not legally allowed, but because Thom couldn't prove that he paid it. So Thom's dispute with the IRS is over the factual issue of whether he paid $3,800—not whether it's a legitimate business expense.

At the Tax Court hearing, Thom starts by explaining what happened in his own words. Thom brings in a witness to back up his story. Thom presents Deena, a friend, who observed the flood damage and saw Jim do the work. Even though Deena didn't see Thom pay Jim, she can tell the judge that Thom needed help fast, that Jim came along and that Jim worked seven full days and provided materials. The judge can easily infer that Jim didn't work without pay.

Thom also shows the judge documents supporting his case, such as a news clipping and photos of the flooded store. It is up to the judge to determine if Thom, Deena and the documentation are believable enough to overturn all or some of the auditor's findings.

Watch and learn. On the day of your trial, there may be other cases heard before yours. You may find it enlightening (or stupefying) to spend a few hours watching and learning about the judge's habits and courtroom procedures firsthand.

b. Cases Over $50,000 Only

If the IRS claims you owe more than $50,000 per tax year and you go before a judge, you will not have such an easy time. You must be familiar with tax law and Tax Court procedures if you hope to win. Start by consulting the books listed at the end of this chapter, or bring in a tax lawyer.

7. Tax Court Decisions

Unlike Judge Wapner, who wraps it all up in 15 minutes and rules on the spot, Tax Court judges usually mail out their decisions a few weeks or months after a trial.

Small case (under $50,000) Tax Court decisions are final; they cannot be appealed by you or by the IRS.

Regular Tax Court decisions (cases over $50,000), may be appealed to a higher court, the U.S. Court of Appeals. Appealing a Tax Court decision definitely requires an attorney. Fewer than 15% of all Tax Court decisions are reversed.

Assuming you don't win outright, it will be several months after receiving the judge's decision before you get a tax bill. Interest is added to the bill starting from the time the original tax return was filed—or the date it should have been filed, if later.

Resources

- IRS Publication 1, Your Rights as a Taxpayer.
- IRS Publication 5, Appeal Rights and Preparation of Unagreed Cases.
- IRS Publication 556, Examination of Returns, Appeal Rights and Claims for Refund.
- *Stand Up to the IRS*, by Frederick W. Daily (Nolo). This companion book has detailed information and tips on handling appeals and Tax Court cases.
- *Represent Yourself in Court*, by Paul Bergman and Sara J. Berman-Barrett (Nolo). This book is full of practical tips on how to present documents to a court and what to say (and not to say) to a judge.
- Rules of Practice and Procedure, United States Tax Court. If you are handling a regular Tax Court case (over $50,000 contested per tax year) on your own, you must familiarize yourself with the rules of court. This book is available through the Tax Court Clerk, 400 Second St., NW, Washington, DC 20217, 202-606-8754. Call to find out the current price. These rules are also available in Adobe Acrobat® format on the U.S. Tax Court's website, http://www.ustaxcourt.gov/ustcweb. htm. You can also find the rules in most federal court buildings and law school libraries.

Penalties and Interest

"Laws and institutions require to be adapted, not to good men, but to bad."

— John Stuart Mill

When the IRS hits you or your business with a tax bill, it usually adds penalties and interest. These extra charges can be shocking—a $7,000 tax bill could have $15,000 in penalties and interest tacked on to it. Some penalties, such as late payments, are added automatically by IRS computers. IRS personnel may also impose penalties if they find that you violated a tax code provision—for example, you paid taxes or filed a return late, or owe from an audit. The IRS doesn't just dream up penalties—each one has been authorized by our elected representatives in Washington.

Once penalties are decreed, if you don't take steps to refute them, the IRS assumes you accept them. Happily, the IRS can remove a penalty from your bill just as easily as it added one. The key to the kingdom of tax penalty relief is showing a "reasonable cause" for your failure to comply with tax law.

And by the way, tax penalties are not tax-deductible when you pay them.

Penalties and Interest in a Nutshell

1. Whenever the IRS finds a business or its owner was late in filing a return or making a payment or otherwise breached the tax laws, it is likely to impose a penalty.
2. If your business is hit with a penalty, it may be canceled if you can show "reasonable cause."
3. You are entitled to a full explanation from the IRS of any penalty imposed and how it was calculated.
4. It is difficult, but not impossible, to get the IRS to drop interest charges on tax bills.

A. Common Reasons for Penalties

The number of different tax code penalties to punish wrongdoers is staggering. This section covers only the penalties most likely to be imposed on a small business person.

1. Inaccuracies

The IRS can hit you with a 20% penalty if it finds you were negligent (unreasonably careless) or substantially understated your taxes. This "accuracy-related" penalty is applied when you can't prove a deduction on an audit, or you didn't report all of your income and the IRS discovers it.

2. Civil Fraud

If the IRS finds that you underreported your income with a fraudulent intent (it doesn't look like an honest mistake to the IRS), a fine of 75% can be added to the resulting tax deficiency. (IRC § 6651(f).) Breathe easy—this civil (noncriminal) tax fraud penalty is imposed in fewer than 2% of all audits. (You may also be charged with the crime of tax fraud, which is even rarer (IRC § 7201).)

3. Failure to Pay on Time

The IRS usually adds a penalty of ½% to 1% per month to an income tax bill that's not paid on time. This late payment penalty is automatically tacked on by the IRS computer whenever you file a return without paying the balance owed, or pay it late. (IRC § 665(a).)

Late payment penalties for failing to make payroll tax deposits on time are much higher.

4. Filing Late

If you're late in filing certain income tax returns or other forms, the IRS can penalize you an additional 5% per month on any balance due. However, this penalty can be applied only for the first five months following the return's due date, up to a 25% maximum charge. If there is no balance due on a late return, the IRS can't impose this penalty.

5. Filing and Paying Late

A special rule applies if you both file late and underpay. The IRS can (and probably will) impose a "combined penalty" of 25% of the amount owed if not paid in the first five months after the return and tax are due. After five months, the "failure to pay" penalty continues at ½% per month until the two penalties reach a combined maximum of 47½%. This is a slightly lower (2½% less overall) penalty than if the two penalties were applied separately. Wow, those IRS folks sure can be generous. (IRC § 665(c).)

> **EXAMPLE:** Mortimer the mortician lets April 15 pass without filing his tax return or making any payment. He finally gets around to filing on September 16 and owes $4,000. The IRS will tack on a 25% penalty ($1,000), bringing the bill up to $5,000. Interest will be charged as well. Typically, the IRS charges 8–10% interest annually.

! **IRS penalties are "stackable."** Late filing and paying penalties can be imposed by the IRS in addition to any other penalties, such as for fraud and filing an inaccurate return. Congress and the IRS believe the more the merrier when it comes to penalizing delinquent or erring taxpayers.

6. Underpaying Estimated Taxes

Many, if not most, self-employed folks occasionally get dinged for the "estimated tax penalty." All self-employed individuals must estimate their income tax for the year and pay it in quarterly installments throughout that year. You must come pretty close to paying everything you will owe, although you don't have to guess the total amount precisely.

Here are the rules for avoiding the penalty:

- If you earn less than $150,000, your quarterly tax payments must equal at least 90% of your final income tax bill, or at least 100% of your last year's tax bill.
- If you earn more than $150,000, you must pay at least 110% of your last year's tax bill in estimated payments or risk the underpayment penalty on whatever amount you come up short.

The penalty for not complying is currently an 8% annual addition to the amount underpaid for each quarter. Quarterly payments should be equal—you can't play catch-up with larger payments later in the year and still avoid this penalty.

Quarterly estimated tax payments are due on April 15, June 15, September 15 and January 15 of each year.

B. Interest on Tax Bills

Congress requires the IRS to charge interest on delinquent tax bills, and has given the IRS very limited discretion in canceling interest charges. The interest rate is adjusted every quarter by a formula and compounded daily—currently it's 8% annually. It is charged on a monthly basis. If you are audited and end up owing more tax, interest is charged starting on the original date the tax return was due.

C. Understanding Penalty and Interest Notices

If you receive a tax bill with a penalty and interest charges, it may not be clear how these charges were computed. Calling or visiting your local IRS

Part 6

Dealing With the IRS

office to ask for an explanation may not help; many IRS staffers don't understand these computer-generated and heavily coded notices. It's best to call the IRS taxpayer assistance line (800-829-1040) with your questions, or simply request that a Penalty and Interest Explanation Notice (PINEX) be sent to you.

A PINEX is a multi-paged computer printout that includes:

- A listing of your business (or personal) tax accounts for the specific years you request, showing all tax penalty and interest computations.
- Dates, interest rates, penalties assessed and any credits to your account, such as your quarterly payments, abatements (reductions) by the IRS or any refunds applied.
- Explanations of why particular penalties were charged, with tax code citations authorizing each penalty.
- A summary of your account with balance due, including up-to-date penalty and interest amounts.

D. How to Get Penalties Reduced or Eliminated

Once you understand why and how the IRS hit you with penalties, you may request that they be reduced or eliminated. The IRS term for this process is "abatement." About one-third of all penalties are eventually abated, according to IRS statistics. I suspect that even more penalties would be canceled if people knew how to contest them.

Just telling the IRS that you don't like a penalty, or can't afford to pay it, won't work. You must show "reasonable cause," meaning a good excuse. The IRS instruction book for its agents, called The Internal Revenue Manual (IRM), says, *"Any sound reason advanced by a taxpayer as the cause for delay in filing a return, making deposits ... or paying tax when due will be carefully analyzed."*

The IRM lists seven categories of excuses for abating any tax penalty except fraud:

1. Death or serious illness of the taxpayer or immediate family

2. Unavoidable absence

3. Destruction by fire or other casualty of the business or records

4. Inability to determine the tax because of reasons beyond the taxpayer's control

5. Civil disturbances

6. Lack of funds, but only when the taxpayer can demonstrate the exercise of ordinary business care and prudence, and

7. Other reasons establishing that the taxpayer exercised ordinary business care but couldn't comply within the time limits.

When requesting an abatement, try to fit your excuse into categories 1 to 6 first. If you honestly can't, try the catch-all number 7. This category covers mistaken reliance on bad advice from a tax pro or from the IRS, or just about any other excuse you can come up with.

 If in doubt, try for an abatement. It is always worth a try to get a penalty abated. I have seen people with all sorts of excuses—some a tad farfetched—succeed. And one thing is for certain: if you don't ask, you don't get.

1. How to Request a Penalty Abatement

As soon as you receive a tax notice with penalties, request an abatement in writing, following the form letter below. Be brief and straightforward. State that you are requesting an abatement of penalties, identify the tax bill and tell the IRS what your reasonable cause is. Attach a photocopy of the IRS notice showing the penalty, along with any documentation supporting your request. Keep several copies of your letters and attachments.

Most penalties are imposed by the IRS Service Center that sent the tax bill, so mail your abatement request there—not to the local IRS office. The IRS is notorious for ignoring, losing or taking seemingly forever to answer correspondence, so you may need to send additional copies later. Wait about 45 days before sending your follow-up request. Photocopies of your first request and documents should be sufficient—just change the date of the request.

Sample Letter Requesting Abatement of Penalties

To: Adjustments/Correspondence Branch
IRS Service Center
P.O. Box 9941
Ogden, UT 84409

Re: Request for Penalty Abatement

From: Sanford Majors
43 Valley Road
Salt Lake City, UT 84000

SSN: 555-55-5555

November 3, 20xx

To Whom It May Concern:

I am requesting an abatement of penalties asserted in the IRS notice enclosed dated 5/5/xx of $2,312.10.

The reason I *[select one]*: filed late, paid late, didn't report some income was that *[fill in your reason, such as]*:

- I was suffering from a nervous breakdown
- My wife had just passed away
- My house burned down on April 14 with all of my tax records
- I was a hostage in Lebanon
- any other excuse

Enclosed is a *[describe your documents, such as]*:

- Letter from Dr. Freud explaining my condition which prevented me from filing my tax return on time
- Death certificate confirming my wife's passing
- Report from the fire department
- Letter from the U.S. State Department confirming my status as a hostage
- any other documentation

I have also enclosed payment that covers the amount of the underlying taxes I owe. *[Optional, but a good idea if you can afford to make the payment.]*

Please abate these penalties for "reasonable cause." I can be reached at 801-555-3444 during daytime hours.

Thank you,

Sanford Majors

Sanford Majors

Enclosed: IRS Tax Notice; Doctor's letter, death certificate, fire report, letter
from State Department *[or whatever]*

Stress your clean IRS record. If you can do so honestly, emphasize that you have never before had a penalty, been behind in paying taxes or asked for an abatement. Even if such claims are not exactly true, the IRS penalty examiner may let it go, so let your conscience be your guide.

2. If Your Abatement Request Is Rejected

If the IRS Service Center officially rejects your request, it will send you a written notice of its decision. To go farther, take one or more of these actions:

1. Write to the Service Center and ask for penalty appeals consideration. There is no IRS form for this—just write a clear letter headed "Penalty Appeal" and explain your "reasonable cause." Attach the tax bill in question and any documentation supporting your case.

2. Call or visit your local IRS office and speak with a Taxpayer Service Representative or a Collection employee. They are authorized to consider "reasonable cause" applications and cancel penalties. Don't mention that a Service Center turned you down. If you're turned down again, request in writing that they forward your case for appeals consideration.

3. File an Offer in Compromise on IRS Form 656 based on doubt as to your liability for the penalty. This is a formal procedure for contesting or negotiating any unpaid IRS bill, including a penalty charge. Don't offer any money when contesting a penalty because you are claiming that you aren't liable for it at all. Follow the directions accompanying Form 656 precisely. Attach your explanation and documents supporting your position, if any. (Offers in Compromise are discussed in Chapter 18, When You Can't Pay Your Taxes.)

4. Pay the penalty and then file IRS Form 843, Claim for Refund and Request of Abatement. Attach a letter and substantiating documents (as you did to your abatement request letter), or write your explanation in the space provided on the form. If your claim is refused illegally, you can sue in U.S. District Court or the Court of Federal Claims for a refund. Seldom are tax penalties large enough to justify the expense of a lawsuit, however.

E. How to Get Interest Charges Removed

It is never easy to get interest removed from a tax bill, unless it resulted from an IRS error. In four instances, however, you might have a chance.

1. Logically enough, if a tax or penalty is abated, interest on that amount should be canceled, too. The IRS computer should do this automatically, but always check a tax bill to verify that the excess interest was removed. If you suspect a mistake, call the IRS at the number on the notice or at 800-829-1040. Ask them to explain on the phone or send you a PINEX. (See Section C, above.) If you continue to get incorrect bills, complain to the IRS office that sent the bill.

2. Did the interest charges result from delays by the IRS? For instance, say you settled an audit agreeing to pay more tax, and the IRS didn't send a bill until a year later. The interest should be canceled, because it accrued because the IRS didn't promptly bill you. However, you can't get interest abated if it accumulated while you were (unsuccessfully) challenging an IRS bill in an audit appeal or in court.

3. If the IRS concludes that you will never be able to pay the tax and interest charges, it may accept less in an Offer in Compromise. (See Chapter 18, When You Can't Pay Your Taxes.)

4. Interest, along with the tax and penalties, may be reduced or eliminated through bankruptcy. (See Chapter 18, When You Can't Pay Your Taxes.)

F. Designating Payments on Delinquent Tax Bills

When making payments on tax bills that include both penalties and interest, you may tell the IRS how to apply the payments. It might make a difference. For instance, if the bill is for a business-related tax, you should designate that the payment be first applied to interest. The reason is that the interest is a deductible business expense. (Tax penalties, however, are never deductible, and neither is interest on a personal (nonbusiness) tax bill.)

One exception to the "first to interest" designation is for past due payroll or employment taxes. With payroll taxes for your incorporated business, payments should be designated to be first applied to the "trust fund portion" of the delinquent payroll tax. (See Chapter 5, Tax Concerns of Employers, for the reason why.)

You should also direct the IRS to apply payments to specific tax periods, if there is more than one for which you are delinquent. Generally, you want payments first applied to the most recent—not the oldest—tax period, because:

- The heaviest penalties are charged in the first few months after a tax return is due.
- The older a tax bill gets, the more likely the IRS is to compromise it, lose it in the shuffle or let the ten-year statute of limitations on collection run out.
- Tax bills over three years old may qualify for discharge in bankruptcy.

If you don't tell the IRS which tax period to apply the payment to, it will automatically apply it to the oldest tax period.

To designate payments, write the tax period on the face of the payment check, along with your taxpayer identification number (your Social Security number or the Employer Identification Number of your business). Also, send a letter with the check stating specifically which tax period the payment is to be applied to.

Resources

- *Stand Up to the IRS,* by Frederick W. Daily (Nolo). This book discusses penalties, interest and how to deal with them in greater detail than we go into in this chapter.
- IRS Notice 746, Information About Your Notice, Penalty and Interest. This notice is usually sent with your first tax bill that contains a penalty or interest charge. If you need a copy, download it from the IRS's website at http://www.irs.gov, call 800-829-1040 or go to your local IRS office.

Part

6

Dealing With the IRS

Help Beyond the Book

"The avoidance of taxes is the only intellectual pursuit that still carries any reward."

— **John Maynard Keynes**

Our tax code is a moving target; tax laws are always being reworked by Congress. Keeping up with changes affecting you, your business or industry can be a challenge.

The average small business person can't afford to call a tax pro with every question. Fortunately, much tax information is available for free (or close to it), if you are willing to look. The IRS provides free publications on basic tax law—always from the IRS's point of view, of course. Trade associations publish specialized newsletters and magazines covering tax concerns common to their members. General tax newsletters, books and annual tax preparation publications are plentiful, and small business tax material is widely available in libraries.

You should also have a good tax advisor on call. Keep professional fees under control by learning as much as you can on your own. The more you know before meeting the tax pro, the better position you will be in to judge his capabilities. And, of course, the less tax education you will require. Throughout this book I alert you to the occasions it makes economic sense to get help.

A tax pro can help set up your recordkeeping system and choose an accounting method. You may want to use a pro if you don't feel comfortable doing your own tax return. (Who does?) Everyone's business and individual tax situation is unique; like

your wardrobe, some custom fitting always works better than off-the-rack. Here are some places to do your shopping.

Tax Help in a Nutshell

1. There are a lot of good resources for answering tax questions, starting with free IRS publications.
2. Tax advice from the IRS is not legally binding on the IRS.
3. Small business owners should establish a working relationship with a tax professional.

A. Finding Answers to Tax Questions

The income tax law is a product of all three branches of our federal government. And all three provide services for answering your tax questions. The legislative branch, Congress, writes the Internal Revenue Code (IRC).

The executive branch, specifically the Treasury Department, of which the Internal Revenue Service is a part, publishes interpretations of many tax code provisions. These interpretations serve as guides as to how the IRS will apply the law.

The judicial branch, the federal courts, interpret the tax code in light of the Constitution and what they divine as Congress's intent. When the IRS applies the tax code contrary to the Constitution or differently than Congress intended, it may be overturned by the federal courts. These court decisions are published ("reported") and serve to guide taxpayers on how to interpret the tax code.

This section discusses the many resources available to augment the tax information in this book: IRS publications, self-help tax preparation guides, textbooks, court decisions and periodicals. Some are free, and most others are reasonably priced. Tax publications for professionals are expensive, but are often available at public or law libraries.

IRS Launches Small Business Website

In March, 2001, the IRS unveiled a promising new small business community website to assist the nation's 45 million business and self-employed taxpayers. The goal is to improve IRS service to these folks through accessibility of helpful info. The site provides:

- answers to basic tax questions and calendar of tax deadlines
- online access to most IRS forms
- industry-specific tax info for specific industries like construction and food service
- tips to avoid common tax problems
- links to court opinions and to rulings and regulations on specific industries
- links to non-IRS sites for general tax information, and
- links to helpful small business resources.

Access this site through the IRS home page (http://www.irs.gov). Click on "Small Business and Self-Employed Community" to connect to this site. The best part about it is the cost; it's free.

1. IRS Booklets and CD-ROM

The IRS publishes over 350 free booklets explaining the tax code; some are incomprehensible and others are fairly straightforward. But where there is a gray area in the law, you can bet you'll get only the IRS's interpretation—even if federal courts have made contrary rulings.

These booklets, called IRS Publications ("Pubs," for short), range from several pages to several hundred pages in length. Get them at IRS offices; download them online at http://www.irs.gov; by calling 800-829-FORM (3676); or by sending in an order form. There is no charge, not even postage. (A list of free IRS tax publications for small businesses is in the Appendix.)

Every small business person should order a package of IRS forms and publications called Your Business Tax Kit. The kit includes Forms SS-4, Application for Employer Identification Number and 1040-ES, Estimated Tax for Individuals. And it includes several key publications mentioned throughout this book:

- Pub 334, Tax Guide for Small Business (at 325 pages, the largest booklet)
- Pub 583, Taxpayers Starting a Business
- Pub 910, Guide to Free Tax Services
- Pub 1057, Small Business Tax Education Program Brochure
- Pub 1544, Reporting Cash Payments of Over $10,000, and
- Pub 1779, Employee or Independent Contractor.

If you have a computer with a CD-ROM and don't mind spending $21 (it's a deductible business expense), you can get all IRS publications, plus 600 forms, IRS Regulations and back year tax forms (to 1991) on CD-ROM Publication 1796 (Stock Number 648-095-00004-0). Call the Superintendent of Documents to order, at 202-512-1800 or order online at http://www.irs.gov. The IRS also offers a free CD-ROM product called the Small Business Resource Guide—2001 CD-ROM, Publication 3207. According to the IRS, this publication contains:

- information on small business topics from various regulatory agencies
- business tax forms, instructions and publications
- valuable insight on a wide range of topics, from preparing a business plan to keeping records of financing and retirement plans, and
- informative tutorials, updates and a multi-agency electronic newsletter.

You can order a single free copy of the CD-ROM from the IRS's website at http://www.irs.gov/prod/businfo/sm_bus/smbus-cd.html or by calling 800-829-3676.

Don't rely exclusively on the IRS for information. The IRS's free publications run the gamut from good to bad to plain ugly. While some are clearly written and useful, others are misleading, and a few are in an unknown language. I am always amused to see IRS publications with disclaimers

Part

6

Dealing With the IRS

warning you against relying on them. The IRS is not legally bound to follow its own writings that explain the tax law. Amazing, isn't it?

2. Free IRS and Social Security Telephone Information

The IRS offers prerecorded tapes on tax topics on its toll-free telephone service (TELETAX) at 800-829-4477. See IRS Publication 910 for a list of topics.

You may talk to a live IRS taxpayer service representative at 800-829-1040. Expect difficulty getting through from January to May. Avoid calling on Mondays or during lunchtime.

The Social Security Administration also has an 800 number: 800-772-1213. It is staffed 7 a.m. to 7 p.m., and has prerecorded business-related topics 24 hours a day. Among other info available from the SSA, you or an employee of your business can get a statement of earnings, Form W-2 and Form 1099 income information for past years, an estimate of benefits and new or replacement Social Security cards.

Be alert for bad advice. The IRS is notorious for giving misleading or outright wrong answers to tax questions. In the IRS's defense, often taxpayers don't know how to ask the right questions, or really understand the answers given. Our overly complex tax code is as much to blame as the IRS. Unfortunately, the IRS does not stand behind oral advice that turns out to be incorrect. If you rely on what someone at the IRS tells you and it is wrong, you'll be liable for any resulting tax plus interest and penalties. If it's important, always check what the IRS tells you with a tax pro.

3. Free IRS Programs

In larger metropolitan areas, the IRS offers small business seminars on various topics, such as payroll tax reporting. You can ask questions at these half-day meetings given at schools and federal buildings. Call the IRS at 800-829-1040 to see if programs are offered near you and to get on the IRS small business mailing list.

4. IRS Written Advice

The IRS is legally bound by specific advice it gives in writing in an "IRS Letter Ruling." If you want one, you'll have to pay $500 to $3,000; expect to wait many months for your answer. If you are still interested, you had best hire a tax pro.

A better (and far cheaper) bet is to look up letter rulings issued to other taxpayers with a similar question—if you can find one. Letter rulings are published in the Internal Revenue Cumulative Bulletin, and in private tax service publications found in larger public and law libraries. I won't kid you; it is not easy to research letter rulings, and even harder to find one on point. (See Section 7 below for more information.) However, if you want to try, you should know how these rulings are identified and indexed. For example, "Ltr. Rul. 892012" refers to a ruling issued in 1989, in the 20th week and which was the 12th letter ruling issued that week. My suggestion is that you ask a tax pro to do this for you.

5. Internal Revenue Code

The Internal Revenue Code (IRC) is written by Congress and is nicknamed "the code" or "the tax code." It's a thick book with tiny print and is found in the reference section of most libraries, IRS offices, tax pros' offices and larger bookstores. The IRC is revised once (or twice) a year, mostly minor changes by Congress. On average, significant revisions to the tax code are made every three to four years.

The IRC is found in Title 26 of the United States Code (USC for short). The USC encompasses all of our federal laws. "Title" simply refers to the place within the massive USC where the IRC is found.

The IRC is divided up into sections, which, in turn, are subdivided into more parts, ad infinitum. The tax code is a crazy-quilt of laws that apply to everyone next to provisions just for left-handed sheep breeders in New Jersey.

> **EXAMPLE:** "IRC § 179(b)(4)(A)" means that this particular tax law is found in Title 26 of the USC, the Internal Revenue Code, Section 179, subsection b, paragraph 4, subparagraph A.

Most folks can live their entire lives without ever looking at the IRC. It is available at larger bookstores for about $25. (See order information at the back of this book.) The USC (including the IRC) is also available on CD-ROM from the Government Printing Office for under $40. And some, but not all, of the IRC can be found at the IRS website.

6. IRS Interpretations of the Tax Code

Congress, when enacting a broadly applicable tax law, can't foresee all possible situations. So the Treasury Department (the IRS is a part of it) is authorized to issue interpretations of broad tax code provisions.

a. Regulations

The most authoritative IRS interpretations are called "Treasury Regulations" or just "Regulations" or "Regs." Regulations provide the mechanics of how many (but not all) tax code provisions operate. Regulations often include examples, like the ones in this book. They are usually bound in a four- to six-volume set and are found in most larger libraries and some bookstores. Many regulations are downloadable from the IRS website. Regulations are marginally easier to read than the tax code on which they are based.

To go beyond the IRC, first check to see if there is a matching regulation. Start with the number of the IRC section; if there is a corresponding regulation, it will bear the same number, usually preceded by the numeral "1."

> **EXAMPLE:** "Reg. 1.179" refers to a Treasury regulation interpreting IRC Section 179.

b. Other IRS Pronouncements

The IRS publishes several types of statements of its position on various tax matters. These pronouncements guide IRS personnel and taxpayers as to how specific tax laws will be applied by the IRS.

IRS Revenue Rulings (Rev. Rul.) are IRS announcements of how the tax law applies to a hypothetical set of facts. Tax book publishers Prentice-Hall, Commerce Clearing House and Research Institute of America reprint IRS Revenue Rulings. They are indexed by IRC section and subject matter. A Revenue Ruling usually contains a factual example, followed by an explanation of how the tax code applies to those facts. While looking for a Revenue Ruling might pay off, it is not always easy to find one that precisely covers your situation.

> **EXAMPLE:** "Rev. Rul. 92-41" refers to IRS Revenue Ruling number 41, issued in 1992.

IRS Letter Rulings are IRS answers to specific written questions about more complex tax situations posed by taxpayers. (See Section 4, above.)

IRS Revenue Procedures (Rev. Procs.) are another way the IRS tells taxpayers exactly how to comply with certain tax code provisions. Rev. Procs. are primarily relied on by tax return preparers. They often explain when and how to report tax items, such as claiming a net operating loss on a tax form or return. They are contained in the Internal Revenue Cumulative Bulletin, found in larger public and law libraries, and also are reprinted by the tax book publishers mentioned above.

> **EXAMPLE:** "Rev. Proc. 91-15" refers to a published Revenue Procedure number 15, issued in 1991.

From time to time, the IRS gives general guidance and statements of policy in official "announcements" and "notices" similar to press releases. They appear in the weekly Internal Revenue Cumulative Bulletin. Seldom does it pay to search IRS announcements or notices, as they are too broad to answer specific questions.

The Internal Revenue Manual (IRM) is a series of handbooks that serve as guides to IRS employees on tax law and procedure. The IRM tells IRS employees —usually auditors or collectors—how specific tax code provisions should be enforced. The manual is for IRS internal use, but most of it is public and reprinted by private tax book publishers. It is also available to the public in larger IRS offices in their Freedom of Information Act reading rooms, and in law libraries and some tax pros' offices. Portions of the IRM are also downloadable from the IRS website.

The IRM can be very revealing of IRS attitudes in certain areas—for example, the criteria the IRS uses to determine whether "reasonable cause" exists for the abatement of a tax penalty. I have used material from the IRM throughout this book.

IRS Forms are well known to us all, especially Form 1040, the annual personal income tax return. There are more than 650 other forms, listed in Publication 676, Catalog of Federal Tax Forms. They are free at IRS offices or by calling 800-829-FORM or 800-829-1040. They also can be downloaded off the IRS website at http://www.irs.gov. Many IRS forms come with instructions and explanations of the tax law.

7. Court Cases

Federal courts have interpreted the tax law in thousands of court cases. Published (reported) Tax Court decisions are found in books called the *Tax Court Reports*. Also, U.S. District Courts, U.S. Courts of Appeal, Court of Federal Claims, U.S. Bankruptcy Courts and the Supreme Court all rule on tax issues. Decisions of these courts are published, along with explanations and discussions of the tax law. Chances are that at least one of these courts has adjudged the point you are interested in; the trick is finding it.

Researching court decisions goes beyond this book, but I can make a few suggestions. Go to Nolo's Legal Research Center at http://www.nolo.com and find your nearest law library with public access. Call your nearest federal court, college library or a

lawyer's office to find out where to go. Beyond the volumes that simply reprint court decisions, look for books by private tax services that summarize the cases and put them into a coherent order.

The key to accessing tax case books is to start looking for the number of an IRC section, or a court case reference you have run across, or a general topic, such as "depreciation." Head for the tax section or, better, ask the law library staff for help. A friendly librarian may take pity (if she knows her way around the tax section) and show you how to use the books and any computer research services that the library can access. Also look at the legal research books listed at the end of this chapter, which are available from their publishers or at bookstores.

8. Federal Small Business Programs

The Small Business Administration (SBA) guarantees business loans and also puts out some good publications. Personal counseling is offered by the Service Corps of Retired Executives (SCORE) program, under the SBA. These folks are not necessarily tax experts, but if they were successful in business, they know a thing or two about the tax game. Call the SBA at 800-827-5722, or visit the SBA office nearest you. The SBA also has a very helpful and informative website at http://www.sba.gov. Or write to the SBA at 1441 L Street, NW, Washington, DC 20461.

Small Business Development Centers (SBDCs) are sponsored by the SBA and state governments. They are usually affiliated with major state universities and provide free or low-cost seminars and counseling to small business people. To locate an SBDC near you, call the SBA at 800-827-5722.

Other federal agencies offer publications—either free or at reasonable prices—to assist small businesses. For a list of federal publications, write to:

Superintendent of Documents
U.S. Government Printing Office
P.O. Box 371954
Pittsburgh, PA 15250-7954.

9. Private Tax Guides and Software

There is a multitude of commercially published tax guides and newsletters. Annual tax preparation guidebooks sell for $20 or less. Most are directed at taxes for individuals, but many deal with small business tax issues as well. Some of my favorites are listed at the end of this chapter.

Tax professional desk books are one-volume guides with more detailed tax information than the preparation guides. They presume some basic tax knowledge on the reader's part and are priced at under $35. See the "Resources" list at the end of the chapter.

Tax-preparation computer programs usually include basic tax guidance. If you are computer literate, *TurboTax for Business* and *TurboTax for Home and Business* (Intuit) are recommended. This book is an interactive feature of both programs. I've tried the other programs such as *TaxCut*, and they just don't match up to *TurboTax* for ease of use!

10. Trade Association Publications

Every business or trade has specialized publications and newsletters that track tax issues of common interest. You might learn about specific tax issues in your industry that your tax pro might not know of—perhaps a new case or IRS ruling. Also, speakers on tax topics are often found on programs offered to members at conventions and trade shows.

11. Tax Info Online

There has been an explosion of tax information available on the Internet in the last year or two. Surprisingly, the IRS has a solid entry into the electronic world, and there are some good private sources as well.

Start your Internet search with the IRS home page at http://www.irs.gov. If you have problems, call the IRS help desk at 703-487-4608. You can download over 600 IRS forms and publications and peruse summaries of 150 tax topics. You can email simple tax questions to the IRS (but remember what I have said about taking tax advice from the IRS with a block of salt).

Commercial online services—America Online, CompuServe and Prodigy—offer tax information to subscribers from a number of good sources, including the National Association of Enrolled Agents. Many of these sites are interactive, allowing you to post tax questions to experts and receive answers. Keep in mind that you don't know the person giving the answer, and they don't know you and your tax history. The "right" tax answer is usually the one tailored to your individual situation—and for that you need the more personal touch of a meeting with a tax pro.

Here are some other helpful tax sites:
- http://www.unclefed.com includes all IRS forms (downloadable) as well as tax articles from private tax pros (including yours truly).
- http://www.sisterstates.com has state tax forms and info.

To go still deeper into cyberspace, simply type "tax" into one of the popular search engines such as Yahoo. Be prepared for thousands of listings to pop up. There is a lot of tax nonsense on the chaotic World Wide Web. People can express their views or promote harebrained "untax yourself" schemes. So, watch out.

B. Finding and Using a Tax Pro

Mastering the tax rules is a Herculean task, given everything else a businessperson has to do. Armed with some basic understanding of how your business is taxed (from reading this book and other resources), it makes sense to get to know a tax professional. Form a long-term relationship with a tax pro, calling any time when you really need her (and, of course, paying her promptly). Just what are tax pros and how can you find one? Read on for the answers.

1. Types of Tax Advisors

Tax advisors are of many varieties, and not all professionals are created equal. Just about anyone can claim to be a "tax expert."

Part

6

Dealing With the IRS

Look for someone specifically knowledgable in helping small businesses—usually not the outfit that advertises "rapid refunds" or a "big five" national CPA firm. Ideally, pick a professional who already understands your particular type of business—whether you are a manufacturer, a restaurateur or retail clothing seller. She should fall into one of the following categories of tax pros:

- **Tax Return Preparer.** The law does not require people who prepare tax returns to be tested or licensed in most states—which in my opinion is a big mistake. I am talking about both the mom-and-pop operations as well as the familiar chains. Unless your tax preparer is in one of the three categories below, be careful about relying on her for business tax help.

- **Enrolled Agent (EA).** An EA is a tax advisor and preparer who is licensed by the IRS. This professional designation is earned by either passing a difficult IRS test or at least five years of experience working for the IRS. There are 24,000 EAs in the United States. Enrolled Agents are the least expensive of the tax pros. They offer good value and are reliable for tax return preparation and routine tax matters. Many EAs offer bookkeeping and accounting assistance.

- **Tax Attorney.** A tax attorney is a lawyer with either a special tax law degree (LL.M. in taxation), or a tax specialization certification from a state Bar association. If you have a serious tax or IRS problem, require legal representation in court or need complex tax and estate planning, go to a tax attorney.

- **Certified Public Accountant (CPA) and other accountants.** CPAs are licensed and regulated by each state, like attorneys. They perform sophisticated accounting and business-related tax work and prepare tax returns. CPAs should be considered by larger businesses or for complex business tax returns. CPAs are found in large national firms or in small local outfits. Some states also license Public Accountants. These folks are competent, but are not as highly regarded as CPAs.

Speak to several tax pros to get a feel for their expertise before hiring one. For typical small business accounting needs I lean toward EAs and small CPA firms. Bigger CPA firms and tax attorneys are overkill, and too costly.

2. How Tax Pros Can Help

A tax pro can assist you with:

Information and Advice. A good tax pro can be a very effective teacher. (If your present advisor told you about this book or gave it to you, hurrah! You are working with someone who respects your ability to help yourself.) She can help make key tax decisions, such as choosing the best entity form for your business and preparing financial statements necessary for obtaining loans.

Recordkeeping. Some people would do about anything to avoid recordkeeping. That's why God created bean counters and small business software that makes recordkeeping (almost) fun. See Chapter 3, Recordkeeping and Accounting, to see what recordkeeping entails before deciding what's best. Or see a pro for setting up a system tailored for your business.

Tax Form Preparation. Once you get past the recordkeeping, you'll face various tax filings. Congress talks about tax simplification, but don't hold your breath. Until that day, seriously consider professional assistance for your business tax returns. If you insist on doing your own tax return, have it reviewed by a tax pro before filing it. For do-it-yourselfers, I recommend Intuit's *TurboTax for Business* or *TurboTax for Home and Business*—whether sole proprietorship, S or C corporation, partnership or limited liability company. However, self-prepared tax returns often cheat their makers; a tax pro can point out tax deductions or other benefits that you and your computer might miss, as well as keep you out of trouble.

Advice in Dealing With the IRS. If you ever need help in dealing with the IRS, a tax pro can be your coach. Some thorny questions may be answered in a minute or two by a canny tax pro.

Representation. You don't have to deal with the IRS at all if you hire an attorney, CPA or Enrolled Agent to represent you. They are costly, but they know how to handle IRS bureaucracy. A tax pro can neutralize the intimidation factor the IRS knows that it holds over you. If you have something to hide, a pro might be able to keep the lid on it.

3. How to Choose a Tax Pro for Your Business

There are several ways to find a good tax pro; asking the IRS is not one of them. Instead, try the following:

- **Personal referrals.** Ask friends, family, your attorney or banker, business associates or even competitors for the names of tax pros.
- **Advertising.** Trade journals, directories, phone books and newspapers carry lists of tax pros. Look under "accountants," "tax return preparers" and "attorneys—tax." Some offer free initial consultations. If they are advertising, they have time for new clients.
- **Professional associations and referral panels.** Most local bar associations and CPA societies can refer you to an attorney or accountant. They refer from a list on a rotation basis, so a referral shouldn't be construed as a recommendation or certification of competence. The National Association of Enrolled Agents (800-424-4339) can help you locate an EA in your area.

Once you have the names of tax pros, start weeding through them. Interview at least three pros to see how well you relate to each other. Break the ice by telling the pro where you got his name. Then discuss your situation, and ask if he has clients in similar businesses. Ask if he is too busy or doesn't have the experience you are looking for. If so, ask him to recommend someone who fits the bill.

If you worked with a tax preparer before you went into business, maybe this is the person you want to stick with, but maybe not. Ask about her experience with small businesses like yours.

Test a tax pro's attitude toward dealing with the IRS and knowledge of small business taxes by pulling out questions from this book. Someone with prior IRS work experience is not necessarily desirable—they may have been permanently imprinted with the IRS point of view.

Don't be in a hurry to hire a tax pro. It should be more like looking for a mate for life than a casual date. After all, complying with the tax laws is a key to whether your business lives or dies. You should be asking yourself some questions as you go through the selection process: Does the tax pro give you a feeling of confidence? Is she knowledgeable? How long has she been doing tax work? Can you envision her going to bat for you in front of the IRS?

4. Tax Pros' Fees

Good tax pros aren't cheap. A start-up business without much cash flow may be tempted to price shop. But an expensive expert who saves you from getting in trouble is a bargain in the long run.

Get a clear understanding of professional fees at your first meeting. Does the pro charge by the hour or have flat (fixed) fees for bookkeeping, accounting and tax form preparation? Professionals working on an hourly basis charge from a low of $50 per hour up to $500 for top CPAs and tax attorneys.

Ask for a written fee agreement so you have a basis for disputing a tax pro bill if necessary.

To some extent, you control costs here. Tax pros can be consulted as needed or hired to take over tasks from bookkeeping to IRS filings and representation.

Everything is negotiable. If you like the tax pro, but not her fee, ask if she can do it for less. Try something like, "I am new in business and need to watch my pennies." If she believes you'll be a long-term client, or you catch her in a slow period, she may discount her normal rates. The best time to hire a tax pro is after the "tax season"—meaning the summer or fall.

Resources

- At the end of each chapter is a list of resources specific to that topic. Start there first, and then go to the more general list here.
- *Internal Revenue Code (IRC).* This book has more fine print than you ever thought you would find in one place, but it is the starting point for most tax research.
- *Regulations (Federal Income Tax Regulations).* Only slightly more comprehensible than the IRC, Regulations are written by the Treasury Department to elaborate on the tax code. IRS homepage at http://www.irs.gov.
- *Legal Research: How to Find and Understand the Law,* by Stephen Elias and Susan Levinkind (Nolo). This book is not directed toward tax research, but is an excellent guide to law library research. Also see Nolo's Legal Research Center at http://www.nolo.com.
- *The Ernst and Young Tax Guide* (John Wiley & Sons). This is my favorite annual tax preparation guidebook. It includes tips and explanations of the tax law far superior to the IRS's publications.
- *Master Tax Guide* (Commerce Clearing House), *Master Federal Tax Manual* (Research Institute of America) and *Federal Tax Guide* (Prentice-Hall). Probably your best chance of understanding most tax issues is reading one of these lengthy, privately published professional tax desk books.
- *Legal Guide for Starting and Running a Small Business,* by Fred Steingold (Nolo). This is a good companion book to the one in your hand; it covers the non-tax aspects of small business as well as any book I have ever seen.

- *Stand Up to the IRS,* by Frederick W. Daily (Nolo). This book contains more detailed information on dealing with the IRS.
- *The Employer's Legal Handbook,* by Fred Steingold (Nolo). This book covers all aspects of being an employer, including tax obligations, in greater detail than covered here.
- *Hiring Independent Contractors,* by Stephen Fishman (Nolo). Explains how to reap the benefits—and avoid the pitfalls—of using independent contractors.
- *The Home Office and Small Business Answer Book,* by Janet Attard (Henry Holt Publishing). Lists guilds, associations and societies that might have publications that touch on specialized tax issues.
- *Representation Before the Collection Division of the IRS, Representing the Audited Taxpayer Before the IRS* and *Representation Before the Appeals Division of the IRS* (Clark, Boardman & Callaghan). Tax pros should have these three excellent looseleaf books in their libraries, and they are also written clearly enough to be of use to most anyone else. (800-328-9352.)
- *Tax Hotline,* P.O. Box 58477, Boulder, CO 83028 (800-288-1051). This inexpensive monthly newsletter is full of current tax tips from experts all over the U.S., including me.
- *TurboTax for Business* (Intuit). This software will make your life much easier at tax preparation time.

23

Answers to Frequently Asked Tax Questions

1. Do I have to file a federal income tax return for a business I operated that lost money?

If the business was a sole proprietorship, LLC or partnership, you do not need to report the loss on your personal tax return. But why not do it anyway? It could provide you with a tax benefit by reducing your other taxable income in that year or future years. To report this loss, either attach a written statement to the loss year's tax return, or attach IRS Form 3621, Net Operating Loss Carry-Over. (Note: If you weren't active in the business, but merely an investor, your ability to deduct a business loss is more limited.) If your business is incorporated, you *must* file an annual tax return whether or not you have any income. However, the loss rules for small corporate shareholders are more generous. See your tax advisor for help.

2. What does the term "depreciation" mean?

Depreciation refers to the annual tax deduction the IRS allows for an asset used in a business that has a useful life of more than a year. The theory is that an asset loses value as it wears out over time and you get a tax break reflecting that. The amount you may deduct per year, and the length of time over which you must take these deductions, depends on how the tax code classifies the property. Unfortunately, depreciation only works for things. We can't depreciate our bodies as they wear out. Sigh.

3. How long do I have to keep my business records?

The bare minimum period for keeping those dust-catching boxes is three years from the date you file your tax return. This coincides with the normal IRS statute of limitations on audits. However, some state tax agencies have longer periods to audit, and the IRS can go beyond three years in questions of serious underreporting. For this reason, as much as it may pain you to keep this clutter, hold on to those boxes of paper for at least six years.

4. I'm a doctor and I had patients who didn't pay approximately $7,400 of their medical bills. Can I deduct this as bad debt expense?

The prognosis is not favorable, doctor. The tax code specifically excludes the value of services provided from the definition of tax deductible bad debts. However, if you incurred out of pocket expenses (medications, needles or supplies) in connection with providing these services to deadbeat patients, those amounts are deductible.

5. My tax advisor told me that if I incorporate my one-man consulting operation, I will reduce my audit risks. Is this true?

If history holds true, the answer is yes. In the past, the IRS audit rate for incorporated small businesses with under $1,000,000 gross receipts has been less than half of similar unincorporated ventures. The IRS vows that it will equalize audit rates in the future, but who can believe what the IRS says? For now, I'd say your tax advisor is correct. However, make sure you investigate the costs and expenses of incorporating before you rush out and add "Inc." to your name—operating a corporation is more complex, and a bit more expensive, than operating as a sole proprietor.

6. Do I need any kind of prior IRS approval or registration before I start my business?

Not if you are starting off as a sole proprietor and have no employees. Then, you would use your own Social Security number when corresponding or filing anything with the IRS. But if you form any kind of business entity (a corporation, partnership or LLC) or have one or more employees you must get a federal Employer Identification Number at the time you begin operations. You can obtain a federal Employer Identification Number using IRS Form SS-4. You will use this number on any forms you file with the IRS. Also, check with your state employment and tax authorities for their requirements.

7.   I make dollhouse furniture in my spare time. Occasionally I sell a few items to friends and at craft fairs. Overall, I lose money every year but have a good time at it. Are my losses tax deductible?

Possibly, as long as you comply with a few IRS rules. The best way to pass muster with the IRS is to show that you had a "profit motive" and operated in a businesslike fashion. That's because if you are ever audited, the auditor may try to argue that the dollhouse "business" was really a non-deductible hobby, and disallow your losses. Keep good records to show your efforts to turn a profit, and do some advertising or business promotion, just like any real business. However, keep in mind that you only have to show that you *tried* to make a profit—it doesn't matter whether you actually did (although an IRS auditor might try to tell you otherwise).

8.   Do IRA, SEP, 401K and other retirement plans for the self-employed really provide much of a tax break?

Absolutely. There is no better tax benefit available to the small businessperson than one of these retirement plans. You'll get an immediate tax savings for every year you contribute, and the money you invest in your plan will accumulate interest, dividends and capital gains—with the tax deferred until you withdraw it. Don't wait—the sooner you start contributing to a plan, the sooner your money can start making money for you.

9.   Should I choose a fiscal year or calendar tax year accounting period for my business?

For most small time operators, the accounting period is rarely a big deal either way. The IRS requires most businesses to use a calendar year (January 1 to December 31) as their fiscal or tax year anyway. If you want to use any other tax period, you must have a good reason and get permission from the IRS. If, for instance, your business is seasonal and you think you might benefit from a non-calendar fiscal year, see an accountant to discuss the ramifications.

10.   If I claim a home office deduction for my consulting business will I be audited?

Several years ago, home offices were IRS targets. But in 1998 Congress passed liberalized home office rules. However, Congress also passed rules that mandate that home office depreciation deductions for property owners are "recaptured" (taxed) in the year the property is sold. So the home office deduction is a double-edged sword for home owners but generally still worth taking. For renters, however, the home office deduction is a no-brainer, since there is no tax recapture issue. So, while a home office deduction increases your chances of audit, it's only a slight increase—unless the deduction is particularly large (50% or more) relative to your business income.

11.   I use my car everyday to call on customers and make deliveries. Am I better off leasing a vehicle or buying it?

As a rule, the more expensive the car, the bigger tax deduction you get from leasing. The price point at which leasing becomes more favorable is about $15,800. That's because the tax code allows very stingy write-offs for cars over that amount. When you get up in Mercedes and Jaguar territory, the lease deductions are much greater than with buying. However, if you are thinking of a truck or a heavy SUV, you might be better off buying because the annual tax deductions are far bigger than with passenger car tax rules. See a tax pro for details on how to get mega-tax breaks from vehicles—up to $23,000 for buying an SUV in the first year.

12. There is a trade show in San Francisco coming up and I'd like to take my wife and spend a few extra days after the show. Can I still deduct the trip expenses?

You can't deduct any expenses (such as airfare and food) solely attributable to your wife unless she is an employee of your business and is there for business reasons, too. (Hint, hint.) However, you can deduct all of your airfare, the full cost of your shared hotel room (for the business days, but not the extra days) and the rental car for the business days. And, if you can find one of those "companion flies free" deals, you don't have to account for your wife's airfare at all. Make sure to take her for a drink at the Cliff House at sunset.

13. Two friends and I want to go into business building and fixing stock cars for racing. What's the simplest way to do this tax-wise?

For simplicity's sake, you should consider forming a limited liability company (LLC). Your other alternatives are a partnership or corporation, both of which require tougher formalities and more complicated recordkeeping and tax reporting. The best advice I can give you is to meet with a business lawyer in your state and tell him your plans and get advice that's tailored to your situation—in some cases, simple may not be best. See you at Daytona.

14. Will the IRS be upset if I hire my 12- and 14- year old kids to help in my video store after school, sweeping floors, answering the phone and so on. I would pay them about $50 a week. Will this be a problem with IRS?

Hiring Junior and Little Susie is perfectly okay with the IRS (and it keeps the kids off the streets and under your eye). In fact, it's a good family tax saver since it takes income from your tax bracket and transfers it to the child's bracket, which is usually lower. The only concern here is that the kids do real work and don't get overpaid—that their (tax-deductible) salaries aren't just disguised weekly allowances or clothes money. They should file their own tax returns, but will probably not owe any income tax at their income levels. Even better, they can contribute to retirement plans and deduct the contributions, which lowers their income tax even more and can make good tax sense even if they take the money out for college.

15. My cousin Luigi and his wife own a multi-million dollar floor covering business. His health is failing and he is thinking about retiring to Florida. His daughter and one son work in the business. Right now, he and his wife are operating the business as a sole proprietorship. I read that operating the business as a family limited partnership could save estate taxes on his death. Is this true?

If Luigi plans far enough ahead and follows the tax rules, yes, putting the floor covering operation into a family limited partnership (FLP) can not only reduce the size of his taxable estate, but can cut probate time and costs. The idea is to gradually transfer as much ownership of the business as possible to his children over a period of years through annual tax-free gifts (right now, the maximum amount you can contribute tax-free is $10,000 per person per year). Get Luigi to an estate-planning attorney so that he can start implementing this plan as soon as possible.

16. I frequently give my employees gift certificates and other "special occasion" items to keep them loyal. What are the tax rules for deducting the costs of these things?

First, congratulations for your enlightened approach to holding on to valuable employees. You can deduct all the costs of gifts to employees; the catch is that anything totaling more than $25 per year must be reported as additional income by the employee. However, if yours is a service business, you can provide "excess capacity" things (services that wouldn't be used anyway, such as a hotel room) to your employees tax-free. And, if you follow special tax code rules you can give "good habit" rewards of up to $400 per year, or if your business follows the rules with a "qualified award plan" you can give items valued up to $1600 per year. Check with your tax pro for more information.

17. I'm buying a small injection molding company that has gross profits of about $500,000 per year. I've never owned a business before. Do I have to tell the IRS about this deal?

If you are buying an unincorporated business, both you and the seller must agree on an allocation of the value of each category of assets that is being transferred. This means allocating a value to things like equipment, real property, goodwill, the seller's covenant not to compete and so on. Both parties report these allocations to the IRS with their annual tax return filings on an IRS Form 8954, Asset Acquisition Statement. However, if you buy shares of stock in a corporation, then there is no special IRS reporting form for the buyer to file. Tax life is more complicated for the seller, but that story is too long for a short answer here.

18. My auto dealership went through some rough times last year. I got behind in payroll tax deposits for $120,000. I owe suppliers, the landlord and others even more and things are getting worse. I'm thinking of filing bankruptcy. Will these payroll taxes be wiped out in my bankruptcy?

Congress (in conjunction with the IRS, no doubt) has decided that payroll taxes are one of the debts that can never be discharged in a bankruptcy. If you're in a financial bind, the best thing to do is use whatever assets you can to make the payroll tax payments and then file bankruptcy. The suppliers' bills are most likely dischargeable, so pay the IRS first. Whether or not you end up in bankruptcy, if you can't pay your payroll taxes, get help from a tax pro. The IRS is tenacious when it comes to collecting payroll taxes, and you could lose more than just your business.

19. I am a psychologist and being audited by the IRS. The auditor says a number of my business expenses will be disallowed in his report. Do I have to accept this?

Absolutely not. The IRS has an administrative process that allows you to appeal an auditor's decision to the IRS Appeals Office—a completely separate division of the IRS. Their job is to settle the dispute with you so you don't take the IRS to Tax Court. And, in most cases, they will compromise an audit report—although your odds of being let off the hook completely are slim. If you can't reach a compromise, the filing fee for Tax Court is only $60 and if the amount you are contesting is less than $50,000, the procedures are fairly simple.

20. I've found I am I better off tax-wise hiring hourly independent contractors for my print shop instead of employees. I've been doing it this way for several years but my accountant says I'm crazy to take the risk that they'll be reclassified as employees. What do you think?

Most small business owners love the tax savings they get from hiring independent contractors—they don't pay the employer's share of payroll taxes or unemployment taxes, or withhold income taxes as required by law. That's fine if the workers are actually independent contractors. But if you are providing a work place on your premises, setting the hours of work and presumably directing the workers, then they probably aren't independent contractors, but employees—and you could be in big trouble with the IRS. The IRS is very aware of the tax benefits of hiring independent contractors and makes a habit of auditing businesses that hire a lot of independent contractors. And worker misclassification is not just an issue with the IRS. Watch out for fines and penalties from your state tax agency as well if—and when—you are caught.

21. I'm thinking of opening a cosmetic store and I project about $250,000 in sales the first year. Should I try to keep records by hand or with my computer?

Unless you are completely hopeless with a computer—and most people can pick up at least a few skills with a couple of classes—you should definitely use a computer. Tracking many relatively small sales, keeping inventory, sales tax reporting and other such items is time-consuming enough without having to worry about doing it by hand. Most small business owners wouldn't dream of operating their business without a computer and a program like Intuit's *Quickbooks*.

22. Should my fiancée and I run our computer repair shop as a sole proprietorship or do we have to be a partnership?

Until you're married, you and your fiancée can't legally operate the business as a sole proprietorship. Until then, you must tax report as a partnership if you don't form an LLC or incorporate. Once you have tied the knot, things become simpler. One spouse can be an employee of the business and on the payroll or can "volunteer" their services to the business without taking a salary (this would save the business employment taxes). And, if you and hubby file a joint tax return it would reduce the overall family tax bill in most cases. You'll just have to see how it "computes" at tax time. ∎

Glossary

The terms in this glossary are defined as they are used by the IRS or by the author. Some terms may have different meanings in other contexts.

Abatement. The IRS's partial or complete cancellation of taxes, penalties or interest owed by a taxpayer.

Accelerated Depreciation. A method of tax deducting the cost of a business-used asset more rapidly than by using straight-line depreciation. (*See* Depreciation.)

Accountant. Someone who works with financial data. Often denotes a person with special training, such as a Certified Public Accountant.

Accounting. Process by which financial information about a business is recorded.

Accounting Methods. *See* Cash Method and Accrual Method.

Accounting Period. *See* Calendar Year Accounting Period and Fiscal Year Accounting Period.

Accounts Payable. Money owed by a business to suppliers, vendors and other creditors.

Accounts Receivable. Money owed to a business for goods or services rendered. A business asset.

Accrual Method of Accounting (also called Accrual Basis). Accounting for income in the period earned, and for expenses when the liability was incurred. This is not necessarily in the period when it is received or paid. *See also* Cash Method.

Adjusted Basis. *See* Basis (Tax Basis).

Adjusted Gross Income (AGI). On personal income tax returns, Form 1040, this figure is the result of reducing a taxpayer's total income by certain adjustments allowed by the tax code, such as a contribution to a traditional IRA. From this figure, personal deductions are subtracted to arrive at taxable income.

Adjustment. (1) An IRS change, usually by an auditor, to a tax liability as reported originally on a tax return. (2) Deductions from an individual taxpayer's total income on Form 1040, lines 23 through 30.

Alternative Minimum Tax (AMT). A federal flat tax on income of individuals or corporations that may apply when a taxpayer claims certain tax benefits that reduce tax liabilities below specified levels. Its intent is to prevent higher-income taxpayers from realizing too many tax benefits from accelerated depreciation or investments in nontaxed items such as municipal bonds.

Amended Tax Return. Generally, amended tax returns may be filed by an individual or entity to correct an error made on a previously filed return or to get a refund of taxes paid.

Amortization. A tax method of recovering costs of certain assets by taking deductions evenly over time. This is similar to straight-line depreciation and unlike an accelerated depreciation method. For example, the Internal Revenue Code directs that business goodwill costs must be amortized over 15 years.

Appeal. Administrative process allowing taxpayers to contest certain decisions, typically audits, within the IRS.

Assess. The IRS process of recording a tax liability in the account of a taxpayer.

Asset (Business). Any property with a value and useful life of at least one year that is used in a trade or business. Examples: machinery, buildings, vehicles, equipment patents and monies held or owed to a business. *See also* Accounts Receivable.

Audit. A review of financial records. An IRS audit is the examination of a taxpayer, his or her tax return and supporting data to determine whether he or she has violated the tax laws.

Auditor. An IRS Examination Division employee who reviews the correctness of a tax return. *See also* Revenue Agent, Tax Auditor (Examiner).

Bad Debt (Business). Money owed for a business debt that cannot be collected and can be deducted as an operating expense.

Balance Sheet. A statement listing a business's assets (what it owns), liabilities (what it owes) and net worth (the difference between the assets and liabilities). A balance sheet shows the financial position of a business at a given point in time.

Bankruptcy. A federal law providing a way for individuals or businesses to wipe out certain debts. There are different kinds of bankruptcy. A defunct business will likely file Chapter 7 bankruptcy, wherein its assets are distributed to creditors and any remaining debts are canceled. Chapters 11 and 13 bankruptcy allow businesses and individuals to repay debts over time while remaining in operation.

Basis (Tax Basis). The tax cost of an asset, which may be adjusted upward by improvements or downward by depreciation. Basis is used to calculate depreciation and amortization deductions and to determine gain or loss on the sale or other disposition of an asset.

Bookkeeper. Someone who records financial data in the accounting records of a business and maintains the accounting system.

Books (Business). The collection of records of financial accounting of business activity kept on paper or in a computer file.

Business. An activity carried on with the intent to make a profit.

Business License. A permit issued by a local or state governmental agency for a business to operate. Most enterprises are required to have one or more licenses and must go through an application process and pay a fee for this privilege. A business license is not issued by the IRS or required to qualify as a taxable entity, however.

Calendar Year Accounting Period. A 12-month period for tax purposes that ends on December 31. *See also* Fiscal Year Accounting Period.

Capital. The investment in a business by its owners. *See also* Equity.

Capital Asset. Any type of property, either held for investment or used in a business, that has a useful life of more than one year.

Capital Expenditure. Cost to acquire an asset or make improvements to an assets which increases its value or adds to its useful life. (*See also* Basis).

Capital Gain or Loss. A gain or loss from the sale or exchange of a capital asset—the difference between the amount realized on the sale or exchange of an asset and the amount of the adjusted basis of the asset.

Capitalized Expenditure. An expenditure for a capital asset that must be tax-deducted over more than one year, as opposed to an ordinary expense. For example, repairing a broken window is an ordinary expense, but remodeling a storefront is an expense that must be capitalized.

Carryovers. Tax rules often limit the ability of a taxpayer to use deductions, losses and credits in the year incurred. The excess of a tax deduction, loss or credit over what can be used in a current year is called a carryover, which may be taken in past or future years.

Cash Method of Accounting. Accounting for income by reporting it when actually or constructively received, and reporting expenses when paid. Also called cash basis method. *See also* Accrual Method, Constructive Receipt of Income.

Certified Public Accountant (CPA). The most highly qualified of all accounting professionals. CPAs are licensed by the state and must meet rigorous educational and testing requirements.

Chart of Accounts. A complete list of a business's expense and income accounts by category. It includes all accounts that appear on the business's balance sheet, as well as the accounts that track particular kinds of expenses or income.

Cohan Rule. A federal court decision allowing taxpayers to use reasonable approximations of expenses when records are missing. The Cohan rule has its limitations and cannot be used to approximate travel and entertainment business expenses.

Constructive Receipt of Income. Income not physically received but treated by the tax code as if it had been because it is accessible to the recipient without qualification. *See also* Cash Method.

Corporation. A state-registered business that is owned by shareholders and reports taxes separately from its owners. The tax code considers all corporations to be taxable entities, called C corporations, unless the corporation has properly elected "S" status. *See* S Corporation.

Cost of Goods Sold (CGS). The amount paid by a business for inventory that is sold during a tax year. The formula for determining the CGS is: the beginning inventory plus the cost of purchases during the period, minus the ending inventory at the end of the period. Also called "cost of sales."

Death Benefit. A fringe benefit payment that is tax-deductible to a C corporation, within dollar limitations, and not taxable to the recipient.

Deductible Business Expense. An expenditure by a business that may be deducted from the business's taxable income under the tax code.

Deduction. An expense that the IRC allows an individual or business to subtract from its gross income to determine its adjusted gross income or taxable income. Example: The cost of this book if you are in business.

Deferred Compensation. Earned income of a taxpayer that is put into a retirement account and not taxable until removed from the account.

Deficiency (Tax). Any difference found by the IRS between a taxpayer's reported tax liability and the amount of tax the IRS says that the taxpayer should have reported.

Dependent Care Plan. A fringe benefit that can be given tax-free to eligible employees of a business to care for their dependents and is deductible to the business, within limitations.

Depreciable Asset. Property used in a business with a useful life of at least one year and deductible over a period set by the IRC. Includes buildings, vehicles and equipment used in a business, but not land, which is never depreciable.

Depreciable Basis. *See* Basis.

Depreciation. An annual tax deduction allowed for the loss of value of an asset due to wear over a period of years, such as a business auto or real estate improvement. The amount of the deduction each year depends on which of the depreciation methods allowed in the tax code for the kind of asset is applied.

Disallowance (Audit). An IRS finding at audit that a taxpayer was not entitled to a deduction or other tax benefit claimed on a tax return.

Dividend. Corporation profits distributed to shareholders as a return on their investment in the corporation. *See also* Unearned Income.

Documentation. Any tangible proof that substantiates an item on a tax return, such as for an expense claimed as a deduction.

Double-Entry System. A system of accounting that records each business transaction twice (once as a debit and once as a credit), and is more accurate than single-entry accounting.

Earned Income. Compensation for services rendered, such as wages, commissions and tips. *See also* Unearned Income.

Education Benefits. Financial assistance to an employee that is tax-free to the recipient and a tax-deductible expense to the business, within tax code limitations.

Employee. A worker under the direction or control of an employer, and subject to payroll tax code rules. *See also* Independent Contractor.

Employer Identification Number (EIN). A 13-digit number assigned to a business by the IRS, upon application. *See also* Taxpayer Identification Number.

Employment Taxes. *See* Payroll Taxes.

Enrolled Agent (EA). A type of tax professional permitted to practice before the IRS along with attorneys and CPAs. An EA must demonstrate competence by passing an IRS test or have at least five years' work experience with the IRS.

Entry. A transaction recorded in the accounting records of a business.

Equity. The net worth of a business, equal to its assets minus its liabilities. Also refers to an owner's investment in the business.

ERISA (Employees' Retirement Security Act). A federal law that governs employee benefits, such as pension and retirement plans. *See also* Pension Plan.

Estate Tax. A tax imposed by the federal government (and some states) on the net value of a decedent's assets.

Estimated Taxes (ES). Tax payments to the IRS by self-employed individuals, quarterly, for their anticipated income tax liability for the year. If payments are not made timely a penalty may be imposed by the IRS.

Examination. *See* Audit.

Examination Report. The findings issued by an IRS auditor after an audit is concluded.

Excise Tax (Federal). A tax, usually at a flat rate, imposed on some businesses for a certain type of transaction, manufacturing, production or consumption.

Exemption. An annual amount allowed to a taxpayer as a deduction for herself and for each dependent.

Expense. A business cost. *See also* Deductible Business Expense.

Fair Market Value. The price a buyer and seller of any kind of property agree on as just, when neither is under any compulsion to buy or sell.

Family Limited Partnership. A business that is a limited partnership of only related members. It can be used to shift present business income and to transfer a business to succeeding generations at a tax savings. *See also* Limited Partnership.

Federal Insurance Contributions Act (FICA). Social Security and Medicare taxes, which are generally applicable to everyone with earned income. Employers and employees split the tax; self-employeds pay the entire tax. *See also Payroll* Taxes, Self-Employment Tax.

Federal Tax Deposits (FTD). An employer is required to place payroll taxes withheld from employees, as well as employer contributions for Social Security and Medicare taxes, in a federal depository (bank).

File (a return). To mail or electronically transmit to the IRS the taxpayer's information in a specified format about income and tax liability.

Fiscal Year Accounting Period. A 12-month period ending on the last day of any month except December. *See also* Calendar Year Accounting Period.

Fixed Asset. A business asset with a useful life of greater than one year as determined by the Internal Revenue Code. *See also* Depreciable Asset.

401(k) Plan. A tax-advantaged deferred compensation arrangement in which a portion of a worker's pay is withheld by the business and invested in a plan to earn income tax-deferred until withdrawn.

Fraud. *See* Tax Fraud.

Fringe Benefit. Any tax-advantaged benefit allowed a business owner or employee. A fringe benefit may be partially or totally tax-free to the recipient and tax-deductible to the business. Prime examples are health and retirement plans.

FUTA (Federal Unemployment Tax Act). An annually paid tax on all employers for unemployment insurance.

General Journal. A book or computer file where all financial transactions of a business are recorded. Also called General Ledger.

Goodwill. The excess value of a going business, over and above the worth of all of its other assets.

Gross Income. Money, goods and property received from all sources required to be reported on a tax return, before subtracting any adjustments, exemptions or deductions allowed by law.

Group Life Insurance Benefit. *See* Fringe Benefit.

Hobby Loss Provision (IRC § 183). An IRC limitation on tax-deducting losses or expenses of any activity that is not carried on with a profit motive.

Home Office. That portion of a taxpayer's home in which he or she carries on a business activity. If the home office is used regularly and exclusively for business and meets other tax code tests, then a deduction—up to the amount of business income—may be taken for the business portion of the home, for depreciation on the structure or rent paid.

Improvements. Additions to or alterations of a capital asset, which either increase its value or extend its useful life. *See also* Capitalized Expenditure.

Income. All money and other things of value received, except items specifically exempted by the tax code. *See also* Gross Income.

Income Statement. *See* Profit and Loss Statement.

Income Taxes. Federal and state taxes, levied on an individual or corporation for earned (such as, wages) and unearned (such as, dividends) income.

Independent Contractor. A self-employed individual whose work hours and methods are not controlled by anyone else, and is not subject to payroll tax rules. *See also* Employee.

Individual Retirement Account (IRA). A retirement plan established by an individual allowing up to $2,000 in annual contributions of earned income per year, and tax-deferred accumulation of income in the account. Contributions may or may not be tax deductible, depending on your income level.

Information Return (Income). A report filed with the IRS by a business showing amounts paid to a taxpayer, such as Form W-2 (wages) or Form 1099 (independent contractor and other types of income). No tax is due with an information return, but there are penalties for not filing one or for filing late.

Installment Payment Agreement (IA). An IRS monthly payment plan for unpaid federal taxes.

Installment Sale. The purchaser of an asset pays the seller over a number of years, allowing the tax liability on any gain to be spread over a period of time instead of being incurred in the year of the sale.

Intangible Property. Assets that consist of rights rather than something material. For example, the accounts receivable of a business is an intangible asset because it is the right to receive payment rather than the money itself. The funds, when received, become a tangible asset.

Intent to Levy. A notice to a delinquent taxpayer that the IRS intends to seize (levy) his or her property to satisfy a tax obligation. This warning is usually issued at least 30 days prior to any confiscation. Intent to Levy notices don't necessarily mean the IRS will actually make any seizures. *See* Levy.

Interest. Cost of borrowing or owing money, usually a tax-deductible business expense. The IRS adds interest to overdue tax bills.

Internal Revenue Code (IRC). The tax laws of the U.S. as enacted by Congress. Also called the "tax code" or simply the "code."

Internal Revenue Service (IRS). The branch of the U.S. Treasury Department that administers the federal tax law. Also called "the Service" by tax professionals, and worse by most other folks.

Inventory. Goods a business has on hand for sale to customers, and raw materials that will become part of merchandise.

Investment. Money spent to acquire an asset, such as the purchase of a partnership interest or stock in a corporation.

IRC § 179. A tax rule allowing a deduction for the purchase of certain trade or business property in the year the property is placed in service.

IRC § 1244 Stock. Corporation stock issued under the rules of IRC § 1244, which allows an ordinary tax loss to be claimed, within tax code limitations, by the shareholder.

Itemized Deductions. Expenses allowed by the tax code to be subtracted from your adjusted gross income and claimed on an individual income tax return, such as medical expenses, mortgage interest and charitable expenses.

Joint Tax Return. A combined income tax return filed by two spouses. Alternatively, a spouse may file a separate tax return.

Journal. *See* General Journal.

Keogh Plan. A type of retirement plan for self-employed people, allowing part of their earnings to be taken from their income and accumulate tax-deferred in an investment account until withdrawn after age 59½.

Lease. A rental agreement for the use of property, such as buildings or equipment. Lease payments are deductible if the property is used in a trade or business.

Levy. An IRS seizure of property or wages from an individual or business to satisfy a delinquent tax debt. *See* Intent to Levy.

Liability (Business). Money owed by a business to others, such as a mortgage debt, payroll taxes or an Account Payable.

Lien. *See* Tax Lien.

Limited Liability Company (LLC). A relatively new form of business recognized by the IRS that is taxed much like a partnership, and shields its owners from liability for business debts, like a corporation.

Limited Partnership. A type of partnership that consists of at least one general partner with unlimited liability for business debts, and one or more limited partners whose liability is limited to their investment in the partnership. *See also* Limited Liability Company.

Listed Property. Certain types of depreciable assets used in a business on which the IRC requires special recordkeeping, such as cellular phones, home-based computers, boats, airplanes and personal cars used for business.

Loss (Operating). An excess of a business's expenses over its income in a given period of time, usually a tax year.

Loss Carryover. *See* Carryovers, Loss (Operating).

MACRS (Modified Accelerated Cost Recovery System). An IRC-established method for rapidly claiming depreciation tax deductions.

Manual Accounting System. An accounting system maintained by hand, using paper.

Medical Expense Reimbursement Benefit. *See Fringe* Benefits.

Medicare Tax. A portion of the Social Security tax of 2.9% on all of an individual's net earned income. *See* Self-Employment Tax, Payroll Taxes.

Mileage Log. A record of miles traveled in a vehicle used for business.

Net Income. Gross income less expenses; a business's profit for a given tax year.

Net Loss. *See* Loss (Operating), Net Operating Loss.

Net Operating Loss (NOL). An annual net loss from a business operation. For tax-reporting purposes, an NOL may be used to offset income of unincorporated business owners from other sources in the year of the loss. An NOL may be carried back two years to reduce tax liabilities or secure refunds of taxes. *See* Carryovers.

Net Worth. *See* Equity.

Ninety-Day Letter. Official notice from the IRS that a taxpayer has 90 days to contest an IRS audit by filing a Petition to the United States Tax Court, or else the decision will become final.

Notice of Deficiency. *See* Ninety-Day Letter.

Notice of Tax Lien. *See* Tax Lien.

Offer in Compromise. A formal written proposal to the IRS to settle a tax debt for less than the amount the IRS claims is owed.

Operating Expense. A normal out-of-pocket cost incurred in a business operation, not including depreciation or amortization expenses. Examples are rent, wages and supplies.

Ordinary Income. Any earned income, such as from work, and not from the sale of a capital asset or from an investment. *See* Unearned Income.

Partnership. A business of two or more individuals (or other entities) which passes its income or losses to its individual partners. A partnership does not pay taxes but is required to file an annual tax return.

Payroll Taxes. The federal income taxes withheld by employers and FICA contributions—including both Social Security and Medicare—that must be deposited to an IRS account for their employees. States may also impose payroll taxes.

Penalties (Tax). Fines imposed by the IRS on taxpayers who disobey tax rules.

Pension Plan. A tax-advantaged arrangement under which annual deposits are made to a tax code-approved account for an owner's or employee's benefit on retirement. Income tax on the accumulated funds is deferred until the year in which they are withdrawn.

Personal Asset. Property owned by an individual, which may also be used in a business.

Personal Income Tax. Annual tax based on an individual's taxable income, less adjustments, deductions and exemptions allowed by the tax code.

Personal Property. Anything of value that is not real estate—such as cash, equipment or vehicles. *See also* Real Property.

Personal Service Corporation (PSC). A tax code-qualified incorporated business composed of one or more members of a specific profession. It must file an annual tax return.

Posting. The act of entering financial transactions into an accounting record, or transferring data from a book of original entry to a ledger.

Profit and Loss Statement (Income Statement). A writing showing a business's gross income, and subtracting from that figure its expenses and the cost of goods sold to reveal a net profit or loss for a specific period.

Profit Motive. An intention to make a profit is imposed by the IRC on anyone going into business. *See also* Hobby Loss Provision.

Proprietorship. A business structure owned by an individual (or married couple) that is not a partnership, an LLC, corporation nor any other type of legal tax entity.

Prorate. To allocate or split one figure between two items, such as prorating business and personal use of an asset.

Protest. A request to appeal a decision within the IRS. *See* Appeal.

Qualified Plan. A tax code-qualified and IRS-approved employee benefit plan, such as a pension or profit-sharing plan. *See* ERISA.

Real Property. Real estate, consisting of land and structures attached to it. *See also* Personal Property.

Recordkeeping. The listing of financial transactions for a business. *See also* Records.

Records. Tangible evidence, usually in writing, of the income, expenses and financial transactions of a business or individual.

Regulations (Regs). Treasury Department interpretations of selected Internal Revenue Code provisions.

Representative. A tax professional who is permitted to represent a taxpayer before the IRS. He or she must be a Certified Public Accountant, Tax Attorney or Enrolled Agent.

Research and Development Expenses. Certain tax-deductible costs for developing new products or services.

Retained Earnings. The accumulated and undistributed profits of a corporation. Retained earnings are subject to tax.

Retirement Plan. *See* Pension Plan.

Revenue Agent. An IRS examiner who performs audits of taxpayers or business entities in the field, meaning outside IRS offices. *See* Tax Auditor.

Revenue Officer. Certain IRS tax collectors.

Sales Tax. A state (not federal) imposed tax on sales of retail products based on a percentage of the price.

S Corporation (Sub-Chapter S Corporation). A state-incorporated business that elects special tax treatment to pass through its income or loss to shareholders instead of being taxed on its income. *See* Corporation, Partnership.

Schedule. A form on which taxpayers report details about an item, usually income or expense, summarized on the associated general return form.

Section 1231 Assets. Property used in a trade or business which is depreciable and when sold, gains are taxed at capital gains rates, while losses are treated as ordinary losses.

Seizure (IRS). *See* Levy.

Self-Employed. A person who works in his or her own business, either full- or part-time.

Self-Employment (SE) Tax. Social Security and Medicare taxes on net self-employment income. The SE tax is reported on the individual's income tax return and is subject to annual revisions by law. (*See* Appendix.)

Service Business. Any enterprise that derives income primarily from providing personal services, not goods, to its customers. Examples: consultants, physicians and accountants.

Shareholder (Stockholder). An investor in a corporation whose ownership is represented by a stock certificate. A shareholder may or may not be an officer or employee of the corporation.

Sideline Business. A for-profit activity carried on in addition to an individual's full-time employment or principal trade or business.

Simplified Employee Pension (SEP, SARSEP or SEP-IRA). A pension plan allowing self-employed business owners and their employees to deduct and put part of their earnings into a retirement account to accumulate tax-deferred until withdrawn. *See also* Individual Retirement Account (IRA), Keogh Plan.

Single-Entry Accounting. A system of tracking business income and expenses that requires only one recording of each financial transaction. *See also* Double-Entry System.

Sole Proprietorship. *See* Proprietorship.

***Soliman* Rule.** A U.S. Supreme Court decision that limits the use of the tax deduction for home offices for some businesses. Changed by 1997 Taxpayer Relief Act.

Standard Deduction. An annual tax deduction granted to each taxpayer who does not choose to itemize deductions. The amount depends on your age, filing status and whether you can be claimed as a dependent on someone else's tax return.

Standard Mileage Rate Deduction. A method for deducting automobile expenses based on the mileage driven for business, used in lieu of claiming actual operating and depreciation expenses.

Statutes of Limitation (Tax). Varying limits imposed by Congress on assessing and collecting taxes, charging tax crimes and claiming tax refunds.

Stock Dividend. *See* Dividend.

Straight-Line Depreciation. A tax code method of depreciating assets of a business by deductions in equal annual amounts. The period of time is specified by the tax code for each category of property.

Summons. A legally enforceable order issued by the IRS compelling an individual taxpayer or business to provide information, usually financial records.

Tangible Personal Property (Asset). Anything of value that is physically movable, such as equipment, vehicles, machinery and fixtures not attached to a building or land.

Tax. Required payment of money to governments to provide public goods and services.

Tax Attorney. A lawyer who specializes in tax-related legal work and has a special degree

(LL.M.—Tax) or certification from a state bar association.

Tax Auditor (Examiner). An IRS employee who determines the correctness of tax returns filed by individual taxpayers and business entities at the IRS offices. *See also* Revenue Agent, Audit.

Tax Basis. *See* Basis.

Tax Bracket. The percentage rate on which an individual's or taxable entity's last dollar of income is taxed. At present there are five brackets for individuals: 15%, 28%, 31%, 36% and 39.6%.

Tax Code. *See* Internal Revenue Code (IRC).

Tax Court (U.S.). A federal court where an individual or business taxpayer can contest an IRS tax assessment without first paying the taxes claimed due.

Tax Deduction. *See* Deduction.

Tax Exempt Income. Receipt of income that is specifically made exempt from taxation by Congress. Example: municipal bond interest.

Tax Fraud. Conduct meant to deceive the IRS or cheat in the assessment or payment of any tax liability. Tax fraud can be punished by both civil penalties (money) and criminal ones (imprisonment and fines).

Tax Law. The Internal Revenue Code (IRC) and the decisions of federal courts interpreting it.

Tax Lien Notice (Federal). An IRS announcement of a tax debt placed in the public records where the debtor resides or the business is located.

Tax Loss Carryover. *See* Carryovers.

Tax Pro. An expert working privately in the tax field. *See* Certified Public Accountant, Enrolled Agent, Tax Attorney.

Tax Rate. A percentage of tax applied to income, which may be fixed or may change at different income levels, and is set by Congress.

Tax Withholding. *See* Withholding.

Taxable Income. An individual's or entity's gross income minus all allowable deductions, adjustments and exemptions. Tax liability is figured on the net result.

Taxpayer Bill of Rights. Federal tax laws restricting IRS conduct and establishing taxpayer rights in dealing with the IRS. Highlights of this law are contained in IRS Publication 1.

Taxpayer Identification Number (TIN). An IRS-assigned number used for computer tracking of tax accounts. For sole proprietors without employees, it is their Social Security number. For other business entities the TIN is a separate 13-digit number called an Employer Identification Number. *See* Employer Identification Number.

Three-of-Five Test. A rebuttable IRS presumption that a business venture that doesn't make a profit in three out of five consecutive years of operation is a not a business for tax purposes. *See also* Profit Motive, Hobby Loss Provision.

Transaction. A financial event in the operation of a business. Examples: paying an expense, making a deposit or receiving payment for selling a service.

Trust Fund Recovery Penalty. Also known as the 100% Penalty. A tax code procedure for shifting payroll tax obligations from a business (usually a corporation) to individuals associated with the business.

Unearned Income. Income from investments, such as interest, dividends and capital gains or other income that isn't compensation for services. *See* Earned Income, Dividend.

Useful Life. The period of months or years the tax code directs to be used to write off a business asset.

Withholding. The amount required to be held back by an employer from an employee's wages to pay Social Security, Medicare and income taxes. Withholding is required by the federal government and most states as well.

Write-Off. An expression for a tax-deductible expense, usually referring to depreciating or taking an IRC § 179 expense for an asset used in business. *See* Depreciation.

∎

Appendix

IRS Publications List

Forms Checklist

How to Get IRS Forms and Publications (Publication 2053A)

Your Rights as a Taxpayer (Publication 1)

Recordkeeping for Individuals (Publication 552)

Business Owner Tax Information (Publication 910)

Interest and Penalty Information (Notice 433)

Deposit Requirements for Employment Taxes (Notice 931)

Form 2553, Election by a Small Business Corporation

Form 4506, Request for a Copy or Transcript of Tax Form

Form 4797, Sales of Business Property

Form 7018, Employer's Order Blank for Forms

Form 8594, Asset Acquisition Statement

Form 8822, Change of Address

Form SS-4, Application for Employer Identification Number

Form W-4, Employees Withholding Allowance Certificate

Form W-9, Request for Taxpayer Identification Number and Certification

Schedule SE, Self-Employment Tax

IRS Publications List

General Guides

1	Your Rights as a Taxpayer
17	Your Federal Income Tax (For Individuals)
225	Farmer's Tax Guide
334	Tax Guide for Small Business
509	Tax Calendars for 1999
595	Tax Guide for Commercial Fishermen
910	Guide to Free Tax Services

Employer's Guides

15	Employer's Tax Guide (Circular E)
15-A	Employer's Supplemental Tax Guide
51	Agricultural Employer's Tax Guide (Circular A)
80	Federal Tax Guide for Employers in the Virgin Islands, Guam, American Samoa, and the Commonwealth of the Northern Mariana Islands (Circular SS)

Specialized Publications

55	Recordkeeping for Individuals
349	Federal Highway Use Tax on Heavy Vehicles
378	Fuel Tax Credits and Refunds
463	Travel, Entertainment, and Gift Expenses
505	Tax Withholding and Estimated Tax
510	Excise Taxes for 1999
515	Withholding of Tax on Nonresident Aliens and Foreign Corporations
517	Social Security and Other Information for Members of the Clergy and Religious Workers
521	Moving Expenses
523	Selling Your Home
525	Taxable and Nontaxable Income
526	Charitable Contributions
527	Residential Rental Property
529	Miscellaneous Deductions
533	Self-Employment Tax
534	Depreciation
535	Business Expenses
536	Net Operating Losses
537	Installment Sales
538	Accounting Periods and Methods
541	Tax Information on Partnerships
542	Tax Information on Corporations
544	Sales and Other Dispositions of Assets
550	Investment Income and Expenses
551	Basis of Assets
555	Federal Tax Information on Community Property
556	Examination of Returns, Appeal Rights, and Claims for Refund
557	Tax-Exempt Status for Your Organization
560	Retirement Plans for the Self-Employed
561	Determining the Value of Donated Property
575	Pension and Annuity Income (Including Simplified General Rule)
583	Taxpayers Starting a Business
587	Business Use of Your Home
589	Tax Information on S Corporations
590	Individual Retirement Arrangements (IRAs)
594	Understanding the Collection Process
596	Earned Income Credit
597	Information on the United States–Canada Income Tax Treaty
598	Tax on Unrelated Business Income of Exempt Organizations
901	U.S. Tax Treaties
907	Tax Highlights for Persons with Disabilities
908	Bankruptcy and Other Debt Cancellation
911	Tax Information for Direct Sellers
917	Business Use of a Car
924	Reporting of Real Estate Transactions to IRS
925	Passive Activity and At-Risk Rules
926	Employment Taxes for Household Employers
937	Employment Taxes and Information Returns
939	Pension General Rule
946	How to Depreciate Your Property
947	Practice Before the IRS and Power of Attorney
953	International Tax Information for Business
1045	Information and Order Blanks for Preparers of Federal Income Tax Returns
1542	Per Diem Rates
1544	Reporting Cash Payments of Over $10,000
1546	How to Use the Problem Resolution Program of the IRS

Spanish Language Publications

1SP	Derechos del Contribuyente
556SP	Revisión de las Declaraciones de Impuesto, Derecho de Apelación y Reclamaciones de Reembolsos
579SP	Cómo Preparar la Declaración de Impuesto Federal
594SP	Comprendiendo el Proceso de Cobro
596SP	Crédito por Ingreso del Trabajo
850	English–Spanish Glossary of Words and Phrases Used in Publications Issued by the Internal Revenue Service

Forms Checklist

Some of the federal taxes for which a sole proprietor, a corporation or a partnership may be liable are listed below. If a due date falls on a Saturday, Sunday or legal holiday, it is postponed until the next day that is not a Saturday, Sunday or legal holiday. A statewide legal holiday delays a due date only if the IRS office where you are required to file is located in that state.

You May Be Liable For	If You Are	Use Form	Due On or Before
Income tax	Sole proprietor	Schedule C or C–EZ (Form 1040)	Same day as Form 1040
	Individual who is a partner, S corporation shareholder or LLC member	1040	15th day of 4th month after end of tax year
	Corporation	1120 or 1120–A	15th day of 3rd month after end of tax year
	S corporation	1120S	15th day of 3rd month after end of tax year
Self-employment tax	Sole proprietor, corporation, S corporation, partnership or LLC member	Schedule SE (Form 1040)	Same day as Form 1040
Estimated tax	Sole proprietor, or individual who is a partner, LLC member or S corporation shareholder	1040–ES	15th day of 4th, 6th and 9th months of tax year, and 15th day of 1st month after the end of tax year
	Corporation	1120–W	15th day of 4th, 6th, 9th and 12th months of tax year
Annual return of income	Partnership or LLC	1065	15th day of 4th month after end of tax year
Social Security and Medicare taxes (FICA taxes) and the withholding of income tax	Sole proprietor, corporation, S corporation, partnership or LLC member	941	4-30, 7-31, 10-31 and 1-31
		8109 (to make deposits)	See IRS Publication 334, Chapter 34
Providing information on Social Security and Medicare taxes (FICA taxes) and the withholding of income tax	Sole proprietor, corporation, S corporation, partnership or LLC member	W–2 (to employee)	1-31
		W–2 and W–3 (to the Social Security Administration)	Last day of February
Federal unemployment (FUTA) tax	Sole proprietor, corporation, S corporation, partnership or LLC	940–EZ or 940	1-31
		8109 (to make deposits)	4-30, 7-31, 10-31 and 1-31, but only if the liability for unpaid tax is more than $100
Information returns for payments to non-employees and transaction with other persons	Sole proprietor, corporation, S corporation, partnership or LLC	See IRS Publication 334, Chapter 36	Form 1099—to the recipient by 1-31, and to the IRS by 2-28. See also IRS Publication 334, Chapter 34
Excise taxes		See IRS Publication 334, Chapter 37	See the instructions to the forms

Quick and Easy Access to IRS Tax Help and Tax Products

Personal Computer

*Access the IRS's web site at **www.irs.gov** to:*

- Obtain Frequently Asked Tax Questions
- Download Electronically Fillable Forms
- Search Publications by Topic or Keyword
- Request Help via E-mail
- Receive Hot Tax News via E-mail

You can also reach us using:
- File Transfer Protocol at **ftp.irs.gov**

TaxFax Service

*Dial **703-368-9694** from your fax machine to get up to 3 items per call. Follow the directions of the prompts and your items will be immediately faxed back to you.*

Phone

Obtain forms, instructions, and publications 24 hours a day, 7 days a week, by calling:

- **1-800-829-3676** to order current and prior year forms, instructions and publications. You should receive your order within 10 days.

Walk-In

Pick up certain forms, instructions, and publications at many post offices, libraries, and IRS offices. Some IRS offices, libraries, grocery stores, copy centers, and office supply stores have an extensive collection of products available to photocopy or print from a CD-ROM.

Mail

Send your order for tax products to the Distribution Center nearest to you. You should receive your products within 10 days after we receive your order.

- **Western part of U.S.**
  Western Area Distribution Center
  Rancho Cordova, CA   95743-0001

- **Central part of U.S.**
  Central Area Distribution Center
  P.O. Box 8903
  Bloomington, IL   61702-8903

- **Eastern part of U.S. and foreign addresses:**
  Eastern Area Distribution Center
  P.O. Box 85074
  Richmond, VA   23261-5074

CD-ROM

Order IRS Publication 1796, Federal Tax Products on CD-ROM, and obtain:

- Current tax forms, instructions and publications
- Prior-year tax forms and instructions
- Popular tax forms which may be filled-in electronically, printed out for submission, and saved for recordkeeping
- Internal Revenue Bulletin

Purchase the CD-ROM via Internet at **http://www.irs.gov/cdorders** from the National Technical Information Service (NTIS) for $21 (no handling fee). Order by phone at 1-877-CDFORMS (1-877-233-6767) for $21 (plus a $5 handling fee). The price for 25 or more copies is $15.75 per CD plus a $5.00 handling fee.

Availability: First release—late December
Final release—late January

Minimum System Requirements:

- Microsoft Windows 95, Windows 98, Windows NT 4.0 with service pack 3 or later
  - i486 or Pentium-based personal computer (Pentium recommended);
  - 16 MB of RAM Windows 95, Windows 98, 24 MB of RAM Windows NT 4.0 (32 MB recommended);
  - 75 MB of available hard disk space;
  - VGA or higher resolution display adaptor supported by Windows;
  - Microsoft CD Extensions with a CD controller board;
  - Windows-compatible printer with at least 1 MB of user RAM
- Macintosh
  - Power Macintosh
  - Apple System Software version 7.5.3 or later
  - 6 MB RAM (12 MB Recommended)
  - 60 MB available hard disk space

Department of the Treasury
Internal Revenue Service
www.irs.gov

Publication 2053A (2000)
Cat. No. 23267Z

IRS

Department of the Treasury
Internal Revenue Service

Publication 1

(Rev. August 2000)

Catalog Number 64731W

www.irs.gov

Your Rights as a Taxpayer

The first part of this publication explains some of your most important rights as a taxpayer. The second part explains the examination, appeal, collection, and refund processes. This publication is also available in Spanish.

THE IRS MISSION

PROVIDE AMERICA'S TAXPAYERS TOP QUALITY SERVICE BY HELPING THEM UNDERSTAND AND MEET THEIR TAX RESPONSIBILITIES AND BY APPLYING THE TAX LAW WITH INTEGRITY AND FAIRNESS TO ALL.

Declaration of Taxpayer Rights

I. Protection of Your Rights

IRS employees will explain and protect your rights as a taxpayer throughout your contact with us.

II. Privacy and Confidentiality

The IRS will not disclose to anyone the information you give us, except as authorized by law. You have the right to know why we are asking you for information, how we will use it, and what happens if you do not provide requested information.

III. Professional and Courteous Service

If you believe that an IRS employee has not treated you in a professional, fair, and courteous manner, you should tell that employee's supervisor. If the supervisor's response is not satisfactory, you should write to the IRS director for your area or the center where you file your return.

IV. Representation

You may either represent yourself or, with proper written authorization, have someone else represent you in your place. Your representative must be a person allowed to practice before the IRS, such as an attorney, certified public accountant, or enrolled agent. If you are in an interview and ask to consult such a person, then we must stop and reschedule the interview in most cases.

You can have someone accompany you at an interview. You may make sound recordings of any meetings with our examination, appeal, or collection personnel, provided you tell us in writing 10 days before the meeting.

V. Payment of Only the Correct Amount of Tax

You are responsible for paying only the correct amount of tax due under the law—no more, no less. If you cannot pay all of your tax when it is due, you may be able to make monthly installment payments.

VI. Help With Unresolved Tax Problems

The Taxpayer Advocate Service can help you if you have tried unsuccessfully to resolve a problem with the IRS. Your local Taxpayer Advocate can offer you special help if you have a significant hardship as a result of a tax problem. For more information, call toll free 1–877–777–4778 (1–800–829–4059 for TTY/TDD) or write to the Taxpayer Advocate at the IRS office that last contacted you.

VII. Appeals and Judicial Review

If you disagree with us about the amount of your tax liability or certain collection actions, you have the right to ask the Appeals Office to review your case. You may also ask a court to review your case.

VIII. Relief From Certain Penalties and Interest

The IRS will waive penalties when allowed by law if you can show you acted reasonably and in good faith or relied on the incorrect advice of an IRS employee. We will waive interest that is the result of certain errors or delays caused by an IRS employee.

Examinations, Appeals, Collections, and Refunds

Examinations (Audits)

We accept most taxpayers' returns as filed. If we inquire about your return or select it for examination, it does not suggest that you are dishonest. The inquiry or examination may or may not result in more tax. We may close your case without change; or, you may receive a refund.

The process of selecting a return for examination usually begins in one of two ways. First, we use computer programs to identify returns that may have incorrect amounts. These programs may be based on information returns, such as Forms 1099 and W-2, on studies of past examinations, or on certain issues identified by compliance projects. Second, we use information from outside sources that indicates that a return may have incorrect amounts. These sources may include newspapers, public records, and individuals. If we determine that the information is accurate and reliable, we may use it to select a return for examination.

Publication 556, *Examination of Returns, Appeal Rights, and Claims for Refund*, explains the rules and procedures that we follow in examinations. The following sections give an overview of how we conduct examinations.

By Mail

We handle many examinations and inquiries by mail. We will send you a letter with either a request for more information or a reason why we believe a change to your return may be needed. You can respond by mail or you can request a personal interview with an examiner. If you mail us the requested information or provide an explanation, we may or may not agree with you, and we will explain the reasons for any changes. Please do not hesitate to write to us about anything you do not understand.

By Interview

If we notify you that we will conduct your examination through a personal interview, or you request such an interview, you have the right to ask that the examination take place at a reasonable time and place that is convenient for both you and the IRS. If our examiner proposes any changes to your return, he or she will explain the reasons for the changes. If you do not

agree with these changes, you can meet with the examiner's supervisor.

Repeat Examinations

If we examined your return for the same items in either of the 2 previous years and proposed no change to your tax liability, please contact us as soon as possible so we can see if we should discontinue the examination.

Appeals

If you do not agree with the examiner's proposed changes, you can appeal them to the Appeals Office of IRS. Most differences can be settled without expensive and time-consuming court trials. Your appeal rights are explained in detail in both Publication 5, *Your Appeal Rights and How To Prepare a Protest If You Don't Agree*, and Publication 556, *Examination of Returns, Appeal Rights, and Claims for Refund*.

If you do not wish to use the Appeals Office or disagree with its findings, you may be able to take your case to the U.S. Tax Court, U.S. Court of Federal Claims, or the U.S. District Court where you live. If you take your case to court, the IRS will have the burden of proving certain facts if you kept adequate records to show your tax liability, cooperated with the IRS, and meet certain other conditions. If the court agrees with you on most issues in your case and finds that our position was largely unjustified, you may be able to recover some of your administrative and litigation costs. You will not be eligible to recover these costs unless you tried to resolve your case administratively, including going through the appeals system, and you gave us the information necessary to resolve the case.

Collections

Publication 594, *The IRS Collection Process*, explains your rights and responsibilities regarding payment of federal taxes. It describes:

- What to do when you owe taxes. It describes what to do if you get a tax bill and what to do if you think your bill is wrong. It also covers making installment payments, delaying collection action, and submitting an offer in compromise.
- IRS collection actions. It covers liens, releasing a lien, levies, releasing a levy, seizures and sales, and release of property.

Your collection appeal rights are explained in detail in Publication 1660, *Collection Appeal Rights*.

Innocent Spouse Relief

Generally, both you and your spouse are responsible, jointly and individually, for paying the full amount of any tax, interest, or penalties due on your joint return. However, if you qualify for innocent spouse relief, you may not have to pay the tax, interest, and penalties related to your spouse (or former spouse). For information on innocent spouse relief and two other ways to get relief, see Publication 971, *Innocent Spouse Relief*, and Form 8857, *Request for Innocent Spouse Relief (And Separation of Liability and Equitable Relief)*.

Refunds

You may file a claim for refund if you think you paid too much tax. You must generally file the claim within 3 years from the date you filed your original return or 2 years from the date you paid the tax, whichever is later. The law generally provides for interest on your refund if it is not paid within 45 days of the date you filed your return or claim for refund. Publication 556, *Examination of Returns, Appeal Rights, and Claims for Refund*, has more information on refunds.

If you were due a refund but you did not file a return, you must file within 3 years from the date the return was originally due to get that refund.

Tax Information

The IRS provides a great deal of free information. The following are sources for forms, publications, and additional information.

- ***Tax Questions: 1-800-829-1040*** (1–800–829–4059 for TTY/TDD)
- ***Forms and Publications: 1-800-829-3676*** (1–800–829–4059 for TTY/TDD)
- ***Internet: www.irs.gov***
- ***TaxFax Service:*** From your fax machine, dial **703-368-9694.**
- ***Small Business Ombudsman:*** If you are a small business entity, you can participate in the regulatory process and comment on enforcement actions of IRS by calling **1–888–REG–FAIR.**
- ***Treasury Inspector General for Tax Administration:*** If you want to confidentially report misconduct, waste, fraud, or abuse by an IRS employee, you can call **1-800-366-4484** (1–800–877–8339 for TTY/TDD). You can remain anonymous.

Department of the Treasury
Internal Revenue Service

Publication 552
(Rev. October 1999)
Cat. No. 15100V

Recordkeeping for Individuals

Contents

Introduction

This publication discusses why you should keep records, what kinds of records you should keep, and how long to keep them.

You probably already keep records in your daily routine. This includes keeping receipts for purchases and recording information in your checkbook. Use this publication to determine if you need to keep additional information in your records.

Throughout this publication we refer you to other IRS publications for additional information. See *How To Get More Information* near the end of this publication for information about getting publications and forms.

This publication does not discuss the records you should keep when operating a business. For information on business records, see Publication 583, *Starting a Business and Keeping Records.*

Why Keep Records?

There are many reasons to keep records. In addition to tax purposes, you may need to keep records for insurance purposes or for getting a loan. Good records will help you:

• **Identify sources of income.** You may receive money or property from a variety of sources. Your records can identify the sources of your income. You need this information to separate business from nonbusiness income and taxable from nontaxable income.

• **Keep track of expenses.** You may forget an expense unless you record it when it occurs. You can use your records to identify expenses for which you can claim a deduction. This will help you determine if you can itemize deductions on your tax return.

• **Keep track of the basis of property.** You need to keep records that show the basis of your property. This includes the original cost or other basis of the property and any improvements you made.

• **Prepare tax returns.** You need records to prepare your tax return. Good records help you to file quickly and accurately.

• **Support items reported on tax returns.** You must keep records in case the IRS has a question about an item on your return. If the IRS examines your tax return, you may be asked to explain the items reported. Good records will help you explain any item and arrive at the correct tax with a minimum of effort. If you do not have records, you may have to spend time getting statements and receipts from various sources. If you cannot produce the correct documents, you may have to pay additional tax and be subject to penalties.

Kinds of Records To Keep

The IRS does not require you to keep your records in a particular way. Keep them in a manner that allows you and the IRS to determine your correct tax.

You can use your checkbook to keep a record of your income and expenses. In your checkbook you should record amounts, sources of deposits, and types of expenses. You also need to keep documents, such as receipts and sales slips, that can help prove a deduction.

You should keep your records in an orderly fashion and in a safe place. Keep them by year and type of income or expense. One method is to keep all records related to a particular item in a designated envelope.

In this section you will find guidance about basic records that everyone should keep. The section also provides guidance about specific records you should keep for certain items.

Computerized records. Many retail stores sell computer software packages that you can use for recordkeeping. These packages are relatively easy to use and require little knowledge of bookkeeping and accounting.

If you use a computerized system, you must be able to produce legible records of the information needed to determine your correct tax liability. In addition to your computerized records, you must keep proof of payment, receipts, and other documents to prove the amounts shown on your tax return.

Copies of tax returns. You should keep copies of your tax returns as part of your tax records. They can help you prepare future tax returns, and you will need them if you file an amended return. Copies of your returns and other records can be helpful to your survivor or the executor or administrator of your estate.

If necessary, you can request a copy of a return and all attachments (including Form W–2) from the IRS by using Form 4506, *Request for Copy or Transcript of Tax Form.* For information on the cost and where to file, see the Form 4506 instructions.

Basic Records

Basic records are documents that everybody should keep. These are the records that prove your income and expenses. If you own a home or investments, your basic records should contain documents related to those items. This table lists documents you should keep as basic records. Following the table are examples of information you can get from these records.

FOR items concerning your...	KEEP as basic records...
Income	• Form(s) W-2
	• Form(s) 1099
	• Bank statements
	• Brokerage statements
	• Form(s) K-1
Expenses	• Sales slips
	• Invoices
	• Receipts
	• Canceled checks or other proof of payment
Home	• Closing statements
	• Purchase and sales invoices
	• Proof of payment
	• Insurance records
	• Form 2119 (if you sold a home before 1998)
Investments	• Brokerage statements
	• Mutual fund statements
	• Form(s) 1099
	• Form(s) 2439

Income. Your basic records prove the amounts you report as income on your tax return. Your income may include wages, dividends, interest, and partnership or S corporation distributions. Your records also can prove that certain amounts are not taxable, such as tax-exempt interest.

Note. Keep Copy C of Form W-2 for at least 3 years after the due date for filing your tax return. However, to help protect your social security benefits, keep Copy C until you begin receiving social security benefits, just in case there is a question about your work record or earnings in a particular year.

Expenses. Your basic records prove the expenses for which you claim a deduction (or credit) on your tax return. Your deductions may include alimony, charitable contributions, mortgage interest, and real estate taxes. You may also have child care expenses for which you can claim a credit.

Home. Your basic records should enable you to determine the basis or adjusted basis of your home. You need this information to determine if you have a gain or loss when you sell your home or to figure depreciation if you use part of your home for business purposes or for rent. Your records should show the purchase price, settlement or closing costs, and the cost of any improvements. They may also show any casualty losses deducted, insurance reimbursements for casualty losses, and postponed gain from the sale of a previously-owned home.

For information on which settlement or closing costs are included in the basis of your home, see Publication 530, *Tax Information for First-Time Homeowners.* For information on basis, including the basis of property you receive other than by purchase, see Publication 551, *Basis of Assets.*

When you sell your home, your records should show the sales price and any selling expenses, such as commissions. For information on selling your home, see Publication 523, *Selling Your Home.*

Investments. Your basic records should enable you to determine your basis in an investment and whether you have a gain or loss when you sell it. Investments include stocks, bonds, and mutual funds. Your records should show the purchase price, sales price, and commissions. They may also show any reinvested dividends, stock splits and dividends, load charges, and original issue discount (OID).

For information on stocks and bonds, see Publication 550, *Investment Income and Expenses.* For information on mutual funds, see Publication 564, *Mutual Fund Distributions.*

Proof of Payment

One of your basic records is proof of payment. You should keep these records to support certain amounts shown on your tax return. Proof of payment alone is not proof that the item claimed on your return is allowable. You should also keep other documents that will help prove that the item is allowable.

Generally, you prove payment with a canceled check or cash receipt. If you do not have a canceled check because your bank does not return canceled checks or if you make payments by credit card or electronic funds transfer, you may be able to prove payment with an account statement.

If you make payments in cash, you should get a dated and signed receipt showing the amount and the reason for the payment.

Account statements. You may be able to prove payment with a legible financial account statement prepared by your bank or other financial institution. These statements are accepted as proof of payment if they show the items in the following table.

Pay statements. If you have deductible expenses withheld from your paycheck, such as union dues or medical insurance premiums, keep your pay statements as proof of payment of these expenses.

IF payment is by...	THEN the statement must show the...
Check	• Check number • Amount • Payee's name • Date the check amount was posted to the account by the financial institution
Electronic funds transfer	• Amount transferred • Payee's name • Date the transfer was posted to the account by the financial institution
Credit card	• Amount charged • Payee's name • Transaction date

Specific Records

This section is an alphabetical list of some items that require specific records in addition to your basic records.

Alimony

If you receive or pay alimony, you should keep a copy of your written separation agreement or the divorce, separate maintenance, or support decree. If you pay alimony, you will also need to know your former spouse's social security number. For information on alimony, see Publication 504, *Divorced or Separated Individuals.*

Business Use of Your Home

You may be able to deduct certain expenses connected with the business use of your home. You should keep records that show the part of your home that you use for business and the expenses related to that use. For information on how to allocate expenses between business and personal use, see Publication 587, *Business Use of Your Home.*

Casualty and Theft Losses

To deduct a casualty or theft loss, you must be able to prove that you had a casualty or theft. Your records also must be able to support the amount you claim.

For a *casualty loss,* your records should show:

• The type of casualty (car accident, fire, storm, etc.) and when it occurred.

• That the loss was a direct result of the casualty.

• That you were the owner of the property.

For a *theft loss,* your records should show:

• When you discovered your property was missing,

• That your property was stolen, and

• That you were the owner of the property.

For more information, see Publication 547, *Casualties, Disasters, and Thefts (Business and Nonbusiness)*. For a workbook designed to help you figure your loss, see Publication 584, *Casualty, Disaster, and Theft Loss Workbook (Personal-Use Property)*.

Child Care Credit

You must give the name, address, and taxpayer identification number for all persons or organizations that provide care for your child or dependent. You can use Form W-10 or various other sources to get the information from the care provider. Keep this information with your tax records. For information on the credit, see Publication 503, *Child and Dependent Care Expenses*.

Contributions

The kinds of records you must keep for charitable contributions depend on the amount of the contribution and whether the contribution is in cash. For information on contributions, see Publication 526, *Charitable Contributions*.

Contributions from which you benefit. Generally, if you make a charitable contribution that is more than $75 and is partly for goods or services, the organization must give you a written statement that you should keep.

Cash. Cash contributions include those paid by cash, check, credit card, or payroll deduction. For each cash contribution, you must keep one of the following:

- A canceled check or a financial account statement,

- A receipt from the organization showing the name of the organization, the amount, and date of the contribution, or

- Other reliable written records that are reasonable under the circumstances and that include the name of the organization, the amount, and the date of the contribution.

Contributions of $250 or more. You can deduct a contribution of $250 or more only if you have a written acknowledgment of your contribution from the organization.

Out-of-pocket expenses. You should keep records of your out-of-pocket expenses when you perform services for a charitable organization. You can record these expenses in a diary. For example, if you use your car when doing volunteer work, you should record the name of the organization and the unreimbursed gas and oil expenses directly related to the volunteer work. If you do not want to keep records of your actual expenses, you can keep a log of the miles you drove your car for the charitable purpose and use the standard mileage rate shown in Publication 526. You should also keep records of any parking fees, tolls, taxi fares, and bus fares.

Property. For each contribution of property, you must keep a receipt from the organization showing:

- The name of the organization,
- The date and location of the contribution, and
- A reasonably detailed description of the property.

A letter or other written communication from the organization containing the above information will serve as a receipt.

You also must keep reliable written records for each item of donated property. These records must include the:

- Fair market value of the property at the time of the contribution,
- Cost or other basis of the property, and
- Terms of any conditions attached to the contribution.

For more information on donated property, see Publication 526.

Credit for the Elderly or the Disabled

If you are under age 65, you must have your physician complete a statement certifying that you were permanently and totally disabled on the date you retired.

You do not have to file this statement with your Form 1040 or Form 1040A, but you **must** keep it for your records.

Veterans. If the Department of Veterans Affairs (VA) certifies that you are permanently and totally disabled, you can substitute VA Form 21–0172, *Certification of Permanent and Total Disability,* for the physician's statement you are required to keep. See Publication 524, *Credit for the Elderly or the Disabled,* for more information.

Employee Business Expenses

If you have employee business expenses, see Publication 463, *Travel, Entertainment, Gift, and Car Expenses,* for a discussion of what records to keep.

Gambling Winnings and Losses

You must keep an accurate diary of your winnings and losses that includes the:

- Date and type of gambling activity,
- Name and address or location of the gambling establishment,
- Names of other persons present with you at the gambling establishment, and
- Amount you won or lost.

In addition to your diary, you should keep other documents. See the discussion related to gambling losses in Publication 529, *Miscellaneous Deductions,* for documents you should keep.

Individual Retirement Arrangements (IRAs)

Keep copies of the following forms and records until all distributions are made from your IRA(s).

- Form 5498 or similar statement received for each year showing contributions you made, distributions you received, and the value of your IRA(s),
- Form 1099–R received for each year you received a distribution, and
- Form 8606 for each year you made a nondeductible contribution to your IRA or received distributions from an IRA if you ever made nondeductible contributions.

For a worksheet you can use to keep a record of yearly contributions and distributions, see Publication 590, *Individual Retirement Arrangements (IRAs) (Including Roth IRAs and Education IRAs)*.

Medical and Dental Expenses

In addition to records you keep of regular medical expenses, you should keep records on transportation expenses that are primarily for and essential to medical care. You can record these expenses in a diary. You should record gas and oil expenses directly related to that transportation. If you do not want to keep records of your actual expenses, you can keep a log of the miles you drive your car for medical purposes and use the standard mileage rate. You should also keep records of any parking fees, tolls, taxi fares, and bus fares.

For information on medical expenses and the standard mileage rate, see Publication 502, *Medical and Dental Expenses*.

Medical Savings Account

For each qualified medical expense you deduct or pay with a distribution from your medical savings account, you must keep a record of the name and address of each person you paid and the amount and date of the payment. For more information on medical savings accounts, see Publication 969, *Medical Savings Accounts (MSAs)*.

Mortgage Interest

If you paid mortgage interest of $600 or more, you should receive Form 1098, *Mortgage Interest Statement*. Keep this form and your mortgage statement and loan information in your records. For information on mortgage interest, see Publication 936, *Home Mortgage Interest Deduction*.

Pensions and Annuities

Use the worksheet in your tax return instructions to figure the taxable part of your pension or annuity. Keep a copy of the completed worksheet until you fully recover your contributions. For information on pensions and annuities, see Publication 575, *Pension and Annuity Income,* or Publication 721, *Tax Guide to U.S. Civil Service Retirement Benefits*.

Taxes

Your Form W–2 shows the state income tax withheld from your wages. If you made estimated state income tax payments, you need to keep a copy of the form. You also need to keep copies of your state income tax returns. If you received a refund of state income taxes, the state may send you Form 1099–G, *Certain Government and Qualified State Tuition Program Payments*.

Keep mortgage statements, tax assessments, or other documents as records of the real estate and personal property taxes you paid.

Tips

You must keep a daily record to accurately report your tips on your return. You can use Form 4070A, *Employee's Daily Record of Tips,* which is found in Publication 1244, *Employee's Daily Record of Tips and Report to Employer,* to record your tips. For information on tips, see Publication 531, *Reporting Tip Income*.

How Long To Keep Records

You must keep your records as long as they may be needed for the administration of any provision of the Internal Revenue Code. Generally, this means you must keep records that support items shown on your return until the period of limitations for that return runs out.

The period of limitations is the period of time in which you can amend your return to claim a credit or refund or the IRS can assess additional tax. The following table contains the periods of limitations that apply to income tax returns. Unless otherwise stated, the years refer to the period beginning after the return was filed. Returns filed before the due date are treated as being filed on the due date.

	IF you...	THEN the period is...
1	Owe additional tax and (2), (3), and (4) do not apply to you	3 years
2	Do not report income that you should and it is more than 25% of the gross income shown on your return	6 years
3	File a fraudulent return	No limit
4	Do not file a return	No limit
5	File a claim for credit or refund after you filed your return	Later of 3 years or 2 years after tax was paid.
6	File a claim for a loss from worthless securities	7 years

Property. Keep records relating to property until the period of limitations expires for the year in which you dispose of the property in a taxable disposition. You must keep these records to figure your basis for computing gain or loss when you sell or otherwise dispose of the property.

Generally, if you received property in a nontaxable exchange, your basis in that property is the same as the basis of the property you gave up. You must keep the records on the old property, as well as the new property, until the period of limitations expires for the year in which you dispose of the new property in a taxable disposition.

Keeping records for nontax purposes. When your records are no longer needed for tax purposes, do not disgard them until you check to see if they should be kept longer for other purposes. Your insurance company or creditors may require you to keep certain records longer than the IRS does.

Business Tax Services and Information

The IRS has many publications containing information about the federal tax laws that apply to businesses. Publication 334, *Tax Guide for Small Business,* is a good place to start to learn more about sole proprietors and statutory employees. Publication 583, *Starting a Business and Keeping Records,* covers basic tax information for those who are starting a business. Look in section **Tax Publications** for other materials that can explain your business tax responsibilities. For electronic assistance, you may go to the *IRS Digital Daily* Web site at www.irs.gov and access "Electronic Services." Then look for "IRS *e-file* Options for Business."

IRS *e-file* Programs for Businesses

File Form 941 by Telephone

Employers nationwide have the opportunity to file Form 941, *Employer's Quarterly Federal Tax Return,* using a Touch-Tone telephone, toll-free telephone number, and simple instructions. Businesses that meet certain qualifications are invited to participate in the paperless, 941TeleFile program. Eligible filers will receive a special 941TeleFile Tax Record and instructions with their Form 941 tax package.

If you receive the purple tax package in the mail with your traditional Form 941 and meet the qualifications in the instructions, you can use 941TeleFile. It's easy and **Free**. File your 941 in three easy steps:
- complete the 941TeleFile Tax Record
- with a Touch-Tone telephone, call the toll-free TeleFile number provided in the 941TeleFile tax package
- keep the 941TeleFile Tax Record as part of your permanent business records.

The 941TeleFile system automatically calculates your tax liability and any overpayment or balance due during the call. It also gives you a confirmation number as proof of filing your return. The call only takes about 10 minutes. The system is available 24 hours a day, 7 days a week. And, there is nothing to mail to the IRS.

File Form 941 Using a Reporting Agent

The 941*e-file* program accepts and processes Forms 941, Employer's Quarterly Federal Tax Return in the Electronic Data Interchange (EDI) format. Returns are transmitted nationwide via dial-up phone lines and menu-driven software directly to the IRS where they are processed at the Tennessee Computing Center (TCC) or the Austin Service Center (AUSC). An electronic acknowledgment is returned within 48 hours of receipt of the return. 941*e-file* accepts both timely filed returns, and late filed returns for the current tax year as well as for one (1) preceding tax year.

Large payroll processing companies, bulk-filer reporting agents, and/or large businesses capable of developing their own software are ideally suited to participate in this 941*e-file* program. Small businesses or reporting agents may also participate by developing their own software or by purchasing off-the-shelf software. With the appropriate software, almost any 941 filer can transmit his/her return.

To file using the IRS 941*e-file* program, an applicant should obtain a copy of Publication 1911, *Instructions for Preparing and Submitting Form 8655, Reporting Agent Authorization,* and Publication 3062, *Requirements of the Electronic Filing Program for Reporting of Form 941, Employer's Quarterly Federal Tax Return.* You can order these items free of charge through an IRS Area Distribution Center by calling the IRS at 1-800-829-3676. Additional information on how to participate in 941*e-file* can be obtained by contacting the IRS electronic filing TCC Help Desk on 901-546-2690, ext 7519 or the AUSC Help Desk on 512-460-4069.

File Form 941 Using a Personal Computer

Businesses that have a computer, modem, and off-the-shelf tax preparation software can transmit tax return information to a third party transmitter. The third party transmitter will batch, and then electronically forward, the return to the Austin Service Center. This program accepts and processes Form 941 in Electronic Data Interchange (EDI) format. The program also automatically conducts security checks, sends acknowledgments, and formats records to be processed by current IRS computer systems.

Business filers are responsible for obtaining a personal identification number (PIN) to be used as the electronic signature. You may request a PIN through a *Letter of Application.* The *Letter of Application* is included in the software and can be electronically transmitted to the Austin Service Center via the third party transmitter.

Payment options are available through the Federal Tax Deposit (FTD) coupon system or through the Electronic Federal Tax Payment System (EFTPS). For more information on the newer EFTPS system, see the EFTPS section below.

Electronic Federal Tax Payment System (EFTPS)

Several year ago, the U.S. Department of Treasury designed EFTPS to modernize 'making tax payments' — from a paper-based payment system to an electronic one. Today, 2.5M business taxpayers are enrolled in EFTPS. This tax payment system helps individuals and business owners save time and money in paying their federal business taxes and in making their federal tax payments electronically — either by telephone, personal computer, or through the transfer of funds offered by their financial institution. **All** federal tax payments (including payroll taxes, corporate income taxes, partnership, and fiduciary taxes) can be made using EFTPS.

You will find that EFTPS is easy to use, convenient, accurate, fast, and economical.

- Individuals and business owners can use **EFTPS-Direct** to make their tax payments by telephone or personal computer, 24 hours a day, seven days a week. For your computer, free Windows-based software is available when you enroll in EFTPS and use EFTPS-Direct. Using EFTPS-Direct only takes a few minutes — no check writing; no trips to the bank; and no courier, checks, stamps, and envelope expenses. And as an added convenience, EFTPS-Direct lets taxpayers **'warehouse'** their tax payment instructions up to 30 days in advance of a tax due date to **automatically make their payments on the tax due date.**
- Financial institutions are integrating EFTPS into the many services they offer their clients. Under the client's direction, funds can be transferred from the client's account into Treasury's account on a specified date.
- Tax professionals have a number of options to make federal tax payments for their clients:
  - ✓ EFTPS Voice Response System — make multiple payments with a single telephone call
  - ✓ EFTPS PC Debit — use Windows-based software to send payments
  - ✓ EFTPS Batch — use Windows-based software to send batches of payments electronically
  - ✓ EFTPS Bulk — make frequent consolidated payments from an EDI-compatible system

To participate in EFTPS, you must first enroll. For an enrollment form and for more information on EFTPS, call EFTPS Customer Service at 1-800-945-8400 or 1-800-555-4477. En Espanol communication, call 1-800-945-8600 or 1-800-244-4829. With access to teletypewriter/telecommunications device for the deaf (TTY/TDD) equipment only, call 1-800-945-8900 or 1-800-733-4829.

The IRS produces a number of print materials that can provide you with additional information on EFTPS. You can order these forms and publications free through the IRS Area Distribution Centers by calling 1-800-829-3676.

- Form 9779, *Business Enrollment Form and Instructions*
- Form 9783, *Individual Enrollment Form and Instructions*
- Publication 966, *The Easiest Way to Pay Your Federal Taxes*
- Publication 3110, *EFTPS Information Stuffer*
- Publication 3127, *EFTPS* Fact Sheet
- Publication 3425, *4 Easy Ways to Use EFTPS* — for tax professionals, accountants, and payroll companies

Some forms can be downloaded from the IRS Web site at www.irs.gov, and you can also get some forms via the IRS Tax Fax by dialing (703) 368-9694 from a fax machine and following the voice prompts to get tax forms faxed back to you.

Independent Contractor or Employee

For Federal tax purposes, this is an important distinction. Worker classification affects how you pay your Federal income tax, social security and Medicare taxes, and how you file your return. Classification affects your eligibility for employer and social security and Medicare benefits and your tax responsibilities.

A worker is either an **independent contractor** or an **employee**. The classification is determined by relevant facts that fall into three main categories: behavioral control; financial control; and relationship of the parties. In each case, it is very important to consider all the facts — no single fact provides the answer.

Publication 1779, *Independent Contractor or Employee,* has detailed information about these facts.

- An independent contractor will usually maintain an office and staff, advertise, and have a financial investment risk. Independent contractors will generally file a Schedule C and may be able to deduct certain expenses that an employee would not.
- Generally, an **employee** is controlled by an employer in ways that a true independent contractor is not. If the employer has the legal right to control the details of how the services are performed, the worker is generally an employee, not an independent contractor.

Those who should be classified as employees, but aren't, may lose out on social security and Medicare benefits, workers' compensation, unemployment benefits, and, in many cases, group insurance (including life and health), and retirement benefits.

If you are not sure whether you are an independent contractor or an employee, get Form SS-8, *Determination of Employee Work Status for Purposes of Federal Employment Taxes and Income Tax Withholding.*

Publication 1779, *Independent Contractor or Employee,* and Publication 15-A, *Employer's Supplemental Tax Guide,* provide additional information on independent contractor or employee status.

IRS publications and forms can be downloaded from the Internet at www.irs.gov. You can also order a free copy of IRS publications and forms when you call the IRS at 1-800-829-3676.

Publication 1518, *Year 2000 Tax Calendar for Small Businesses*

Business owners who are opening their doors for the first time or are hiring their first employees may benefit from this 12-month wall calendar. Publication 1518 shows all the 2000 due dates for making payroll deposits, paying estimated taxes, and for filing business tax forms. It also includes general information on basic business tax law, where to go for assistance, helpful bookkeeping and recordkeeping hints, and facts about IRS notices and penalties. Call the IRS at 1-800-829-3676 to order a free copy of this calendar.

Office of Public Liaison and Small Business Affairs

As a national public liaison for small businesses, this office maintains daily contact and exchanges business tax information with IRS external stakeholders — national organizations representing tax professionals, payroll processors, volunteers and social services, electronic commerce, state departments of revenue, small business organizations, and large corporate taxpayers. This office also works with the Small Business Administration and other government agencies to initiate and foster programs and actions to reduce small business burdens government-wide.

The Office of Public Liaison and Small Business Affairs provides 'one-stop' service for sharing 'small business' information. Some of these services include:

- working to establish partnering opportunities
- providing forums to discuss new ideas and feedback
- tracking issues and sharing information
- coordinating liaison meetings
- coordinating IRS participation at meetings and conferences

You can write to the IRS Office of Public Liaison and Small Business Affairs if you have **suggestions regarding tax laws, regulations, or policy.**

Internal Revenue Service
The Office of Public Liaison and
  Small Business Affairs CL:PL
IR Room 7559
1111 Constitution Avenue NW
Washington, DC 20224
*public_liaison@m1.irs.gov

This office **does not** handle small business owners' individual tax problems. If a problem has not been resolved after repeated attempts through normal IRS

channels, small business owners should contact their local IRS Taxpayer Advocate Service for assistance. See section in this booklet on Taxpayer Advocate Service (TAS) under **Taxpayer Assistance Programs** for more information.

The IRS produces a number of print and electronic information materials to help new businesses. The following IRS tax publications and small business CD-ROM can be ordered free through the IRS by calling 1-800-829-3676.

- Publication 334, *Tax Guide for Small Business (For Individuals Who Use Schedule C or C-EZ)*
- Publication 583, *Starting a Business and Keeping Records*
- Publication 1066, *Small Business Tax Workshop* (booklet), provides general information about different types of business organizations, record-keeping requirements, and business tax returns. This booklet is used as an education tool in small business workshops given by local IRS offices.
- Publication 1518, *Year 2000 Tax Calendar for Small Businesses,* notes the most common tax filing dates. A specific tax tip is highlighted each month, in the calendar, to help small businesses not only during the tax-filing season, but also throughout the year.
- Publication 1853, *Small Business Talk,* tells of the Office of Public Liaison and Small Business Affairs, and lists services and tax materials available to small businesses.
- Publication 3207, *Small Business Resource Guide 2000: What You Need to Know About Taxes and Other Topics* (CD-ROM). This CD-ROM includes tax information, provided by multiple government agencies, to help small business entrepreneurs meet regulatory requirements.

Many IRS information products are also available on the small business corner of the IRS Web site @ www.irs.gov/prod/bus_info/sm_bus/index.html.

SSA/IRS *(Social Security Administration/Internal Revenue Service) Reporter* (newsletter)

If you are an employer and have not been receiving a copy of the *SSA/IRS Reporter,* tell your local IRS Public Affairs Officer/Communications Manager.

The *SSA/IRS Reporter* is a quarterly newsletter that keeps you up-to-date on changes to taxes and employee wage obligations. This newsletter, produced jointly by the Social Security Administration and the IRS, is mailed to approximately seven million employers along with each quarterly Form 941, *Employer's Quarterly Federal Tax Return,* and instructions.

Small Business Tax Education Program (STEP)

Small business owners and other self-employed individuals can learn about business taxes through a unique partnership between the IRS and local organizations. Through workshops or in-depth tax courses, instructors provide training on starting a business, recordkeeping, preparing business tax returns, self-employment tax issues, and employment taxes.

Some courses are offered free as a community service. Courses given by an educational facility may include costs for materials and tuition. Other courses may have a nominal fee to offset administrative costs of sponsoring organizations.

Your Business Tax Kit (YBTK)

The *YBTK,* in booklet format, contains various IRS business tax forms and publications that may be used to prepare and file business tax returns. Besides forms and publications, the kit includes information on quick and easy access to IRS tax help. To order, call 1-800-829-3676 and ask for Publication 454, *Your Business Tax Kit.*

Department of the Treasury
Internal Revenue Service
www.irs.gov

Notice 433 (Rev. 8-1999)
Catalog Number 26242I

Interest and Penalty Information

The interest rate on underpayment and overpayment of taxes and the penalty for underpayment of estimated tax are as follows:

Period	Estimated Tax Underpayment	Interest Rate and Penalty Rate Overpayment
10/1/88–3/31/89	11%	10%
4/1/89–9/30/89	12%	11%
10/1/89–3/31/91	11%	10%
4/1/91–12/31/91	10%	9%
1/1/92–3/31/92	9%	8%
4/1/92–9/30/92	8%	7%
10/1/92–6/30/94	7%	6%
7/1/94–9/30/94	8%	7%
10/1/94–3/31/95	9%	8%
4/1/95–6/30/95	10%	9%
7/1/95–3/31/96	9%	8%
4/1/96–6/30/96	8%	7%
7/1/96–3/31/98	9%	8%
4/1/98–12/31/98	8%	7%
1/1/99–3/31/99	7%	7%
4/1/99–12/31/99	8%	8%

The law requires us to redetermine these interest rates quarterly. We compound interest daily except on late or underpaid estimated taxes for individuals or corporations.

We charge 120% of the underpayment interest rate if: (1) the return is due before January 1, 1990, excluding extensions; (2) the underpayment is over $1,000; and (3) the underpayment was from a tax-motivated transaction.

For large (C) Corporations with underpayments over $100,000, we charge the underpayment interest rate plus 2%.

We'll continue to charge interest until you pay the amount you owe in full.

The penalty for late filing is 5% of the tax due on the return you filed late for each month or part of a month you filed late, up to 25% of the tax due. If you don't file your tax return within 60 days of the due date, the penalty is $100 or 100% of the tax due on your return, whichever is less.

The penalty for late payment is 1/2% of the tax due for each month or part of a month your payment is late, up to 25% of the tax due. The penalty increases to 1% per month if we send a notice of intent to levy, and you don't pay the tax due within 10 days from the date of the notice.

The combined late filing and the late payment penalties are limited to 5% of the unpaid tax for that month.

The deposit penalty for employment, excise, or railroad retirement tax varies from 2% to 15% depending on how late the deposit is.

The penalty for filing an exempt organization return late prior to 1998 is $10 a day for each day the return is late, but not more than $5,000 or 5% of the gross receipts for the year, whichever is less. For 1998 and subsequent, if gross receipts are equal to or less than $1 million, the penalty is $20 a day for each day the return is late, not to exceed $10,000 or 5% of gross receipts for the year, whichever is less. If gross receipts exceed $1 million the penalty is $100 a day for each day the return is late, not to exceed $50,000.

Appeal Rights—Arithmetic Error

You may appeal the changes shown on the enclosed notice within 60 days from your notice date. Send your explanation with a copy of the notice to the address shown on your notice.

We'll notify you if we don't accept your explanation. If we accept it, we'll reduce any tax increase due to the change. We'll refund any tax you overpaid if you owe no other tax or have no other debts the law requires us to collect.

We'll continue to charge interest if you don't pay the balance you owe by the date requested in this enclosed notice.

Interest on Certain Penalties

We charge interest on penalties from the return due date for late filing, valuation overstatements or understatements and substantial understatement of the tax due. The interest rate on penalties is the same as the underpayment interest rate. On fraud and negligence penalties for returns due after December 31, 1988, we charge interest from the return due date.

Removal of Penalty and Interest

Reasonable Cause

The law allows us to remove or reduce a penalty based on reasonable cause. This procedure doesn't apply to interest. To request a penalty reduction, send a statement to us fully explaining the facts. You or your representative with your power of attorney must sign your statement under penalty of perjury. In some cases, we may request that you pay the tax in full before we remove or reduce the late payment penalty.

Erroneous Written Advice from IRS

We'll remove the penalty (but not the interest) if: (1) you wrote to us and asked for advice on a specific issue; (2) you gave us complete and accurate information; (3) we wrote back to you and told you what to do or explained what not to do; (4) you followed our written advice in the way we told you to; and (5) you received a penalty for the action we advised you to take.

If you meet this criteria, complete Form 843, Claim for Refund and Request for Abatement, and ask us to remove the penalty.

Attach to your Form 843: (1) a copy of your original request for advice; (2) a copy of the written advice we gave you; and (3) the notice (if any) showing the penalty we charged.

Send Form 843 to the IRS Service Center where you filed your return for the year you relied on erroneous advice from us.

Interest on Erroneous Refunds

The law requires us to remove interest up to the date we request you to repay the erroneous refund when: (1) you did not cause the erroneous refund in any way; and (2) the refund doesn't exceed $50,000.

IRS may remove or reduce interest on other erroneous refunds or on errors due to an IRS ministerial act, based on the facts and circumstances of each case.

If we reduce interest that you previously reported as a deduction on your tax return, you must report this reduction of interest as income on your tax return for the year we reduce it.

Notice 931
(Rev. October 1998)

Deposit Requirements for Employment Taxes

There are two deposit schedules—monthly or semiweekly—for determining when you deposit social security and Medicare taxes and withheld income tax. These schedules tell you when a deposit is due after a tax liability arises (e.g., when you have a payday). Prior to the beginning of each calendar year, you must determine which of the two deposit schedules you are required to use. The deposit schedule you must use is based on the total tax liability you reported on Form 941 during a four-quarter *lookback period* as discussed below. Your deposit schedule is **not** determined by how often you pay your employees or make deposits (see **Application of Monthly and Semiweekly Schedules** on the back).

Similar rules apply for Federal income tax withholding for nonpayroll items such as backup withholding, voluntary withholding on certain government payments, and withholding on pensions, annuities, and gambling winnings. These rules do not apply to Federal unemployment (FUTA) tax. See the **Instructions for Form 940** for information on depositing FUTA tax.

Electronic deposit requirement. If your total deposits of social security, Medicare, and withheld income taxes were more than $50,000 in 1997, you must make electronic deposits for all depository tax liabilities that occur after 1998. For details, see **Circular E**, Employer's Tax Guide.

Lookback period. Your deposit schedule for a calendar year is determined from the total taxes (not reduced by any advance earned income credit payments) reported on your Forms 941 (line 11) in a four-quarter lookback period. The lookback period begins July 1 and ends June 30 as shown in the chart below. If you reported $50,000 or less of Form 941 taxes for the lookback period, you are a monthly schedule depositor; if you reported more than $50,000, you are a semiweekly schedule depositor. There are two exception rules—the $1,000 rule and the $100,000 next-day deposit rule. The deposit rules and exceptions are discussed below.

Lookback Period For Calendar Year 1999

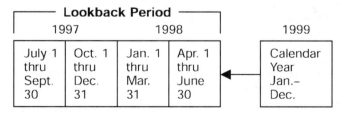

Monthly Deposit Schedule

Under the **monthly deposit schedule,** Form 941 taxes on payments made during a calendar month must be deposited by the 15th day of the following month.

Monthly schedule depositors are **not** required to file Form 941 on a monthly basis. Do not file **Form 941-M,** Employer's Monthly Federal Tax Return, unless you are instructed to do so by an IRS representative.

New employers. During the first calendar year of your business, your tax liability for each quarter in the lookback period is considered to be zero. Therefore, you are a monthly schedule depositor for the first year of your business (but see the **$100,000 Next-Day Deposit Rule** on the back).

Semiweekly Deposit Schedule

Under the **semiweekly deposit schedule,** Form 941 taxes on payments made on Wednesday, Thursday, and/or Friday must be deposited by the following Wednesday. Taxes on payments made on Saturday, Sunday, Monday, and/or Tuesday must be deposited by the following Friday.

Deposit Period (Payment Days)	Deposit By
Wednesday, Thursday, and/or Friday	Following Wednesday
Saturday, Sunday, Monday, and/or Tuesday	Following Friday

The end of the quarterly return period always ends a semiweekly deposit period and begins a new one. For example, if the quarter ends on Thursday, then Wednesday and Thursday are one deposit period in the quarter just ended and Friday becomes a separate deposit period in the new quarter. Taxes accumulated on Wednesday and Thursday are subject to one deposit obligation and taxes accumulated on Friday are subject to a separate deposit obligation. Separate deposits are required because two different quarters are affected.

Example of Monthly and Semiweekly Schedules

Elm Co. reported Form 941 tax liability as follows:

1998 Lookback Period	1999 Lookback Period
3rd Quarter 1996 - $12,000	3rd Quarter 1997 - $12,000
4th Quarter 1996 - $12,000	4th Quarter 1997 - $12,000
1st Quarter 1997 - $12,000	1st Quarter 1998 - $12,000
2nd Quarter 1997 - $12,000	2nd Quarter 1998 - $15,000
$48,000	$51,000

Elm Co. is a monthly schedule depositor for 1998 because its tax liability for the four quarters in its lookback period (3rd quarter 1996 through 2nd quarter 1997) was not more than $50,000. However, for 1999, Elm Co. must follow the semiweekly deposit rule described above because its liability exceeded $50,000 for the four quarters in its lookback period (3rd quarter 1997 through 2nd quarter 1998).

Deposits on Banking Days Only

If a deposit is due on a day that is not a banking day, the deposit is considered to have been made timely if it is made by the close of the next banking day. In addition to Federal and state bank holidays, Saturdays and Sundays are treated as nonbanking days. For example, if a deposit is due on a Friday and Friday is not a banking day, the deposit will be considered timely if it is made by the following Monday (if that Monday is a banking day).

A special rule is provided for **semiweekly schedule depositors** that allows at least 3 banking days to make a deposit. For example, if a semiweekly schedule depositor has Form 941 taxes accumulated for payments made on Friday and the following Monday is not a banking day, deposits made by the following Thursday are considered timely (allowing 3 banking days to make the deposit).

Application of Monthly and Semiweekly Schedules

The terms "monthly schedule depositor" and "semiweekly schedule depositor" **do not** refer to how often your business pays its employees, or even how often you are required to make deposits. The terms identify which set of deposit rules you must follow when a Form 941 tax liability arises. The deposit rules are based on the dates wages are paid; **not** on when employment tax liabilities are accrued.

Monthly schedule example: Pine Co. has a monthly deposit schedule. It paid wages each Friday during January but did not pay any wages during February. Under the monthly schedule, Pine Co. must deposit the combined tax liabilities for the January paydays by February 16 (February 15 is a nonbanking day). Pine Co. does not have a deposit requirement for February (due by March 16) because no wages were paid and, therefore, it did not have a tax liability for the month.

Semiweekly schedule example: Green Inc., which has a semiweekly deposit schedule, pays wages once each month on the last day of the month. Although Green Inc. has a semiweekly deposit schedule, it will deposit just once a month because it pays wages only once a month. The deposit, however, will be made under the semiweekly deposit schedule as follows: Green Inc.'s tax liability for the March 31 (Wednesday) payday must be deposited by April 7 (Wednesday). Under the semiweekly deposit schedule, liabilities arising on Wednesday through Friday must be deposited by the following Wednesday.

$1,000 Rule

If an employer accumulates a Form 941 tax liability of less than $1,000 during a quarter, no deposits are required and this liability may be paid with Form 941 for the quarter. However, if you are unsure that you will accumulate less than $1,000, deposit under the appropriate deposit rules so that you will not be subject to failure-to-deposit penalties.

$100,000 Next-Day Deposit Rule

If the total accumulated tax reaches $100,000 or more on any day during a deposit period, it must be deposited by the next banking day, whether an employer is a monthly or semiweekly schedule depositor. For monthly schedule depositors, the deposit period is a calendar month. The deposit periods for a semiweekly schedule depositor are Wednesday through Friday and Saturday through Tuesday. For purposes of the $100,000 next-day deposit rule, do not continue accumulating Form 941 tax liability after the end of a deposit period. For example, if a semiweekly schedule depositor has accumulated a liability of $95,000 on a Tuesday (of a Saturday-through-Tuesday deposit period) and accumulated a $10,000 liability on Wednesday, the $100,000 next-day deposit rule does not apply. Therefore, $95,000 must be deposited by Friday and $10,000 by the following Wednesday.

If a monthly schedule depositor accumulates a $100,000 Form 941 tax liability on any day during a calendar month, it becomes a semiweekly schedule depositor on the next day and remains so for at least the remainder of the calendar year and for the following calendar year.

Example of $100,000 next-day deposit rule. Fir Co. started its business on April 8, 1999. On April 15, it paid wages for the first time and accumulated a tax liability of $40,000. On April 22, Fir Co. paid wages and accumulated a liability of $60,000, bringing its accumulated Form 941 tax liability to $100,000. Because this was the first year of its business, the tax liability for its lookback period is considered to be zero, and it would be a monthly schedule depositor based on the lookback rules. However, because Fir Co. accumulated $100,000 on April 22, it became a semiweekly schedule depositor on April 23. It will be a semiweekly schedule depositor for the remainder of 1999 and for 2000. Fir Co. is required to deposit $100,000 by April 23, the next banking day.

Adjustments and the Lookback Rule

Determine your tax liability for the quarters in the lookback period based on the tax liability as **originally** reported. If you made adjustments to correct errors on previously filed Forms 941, these adjustments do not affect the amount of tax liability for purposes of the lookback rule. If you report adjustments on your current Form 941 to correct errors on prior period returns, include these adjustments as part of your tax liability for the current quarter. If you filed **Form 843**, Claim for Refund and Request for Abatement, to claim a refund for a prior period overpayment, your tax liability does not change for either the prior period or the current period quarter for purposes of the lookback rule.

Example of adjustments and the lookback rule. An employer originally reported a tax liability of $45,000 for the four quarters in the lookback period ending June 30, 1998. The employer discovered during January 1999 that the tax during one of the lookback period quarters was understated by $10,000 and corrected this error with an adjustment on the 1999 first quarter Form 941. This employer is a monthly schedule depositor for 1999 because the lookback period tax liabilities are based on the amounts originally reported and they were less than $50,000. The $10,000 adjustment is part of the 1999 first quarter tax liability.

Accuracy of Deposits Rule

You are required to deposit 100% of your tax liability on or before the deposit due date. However, penalties will not be applied for depositing less than 100% if **both** of the following conditions are met:

1. Any deposit shortfall does not exceed the greater of $100 or 2% of the amount of taxes otherwise required to be deposited and

2. The deposit shortfall is paid or deposited by the shortfall makeup date as described below.

● **Monthly schedule depositor.** Deposit or pay the shortfall with your return by the due date of the Form 941 for the period in which the shortfall occurred. You may pay the shortfall with Form 941 even if the amount is $1,000 or more.

● **Semiweekly schedule depositor.** Deposit the shortfall by the first Wednesday or Friday, whichever is earlier, falling on or after the 15th day of the month following the month in which the shortfall occurred, or, if earlier, the due date of the return. For example, if a semiweekly schedule depositor has a deposit shortfall during February 1999, the shortfall makeup date is March 17, 1999 (Wednesday). However, if the shortfall occurred on the required April 2 deposit date for a March 29, 1999, pay date, the return due date for the March 29 tax liability (April 30) would come before the May 19 (Wednesday) shortfall makeup date. In this case, the shortfall would have to be deposited by April 30.

Notice 931
(Rev. October 1998)

Form **2553**
(Rev. January 2001)

Department of the Treasury
Internal Revenue Service

Election by a Small Business Corporation
(Under section 1362 of the Internal Revenue Code)
▶ See Parts II and III on back and the separate instructions.
▶ The corporation may either send or fax this form to the IRS. See page 1 of the instructions.

OMB No. 1545-0146

Notes:
1. This election to be an S corporation can be accepted only if all the tests are met under **Who May Elect** on page 1 of the instructions; all signatures in Parts I and III are originals (no photocopies); and the exact name and address of the corporation and other required form information are provided.
2. Do not file **Form 1120S,** U.S. Income Tax Return for an S Corporation, for any tax year before the year the election takes effect.
3. If the corporation was in existence before the effective date of this election, see **Taxes an S Corporation May Owe** on page 1 of the instructions.

Part I	**Election Information**	

Please Type or Print

Name of corporation (see instructions)	**A** Employer identification number
Number, street, and room or suite no. (If a P.O. box, see instructions.)	**B** Date incorporated
City or town, state, and ZIP code	**C** State of incorporation

D Election is to be effective for tax year beginning (month, day, year) . . . . ▶ / /

E Name and title of officer or legal representative who the IRS may call for more information

F Telephone number of officer or legal representative ( )

G If the corporation changed its name or address after applying for the EIN shown in **A** above, check this box . . . . ▶ ☐

H If this election takes effect for the first tax year the corporation exists, enter month, day, and year of the **earliest** of the following: (1) date the corporation first had shareholders, (2) date the corporation first had assets, or (3) date the corporation began doing business . . . . ▶ / /

I Selected tax year: Annual return will be filed for tax year ending (month and day) ▶ -

If the tax year ends on any date other than December 31, except for an automatic 52-53-week tax year ending with reference to the month of December, you **must** complete Part II on the back. If the date you enter is the ending date of an automatic 52-53-week tax year, write "52-53-week year" to the right of the date. See Temporary Regulations section 1.441-2T(e)(3).

J Name and address of each shareholder; shareholder's spouse having a community property interest in the corporation's stock; and each tenant in common, joint tenant, and tenant by the entirety. (A husband and wife (and their estates) are counted as one shareholder in determining the number of shareholders without regard to the manner in which the stock is owned.)	**K** Shareholders' Consent Statement. Under penalties of perjury, we declare that we consent to the election of the above-named corporation to be an S corporation under section 1362(a) and that we have examined this consent statement, including accompanying schedules and statements, and to the best of our knowledge and belief, it is true, correct, and complete. We understand our consent is binding and may not be withdrawn after the corporation has made a valid election. (Shareholders sign and date below.)		**L** Stock owned		**M** Social security number or employer identification number (see instructions)	**N** Shareholder's tax year ends (month and day)
	Signature	Date	Number of shares	Dates acquired		

Under penalties of perjury, I declare that I have examined this election, including accompanying schedules and statements, and to the best of my knowledge and belief, it is true, correct, and complete.

Signature of officer ▶   Title ▶   Date ▶

For Paperwork Reduction Act Notice, see page 4 of the instructions.   Cat. No. 18629R   Form **2553** (Rev. 1-2001)

Part II **Selection of Fiscal Tax Year** (All corporations using this part must complete item O and item P, Q, or R.)

O Check the applicable box to indicate whether the corporation is:

1. ☐ A new corporation adopting the tax year entered in item I, Part I.

2. ☐ An existing corporation retaining the tax year entered in item I, Part I.

3. ☐ An existing corporation changing to the tax year entered in item I, Part I.

P Complete item P if the corporation is using the expeditious approval provisions of Rev. Proc. 87-32, 1987-2 C.B. 396, to request **(1)** a natural business year (as defined in section 4.01(1) of Rev. Proc. 87-32) or **(2)** a year that satisfies the ownership tax year test in section 4.01(2) of Rev. Proc. 87-32. Check the applicable box below to indicate the representation statement the corporation is making as required under section 4 of Rev. Proc. 87-32.

1. Natural Business Year ▶ ☐ I represent that the corporation is retaining or changing to a tax year that coincides with its natural business year as defined in section 4.01(1) of Rev. Proc. 87-32 and as verified by its satisfaction of the requirements of section 4.02(1) of Rev. Proc. 87-32. In addition, if the corporation is changing to a natural business year as defined in section 4.01(1), I further represent that such tax year results in less deferral of income to the owners than the corporation's present tax year. I also represent that the corporation is not described in section 3.01(2) of Rev. Proc. 87-32. (See instructions for additional information that must be attached.)

2. Ownership Tax Year ▶ ☐ I represent that shareholders holding more than half of the shares of the stock (as of the first day of the tax year to which the request relates) of the corporation have the same tax year or are concurrently changing to the tax year that the corporation adopts, retains, or changes to per item I, Part I. I also represent that the corporation is not described in section 3.01(2) of Rev. Proc. 87-32.

Note: *If you do not use item P and the corporation wants a fiscal tax year, complete either item Q or R below. Item Q is used to request a fiscal tax year based on a business purpose and to make a back-up section 444 election. Item R is used to make a regular section 444 election.*

Q Business Purpose—To request a fiscal tax year based on a business purpose, you must check box Q1 and pay a user fee. See instructions for details. You may also check box Q2 and/or box Q3.

1. Check here ▶ ☐ if the fiscal year entered in item I, Part I, is requested under the provisions of section 6.03 of Rev. Proc. 87-32. Attach to Form 2553 a statement showing the business purpose for the requested fiscal year. See instructions for additional information that must be attached.

2. Check here ▶ ☐ to show that the corporation intends to make a back-up section 444 election in the event the corporation's business purpose request is not approved by the IRS. (See instructions for more information.)

3. Check here ▶ ☐ to show that the corporation agrees to adopt or change to a tax year ending December 31 if necessary for the IRS to accept this election for S corporation status in the event (1) the corporation's business purpose request is not approved and the corporation makes a back-up section 444 election, but is ultimately not qualified to make a section 444 election, or (2) the corporation's business purpose request is not approved and the corporation did not make a back-up section 444 election.

R Section 444 Election—To make a section 444 election, you must check box R1 and you may also check box R2.

1. Check here ▶ ☐ to show the corporation will make, if qualified, a section 444 election to have the fiscal tax year shown in item I, Part I. To make the election, you must complete **Form 8716**, Election To Have a Tax Year Other Than a Required Tax Year, and either attach it to Form 2553 or file it separately.

2. Check here ▶ ☐ to show that the corporation agrees to adopt or change to a tax year ending December 31 if necessary for the IRS to accept this election for S corporation status in the event the corporation is ultimately not qualified to make a section 444 election.

Part III **Qualified Subchapter S Trust (QSST) Election Under Section 1361(d)(2)***

Income beneficiary's name and address	Social security number
Trust's name and address	Employer identification number

Date on which stock of the corporation was transferred to the trust (month, day, year) . . . . ▶   /   /

In order for the trust named above to be a QSST and thus a qualifying shareholder of the S corporation for which this Form 2553 is filed, I hereby make the election under section 1361(d)(2). Under penalties of perjury, I certify that the trust meets the definitional requirements of section 1361(d)(3) and that all other information provided in Part III is true, correct, and complete.

_____   _____

Signature of income beneficiary or signature and title of legal representative or other qualified person making the election   Date

*Use Part III to make the QSST election only if stock of the corporation has been transferred to the trust on or before the date on which the corporation makes its election to be an S corporation. The QSST election must be made and filed separately if stock of the corporation is transferred to the trust after the date on which the corporation makes the S election.

Form 4506
(Rev. May 1997)

Department of the Treasury
Internal Revenue Service

Request for Copy or Transcript of Tax Form

▶ Read instructions before completing this form.

▶ Type or print clearly. Request may be rejected if the form is incomplete or illegible.

OMB No. 1545-0429

Note: Do not use this form to get tax account information. Instead, see instructions below.

1a Name shown on tax form. If a joint return, enter the name shown first.	**1b** First social security number on tax form or employer identification number (see instructions)
2a If a joint return, spouse's name shown on tax form	**2b** Second social security number on tax form

3 Current name, address (including apt., room, or suite no.), city, state, and ZIP code

4 Address, (including apt., room, or suite no.), city, state, and ZIP code shown on the last return filed if different from line 3

5 If copy of form or a tax return transcript is to be mailed to someone else, enter the third party's name and address

6 If we cannot find a record of your tax form and you want the payment refunded to the third party, check here . . . . . . ▶ ☐

7 If name in third party's records differs from line 1a above, enter that name here (see instructions) ▶

8 Check only one box to show what you want. There is **no charge** for items 8a, b, and c:

a ☐ Tax return transcript of Form 1040 series filed during the **current calendar year** and the **3 prior calendar years** (see instructions).

b ☐ Verification of nonfiling.

c ☐ Form(s) W-2 information (see instructions).

d ☐ Copy of tax form and all attachments (including Form(s) W-2, schedules, or other forms). **The charge is $23 for each period requested.**
   Note: If these copies must be certified for court or administrative proceedings, see instructions and check here . . . . . ▶ ☐

9 If this request is to meet a requirement of one of the following, check all boxes that apply.
☐ Small Business Administration   ☐ Department of Education   ☐ Department of Veterans Affairs   ☐ Financial institution

10 Tax form number (Form 1040, 1040A, 941, etc.)	**12** Complete only if **line 8d** is checked. Amount due:
11 Tax period(s) (year or period ended date). If more than four, see instructions.	**a** Cost for each period . . . . $ 23.00
	b Number of tax periods requested on line 11
	c Total cost. Multiply line 12a by line 12b. . $
	Full payment must accompany your request. Make check or money order payable to "Internal Revenue Service."

Caution: Before signing, make sure all items are complete and the form is dated.

I declare that I am either the taxpayer whose name is shown on line 1a or 2a, or a person authorized to obtain the tax information requested. I am aware that based upon this form, the IRS will release the tax information requested to any party shown on line 5. The IRS has no control over what that party does with the information.

Please Sign Here

▶ Signature. See instructions. If other than taxpayer, attach authorization document.   Date

Telephone number of requester ( )

Best time to call

▶ Title (if line 1a above is a corporation, partnership, estate, or trust)

TRY A TAX RETURN TRANSCRIPT (see line 8a instructions)

▶ Spouse's signature   Date

Instructions

Section references are to the Internal Revenue Code.

TIP: If you had your tax form filled in by a paid preparer, check first to see if you can get a copy from the preparer. This may save you both time and money.

Purpose of Form.—Use Form 4506 to get a tax return transcript, verification that you did not file a Federal tax return, Form W-2 information, or a copy of a tax form. Allow 6 weeks after you file a tax form before you request a copy of it or a transcript. For W-2

information, wait 13 months after the end of the year in which the wages were earned. For example, wait until Feb. 1999 to request W-2 information for wages earned in 1997.

Do not use this form to request Forms 1099 or tax account information. See this page for details on how to get these items.

Note: Form 4506 must be received by the IRS within 60 calendar days after the date you signed and dated the request.

How Long Will It Take?—You can get a tax return transcript or verification of nonfiling within 7 to 10 workdays after the IRS receives your request. It can take up to 60 calendar

days to get a copy of a tax form or W-2 information. To avoid any delay, be sure to furnish all the information asked for on Form 4506.

Forms 1099.—If you need a copy of a Form 1099, contact the payer. If the payer cannot help you, call or visit the IRS to get Form 1099 information.

Tax Account Information.—If you need a statement of your tax account showing any later changes that you or the IRS made to the original return, request tax account information. Tax account information lists

(Continued on back)

For Privacy Act and Paperwork Reduction Act Notice, see back of form.   Cat. No. 41721E   Form **4506** (Rev. 5-97)

Part V **Listed Property** (Include automobiles, certain other vehicles, cellular telephones, certain computers, and property used for entertainment, recreation, or amusement.)

Note: *For any vehicle for which you are using the standard mileage rate or deducting lease expense, complete **only** 23a, 23b, columns (a) through (c) of Section A, all of Section B, and Section C if applicable.*

Section A—Depreciation and Other Information (Caution: *See page 7 of the instructions for limits for passenger automobiles.*)

23a Do you have evidence to support the business/investment use claimed? ☐ **Yes** ☐ **No**   **23b** If "Yes," is the evidence written? ☐ **Yes** ☐ **No**

(a) Type of property (list vehicles first)	(b) Date placed in service	(c) Business/ investment use percentage	(d) Cost or other basis	(e) Basis for depreciation (business/investment use only)	(f) Recovery period	(g) Method/ Convention	(h) Depreciation deduction	(i) Elected section 179 cost
24 Property used more than 50% in a qualified business use (See page 6 of the instructions.):								
		%						
		%						
		%						
25 Property used 50% or less in a qualified business use (See page 6 of the instructions.):								
		%				S/L –		
		%				S/L –		
		%				S/L –		

26 Add amounts in column (h). Enter the total here and on line 20, page 1 . . . . . **26**

27 Add amounts in column (i). Enter the total here and on line 7, page 1 . . . . **27**

Section B—Information on Use of Vehicles

Complete this section for vehicles used by a sole proprietor, partner, or other "more than 5% owner," or related person.

If you provided vehicles to your employees, first answer the questions in Section C to see if you meet an exception to completing this section for those vehicles.

	(a) Vehicle 1		(b) Vehicle 2		(c) Vehicle 3		(d) Vehicle 4		(e) Vehicle 5		(f) Vehicle 6	
28 Total business/investment miles driven during the year (**do not** include commuting miles— see page 1 of the instructions)												
29 Total commuting miles driven during the year												
30 Total other personal (noncommuting) miles driven												
31 Total miles driven during the year. Add lines 28 through 30												
	Yes	No	Yes	No	Yes	No	Yes	No	Yes	No	Yes	No
32 Was the vehicle available for personal use during off-duty hours?												
33 Was the vehicle used primarily by a more than 5% owner or related person?												
34 Is another vehicle available for personal use?												

Section C—Questions for Employers Who Provide Vehicles for Use by Their Employees

Answer these questions to determine if you meet an exception to completing Section B for vehicles used by employees who **are not** more than 5% owners or related persons. See page 8 of the instructions.

		Yes	No
35	Do you maintain a written policy statement that prohibits all personal use of vehicles, including commuting, by your employees?		
36	Do you maintain a written policy statement that prohibits personal use of vehicles, except commuting, by your employees? See page 8 of the instructions for vehicles used by corporate officers, directors, or 1% or more owners		
37	Do you treat all use of vehicles by employees as personal use?		
38	Do you provide more than five vehicles to your employees, obtain information from your employees about the use of the vehicles, and retain the information received?		
39	Do you meet the requirements concerning qualified automobile demonstration use? See page 8 of the instructions . .		

Note: *If your answer to 35, 36, 37, 38, or 39 is "Yes," do not complete Section B for the covered vehicles.*

Part VI **Amortization**

(a) Description of costs	(b) Date amortization begins	(c) Amortizable amount	(d) Code section	(e) Amortization period or percentage	(f) Amortization for this year
40 Amortization of costs that begins during your 2000 tax year (See page 8 of the instructions.):					

41 Amortization of costs that began before 2000 . . . . **41**

42 **Total.** Add amounts in column (f). See page 9 of the instructions for where to report . . . **42**

Form **4797**

Department of the Treasury
Internal Revenue Service (99)

Sales of Business Property

(Also Involuntary Conversions and Recapture Amounts
Under Sections 179 and 280F(b)(2))

▶ **Attach to your tax return.**   ▶ **See separate instructions.**

OMB No. 1545-0184

2000

Attachment
Sequence No. **27**

Name(s) shown on return

Identifying number

| 1 | Enter the gross proceeds from sales or exchanges reported to you for 2000 on Form(s) 1099-B or 1099-S (or substitute statement) that you are including on line 2, 10, or 20 (see instructions) . . . . | **1** | |

Part I   Sales or Exchanges of Property Used in a Trade or Business and Involuntary Conversions From Other Than Casualty or Theft—Most Property Held More Than 1 Year (See instructions.)

(a) Description of property	(b) Date acquired (mo., day, yr.)	(c) Date sold (mo., day, yr.)	(d) Gross sales price	(e) Depreciation allowed or allowable since acquisition	(f) Cost or other basis, plus improvements and expense of sale	(g) Gain or (loss) Subtract (f) from the sum of (d) and (e)
2						

3	Gain, if any, from Form 4684, line 39	**3**	
4	Section 1231 gain from installment sales from Form 6252, line 26 or 37	**4**	
5	Section 1231 gain or (loss) from like-kind exchanges from Form 8824	**5**	
6	Gain, if any, from line 32, from other than casualty or theft	**6**	
7	Combine lines 2 through 6. Enter the gain or (loss) here and on the appropriate line as follows:	**7**	

Partnerships (except electing large partnerships). Report the gain or (loss) following the instructions for Form 1065, Schedule K, line 6. Skip lines 8, 9, 11, and 12 below.

S corporations. Report the gain or (loss) following the instructions for Form 1120S, Schedule K, lines 5 and 6. Skip lines 8, 9, 11, and 12 below, unless line 7 is a gain and the S corporation is subject to the capital gains tax.

All others. If line 7 is zero or a loss, enter the amount from line 7 on line 11 below and skip lines 8 and 9. If line 7 is a gain and you did not have any prior year section 1231 losses, or they were recaptured in an earlier year, enter the gain from line 7 as a long-term capital gain on Schedule D and skip lines 8, 9, and 12 below.

| 8 | Nonrecaptured net section 1231 losses from prior years (see instructions) . . . . | **8** | |
| 9 | Subtract line 8 from line 7. If zero or less, enter -0-. Also enter on the appropriate line as follows (see instructions): | **9** | |

S corporations. Enter any gain from line 9 on Schedule D (Form 1120S), line 15, and skip lines 11 and 12 below.

All others. If line 9 is zero, enter the gain from line 7 on line 12 below. If line 9 is more than zero, enter the amount from line 8 on line 12 below, and enter the gain from line 9 as a long-term capital gain on Schedule D.

Part II   Ordinary Gains and Losses

10	Ordinary gains and losses not included on lines 11 through 17 (include property held 1 year or less):						

11	Loss, if any, from line 7	**11**	( )
12	Gain, if any, from line 7 or amount from line 8, if applicable	**12**	
13	Gain, if any, from line 31	**13**	
14	Net gain or (loss) from Form 4684, lines 31 and 38a	**14**	
15	Ordinary gain from installment sales from Form 6252, line 25 or 36	**15**	
16	Ordinary gain or (loss) from like-kind exchanges from Form 8824	**16**	
17	Recapture of section 179 expense deduction for partners and S corporation shareholders from property dispositions by partnerships and S corporations (see instructions)	**17**	
18	Combine lines 10 through 17. Enter the gain or (loss) here and on the appropriate line as follows:	**18**	
a	For all except individual returns: Enter the gain or (loss) from line 18 on the return being filed.		
b	For individual returns:		
	(1) If the loss on line 11 includes a loss from Form 4684, line 35, column (b)(ii), enter that part of the loss here. Enter the part of the loss from income-producing property on Schedule A (Form 1040), line 27, and the part of the loss from property used as an employee on Schedule A (Form 1040), line 22. Identify as from "Form 4797, line 18b(1)." See instructions	**18b(1)**	
	(2) Redetermine the gain or (loss) on line 18 excluding the loss, if any, on line 18b(1). Enter here and on Form 1040, line 14	**18b(2)**	

For Paperwork Reduction Act Notice, see page 7 of the instructions.   Cat. No. 13086I   Form **4797** (2000)

Part III   Gain From Disposition of Property Under Sections 1245, 1250, 1252, 1254, and 1255

19	(a) Description of section 1245, 1250, 1252, 1254, or 1255 property:	(b) Date acquired (mo., day, yr.)	(c) Date sold (mo., day, yr.)
A			
B			
C			
D			

	These columns relate to the properties on lines 19A through 19D. ▶		Property A	Property B	Property C	Property D
20	Gross sales price (**Note:** *See line 1 before completing.*)	20				
21	Cost or other basis plus expense of sale	21				
22	Depreciation (or depletion) allowed or allowable	22				
23	Adjusted basis. Subtract line 22 from line 21	23				
24	Total gain. Subtract line 23 from line 20	24				
25	**If section 1245 property:**					
a	Depreciation allowed or allowable from line 22	25a				
b	Enter the **smaller** of line 24 or 25a	25b				
26	**If section 1250 property:** If straight line depreciation was used, enter -0- on line 26g, except for a corporation subject to section 291.					
a	Additional depreciation after 1975 (see instructions)	26a				
b	Applicable percentage multiplied by the **smaller** of line 24 or line 26a (see instructions)	26b				
c	Subtract line 26a from line 24. If residential rental property or line 24 is not more than line 26a, skip lines 26d and 26e	26c				
d	Additional depreciation after 1969 and before 1976	26d				
e	Enter the **smaller** of line 26c or 26d	26e				
f	Section 291 amount (corporations only)	26f				
g	Add lines 26b, 26e, and 26f	26g				
27	**If section 1252 property:** Skip this section if you did not dispose of farmland or if this form is being completed for a partnership (other than an electing large partnership).					
a	Soil, water, and land clearing expenses	27a				
b	Line 27a multiplied by applicable percentage (see instructions)	27b				
c	Enter the **smaller** of line 24 or 27b	27c				
28	**If section 1254 property:**					
a	Intangible drilling and development costs, expenditures for development of mines and other natural deposits, and mining exploration costs (see instructions)	28a				
b	Enter the **smaller** of line 24 or 28a	28b				
29	**If section 1255 property:**					
a	Applicable percentage of payments excluded from income under section 126 (see instructions)	29a				
b	Enter the **smaller** of line 24 or 29a (see instructions)	29b				

Summary of Part III Gains. Complete property columns A through D through line 29b before going to line 30.

30	Total gains for all properties. Add property columns A through D, line 24	30	
31	Add property columns A through D, lines 25b, 26g, 27c, 28b, and 29b. Enter here and on line 13	31	
32	Subtract line 31 from line 30. Enter the portion from casualty or theft on Form 4684, line 33. Enter the portion from other than casualty or theft on Form 4797, line 6	32	

Part IV   Recapture Amounts Under Sections 179 and 280F(b)(2) When Business Use Drops to 50% or Less (See instructions.)

			(a) Section 179	(b) Section 280F(b)(2)
33	Section 179 expense deduction or depreciation allowable in prior years	33		
34	Recomputed depreciation. See instructions	34		
35	Recapture amount. Subtract line 34 from line 33. See the instructions for where to report	35		

Form **7018**
(Rev. August 2000)
Department of the Treasury
Internal Revenue Service

Employer's Order Blank for Forms

Visit IRS Web Site @ www.irs.gov

▶ Please send your order to IRS as soon as possible

OMB No. 1545–1059

Instructions.— Enter the quantity next to the form you are ordering. Type or print your name and complete mail delivery address in the space provided below. An accurate mail delivery address is necessary to ensure delivery of your order. Use the top portion for ordering 2000 forms **ONLY.** Use the bottom portion for ordering 2001 forms **ONLY. PLEASE ORDER THE NUMBER OF FORMS NEEDED, NOT THE NUMBER OF SHEETS. Note:** None of the items on the order blank are available from the IRS in continuous feed version. You will automatically receive one instruction with any form on this order blank.

USE THIS PORTION FOR 2000 FORMS ONLY

QUANTITY	ITEM	TITLE	QUANTITY	ITEM	TITLE
	W-2	Wage and Tax Statement		1098-T	Tuition Payment Statement
	W-2c	Corrected Wage and Tax Statement		1099-A	Acquisition or Abandonment of Secured Property
	W-2G	Statement for Recipients of Certain Gambling Winnings		1099-B	Proceeds From Broker and Barter Exchange Transactions
	W-3	Transmittal of Wage and Tax Statements		1099-C	Cancellation of Debt
	W-3c	Transmittal of Corrected Wage and Tax Statements		1099-DIV	Dividends and Distributions
	W-4	Employee's Withholding Allowance Certificate (2000)		1099-G	Certain Government and Qualified State Tuition Program Payments
	W-4P	Withholding Certificate for Pension or Annuity Payments		1099-INT	Interest Income
	W-4S	Request for Federal Income Tax Withholding From Sick Pay		1099-LTC	Long-Term Care and Accelerated Death Benefits
	W-5	Earned Income Credit Advance Payment Certificate		1099-MISC	Miscellaneous Income
	941	Employer's Quarterly Federal Tax Return		1099-MSA	Distributions From an MSA or Medicare+Choice MSA
	941 SCH B	Supplemental Record of Federal Tax Liability		1099-OID	Original Issue Discount
	941c	Supporting Statement To Correct Information		1099-PATR	Taxable Distribution Received From Cooperatives
	943	Employer's Annual Tax Return for Agricultural Employees		1099-R	Distributions From Pensions, Annuities, Retirement or Profit-Sharing Plans, IRAs, Insurance Contracts, etc.
	943-A	Agricultural Employer's Record of Federal Tax Liability		1099-S	Proceeds From Real Estate Transactions
	945	Annual Return of Withheld Federal Income Tax Liability		5498	IRA Contribution Information
	945-A	Annual Record of Federal Tax Liability		5498-MSA	MSA or Medicare+Choice MSA Information
	1096	Annual Summary and Transmittal of U.S. Information Returns		Pub 213	You May Need to Check Your Withholding
	1098	Mortgage Interest Statement		Pub 1494	Table for Figuring Amount Exempt From Levy On Wages, Salary, and Other Income (Forms 668-W and 668-W(c))
	1098-E	Student Loan Interest Statement			

USE THIS PORTION FOR 2001 FORMS ONLY

NOTE: An accurate mail delivery address is necessary to ensure delivery of your order.

Attention:

QUANTITY

_____ W-4

_____ W-4P

_____ W-4S

_____ W-5

(2001 Revisions)

Company Name

Postal Mailing Address

City   State   Zip Code

Foreign Country   International Postal Code

Daytime Telephone Number

Cat. No. 43708F

Where To Send Your Order

Send your order to the Internal Revenue Service address for the Area Distribution Center closest to your state.

Central Area Distribution Center
P.O. Box 8908
Bloomington, IL 61702-8908

Western Area Distribution Center
Rancho Cordova, CA 95743-0001

Eastern Area Distribution Center
P.O. Box 85075
Richmond, VA 23261-5075

Paperwork Reduction Act Notice. We ask for the information on this form to carry out the Internal Revenue laws of the United States. Your response is voluntary.

You are not required to provide the information requested on a form that is subject to the Paperwork Reduction Act unless the form displays a valid OMB control number. Books or records relating to a form or its instructions must be retained as long as their contents may become material in the administration of any Internal Revenue law. Generally, tax returns and return information are confidential, as required by Code section 6103.

The time needed to complete this form will vary depending on the individual circumstances. The estimated average time is 3 minutes. If you have comments concerning the accuracy of this time estimate or suggestions for making this form simpler, we would be happy to hear from you. You can write to the Tax Forms Committee, Western Area Distribution Center, Rancho Cordova, CA 95743-0001.

Please **DO NOT** send your order Form 7018 to the Tax Forms Committee. Send your forms order to the IRS Area Distribution Center closest to your state.

Form **8594**
(Rev. July 1998)
Department of the Treasury
Internal Revenue Service

Asset Acquisition Statement
Under Section 1060

▶ **Attach to your Federal income tax return.**

OMB No. 1545-1021

Attachment
Sequence No. **61**

Name as shown on return	Identification number as shown on return

Check the box that identifies you: ☐ Buyer ☐ Seller

Part I General Information—To be completed by all filers.

1 Name of other party to the transaction	Other party's identification number

Address (number, street, and room or suite no.)

City or town, state, and ZIP code

2 Date of sale	3 Total sales price

Part II Assets Transferred—To be completed by all filers of an original statement.

4 Assets	Aggregate Fair Market Value (Actual Amount for Class I)	Allocation of Sales Price
Class I	$	$
Class II	$	$
Class III	$	$
Classes IV and V	$	$
Total	$	$

5 Did the buyer and seller provide for an allocation of the sales price in the sales contract or in another written document signed by both parties? . . . . ☐ Yes ☐ No

If "Yes," are the aggregate fair market values listed for each of asset Classes I, II, III, IV and V the amounts agreed upon in your sales contract or in a separate written document? . . . . ☐ Yes ☐ No

6 In connection with the purchase of the group of assets, did the buyer also purchase a license or a covenant not to compete, or enter into a lease agreement, employment contract, management contract, or similar arrangement with the seller (or managers, directors, owners, or employees of the seller)? . . . . ☐ Yes ☐ No

If "Yes," specify (a) the type of agreement, and (b) the maximum amount of consideration (not including interest) paid or to be paid under the agreement. See the instructions for line 6.

For Paperwork Reduction Act Notice, see instructions.   Cat. No. 63768Z   Form **8594** (Rev. 7-98)

Part III   **Supplemental Statement**—To be completed only if amending an original statement or previously filed supplemental statement because of an increase or decrease in consideration.

7 Assets	Allocation of Sales Price as Previously Reported	Increase or (Decrease)	Redetermined Allocation of Sales Price
Class I	$	$	$
Class II	$	$	$
Class III	$	$	$
Classes IV and V	$	$	$
Total	$		$

8   Reason(s) for increase or decrease. Attach additional sheets if more space is needed.

\
\
\
\
\
\
\
\
\

9   Tax year and tax return form number with which the original Form 8594 and any supplemental statements were filed.

Form **8822**
(Rev. Oct. 2000)
Department of the Treasury
Internal Revenue Service

Change of Address

▶ Please type or print.

▶ See instructions on back.　　▶ Do not attach this form to your return.

OMB No. 1545-1163

Part I　Complete This Part To Change Your Home Mailing Address

Check **all** boxes this change affects:

1 ☐　Individual income tax returns (Forms 1040, 1040A, 1040EZ, TeleFile, 1040NR, etc.)

　　▶ If your last return was a joint return and you are now establishing a residence separate
　　　from the spouse with whom you filed that return, check here . . . . ▶ ☐

2 ☐　Gift, estate, or generation-skipping transfer tax returns (Forms 706, 709, etc.)

　　▶ For Forms 706 and 706-NA, enter the decedent's name and social security number below.

▶ Decedent's name　　　　　　　　　　　　　　　▶ Social security number

3a Your name (first name, initial, and last name)	3b Your social security number

4a Spouse's name (first name, initial, and last name)	4b Spouse's social security number

5　Prior name(s). See instructions.

6a Old address (no., street, city or town, state, and ZIP code). If a P.O. box or foreign address, see instructions.	Apt. no.

6b Spouse's old address, if different from line 6a (no., street, city or town, state, and ZIP code). If a P.O. box or foreign address, see instructions.	Apt. no.

7　New address (no., street, city or town, state, and ZIP code). If a P.O. box or foreign address, see instructions.	Apt. no.

Part II　Complete This Part To Change Your Business Mailing Address or Business Location

Check **all** boxes this change affects:

8 ☐　Employment, excise, and other business returns (Forms 720, 940, 940-EZ, 941, 990, 1041, 1065, 1120, etc.)
9 ☐　Employee plan returns (Forms 5500 and 5500-EZ).
10 ☐　Business location

11a Business name	11b Employer identification number

12　Old mailing address (no., street, city or town, state, and ZIP code). If a P.O. box or foreign address, see instructions.	Room or suite no.

13　New mailing address (no., street, city or town, state, and ZIP code). If a P.O. box or foreign address, see instructions.	Room or suite no.

14　New business location (no., street, city or town, state, and ZIP code). If a foreign address, see instructions.	Room or suite no.

Part III　Signature

Daytime telephone number of person to contact (optional) ▶ (　　　)

Sign Here ▶

Your signature	Date	▶ If Part II completed, signature of owner, officer, or representative	Date

If joint return, spouse's signature	Date	Title	

For Privacy Act and Paperwork Reduction Act Notice, see back of form.　　Cat. No. 12081V　　Form **8822** (Rev. 10-2000)

Purpose of Form

You may use Form 8822 to notify the Internal Revenue Service if you changed your home or business mailing address or your business location. If this change also affects the mailing address for your children who filed income tax returns, complete and file a separate Form 8822 for each child. If you are a representative signing for the taxpayer, attach to Form 8822 a copy of your power of attorney.

Changing Both Home and Business Addresses? If you are, use a separate Form 8822 to show each change unless the service center under **Where To File** is the same for both home and business.

Prior Name(s)

If you or your spouse changed your name because of marriage, divorce, etc., complete line 5. Also, be sure to notify the **Social Security Administration** of your new name so that it has the same name in its records that you have on your tax return. This prevents delays in processing your return and issuing refunds. It also safeguards your future social security benefits.

Addresses

Be sure to include any apartment, room, or suite number in the space provided.

P.O. Box

Enter your box number instead of your street address **only** if your post office does not deliver mail to your street address.

Foreign Address

Enter the information in the following order: city, province or state, and country. Follow the country's practice for entering the postal code. Please **do not** abbreviate the country name.

Signature

If you are completing Part II, the owner, an officer, or a representative must sign. An officer is the president, vice president, treasurer, chief accounting officer, etc. A representative is a person who has a valid power of attorney to handle tax matters.

Where To File

Send this form to the **Internal Revenue Service Center** shown below that applies to you.

Filers Who Completed Part I

IF your old home mailing address was in. . .	THEN use this address. . .
Florida, Georgia, South Carolina, West Virginia	Atlanta, GA 39901
Colorado, Idaho, Montana, New Mexico, Oklahoma, Texas, Wyoming	Austin, TX 73301
Delaware, New Jersey, New York (New York City and counties of Nassau, Rockland, Suffolk, and Westchester)	Holtsville, NY 00501
New York (all other counties), Connecticut, Maine, Massachusetts, New Hampshire, Rhode Island, Vermont	Andover, MA 05501
Arizona, California (counties of Alpine, Amador, Butte, Calaveras, Colusa, Contra Costa, Del Norte, El Dorado, Glenn, Humboldt, Lake, Lassen, Marin, Mendocino, Modoc, Napa, Nevada, Placer, Plumas, Sacramento, San Joaquin, Shasta, Sierra, Siskiyou, Solano, Sonoma, Sutter, Tehama, Trinity, Yolo, and Yuba), Nevada, North Dakota, South Dakota, Utah, Washington	Ogden, UT 84201
Alaska, California (all other counties), Hawaii	Fresno, CA 93888
Michigan, Ohio	Cincinnati, OH 45999
District of Columbia, Indiana, Maryland, Pennsylvania, Virginia	Philadelphia, PA 19255
Alabama, Arkansas, Kentucky, Louisiana, Mississippi, Nebraska, North Carolina, Tennessee	Memphis, TN 37501
Illinois, Iowa, Kansas, Minnesota, Missouri, Oregon, Wisconsin	Kansas City, MO 64999
American Samoa	Philadelphia, PA 19255
Guam: Permanent residents	Department of Revenue and Taxation Government of Guam P.O. Box 23607 GMF, GU 96921
Guam: Nonpermanent residents Puerto Rico (or if excluding income under Internal Revenue Code section 933) Virgin Islands: Nonpermanent residents	Philadelphia, PA 19255
Virgin Islands: Permanent residents	V. I. Bureau of Internal Revenue 9601 Estate Thomas Charlotte Amalie St. Thomas, VI 00802
Foreign country: U.S. citizens and those filing Form 2555, Form 2555-EZ, or Form 4563 All APO and FPO addresses	Philadelphia, PA 19255

Filers Who Completed Part II

IF your old business address was in. . .	THEN use this address. . .
Virginia or Outside the United States	Philadelphia, PA 19255
Delaware, District of Columbia, Indiana, Kentucky, Maryland, Michigan, New Jersey, North Carolina, Ohio, Pennsylvania, South Carolina, West Virginia, Wisconsin	Cincinnati, OH 45999
Kansas, New Mexico, Oklahoma	Austin, TX 73301
Alabama, Tennessee	Memphis, TN 37501
Illinois	Kansas City, MO 64999
Alaska, Arizona, Arkansas, California (counties of Alpine, Amador, Butte, Calaveras, Colusa, Contra Costa, Del Norte, El Dorado, Glenn, Humboldt, Lake, Lassen, Marin, Mendocino, Modoc, Napa, Nevada, Placer, Plumas, Sacramento, San Joaquin, Shasta, Sierra, Siskiyou, Solano, Sonoma, Sutter, Tehama, Trinity, Yolo, and Yuba), Colorado, Hawaii, Idaho, Iowa, Louisiana, Minnesota, Mississippi, Missouri, Montana, Nebraska, Nevada, North Dakota, Oregon, South Dakota, Texas, Utah, Washington, Wyoming	Ogden, UT 84201
California (all other counties)	Fresno, CA 93888
Florida, Georgia	Atlanta, GA 39901
New York (New York City and counties of Nassau, Rockland, Suffolk, and Westchester)	Holtsville, NY 00501
New York (all other counties), Connecticut, Maine, Massachusetts, New Hampshire, Rhode Island, Vermont	Andover, MA 05501

Privacy Act and Paperwork Reduction Act Notice. We ask for the information on this form to carry out the Internal Revenue laws of the United States. We may give the information to the Department of Justice and to other Federal agencies, as provided by law. We may also give it to cities, states, the District of Columbia, and U.S. commonwealths or possessions to carry out their tax laws. And we may give it to foreign governments because of tax treaties they have with the United States.

You are not required to provide the information requested on a form that is subject to the Paperwork Reduction Act unless the form displays a valid OMB control number. Books or records relating to a form or its instructions must be retained as long as their contents may become material in the administration of any Internal Revenue law. Generally, tax returns and return information are confidential, as required by Internal Revenue Code section 6103.

The use of this form is voluntary. However, if you fail to provide the Internal Revenue Service with your current mailing address, you may not receive a notice of deficiency or a notice and demand for tax. Despite the failure to receive such notices, penalties and interest will continue to accrue on the tax deficiencies.

The time needed to complete and file this form will vary depending on individual circumstances. The estimated average time is 16 minutes.

If you have comments concerning the accuracy of this time estimate or suggestions for making this form simpler, we would be happy to hear from you. You can write to the Tax Forms Committee, Western Area Distribution Center, Rancho Cordova, CA 95743-0001. **Do not** send the form to this address. Instead, see **Where To File** on this page.

Form **SS-4**	**Application for Employer Identification Number**	**EIN**

Form **SS-4**
(Rev. April 2000)
Department of the Treasury
Internal Revenue Service

Application for Employer Identification Number
(For use by employers, corporations, partnerships, trusts, estates, churches, government agencies, certain individuals, and others. See instructions.)
▶ Keep a copy for your records.

EIN

OMB No. 1545-0003

Please type or print clearly.

1 Name of applicant (legal name) (see instructions)

2 Trade name of business (if different from name on line 1)

3 Executor, trustee, "care of" name

4a Mailing address (street address) (room, apt., or suite no.)

5a Business address (if different from address on lines 4a and 4b)

4b City, state, and ZIP code

5b City, state, and ZIP code

6 County and state where principal business is located

7 Name of principal officer, general partner, grantor, owner, or trustor—SSN or ITIN may be required (see instructions) ▶

8a Type of entity (Check only one box.) (see instructions)

Caution: *If applicant is a limited liability company, see the instructions for line 8a.*

☐ Sole proprietor (SSN) _____
☐ Partnership   ☐ Personal service corp.
☐ REMIC   ☐ National Guard
☐ State/local government   ☐ Farmers' cooperative
☐ Church or church-controlled organization
☐ Other nonprofit organization (specify) ▶ _____
☐ Other (specify) ▶

☐ Estate (SSN of decedent) _____
☐ Plan administrator (SSN) _____
☐ Other corporation (specify) ▶ _____
☐ Trust
☐ Federal government/military
(enter GEN if applicable) _____

8b If a corporation, name the state or foreign country (if applicable) where incorporated

State

Foreign country

9 Reason for applying (Check only one box.) (see instructions)
☐ Started new business (specify type) ▶_____
☐ Hired employees (Check the box and see line 12.)
☐ Created a pension plan (specify type) ▶

☐ Banking purpose (specify purpose) ▶ _____
☐ Changed type of organization (specify new type) ▶ _____
☐ Purchased going business
☐ Created a trust (specify type) ▶ _____
☐ Other (specify) ▶

10 Date business started or acquired (month, day, year) (see instructions)

11 Closing month of accounting year (see instructions)

12 First date wages or annuities were paid or will be paid (month, day, year). **Note:** *If applicant is a withholding agent, enter date income will first be paid to nonresident alien. (month, day, year)* . . . . ▶

13 Highest number of employees expected in the next 12 months. **Note:** *If the applicant does not expect to have any employees during the period, enter -0-. (see instructions)* . . . . ▶	Nonagricultural	Agricultural	Household

14 Principal activity (see instructions) ▶

15 Is the principal business activity manufacturing? . . . . ☐ **Yes** ☐ **No**
If "Yes," principal product and raw material used ▶

16 To whom are most of the products or services sold? Please check one box. ☐ Business (wholesale)
☐ Public (retail)   ☐ Other (specify) ▶   ☐ N/A

17a Has the applicant ever applied for an employer identification number for this or any other business? . . . . ☐ **Yes** ☐ **No**
Note: *If "Yes," please complete lines 17b and 17c.*

17b If you checked "Yes" on line 17a, give applicant's legal name and trade name shown on prior application, if different from line 1 or 2 above.
Legal name ▶   Trade name ▶

17c Approximate date when and city and state where the application was filed. Enter previous employer identification number if known.
Approximate date when filed (mo., day, year) | City and state where filed | Previous EIN

Under penalties of perjury, I declare that I have examined this application, and to the best of my knowledge and belief, it is true, correct, and complete.

Business telephone number (include area code)
( )

Fax telephone number (include area code)
( )

Name and title (Please type or print clearly.) ▶

Signature ▶   Date ▶

Note: *Do not write below this line. For official use only.*

Please leave blank ▶	Geo.	Ind.	Class	Size	Reason for applying

For Privacy Act and Paperwork Reduction Act Notice, see page 4.   Cat. No. 16055N   Form **SS-4** (Rev. 4-2000)

General Instructions

Section references are to the Internal Revenue Code unless otherwise noted.

Purpose of Form

Use Form SS-4 to apply for an employer identification number (EIN). An EIN is a nine-digit number (for example, 12-3456789) assigned to sole proprietors, corporations, partnerships, estates, trusts, and other entities for tax filing and reporting purposes. The information you provide on this form will establish your business tax account.

Caution: *An EIN is for use in connection with your business activities only. Do **not** use your EIN in place of your social security number (SSN).*

Who Must File

You must file this form if you have not been assigned an EIN before and:

● You pay wages to one or more employees including household employees.

● You are required to have an EIN to use on any return, statement, or other document, even if you are not an employer.

● You are a withholding agent required to withhold taxes on income, other than wages, paid to a nonresident alien (individual, corporation, partnership, etc.). A withholding agent may be an agent, broker, fiduciary, manager, tenant, or spouse, and is required to file **Form 1042,** Annual Withholding Tax Return for U.S. Source Income of Foreign Persons.

● You file **Schedule C,** Profit or Loss From Business, **Schedule C-EZ,** Net Profit From Business, or **Schedule F,** Profit or Loss From Farming, of **Form 1040,** U.S. Individual Income Tax Return, **and** have a Keogh plan or are required to file excise, employment, or alcohol, tobacco, or firearms returns.

The following must use EINs even if they do not have any employees:

● State and local agencies who serve as tax reporting agents for public assistance recipients, under Rev. Proc. 80-4, 1980-1 C.B. 581, should obtain a separate EIN for this reporting. See **Household employer** on page 3.

● Trusts, except the following:

　1. Certain grantor-owned trusts. (See the **Instructions for Form 1041,** U.S. Income Tax Return for Estates and Trusts.)

　2. Individual retirement arrangement (IRA) trusts, unless the trust has to file **Form 990-T,** Exempt Organization Business Income Tax Return. (See the **Instructions for Form 990-T.**)

● Estates

● Partnerships

● REMICs (real estate mortgage investment conduits) (See the **Instructions for Form 1066,** U.S. Real Estate Mortgage Investment Conduit (REMIC) Income Tax Return.)

● Corporations

● Nonprofit organizations (churches, clubs, etc.)

● Farmers' cooperatives

● Plan administrators (A plan administrator is the person or group of persons specified as the administrator by the instrument under which the plan is operated.)

When To Apply for a New EIN

New Business. If you become the new owner of an existing business, **do not** use the EIN of the former owner. **If you already have an EIN, use that number.** If you do not have an EIN, apply for one on this form. If you become the "owner" of a corporation by acquiring its stock, use the corporation's EIN.

Changes in Organization or Ownership. If you already have an EIN, you may need to get a new one if either the organization or ownership of your business changes. If you incorporate a sole proprietorship or form a partnership, you must get a new EIN. However, **do not** apply for a new EIN if:

● You change only the name of your business,

● You elected on **Form 8832,** Entity Classification Election, to change the way the entity is taxed, or

● A partnership terminates because at least 50% of the total interests in partnership capital and profits were sold or exchanged within a 12-month period. (See Regulations section 301.6109-1(d)(2)(iii).) The EIN for the terminated partnership should continue to be used.

Note: *If you are electing to be an "S corporation," be sure you file **Form 2553,** Election by a Small Business Corporation.*

File Only One Form SS-4. File only one Form SS-4, regardless of the number of businesses operated or trade names under which a business operates. However, each corporation in an affiliated group must file a separate application.

EIN Applied for, But Not Received. If you do not have an EIN by the time a return is due, write "Applied for" and the date you applied in the space shown for the number. **Do not** show your social security number (SSN) as an EIN on returns.

If you do not have an EIN by the time a tax deposit is due, send your payment to the Internal Revenue Service Center for your filing area. (See **Where To Apply** below.) Make your check or money order payable to "United States Treasury" and show your name (as shown on Form SS-4), address, type of tax, period covered, and date you applied for an EIN. Send an explanation with the deposit.

For more information about EINs, see **Pub. 583,** Starting a Business and Keeping Records, and **Pub. 1635,** Understanding Your EIN.

How To Apply

You can apply for an EIN either by mail or by telephone. You can get an EIN immediately by calling the Tele-TIN number for the service center for your state, or you can send the completed Form SS-4 directly to the service center to receive your EIN by mail.

Application by Tele-TIN. Under the Tele-TIN program, you can receive your EIN by telephone and use it immediately to file a return or make a payment. To receive an EIN by telephone, complete Form SS-4, then call the Tele-TIN number listed for your state under **Where To Apply.** The person making the call must be authorized to sign the form. (See **Signature** on page 4.)

An IRS representative will use the information from the Form SS-4 to establish your account and assign you an EIN. Write the number you are given on the upper right corner of the form and sign and date it.

*Mail or fax (facsimile) the signed Form SS-4 **within 24 hours** to the Tele-TIN Unit at the service center address for your state.* The IRS representative will give you the fax number. The fax numbers are also listed in Pub. 1635.

Taxpayer representatives can receive their client's EIN by telephone if they first send a fax of a completed **Form 2848,** Power of Attorney and Declaration of Representative, or **Form 8821,** Tax Information Authorization, to the Tele-TIN unit. The Form 2848 or Form 8821 will be used solely to release the EIN to the representative authorized on the form.

Application by Mail. Complete Form SS-4 at least 4 to 5 weeks before you will need an EIN. Sign and date the application and mail it to the service center address for your state. You will receive your EIN in the mail in approximately 4 weeks.

Where To Apply

The Tele-TIN numbers listed below will involve a long-distance charge to callers outside of the local calling area and can be used only to apply for an EIN. **The numbers may change without notice.** Call 1-800-829-1040 to verify a number or to ask about the status of an application by mail.

If your principal business, office or agency, or legal residence in the case of an individual, is located in:	Call the Tele-TIN number shown or file with the Internal Revenue Service Center at:
Florida, Georgia, South Carolina	Attn: Entity Control Atlanta, GA 39901 770-455-2360
New Jersey, New York (New York City and counties of Nassau, Rockland, Suffolk, and Westchester)	Attn: Entity Control Holtsville, NY 00501 631-447-4955
New York (all other counties), Connecticut, Maine, Massachusetts, New Hampshire, Rhode Island, Vermont	Attn: Entity Control Andover, MA 05501 978-474-9717
Illinois, Iowa, Minnesota, Missouri, Wisconsin	Attn: Entity Control Stop 6800 2306 E. Bannister Rd. Kansas City, MO 64999 816-823-7777
Delaware, District of Columbia, Maryland, Pennsylvania, Virginia	Attn: Entity Control Philadelphia, PA 19255 215-516-6999
Indiana, Kentucky, Michigan, Ohio, West Virginia	Attn: Entity Control Cincinnati, OH 45999 859-292-5467

Kansas, New Mexico, Oklahoma, Texas	Attn: Entity Control Austin, TX 73301 512-460-7843
Alaska, Arizona, California (counties of Alpine, Amador, Butte, Calaveras, Colusa, Contra Costa, Del Norte, El Dorado, Glenn, Humboldt, Lake, Lassen, Marin, Mendocino, Modoc, Napa, Nevada, Placer, Plumas, Sacramento, San Joaquin, Shasta, Sierra, Siskiyou, Solano, Sonoma, Sutter, Tehama, Trinity, Yolo, and Yuba), Colorado, Idaho, Montana, Nebraska, Nevada, North Dakota, Oregon, South Dakota, Utah, Washington, Wyoming	Attn: Entity Control Mail Stop 6271 P.O. Box 9941 Ogden, UT 84201 801-620-7645
California (all other counties), Hawaii	Attn: Entity Control Fresno, CA 93888 559-452-4010
Alabama, Arkansas, Louisiana, Mississippi, North Carolina, Tennessee	Attn: Entity Control Memphis, TN 37501 901-546-3920
If you have no legal residence, principal place of business, or principal office or agency in any state	Attn: Entity Control Philadelphia, PA 19255 215-516-6999

Specific Instructions

The instructions that follow are for those items that are not self-explanatory. Enter N/A (nonapplicable) on the lines that do not apply.

Line 1. Enter the legal name of the entity applying for the EIN exactly as it appears on the social security card, charter, or other applicable legal document.

Individuals. Enter your first name, middle initial, and last name. If you are a sole proprietor, enter your individual name, not your business name. Enter your business name on line 2. Do not use abbreviations or nicknames on line 1.

Trusts. Enter the name of the trust.

Estate of a decedent. Enter the name of the estate.

Partnerships. Enter the legal name of the partnership as it appears in the partnership agreement. **Do not** list the names of the partners on line 1. See the specific instructions for line 7.

Corporations. Enter the corporate name as it appears in the corporation charter or other legal document creating it.

Plan administrators. Enter the name of the plan administrator. A plan administrator who already has an EIN should use that number.

Line 2. Enter the trade name of the business if different from the legal name. The trade name is the "doing business as" name.

Note: *Use the full legal name on line 1 on all tax returns filed for the entity. However, if you enter a trade name on line 2 and choose to use the trade name instead of the legal name, enter the trade name on all returns you file. To prevent processing delays and errors, **always** use either the legal name only or the trade name only on all tax returns.*

Line 3. Trusts enter the name of the trustee. Estates enter the name of the executor, administrator, or other fiduciary. If the entity applying has a designated person to receive tax information, enter that person's name as the "care of" person. Print or type the first name, middle initial, and last name.

Line 7. Enter the first name, middle initial, last name, and SSN of a principal officer if the business is a corporation; of a general partner if a partnership; of the owner of a single member entity that is disregarded as an entity separate from its owner; or of a grantor, owner, or trustor if a trust. If the person in question is an alien individual with a previously assigned individual taxpayer identification number (ITIN), enter the ITIN in the space provided, instead of an SSN. You are not required to enter an SSN or ITIN if the reason you are applying for an EIN is to make an entity classification election (see Regulations section 301.7701-1 through 301.7701-3), and you are a nonresident alien with no effectively connected income from sources within the United States.

Line 8a. Check the box that best describes the type of entity applying for the EIN. If you are an alien individual with an ITIN previously assigned to you, enter the ITIN in place of a requested SSN.

Caution: *This is not an election for a tax classification of an entity. See "Limited liability company (LLC)" below.*

If not specifically mentioned, check the "Other" box, enter the type of entity and the type of return that will be filed (for example, common trust fund, Form 1065). Do not enter N/A. If you are an alien individual applying for an EIN, see the **Line 7** instructions above.

Sole proprietor. Check this box if you file Schedule C, C-EZ, or F (Form 1040) and have a qualified plan, or are required to file excise, employment, or alcohol, tobacco, or firearms returns, or are a payer of gambling winnings. Enter your SSN (or ITIN) in the space provided. If you are a nonresident alien with are a nonresident alien with no effectively

connected income from sources within the United States, you do not need to enter an SSN or ITIN.

REMIC. Check this box if the entity has elected to be treated as a real estate mortgage investment conduit (REMIC). See the Instructions for Form 1066 for more information.

Other nonprofit organization. Check this box if the nonprofit organization is other than a church or church-controlled organization and specify the type of nonprofit organization (for example, an educational organization).

If the organization also seeks tax-exempt status, you must file either **Package 1023,** Application for Recognition of Exemption, or **Package 1024,** Application for Recognition of Exemption Under Section 501(a). Get **Pub. 557,** Tax Exempt Status for Your Organization, for more information.

Group exemption number (GEN). If the organization is covered by a group exemption letter, enter the four-digit GEN. (Do not confuse the GEN with the nine-digit EIN.) If you do not know the GEN, contact the parent organization. Get Pub. 557 for more information about group exemption numbers.

Withholding agent. If you are a withholding agent required to file Form 1042, check the "Other" box and enter "Withholding agent."

Personal service corporation. Check this box if the entity is a personal service corporation. An entity is a personal service corporation for a tax year only if:

● The principal activity of the entity during the testing period (prior tax year) for the tax year is the performance of personal services substantially by employee-owners, and

● The employee-owners own at least 10% of the fair market value of the outstanding stock in the entity on the last day of the testing period.

Personal services include performance of services in such fields as health, law, accounting, or consulting. For more information about personal service corporations, see the **Instructions for Forms 1120 and 1120-A,** and **Pub. 542,** Corporations.

Limited liability company (LLC). See the definition of limited liability company in the **Instructions for Form 1065,** U.S. Partnership Return of Income. An LLC with two or more members can be a partnership or an association taxable as a corporation. An LLC with a single owner can be an association taxable as a corporation or an entity disregarded as an entity separate from its owner. See Form 8832 for more details.

Note: *A domestic LLC with at least two members that does not file Form 8832 is classified as a partnership for Federal income tax purposes.*

● If the entity is classified as a partnership for Federal income tax purposes, check the "partnership" box.

● If the entity is classified as a corporation for Federal income tax purposes, check the "Other corporation" box and write "limited liability co." in the space provided.

● If the entity is disregarded as an entity separate from its owner, check the "Other" box and write in "disregarded entity" in the space provided.

Plan administrator. If the plan administrator is an individual, enter the plan administrator's SSN in the space provided.

Other corporation. This box is for any corporation other than a personal service corporation. If you check this box, enter the type of corporation (such as insurance company) in the space provided.

Household employer. If you are an individual, check the "Other" box and enter "Household employer" and your SSN. If you are a state or local agency serving as a tax reporting agent for public assistance recipients who become household employers, check the "Other" box and enter "Household employer agent." If you are a trust that qualifies as a household employer, you do not need a separate EIN for reporting tax information relating to household employees; use the EIN of the trust.

QSub. For a qualified subchapter S subsidiary (QSub) check the "Other" box and specify "QSub."

Line 9. Check only **one** box. Do not enter N/A.

Started new business. Check this box if you are starting a new business that requires an EIN. If you check this box, enter the type of business being started. **Do not** apply if you already have an EIN and are only adding another place of business.

Hired employees. Check this box if the existing business is requesting an EIN because it has hired or is hiring employees and is therefore required to file employment tax returns. **Do not** apply if you already have an EIN and are only hiring employees. For information on the applicable employment taxes for family members, see **Circular E,** Employer's Tax Guide (Publication 15).

Created a pension plan. Check this box if you have created a pension plan and need an EIN for reporting purposes. Also, enter the type of plan.

Note: *Check this box if you are applying for a trust EIN when a new pension plan is established.*

Banking purpose. Check this box if you are requesting an EIN for banking purposes only, and enter the banking purpose (for example, a bowling league for depositing dues or an investment club for dividend and interest reporting).

Changed type of organization. Check this box if the business is changing its type of organization, for example, if the business was a sole proprietorship and has been incorporated or has become a partnership. If you check this box, specify in the space provided the type of change made, for example, "from sole proprietorship to partnership."

Purchased going business. Check this box if you purchased an existing business. **Do not** use the former owner's EIN. **Do not** apply for a new EIN if you already have one. Use your own EIN.

Created a trust. Check this box if you created a trust, and enter the type of trust created. For example, indicate if the trust is a nonexempt charitable trust or a split-interest trust.

Note: *Do not check this box if you are applying for a trust EIN when a new pension plan is established. Check "Created a pension plan."*

Exception. Do **not** file this form for certain grantor-type trusts. The trustee does not need an EIN for the trust if the trustee furnishes the name and TIN of the grantor/owner and the address of the trust to all payors. See the Instructions for Form 1041 for more information.

Other (specify). Check this box if you are requesting an EIN for any other reason, and enter the reason.

Line 10. If you are starting a new business, enter the starting date of the business. If the business you acquired is already operating, enter the date you acquired the business. Trusts should enter the date the trust was legally created. Estates should enter the date of death of the decedent whose name appears on line 1 or the date when the estate was legally funded.

Line 11. Enter the last month of your accounting year or tax year. An accounting or tax year is usually 12 consecutive months, either a calendar year or a fiscal year (including a period of 52 or 53 weeks). A calendar year is 12 consecutive months ending on December 31. A fiscal year is either 12 consecutive months ending on the last day of any month other than December or a 52-53 week year. For more information on accounting periods, see **Pub. 538,** Accounting Periods and Methods.

Individuals. Your tax year generally will be a calendar year.

Partnerships. Partnerships generally must adopt one of the following tax years:
- The tax year of the majority of its partners,
- The tax year common to all of its principal partners,
- The tax year that results in the least aggregate deferral of income, or
- In certain cases, some other tax year.

See the Instructions for Form 1065 for more information.

REMIC. REMICs must have a calendar year as their tax year.

Personal service corporations. A personal service corporation generally must adopt a calendar year unless:
- It can establish a business purpose for having a different tax year, or
- It elects under section 444 to have a tax year other than a calendar year.

Trusts. Generally, a trust must adopt a calendar year except for the following:
- Tax-exempt trusts,
- Charitable trusts, and
- Grantor-owned trusts.

Line 12. If the business has or will have employees, enter the date on which the business began or will begin to pay wages. If the business does not plan to have employees, enter N/A.

Withholding agent. Enter the date you began or will begin to pay income to a nonresident alien. This also applies to individuals who are required to file Form 1042 to report alimony paid to a nonresident alien.

Line 13. For a definition of agricultural labor (farmwork), see **Circular A,** Agricultural Employer's Tax Guide (Publication 51).

Line 14. Generally, enter the exact type of business being operated (for example, advertising agency, farm, food or beverage establishment, labor union, real estate agency, steam laundry, rental of coin-operated vending machine, or investment club). Also state if the business will involve the sale or distribution of alcoholic beverages.

Governmental. Enter the type of organization (state, county, school district, municipality, etc.).

Nonprofit organization (other than governmental). Enter whether organized for religious, educational, or humane purposes, and the principal activity (for example, religious organization—hospital, charitable).

Mining and quarrying. Specify the process and the principal product (for example, mining bituminous coal, contract drilling for oil, or quarrying dimension stone).

Contract construction. Specify whether general contracting or special trade contracting. Also, show the type of work normally performed (for example, general contractor for residential buildings or electrical subcontractor).

Food or beverage establishments. Specify the type of establishment and state whether you employ workers who receive tips (for example, lounge—yes).

Trade. Specify the type of sales and the principal line of goods sold (for example, wholesale dairy products, manufacturer's representative for mining machinery, or retail hardware).

Manufacturing. Specify the type of establishment operated (for example, sawmill or vegetable cannery).

Signature. The application must be signed by (a) the individual, if the applicant is an individual, (b) the president, vice president, or other principal officer, if the applicant is a corporation, (c) a responsible and duly authorized member or officer having knowledge of its affairs, if the applicant is a partnership or other unincorporated organization, or (d) the fiduciary, if the applicant is a trust or an estate.

How To Get Forms and Publications

Phone. You can order forms, instructions, and publications by phone 24 hours a day, 7 days a week. Just call 1-800-TAX-FORM (1-800-829-3676). You should receive your order or notification of its status within 10 workdays.

Personal computer. With your personal computer and modem, you can get the forms and information you need using IRS's Internet Web Site at **www.irs.gov** or File Transfer Protocol at **ftp.irs.gov.**

CD-ROM. For small businesses, return preparers, or others who may frequently need tax forms or publications, a CD-ROM containing over 2,000 tax products (including many prior year forms) can be purchased from the National Technical Information Service (NTIS).

To order **Pub. 1796,** Federal Tax Products on CD-ROM, call **1-877-CDFORMS** (1-877-233-6767) toll free or connect to **www.irs.gov/cdorders**

Form W-4 (2001)

Purpose. Complete Form W-4 so your employer can withhold the correct Federal income tax from your pay. Because your tax situation may change, you may want to refigure your withholding each year.

Exemption from withholding. If you are exempt, complete only lines 1, 2, 3, 4, and 7, and sign the form to validate it. Your exemption for 2001 expires February 18, 2002.

Note: *You cannot claim exemption from withholding if (1) your income exceeds $750 and includes more than $250 of unearned income (e.g., interest and dividends) and (2) another person can claim you as a dependent on their tax return.*

Basic instructions. If you are not exempt, complete the **Personal Allowances Worksheet** below. The worksheets on page 2 adjust your withholding allowances based on itemized deductions, certain credits, adjustments to income, or two-earner/two-job situations. Complete all worksheets that apply. They will help you figure the number of withholding allowances you are entitled to claim. However, **you may claim fewer (or zero) allowances.**

Head of household. Generally, you may claim head of household filing status on your tax return only if you are unmarried and pay more than 50% of the costs of keeping up a home for yourself and your dependent(s) or other qualifying individuals. See line **E** below.

Tax credits. You can take projected tax credits into account in figuring your allowable number of withholding allowances. Credits for child or dependent care expenses and the child tax credit may be claimed using the **Personal Allowances Worksheet** below. See **Pub. 919,** How Do I Adjust My Tax Withholding? for information on converting your other credits into withholding allowances.

Nonwage income. If you have a large amount of nonwage income, such as interest or dividends, consider making estimated tax payments using **Form 1040-ES,** Estimated Tax for Individuals. Otherwise, you may owe additional tax.

Two earners/two jobs. If you have a working spouse or more than one job, figure the total number of allowances you are entitled to claim on all jobs using worksheets from only one Form W-4. Your withholding usually will be most accurate when all allowances are claimed on the Form W-4 for the highest paying job and zero allowances are claimed on the others.

Check your withholding. After your Form W-4 takes effect, use Pub. 919 to see how the dollar amount you are having withheld compares to your projected total tax for 2001. Get Pub. 919 especially if you used the **Two-Earner/Two-Job Worksheet** on page 2 and your earnings exceed $150,000 (Single) or $200,000 (Married).

Recent name change? If your name on line 1 differs from that shown on your social security card, call 1-800-772-1213 for a new social security card.

Personal Allowances Worksheet (Keep for your records.)

A	Enter "1" for **yourself** if no one else can claim you as a dependent	**A** _____
B	Enter "1" if: • You are single and have only one job; or • You are married, have only one job, and your spouse does not work; or • Your wages from a second job or your spouse's wages (or the total of both) are $1,000 or less.	**B** _____
C	Enter "1" for your **spouse.** But, you may choose to enter -0- if you are married and have either a working spouse or more than one job. (Entering -0- may help you avoid having too little tax withheld.)	**C** _____
D	Enter number of **dependents** (other than your spouse or yourself) you will claim on your tax return	**D** _____
E	Enter "1" if you will file as **head of household** on your tax return (see conditions under **Head of household** above)	**E** _____
F	Enter "1" if you have at least $1,500 of **child or dependent care expenses** for which you plan to claim a credit (**Note:** Do **not** include child support payments. See **Pub. 503,** Child and Dependent Care Expenses, for details.)	**F** _____
G	**Child Tax Credit** (including additional child tax credit): • If your total income will be between $18,000 and $50,000 ($23,000 and $63,000 if married), enter "1" for each eligible child. • If your total income will be between $50,000 and $80,000 ($63,000 and $115,000 if married), enter "1" if you have two eligible children, enter "2" if you have three or four eligible children, or enter "3" if you have five or more eligible children.	**G** _____
H	Add lines A through G and enter total here. (**Note:** This may be different from the number of exemptions you claim on your tax return.) ▶	**H** _____

For accuracy, complete all worksheets that apply.
- If you plan to **itemize or claim adjustments to income** and want to reduce your withholding, see the **Deductions and Adjustments Worksheet** on page 2.
- If you are **single,** have **more than one job** and your combined earnings from all jobs exceed $35,000, **or** if you are **married** and have a **working spouse or more than one job** and the combined earnings from all jobs exceed $60,000, see the **Two-Earner/Two-Job Worksheet** on page 2 to avoid having too little tax withheld.
- If **neither** of the above situations applies, **stop here** and enter the number from line H on line 5 of Form W-4 below.

- - - - - - - - - - - - - - -   **Cut here and give Form W-4 to your employer. Keep the top part for your records.**   - - - - - - - - - - - - - - -

Form **W-4** Department of the Treasury Internal Revenue Service	**Employee's Withholding Allowance Certificate** ▶ **For Privacy Act and Paperwork Reduction Act Notice, see page 2.**	OMB No. 1545-0010 **2001**

1 Type or print your first name and middle initial	Last name		**2** Your social security number
Home address (number and street or rural route)		**3** ☐ Single ☐ Married ☐ Married, but withhold at higher Single rate. **Note:** If married, but legally separated, or spouse is a nonresident alien, check the Single box.	
City or town, state, and ZIP code		**4** If your last name differs from that on your social security card, check here. You must call 1-800-772-1213 for a new card. ▶ ☐	

5	Total number of allowances you are claiming (from line **H** above **or** from the applicable worksheet on page 2)	**5**	
6	Additional amount, if any, you want withheld from each paycheck	**6**	$
7	I claim exemption from withholding for 2001, and I certify that I meet **both** of the following conditions for exemption: • Last year I had a right to a refund of **all** Federal income tax withheld because I had **no** tax liability **and** • This year I expect a refund of **all** Federal income tax withheld because I expect to have **no** tax liability. If you meet both conditions, write "Exempt" here ▶	**7**	

Under penalties of perjury, I certify that I am entitled to the number of withholding allowances claimed on this certificate, or I am entitled to claim exempt status.

Employee's signature
(Form is not valid
unless you sign it.) ▶ _____ Date ▶ _____

8 Employer's name and address (Employer: Complete lines 8 and 10 only if sending to the IRS.)	**9** Office code (optional)	**10** Employer identification number

Cat. No. 10220Q

Deductions and Adjustments Worksheet

Note: *Use this worksheet only if you plan to itemize deductions, claim certain credits, or claim adjustments to income on your 2001 tax return.*

1	Enter an estimate of your 2001 itemized deductions. These include qualifying home mortgage interest, charitable contributions, state and local taxes, medical expenses in excess of 7.5% of your income, and miscellaneous deductions. (For 2001, you may have to reduce your itemized deductions if your income is over \$132,950 (\$66,475 if married filing separately). See **Worksheet 3** in Pub. 919 for details.) . . .	**1** \$ _____

2	Enter:	\$7,600 if married filing jointly or qualifying widow(er) \$6,650 if head of household \$4,550 if single \$3,800 if married filing separately	**2** \$ _____

3 Subtract line 2 from line 1. If line 2 is greater than line 1, enter -0- . . . . **3** \$ _____

4 Enter an estimate of your 2001 adjustments to income, including alimony, deductible IRA contributions, and student loan interest **4** \$ _____

5 **Add** lines 3 and 4 and enter the total (Include any amount for credits from **Worksheet 7** in Pub. 919.) . **5** \$ _____

6 Enter an estimate of your 2001 nonwage income (such as dividends or interest) . . . . **6** \$ _____

7 **Subtract** line 6 from line 5. Enter the result, but not less than -0- . . . . **7** \$ _____

8 **Divide** the amount on line 7 by \$3,000 and enter the result here. Drop any fraction . . . . . . **8** _____

9 Enter the number from the **Personal Allowances Worksheet,** line H, page 1 . . . . . . **9** _____

10 **Add** lines 8 and 9 and enter the total here. If you plan to use the **Two-Earner/Two-Job Worksheet,** also enter this total on line 1 below. Otherwise, **stop here** and enter this total on Form W-4, line 5, page 1 . **10** _____

Two-Earner/Two-Job Worksheet

Note: *Use this worksheet only if the instructions under line H on page 1 direct you here.*

1 Enter the number from line H, page 1 (or from line 10 above if you used the **Deductions and Adjustments Worksheet**) **1** _____

2 Find the number in **Table 1** below that applies to the **lowest** paying job and enter it here . . . . . **2** _____

3 If line 1 is **more than or equal to** line 2, subtract line 2 from line 1. Enter the result here (if zero, enter -0-) and on Form W-4, line 5, page 1. **Do not** use the rest of this worksheet . . . . **3** _____

Note: *If line 1 is **less than** line 2, enter -0- on Form W-4, line 5, page 1. Complete lines 4–9 below to calculate the additional withholding amount necessary to avoid a year end tax bill.*

4 Enter the number from line 2 of this worksheet . . . . **4** _____

5 Enter the number from line 1 of this worksheet . . . . **5** _____

6 **Subtract** line 5 from line 4 . . . . **6** _____

7 Find the amount in **Table 2** below that applies to the **highest** paying job and enter it here . . . . . **7** \$ _____

8 **Multiply** line 7 by line 6 and enter the result here. This is the additional annual withholding needed . . **8** \$ _____

9 Divide line 8 by the number of pay periods remaining in 2001. For example, divide by 26 if you are paid every two weeks and you complete this form in December 2000. Enter the result here and on Form W-4, line 6, page 1. This is the additional amount to be withheld from each paycheck . . . . **9** \$ _____

Table 1: Two-Earner/Two-Job Worksheet

Married Filing Jointly				All Others			
If wages from **LOWEST** paying job are—	Enter on line 2 above	If wages from **LOWEST** paying job are—	Enter on line 2 above	If wages from **LOWEST** paying job are—	Enter on line 2 above	If wages from **LOWEST** paying job are—	Enter on line 2 above
\$0 - \$4,000	0	42,001 - 47,000	8	\$0 - \$6,000	0	65,001 - 80,000	8
4,001 - 8,000	1	47,001 - 55,000	9	6,001 - 12,000	1	80,001 - 105,000	9
8,001 - 14,000	2	55,001 - 65,000	10	12,001 - 17,000	2	105,001 and over	10
14,001 - 19,000	3	65,001 - 70,000	11	17,001 - 22,000	3		
19,001 - 25,000	4	70,001 - 90,000	12	22,001 - 28,000	4		
25,001 - 32,000	5	90,001 - 105,000	13	28,001 - 40,000	5		
32,001 - 38,000	6	105,001 - 115,000	14	40,001 - 50,000	6		
38,001 - 42,000	7	115,001 and over	15	50,001 - 65,000	7		

Table 2: Two-Earner/Two-Job Worksheet

Married Filing Jointly		All Others	
If wages from **HIGHEST** paying job are—	Enter on line 7 above	If wages from **HIGHEST** paying job are—	Enter on line 7 above
\$0 - \$50,000	\$440	\$0 - \$30,000	\$440
50,001 - 100,000	800	30,001 - 60,000	800
100,001 - 130,000	900	60,001 - 120,000	900
130,001 - 250,000	1,000	120,001 - 270,000	1,000
250,001 and over	1,100	270,001 and over	1,100

Form **W-9**
(Rev. December 2000)
Department of the Treasury
Internal Revenue Service

Request for Taxpayer
Identification Number and Certification

Give form to the requester. Do not send to the IRS.

Please print or type

Name (See **Specific Instructions** on page 2.)

Business name, if different from above. (See **Specific Instructions** on page 2.)

Check appropriate box: ☐ Individual/Sole proprietor ☐ Corporation ☐ Partnership ☐ Other ▶ ------------------------

Address (number, street, and apt. or suite no.)

Requester's name and address (optional)

City, state, and ZIP code

Part I Taxpayer Identification Number (TIN)

List account number(s) here (optional)

Enter your TIN in the appropriate box. For individuals, this is your social security number (SSN). **However, for a resident alien, sole proprietor, or disregarded entity, see the Part I instructions on page 2.** For other entities, it is your employer identification number (EIN). If you do not have a number, see **How to get a TIN** on page 2.

Note: *If the account is in more than one name, see the chart on page 2 for guidelines on whose number to enter.*

Social security number

or

Employer identification number

Part II For U.S. Payees Exempt From Backup Withholding (See the instructions on page 2.)

▶

Part III Certification

Under penalties of perjury, I certify that:

1. The number shown on this form is my correct taxpayer identification number (or I am waiting for a number to be issued to me), **and**

2. I am not subject to backup withholding because: **(a)** I am exempt from backup withholding, or **(b)** I have not been notified by the Internal Revenue Service (IRS) that I am subject to backup withholding as a result of a failure to report all interest or dividends, or **(c)** the IRS has notified me that I am no longer subject to backup withholding, **and**

3. I am a U.S. person (including a U.S. resident alien).

Certification instructions. You must cross out item **2** above if you have been notified by the IRS that you are currently subject to backup withholding because you have failed to report all interest and dividends on your tax return. For real estate transactions, item **2** does not apply. For mortgage interest paid, acquisition or abandonment of secured property, cancellation of debt, contributions to an individual retirement arrangement (IRA), and generally, payments other than interest and dividends, you are not required to sign the Certification, but you must provide your correct TIN. (See the instructions on page 2.)

Sign Here | Signature of U.S. person ▶

Date ▶

Purpose of Form

A person who is required to file an information return with the IRS must get your correct taxpayer identification number (TIN) to report, for example, income paid to you, real estate transactions, mortgage interest you paid, acquisition or abandonment of secured property, cancellation of debt, or contributions you made to an IRA.

Use Form W-9 only if you are a U.S. person (including a resident alien), to give your correct TIN to the person requesting it (the requester) and, when applicable, to:

1. Certify the TIN you are giving is correct (or you are waiting for a number to be issued),

2. Certify you are not subject to backup withholding, or

3. Claim exemption from backup withholding if you are a U.S. exempt payee.

If you are a foreign person, use the appropriate Form W-8. See Pub. 515, Withholding of Tax on Nonresident Aliens and Foreign Corporations.

Note: *If a requester gives you a form other than Form W-9 to request your TIN, you must use the requester's form if it is substantially similar to this Form W-9.*

What is backup withholding? Persons making certain payments to you must withhold and pay to the IRS 31% of such payments under certain conditions. This is called "backup withholding." Payments that may be subject to backup withholding include interest, dividends, broker and barter exchange transactions, rents, royalties, nonemployee pay, and certain payments from fishing boat operators. Real estate transactions are not subject to backup withholding.

If you give the requester your correct TIN, make the proper certifications, and report all your taxable interest and dividends on your tax return, payments you receive will not be subject to backup withholding. **Payments you receive will be subject to backup withholding if:**

1. You do not furnish your TIN to the requester, or

2. You do not certify your TIN when required (see the Part III instructions on page 2 for details), or

3. The IRS tells the requester that you furnished an incorrect TIN, or

4. The IRS tells you that you are subject to backup withholding because you did not report all your interest and dividends on your tax return (for reportable interest and dividends only), or

5. You do not certify to the requester that you are not subject to backup withholding under 4 above (for reportable interest and dividend accounts opened after 1983 only).

Certain payees and payments are exempt from backup withholding. See the Part II instructions and the separate **Instructions for the Requester of Form W-9.**

Penalties

Failure to furnish TIN. If you fail to furnish your correct TIN to a requester, you are subject to a penalty of $50 for each such failure unless your failure is due to reasonable cause and not to willful neglect.

Civil penalty for false information with respect to withholding. If you make a false statement with no reasonable basis that results in no backup withholding, you are subject to a $500 penalty.

Criminal penalty for falsifying information. Willfully falsifying certifications or affirmations may subject you to criminal penalties including fines and/or imprisonment.

Misuse of TINs. If the requester discloses or uses TINs in violation of Federal law, the requester may be subject to civil and criminal penalties.

Specific Instructions

Name. If you are an individual, you must generally enter the name shown on your social security card. However, if you have changed your last name, for instance, due to marriage without informing the Social Security Administration of the name change, enter your first name, the last name shown on your social security card, and your new last name.

If the account is in joint names, list first and then circle the name of the person or entity whose number you enter in Part I of the form.

Sole proprietor. Enter your **individual** name as shown on your social security card on the "Name" line. You may enter your business, trade, or "doing business as (DBA)" name on the "Business name" line.

Limited liability company (LLC). If you are a single-member LLC (including a foreign LLC with a domestic owner) that is disregarded as an entity separate from its owner under Treasury regulations section 301.7701-3, **enter the owner's name on the "Name" line.** Enter the LLC's name on the "Business name" line.

Caution: *A disregarded domestic entity that has a foreign owner must use the appropriate Form W-8.*

Other entities. Enter your business name as shown on required Federal tax documents on the "Name" line. This name should match the name shown on the charter or other legal document creating the entity. You may enter any business, trade, or DBA name on the "Business name" line.

Part I—Taxpayer Identification Number (TIN)

Enter your TIN in the appropriate box.

If you are a **resident alien** and you do not have and are not eligible to get an SSN, your TIN is your IRS individual taxpayer identification number (ITIN). Enter it in the social security number box. If you do not have an ITIN, see **How to get a TIN** below.

If you are a **sole proprietor** and you have an EIN, you may enter either your SSN or EIN. However, the IRS prefers that you use your SSN.

If you are an **LLC** that is **disregarded as an entity** separate from its owner (see **Limited liability company (LLC)** above), and are owned by an individual, enter your SSN (or "pre-LLC" EIN, if desired). If the owner of a disregarded LLC is a corporation, partnership, etc., enter the owner's EIN.

Note: *See the chart on this page for further clarification of name and TIN combinations.*

How to get a TIN. If you do not have a TIN, apply for one immediately. To apply for an SSN, get **Form SS-5,** Application for a Social Security Card, from your local Social Security Administration office. Get **Form W-7,** Application for IRS Individual Taxpayer Identification Number, to apply for an ITIN or **Form SS-4,** Application for Employer Identification Number, to apply for an EIN. You can get Forms W-7 and SS-4 from the IRS by calling 1-800-TAX-FORM (1-800-829-3676) or from the IRS's Internet Web Site at **www.irs.gov.**

If you do not have a TIN, write "Applied For" in the space for the TIN, sign and date the form, and give it to the requester. For interest and dividend payments, and certain payments made with respect to readily tradable instruments, generally you will have 60 days to get a TIN and give it to the requester before you are subject to backup withholding on payments. The 60-day rule does not apply to other types of payments. You will be subject to backup withholding on all such payments until you provide your TIN to the requester.

Note: *Writing "Applied For" means that you have already applied for a TIN **or** that you intend to apply for one soon.*

Part II—For U.S. Payees Exempt From Backup Withholding

Individuals (including sole proprietors) are **not** exempt from backup withholding. Corporations are exempt from backup withholding for certain payments, such as interest and dividends. For more information on exempt payees, see the separate Instructions for the Requester of Form W-9.

If you are exempt from backup withholding, you should still complete this form to avoid possible erroneous backup withholding. Enter your correct TIN in Part I, write "Exempt" in Part II, and sign and date the form.

If you are a nonresident alien or a foreign entity not subject to backup withholding, give the requester the appropriate completed Form W-8.

Part III—Certification

To establish to the withholding agent that you are a U.S. person, or resident alien, sign Form W-9. You may be requested to sign by the withholding agent even if items 1, 3, and 5 below indicate otherwise.

For a joint account, only the person whose TIN is shown in Part I should sign (when required).

1. Interest, dividend, and barter exchange accounts opened before 1984 and broker accounts considered active during 1983. You must give your correct TIN, but you do not have to sign the certification.

2. Interest, dividend, broker, and barter exchange accounts opened after 1983 and broker accounts considered inactive during 1983. You must sign the certification or backup withholding will apply. If you are subject to backup withholding and you are merely providing your correct TIN to the requester, you must cross out item **2** in the certification before signing the form.

3. Real estate transactions. You must sign the certification. You may cross out item **2** of the certification.

4. Other payments. You must give your correct TIN, but you do not have to sign the certification unless you have been notified that you have previously given an incorrect TIN. "Other payments" include payments made in the course of the requester's trade or business for rents, royalties, goods (other than bills for merchandise), medical and health care services (including payments to corporations), payments to a nonemployee for services, payments to certain fishing boat crew members and fishermen, and gross proceeds paid to attorneys (including payments to corporations).

5. Mortgage interest paid by you, acquisition or abandonment of secured property, cancellation of debt, qualified state tuition program payments, IRA or MSA contributions or distributions, and pension distributions. You must give your correct TIN, but you do not have to sign the certification.

Privacy Act Notice

Section 6109 of the Internal Revenue Code requires you to give your correct TIN to persons who must file information returns with the IRS to report interest, dividends, and certain other income paid to you, mortgage interest you paid, the acquisition or abandonment of secured property, cancellation of debt, or contributions you made to an IRA or MSA. The IRS uses the numbers for identification purposes and to help verify the accuracy of your tax return. The IRS may also provide this information to the Department of Justice for civil and criminal litigation, and to cities, states, and the District of Columbia to carry out their tax laws.

You must provide your TIN whether or not you are required to file a tax return. Payers must generally withhold 31% of taxable interest, dividend, and certain other payments to a payee who does not give a TIN to a payer. Certain penalties may also apply.

What Name and Number To Give the Requester

For this type of account:	Give name and SSN of:
1. Individual	The individual
2. Two or more individuals (joint account)	The actual owner of the account or, if combined funds, the first individual on the account [1]
3. Custodian account of a minor (Uniform Gift to Minors Act)	The minor [2]
4. a. The usual revocable savings trust (grantor is also trustee)	The grantor-trustee [1]
b. So-called trust account that is not a legal or valid trust under state law	The actual owner [1]
5. Sole proprietorship	The owner [3]

For this type of account:	Give name and EIN of:
6. Sole proprietorship	The owner [3]
7. A valid trust, estate, or pension trust	Legal entity [4]
8. Corporate	The corporation
9. Association, club, religious, charitable, educational, or other tax-exempt organization	The organization
10. Partnership	The partnership
11. A broker or registered nominee	The broker or nominee
12. Account with the Department of Agriculture in the name of a public entity (such as a state or local government, school district, or prison) that receives agricultural program payments	The public entity

[1] List first and circle the name of the person whose number you furnish. If only one person on a joint account has an SSN, that person's number must be furnished.

[2] Circle the minor's name and furnish the minor's SSN.

[3] You must show your individual name, but you may also enter your business or "DBA" name. You may use either your SSN or EIN (if you have one).

[4] List first and circle the name of the legal trust, estate, or pension trust. (Do not furnish the TIN of the personal representative or trustee unless the legal entity itself is not designated in the account title.)

Note: *If no name is circled when more than one name is listed, the number will be considered to be that of the first name listed.*

SCHEDULE SE
(Form 1040)

Department of the Treasury
Internal Revenue Service (99)

Self-Employment Tax

▶ See Instructions for Schedule SE (Form 1040).

▶ Attach to Form 1040.

OMB No. 1545-0074

2000

Attachment
Sequence No. **17**

Name of person with **self-employment** income (as shown on Form 1040)

Social security number of person
with **self-employment** income ▶

Who Must File Schedule SE

You must file Schedule SE if:

● You had net earnings from self-employment from **other than** church employee income (line 4 of Short Schedule SE or line 4c of Long Schedule SE) of $400 or more **or**

● You had church employee income of $108.28 or more. Income from services you performed as a minister or a member of a religious order **is not** church employee income. See page SE-1.

Note. Even if you had a loss or a small amount of income from self-employment, it may be to your benefit to file Schedule SE and use either "optional method" in Part II of Long Schedule SE. See page SE-3.

Exception. If your only self-employment income was from earnings as a minister, member of a religious order, or Christian Science practitioner **and** you filed Form 4361 and received IRS approval not to be taxed on those earnings, **do not** file Schedule SE. Instead, write "Exempt–Form 4361" on Form 1040, line 52.

May I Use Short Schedule SE or Must I Use Long Schedule SE?

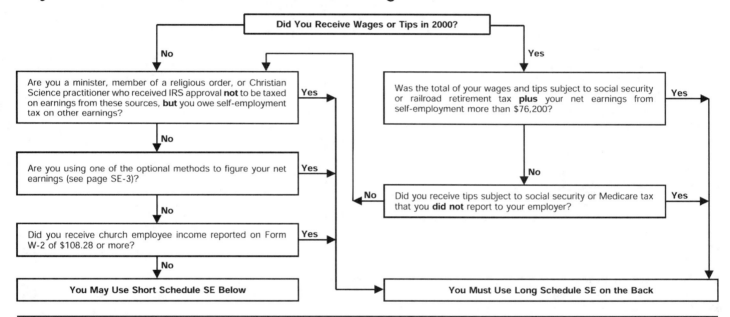

Section A—Short Schedule SE. Caution: *Read above to see if you can use Short Schedule SE.*

1	Net farm profit or (loss) from Schedule F, line 36, and farm partnerships, Schedule K-1 (Form 1065), line 15a	**1**	
2	Net profit or (loss) from Schedule C, line 31; Schedule C-EZ, line 3; Schedule K-1 (Form 1065), line 15a (other than farming); and Schedule K-1 (Form 1065-B), box 9. Ministers and members of religious orders, see page SE-1 for amounts to report on this line. See page SE-2 for other income to report	**2**	
3	Combine lines 1 and 2	**3**	
4	**Net earnings from self-employment.** Multiply line 3 by 92.35% (.9235). If less than $400, **do not** file this schedule; you do not owe self-employment tax . . . . ▶	**4**	
5	**Self-employment tax.** If the amount on line 4 is: ● $76,200 or less, multiply line 4 by 15.3% (.153). Enter the result here and on **Form 1040, line 52.** ● More than $76,200, multiply line 4 by 2.9% (.029). Then, add $9,448.80 to the result. Enter the total here and on **Form 1040, line 52.**	**5**	

| 6 | **Deduction for one-half of self-employment tax.** Multiply line 5 by 50% (.5). Enter the result here and on **Form 1040, line 27** . . . . | 6 | |

For Paperwork Reduction Act Notice, see Form 1040 instructions.   Cat. No. 11358Z   Schedule SE (Form 1040) 2000

Name of person with **self-employment** income (as shown on Form 1040)	Social security number of person with **self-employment** income ▶	

Section B—Long Schedule SE

Part I   Self-Employment Tax

Note. If your only income subject to self-employment tax is **church employee income,** skip lines 1 through 4b. Enter -0- on line 4c and go to line 5a. Income from services you performed as a minister or a member of a religious order **is not** church employee income. See page SE-1.

A   If you are a minister, member of a religious order, or Christian Science practitioner **and** you filed Form 4361, but you had $400 or more of **other** net earnings from self-employment, check here and continue with Part I . . . . . . ▶ ☐

1	Net farm profit or (loss) from Schedule F, line 36, and farm partnerships, Schedule K-1 (Form 1065), line 15a. **Note.** Skip this line if you use the farm optional method. See page SE-3 . .	**1**	
2	Net profit or (loss) from Schedule C, line 31; Schedule C-EZ, line 3; Schedule K-1 (Form 1065), line 15a (other than farming); and Schedule K-1 (Form 1065-B), box 9. Ministers and members of religious orders, see page SE-1 for amounts to report on this line. See page SE-2 for other income to report. **Note.** Skip this line if you use the nonfarm optional method. See page SE-3 .	**2**	
3	Combine lines 1 and 2	**3**	
4a	If line 3 is more than zero, multiply line 3 by 92.35% (.9235). Otherwise, enter amount from line 3	**4a**	
b	If you elect one or both of the optional methods, enter the total of lines 15 and 17 here . . .	**4b**	
c	Combine lines 4a and 4b. If less than $400, **do not** file this schedule; you do not owe self-employment tax. **Exception.** If less than $400 and you had **church employee income,** enter -0- and continue ▶	**4c**	
5a	Enter your **church employee income** from Form W-2. **Caution:** See page SE-1 for definition of church employee income	**5a**			
b	Multiply line 5a by 92.35% (.9235). If less than $100, enter -0-	**5b**	
6	**Net earnings from self-employment.** Add lines 4c and 5b	**6**	
7	Maximum amount of combined wages and self-employment earnings subject to social security tax or the 6.2% portion of the 7.65% railroad retirement (tier 1) tax for 2000	**7**	76,200	00
8a	Total social security wages and tips (total of boxes 3 and 7 on Form(s) W-2) and railroad retirement (tier 1) compensation	**8a**			
b	Unreported tips subject to social security tax (from Form 4137, line 9)	**8b**			
c	Add lines 8a and 8b	**8c**	
9	Subtract line 8c from line 7. If zero or less, enter -0- here and on line 10 and go to line 11 . ▶	**9**	
10	Multiply the **smaller** of line 6 or line 9 by 12.4% (.124)	**10**	
11	Multiply line 6 by 2.9% (.029)	**11**	
12	**Self-employment tax.** Add lines 10 and 11. Enter here and on **Form 1040, line 52**	**12**	
13	**Deduction for one-half of self-employment tax.** Multiply line 12 by 50% (.5). Enter the result here and on **Form 1040, line 27**	**13**			

Part II   Optional Methods To Figure Net Earnings (See page SE-3.)

Farm Optional Method. You may use this method **only** if:

● Your gross farm income[1] was not more than $2,400 **or**

● Your net farm profits[2] were less than $1,733.

14	Maximum income for optional methods	**14**	1,600	00
15	Enter the **smaller** of: two-thirds (⅔) of gross farm income[1] (not less than zero) or $1,600. Also include this amount on line 4b above	**15**	

Nonfarm Optional Method. You may use this method **only** if:

● Your net nonfarm profits[3] were less than $1,733 and also less than 72.189% of your gross nonfarm income[4] **and**

● You had net earnings from self-employment of at least $400 in 2 of the prior 3 years.

Caution: *You may use this method no more than five times.*

16	Subtract line 15 from line 14	**16**	
17	Enter the **smaller** of: two-thirds (⅔) of gross nonfarm income[4] (not less than zero) or the amount on line 16. Also include this amount on line 4b above	**17**	

[1]From Sch. F, line 11, and Sch. K-1 (Form 1065), line 15b.   [3]From Sch. C, line 31; Sch. C-EZ, line 3; Sch. K-1 (Form 1065), line 15a; and Sch. K-1 (Form 1065-B), box 9.
[2]From Sch. F, line 36, and Sch. K-1 (Form 1065), line 15a.   [4]From Sch. C, line 7; Sch. C-EZ, line 1; Sch. K-1 (Form 1065), line 15c; and Sch. K-1 (Form 1065-B), box 9.

Index

G

H

Q

R

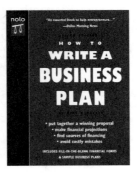

Take 2 Minutes & Give Us Your 2 cents

Your comments make a big difference in the development and revision of Nolo books and software. Please take a few minutes and register your Nolo product—and your comments—with us. Not only will your input make a difference, you'll receive special offers available only to registered owners of Nolo products on our newest books and software. Register now by:

PHONE
1-800-992-6656

FAX
1-800-645-0895

EMAIL
cs@nolo.com

or **MAIL** us
this registration card

REMEMBER:
Little publishers have big ears. We really listen to you.

- fold here -

REGISTRATION CARD

NAME _____ DATE _____

ADDRESS _____

_____

CITY _____ STATE _____ ZIP _____

PHONE _____ E-MAIL _____

WHERE DID YOU HEAR ABOUT THIS PRODUCT? _____

WHERE DID YOU PURCHASE THIS PRODUCT? _____

DID YOU CONSULT A LAWYER? (PLEASE CIRCLE ONE)   YES   NO   NOT APPLICABLE

DID YOU FIND THIS BOOK HELPFUL?   (VERY)   5   4   3   2   1   (NOT AT ALL)

COMMENTS _____

_____

_____

WAS IT EASY TO USE?   (VERY EASY)   5   4   3   2   1   (VERY DIFFICULT)

DO YOU OWN A COMPUTER? IF SO, WHICH FORMAT? (PLEASE CIRCLE ONE)   WINDOWS   DOS   MAC

We occasionally make our mailing list available to carefully selected companies whose products may be of interest to you.
☐ If you do not wish to receive mailings from these companies, please check this box.
☐ You can quote me in future Nolo promotional materials. Daytime phone number _____.

SAVVY 5.0

NOLO IN THE NEWS

"Nolo helps lay people perform legal tasks without the aid—or fees—of lawyers."

—**USA TODAY**

Nolo books are ..."written in plain language, free of legal mumbo jumbo, and spiced with witty personal observations."

—**ASSOCIATED PRESS**

"...Nolo publications...guide people simply through the how, when, where and why of law."

—**WASHINGTON POST**

"Increasingly, people who are not lawyers are performing tasks usually regarded as legal work... And consumers, using books like Nolo's, do routine legal work themselves."

—**NEW YORK TIMES**

"...All of [Nolo's] books are easy-to-understand, are updated regularly, provide pull-out forms...and are often quite moving in their sense of compassion for the struggles of the lay reader."

—**SAN FRANCISCO CHRONICLE**

fold here

- -

Place
stamp here

nolo
950 Parker Street
Berkeley, CA 94710-9867

Attn: SAVVY 5.0